THE DIARY
OF
SAMUEL PEPYS
Selections

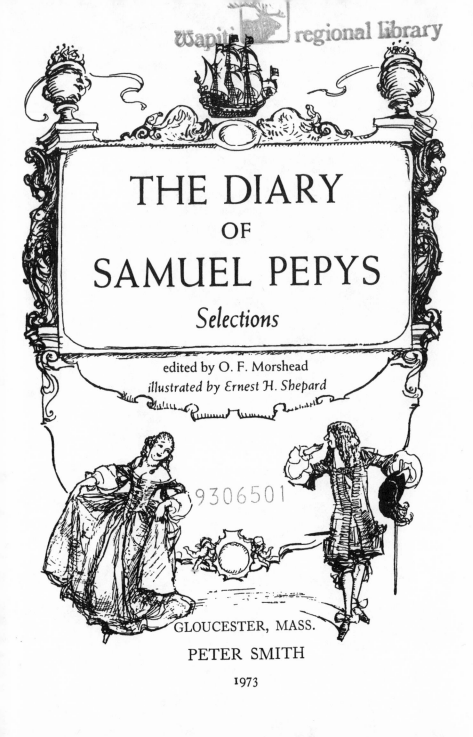

THE DIARY
OF
SAMUEL PEPYS
Selections

edited by O. F. Morshead
illustrated by *Ernest H. Shepard*

GLOUCESTER, MASS.

PETER SMITH

1973

Reprinted 1973, by Peter Smith Publisher, Inc.
Gloucester, Mass.
ISBN: 0-8446-2727-5

CONTENTS

LIST OF ILLUSTRATIONS

INTRODUCTION

SAMUEL PEPYS was born in London on February 23, 1633. His father was a needy tailor in Salisbury Court, off Fleet Street; his mother had been a domestic servant. The Pepys family had been substantial enough in their native counties of Huntingdon and Cambridge, where they had been established for many generations as small squires or yeomen. Pepys' uncle Robert, who died in the year after the Diary begins, left them property valued at £80 a year at Brampton, just outside Huntingdon; and this, we are told, caused great store of tattle in Salisbury Court between the old women and Pepys' mother, who thought there was 'God knows what fallen to her.'

But things were different in Pepys' childhood, when his improvident father was struggling to cope with the eleven children with which fortune had blessed him. The Pepys we know no doubt owed much of his positive character to this environment. Somehow or other he became an exhibitioner at St. Paul's School, where, he has told us, he roundly declared to his fellows on the day of Charles I.'s execution, that if he should preach upon the late King his text should be "the memory of the wicked should rot." It troubled him a good deal later on, as in those days it must have troubled many others, to reflect how he had once shouted with the crowd, as truculent a Roundhead as any. We get a similar glimpse of character in the moulding from the only record of him at Magdalene College, Cambridge, whither, his Iick accompanying him, he proceeded as a scholar in 1650; for it appears from an entry in the College Order Book that he and his friend Hinde incurred a severe rebuke for being 'scandalously overseene in drink' one October night. A few years later he returned to Cambridge for a week-end, which he celebrated by drinking copiously with each of his former judges in turn; and then, such is the contrariness of human nature, he turned on them in judgment to 'find that there was nothing at all left of the old preciseness in their discourse, specially on Saturday nights.'

He took his degree in 1653, and there is no trace of him for the next two years. In 1655 he married. He was then twenty-two, and she fifteen; and they had not a penny between them. His very lute was pawned for forty shillings. Her parents, though a good deal above the social standing of his, were fully as penurious; for Elizabeth St. Michel's father had forfeited one fortune in his native France by an unhappy preference for Protestantism, and had failed to make another in England, either as Gentleman Carver to Queen Henrietta Maria or by his discovery of King Solomon's gold and silver mines—'now much fuller than they were in that king's times.'

At Brampton Pepys' relatives had never been people of great social consequence. The fine property of Hinchingbrooke in this village had formerly belonged to the Cromwells; but in 1627 it had been sold by Oliver Cromwell's uncle to Sir Sydney Montagu, a well-known Royalist, and member for Huntingdonshire in the Long Parliament. He had married Paulina Pepys, who was aunt to the tailor; and her son Edward Montagu, afterwards created Earl of Sandwich, was therefore the tailor's first cousin. This relationship is important, for it is the key to Samuel Pepys' career.

Edward Montagu was a close personal friend of Oliver Cromwell. Without any remarkable ability, and despite his ignorance of naval matters, he had been put in joint command of the Commonwealth fleet when he was thirty. His appointment took place only a month after Pepys' wedding; and it is not unlikely that Pepys married on his prospects, for he was at once engaged by Montagu in the capacity of secretary, or steward, with the duty of supervising Montagu's affairs and controlling his household in London whilst he was at sea. 'My Lord,' as Pepys always calls him, had already been married for thirteen years and had a rising family. By 'my Lady' and by the Crewe family, her relatives, Pepys was well received; and from many chance remarks in the Diary it is clear that he performed his delicate task with a diligence and discretion that brought him the affection of Lady Sandwich and her numerous children. It earned him also the entire confidence of my Lord, who presently secured his entry into the Navy Office with the result that we see in the pages that follow.

Of the events of the next nine years the Diary may well be left to tell the tale. Towards the end of the period which it covers Pepys complains with increasing frequency of the pain which his eyes give him, especially at night; and indeed one cannot wonder at it. For he would frequently keep late hours poring by candle-light over his ledgers at the Navy Office, and would then proceed to detail the day's doings in his journal. The Diary was written in shorthand; in the early volumes the characters are neat and small, but for some time before the end, coincidentally with his complaints of eye trouble, the quality of his script falls off, and on May 31, 1669, he was forced to abandon it, to his own grief and our great loss.

In a moving passage at its close he writes: "And thus ends all that I doubt I shall ever be able to do with my own eyes in the keeping of my journal, I being not able to do it any longer, having done now so long as to undo my eyes almost every time that I take a pen in my hand, and therefore whatever comes of it I must forbear; and resolve from this time forward to have it kept by my people in long-hand, and must therefore be contented to set down no more than is fit for them and all the world to know. . . . And so I betake myself to that course, which is almost as much as to see myself go into my grave; for which, and for all the discomforts that will accompany my being blind, the good God prepare me!"

He did not in fact become blind, for fifteen years later he took down in shorthand, at Charles the Second's dictation, the narrative of the king's hiding in the oak; and though this script lacks the precision which is so remarkable a feature of the earlier volumes of the Diary, the disparity between the two is not greater than would be accounted for by the different circumstances in which each was written. But the thread of the Diary was broken, and the only sequel was a somewhat tedious record of a journey to Tangier undertaken late in life, which lacks the authentic Pepysian flavour.

Upon the conclusion of his Diary Pepys took his wife for a tour in Holland and France; but immediately after their return Mrs. Pepys was taken ill and died. She was buried in the church of St. Olave's, Hart Street, where her bust in marble may still be seen. After fourteen years of married life she was still only twenty-nine, and Pepys, a childless widower at thirty-six, did not marry again. He had been a trying husband, and she a refractory girl; but there is no doubt that the marriage was on the whole a happy one. It had the singular merit for those days of having been based originally upon genuine affection—for we are safe in assuming that it was not promoted by the parents of either party. It is very remarkable that for a period of nearly ten years Pepys should never have disclosed, even in the intimacy of his Diary, what name he called his wife by. She appears to have been a playful and attractive girl, with a distinct will of her own. Her diary also would have made good reading.

In 1673 the passing of the Test Act was followed by the retirement of James, Duke of York, from the office of Lord High Admiral. Naval affairs were thereafter entrusted to a Commission over which the King presided, and Pepys' thirteen years of service as Clerk of the Acts were recognized by his appointment as Secretary of the Admiralty, a post of considerable honour. True his salary was only advanced from £350 to £500, but the last words on this subject had fallen from the lips of Lord Sandwich when originally introducing Pepys to the King's service. "It was not," he had observed, "the salary of any place that did make a man rich, but the opportunity of getting money while he is in the place." And perhaps the secretary now said as much to his brother John, who discarded his cassock and succeeded, jointly with Pepys' former clerk, to the Clerkship of the Acts.

For six years Pepys retained the secretaryship; but times were difficult, and he had not been a public official for so many years without making enemies. These now sought occasion to upset him, and he became the object of an infamous attack upon his supposed Papist tendencies—a subject upon which popular feeling ran high owing to the recent Popish Plot. His administration was attacked also in the Press. In 1679 he and Sir Antony Deane, the great shipbuilder, were actually imprisoned for six weeks in the Tower, pending their acquittal in the Public Courts. Just prior to his imprisonment he had resigned his secretaryship, and on his release he went to live with his former clerk Will Hewer, in a substantial house in York Buildings, overlooking the Thames, near the present site of Hungerford Bridge. For five years he remained in retirement, abandoning himself to his intellectual interests, travelling a little, and visiting the Court at Newmarket, where he still retained the favour of the King and the Duke of York.

In 1684 Charles II. abolished the Admiralty Commission and himself assumed the office of Lord High Admiral, appointing Pepys Secretary for the Affairs of the Admiralty of England. The King's death six months later was followed by the accession of Pepys' old chief at the Naval Office as King James II.; and with his assistance once more the new secretary was able to place the administration of the Navy on a sound basis after the mishandling of the inexperienced Commissioners. But his second tour as secretary was to be cut short after four years by the Revolution, and a few weeks after the abdication of James II. Pepys again retired, this time for good.

During most of the fourteen years that remained to him he continued to live in York Buildings, where on Saturday evenings for many years he used to entertain his fellow-members of the Royal Society. "If I should be put out of my office," he had written twenty years earlier, "I do take great content in the liberty I shall be at, of frequenting these gentlemen's company." He became known as a patron of the Arts and Letters, and conducted an extensive correspondence with many of the leading savants of the day. Perhaps his chief interest in these later years centred upon the library which he bequeathed to Magdalene College, into the collection and arrangement of which he threw all that energy which had characterized his official life. Everything was grist that came to his mill, books and manuscripts, engraved portraits and landscapes, pamphlets, broadside ballads and music. Nor did he confine himself to English works, for his nephew John Jackson, the second son of his slighted sister Pall, was commissioned to make purchases for him in the course of an extensive European tour undertaken at Pepys' expense. His library abounds in French, Spanish and Italian works, besides many in Latin and Greek. Of German books he possessed none.

From 1700 onwards he lived at Clapham under the care of his loyal friend William Hewer. His long life was drawing to its close and his old enemy the stone made periodical and painful inroads upon his health. He died on May 26, 1703, at the age of seventy, and was buried beneath his wife's monument in St. Olave's church.

"If I were worth £2000," he had said to his wife in the early days of the Diary, "I would (and I could), be a Knight, and keep my coach." The second intention had long been realized, but the knighthood never came. Many other honours had fallen to him: he was elected President of the Royal Society in 1684 and 1685; he was Master of the Trinity House in 1676 and again in 1699; Master of the Clothworkers Company in 1677; Governor (1676) and Vice-President (1699) of Christ's Hospital; Baron of the Cinque Ports (1685); Deputy Lieutenant for Huntingdonshire (1685); Justice of the Peace for Middlesex, Essex, Kent and Southampton; Freeman of Portsmouth (1662), Newcastle (1682), and London (1699). In 1681 he was asked to stand for the Provostship of King's College, Cambridge. He was on several occasions returned as a 'Parliament man'; for Castle Rising in 1673, and for Harwich in 1679 and again in 1685. Nor were the consolations of wealth denied him; for the growth of his fortune, so faithfully recorded in the Diary, was continued in growing measure as time went on. At the opening of his career we see Pepys laying the cloth and his wife larding the pullets: at its close he was living in affluence, collecting rare books and commissioning the leading artist of the day to paint portraits of himself and his friends; and his financial condition was such that he could afford to write off as a bad debt the modern equivalent of £140,000, which he had been constrained to lend to the Stuart Kings—a debt which had been repudiated by the Crown after the Revolution.[1]

In appearance we may picture Pepys as a smallish man, bright-eyed and sprucely dressed. Dapper Dickey, he signed himself to Mrs. Knipp. He does not seem to have claimed a greater degree of beauty than his portraits warrant, for when his aunt commends the Queen's features he retorts "if my nose be handsome, then is hers." He probably never entirely shook off his country speech; at any rate he was past thirty when he admired Dr. Pierce on the ground that he was the only man that he could learn to pronounce by.

Of his many qualities the most marked were his astonishing physical energy and his industry. "For myself," he writes, "chance without merit brought me in, and diligence only keeps me so, and will, living as I do among so many lazy people that the diligent man becomes necessary." His day frequently begins at four in the morning; the one substantial meal of the day comes at noon, and we often find him still working at midnight. At any moment in this active life he is ready to get into the saddle and ride fifty miles along miry and unmetalled roads to Cambridge; on to Huntingdon the next day and back to London on the third, exclaiming next morning that he never felt better in his life.

Nor was his the phlegmatic temperament that makes little demand upon the physical constitution. Highly emotional, readily moved alike to a 'great transport of grief and cries' and to outbursts of passionate anger, susceptible in the highest degree to musical sounds, agape with a breathless curiosity, he lived his seventy years at a pace which must have broken a man not endowed

---

[1] It may be convenient here to note that the sums of money mentioned throughout the Diary should, on the average, be multiplied by five in order to arrive at their present-day value. Foodstuffs were cheaper, with the exception of bread, which was about the same; clothes, especially silks and finery, were vastly more expensive.

with quite unusual strength. What, not want to see the lions at the other end of the town? he would cry to honest Will Stankes up from the country, footsore and tired; great God, how could a man be so incurious! For himself he was with child to see any strange thing.

The fact is that in spite of his susceptibilities to female charms his was not the self-indulgent life that it is too often represented to have been. In an age of licence we see Pepys forswearing his fondness for wine, and looking 'something askew' upon dancing, gaming and swearing, the lax observance of Sunday, and the broad humour that marked the wedding frivolities of the day. The profligacy of the Court which had infected the stratum of society into which his natural abilities had led him, he regarded with the eye of one born to a straiter rule of life. True Londoner though he was in many respects, his spiritual home remained in those country parts which had produced a Cromwell and worshipped still a jealous God.

The original Diary is contained in six leather-bound octavo volumes, which stand on the shelves of the Pepys Library at Magdalene College. For a hundred years after Pepys' death it remained undeciphered. But the publication of Evelyn's Diary in 1818 suggested that equally interesting matter might lie concealed here, and one of the volumes was shown to Lord Grenville, who, if tradition in the College is correct, took it up to bed one evening and appeared at breakfast with the key. The original Diary was then handed over to John Smith, an undergraduate of St. John's College, who produced a complete transcription. The deciphering of three thousand pages of close and somewhat faint shorthand took him three years, working twelve hours a day— 'very trying and injurious indeed to the visual organs,' he said it was. The first edition, edited by the third Lord Braybrooke, brother of the Master of Magdalene, appeared in 1825; a second edition in 1828, a third, much enlarged, in 1848, and a fourth in 1854. This edition of 1854 is what is now known as the Braybrooke text. It comprises only a fraction of the whole Diary, and as an abridgment it faithfully reflects the taste of the period from which it dates.

The only other text now obtainable (if we except the Mynors Bright edition of 1875, of which only one thousand copies were printed) is that of the Wheatley edition, first published in ten volumes in 1893–1899, and reissued in 1923 in three volumes on India paper. This is, and will probably remain, the standard edition of Pepys' Diary. It runs to over three thousand pages, and contains the full text, with the exception of an occasional word or phrase which it is safe to say will never be put into print.

Its style, so artless and so effective, blossoms upon occasion into passages of extreme beauty. The description of the Great Fire is a *tour de force* by reason of its headlong narration of an event which in itself stirs the imagination. But in another vein the story of the courtship of Philip Carteret; the famous passage, beloved of Stevenson, in which Pepys describes the life of a shepherd on Epsom Downs; the intensely moving incident at the funeral of Sir Christopher Mings; the stereoscopic portraits such as that of poor Major Waters ("a deaf and most amorous melancoly gentleman, under a despayr in love, which makes him bad company, though a most good-natured man"); and not least the delicate glimpses of children with which the Diary abounds: these are the fruits of a mind keenly alive to the beauty and the poetry, as well as the humour, of life. In the six volumes of the original Diary there is scarcely a single erasure, and one cannot regard it as a fair copy in shorthand of a preliminary draft. Passages such as these derive their high impressiveness from the obvious sincerity with which Pepys sets down his reaction to the incidents which he records. Not for him the mental corsets of his friend John Evelyn, who had a part to sustain throughout the pages of his Diary. Writing for himself alone Pepys could afford to disregard the opinions of posterity: he needed not to refrain from sowing on account of the birds.

But the very frankness of the book challenges an equal degree of scrupulousness in those who dip with delight into its pages to-day. It is easy to compare Pepys as a public administrator with his modern counterpart without realizing that standards were very different in his day when, he says, "a purser without professed cheating is a professed loser, twice as much as he gets." "Good God!" he exclaims over a £3000 contract for masts, "to see what a man might do, were I a knave! the whole business from beginning to end done by me . . . but I hope my pains was such as the king has the best bargain of masts has been bought these 27 years."

Again, we are sometimes inclined to think and speak of the diarist as Old Pepys, and to regard many of his peculiarities as the foibles of an elderly man. But this he was not. He was twenty-seven when we are introduced, and only thirty-six when we part. If the book had been called from the first The Diary of a Young Man, Pepys would have been seen in a truer perspective. Nelson's diary, to take a hypothetical case, would do him less than justice if it ceased at the point where he was promoted lieutenant: Pepys perhaps suffers more, for the career of the most devoted civil servant lacks the lustre which surrounds the memory of a great commander. When we call him Old Pepys, even as a term of endearment, we are apt to deceive ourselves into taking his measure by the stature which he had attained in early middle age, to regard his youthful indiscretions in the wrong perspective, and to invest his hasty opinions with the balanced judgment of an experienced administrator. He lived, we know, to enjoy an honourable old age, in which his advice on many subjects was frequently sought; but those are not the years in which he stands stripped before us.

Moreover, the intimate form of a diary is not designed to exhibit the best side of its writer. If a man is no hero to his valet it is certain he will be still less so to his diary—unless he is writing for publication, which we are forced to believe that Pepys was not. To give him credit then for such actions as may reflect the finer side of his nature is only his due, for they are hidden almost as if by artifice beneath a pitiless chronicle of petty misdemeanours. When for instance irregularities in the private life of Lord Sandwich came to be spoken of at Court, Pepys staked his whole future, as he thought, upon a noble letter of reproof to his patron, basing it upon 'the duty which every bit of bread I eat tells me I owe to your Lordship.' During the Dutch Wars, when his colleagues had fled from the plague-stricken city, Pepys, alone at the Navy Office, wrote to Sir William Coventry, who was then serving with the fleet: "The sickness in general thickens round us, and particularly upon our neighbourhood. You, Sir, took your turn of the sword; I must not therefore grudge to take mine of the pestilence." These are not the words of a mean man; nor did he show himself lacking in fine qualities when on another occasion he approached the King himself on behalf of his cousin Kate Joyce, whose innkeeper husband had committed suicide, and would without Pepys' intervention thereby have forfeited his worldly goods.

Had Pepys realized that his Diary would come to be read not only by the townsfolk of the little timbered city which he knew, but wherever the English language is spoken, in lands of whose very existence he was ignorant, he would surely have given a different account of himself. For it is not possible to believe that he ever foresaw the extent to which the Diary would appeal to posterity. It may be that he meant to destroy the incriminating volumes, but was overtaken by death before he had steeled himself to the deed; but if so it is significant that he should have had them uniformly bound with the rest of his books, in the orderly sequence of which he had allotted them their due place according to their size. Conceivably he thought that they would never be deciphered; or more likely (for two clues to the shorthand exist in the Library) that their historical significance, dimly realized perhaps by himself, would remain in the cloistered seclusion of a college library, yielding some of their secrets to an occasional scholar as the centuries passed. Possibly in his later years he looked back with roguish complacency to this record of his salad days, reading it over and liking it very well, and wondering a little at himself at his vein at that time when he wrote it, as he says upon reviewing the romance which he wrote as an undergraduate. Who can say what reason operated thus to our great good fortune? The one thing that emerges, surely with unmistakable clarity, is that the Diary was not written with one eye on the reading public of the twentieth century—and it is safe to say that the reading public would not have read it had it been so.

O. F. M.

NOTE ON THE PEPYS FAMILY

OF Samuel Pepys' *brothers and sisters* three survived infancy:

1. THOMAS, whose death at the age of 30 is recorded in the Diary, took over the
tailor's shop from his father upon the retirement of the latter. But his
methods were fully as dilatory as his predecessor's had been, and upon his
death his brother had to pay £90 worth of his debts.

2. JOHN, who was born in 1641. He was educated at St. Paul's School and
Christ's College, Cambridge. Abandoning the intention of taking Holy
Orders he succeeded, jointly with Samuel's former clerk, to the Clerkship
of the Acts; and in 1670 he became Clerk to the Trinity House. But he
died unmarried in 1677, aged 36, leaving his brother to pay a debt of £300
to his employers.

3. PAULINA, born in 1640, and who, despite the uncomplimentary references to
her in the Diary, was the only one of the family to leave children. She married, in the Diary years, John Jackson of Brampton; her second son, John
Jackson, became Samuel Pepys' heir, and is the ancestor of the Pepys-Cock-
erell family.

Of Samuel Pepys' *aunts*, Mary Pepys married a fishmonger in London. William
WIGHT; Edith Pepys married one TRICE and caused trouble to Pepys at the time of
his Uncle Robert's death; Elizabeth Pepys married Richard BELL: and Jane
Pepys married John PERKIN, with whom she lived in poverty at Parson's Drove,
'a heathen place': all of these families are frequently mentioned in the Diary.
He had two *uncles*, ROBERT Pepys, who owned the estate at Brampton, and THOMAS
Pepys, who, with his son Thomas (who kept a hardware shop in St. Paul's Church-
yard) disputed Uncle Robert's will.

Samuel Pepys' *grandfather* had married a Day, and that name occurs in the
Diary; it was his sister Paulina, Pepys' Great-Aunt, who became the mother of
Lord SANDWICH, who was thus Pepys' first cousin once removed. Another brother
of that generation was TALBOT Pepys of Impington (Pepys' great-uncle) with whose
son ROGER (Pepys' first cousin once removed) we are brought in frequent contact;
and lastly, through the eldest brother came in the various second cousins SCOTT,
STRADWICK, and WRIGHT, whose names occur also from time to time.

The relationship with JANE TURNER and her daughter THE(ophila) Turner,
though more cordial, was far more remote. Jane Turner had been a Pepys, a
fourth cousin, only, of Samuel. There is a penumbra of remoter relations still;
Uncle FENNER and his daughter Kate JOYCE, for instance, who appear to have had
no ties of consanguinity.

THE NAVY BOARD

1. Lord High Admiral: JAMES, DUKE OF YORK, afterwards King James II.
2. The Treasurer: Sir George CARTERET till 1667, described by Clarendon as "undoubtedly as good, if not the best, seaman in England."

   The Earl of ANGLESEY, 1667-8, a painstaking and experienced finance minister.

   Sir Thomas OSBORNE
   Sir Thomas LITTLETON } 1668 onwards.

3. The Comptroller: Sir Robert SLYNGSBIE till 1661, the son of a former Comptroller, and a sea captain as early as 1663.
   Sir John MINNES, 1661 onwards, an experienced naval commander.
4. The Surveyor: Sir William BATTEN till 1677, surveyor also in King Charles I.'s reign, and an active naval commander. Col. Thomas MIDDLETON, 1677 onwards. Formerly resident Commissioner for Portsmouth.
5. The Clerk of the Acts: Samuel PEPYS.
6. Extra Commissioners:

   (a) Lord BERKELEY of Stratton, till 1665, an illustrious general.
       Sir Thomas HARVEY, 1665 onwards.

   (b) Sir William PENN, a distinguished admiral.

   (c) Peter PETT, a famous shipbuilder.

   (d) Sir William COVENTRY, M.P., secretary to the Duke of York.

   (e) Lord BROUNCKER, first President of the Royal Society.

To this Board Pepys was secretary, or Clerk of the Acts, and with the exception of Slingsbie and Coventry he has scarcely a good word to say for them, individually or collectively. Thus of the 'two doating knights,' Batten and Penn, the one is a knave and a sot, the other a counterfeit rogue; Lord Berkeley is a great vapourer; Lord Brouncker a rotten-hearted, false man; Sir Thomas Harvey a very droll; and Sir John Minnes, though a fine gentleman and a scholar, is nothing but a jester. Pepys found them excellent company at dinner; but professionally they are either dismissed as incompetent idlers or plied with invective when they stir. History does not bear out this view of Pepys' colleagues, amongst whom he alone, though extremely efficient, was ignorant of naval matters—the 'business man' in a council of able and experienced experts.

ROYALTY

King CHARLES II. (1630–1685). Married in 1662 to Katherine, daughter of John, Duke of Braganza, later King John IV. of Portugal. She bore him no children.

JAMES, Duke of York (1633–1701), brother of Charles II. Married secretly in 1660 Anne Hyde, daugher of Lord Clarendon. Of their children only two survived childhood: Mary (b. 1662), wife of William III., and Anne (b. 1665), who succeeded her sister on the throne.

HENRY, Duke of Gloucester (1639–1660), younger brother of Charles and James; his death from smallpox is recorded in the Diary.

MARY, Princess Royal (1631–1660), eldest sister of the above. She married William Prince of Orange, and became the mother of King William III., who thus married his first cousin. She died at Whitehall of smallpox while on a visit to England.

HENRIETTA MARIA, the Queen-Mother (1609–1669), aunt of Louis XIV. Married Charles I., 1625.

Prince RUPERT (1619–1682), first cousin to Charles II. and the Duke of York: son of Charles I.'s sister Elizabeth, Queen of Bohemia. An illustrious commander, both on land during the Civil Wars and at sea against the Dutch after the Restoration.

JAMES, Duke of Monmouth (1649–1685), natural son of Charles II. by Lucy Walters. Known in boyhood as James Crofts. Married in 1663 Anne Scott, Countess of Buccleuch, took the name Scott and was made Duke of Buccleuch. He was executed upon the failure of his attempt to seize the throne in 1685.

FIRST YEAR

1660

BLESSED be God, at the end of the last year I was in very good health, without any sense of my old pain,[1] but upon taking of cold. I lived in Axe Yard,[2] having my wife and servant Jane, and no more in family than us three.

The condition of the State was thus; viz. the Rump, after being disturbed by my Lord Lambert, was lately returned to sit again. The officers of the Army all forced to yield. Lawson lies still in the river, and Monk is with his army in Scotland. The new Common Council of the City do speak very high; and had sent to Monk their sword-bearer, to acquaint him with their desires for a free and full Parliament. My own private condition very handsome, and esteemed rich, but indeed very poor; besides my goods of my house, and my office, which at present is somewhat uncertain. Mr. Downing master of my office.[3]

January 1st. (Lord's Day.) This morning (we living lately in the garret) I rose, put on my suit with great skirts, having not lately worn any other clothes but them. Went to Mr. Gunning's chapel at Exeter House, where he made a very good sermon. Dined at home in the garret, where my wife dressed the remains of a turkey, and in the doing of it she burned her hand.

2nd. In the morning before I went forth old East brought me a dozen of bottles of sack, and I gave him a shilling for his pains. Then I went to Mr. Sheply,[4] who was drawing of sack in the wine cellar to send to other places as a gift from my Lord,[5] and told me that my Lord had given him order to give me the dozen of bottles. Then I went to Mr. Crew's[6] and borrowed £10 of Mr. Andrewes for my own use, and so went to my office, where there was nothing to do.

[1] Pepys had been cut for the stone on March 26, 1658.   [2] In Westminster.
[3] Pepys was a clerk in the Receipt of the Exchequer office.
[4] A servant of "my Lord's" and steward at his country seat, Hinchingbrooke.
[5] Sir Edward Montagu, afterwards created Earl of Sandwich. Through his mother (Paulina Pepys) he was a cousin of Pepys'. At this time he was a man of thirty-five.
[6] John Crew, afterwards Baron Crew of Stene, Sir Edward Montagu's father-in-law.

1

5th. Dined with Mr. Sheply, at my Lord's lodgings, upon his turkey-pie. And so to my office again, where the Excise money was brought, and some of it told to soldiers till it was dark. Then I went home, and after writing a letter to my Lord, and told him the news that Monk and Fairfax were commanded up to town, and that the Prince's lodgings were to be provided for Monk at Whitehall.

8th. (Sunday.) In the morning I went to Mr. Gunning's, where a good sermon, wherein he showed the life of Christ, and told us good authority for us to believe that Christ did follow his father's trade, and was a carpenter till thirty years of age. From thence to my father's to dinner, where I found my wife, who was forced to dine there, we not having one coal of fire in the house and it being very hard frosty weather.

9th. For these two or three days I have been much troubled with thoughts how to get money to pay them that I have borrowed money of, by reason of my money being in my uncle's hands.

13th. To my office, where nothing to do. So to Will's with Mr. Pinkney,[1] who invited me to their feast at his Hall the next Monday. Thence I went home and took my wife and dined at Mr. Wade's. From thence home again, and my wife was very unwilling to let me go forth, but with some discontent would go out if I did, and I going forth towards Whitehall I saw she followed me, and so I staid and took her round through Whitehall, and so carried her home angry.

15th. Having been exceedingly disturbed in the night with the barking of a dog of one of our neighbours that I could not sleep for an hour or two I slept late, and then in the morning took physic, and so staid within all day. At noon my brother John [2] came to me, and I corrected as well as I could his Greek speech to say at the Apposition, though I believe he himself was as well able to do it as myself.

16th. In the morning I went up to Mr. Crew's, and at his bedside he did talk to me concerning things of state, and expressed his mind how just it was that the secluded members should come to sit again. I went from thence, and in my way went into an alehouse and drank my morning draft with Matthew Andrews and two or three more of his friends, coachmen. From thence to my office, where nothing to do. At noon, Harry Ethall came to

---

[1] A Teller of the Receipt of the Exchequer.
[2] John Pepys, then a schoolboy at St. Paul's.

"DINED AT HOME IN THE GARRET"

me and we went to the Clerks, where in a closet we had a very good dinner by Mr. Pinkney's courtesy, and after dinner we went to the Green Dragon, on Lambeth Hill, and there we sang of all sorts of things, and I ventured with good success upon things at first sight; and after that I played on my flageolet, and staid there till nine o'clock, very merry and drawn on with one song after another till it came to be so late. So parted, and thence home, where I found my wife and maid a-washing. I staid up till the bell-man came by with his bell just under my window as I was writing of this very line, and cried, "Past one of the clock, and a cold, frosty, windy morning." I then went to bed, and left my wife and the maid a-washing still.

17th. To Whitehall, and coming back turned in at Harper's, where Jack Price was, and I drank with him and he told me among other things how much the Protector [1] is altered, though he would seem to bear out his trouble very well, yet he is scarce able to talk sense with a man; and how he will say that "Who should a man trust, if he may not trust to a brother and an uncle"; and "How much those men have to answer before God Almighty, for their playing the knave with him as they did." He told me also, that there was £100,000 offered, and would have been taken, for his restitution, had not the Parliament come in as they did again; and that he do believe that the Protector will live to give a tes- timony of his valour and revenge yet before he dies, and that the Protector will say so himself sometimes.

19th. This morning I was sent for to Mr. Downing, and at his bed side he told me that he had a kindness for me, and that he thought that he had done me one; and that was that he had got me to be one of the Clerks of the Council, at which I was a little stumbled, and could not tell what to do, whether to thank him or no; but by and by I did, but not very heartily, for I feared that his doing of it was but only to ease himself of the salary [2] which he gives me. Thence to my office, and so with Mr. Sheply and Moore [3] to dine upon a turkey with Mrs. Jem[4]; and after that to the French Ordinary, where Mr. Downing this day feasted Sir Arth. Hasel- rigge and a great many more of the Parliament, and did stay to put him in mind of me.

---

[1] Richard, third son of Oliver Cromwell.
[2] The salary appears to have been £50 a year.
[3] Mr. Moore was a poor relation of Sir Edward Montagu's.
[4] Jemimah, daughter of Sir Edward Montagu, afterwards Lady Carteret. She was only twelve at this time. "Mrs." was used indiscriminately for girls and married women.

22nd. I went in the morning to Mr. Messum's,[1] where I met with W. Thurburn and sat with him in his pew. A very eloquent sermon about the duty of all to give good example in our lives and conversation, which I fear he himself was most guilty of not doing. After sermon, at the door by appointment my wife met me, and so to my father's [2] to dinner, where we had not been to my shame in a fortnight before.

23rd. To my office, and there did nothing but make up my balance. Came home and found my wife dressing of the girl's head, by which she was made to look very pretty. I went out and paid Wilkinson what I did owe him, and brought a piece of beef home for dinner. Went to see Mrs. Jem, where I found my Lady Wright.[3] Here I staid and made up Mrs. Ann's [4] bills, and played a game or two at cards, and thence to Westminster Hall, it being very dark.

24th. Took my wife to Mr. Pierce's,[5] she in the way being exceedingly troubled with a pair of new pattens, and I vexed to go so slow, it being late. There when we came we found Mrs. Carrick very fine, and one Mr. Lucy, who called one another husband and wife, and after dinner a great deal of mad stir. There was pulling of Mrs. bride's and Mr. bridegroom's ribbons, with a great deal of fooling among them that I and my wife did not like. Mr. Lucy and several other gentlemen coming in after dinner, swearing and singing as if they were mad, only he singing very handsomely. Taking leave I went to speak with Mr. Crumlum.[6] He gave directions what to do about getting my brother an exhibition, and spoke very well of my brother. Thence back with my father home, where he and I spoke privately in the little room to my sister Pall [7] about stealing of things as my wife's scissars and my maid's book, at which my father was much troubled.

This day the Parliament gave order that the late Committee of Safety should come before them this day se'n-night, and all their papers and their model of Government that they had made to be brought in with them. So home and talked with my wife about our dinner on Thursday.

25th. To my Lady Wright to speak with her, but she was abroad, so Mr. Evans, her butler, had me into his buttery, and gave me sack and a lesson on his lute, which he played very well.

[1] Dr. Robert Mossum: later Bishop of Derry.   [2] John Pepys, a tailor.
[3] Sister to Lady Montagu.   [4] Lady Jem's maid.
[5] Mr. James Pierce, a surgeon, who had operated on Pepys for the stone.
[6] Samuel Cromleholme, Master of St. Paul's School.   [7] Paulina Pepys.

Thence I went to my Lord's and got most things ready against to-morrow, as fires and laying the cloth, and my wife was making of her tarts and larding of her pullets till eleven o'clock.

26th. Home from my office to my Lord's lodgings where my wife had got ready a very fine dinner—viz. a dish of marrow bones; a leg of mutton; a loin of veal; a dish of fowl, three pullets, and two dozen of larks all in a dish; a great tart, a neat's tongue, a dish of anchovies; a dish of prawns and cheese. My company was my father, my uncle Fenner, his two sons,[1] Mr. Pierce, and all their wives, and my brother Tom. We were as merry as I could frame myself to be in the company. W. Joyce, talking after the old rate and drinking hard, vexed his father and mother and wife. And I did perceive that Mrs. Pierce her coming so gallant, that it put the two young women quite out of courage.

29th. Spent the afternoon in casting up my accounts, and do find myself to be worth £40 and more, which I did not think, but am afraid that I have forgot something.

30th. This morning, before I was up, I fell a-singing of my song, "Great, good, and just," [2] &c., and put myself thereby in mind that this was the fatal day, now ten years since, his Majesty died. There seems now to be a general cease of talk, it being taken for granted that Monk do resolve to stand to the Parliament, and nothing else. Spent a little time this night in knocking up nails for my hat and cloaks in my chamber.

February 3rd. Mrs. Turner [3] and I and Joyce went walking all over White Hall, whither General Monk was newly come, and we saw all his forces march by in very good plight and stout officers. Thence to my house where we dined, but with a great deal of patience, for the mutton came in raw, and so we were fain to stay the stewing of it. In the meantime we sat studying a Posy [4] for a ring for her which she is to have at Roger Pepys [5] his wedding. After dinner I left them and went to hear news, but only found that the Parliament House was most of them with Monk at White Hall, and that in his passing through the town he had many calls to him for a free Parliament, but little other welcome. The town and guards are already full of Monk's soldiers. I returned, and it growing dark I and they went to take a turn

---

[1] *i. e.* his sons-in-law Anthony and William Joyce.
[2] The opening lines of the Marquis of Montrose's verses on the execution of King Charles I.
[3] The wife of Sergeant John Turner and a descendant of William Pepys of Cottenham.
[4] A motto to be engraved on the ring.
[5] A cousin, at this time aged about thirty-nine. Son of Talbot Pepys of Impington.

in the park, where Theoph.[1] (who was sent for to us to dinner) outran my wife and another poor woman, that laid a pot of ale with me that she would outrun her. After that I set them as far as Charing Cross, and there left them and my wife, and I went to see Mrs. Ann, who began very high about a flock bed I sent her, but I took her down. Here I played at cards till 9 o'clock. So home and to bed.

9th. To Westminster up and down the Hall, where I heard an action very finely pleaded between my Lord Dorset and some other noble persons, his lady and other ladies of quality being here, and it was about £330 per annum that was to be paid to a poor Spittal,[2] which was given by some of his predecessors; and given on his side.

11th. At noon I walked in the Hall, where I heard the news of a letter from Monk, who did resolve to stand for the sudden filling up of the House, and it was very strange how the countenance of men in the Hall was all changed with joy in half an hour's time. I went alone to Guildhall to see whether Monk was come or no, and met with him coming out of the chamber where he had been with the Mayor and Aldermen, but such a shout I never heard in all my life, crying out, "God bless your Excellence." Here I met with Mr. Lock,[3] and took him to an alehouse, and left him there to fetch Chetwind; when we were come together, Lock told us the substance of the letter that went from Monk to the Parliament, wherein, he [Monk] do desire that all writs for filling up of the House be issued by Friday next.

14th. Called out in the morning by Mr. Moore, whose voice my wife hearing in my dressing-chamber with me, got herself ready, and came down and challenged him for her valentine, this being the day.

16th. To my office, where I wrote by the carrier to my Lord and sealed my letter at Will's. Here I met with Osborne and with Shaw and Spicer, and we went to the Sun Tavern, where we had sent us only two trenchers full of meat, and here we staid till seven at night, I winning a quart of sack of Shaw that one trencherfull that was sent us was all lamb and he that it was veal. I by having but 3*d.* in my pocket made shift to spend no more, whereas if I had had more I had spent more as the rest did, so that I see it is an

---

[1] Theophila, Mrs. Turner's daughter.
[2] Sackville College for the poor, at East Grinstead.
[3] Matthew Lock, the musician, later composer in ordinary to the king.

advantage to a man to carry little in his pocket. Home, and after supper, and a little at my flute, I went to bed.

19th. (Lord's Day.) Met with Mr. Moore, and went home with him to dinner. He told me that there is great likelihood that the secluded members will come in, and so Mr. Crew and my Lord are likely to be great men, at which I was very glad.

20th. My brother John came to dine with me. After dinner I took him to my study at home and at my Lord's, and gave him some books and other things against his going to Cambridge.

21st. Mr. Crew bid me come to his house, which I did, and he would have me dine with him, which I did; and he very joyful told me that the House had made General Monk General of all the Forces in England, Scotland, and Ireland; and that upon Monk's desire, for the service that Lawson had lately done in pulling down the Committee of Safety, he had the command of the Sea for the time being. He advised me to send for my Lord forthwith, and told me that there is no question that, if he will, he may now be employed again; and that the House do intend to do nothing more than to issue writs, and to settle a foundation for a free Parliament. After dinner I back to Westminster Hall with him in his coach. Here I met with Mr. Lock and Pursell,[1] Masters of Music, and with them to the Coffee House, into a room next the water. Here we had variety of brave Italian and Spanish songs, and a canon for eight voices which Mr. Lock had lately made on these words: "Domine salvum fac Regem," an admirable thing. Here out of the window it was a most pleasant sight to see the City from one end to the other with a glory about it, so high was the light of the bonfires, and so thick round the City, and the bells rang everywhere. Hence home and wrote to my Lord.

22nd. In the morning intended to have gone to Mr. Crew's to borrow some money, but it raining I forbore, and went to my Lord's lodging and look that all things were well there. Then home and sang a song to my viall, so to my office and to Will's, where Mr. Pierce found me out, and told me that he would go with me to Cambridge, where Colonel Ayre's regiment, to which he was surgeon, lieth. Walking in the Hall, I saw Major-General Brown, who had a long time been banished by the Rump, but now with his beard overgrown he comes abroad and sat in the House. To my father's to dinner, where nothing but a small dish of pow-

---

[1] Henry Purcell, father of the composer.

dered [1] beef and dish of carrots, they being all busy to get things ready for my brother John to go. After dinner, my wife staying there, I went to Mr. Crew's, and got £5 of Mr. Andrews. Home for my lanthorn and so to my father's, where I directed John what books to put for Cambridge. After that to supper, where my Uncle Fenner and my Aunt, The. Turner, and Joyce, at a brave leg of veal roasted, and were very merry against John's going to Cambridge.

23rd. Thursday, my birthday, now twenty-seven years. A pretty fair morning, I rose and after writing a while in my study I went forth. To my office, where I told Mr. Hawly of my thoughts to go out of town to-morrow. Hither Mr. Fuller comes to me and my Uncle Thomas [2] too, thence I took them to drink, and so put off my uncle. So with Mr. Fuller home to my house, where he dined with me, and I to Whitehall, where I was to see my horse which Mr. Garthwayt lends me to-morrow. So home, where Mr. Pierce comes to me about appointing time and place where and when to meet to-morrow. So to Westminster Hall, where, after the House rose, I met with Mr. Crew, who told me that my Lord was chosen by 73 voices, to be one of the Council of State. Home and wrote to my Lord the news of the choice of the Council by the post, and so to bed.

24th. I rose very early, and taking horse at Scotland Yard I rode to Mr. Pierce's; and so we set forth about seven of the clock, the day and the way very foul. At Puckeridge we baited. Then up again and as far as Foulmer, within six miles of Cambridge, where we lay at the Chequer. Next morning we come to Cambridge by eight o'clock.

25th. To the Falcon, in the Petty Cury. After dressing myself, about ten o'clock, my father, brother, and I to Mr. Widdrington, at Christ's College, who received us very civilly, and caused my brother to be admitted, while my father, he, and I, sat talking. After that done, we take leave. My father and brother went to visit some friends, Pepys's, scholars in Cambridge, while I went to Magdalene College, to Mr. Hill, with whom I found Mr. Zanchy, Burton, [3] and Hollins, and was exceedingly civilly received by them. I took leave on promise to sup with them, and to my Inn again, where I dined with some others that were there at an ordinary. After dinner my brother to the College, and my father and I to my

---

[1] Salted. [2] Thomas Pepys.
[3] Hill, Zanchy and Burton were Fellows of Magdalene College.

Cozen Angier's, to see them, where Mr. Fairbrother [1] came to us. Here we sat a while talking. My father he went to look after his things at the carrier's, and my brother's chamber, while Mr. Fairbrother, my Cozen Angier, and Mr. Zanchy, whom I met at Mr. Merton's shop (where I bought *Elenchus Motuum*, having given my former to Mr. Downing when he was here), to the Three Tuns, where we drank pretty hard and many healths to the King, etc., till it began to be darkish: then we broke up and I and Mr. Zanchy went to Magdalene College, where a very handsome supper at Mr. Hill's chambers, I suppose upon a club [2] among them, where in their discourse I could find that there was nothing at all left of the old preciseness in their discourse, especially on Saturday nights. And Mr. Zanchy told me that there was no such thing now-a-days among them at any time. After supper and some discourse, then to my Inn.

26th. (Sunday.) My brother went to the College to Chapel. My father and I went out in the morning, and walked out in the fields behind King's College, and in King's College Chapel Yard, where we met with Mr. Fairbrother, who took us to Botolph's Church, where we heard Mr. Nicholas, of Queen's College, who I knew in my time to be Tripos,[3] with great applause, upon this text, "For thy commandments are broad." Thence my father and I to Mr. Widdrington's chamber to dinner, where he used us very courteously again. By and by my father, Mr. Zanchy, and I to my Cosen Angier to supper, where I caused two bottles of wine to be carried from the Rose Tavern; that was drunk up, and I had not the wit to let them know at table that it was I that paid for them, and so I lost my thanks for them. After supper we sat down and talked; I took leave of all my friends, and so to my Inn, and so to bed.

27th. Up by four o'clock, and after I was ready, took my leave of my father, whom I left in bed, and the same of my brother John, to whom I gave 10*s.* Mr. Blayton and I took horse and straight to Saffron Walden, where at the White Hart we set up our horses, and took the master of the house to shew us Audley End House, who took us on foot through the park, and so to the house, where the housekeeper shewed us all the house, in which the stateliness of the ceilings, chimney-pieces, and form of the whole was exceedingly worth seeing. He took us into the cellar,

---

[1] William Fairbrother: Fellow of King's College.   [2] *i. e.* sharing the expense.
[3] The Tripos, or Bachelor of the Stool, who made a speech on Ash Wednesday at the bidding of the Senior Proctor.

where we drank most admirable drink, a health to the King. Here I played on my flageolette, there being an excellent echo. He shewed us excellent pictures; two especially, those of the four Evangelists and Henry VIII. After that I gave the man 2s. for his trouble, and went back again. In our going, my landlord carried us through a very old hospital or almshouse,[1] where forty poor people was maintained; a very old foundation; and over the chimney in the mantel-piece was an inscription in brass: "Orate pro animâ Thomæ Bird", &c.; and the poor box also was on the same chimney-piece, with an iron door and locks to it, into which I put 6d. They brought me a draft of their drink in a brown bowl, tipt with silver, which I drank off, and at the bottom was a picture of the Virgin and the Child in her arms, done in silver. So we went to our Inn, and after eating of something, and kissed the daughter of the house, she being very pretty, we took leave; and so that night, the road pretty good but the weather rainy, to Epping, where we sat and played a game at cards, and after supper, and some merry talk with a plain bold maid of the house, we went to bed.

28th. Up in the morning, and had some red herrings to our breakfast, while my boot-heel was a-mending; by the same token the boy left the hole as big as it was before. Then to horse, and for London through the forest. We found the shops all shut, and the militia of the red regiment in arms at the Old Exchange, among whom I found and spoke to Nich. Osborne, who told me that it was a thanksgiving-day through the City for the return of the Parliament. So home, where my wife and all well. Shifted myself, and so to Mr. Crew's, and then to Sir Harry Wright's, where I found my Lord at dinner, who called for me in, and was glad to see me.

29th. To my office, and drank at Will's with Mr. Moore, who told me how my Lord is chosen General at Sea by the Council, and that it is thought that Monk will be joined with him therein.

March 2nd. This morning I went early to my Lord at Mr. Crew's where I spoke to him. Here were a great many come to see him, as Secretary Thurlow who is now by this Parliament chosen again Secretary of State. There were also General Monk's trumpeters to give my Lord a sound of their trumpets this morning. Thence I went to my office, and wrote a letter to Mr. Downing

---

[1] King Edward VI.'s almshouses, Saffron Walden.

about the business of his house. Great is the talk of a single person, and that it would now be Charles, George, or Richard again.[1] For the last of which, my Lord St. John is said to speak high. Great also is the dispute now in the House, in whose name the writs shall run for the next Parliament; and it is said that Mr. Prin, in open House, said, "In King Charles's."

3rd. After dinner I to Warwick House, in Holborn, to my Lord, where he dined with my Lord of Manchester, Sir Dudley North, my Lord Fiennes, and my Lord Barkly. I staid in the great hall, talking with some gentlemen there, till they all come out. Then I, by coach with my Lord, to Mr. Crew's, in our way talking of publick things, and how I should look after getting of his Commissioner's despatch. He told me he feared there was new design hatching, as if Monk had a mind to get into the saddle.

5th. To Westminster by water, seeing Mr. Pinkney at his own house, where he shewed me how he had alway kept the Lion and Unicorn, in the back of his chimney bright, in expectation of the King's coming again. At home I found Mr. Hunt, who told me how the Parliament had voted that the Covenant be printed and hung in churches again. Great hopes of the King's coming again. To bed.

6th. (Shrove Tuesday.) I called Mr. Sheply and we both went up to my Lord's lodgings at Mr. Crew's, where he bade us to go home again, and get a fire against an hour after. Which we did at White Hall, whither he came, and after talking with him and me about his going to sea, he called me by myself to go along with him into the garden, where he asked me how things were with me, and what he had endeavoured to do with my uncle [2] to get him to do something for me but he would say nothing too. He likewise bade me look out now at this turn some good place, and he would use all his own, and all the interest of his friends that he had in England, to do me good. And asked me whether I could, without too much inconvenience, go to sea as his secretary, and bid me think of it. He told me also, that he did believe the King would come in, and did discourse with me about it, and about the affection of the people and City, at which I was full glad.

After he was gone, I went up to my office. Here comes my uncle Tom, whom I took to Will's and drank with; poor man, he comes to inquire about the knights of Windsor,[3] of which he desires

[1] Charles II., George Monk, or Richard Cromwell.
[2] Robert Pepys, who lived at Brampton, near "my Lord's" country seat, Hinchingbroke.
[3] The Poor Knights of Windsor, instituted by King Edward III.

to get to be one. While we were drinking, in comes Mr. Day, a carpenter in Westminster, to tell me that it was Shrove Tuesday, and that I must go with him to their yearly Club upon this day, which I confess I had quite forgot. So I went to the Bell, where were Mr. Eglin, Veezy, Vincent a butcher, one more, and Mr. Tanner, with whom I played upon a viall, and he a viallin, after dinner, and were very merry, with a special good dinner, a leg of veal and bacon, two capons and sausages and fritters, with abundance of wine. After that I went to see Mrs. Jem, at whose chamber door I found a couple of ladies, but she not being there, we hunted her out, and found that she and another had hid themselves behind a door. Well, they all went down into the dining-room, where it was full of tag, rag, and bobtail, dancing, singing, and drinking, of which I was ashamed; and after I had staid a dance or two I went away.

This day I hear that the Lords do intend to sit, and great store of them are now in town, and I see in the Hall to-day. Overton at Hull do stand out, but can, it is thought, do nothing; and Lawson, it is said, is gone with some ships thither, but all that is nothing. My Lord told me that there was great endeavours to bring in the Protector again; but he told me too that he did believe it would not last long if he were brought in; no, nor the King neither (though he seems to think that he will come in), unless he carry himself very soberly and well. Every body now drinks the King's health without any fear, whereas before it was very private that a man dare do it. Monk this day is feasted at Mercer's Hall, and is invited one after another to all the twelve halls in London. Many think that he is honest yet, and some or more think him to be a fool that would raise himself, but think that he will undo himself by endeavouring it. My mind, I must needs remember, has been very much eased and joyed at my Lord's great expressions of kindness this day, and in discourse thereupon my wife and I lay awake an hour or two in our bed.

7th. (Ash Wednesday.) In the morning I went to my Lord at Mr. Crew's. In my way Washington overtook me and told me upon my question whether he knew of any place now void that I might have, by power over friends, that this day Mr. G. Montagu [1] was to be made Custos Rotulorum for Westminster, and that by friends I might get to be named by him Clerk of the Peace, with

---

[1] George Montagu, brother of Lord Manchester, and father of the first Earl of Halifax. Later M. P. for Dover.

"TO MY FATHER'S, WHOM I TOOK IN HIS CUTTING HOUSE"

which I was, as I am at all new things, very much joyed. So when I came to Mr. Crew's, I spoke to my Lord about it, who told me he believed Mr. Montagu had already promised it, and that it was given him only that he might gratify one person with the place I look for. He did give me the best advice that he could what was best for me, whether to stay or go with him, and offered all the ways that could be, how he might do me good, with the greatest liberty and love that could be.

My father newly come home from Brampton very well. He left my uncle with his leg very dangerous, and do believe he cannot continue in that condition long. He tells me that my uncle did acquaint him very largely what he did intend to do with his estate, to make me his heir and give my brother Tom something, and that my father and mother should have likewise something, to raise portions for John and Pall. I pray God he may be as good as his word. Going home I called at Wotton's and took home a piece of cheese. At home Mr. Sheply sat with me a little while, and so we all to bed. This news and my Lord's great kindness makes me very cheerful within. I pray God make me thankful.

9th. To my Lord at his lodging, and came to Westminster with him in the coach, and he in the Painted Chamber walked a good while; and I telling him that I was willing and ready to go with him to sea, he agreed that I should, and advised me what to write to Mr. Downing about it, which I did at my office, that by my Lord's desire I offered that my place might for a while be supplied by Mr. Moore, and that I and my security should be bound by the same bond for him. All night troubled in my thoughts how to order my business upon this great change with me that I could not sleep, and being overheated with drink I made a promise the next morning to drink no strong drink this week, for I find that it makes me sweat and puts me quite out of order. I hear that it is resolved privately that a treaty be offered with the King.

10th. In the morning went to my father's, whom I took in his cutting house, and there I told him my resolution to go to sea with my Lord, and consulted with him how to dispose of my wife, and we resolve of letting her be at Mr. Bowyer's.[1] By coach home, where I took occasion to tell my wife of my going to sea, who was much troubled at it, and was with some dispute at last willing to continue at Mr. Bowyer's in my absence. She was late

---

1 Of Huntsmore, Bucks, an old friend of Pepys.

making of caps for me, and the wench making an end of a pair of stockings that she was knitting of. So to bed.

12th. This day the wench rose at two in the morning to wash, and my wife and I lay talking a great while. My wife and I to the Exchange,[1] where we bought a great many things, where I left her and went into London.

13th. Eight o'clock at my Lord's lodgings, who told me that I was to be secretary, and Creed [2] to be deputy treasurer to the Fleet, at which I was troubled, but I could not help it. Things seem very doubtful what will be the end of all; for the Parliament seems to be strong for the King, while the soldiers do all talk against.

14th. To my Lord, where infinity of applications to him and to me. To my great trouble, my Lord gives me all the papers that was given to him, to put in order and give him an account of them. I went hence to St. James's and Mr. Pierce the surgeon with me, to speak with Mr. Clerke, Monk's secretary, about getting some soldiers removed out of Huntingdon to Oundle, which my Lord told me he did to do a courtesy to the town. This done (where I saw General Monk and methought he seemed a dull heavy man), he and I to Whitehall, where with Luellin [3] we dined at Marsh's. Went to the Admiralty, where a strange thing how I am already courted by the people. This morning among others that came to me I hired a boy of Jenkins of Westminster, and Burr to be my clerk. This night I went to Mr. Creed's chamber where he gave me the former book of the proceedings in the fleet and the Seal.

15th. Early packing up my things to be sent by cart with the rest of my Lord's. So to Will's, where I took leave of some of my friends. Here I met Tom Alcock, one that went to school with me at Huntingdon, but I had not seen him these sixteen years.

16th. To Westminster Hall, where I heard how the Parliament had this day dissolved themselves, and did pass very cheerfully through the Hall, and the Speaker without his mace. The whole Hall was joyful thereat, as well as themselves, and now they begin to talk loud of the King. From the Hall I went home to bed, very sad in mind to part with my wife, but God's will be done.

---

[1] In the Strand. It was built with cellars below, a walk above, and rows of shops over that, chiefly milliners, sempstresses, and the like.
[2] John Creed of Oundle: a protégé of "my Lord's," of whom Pepys was always jealous.
[3] Peter Luellin, a clerk of the Council.

17th. This morning bade adieu in bed to the company of my wife. We rose and I gave my wife some money to serve her for a time, and what papers of consequence I had. Then I left her to get her ready and went to my Lord's with my boy Eliezer to my Lord's lodging at Mr. Crew's. Here I had much business with my Lord, and papers, great store, given me by my Lord to dispose of as of the rest. After that, with Mr. Moore home to my house and took my wife by coach to the Chequer in Holborn, where, after we had drank, &c., she took coach and so farewell. This day (in the presence of Mr. Moore who made it, and Mr. Hawly), I did before I went out with my wife, seal my will to her, whereby I did give her all that I have in the world, but my books which I give to my brother John, excepting only French books, which my wife is to have.

18th. I rose early and went to the barber's (Jervas) in Palace Yard and I was trimmed by him, and afterwards drank with him a cup or two of ale, and did begin to hire his man to go with me to sea. Called at Mr. Blagrave's, where I took up my note that he had of mine for 40*s.*, which he two years ago did give me as a pawn while he had my lute. So that all things are even between him and I.

19th. Early to my Lord, where infinity of business to do, which makes my head full; and indeed for these two or three days I have not been without a great many cares and thoughts concerning them. My mind is still much troubled for my poor wife, but I hope that this undertaking will be worth my pains. To Whitehall and staid about business at the Admiralty late.

23rd. Up early, carried my Lord's will in a black box to Mr. William Montagu [1] for him to keep for him. Then to the barber's and put on my cravat there. So to my Lord again, who was almost ready to be gone and had staid for me. Hither came Gilb. Holland, and brought me a stick rapier, and Shelston a sugar-loaf, and had brought his wife who he said was a very pretty woman to the Ship tavern hard by for me to see but I could not go. Young Reeve also brought me a little perspective glass which I bought for my Lord; it cost me 8*s.* So after that to the Tower, where the barges staid for us; my Lord and the Captain in one, and W. Howe and I, &c., in the other, to the Long Reach,[2] where the Swiftsure lay at anchor. Soon as my Lord on board, the guns went off bravely from the ships. And a little while after comes the Vice-Admiral Lawson,

---

[1] First cousin to Sir Edward.   [2] Between Erith and Gravesend.

and seemed very respectful to my Lord, and so did the rest of the Commanders of the frigates that were thereabouts. I to the cabin allotted for me, which was the best that any had that belonged to my Lord. I got out some things out of my chest for writing and to work presently, Mr. Burr and I both. I supped at the deck table with Mr. Sheply. After that to bed in my cabin, which was but short; however, I made shift with it and slept very well, and the weather being good I was not sick at all, yet I know not what I shall be.

24th. At work hard all the day writing letters to the Council, &c. The boy Eliezer flung down a can of beer upon my papers which made me give him a box of the ear, it having all spoiled my papers and cost me a great deal of work. So to bed.

25th. (Lord's Day.) About two o'clock in the morning, letters came from London by our coxon, so they waked me, but I would not rise but bid him stay till morning, which he did, and then I rose and carried them in to my Lord, who read them a-bed. There was also one for me from Mr. Blackburne,[1] who with his own hand superscribes it to S. P. Esq., of which God knows I was not a little proud. Up into the great cabin above to dinner with the Captain, where was Captain Isham and all the officers of the ship. I took place of all but the Captains. After dinner I wrote a great many letters to my friends at London.

26th. This day it is two years since it pleased God that I was cut of the stone at Mrs. Turner's in Salisbury Court, and did resolve while I live to keep it a festival, as I did the last year at my house, and for ever to have Mrs. Turner and her company with me. But now it pleases God that I am where I am and so prevented to do it openly; only within my soul I can and do rejoice, and bless God, being at this time, blessed be his holy name, in as good health as ever I was in my life. This morning I rose early, and went about making of an establishment of the whole Fleet, and a list of all the ships, with the number of men and guns. Captain Cuttance[2] came and sat drinking a bottle of wine till eleven, a kindness he do not usually do the greatest officer in the ship. After that to bed.

30th. I was saluted in the morning with two letters, from some that I had done a favour to, which brought me in each a piece of gold. This day, while my Lord and we were at dinner, the Nazeby came in sight towards us, and at last came to anchor

---

[1] Secretary to the Admiralty.   [2] Captain, later Sir Roger, Cuttance, commander of the *Nazeby*.

close by us. After dinner my Lord and many others went on board
her, where every thing was out of order, and a new chimney made
for my Lord in his bedchamber, which he was much pleased with.
My Lord, in his discourse, discovered a great deal of love to this
ship.

31st. This morning, Mr. Hill that lives in Axe-yard was here
on board with the Vice-Admiral. I did give him a bottle of wine,
and was exceedingly satisfied of the power that I have to make
my friends welcome.

April 2nd. Up very early, and to get all my things and my
boy's [1] packed up. Great concourse of commanders here this
morning to take leave of my Lord upon his going into the Nazeby,
so that the table was full, so there dined below many commanders.
After dinner I went in one of the boats with my boy before my
Lord, and made shift before night to get my cabin in pretty good
order. It is but little, but very convenient, having one window to
the sea and another to the deck, and a good bed.

3rd. My heart exceeding heavy for not hearing of my dear
wife, and indeed I do not remember that ever my heart was so
apprehensive of her absence as at this very time.

4th. This morning I dispatch many letters of my own private
business to London. There come Colonel Thomson with the
wooden leg, and General Pen,[2] and dined with my Lord, and Mr.
Blackburne, who told me that it was certain now that the King
must of necessity come in, and that one of the Council told him
there is something doing in order to a treaty already among
them.

6th. This morning came my brother-in-law Balty [3] to see me,
and to desire to be here with me as Reformado,[4] which did much
trouble me. But after dinner (my Lord using him very civilly,
at table), I spoke to my Lord, and he presented me a letter to
Captain Stokes for him that he should be there. All the day with
him walking and talking, we under sail as far as the Spitts. In the
evening, it being fine moonshine, I staid late walking upon the
quarter-deck with Mr. Cuttance, learning of some sea terms.

7th. This day, about nine o'clock in the morning, the wind
grew high, and we being among the sands lay at anchor; I began to
be dizzy and squeamish. Before dinner my Lord sent for me down

---

[1] Eliezer; not to be confused with "my Lord's" son, whom Pepys alludes to later as "my boy" or
"the child."

[2] Admiral (afterwards Sir William) Penn, at this time aged thirty-nine.

[3] Balthasar St. Michel (aged about twenty), Mrs. Pepys' brother.

[4] A volunteer, serving without a commission but with the rank of an officer..

to eat some oysters, the best my Lord said that ever he ate in his life, though I have ate as good at Bardsey. After dinner, and all the afternoon, I walked upon the deck to keep myself from being sick, and at last about five o'clock, went to bed and got a caudle made me, and sleep upon it very well.

8th. (Lord's Day.) Very calm again, and I pretty well, but my head aked all day. About noon set sail; in our way I see many vessels and masts, which are now the greatest guides for ships.

9th. We having sailed all night, were come in sight of the Nore and South Forelands in the morning, and so sailed all day. In the afternoon we had a very fresh gale, which I brooked better than I thought I should be able to do. This afternoon I first saw France and Calais, with which I was much pleased, though it was at a distance. About five o'clock we came to the Goodwin, so to the Castles about Deal, where our Fleet lay, among whom we anchored. Great was the shout of guns from the castles and ships, and our answers, that I never heard yet so great rattling of guns. Nor could we see one another on board for the smoke that was among us, nor one ship from another.

10th. This morning many or most of the commanders in the Fleet came on board and dined here, so that some of them and I dined together in the Round-house, where we were very merry. Hither came the Vice-Admiral to us, and sat and talked and seemed a very good-natured man. At night as I was all alone in my cabin, in a melancholy fit playing on my viallin, my Lord and Sir R. Stayner [1] came into the coach [2] and supped there, and called me out to supper with them.

11th. I ate a good breakfast by my Lord's orders with him in the great cabin below. The wind all this day was very high, so that a gentleman that was at dinner with my Lord that came along with Sir John Bloys [3] (who seemed a fine man) was forced to rise from table. This afternoon came a great packet of letters from London directed to me, among the rest two from my wife, the first that I have since coming away from London. All the news from London is that things go on further towards a King. That the Skinners' Company the other day at their entertaining of General Monk had took down the Parliament Arms in their Hall, and set up the King's. In the evening my Lord and I had a great deal of discourse about the several Captains of the Fleet and his

[1] Rear-Admiral.
[2] Name for the quarters commonly assigned to the Flag-captain in a large warship.
[3] Probably Boys, the Royalist commander.

"A GENTLEMAN THAT WAS AT DINNER WITH MY LORD . . . WAS FORCED TO RISE FROM TABLE"

interest among them, and had his mind clear to bring in the King. He confessed to me that he was not sure of his own Captain [Cuttance] to be true to him, and that he did not like Captain Stokes.

It comes into my mind to observe that I am sensible that I have been a little too free to make mirth with the minister of our ship, he being a very sober and an upright man.

18th. I all the afternoon dictating in my cabin (my own head being troubled with multiplicity of business) to Burr, who wrote for me above a dozen letters, by which I have made my mind more light and clear than I have had it yet since I came on board. At night sent a packet to London, and Mr. Cook returned hence bringing me this news, that the Sectaries do talk high what they will do, but I believe all to no purpose; but the Cavaliers are something unwise to talk so high on the other side as they do. That it is evident now that the General and the Council do resolve to make way for the King's coming. And it is now clear that either the Fanatiques [1] must now be undone, or the gentry and citizens throughout England, and clergy, must fall, in spite of their militia and army, which is not at all possible I think. To bed, and W. Howe sat by my bed-side, and he and I sang a psalm or two and so I to sleep.

20th. All the morning I was busy to get my window altered, and to have my table set as I would have it, which after it was done I was infinitely pleased with it, and also to see what a command I have to have every one ready to come and go at my command. To-night Mr. Sheply told me that he heard for certain at Dover that Mr. Edw. Montagu [2] did go beyond sea when he was here first the other day, and I am apt to believe that he went to speak with the King.

21st. This day dined Sir John Boys and some other gentlemen formerly great Cavaliers, and among the rest one Mr. Norwood, for whom my Lord gave a convoy to carry him to the Brill,[3] but he is certainly going to the King, for my Lord commanded me that I should not enter his name in my book. My Lord do show them and that sort of people great civility; all their discourse and others are of the King's coming, and we begin to speak of it very freely. In the afternoon the Captain would by all means have me up to his cabin, and there treated me huge nobly, giving me a barrel of pickled oysters, and opened another for me, and a bottle of wine, which was a very great favour.

[1] See footnote, p. 72.   [2] A cousin of Sir Edward Montagu.   [3] Den Briel, a Dutch seaport.

23rd. In the evening the first time that we had any sport among the seamen, and indeed there was extraordinary good sport after my Lord had done playing at ninepins. After that W. Howe and I went to play two trebles in the great cabin below, which my Lord hearing, after supper he called for our instruments, and played a set of Lock's, two trebles and a base, and that being done he fell to singing of a song made upon the Rump, with which he played himself well, to the tune of "The Blacksmith." After all that done, then to bed.

24th. While I was at dinner with my Lord, the Coxon of the Vice-Admiral came for me to the Vice-Admiral to dinner. So I told my Lord and he gave me leave to go. I rose therefore from table and went, where there was very many commanders, and very pleasant we were on board the London, which hath a state-room much bigger than the Nazeby, but not so rich.

29th. (Sunday.) After sermon in the morning Mr. Cook came from London, bringing news that a letter is come from the King to the House, which is locked up by the Council 'till next Tuesday that it may be read in the open House when they meet again.

30th. W. Howe, Mr. Sheply and I got my Lord's leave to go to see Captain Sparling. So we took boat and first went on shore, it being very pleasant in the fields; but a very pitiful town Deal is. We went to Fuller's (the famous place for ale), but they have none but what was in the vat. After that to Poole's, a tavern in the town, where we drank, and so to boat again, and went to the Assistance, where we were treated very civilly by the Captain, and he did give us such music upon the harp by a fellow that he keeps on board that I never expect to hear the like again, yet he is a drunken simple fellow to look on as any I ever saw.

May 2nd. In the morning at a breakfast of radishes at the Purser's cabin. After that to writing till dinner. At which time comes Dunne from London, with letters that tell us the welcome news of the Parliament's votes yesterday, which will be remembered for the happiest May-day that hath been many a year to England. The King's letter was read in the House, wherein he submits himself and all things to them, as to an Act of Oblivion to all, unless they shall please to except any, as to the confirming of the sales of the King's and Church lands, if they see good. The House upon reading the letter, ordered £50,000 to be forthwith provided to send to His Majesty for his present supply; and a committee chosen to return an answer of thanks to His Majesty for his gracious letter, and that the letter be kept among the records of the Parliament, and in all this not so much as one No. Great joy all yesterday at London, and at night more bonfires than ever, and ringing of bells, and drinking of the King's health upon their knees in the streets, which methinks is a little too much. But every body seems to be very joyfull in the business, insomuch that our sea-commanders now begin to say so too, which a week ago they would not do. And our seamen, as many as had money or credit for drink, did do nothing else this evening.

3rd. This morning my Lord showed me the King's declaration and his letter to the two Generals to be communicated to the fleet. The letter dated at Breda, April $\frac{4}{14}$ 1660, in the 12th year of his reign. Upon the receipt of it this morning by an express (Mr. Phillips, one of the messengers of the Council from General Monk), my Lord summoned a council of war, and in the mean time did dictate to me how he would have the vote ordered which he would have pass this council. Which done, the Commanders all came on board, and the council sat in the coach (the first council of war that had been in my time), where I read the letter and declaration; and while they were discoursing upon it, I seemed to draw up a vote, which being offered, they passed. Not one man seemed to say no to it, though I am confident many in their hearts were against it. After this was done I went up to the quarter-deck with my Lord and the Commanders, and there read both the papers and the vote; which done, and demanding their opinion, the seamen did all of them cry out, "God bless King Charles!" with the greatest joy imaginable. After dinner, to the rest of the ships quite through the fleet. Which was a very brave sight to visit all the ships, and to be received with the respect and honour that I was on board them all; and much more to see the great joy that I brought to all men, not one through the whole fleet showing the least dislike of the business.

This done and finished my Proclamation, I returned to the Nazeby, where my Lord was much pleased to hear how all the fleet took it in a transport of joy, showed me a private letter of the King's to him, and another from the Duke of York in such familiar style as to their common friend, with all kindness imaginable. And I found by the letters, and so my Lord told me too, that there had been many letters passed between them for a great while, and I perceive unknown to Monk. The King speaks of his being courted to come to the Hague, but do desire my Lord's advice whither to come to take ship. And the Duke offers to learn the seaman's trade of him, in such familiar words as if Jack Cole [1] and I had writ them. This was very strange to me, that my Lord should carry all things so wisely and prudently as he do, and I was over joyful to see him in so good condition, and he did not a little please himself to tell me how he had provided for himself so great a hold on the King.

After this to supper, and then to writing of letters till twelve at night, and so up again at three in the morning. My Lord seemed to put great confidence in me, and would take my advice in many things. I perceive his being willing to do all the honour in the world to Monk, and to let him have all the honour of doing the business, though he will many times express his thoughts of him to be but a thick-sculled fool. So that I do believe there is some agreement more than ordinary between the King and my Lord to let Monk carry on the business, for it is he that must do the business, or at least that can hinder it, if he be not flattered and observed. This my Lord will hint himself sometimes.

4th. I wrote this morning many letters, and to all the copies of the vote of the council of war I put my name, that if it should come in print my name may be at it. In the evening came a packet from London, among the rest a letter from my wife, which tells me that she has not been well, which did exceedingly trouble me; but my Lord sending Mr. Cook at night, I wrote to her and sent a piece of gold enclosed to her, and wrote also to Mrs. Bowyer, and enclosed a half piece to her for a token.

In the afternoon came a minister on board, one Mr. Sharpe, who is going to the King; who tells me that Commissioners are chosen both of Lords and Commons to go to the King; and that Dr. Clarges [2] is going to him from the Army, and that he will be here to-morrow. My letters at night tell me, that the House did deliver their letter to Sir John Greenville, in answer to the King's sending, and that they give him £500 for his pains, to buy him a jewel; and that besides the £50,000 ordered to be borrowed of the City for the present use of the King, the twelve companies of the City do give every one of them to his Majesty, as a present, £1,000.

[1] "My old schoole-fellow . . . a great crony of mine."—See May 30, 1665.
[2] Sir Thomas Clarges, brother-in-law to Monk, and physician to the army.

5th. This evening came Dr. Clarges to Deal, going to the King; where the towns-people strewed the streets with herbes against his coming, for joy of his going. Never was there so general a content as there is now. I cannot but remember that our parson did, in his prayer to-night, pray for the long life and happiness of our King and dread Soveraign, that may last as long as the sun and the moon endureth.

7th. My Lord went this morning about the flag-ships in a boat, to see what alterations there must be, as to the arms and flags. He did give me order also to write for silk flags and scarlett waistcloathes,[1] for a rich barge, for a noise of trumpets, and a set of fidlers. Very great deal of company come to-day, among others Captain Titus,[2] whom my Lord showed all our cabins, and I suppose he is to take notice what room there will be for the King's entertainment.

8th. All the morning busy. After dinner come several persons of honour, as my Lord St. John and others, for convoy to Flushing, and great giving of them salutes. My Lord and we at nine-pins: I lost 9*s.* While we were at play Mr. Cook brings me word of my wife. He went to Huntsmore to see her, and brought her and my father[3] Bowyer to London, where he left her at my father's, very well, and speaks very well of her love to me.

10th. In the afternoon comes in a messenger to tell us that Mr. Edward Montagu, my Lord's son,[4] was come to Deal, who afterwards came on board with Mr. Pickering with him. The child was sick in the evening.

11th. This morning we began to pull down all the State's arms in the fleet, having first sent to Dover for painters and others to come to set up the King's. The rest of the morning writing of letters to London. After dinner we set sail from the Downs, I leaving my boy to go to Deal for my linen. It blew very hard all this night that I was afeard of my boy. About 11 at night came the boats from Deal, with great store of provisions (by the same token John Goods told me that above 20 of the fowls are smothered), but my boy was put on board the Northwich.

13th. (Lord's Day.) No sermon all day, we being under sail, only at night prayers, wherein Mr. Ibbott prayed for all that were related to us in a spiritual and fleshly way. We came within sight

---

[1] Painted canvas coverings for hammocks stowed in the waist-nettings.
[2] Gentleman of the Bedchamber to the King. Author of *Killing no Murder*.
[3] A courtesy title only. Similarly, Pepys speaks of "my mother Bowyer" later on.
[4] Later Lord Hinchingbroke.

of Middle's shore.[1] Late at night we writ letters to the King of the news of our coming, and Mr. Edward Pickering [2] carried them.

14th. In the morning when I woke and rose, I saw myself out of the scuttle, close by, the shore, which afterwards I was told to be the Dutch shore; the Hague was clearly to be seen by us. My Lord went up in his nightgown into the cuddy,[3] to see how to dispose thereof for himself and us that belong to him, to give order for our removal to-day. Some nasty Dutchmen came on board to proffer their boats to carry things from us on shore, &c., to get money by us. Before noon some gentlemen came on board from the shore to kiss my Lord's hands. And by and by Mr. North [4] and Dr. Clerke [5] went to kiss the Queen of Bohemia's [6] hands, from my Lord, with twelve attendants from on board to wait on them, among which I sent my boy, who, like myself, is with child to see any strange thing. After noon they came back again after having kissed the Queen of Bohemia's hand, and were sent again by my Lord to do the same to the Prince of Orange.[7] So I got the Captain to ask leave for me to go, which my Lord did give, and I taking my boy and Judge Advocate with me, went in company with them. The weather bad; we were sadly washed when we came near the shore, it being very hard to land there. The rest of the company got a coach by themselves; Mr. Creed and I went in the fore part of a coach wherein were two very pretty ladies, very fashionable and with black patches, who very merrily sang all the way and that very well, and were very free to kiss the two blades that were with them. I took out my flageolette and piped.

The Hague is a most neat place in all respects. Here we walked up and down a great while, the town being now very full of Englishmen. About 10 at night the Prince comes home, and we found an easy admission. His attendance very inconsiderable as for a prince; but yet handsome, and his tutor a fine man, and himself a very pretty boy. It was bright moonshine to-night.

15th. We lay till past three o'clock, then up and down the town, to see it by daylight, where we saw the soldiers of the Prince's guard, all very fine, and the burghers of the town with their arms and muskets as bright as silver. And meeting this morning a schoolmaster that spoke good English and French, he went along with us and shewed us the whole town, and indeed I cannot speak

[1] Probably Middelburg.
[2] "My Lord's" brother-in-law.
[3] "A sort of cabin or cook-room."
[4] Sir Charles, afterwards 5th Lord North.
[5] Sir Timothy Clerke. Physician in Ordinary to King Charles II. He and his wife appear frequently in the Diary as friends of the Pepys'.
[6] Elizabeth, sister to King Charles I.
[7] Afterwards King William III. At this date aged ten.

OFF THE COAST OF HOLLAND

enough of the gallantry of the town. Every body of fashion speaks French or Latin, or both. The women many of them very pretty and in good habits, fashionable and black spots. He went with me to buy a couple of baskets, one of them for Mrs. Pierce, the other for my wife. After that to a bookseller's and bought for the love of the binding three books: the French Psalms in four parts, Bacon's Organon, and Farnab. Rhetor.[1] After that by coach to Scheveling,[2] where we went into a house of entertainment and drank there, the wind being very high; and we saw two boats overset and the gallants forced to be pulled on shore by the heels, while their trunks, portmanteaus, hats, and feathers, were swimming in the sea. We were fain to wait a great while before we could get off from the shore. In the afternoon my Lord called me on purpose to show me his fine cloathes which are now come hither, and indeed are very rich as gold and silver can make them, only his sword he and I do not like. After supper he sent for me, intending to have me play at cards with him, but I not knowing cribbage, we fell into discourse of many things, till it was so rough sea and the ship rolled so much that I was not able to stand, and so he bid me go to bed.

16th. Commissioner Pett [3] come to take care to get all things ready for the King on board. My Lord in his best suit, this the first day, in expectation to wait upon the King. But Mr. Edw. Pickering coming from the King brought word that the King would not put my Lord to the trouble of coming to him; but that he would come to the shore to look upon the fleet to-day, which we expected, and had our guns ready to fire, and our scarlet waist-cloathes out and silk pendants, but he did not come. My Lord and we at ninepins this afternoon upon the Quarter-deck, which was very pretty sport. This afternoon Mr. Edwd. Pickering told me in what a sad, poor condition for clothes and money the king was, and all his attendants, when he came to him first from my Lord, their clothes not being worth forty shillings the best of them. And how overjoyed the King was when Sir J. Greenville brought him some money; so joyful, that he called the Princess Royal [4] and Duke of York to look upon it as it lay in the portmanteau before it was taken out. My Lord told me, too, that the Duke of York is made High Admiral of England.

17th. Before dinner Mr. Edw. Pickering and I, W. Howe,

---

[1] *Index Rhetoricus*, by Thomas Farnaby. This book, printed at Amsterdam in 1648, is still in the Pepys Library.   [2] Scheveningen.
[3] Peter Pett.   [4] His sister Mary, Princess of Orange.

Pim,[1] and my boy,[2] to Scheveling, where we took coach, and so to
the Hague, where walking, intending to find one that might show
us the King incognito, I met with Captain Whittington and he did
promise me to do it. At dinner in came Dr. Cade, a merry mad
parson of the King's. And they two after dinner got the child and
me (the others not being able to crowd in) to see the King, who
kissed the child very affectionately. Then we kissed his, and the
Duke of York's, and the Princess Royal's hands. The King
seems to be a very sober man; and a very splendid Court he hath
in the number of persons of quality that are about him, from the
King to the Lord Chancellor,[3] who did lie bed-rid of the gout. He
spoke very merrily to the child and me. After that we went to
see the Queen, who used us very respectfully; her hand we all
kissed. She seems a very debonaire, but plain lady. We took
wagon to Scheveling and returned between 10 and 11 at night in
the dark with a wagon with one horse to the Hague, where being
come we went to bed, and so to sleep.

18th. Very early up, and hearing that the Duke of York, our
Lord High Admiral, would go on board to-day, Mr. Pickering and
I took waggon for Scheveling, leaving the child in Mr. Pierce's
hands, with directions to keep him within doors all day till he
heard from me. But the wind being very high that no boats could
get off from shore, we returned to the Hague, where I hear that the
child is gone to Delfe to see the town. So we all went after them,
but met them by the way. But however we went forward. It is a
most sweet town, with bridges, and a river in every street. Observing that in every house of entertainment there hangs in every
room a poor-man's box, and desiring to know the reason thereof,
it was told me that it is their custom to confirm all bargains by
putting something into the poor people's box, and that that binds
as fast as any thing. Back by water, where a pretty sober Dutch
lass sat reading all the way, and I could not fasten any discourse
upon her. At our landing we met with Commissioner Pett. I
went along with him and his friends, to the Princess Dowager's
house again. Back to the Hague, where not finding Mr. Edward
I was much troubled, but went to supper to Commissioner Pett.
After that to our lodging, where W. Howe and I exceeding troubled
not to know what is become of our young gentleman. So to bed.

19th. Up early, hearing nothing of the child, and went to

[1] Lord Sandwich's tailor.   [2] "My Lord's" young son.
[3] Edward Hyde, 1st Earl of Clarendon. James Duke of York married his daughter.

Scheveling, where I found no getting on board, though the Duke of York sent every day to see whether he could do it or no. Here I met with Mr. Pinkney and his sons, and with them went back to the Hague. While we were here buying of pictures, we saw Mr. Edward and his company land. Who told me that they had been at Leyden all night, at which I was very angry with Mr. Pierce, and shall not be friends I believe a good while. To our lodging to dinner. After that out to buy some linen to wear against to-morrow, and so to the barber's.

20th. Up early, and with Mr. Pickering and the child by waggon to Scheveling, where it not being yet fit to go off, I went to lie down in a chamber in the house, where in another bed there was a pretty Dutch woman in bed alone; so there I slept an hour or two. At last she rose, and then I rose and talked to her as much as I could, and took occasion to kiss her hand. Commissioner Pett at last came to our lodging and caused the boats to go off; so some in one boat and some in another we all bid adieu to the shore. But through badness of weather we were in great danger, and a great while before we could get to the ship, so that of all the company not one but myself that was not sick.

21st. We expect every day to have the King and Duke on board as soon as it is fair. My Lord do nothing now, but offers all things to the pleasure of the Duke as Lord High Admiral. So that I am at a loss what to do.

22nd. News brought that the two Dukes are coming on board, which by and by they did, in a Dutch boat, the Duke of York in yellow trimmings, the Duke of Gloucester [1] in grey and red. My Lord went in a boat to meet them, the Captain, myself, and others, standing at the entering port. So soon as they were entered we shot the guns off round the fleet. They seem to be both very fine gentlemen. After that done, upon the quarter-deck table, under the awning the Duke of York and my Lord, Mr. Coventry [2] and I, spent an hour at allotting to every ship their service in their return to England; which having done, they went to dinner, where the table was very full: the two Dukes at the upper end, my Lord Opdam [3] next on one side, and my Lord on the other. Two guns given to every man while he was drinking the King's health, and so likewise to the Duke's health. I took down Monsieur d'Esquier to the great cabin below, and dined with him in state

[1] The King's youngest brother, Henry, who died of smallpox four months later, aged twenty.
[2] Mr. (later Sir) William Coventry, secretary to the Duke of York. At this time aged thirty-two.
[3] The celebrated Dutch admiral.

alone with only one or two friends of his. All dinner the harper belonging to Captain Sparling played to the Dukes. After dinner, the Dukes and my Lord to see the Vice and Rear-Admirals, and I in a boat after them. After that done, they made to the shore in the Dutch boat that brought them, and I got into the boat with them; but the shore was so full of people to expect their coming, as that it was as black (which otherwise is white sand), as every one could stand by another. When we came near the shore, my Lord left them and came into his own boat, and General Pen and I with him; my Lord being very well pleased with this day's work.

By the time we came on board again, news is sent us that the King is on shore; so my Lord fired all his guns round twice, and all the fleet after him, which in the end fell into disorder, which seemed very handsome. The gun over against my cabin I fired myself to the King, which was the first time that he had been saluted by his own ships since this change; but holding my head too much over the gun, I had almost spoiled my right eye. Nothing in the world but going of guns almost all this day. In the evening we began to remove cabins; I to the carpenter's cabin, and Dr. Clerke with me, who came on board this afternoon, having been twice ducked in the sea to-day coming from shore. Many of the King's servants came on board to-night, and so many Dutch of all sorts came to see the ship till it was quite dark that we could not pass by one another, which was a great trouble to us all. This afternoon Mr. Downing (who was knighted yesterday by the King) was here on board, and had a ship for his passage into England, with his lady and servants.

23rd. Waked very merry, only my eye was very red and ill in the morning from yesterday's hurt. In the morning came infinity of people on board from the King to go along with him. My Lord, Mr. Crew, and others, go on shore to meet the King as he comes off from shore, where Sir R. Stayner bringing His Majesty into the boat, I hear that His Majesty did with a great deal of affection kiss my Lord upon his first meeting. The King with the two Dukes and Queen of Bohemia, Princess Royal, and Prince of Orange, came on board, where I in their coming in kissed the King's, Queen's, and Princess's hands. Infinite shooting off of the guns, and that in a disorder on purpose, which was better than if it had been otherwise. All day nothing but Lords and persons of honour on board, that we were exceeding full. Dined in a great deal of state, the Royall company by themselves in the coach, which was a blessed sight to see. After dinner the King and Duke altered the name of some of the ships. That done, the Queen, Princess Royal, and Prince of Orange took leave of the King, and the Duke of York went on board the London, and the Duke of Gloucester, the Swiftsure. Which done, we weighed anchor, and with a fresh gale and most happy weather we set sail for England.

All the afternoon the King walked here and there, up and down, very active and stirring. Upon the quarter-deck he fell into discourse of his escape from Worcester,[1] where it made me ready to weep to hear the stories that he told of his difficulties that he had passed through: as his travelling four days and three nights on foot, every step up to his knees in dirt, with nothing but a green coat and a pair of country breeches on, and a pair of country shoes that made him so sore all over his feet that he could scarce stir; yet he was forced to run away from a miller and other company, that took them for rogues. His sitting at table at one place, where the master of the house, that had not seen him in eight years, did know him, but kept it private; when at the same table there was one that had been of his own regiment at Worcester could not know him, but made him drink the King's health, and said that the King was at least four fingers higher than he. At another place he was by some servants of the house made to drink, that they might know him not to be a Roundhead, which they swore he was. In another place at his inn, the master of the house, as the King was standing with his hands upon the back of a chair by the fire-side, kneeled down and kissed his hand privately, saying that he would not ask him who he was, but bid God bless him whither he was going. Then the difficulty of getting a boat to get into France, where he was fain to plot with the master thereof to keep his design from the four men and a boy (which was all his ship's company), and so got to Fécamp in France. At Rouen he looked so poorly that the people went into the rooms before he went away to see whether he had not stole something or other.

We have all the Lords Commissioners on board us, and many others. Under sail all night, and most glorious weather.

24th. Up, and make myself as fine as I could, with the linning stockings on and wide canons [2] that I bought the other day at

---

[1] Twenty years later, at Newmarket, King Charles II. dictated to Pepys the narrative of his hiding in the oak and of his subsequent wanderings; Pepys' script is preserved in his Library at Magdalene College, Cambridge.

[2] Ornamental rolls laid round the ends of the legs of breeches.

Hague. Extraordinary press of noble company and great mirth all the day. There dined with me in my cabin Dr. Earle and Mr. Hollis, the King's Chaplins, Dr. Scarborough, Dr. Quarterman, and Dr. Clerke, Physicians, Mr. Darcy, and Mr. Fox (both very fine gentlemen), the King's servants, where we had brave discourse. Walking upon the decks, where persons of honour all the afternoon, among others Thomas Killigrew [1] (a merry droll, but a gentleman of great esteem with the King), who told us many merry stories.

25th. By the morning we were come close to the land, and every body made ready to get on shore. The King and the two Dukes did eat their breakfast before they went, and there being set some ship's diet before them, only to show them the manner of the ship's diet, they eat of nothing else but pease and pork, and boiled beef. I had Mr. Darcy in my cabin and Dr. Clerke, who eat with me, told me how the King had given £50 to Mr. Sheply for my Lord's servants, and £500 among the officers and common men of the ship. I spoke with the Duke of York about business, who called me Pepys by name, and upon my desire did promise me his future favour. Great expectation of the King's making some Knights, but there was none.

About noon (though the brigantine that Beale made was there ready to carry him) yet he would go in my Lord's barge with the two Dukes. Our Captain steered, and my Lord went along bare with him. I went, and Mr. Mansell, and one of the King's footmen, with a dog that the King loved, and so got on shore when the King did, who was received by General Monk with all imaginable love and respect at his entrance upon the land of Dover. Infinite the crowd of people and the horsemen, citizens, and noblemen of all sorts. The Mayor of the town came and gave him his white staff, the badge of his place, which the King did give him again. The Mayor also presented him from the town a very rich Bible, which he took and said it was the thing that he loved above all things in the world. A canopy was provided for him to stand under, which he did, and talked awhile with General Monk and others, and so into a stately coach there set for him, and so away through the town towards Canterbury, without making any stay at Dover.

The shouting and joy expressed by all is past imagination. My Lord almost transported with joy that he had done all this without

[1] The playwright, always a favourite of King Charles II.

any the least blur or obstruction in the world, that could give an offence to any, and with the great honour he thought it would be to him.

27th. (Lord's Day.) Called up by John Goods to see the Garter and Heralds coat, which lay in the coach, brought by Sir Edward Walker, King at Arms, this morning, for my Lord. My Lord hath summoned all the Commanders on board him, to see the ceremony, which was thus: Sir Edward putting on his coat, and having laid the George and Garter, and the King's letter to my Lord, upon a crimson cushion (in the coach, all the Commanders standing by) makes three congees to him, holding the cushion in his arms. Then laying it down with the things upon it upon a chair, he takes the letter and delivers it to my Lord, which my Lord breaks open and gives him to read. It was directed to our trusty and well beloved Sir Edward Montagu, Knight, one of our Generals at sea, and our Companion elect of our Noble Order of the Garter. The contents of the letter is to show that the Kings of England have for many years made use of this honour, as a special mark of favour to persons of good extraction and virtue (and that many Emperors, Kings and Princes of other countries have borne this honour); and that whereas my Lord is of a noble family, and hath now done the King such service by sea, at this time, as he hath done; he do send him this George and Garter to wear as Knight of the Order, with a dispensation for the other ceremonies of the habit of the Order, and other things, till hereafter, when it can be done. So the herald putting the ribbon about his neck, and the Garter about his left leg, he salutes him with joy as Knight of the Garter, and that was all. After that was done, and the Captain and I had breakfasted with Sir Edward while my Lord was writing of a letter, he took his leave of my Lord, and so to shore again to the King at Canterbury, where he yesterday gave the like honour to General Monk, who are the only two for many years that have had the Garter given them, before they had other honours of Earldom, or the like, excepting only the Duke of Buckingham, who was only Sir George Villiers when he was made Knight of the Garter. A while after Mr. Thos. Crew and Mr. J. Pickering (who had staid long enough to make all the world see him to be a fool), took ship for London. So there now remain no strangers with my Lord, but Mr. Hetley, who had been with us a day before the King went from us.

29th. The King's birthday. Busy all the morning writing

letters to London, among the rest one to Mr. Chetwind to give me an account of the fees due to the Herald for the Order of the Garter, which my Lord desires to know. After dinner got all ready and sent away Mr. Cook to London with a letter and token to my wife. After that abroad to shore with my Lord (which he offered me of himself, saying that I had a great deal of work to do this month, which was very true). On shore we took horses, my Lord and Mr. Edward, Mr. Hetley and I, and three or four servants, and had a great deal of pleasure in riding. It being a pretty fair day we could see above twenty miles, into France.

31st. This day the month ends, I in very good health, and all the world in a merry mood because of the King's coming. This day I began to teach Mr. Edward, who I find to have a very good foundation laid for his Latin by Mr. Fuller. I expect every minute to hear how my poor wife do. I find myself in all things well as to body and mind, but troubled for the absence of my wife.

June 1st. This morning Mr. Sheply disposed of the money that the Duke of York did give my Lord's servants, 22 ducatoons [1] came to my share. At night Mr. Cooke comes from London with letters. My poor wife has not been well a week before, but thanks be to God is well again. She would fain see me and be at her house again, but we must be content. She writes word how the Joyces grow very rich and very proud, but it is no matter, and that there was a talk that I should be knighted by the King, which they (the Joyces) laugh at; but I think myself happier in my wife and estate than they are in theirs. To bed. The Captain come on board, when I was going to bed, quite fuddled; and himself the next morning told me so too, that the Vice-Admiral, Rear-Admiral, and he had been drinking all day.

2nd. Being with my Lord in the morning about business in his cabin, I took occasion to give him thanks for his love to me in the share that he had given me of his Majesty's money, and the Duke's. He told me he hoped to do me a more lasting kindness, if all things stand as they are now between him and the King, but, says he, "We must have a little patience and we will rise together; in the mean time I will do you all the good jobs I can." Which was great content for me to hear from my Lord.

3rd. At sermon in the morning; after dinner into my cabin, to cast my accounts up, and find myself to be worth near £100, for which I bless Almighty God, it being more than I hoped for so

[1] A ducatoon was worth about 5s. 9d.

"I PLAYED AT NINEPINS WITH MY LORD"

soon. Then to set my papers in order, they being increased much upon my hands through want of time to put them in order.

5th. A-bed late. In the morning my Lord went on shore with the Vice-Admiral a-fishing, and at dinner returned. In the afternoon I played at ninepins with my Lord, and after supper my Lord called for the lieutenant's cittern, and with two candlesticks with money in them for symballs, we made barber's music,[1] with which my Lord was well pleased. So to bed.

6th. In the morning I had letters come that told me among other things that my Lord's place of Clerk of the Signet was fallen to him, which he did most lovingly tell me that I should execute, in case he could not get a better employment for me at the end of the year. I had a great deal of talk about my uncle Robert, and he told me that he could not tell how his mind stood as to his estate, but he would do all that lay in his power for me.

My letters tell me, that Mr. Calamy[2] had preached before the King in a surplice (this I heard afterwards to be false); that my Lord, Gen. Monk, and three more Lords, are made Commissioners for the Treasury; that my Lord had some great place conferred on him, and they say Master of the Wardrobe.[3]

7th. W. Howe called me up to give him a letter to carry to my Lord that came to me to-day, which I did and so to sleep again. About three in the morning the people began to wash the deck, and the water came pouring into my mouth, which waked me, and I was fain to rise and get on my gown, and sleep leaning on my table. After dinner come Mr. John Wright and Mr. Moore, with the sight of whom my heart was very glad. They brought an order for my Lord's coming up to London, which my Lord resolved to do to-morrow. All the afternoon getting my things in order tc set forth to-morrow.

8th. Out early, took horses at Deale. Came to Canterbury, dined there. I saw the minster and the remains of Becket's tomb. To Sittingborne and Rochester. At Chatham and Rochester the ships and bridge. Come to Gravesend. A good handsome wench I kissed, the first that I have seen a great while. Supped with my Lord.

9th. Up betimes, and by boats to London. Landed at the Temple. To Mr. Crew's. To my father's and put myself into a

---

[1] *i. e.* idle music dispensed by the person waiting to be shaved.
[2] A celebrated Nonconformist divine.
[3] His duties were to provide the dresses and furnishings for State ceremonies. An official residence was provided, near Blackfriars.

handsome posture to wait upon my Lord; dined there. To White Hall with my Lord and Mr. Edwd. Montagu. Found the King in the Park. There walked. Gallantly great.

10th. (Lord's Day.) At my father's found my wife and to walk with her in Lincoln's Inn Walks.

11th. Betimes to my Lord. Extremely much people and business.

12th. To my Lord and with him to the Duke of Gloucester. The two Dukes dined with the Speaker, and I saw there a fine entertainment and dined with the pages.

15th. My Lord told me how the King has given him the place of the great Wardrobe.

16th. Rose betimes and abroad in one shirt, which brought me a great cold and pain. To my Lord, and so to White Hall with him about the Clerk of the Privy Seal's place, which he is to have. Dined at Mr. Crew's and after dinner with my Lord to Whitehall. Court attendance infinite tedious.

18th. To my Lord's, where much business and some hopes of getting some money thereby. By barge to Stepny with my Lord, where at Trinity House we had great entertainment.[1] With my Lord there went Sir W. Pen, Sir H. Wright, Hetly, Pierce, Creed, Hill, I and other servants. Back again to the Admiralty, and so to my Lord's lodgings, where he told me that he did look after the place of the Clerk of the Acts [2] for me. This evening my wife's brother, Balty, came to me to let me know his bad condition and to get a place for him, but I perceive he stands upon a place for a gentleman, that may not stain his family when, God help him, he wants bread.

This morning my Lord went into the House of Commons, and there had the thanks of the House, in the name of the Parliament and Commons of England, for his late service to his King and Country. A motion was made for a reward for him, but it was quashed by Mr. Annesly,[3] who, above most men, is engaged to my Lord's and Mr. Crew's families. My Lord went at night with the King to Baynard's Castle [4] to supper, and I home to my father's

---

[1] The Trinity House, which figures a great deal in the Diary, was in those days at Deptford.
[2] One of the first acts of King Charles II. upon his return was to revive the former method of government of the navy. His first Navy Board consisted of his brother, James Duke of York (afterwards King James II.) as Lord High Admiral, four Principal Officers and three extra Commissioners. The principal Officers were: the Treasurer (Sir George Carteret), the Comptroller (Sir Robert Slingsby), the Surveyor (Sir Wm. Batten), and the Clerk of the Acts (S. Pepys). The three extra Commissioners were Lord Berkeley, Sir Wm. Penn, and Peter Pett. Of these Pepys alone knew nothing about the sea.
[3] Arthur Annesley, later Earl of Anglesey.
[4] On the Thames near Blackfriars. It was not rebuilt after the Great Fire.

to bed. My wife and the girl and dog came home to-day. When
I came home I found a quantity of chocolate left for me, I know not
from whom.

21st. With my Lord to see the great Wardrobe, where Mr.
Townsend brought us to the governor of some poor children in
tawny clothes, who had been maintained there these eleven years,
which put my Lord to a stand how to dispose of them, that he
may have the house for his use. The children did sing finely, and
my Lord did bid me give them five pieces in gold at his going away.
Thence back to White Hall, where, the King being gone abroad,
my Lord and I walked a great while discoursing of the simplicity of
the Protector, in his losing all that his father had left him. My
Lord told me, that the last words that he parted with the Protector
with (when he went to the Sound), were, that he should rejoice
more to see him in his grave at his return home, than that he should
give way to such things as were then in hatching, and afterwards
did ruin him: and the Protector said that whatever G. Montagu,
my Lord Broghill, Jones, and the Secretary, would have him to do,
he would do it, be it what it would.

22nd. My dear friend Mr. Fuller of Twickenham [1] and I dined
alone at the Sun Tavern, where he told me how he had the grant of
being Dean of St. Patrick's, in Ireland; and I told him my condition, and both rejoiced one for another. Thence to my Lord's.
My Lord abroad, and I to my house and set things in a little order
there. To bed, the first time since my coming from sea, in my own
house, for which God be praised.

23rd. To my Lord's lodgings, and there staid to see the King
touch people for the King's evil. [2] But he did not come at all, it
rayned so; and the poor people were forced to stand all the morning
in the rain in the garden. Afterward he touched them in the
Banquetting-house. With my Lord, to my Lord Frezendorfe's, [3]
where he dined to-day. Where he told me that he had obtained a
promise of the Clerk of the Acts place for me, at which I was glad.

25th. With my Lord at White Hall all the morning. I spoke
with Mr. Coventry about my business, who promised me all the
assistance I could expect. I met with Mr. Kipps, my old friend,
with whom the world is well changed, he being now sealbearer to
the Lord Chancellor, at which my wife and I are well pleased, he
being a very good natured man.

---

[1] William Fuller, a schoolmaster. Later Bishop of Lincoln.
[2] The scrofula, which was popularly held to be cured by the king's touch. The custom died out
early in the eighteenth century.   [3] John Frederic de Friesendorff, Swedish Ambassador.

28th. My brother Tom came to me with patterns to choose for a suit. I paid him all to this day, and did give him £10 upon account. To Sir G. Downing, the first visit I have made him since he came. He is so stingy a fellow I care not to see him; I quite cleared myself of his office, and did give him liberty to take any body in. I went also this morning to see Mrs. Pierce, the chirurgeon ['s wife]. I found her in bed in her house in Margaret churchyard, her husband returned to sea: I did invite her to go to dinner with me and my wife to-day. After all this to my Lord, who lay a-bed till eleven o'clock, it being almost five before he went to bed, they supped so late last night with the King.

After my Lord was awake, I went up to him to the Nursery, where he do lie, and having talked with him a little I took leave and carried my wife and Mrs. Pierce to Clothworkers'-Hall to dinner, where Mr. Pierce, the Purser, met us. We were invited by Mr. Chaplin,[1] the Victualler, where Nich. Osborne was. Our entertainment very good, a brave hall, good company, and very good music. Where among other things I was pleased that I could find out a man by his voice, whom I had never seen before, to be one that sang behind the curtaine formerly at Sir W. Davenant's opera. Here Dr. Gauden and Mr. Gauden the victualler [2] dined with us.

29th. Up and to White Hall, where I got my warrant from the Duke to be Clerk of the Acts. I was told by Mr. Hutchinson at the Admiralty that Mr. Barlow,[3] my predecessor, Clerk of the Acts, is yet alive, and coming up to town to look after his place, which made my heart sad a little. At night told my Lord thereof, and he bade me get possession of my Patent; and he would do all that could be done to keep him out.

July 1st. This morning came home my fine Camlett [4] cloak, with gold buttons, and a silk suit, which cost me much money, and I pray God to make me able to pay for it. In the afternoon to the Abbey, where a good sermon by a stranger, but no Common Prayer yet.

2nd. Infinite of business that my heart and head and all were full. Met with purser Washington, with whom and a lady, a friend of his, I dined at the Bell Tavern in King Street; but the rogue had no more manners than to invite me and to let me pay

---

[1] Afterwards Sir Francis Chaplin. Lord Mayor 1677.
[2] Later Sir Dennis Gauden, Victualler to the Navy; Dr. John Gauden, his brother, was at this time Bishop of Exeter.   [3] He had been appointed in 1638, before Cromwell abolished the office.
[4] A costly fabric of wool and silk.

my club. All the afternoon with my Lord, going up and down the town; at seven at night he went home, and there the principal Officers of the Navy, among the rest myself was reckoned one. We had order to meet to-morrow. At night supped with my Lord, he and I together in the great dining-room alone by ourselves, the first time I ever did it in London.

3rd. All the morning the Officers and Commissioners of the Navy, we met at Sir G. Carteret's [1] chamber and agreed upon orders for the Council to supersede the old ones, and empower us to act. In the afternoon my heart was quite pulled down by being told that Mr. Barlow was to enquire to-day for Mr. Coventry; but at night I met with my Lord, who told me that I need not fear, for he would get me the place against the world. Till 2 in the morning writing letters and things for my Lord to send to sea. So home to my wife to bed.

4th. Commissioner Pett and I went to view the house in Seething Lane,[2] belonging to the Navy, where I find the worst very good, and had great fears in my mind that they will shuffle me out of them, which troubles me. To Westminster Hall, where meeting with Mons. L'Impertinent [3] and W. Bowyer, I took them to the Sun Tavern, and gave them a lobster and some wine, and sat talking like a fool till 4 o'clock. So to my Lord's, and walking all the afternoon in White Hall Court. It was strange to see how all the people flocked together bare, to see the King looking out of the Council window.

5th. This morning my brother Tom brought me my jackanapes coat with silver buttons. It rained this morning, which makes us fear that the glory of this great day will be lost; the King and Parliament being to be entertained by the City to-day with great pomp. Mr. Hater [4] was with me to-day, and I agreed with him to be my clerk. Being at White Hall, I saw the King, the Dukes, and all their attendants go forth in the rain to the City, and it bedraggled many a fine suit of clothes. I was forced to walk all the morning in White Hall, not knowing how to get out because of the rain. Met with Mr. Cooling, my Lord Chamberlain's secretary, who took me to dinner among the gentlemen waiters, and after dinner into the wine-cellar. He told me how he had a project for all us Secretaries to join together, and get money by bringing

---

[1] Treasurer of the Navy. At this time aged sixty-one.
[2] Near the Tower of London.   [3] Pepys' nickname for a Mr. Butler.
[4] Thomas Hater appears to have been a clerk in the Navy Office before Pepys went there. In 1674 he became himself Clerk of the Acts, and five years later Secretary of the Admiralty.

all business into our hands. At my Lord's at night comes Dr. Petty [1] to me, to tell me that Barlow had come to town, and other things, which put me into a despair, and I went to bed very sad.

6th. To my Lord's and dined with W. Howe and Sarah,[2] thinking it might be the last time that I might dine with them together. In the afternoon my Lord and I, and Mr. Coventry and Sir G. Carteret, went and took possession of the Navy Office, whereby my mind was a little cheered, but my hopes not great.

7th. To the Council Chamber, where I took an order for the advance of the salaries of the officers of the Navy, and I find mine to be raised to £350 per annum. Thence to the Change, where I bought two fine prints of Ragotti from Rubens, and afterwards dined with my Uncle and Aunt Wight.

8th. (Lord's Day.) To White Hall chapel, where I got in with ease by going before the Lord Chancellor with Mr. Kipps. Here I heard very good music, the first time that ever I remember to have heard the organs and singing-men in surplices in my life.[3] The Bishop of Chichester preached before the King, and made a great flattering sermon, which I did not like that Clergy should meddle with matters of state. Home, and staid all the afternoon with my wife till after sermon. There till Mr. Fairebrother came to call us out to my father's to supper. He told me how he had perfectly procured me to be made Master in Arts by proxy, which did somewhat please me.

10th. This day I put on first my new silk suit, the first that ever I wore in my life. Took my wife to Dr. Clodius's to a great wedding of Nan Hartlib to Mynheer Roder, which was kept at Goring House [4] with very great state, cost, and noble company. But among all the beauties there my wife was thought the greatest. After dinner I left the company and carried my wife to Mrs. Turner's, not returning, as I said I would, to see the bride put to bed.

11th. With Sir W. Pen by water to the Navy office, where we met, and dispatched business. I was vexed and so was Commissioner Pett, to see a busy fellow come to look out the best lodgings for my Lord Barkley, and the combining between him and Sir W. Pen; and, indeed, was troubled much at it.

12th. To the Privy Seal and got my bill perfected there, and at the Signet: and then to the House of Lords, and met with Mr.

---

[1] Afterwards Sir William Petty.   [2] Lord Sandwich's housekeeper.
[3] Organs and vestments had been abolished during the Commonwealth.
[4] Burnt down in 1674. It occupied the site of Buckingham Palace.

Kipps, who directed me to get my patent engrossed. In great trouble because I heard at Mr. Beale's to-day that Barlow had been there and said that he would make a stop in the business.

13th. Up early. To Mr. Spong, whom I found in his night-gown writing of my patent, and he had done as far as he could "for that &c." by 8 o'clock. It being done, we carried it to Worcester House [1] to the Chancellor, where Mr. Kipps got me the Chancellor's recepi to my bill; and so carried it to Mr. Beale for a docket. After to Worcester House, where I did get my seal passed. Went home and brought my wife with me into London, and some money, with which I paid Mr. Beale £9 in all, and took my patent of him and went to my wife again, whom I had left in a coach at the door of Hinde Court, and presented her with my patent at which she was overjoyed; so to the Navy office, and showed her my house, and were both mightily pleased at all things there, and so to my business. So home with her, leaving her at her mother's door. Late writing letters; and great doings of music at the next house, which was Whally's; the King and Dukes there with Madame Palmer,[2] a pretty woman that they have a fancy to.

14th. To my Lord's, where I staid doing his business and taking his commands. After that to Westminster Hall, where I paid all my debts in order to my going away from hence. Here I met with Mr. Eglin, who would needs take me to the Leg in King Street and gave me a dish of meat to dinner; and so I sent for Mons. L'Impertinent, where we sat long and were merry. After that parted, and I took Mr. Butler [Mons. L'Impertinent] with me into London by coach and shewed him my house at the Navy Office, and did give order for the laying in coals. So into Fenchurch Street, and did give him a glass of wine at Rawlinson's, and was trimmed in the street. So to my Lord's late writing letters, and so home, where I found my wife had packed up all her goods in the house fit for a removal. So to bed.

17th. This morning there came to my house before I went out Mr. Barlow, an old consumptive man, and fair conditioned. After much talk I did grant him what he asked, viz., £50 per annum, if my salary be not increased, and £100 per annum, in case it be to £350, at which he was very well pleased to be paid as I received my money and not otherwise. Going to my Lord's I found my Lord had got a great cold and kept his bed, and so I brought him to my Lord's bedside, and he and I did agree together to this purpose

---

[1] In the Strand.   [2] Barbara Villiers, afterwards Lady Castlemaine.

what I should allow him. That done and the day proving fair I went home and got all my goods packed up and sent away, and my wife and I and Mrs. Hunt went by coach, overtaking the carts a-drinking in the Strand. Being come to my house and set in the goods, and at night sent my wife and Mrs. Hunt to buy something for supper; they bought a Quarter of Lamb, and so we ate it, but it was not half roasted. Will,[1] Mr. Blackburne's nephew, is so obedient, that I am greatly glad of him. At night he and I and Mrs. Hunt home by water to Westminster. I to my Lord, and after having done some business with him, to my home, where I found my wife in bed and Jane washing the house, and Will the boy sleeping, and a great deal of sport I had before I could wake him. I to bed the first night that I ever lay here with my wife.

23rd. After dinner to my Lord, who took me to Secretary Nicholas, and there before him and Secretary Morris, my Lord and I upon our knees together took our oaths of Allegiance and Supremacy, and the Oath of the Privy Seal.

26th. Early to White Hall, thinking to have a meeting of my Lord and the principal officers, but my Lord could not, it being the day that he was to go and be admitted in the House of Lords, his patent being done, which he presented upon his knees to the Speaker; and so it was read in the House, and he took his place.[2]

27th. The last night Sir W. Batten [3] and Sir W. Pen came to their houses at the office. Met this morning and did business till noon. Dined at home, and from thence to my Lord's, where Will, my clerk and I were all the afternoon makir; up my accounts, which we had done by night, and I find myself worth about £100 after all my expenses.

August 2nd. To Westminster by water with Sir W. Batten and Sir W. Pen (our servants in another boat) to the Admiralty; and from thence I went to my Lord's to fetch him thither, where we stayed in the morning about ordering of money for the victuallers, and advising how to get a sum of money to carry on the business of the Navy. From thence dined with Mr. Blackburne at his house with his friends (his wife being in the country and just upon her return to London), where we were very well treated and merry. From thence W. Hewer and I to the office of Privy Seal, where I stayed all the afternoon, and received about £40 for

---

[1] William Hewer (aged eighteen), Pepys' first clerk and his faithful and lifelong friend. He, like his master, rose in the world to positions of importance, and it was in his house in Clapham that Pepys died.   [2] As Earl of Sandwich and Viscount Hinchingbroke.
[3] Surveyor of the Navy.

yesterday and to-day, at which my heart rejoiced for God's blessing to me, to give me this advantage by chance, there being of this £40 about £10 due to me for this day's work. So great is the present profit of this office above what it was in the King's time, there being the last month about 300 bills, whereas in the late King's time it was much to have 40. With my money home by coach.

10th. After dinner I went by water to Whitehall to the Privy Seal, and that done with Mr. Moore and Creed to Hide Park by coach, and saw a fine foot-race three times round the Park between an Irishman and Crow, that was once my Lord Claypoole's footman. Crow beat the other by above two miles. Returned from Hide Park, I went to my Lord's, and took Will (who waited for me there) by coach and went home, taking my lute home with me. It had been all this while since I came from sea at my Lord's for him to play on. For this month or two it is not imaginable how busy my head has been, so that I have neglected to write letters to my uncle Robert in answer to many of his, and to other friends, nor indeed have I done anything as to my own family; and especially this month my waiting at the Privy Seal makes me much more unable to think of anything, because of my constant attendance there after I have done at the Navy Office. But blessed be God for my good chance of the Privy Seal, where I get every day I believe about £3. This place I got by chance, and my Lord did give it me by chance, neither he nor I thinking it to be of the worth that he and I find it to be. Never since I was a man in the world was I ever so great a stranger to public affairs as now I am, having not read a new book or anything like it, or enquiring after any news, or what the Parliament do, or in any wise how things go.

11th. I was vexed this night that W. Hewer was out of doors till ten at night, but was pretty well satisfied again when my wife told me that he wept because I was angry, though indeed he did give me a good reason for his being out, but I thought it a good occasion to let him know that I do expect his being at home.

12th. (Lord's Day.) To my Lord, and with him to White Hall Chappell, where Mr. Calamy preached, and made a good sermon upon these words "To whom much is given, of him much is required." He was very officious with his three reverences to the King, as others do. After sermon a brave anthem of Captain Cooke's,[1] which he himself sung, and the King was well pleased

---

[1] Henry Cooke, Master of the Children of the Chapel Royal.

"MR. MILLS, A VERY GOOD MINISTER"

with it. After dinner I went to walk, and meeting Mrs. Lane of Westminster Hall, I took her to my Lord's, and did give her a bottle of wine in the garden. After that I took her to my house.

14th. My father, Mr. Fairbrother, and Cooke dined with me. My father after dinner takes leave, after I had given him 40s. for the last half year for my brother John at Cambridge. I did also make even with Mr. Fairbrother for my degree of Master of Arts, which cost me about £9 16s. To White Hall, and my wife with me by water, where at the Privy Seal and elsewhere all the afternoon. At night home with her by water, where I made good sport with having the girl and the boy to comb my head before I went to bed, in the kitchen.

15th. The King gone this morning by 5 of the clock to see a Dutch pleasure-boat below bridge, where he dines, and my Lord with him. The King do tire all his people that are about him with early rising since he came.

16th. This morning my Lord (all things being ready) carried me by coach to Mr. Crew's, (in the way talking how good he did hope my place would be to me, and in general speaking that it was not the salary of any place that did make a man rich, but the opportunity of getting money while he is in the place) where he took leave, and went into the coach, and so for Hinchinbroke. My Lady Jemimah and Mr. Thomas Crew [1] in the coach with him.

18th. This morning I took my wife towards Westminster by water and landed her at Whitefriars with £5 to buy her a petticoat, and I to the Privy Seal. By and by comes my wife to tell me that my father has persuaded her to buy a most fine cloth at 26s. a yard, and a rich lace, that the petticoat will come to £5, at which I was somewhat troubled, but she doing it very innocently I could not be angry. I did give her more money and sent her away. To the Cockpitt play,[2] the first that I have had time to see since my coming from sea, "The Loyall Subject," where one Kinaston, a boy, acted the Duke's sister, but made the loveliest lady that ever I saw in my life, only her voice not very good.

19th. (Lord's Day.) This morning Sir W. Batten, Pen, and myself, went to church to the churchwardens, to demand a pew, which at present could not be given us, but we are resolved to have one built. So we staid and heard Mr. Mills,[3] a very good minister. Home to dinner, where my wife had on her new petticoat

---

[1] [Sir] Thomas Crewe, brother of Lady Sandwich. Later succeeded his father as Lord Crewe.
[2] Davenant's theatre in Drury Lane. This play was by Beaumont and Fletcher.
[3] Dr. Daniel Mills, for thirty-two years rector of St. Olave's, Hart Street.

that she bought yesterday, which indeed is a very fine cloth and a fine lace; but that being of a light colour, and the lace all silver, it makes no great show. Mr. Creed and my brother Tom dined with me. After they were gone I went up to put my papers in order, and finding my wife's clothes lie carelessly laid up I was angry with her, which I was troubled for. After that my wife and I went and walked in the garden, and so home to bed.

20th. (Office day.) As Sir W. Pen and I were walking in the garden, a messenger came to me from the Duke of York to fetch me to the Lord Chancellor. So I went by coach to Worcester House, and saw my Lord Chancellor come into his Great Hall, where wonderful how much company there was to expect him at a Seal. Before he would begin any business he took my papers of the state of the debts of the Fleet, and there viewed them before all the people, and did give me his advice privately how to order things to get as much money as we can of the Parliament.

21st. To Westminster Hall, where I met Mr. Crew and dined with him, where there dined one Mr. Hickeman,[1] an Oxford man, who spoke very much against the height of the now old clergy, for putting out many of the religious fellows of Colleges, and inveighing against them for their being drunk, which, if true, I am sorry to hear.

23rd. By water to Doctors' Commons to Dr. Walker, to give him my Lord's papers to view over concerning his being empowered to be Vice-Admiral under the Duke of York.

24th. Office, and thence with Sir William Batten and Sir William Pen to the parish church to find out a place where to build a seat or a gallery to sit in, and did find one which is to be done speedily. At night by land to my father's, where I found my mother not very well. I did give her a pint of sack. My father came in, and Dr. T. Pepys,[2] who talked with me in French about looking out for a place for him. But I found him a weak man, and speaks the worst French that ever I heard of one that had been so long beyond sea.

26th. (Lord's Day.) With Sir W. Pen to the parish church, where we are placed in the highest pew of all, where a stranger preached a dry and tedious long sermon. Dined at home. To church again in the afternoon with my wife; in the garden and on the leads at night, and so to supper and to bed.

27th. This morning comes one with a vessel of Northdown ale

---

1 Henry Hickman. In this year he lost his Fellowship at Magdalen College, Oxford.

2 Thomas Pepys, M.D., son of Pepys' great-uncle Talbot Pepys of the Middle Temple and of Impington, near Cambridge.

from Mr. Pierce, the purser, to me, and after him another with a brave Turkey carpet and a jar of olives from Captain Cuttance, and a pair of fine turtle-doves from John Burr to my wife. These things came up to-day in our smack, and my boy Ely came along with them, and came after office was done to see me. I did give him half a crown because I saw that he was ready to cry to see that he could not be entertained by me here.

28th. At home looking over my papers and books and house as to the fitting of it to my mind till two in the afternoon. Some time I spent this morning beginning to teach my wife some scale in music, and found her apt beyond imagination. To the Privy Seal, where great store of work to-day. This day I heard my poor mother had then two days been very ill, and I fear she will not last long. To bed, a little troubled that I fear my boy is a thief and has stole some money of mine.

29th. (Office day.) To the office. Home at night, and find that my wife had found out more of the boy's stealing 6*s.* out of W. Hewer's closet, and hid it in the house of office, at which my heart was troubled. To bed, and caused the boy's clothes to be brought up to my chamber. But after we were all a-bed, the wench (which lies in our chamber) called us to listen of a sudden, which put my wife into such a fright that she shook every joint of her, and a long time that I could not get her out of it. The noise was the boy, we did believe, got in a desperate mood out of his bed to do himself or William [Hewer] some mischief. But the wench went down and got a candle lighted, and finding the boy in bed, and locking the doors fast, with a candle burning all night, we slept well, but with a great deal of fear.

30th. We found all well in the morning below stairs, but the boy in a sad plight of seeming sorrow; but he is the most cunning rogue that ever I met with of his age.

31st. Early to wait upon my Lord at White Hall, and with him to the Duke's chamber. So to my office in Seething Lane. Dined at home, and after dinner to my Lord again, who told me that he is ordered to go suddenly to sea, and did give me some orders to be drawing up against his going. At night made even at Privy Seal for this month against to-morrow to give up possession, and so home and to bed. Blessed be God all things continue well with and for me. I pray God fit me for a change of my fortune.

September 5th. To the office. Home to dinner, where, (having put away my boy in the morning) his father brought him again, but I did so clear up my boy's roguery to his father, that he could not speak anything against my putting him away. In the evening my wife being a little impatient I went along with her to buy her a necklace of pearl, which will cost £4 10s., which I am willing to comply with her in for her encouragement, and because I have lately got money, having now above £200 in cash beforehand in the world. Home, and having in our way bought a rabbit and two little lobsters, my wife and I did sup late, and so to bed.

8th. At night sent for by Sir W. Pen, with whom I sat late drinking a glass of wine, and I find him to be a very sociable man, and an able man, and very cunning.

11th. Dined at Sir W. Batten's, and by this time I see that we are like to have a very good correspondence and neighbourhood, but chargeable.

21st. (Office day.) There all the morning and afternoon till 4 o'clock. Hence to Whitehall. Back by water about 8 o'clock and went to the Hoop Tavern, and (by a former agreement) sent for Mr. Chaplin, who with Nicholas Osborne and one Daniel came to us and we drank off two or three quarts of wine, which was very good; and we did eat above 200 walnuts. About 10 o'clock we broke up and so home, where I found my boy [1] (my maid's brother) come to-day.

24th. (Office day.) Went to the Temple church, where I had appointed Sir W. Batten to meet him; and there at Sir Heneage Finch Sollicitor General's chambers, before him and Sir W. Wilde, Recorder of London (whom we sent for from his chamber) we were sworn justices of peace for Middlesex, Essex, Kent, and Southampton; with which honour I did find myself mightily pleased, though I am wholly ignorant in the duty of a justice of peace.

25th. To the office, where Sir W. Batten, Colonel Slingsby,[2] and I sat awhile, and Sir R. Ford coming to us about some business, we talked together of the interest of this kingdom to have a peace with Spain and a war with France and Holland. And afterwards I did send for a cup of tee [3] (a China drink) of which I never had drank before, and went away.

29th. This day or yesterday, I hear, Prince Rupert [4] is come to Court; but welcome to nobody.

---

[1] Wayneman, another troublesome boy.
[2] Later Sir Robert Slingsby, Comptroller of the Navy.
[3] Said to have been first introduced into Europe in 1610 and into England (from Holland) about 1650. In 1664, King Charles II. was presented with 2 lbs. of tea.
[4] He was a son of Elizabeth, Queen of Bohemia, and so first cousin to the King and Duke of York. Aged forty; they were thirty and twenty-seven respectively.

October 1st. My layings out upon my house in furniture are so great that I fear I shall not be able to go through them without breaking one of my bags of £100.

2nd. With Sir Wm. Pen by water to Whitehall, being this morning visited before I went out by my brother Tom,[1] who told me that for his lying out of doors a day and a night my father had forbade him to come any more into his house, at which I was troubled, and did soundly chide him for doing so, and upon confessing his fault I told him I would speak to my father. At Will's I met with Mr. Spicer,[2] and with him to the Abbey to see them at vespers. Thence by coach to my father's, and discoursed with him about Tom, and did give my advice to take him home again, which I think he will do in prudence rather than put him upon learning the way of being worse. So home, where my wife tells me what she has bought to-day, namely, a bed and furniture for her chamber.

3rd. With Sir W. Batten and Pen by water to White Hall, where a meeting of the Dukes of York and Albemarle,[3] my Lord Sandwich and all the principal officers about the Winter Guard, but we determined of nothing. To my Lord's, who sent a great iron chest to White Hall; and I saw it carried into the King's closet, where I saw most incomparable pictures. Among the rest a book open upon a desk, which I durst have sworn was a reall book, and back again to my Lord, and dined all alone with him, who do treat me with a great deal of respect; and after dinner did discourse an hour with me, and advise about some way to get himself some money to make up for all his great expenses, saying that he believed that he might have any thing that he would ask of the King. This day Mr. Sheply and all my Lord's goods came from sea, some of them laid at the Wardrobe and some brought to my Lord's house. From thence to our office, where we met and did business, and so home and spent the evening looking upon the painters that are at work in my house. This day I heard the Duke speak of a great design that he and my Lord of Pembroke have, and a great many others, of sending a venture to some parts of Africa to dig for gold ore there. They intend to admit as many as will venture their money, and so make themselves a company.

[1] Pepys' brother Thomas was born in 1634 and died at the age of thirty. He carried on his father's business as a tailor.
[2] A brother clerk of Pepys' at the Privy Seal.
[3] General George Monk had been created Duke of Albemarle in July.

£250 is the lowest share for every man. But I do not find that my Lord do much like it.

4th. I and Lieut. Lambert to Westminster Abbey, where we saw Dr. Frewen translated to the Archbishoprick of York. Here I saw the Bishops of Winchester, Bangor, Rochester, Bath and Wells, and Salisbury, all in their habits, in King Henry Seventh's chappell. But, Lord! at their going out, how people did most of them look upon them as strange creatures, and few with any kind of love or respect.

11th. Mr. Creed and I to walk in St. James's Park, where we observed the several engines at work to draw up water, with which sight I was very much pleased. Above all the rest I liked best that which Mr. Greatorex [1] brought, which is one round thing going within all, with a pair of stairs round; which being laid at an angle of 45°, do carry up the water with a great deal of ease. Here in the Park, we met with Mr. Salisbury,[2] who took Mr. Creed and me to the Cockpitt to see "The Moore of Venice," which was well done. Burt acted the Moore; by the same token a very pretty lady that sat by me called out to see Desdemona smothered.

12th. I went to Westminster to see Lady Sandwich and found her at supper, so she made me sit down all alone with her, and after supper staid and talked with her, she showing me most extraordinary love and kindness, and do give me good assurance of my uncle's resolution to make me his heir. From thence home and to bed.

13th. To my Lord's in the morning, where I met with Captain Cuttance, but my Lord not being up I went out to Charing Cross, to see Major-general Harrison [3] hanged, drawn, and quartered; which was done there, he looking as cheerful as any man could do in that condition. He was presently cut down, and his head and heart shown to the people, at which there was great shouts of joy. It is said that he said that he was sure to come shortly at the right hand of Christ to judge them that now had judged him; and that his wife do expect his coming again. Thus it was my chance to see the King beheaded at White Hall, and to see the first blood shed in revenge for the blood of the King at Charing Cross. After that I went by water home, where I was angry with

---

[1] A famous mathematical instrument maker.   [2] A portrait painter.
[3] Thomas Harrison, son of a butcher at Newcastle-under-Lyme, appointed by Cromwell to convey Charles I. from Windsor to Whitehall, in order to his trial. He signed the warrant for the execution of the King.

my wife for her things lying about, and in my passion kicked the little fine basket, which I bought her in Holland, and broke it, which troubled me after I had done it.

14th. (Lord's Day.) To White Hall chappell, where one Dr. Crofts made an indifferent sermon, and after it an anthem, ill sung, which made the King laugh. Here I first did see the Princess Royal since she came into England. Here I also observed how the Duke of York and Mrs. Palmer did talk to one another very wantonly through the hangings that parts the King's closet and the closet where the ladies sit.

18th. To Mr. Blackburne, where we had a very fine dinner. Mr. Creed was also there. This day by her high discourse I found Mrs. Blackburne to be a very high dame and a costly one. Home with my wife by coach.

19th. Office in the morning. This morning my dining-room was finished with green serge hanging and gilt leather, which is very handsome. Dined with my Lord and Lady; when he was very merry, and did talk very high how he would have a French cook, and a master of his horse, and his lady and child to wear black patches; which methought was strange, but he is become a perfect courtier; and, among other things, my Lady saying that she could get a good merchant for her daughter Jem., he answered, that he would rather see her with a pedlar's pack at her back, so she married a gentleman, than she should marry a citizen.

22nd. Office day. After dinner to my Lord's, where I found all preparing for my Lord's going to sea to fetch the Queen [1] to-morrow.

23rd. We rose early in the morning to get things ready for my Lord, and Mr. Sheply going to put up his pistols (which were charged with bullets) into the holsters, one of them flew off, and it pleased God that, the mouth of the gun being downwards, it did us no hurt, but I think I never was in more danger in my life, which put me into a great fright. I met the Lord Chancellor and all the Judges riding on horseback and going to Westminster Hall, it being the first day of the term, which was the first time I ever saw any such solemnity.

24th. I took occasion to be angry with my wife before I rose about her putting up of half a crown of mine in a paper box, which she had forgot where she had lain it. But we were friends again as we are always. Then I rose to Jack Cole, who came to see me.

---

[1] Henrietta Maria, the Queen-mother. Charles II. was unmarried as yet.

Then to the office, so home to dinner, where I found Captain Murford, who did put £3 into my hands for a friendship I had done him, but I would not take it, but bade him keep it till he has enough to buy my wife a necklace.

Mr. Spong did show me the manner of the lamp-glasses, which carry the light a great way, good to read in bed by, and I intend to have one of them.

26th. Office. My father and Dr. Thomas Pepys dined at my house, the last of whom I did almost fox with Margate ale. My father is mightily pleased with my ordering of my house. I did give him money to pay several bills. After that I to Westminster to White Hall, where I saw the Duke de Soissons [1] go from his audience with a very great deal of state: his own coach all red velvet covered with gold lace, and drawn by six barbes, and attended by twenty pages very rich in clothes.

29th. I up early, it being my Lord Mayor's day (Sir Richd. Browne), and neglecting my office I went to the Wardrobe, where I met my Lady Sandwich and all the children. [We went] to one Mr. Isaacson's, a linen draper at the Key in Cheapside; where there was a company of fine ladies, and we were very civilly treated, and had a very good place to see the pageants, which were many, and I believe good for such kind of things, but in themselves but poor and absurd.

30th. In the afternoon I went to the Cockpit and there saw a very fine play called "The Tamer tamed;" [2] very well acted.

31st. This month I conclude with my mind very heavy for the greatness of my late expenses, insomuch that I do not think that I have above £150 clear money in the world, but I have, I believe, got a great deal of good household stuff. I hear to-day that the Queen is landed at Dover, and will be here on Friday next, November 2nd.

November 1st. This morning Sir W. Pen and I were mounted early, and had very merry discourse all the way, he being very good company. We came to Sir W. Batten's,[3] where he lives like a prince, and we were made very welcome. Among other things he showed us my Lady's closet, where was great store of rarities; as also a chair, which he calls King Harry's chair, where he that sits down is catched with two irons, that come round about him, which makes good sport. Here dined with us two or three more country

[1] Father of the celebrated general, Prince Eugène of Savoy, Barbes were Arab (Barbary) horses.
[2] *The Woman's Prize, or Tamer Tamed.* By John Fletcher.
[3] At Walthamstow.

gentlemen; among the rest Mr. Christmas, my old school-fellow, with whom I had much talk. He did remember that I was a great Roundhead when I was a boy, and I was much afraid that he would have remembered the words that I said the day the King was beheaded (that, were I to preach upon him, my text should be—"The memory of the wicked shall rot"); but I found afterwards that he did go away from school before that time. He did make us good sport in imitating Mr. Case, Ash, and Nye, the ministers; which he did very well; but a deadly drinker he is, and grown exceeding fat.

2nd. I supt with my Lord, he being very merry, telling merry stories of the country mayors; how they entertained the King all the way as he come along; and how the country gentlewomen did hold up their heads to be kissed by the King, not taking his hand to kiss as they should do. I observed this night very few bonfires in the City, not above three in all London, for the Queen's coming; whereby I guess that (as I believed before) her coming do please but very few.

4th. (Lord's Day.) In the morn to our own church,[1] where Mr. Mills did begin to nibble at the Common Prayer, by saying "Glory be to the Father, &c." after he had read the two psalms; but the people had been so little used to it, that they could not tell what to answer. My wife seemed very pretty to-day, it being the first time I had given her leave to wear a black patch.

6th. At night my wife and I did fall out about the dog's being put down into the cellar, which I had a mind to have done because of his fouling the house, and I would have my will; and so we went to bed and lay all night in a quarrel. This night I was troubled all night with a dream that my wife was dead, which made me that I slept ill all night.

7th. (Office day.) By water to my Lord, where I dined with him, and he, in discourse of the great opinion of the virtue—gratitude (which he did account the greatest thing in the world to him) did say it was that did bring him to his obedience to the King; and did also bless himself with his good fortune in comparison to what it was when I was with him in the Sound, when he durst not own his correspondence with the King. After dinner he bid all go out of the room, and did tell me how the King had promised him £4,000 per annum for ever. My Lord did advise

---

[1] St. Olave's, Hart Street. The congregation were unaccustomed to the use of the Book of Common Prayer because it had been totally suppressed since 1645.

"THE COUNTRY GENTLEWOMEN DID HOLD UP THEIR HEADS TO BE KISSED"

with me how to get this received, and to put out £3,000 into safe hands at use, and the other he will make use of for his present occasion. This he did advise with me about with much secresy.

12th. Lay long in bed to-day. Walked to my father's, where I found my wife, who had been with my father to-day, buying of a tablecloth and a dozen of napkins of diaper, the first that ever I bought in my life. My father and I took occasion to go forth, and went and drank at Mr. Standing's, and there discoursed seriously about my sister's coming to live with me, which I have much mind for her good to have, and yet I am much afeard of her ill-nature. Coming home again, he and I, and my wife, my mother and Pall, went all together into the little room, and there I told her plainly what my mind was, to have her come not as a sister in any respect, but as a servant, which she promised me that she would, and with many thanks did weep for joy, which did give me and my wife some content and satisfaction.

14th. (Office day.) This day was the first that we do begin to sit in the afternoon, and not in the forenoon. To the office till late at night, and so Sir W. Pen and I to the Dolphin, where we found Sir W. Batten, and there we did drink a great quantity of sack and did tell many merry stories, and in good humours we were all.

15th. To my Lord's. Here I did leave my wife to dine with my Lord, the first time he ever did take notice of her as my wife, and did seem to have a just esteem for her. [I] to Sir W. Batten's to dinner, he having a couple of servants married to-day; and so there was a great number of merchants, and others of good quality on purpose after dinner to make an offering, which, when dinner was done, we did, and I did give ten shillings and no more, though I believe most of the rest did give more, and did believe that I did so too.

19th. (Office day.) To the office, where we sat all the afternoon till night. So home to my musique and sat up late at it, and so to bed, leaving my wife to sit up till 2 o'clock that she may call the wench up to wash.

20th. About two o'clock my wife wakes me, and comes to bed, and so both to sleep and the wench to wash.

To the new Play-house near Lincoln's-Inn-Fields [1] where the play of "Beggar's Bush" was newly begun; and so we went in and

[1] This was Killigrew's or the King's House, opened for the first time on November 8. The play was by Beaumont and Fletcher. Michael Mohun, or Moone, the celebrated actor, had been a major in the King's army.

saw it, it was well acted: and here I saw the first time one Moone, who is said to be the best actor in the world, lately come over with the King; and indeed it is the finest play-house, I believe, that ever was in England.

21st. This morning my wife and I went to Paternoster Row, and there we bought some green watered moyre for a morning wastecoate. And after that we went to Mr. Cade's[1] to choose some pictures for our house. After that my wife went home, and I to Pope's Head,[2] and bought me an aggate hafted knife, which cost me 5s. So home to dinner, and so to the office all the afternoon, and at night to my viallin (the first time that I have played on it since I came to this house) in my dining room, and afterwards to my lute there, and I took much pleasure to have the neighbours come forth into the yard to hear me. So up to bed, leaving my wife to wash herself, and to do other things against to-morrow to go to court.

22nd. At noon my wife and I walked to the Old Exchange, and there she bought her a white whisk[3] and put it on, and I a pair of gloves, and so we took coach for Whitehall to Mr. Fox's,[4] where we found Mrs. Fox within, and an alderman of London. Mr. Fox came in presently and did receive us with a great deal of respect; and then did take my wife and I to the Queen's presence-chamber, where he got my wife placed behind the Queen's chair, and I got into the crowd; and by and by the Queen and the two Princesses came to dinner. The Queen a very little plain old woman, and nothing more in her presence in any respect nor garb than any ordinary woman. The Princess of Orange I had often seen before. The Princess Henrietta[5] is very pretty, but much below my expectation; and her dressing of herself with her hair frized short up to her ears did make her seem so much the less to me. But my wife standing near her with two or three black patches on, and well dressed, did seem to me much handsomer than she. Dinner being done, we went to Mr. Fox's again, where many gentlemen dined with us, and most princely dinner, all provided for me and my friends; but I bringing none but myself and wife, he did call the company to help to eat up so much good victuals.

---

[1] A stationer in Cornhill.
[2] Pope's Head Alley, linking Cornhill and Lombard Street, famous for its cutlers.
[3] A gorget, or neckerchief.
[4] Stephen (afterwards Sir Stephen) Fox, Clerk of the Green Cloth, and later Paymaster of the Forces. His sons were created Earl of Ilchester and Lord Holland.
[5] Youngest child of King Charles I. Married Philippe, Duc d'Anjou, later Duc d'Orléans, brother of Louis XIV.

26th. (Office day.) Dined at home where my father come and dined with me, who seems to take much pleasure to have a son that is neat in his house. After dinner to the office again and there till night. And that being done the Comptroller and I to the Mitre to a glass of wine, when we fell into a discourse of poetry, and he did repeat some verses of his own making which were very good. Home, there hear that my Lady Batten had given my wife a visit (the first that ever she made her), which pleased me exceedingly.

27th. Mr. Moore told me how the House had this day voted the King to have all the Excise for ever. This day I do also hear that the Queen's going to France is stopt, which do like me well, because then the King will be in town the next month, which is my month again at the Privy Seal.

December 1st. This morning, observing some things to be laid up not as they should be by the girl, I took a broom and basted her till she cried extremely, which made me vexed, but before I went out I left her appeased. So to Whitehall, where I found Mr. Moore attending for me at the Privy Seal, but nothing to do to-day.

3rd. This morning I took a resolution to rise early in the morning, and so I rose by candle, which I have not done all this winter, and spent my morning in fiddling till time to go to the office.

4th. This day the Parliament voted that the bodies of Oliver, Ireton, Bradshaw, &c., should be taken up out of their graves in the Abbey, and drawn to the gallows, and there hanged and buried under it: which (methinks) do trouble me that a man of so great courage as he was, should have that dishonour, though otherwise he might deserve it enough.

5th. After dinner I went to the new Theatre [1] and there I saw "The Merry Wives of Windsor" acted, the humours of the country gentleman and the French doctor very well done, but the rest but very poorly, and Sir J. Falstaffe as bad as any.

8th. Going into Westminster Hall met with Sir G. Carteret and Sir W. Pen (who were in a great fear that we had committed a great error of £100,000 in our late account gone into the Parliament in making it too little); and so I went along with Sir W. Pen by water to the office, and there with Mr. Huchinson [2] we did find that we were in no mistake. And so I went to dinner, with my

---

[1] Killigrew's house.
[2] Richard Hutchinson, predecessor to Sir G. Carteret as Treasurer for the Navy.

"READING MYSELF ASLEEP, WHILE THE WENCH SAT MENDING MY BREECHES"

wife and Mr. and Mrs. Pierce the Surgeon, to Mr. Pierce the Purser (the first time that ever I was at his house) who does live very plentifully and finely. We had a lovely chine of beef and other good things very complete and drank a great deal of wine, and her daughter played after dinner upon the virginals,[1] and at night by lanthorn home again.

10th. Col. Slingsby came and sat with me at my house, and among other discourse he told me that it is expected that the Duke will marry the Lord Chancellor's daughter, which is likely to be the ruin of Mr. Davis [2] and my Lord Barkley,[3] who have carried themselves so high against the Chancellor. Up to bed, having first been into my study, and to ease my mind did go to cast up how my cash stands, and I do find as near as I can that I am worth in money clear £240, for which God be praised.

12th. This morning I went to Whitehall to dine with my Lady, and after dinner to the Exchequer and did give my mother Bowyer a visit and her daughters, the first time that I have seen them since I went last to sea. From thence up with J. Spicer as far as my father's. So to my Lady Batten, and sat an hour or two, and talked with her daughter and people. After that home and to bed, reading myself asleep, while the wench sat mending my breeches by my bedside.

22nd. At noon I went to the Sun tavern to a dinner, where was my Lord Inchiquin, Sir W. Pen, Captn. Cuttance, and other good company, where we had a very fine dinner, good musique, and a great deal of wine. We staid here very late. At last Sir W. Pen and I home together, he so overcome with wine that he could hardly go; I was forced to lead him through the streets and he was in a very merry and kind mood.

24th. In the morning to the office; and Commissioner Pett (who seldom comes there) told me that he had lately presented a piece of plate to Mr. Coventry; but he did not receive them, which also put me upon doing the same too.

31st. At the office all the morning, and after that home; and not staying to dine I went out, and in Paul's Churchyard I bought the play of "Henry the Fourth," and so went to the new Theatre and saw it acted; but my expectation being too great, it did not please me as otherwise I believe it would; and my having a book I believe did spoil it a little.

---

[1] All instruments of the harpsichord and spinet kind were called virginals.
[2] Storekeeper at Deptford.
[3] John, Lord Berkeley of Stratton, one of the three Commissioners for the Navy. Formerly a distinguished Royalist officer in the Civil Wars.

At the end of the last and the beginning of this year, I do live in one of the houses belonging to the Navy Office, as one of the principal officers, and have done now about half a year. After much trouble with workmen I am now almost settled; my family being, myself, my wife, Jane, Will. Hewer, and Wayneman, my girle's brother. Myself in constant good health, and in a most handsome and thriving condition. Blessed be Almighty God for it. I am now taking of my sister to come and live with me. I take myself now to be worth £300 clear in money, and all my goods and all manner of debts paid, which are none at all.

SECOND YEAR

1661

January 2nd. By water to my office, and there all the morning, and so home to dinner, where I found Pall (my sister) was come; but I do not let her sit down at table with me, which I do at first that she may not expect it hereafter from me.

3rd. To the Theatre; and here the first time that ever I saw women come upon the stage. From thence to my father's, where I found my mother gone by Bird, the carrier, to Brampton, upon my uncle's great desire, my aunt being now in despair of life. So home.

6th. (Lord's Day.) To church where, before sermon, a long Psalm was set that lasted an hour, while the sexton gathered his year's contribucion through the whole church. After sermon home, and there I went to my chamber and wrote a letter to send to Mr. Coventry, with a piece of plate along with it, which I do preserve among my other letters.

7th. This morning news was brought to me to my bedside that there had been a great stir in the City this night by the Fanatiques,[1] who had been up and killed six or seven men, but all are fled. My Lord Mayor and the whole City had been in arms, above 40,000. To the office, and after that to dinner, where my brother Tom came and dined with me; and after dinner (leaving 12d. with the servants to buy a cake with at night, this day being kept as Twelfth day) Tom and I and my wife to the Theatre, and there saw "The Silent Woman."[2] The first time that ever I did see it, and it is an excellent play. Among other things here, Kinaston, the boy, had the good turn to appear in three shapes; first as a poor woman in ordinary clothes, to please Morose; then in fine clothes as a gallant, and in them was clearly the prettiest woman in the whole house; and lastly as a man, and then likewise did appear the handsomest man in the house.

[1] Thomas Venner, a cooper and preacher, with a following of about fifty, took up arms on January 6 for the establishment of the Millennium. He was a violent enthusiast, and had persuaded his followers that they were invulnerable. Events proved him wrong, and he was hanged, drawn and quartered on January 19. Many of his followers, known as Fanatiques or Fifth Monarchy Men, shared a similar fate.
[2] By Ben Jonson.

64

9th. Waked in the morning about six o'clock, by people running up and down in Mr. Davis's house, talking that the Fanatiques were up in arms in the City. And so I rose and went forth, where in the street I found every body in arms at the doors. So I returned (though with no good courage at all, but that I might not seem to be afeared), and got my sword and pistol, which, however, I had no powder to charge; and went to the door, where I found Sir R. Ford, and with him I walked up and down as far as the Exchange, and there I left him. In our way the streets full of Trainband, and great stories what mischief these rogues have done; and I think near a dozen have been killed this morning on both sides. Seeing the city in this condition, the shops shut, and all things in trouble, I went home and sat, it being office day, till noon. So home, and dined at home, my father with me; and after dinner he would needs have me go to my uncle Wight's (where I have been so long absent that I am ashamed to go). I found him at home and his wife, and I can see they have taken my absence ill; but all things are past and we good friends; and here I sat with my aunt till it was late, my uncle going forth about business, my aunt being very fearful to be alone. So home to my lute till late, and then to bed, there being strict guards all night in the City, though most of the enemies, they say, are killed or taken.

10th. After dinner Will comes to tell me that he had presented my piece of plate to Mr. Coventry, who takes it very kindly, and sends me a very kind letter, and the plate back again; of which my heart is very glad. So to Mrs. Hunt,[1] where I found a Frenchman, a lodger of her's, at dinner, and just as I came in was kissing my wife, which I did not like, though there could not be any hurt in it. The King is this day come to town.

11th. This morning we had order to see guards set in all the King's yards; and so we do appoint who and who should go to them; Sir Wm. Batten to Chatham, Colonel Slingsby and I to Deptford and Woolwich. Portsmouth, being a garrison, needs none. Dined at home, discontented that my wife do not go neater now she has two maids.

12th. With Colonel Slingsby and a friend of his, Major Waters (a deaf and most amorous melancholy gentleman, who is under a despayr in love, as the Colonel told me, which makes him bad company, though a most good-natured man), by water to Red-

---

[1] Mr. Hunt was a clerk in the Excise. Both he and his wife were always on intimate terms with the Pepys.

riffe,[1] and so on foot to Deptford (our servants by water), where we fell to choosing four captains to command the guards, and choosing the places where to keep them, and other things in order thereunto. We dined at the Globe, having our messenger with us to take care for us. Never till now did I see the great authority of my place, all the captains of the fleet coming cap in hand to us. Having staid very late there talking with the Colonel, I went home with Mr. Davis, storekeeper (whose wife is ill and so I could not see her), and was there most prince-like lodged, with so much respect and honour that I was at a loss how to behave myself.

14th. To Mr. Pett's, the shipwright, and there supped, where he did treat us very handsomely (and strange it is to see what neat houses all the officers of the King's yards have), his wife a proper woman, and has been handsome, and yet has a very pretty hand. Thence I with Mr. Ackworth [2] to his house, where he has a very pretty house, and a very proper lovely woman to his wife, who both sat with me in my chamber, and they being gone, I went to bed, which was also most neat and fine.

15th. Home, where I found my wife and Pall abroad, so I went to see Sir W. Pen, and there found Mr. Coventry come to see him, and now had an opportunity to thank him, and he did express much kindness to me. I sat a great while with Sir Wm. after he was gone, and had much talk with him. I perceive none of our officers care much for one another, but I do keep in with them all as much as I can.

18th. In the afternoon we met at the office and sat till night, and then I to see my father who I found well, and took him to Standing's to drink a cup of ale. He told me my aunt at Brampton is yet alive and my mother well there. In comes Will Joyce to us drunk, and in a talking vapouring humour of his state, and I know not what, which did vex me cruelly. Hence home, and took home with me from the bookseller's Ogilby's Æsop,[3] which he had bound for me, and indeed I am very much pleased with the book.

19th. After dinner I went to the Theatre, where I saw "The Lost Lady," [4] which do not please me much. Here I was troubled to be seen by four of our office clerks, which sat in the half-crown box and I in the 1s. 6d.

---

[1] The usual corruption of the name Rotherhithe.   [2] William Acworth, storekeeper at Woolwich.
[3] Pepys' copy, dated 1665, is bound in parchment and bears the Royal arms; it no doubt superseded the copy referred to in the text.
[4] By Sir Wm. Barclay.

21st. It is strange what weather we have had all this winter; no cold at all, but the ways are dusty, and the flyes fly up and down, and the rose-bushes are full of leaves, such a time of the year as was never known in this world before here. This day many of the Fifth Monarchy men were hanged.

22nd. After a little dinner my wife and I by coach into London and bought some glasses, and then my wife to my mother Bowyer, and I met with Dr. Thomas Fuller,[1] and took him to the Dog, where he tells me of his last and great book that is coming out: that is, his History of all the Families in England; and could tell me more of my own, than I knew myself. And also to what perfection he hath now brought the art of memory; that he did lately to four eminently great scholars dictate together in Latin, upon different subjects of their proposing, faster than they were able to write, till they were tired; and by the way in discourse tells me that the best way of beginning a sentence, if a man should be out and forget his last sentence (which he never was), that then his last refuge is to begin with an Utcunque.

23rd. To the office all the morning. My wife and people at home busy to get things ready for to-morrow's dinner. Meeting with Greatorex, we went and drank a pot of ale. With him to Gresham Colledge [2] (where I never was before), and saw the manner of the house, and found great company of persons of honour there; thence to my bookseller's, for books, and to Stevens, the silversmith, to make clean some plate against to-morrow, and so home, by the way paying many little debts for line and pictures, &c., which is my great pleasure. Home and found all things in a hurry of business, Slater, our messenger, being here as my cook till very late. I in my chamber all the evening looking over my Osborn's works and new Emanuel Thesaurus Patriarchæ.

24th. At home all day. There dined with me Sir William Batten and his lady and daughter, Sir W. Pen, Mr. Fox (his lady being ill could not come), and Captain Cuttance; the first dinner I have made since I came hither. This cost me above £5, and merry we were, only my chimney smokes.

26th. Within all the morning. About noon comes one that had formerly known me and I him, but I know not his name, to borrow £5 of me, but I had the wit to deny him.

[1] Thomas Fuller, D.D., author of *The Worthies of England*.
[2] Gresham College occupied Sir Thomas Gresham's house in Bishopsgate Street. The meeting which Pepys attended was an early one of the Royal Society, which was founded by King Charles II. in 1660. Pepys was admitted a Fellow on February 15, 1665, and was elected President in 1684 and 1685.

28th. At the office all the morning; dine at home, and after dinner to Fleet Street, with my sword to Mr. Brigden to be refreshed. To the Theatre, where I saw again "The Lost Lady" which do now please me better than before; and here I sitting behind in a dark place, a lady spit backward upon me by a mistake, not seeing me; but after seeing her to be a very pretty lady, I was not troubled at it at all.

29th. To Mr. Turner's[1] house, where the Comptroller, Sir William Batten, and Mr. Davis and their ladies; and here we had a most neat little but costly and genteel supper, and after that a great deal of impertinent mirth by Mr. Davis, and some catches, and so broke up, and going away, Mr. Davis's eldest son took up my old Lady Slingsby in his arms, and carried her to the coach, and is said to be able to carry three of the biggest men that were in the company, which I wonder at.

30th. (Fast Day.)[2] The first time that this day hath been yet observed: and Mr. Mills made a most excellent sermon, upon "Lord forgive us our former iniquities;" speaking excellently of the justice of God in punishing men for the sins of their ancestors. To my Lady Batten's, where my wife and she are lately come back again from being abroad, and seeing of Cromwell, Ireton, and Bradshaw hanged and buried at Tyburn.

31st. To my father's to see my mother, who is pretty well after her journey from Brampton. She tells me my aunt is pretty well, yet cannot live long. My uncle pretty well too, and she believes would marry again were my aunt dead, which God forbid. So home.

February 3rd. (Lord's Day.) This day I first begun to go forth in my coat and sword, as the manner now among gentlemen is. To Whitehall. In my way heard Mr Thomas Fuller preach at the Savoy upon our forgiving of other men's trespasses, shewing among other things that we are to go to law never to revenge, but only to repayre, which I think a good distinction. So to White Hall, where I staid to hear the trumpets and kettle-drums, and then the other drums, which are much cried up, though I think it dull, vulgar musique. So to Mr. Fox's, unbid, where I had a good dinner and special company.

4th. To a dinner of Capt. Tayler's, where Sir William Pen and the Comptroller and several others were, men and women, and we

---

[1] Thomas Turner, of the Navy Office; a neighbour of Pepys'.
[2] In commemoration of the martyrdom of King Charles I.

"I TOOK PLEASURE TO TAKE THE FORFEITS OF THE LADIES"

had a very great and merry dinner; and after dinner the Comptroller begun some sports, among others the naming of people round and afterwards demanding questions of them that they are forced to answer their names to, which do make very good sport. And here I took pleasure to take the forfeits of the ladies who would not do their duty by kissing of them; among others a pretty lady, who I found afterwards to be wife to Sir W. Batten's son.

5th. Washing-day. My wife and I by water to Westminster. She to her mother's and I to Westminster Hall, where I found a full term, and here I went to Will's, and there found Shaw [1] and Ashwell [2] and another Bragrave (who knew my mother washmaid to my Lady Veere), who by cursing and swearing made me weary of his company and so I went away. Into the Hall and there saw the heads of Cromwell, Bradshaw, and Ireton, set up upon the further end of the Hall.

7th. To my Lord's, where, while I and my Lady were in her chamber in talk, in comes my Lord from sea, to our great wonder. All my friends his servants well. Dined with my Lord, and then with Mr. Shepley and Creed (who talked very high of France for a fine country) to the tavern, and then I home.

10th. (Lord's Day.) Took physique all day, and, God forgive me, did spend it in reading of some little French romances. At night my wife and I did please ourselves talking of our going into France, which I hope to effect this summer.

13th. At the office all the morning; dined at home, and poor Mr. Wood with me, who after dinner would have borrowed money of me, but I would lend none. Then to Whitehall by coach with Sir W. Pen, where we did very little business, and with him to Sir W. Batten's whither I sent for my wife, and we chose Valentines against to-morrow. My wife chose me, which did much please me; my Lady Batten Sir W. Pen, &c.

14th. (Valentine's day.) Up early and to Sir W. Batten's, but would not go in till I asked whether they that opened the door was a man or a woman, and Mingo,[3] who was there, answered a woman, which, with his tone, made me laugh. So up I went and took Mrs. Martha [4] for my Valentine (which I do only for complacency), and Sir W. Batten he go in the same manner to my

---

[1] Robert Shaw, manager to Alderman Backwell, the great banker and goldsmith.
[2] Formerly a brother clerk of Pepys at the Exchequer. Father of Mary Ashwell, who becomes later companion to Mrs. Pepys.
[3] Sir W. Batten's black servant.
[4] Sir W. Batten's daughter, then aged twenty-four. Two years later she married a Mr. Castle; Pepys did not envy him his wife.

wife, and so we were very merry. About 10 o'clock we, with a great deal of company, went down by our barge to Deptford, the first time I ever carried my wife a-ship-board; as also my boy Wayneman, who hath all this day been called young Pepys, as Sir W. Pen's boy young Pen. So home by barge again; good weather, but pretty cold. The talk of the town now is, who the King is like to have for his Queen: and whether Lent shall be kept with the strictness of the King's proclamation;[1] which it is thought cannot be because of the poor, who cannot buy fish. And also the great preparation for the King's crowning is now much thought upon and talked of.

15th. At the office all the morning, and in the afternoon at making up my accounts for my Lord to-morrow; and that being done I found myself to be clear (as I think) £350 in the world, besides my goods in my house and all things paid for.

16th. Dined with my Lord and then to the Theatre, where I saw "The Virgin Martyr,"[2] a good but too sober a play for the company.

17th. (Lord's Day.) A most tedious, unreasonable, and impertinent sermon, by an Irish Doctor. His text was "Scatter them, O Lord, that delight in war." Sir Wm. Batten and I very much angry with the parson.

18th. At the office all the morning. In the afternoon my wife and I and Mrs. Martha Batten, my Valentine, to the Exchange, and there upon a payre of embroydered and six payre of plain white gloves I laid out 40s. upon her. And at night I got the whole company and Sir Wm. Pen home to my house, and there I did give them Rhenish wine and sugar, and continued together till it was late, and so to bed. It is much talked that the King is already married to the niece of the Prince de Ligne,[3] and that he hath two sons already by her, which I am sorry to hear; but yet am gladder that it should be so, than that the Duke of York and his family should come to the crown, he being a professed friend to the Catholiques.

23rd. This my birthday, 28 years   To my Lord and there spoke to him about his opinion of the Light, the seamark that Captain Murford is about, and do offer me an eighth part to concern myself with it, and my Lord do give me some encouragement

---

[1] A proclamation for restraint of killing dressing, and eating of flesh in Lent had been issued on January 29.   [2] By Massinger and Dekker.
  [3] The Prince de Ligne had no niece. Charles had at one time made an offer of marriage to a niece of Cardinal Mazarin.

in it, and I shall go on. After dinner to Whitehall Chappell with Mr. Child,[1] and there did hear Captain Cooke and his boy make a trial of an Anthem against to-morrow, which was brave musique. Then by water to Whitefriars to the Play-house, and there saw "The Changeling," [2] the first time it hath been acted these twenty years, and it takes exceedingly. Besides, I see the gallants do begin to be tyred with the vanity and pride of the theatre actors who are indeed grown very proud and rich. Then by link home, and there to my book awhile and to bed, blessed be God, in a state of full content, and great hopes to be a happy man in all respects, both to myself and friends.

27th. This being the first day of Lent I do intend to try whether I can keep it or no. My father dined with me and did show me a letter from my brother John, wherein he tells us that he is chosen Schollar of the house,[3] which do please me much.

28th. Took boat at Whitehall for Redriffe, but in my way overtook Captain Cuttance, and walked with him to Deptford, where notwithstanding my resolution, yet for want of other victualls, I did eat flesh this Lent, but am resolved to eat as little as I can.

March 1st. Sat up late, spending my thoughts how to get money to bear me out in my great expense at the Coronacion, against which all provide, and scaffolds setting up in every street. I had many designs in my head to get some, but know not which will take.

2nd. To Salsbury Court, where the house as full as could be; it seems it was a new play, "The Queen's Maske," [4] wherein there are some good humours: among others a good jeer to the old story of the Siege of Troy, making it to be a common country tale. But above all it was strange to see so little a boy as that was to act Cupid, which is one of the greatest parts in it.

18th. This morning early Sir W. Batten went to Rochester, where he expects to be chosen Parliament man. This day I found in the newes-booke that Roger Pepys is chosen at Cambridge for the town, the first place that we hear of to have made their choice yet. To bed with my head and mind full of business, which do a little put me out of order, and I do find myself to become more and more thoughtful about getting of money than ever heretofore.

---

[1] One of the organists of St. George's Chapel, Windsor.
[3] Christ's College, Cambridge.   [2] By Thomas Middleton.
[4] *Love's Mistress, or The Queen's Masque.*   By Thomas Heywood.

23rd. All the morning at home putting papers in order; dined at home, and then out to the Red Bull,[1] and went in, where I was led by a seaman that knew me, but is here as a servant, up to the tireing-room, where strange the confusion and disorder that there is among them in fitting themselves, especially here, where the clothes are very poor, and the actors but common fellows. At last into the pitt, where I think there was not above ten more than myself, and not one hundred in the whole house. And the play, which is called "All's lost by Lust," [2] poorly done; and with so much disorder, among others, that in the musique-room the boy that was to sing a song not singing it right, his master fell about his ears and beat him so that it put the whole house in an uprore.

25th. (Lady Day.) This morning came workmen to begin the making of me a new pair of stairs up out of my parler, which, with other work that I have to do, I doubt will keep me this two months and so long I shall be all in dirt; but the work do please me very well. After dinner I to Mrs. Turner, and there staid talking late. The. Turner being in a great chafe about being disappointed of a room to stand in at the Coronacion. Then to my father's. So homewards and took up a boy that had a lanthorn, that was picking up of rags, and got him to light me home, and had great discourse with him, how he could get sometimes three or four bushells of rags in a day, and got 3*d.* a bushell for them, and many other discourses, what and how many ways there are for poor children to get their livings honestly. So home and I to bed at 12 o'clock at night.

26th. Up early to do business in my study. All this morning I staid at home looking after my workmen to my great content about my stairs, and at noon by coach to my father's, where Mrs. Turner, The., Joyce, Mr. Morrice, Mr. Armiger, Mr. Pierce, the surgeon, and his wife, my father and mother, and myself and my wife. Very merry at dinner; among other things, because Mrs. Turner and her company eat no flesh at all this Lent, and I had a great deal of good flesh which made their mouths water.

27th. To the Dolphin to a dinner of Mr. Harris's,[3] where Sir Williams both[4] and my Lady Batten and her two daughters, and other company, where a great deal of mirth, and there staid till 11 o'clock at night; and in our mirth I sang and sometimes fiddled. At last we fell to dancing, the first time that ever I did in my life,

---

[1] A playhouse at Clerkenwell. [2] By W. Rowley.
[3] John Harris. He supplied sails to the Navy Office.
[4] Sir William Penn and Sir William Batten.

which I did wonder to see myself to do. At last we made Mingo, Sir W. Batten's black, and Jack, Sir W. Pen's, dance, and it was strange how the first did dance with a great deal of seeming skill. Home, where I found my wife all day in her chamber. So to bed.

29th. To the office, where I found Sir W. Pen sent down yesterday to Chatham to get two great ships in readiness presently to go to the East Indies upon some design against the Dutch, we think, at Goa,[1] but it is a great secret yet. After that to Sir W. Batten's, where great store of company at dinner, and hither came letters from above for the fitting of two other ships for the East Indies in all haste, and so we got orders presently for the Hampshire and Nonsuch.

April 1st. To Whitefryars, and there saw part of "Rule a wife and have a wife," [2] which I never saw before, but do not like it. So to my father; and there finding a discontent between my father and mother about the maid, I staid till 10 at night, persuading my mother to understand herself,[3] and that in some high words, which I was sorry for, but she is grown, poor woman, very froward. So leaving them in the same discontent I went away home, it being a brave moonshine, and to bed.

2nd. Among my workmen early, and then along with my wife and Pall to my Father's by coach, there to have them lie a while till my house be done. Then to the Privy Seal and signed some things, and then to the Dolphin to Sir W. Batten, and Pen, and other company; where strange how these men, who at other times are all wise men, do now, in their drink, betwitt and reproach one another with their former conditions and their actions as in public concernments, till I was ashamed to see it. But parted all friends at 12 at night after drinking a great deal of wine. So home and alone to bed.

3rd. Up among my workmen, my head akeing all day from last night's debauch. To the office all the morning, and at noon dined with Sir W. Batten and Pen, who would needs have me drink two drafts of sack to-day to cure me of last night's disease, which I thought strange but I think find it true.

6th. Up among my workmen, then to Whitehall, and there at Privy Seal and elsewhere did business; and among other things met with Mr. Townsend,[4] who told of his mistake the other day,

---

[1] On the Malabar coast of India.
[2] By John Fletcher.
[3] To know one's place, to conduct oneself properly (*O.E.D.*).
[4] An official at the Wardrobe.

to put both his legs through one of his knees of his breeches, and went so all day.

7th.   (Lord's Day.)   Went to Sir W. Batten's and resolved of a journey to-morrow to Chatham, and so home and to bed.

8th.   Up early, my Lady Batten knocking at her door that comes into one of my chambers.   I did give directions to my people and workmen, and so about 8 o'clock we took barge at the Tower.   A very pleasant passage and so to Gravesend, where we dined.   At Rochester, where alight at Mr. Alcock's and there drank, and had good sport with his bringing out so many sorts of cheese.   Then to the Hillhouse at Chatham.[1]   Here we supped very merry, and late to bed; Sir William telling me that Old Edgeborrow, his predecessor, did die and walk in my chamber, did make me somewhat afeard, but not so much as for mirth's sake I did seem.   So to bed in the treasurer's chamber,

9th.   And lay and slept well till 3 in the morning, and then waking, and by the light of the moon I saw my pillow (which overnight I flung from me) stand upright, but not bethinking myself what it might be, I was a little afeard, but sleep overcame all and so lay till high morning, at which time I had a candle brought me and a good fire made; and in general it was a great pleasure all the time I staid here to see how I am respected and honoured by all people; and I find that I begin to know now how to receive so much reverence, which at the beginning I could not tell how to do.   After dinner the ladies and I and Captain Pett and Mr. Castle [2] took barge, and down we went to see the Sovereign, which we did, taking great pleasure therein, singing all the way; and, among other pleasures, I put my Lady,[3] Mrs. Turner, Mrs. Hempson, and the two Mrs. Allens [4] into the lanthorn and I went in and kissed them, demanding it as a fee due to a principall officer, with all which we were exceeding merry, and drunk some bottles of wine and neat's tongue, &c.   Then back again home and so supped, and after much mirth to bed.

10th.   In the morning to see the Dockhouses.   Then to Rochester, and there saw the Cathedrall, which is now fitting for use, and the organ then a-tuning.   Then away thence, observing the great doors of the church, which, they say, was covered with the skins of the Danes.   So to the Salutacion tavern, where Mr. Alcock and

---

1 Now incorporated in the Marine Barracks.
2 William Castle, shipwright, who married Sir W. Batten's daughter Martha.
3 Lady Batten.   Pepys commonly reserves this title for Lady Sandwich.
4 Daughters of Capt. John Allen, formerly Clerk of the Ropeyard at Chatham.

many of the town came and entertained us with wine and oysters and other things. Here much mirth, but I was a little troubled to stay too long, because of going to Hempson's, which afterwards we did. Here we had, for my sake, two fiddles, the one a base viall, on which he that played, played well some lyra lessons, but both together made the worst musique that ever I heard. We had a fine collacion, but I took little pleasure in that, for the illness of the musique and for the intentness of my mind upon Mrs. Rebecca Allen. After we had done eating, the ladies went to dance, and among the men we had I was forced to dance too, and did make an ugly shift. Mrs. R. Allen danced very well, and seems the best humoured woman that ever I saw.

11th. At 2 o'clock, with very great mirth, we went to our lodging and to bed, and lay till 7, and then called up by Sir W. Batten; and then came Captn. Allen, and he and I withdrew and sang a song or two, and among others took pleasure in "Goe and bee hanged, that's good-bye." The young ladies come too, and so I did again please myself with Mrs. Rebecca, and about 9 o'clock, after we had breakfasted, we sett forth for London.

We baited at Dartford, and thence to London, but of all the journeys that ever I made this was the merriest, and I was in a strange mood for mirth. Among other things I got my Lady to let her maid, Mrs. Anne, to ride all the way on horseback, and she rides exceeding well; and so I called her my clerk, that she went to wait upon me. I met two little schoolboys going with pitchers of ale to their school-master to break up against Easter, and I did drink of some of one of them and gave him two pence. By and by we come to two little girls keeping cows, and I saw one of them very pretty, so I had a mind to make her ask my blessing, and telling her that I was her godfather, she asked me innocently whether I was not Ned Wooding, and I said that I was, so she kneeled down and very simply called, "Pray, godfather, pray to God to bless me," which made us very merry, and I gave her two-pence. In several places, I asked women whether they would sell me their children, but they denied me all, but said they would give me one to keep for them, if I would. So home and I found all well, and a deal of work done since I went. I sent to see how my wife do, who is well, and my brother John come from Cambridge.

17th. To the Dolphin by appointment and there I met Sir Wms. both and Mr. Castle, and did eat a barrel of oysters and two lobsters, which I did give them, and were very merry. Here we

"PRAY, GODFATHER, PRAY TO GOD TO BLESS ME"

had great talk of Mr. Warren's [1] being knighted by the King, and Sir W. B. seemed to be very much incensed against him. So home.

20th. Here comes my boy to tell me that the Duke of York had sent for all the principall officers, &c., to come to him to-day. So I went by water to Mr. Coventry's, and there staid and talked a good while with him till all the rest come. We went up and saw the Duke dress himself, and in his night habitt he is a very plain man. Then he sent us to his closett, and after he had told us that the fleet was designed for Algier (which was kept from us till now), we did advise about many things as to the fitting of the fleet, and so went away.

Dined with my Lord. After dinner my Lord looked upon his pages' and footmen's liverys, which are come home to-day, and will be handsome, though not gaudy. Then with my Lady and my Lady Wright to White Hall; and in the Banqueting-house saw the King create my Lord Chancellor and several others, Earls, and Mr. Crew and several others, Barons: the first being led up by Heralds and five old Earls to the King, and there the patent is read, and the King puts on his vest, and sword, and coronet, and gives him the patent. And then he kisseth the King's hand, and rises and stands covered before the king. And the same for the Barons, only he is led up but by three of the old Barons, and are girt with swords before they go to the King. That being done (which was very pleasant to see their habits), I carried my Lady back, and I found my Lord angry, for that his page had let my Lord's new beaver be changed for an old hat.

21st. (Lord's Day.) In the morning we were troubled to hear it rain as it did, because of the great show to-morrow. After I was ready I walked to my father's. Here dined Doctor Thos. Pepys and Dr. Fayrebrother; and all our talk about to-morrow's show, and our trouble that it is like to be a wet day. After dinner comes in my coz. Snow [2] and his wife, and I think stay there till the show be over. Then I went home, and all the way is so thronged with people to see the triumphal arches that I could hardly pass for them.

22nd. (King's going from y Tower to White Hall.[3]) Up early and made myself as fine as I could, and put on my velvet coat, the first day that I put it on, though made half a year ago. And being

---

[1] Sir William Warren, a wealthy tradesman of Wapping. Pepys was much beholden to him for advice later on.
[2] Cousin is here only a term of friendship.
[3] Prior to his progress through the City to his coronation at Westminster Abbey.

ready, Sir W. Batten, my Lady, and his two daughters and his son and wife, and Sir W. Pen and his son and I, went to Mr. Young's, the flag-maker, in Corne-hill; and there we had a good room to ourselves, with wine and good cake, and saw the show very well. In which it is impossible to relate the glory of this day, expressed in the clothes of them that rid, and their horses and horses-clothes, among others, my Lord Sandwich's. Embroidery and diamonds were ordinary among them. The Knights of the Bath was a brave sight of itself; and their Esquires, among which Mr. Armiger was an Esquire to one of the Knights. Remarquable were the two men that represent the two Dukes of Normandy and Aquitane. The Bishops come next after Barons, which is the higher place; which makes me think that the next Parliament they will be called to the House of Lords. My Lord Monk rode bare after the King, and led in his hand a spare horse, as being Master of the Horse. The King, in a most rich embroidered suit and cloak, looked most noble. Wadlow, the vintner at the Devil, in Fleet-street, did lead a fine company of soldiers, all young comely men in white doublets. There followed the Vice-Chamberlain, Sir G. Carteret, a company of men all like Turks, but I know not yet what they are for. The streets all gravelled, and the houses hung with carpets before them, made brave show, and the ladies out of the windows, one of which over against us I took much notice of, and spoke of her, which made good sport among us. So glorious was the show with gold and silver, that we were not able to look at it, our eyes at last being so much overcome with it. Both the King and the Duke of York took notice of us, as he saw us at the window. The show being ended, Mr. Young did give us a dinner, at which we were very merry, and pleased above imagination at what we have seen. Sir W. Batten going home, he and I called and drunk some mum [1] and laid our wager about my Lady Faulconbridge's name,[2] which he says not to be Mary, and so I won above 20s. So home, where Will and the boy staid and saw the show upon Towre Hill, and Jane at T. Pepys's, The. Turner and my wife at Charles Glassecocke's, in Fleet Street. In the evening by water to White Hall to my Lord's, and there I spoke with my Lord. He talked with me about his suit, which was made in France, and cost him £200, and very rich it is with embroidery. I lay with Mr. Shepley, and

---

[1] A kind of beer originally brewed in Brunswick, and largely imported into England in the seventeenth and eighteenth centuries. [2] Mary, third daughter of Oliver Cromwell.

23rd. (Coronaĉon Day) about 4 I rose and got to the Abbey, where I followed Sir J. Denham, the Surveyor, with some company that he was leading in. And with much ado, by the favour of Mr. Cooper, his man, did get up into a great scaffold across the North end of the Abbey, where with a great deal of patience I sat from past 4 till 11 before the King came in. And a great pleasure it was to see the Abbey raised in the middle, all covered with red, and a throne (that is a chair) and footstool on the top of it; and all the officers of all kinds, so much as the very fidlers, in red vests. At last comes in the Dean and Prebends of Westminster, with the Bishops (many of them in cloth of gold copes), and after them the Nobility, all in their Parliament robes, which was a most magnificent sight. Then the Duke, and the King with a scepter (carried by my Lord Sandwich) and sword and mond [1] before him, and the crown too. The King in his robes, bare-headed, which was very fine. And after all had placed themselves, there was a sermon and the service; and then in the Quire at the high altar, the King passed through all the ceremonies of the Coronaĉon, which to my great grief I and most in the Abbey could not see. The crown being put upon his head, a great shout begun, and he came forth to the throne, and there passed more ceremonies, as taking the oath, and having things read to him by the Bishop [2]; and his lords (who put on their caps as soon as the King put on his crown [3]) and bishops come, and kneeled before him. And three times the King at Arms went to the three open places on the scaffold, and proclaimed that if any one could show any reason why Charles Stewart should not be King of England, that now he should come and speak. And a Generall Pardon also was read by the Lord Chancellor, and meddalls flung up and down by my Lord Cornwallis,[4] of silver, but I could not come by any. But so great a noise that I could make but little of the musique; and indeed, it was lost to every body.

I went out a little while before the King had done all his cere-monies, and went round the Abbey to Westminster Hall, all the way within rayles, and 10,000 people, with the ground covered with blue cloth, and scaffolds all the way. Into the Hall I got, where it was very fine with hangings and scaffolds one upon an-other full of brave ladies; and my wife in one little one, on the

[1] Orb.
[2] The place of Juxon, Archbishop of Canterbury, was on this occasion taken by Gilbert Sheldon. Bishop of London; he succeeded Juxon in 1663.
[3] As yet barons had no coronet. Charles II. granted them coronets later, as Elizabeth had previously done to viscounts.   [4] Treasurer of the Household.

right hand. Here I staid walking up and down, and at last upon one of the side stalls I stood and saw the King come in with all the persons (but the soldiers) that were yesterday in the cavalcade; and a most pleasant sight it was to see them in their several robes. And the King came in with his crown on, and his sceptre in his hand, under a canopy borne up by six silver staves, carried by Barons of the Cinque Ports, and little bells at every end. And after a long time he got up to the farther end, and all set themselves down at their several tables; and that was also a brave sight: and the King's first course carried up by the Knights of the Bath. And many fine ceremonies there was of the Heralds leading up people before him, and bowing; and my Lord of Albemarle's going to the kitchin and eat a bit of the first dish that was to go to the King's table. But, above all, was these three Lords,[1] Northumberland, and Suffolk, and the Duke of Ormond, coming before the courses on horseback, and staying so all dinner-time, and at last to bring up [Dymock] [2] the King's Champion, all in armour on horseback, with his spear and targett carried before him. And a Herald proclaims "That if any dare deny Charles Stewart to be lawful King of England, here was a Champion that would fight with him;" and with these words, the Champion flings down his gauntlet, and all this he do three times in his going up towards the King's table. At last when he is come, the King drinks to him, and then sends him the cup which is of gold, and he drinks it off, and then rides back again with the cup in his hand. I went from table to table to see the Bishops and all others at their dinner, and was infinitely pleased with it. And at the Lords' table I met with William Howe, and he spoke to my Lord for me, and he did give me four rabbits and a pullet, and so I got it and Mr. Creed and I got Mr. Michell to give us some bread, and so we at a stall eat it, as every body else did what they could get. I took a great deal of pleasure to go up and down and look upon the ladies, and to hear the musique of all sorts, but above all the 24 violins.

About six at night they had dined, and I went up to my wife, and there met with a pretty lady (Mrs. Frankleyn, a Doctor's wife, a friend of Mr. Bowyer's) and kissed them both, and by and by took them down to Mr. Bowyer's. And strange it is to think, that these two days have held up fair till now that all is done,

---

[1] Acting as Lord High Constable, Earl Marshal, and Lord High Steward, respectively.
[2] Sir Edward Dymock, as Lord of the Manor of Scrivelsby, Lincs.

and the King gone out of the Hall; and then it fell a-raining and thundering and lightening as I have not seen it do for some years: which people did take great notice of, God's blessing of the work of these two days, which is a foolery to take too much notice of such things. I observed little disorder in all this, but only the King's footmen had got hold of the canopy and would keep it from the Barons of the Cinque Ports, which they endeavoured to force from them again but could not do it, till my Lord Duke of Albemarle caused it to be put into Sir R. Pye's hand till to-morrow to be decided. At Mr. Bowyer's a great deal of company, some I knew, others I did not. Here we staid upon the leads and below till it was late, expecting to see the fire-works, but they were not performed to-night: only the City had a light like a glory round about it with bonfires. At last I went to King-street, and there sent Crockford to my father's and my house, to tell them I could not come home to-night, because of the dirt, and a coach could not be had. And so after drinking a pot of ale alone at Mrs. Harper's I returned to Mr. Bowyer's, and after a little stay more I took my wife and Mrs. Frankleyn (who I proffered the civility of lying with my wife at Mrs. Hunt's to-night) to Axe-yard, in which at the further end there were three great bonfires, and a great many great gallants, men and women; and they laid hold of us, and would have us drink the King's health upon our knees, kneeling upon a faggot, which we all did, they drinking to us one after another, which we thought a strange frolique; but these gallants continued thus a great while, and I wondered to see how the ladies did tipple. At last I sent my wife and her bedfellow to bed, and Mr. Hunt and I went in with Mr. Thornbury (who did give the company all their wine, he being yeoman of the wine-cellar to the King) to his house; and there, with his wife and two of his sisters, and some gallant sparks that were there, we drank the King's health and nothing else, till one of the gentlemen fell down stark drunk, and there lay spewing; and I went to my Lord's pretty well. But no sooner a-bed with Mr. Shepley but my head began to hum, and I to vomit, and if ever I was foxed it was now, which I cannot say yet, because I fell asleep, and slept till morning. Thus did the day end with joy every where.

29th. It is determined that I should go to-morrow to Portsmouth.

30th. This morning, after order given to my workmen, my wife and I and Mr. Creed took coach, and in Fish-street took up

Mr. Hater and his wife, who through her mask seemed at first to be an old woman, but afterwards I found her to be a very pretty modest black woman. We got a small bait at Leatherhead, and so to Godlyman,[1] where we lay all night, and were very merry. I am sorry that I am not at London to be at Hide-parke to-morrow, among the great gallants and ladies, which will be very fine.

May 1st. Up early, and bated at Petersfield, in the room which the King lay in lately at his being there. Here very merry, and played, us and our wives, at bowls. Then we set forth again, and so to Portsmouth, seeming to me to be a very pleasant and strong place; and we lay at the Red Lyon, where Haselrigge and Scott and Walton did hold their councill, when they were here, against Lambert and the Committee of Safety.

2nd. Up, and Mr. Creed and I to walk round the town upon the walls. Then to our inn, and there all the officers of the Yard to see me with great respect, and I walked with them to the Dock and saw all the stores, and much pleased with the sight of the place.

4th. Up in the morning and took coach, and so to Gilford, where we lay at the Red Lyon, the best Inn.

7th. In the morning to Mr. Coventry, Sir G. Carteret, and my Lord's to give them an account of my return. Then with Mr. Creed into London, to several places about his and my business, being much stopped in our way by the City trayne-bands, who go in much solemnity and pomp this day to muster before the King and the Duke; and shops in the City are shut up every where all this day.

8th. To-day I received a letter from my uncle, to beg an old fiddle of me for my Cozen Perkin,[2] the miller, whose mill the wind hath lately broke down; and now he hath nothing to live by but fiddling, and he must needs have it against Whitsuntide to play to the country girls; but it vexed me to see how my uncle writes to me, as if he were not able to buy him one. But I intend to-morrow to send him one.

23rd. To the Rhenish wine house, and there came Jonas Moore,[3] the mathematician, to us; and there he did by discourse make us fully believe that England and France were once the same continent, by very good arguments, and spoke very many things, not so much to prove the Scripture false as that the time

---

[1] Godalming.   [2] Frank Perkins, whose mother was the youngest sister of Pepys's father.
[3] Sir Jonas Moore, Surveyor-General of the Ordnance. At one time tutor to James, Duke of York. A founder of the Royal Society.

therein is not well computed nor understood. From thence home by water, and there shifted myself into my black silk suit (the first day I have put it on this year), and so to my Lord Mayor's by coach, with a great deal of honourable company, and great entertainment. At table I had very good discourse with Mr. Ashmole,[1] wherein he did assure me that frogs and many insects do often fall from the sky, ready formed. Dr. Bates's [2] singularity in not rising up nor drinking the King's nor other healths at the table was very much observed. From thence we all took coach, and to our office, and there sat till it was late; and so I home and to bed by day-light. This day was kept a holy-day through the town; and it pleased me to see the little boys walk up and down in procession with their broom-staffs in their hands, as I had myself long ago gone.[3]

24th. At home all the morning making up my private accounts, and this is the first time that I do find myself to be clearly worth £500 in money, besides all my goods in my house, &c. In the afternoon at the office late, and then I went to the Wardrobe, where I found my Lord at supper, and therefore I walked a good while till he had done, and I went in to him, and there he looked over my accounts. Then down to the kitchen to eat a bit of bread and butter, which I did, and there I took one of the maids by the chin, thinking her to be Susan, but it proved to be her sister, who is very like her. From thence home.

26th. (Lord's Day.) Lay long in bed. To church and heard a good sermon at our own church, where I have not been a great many weeks. Dined with my wife alone at home pleasing myself in that my house do begin to look as if at last it would be in good order. To Sir W. Batten's, where I have on purpose made myself a great stranger, only to get a high opinion a little more of myself in them. Here I heard how Mrs. Browne, Sir W. Batten's sister, is brought to bed, and I to be one of the godfathers, which I could not nor did deny.

29th. (King's birth-day.) Rose early and having made myself fine, and put six spoons and a porringer of silver in my pocket to give away to-day, Sir W. Pen and I took coach, and (the weather and ways being foul) went to Walthamstowe, to dinner to Sir William Batten's; and then, after a walk in the fine gardens, we went to Mrs. Browne's, where Sir W. Pen and I were godfathers to

---

[1] Elias Ashmole, the antiquary and astrologer; founder of the Ashmolean Museum, Oxford.
[2] Dr. William Bates, an eminent Puritan divine.
[3] Beating the bounds of the parishes on Maundy Thursday.

her boy. And there, before and after the christening, we were with the woman above in her chamber; but whether we carried ourselves well or ill, I know not; but I was directed by young Mrs. Batten. One passage of a lady that eat wafers with her dog did a little displease me. I did give the midwife 10s. and the nurse 5s. and the maid of the house 2s. But for as much I expected to give the name to the child, but did not (it being called John), I forebore then to give my plate till another time, after a little more advice.

31st. I went to my father's, but to my great grief I found my father and mother in a great deal of discontent one with another, and indeed my mother is grown now so pettish that I know not how my father is able to bear with it. I did talk to her so as did not indeed become me, but I could not help it, she being so unsufferably foolish and simple, so that my father, poor man, is become a very unhappy man.

June 5th. This morning did give my wife £4 to lay out upon lace and other things for herself. After dinner to the office, where we sat and did business, and Sir W. Pen and I went home with Sir R. Slingsby to bowls in his ally, and there had good sport, and afterwards went in and drank and talked. So home Sir William and I, and it being very hot weather I took my flageolette and played upon the leads in the garden, where Sir W. Pen came out in his shirt into his leads, and there we staid talking and singing, and drinking great drafts of claret, and eating botargo [1] and bread and butter till 12 at night, it being moonshine; and so to bed, very near fuddled.

6th. Went and eat and drank and heard musique at the Globe, and saw the simple motion that is there of a woman with a rod in her hand keeping time to the musique while it plays, which is simple, methinks.

9th. (Lord's Day.) This day my wife put on her black silk gown, which is now laced all over with black gimp lace, as the fashion is, in which she is very pretty. She and I walked to my Lady's at the Wardrobe, and there dined and was exceeding much made of.

10th. Early to my Lord's, who privately told me how the King had made him Embassador in the bringing over the Queen. [2]

---

[1] The dried roe of the tunny-fish.
[2] Katherine of Braganza, a Portuguese princess, aged twenty-three. The match had been first proposed by her father when she was seven. She brought the ports of Tangiers and Bombay, together with a dowry of £300,000.

I staid and dined with my Lady; but after we were set, comes in some persons of condition, and so the children and I rose and dined by ourselves, all the children and I, and were very merry and they mighty fond of me.

11th. At the office this morning, Sir G. Carteret with us; and we agreed upon a letter to the Duke of York, to tell him the sad condition of this office for want of money; how men are not able to serve us more without some money; and that now the credit of the office is brought so low, that none will sell us any thing without our personal security given for the same. All the afternoon abroad about several businesses, and at night home and to bed.

12th. To White Hall, where I met my Lord, who told me he must have £300 laid out in cloth, to give in Barbary, as presents among the Turks.

13th. To Alderman Backwell's, but his servants not being up I went home and put on my gray cloth suit and faced white coat, made of one of my wife's pettycoates, and so back again and spoke with Mr. Shaw at the Alderman's, who offers me £300, if my Lord pleases, to buy this cloth with, which pleased me well. So to the Wardrobe and with my Lord to Whitehall by water, and he having taken leave of the King, comes to us at his lodgings and from thence goes to the garden stairs and there takes barge, and at the stairs was met by Sir R. Slingsby, who there took his leave of my Lord, and I heard my Lord thank him for his kindness to me, which Sir Robert answered much to my advantage. I went down with my Lord in the barge to Deptford, and there went on board the Dutch yacht and staid there a good while, W. Howe not being come with my Lord's things, which made my Lord very angry. By and by he comes and so we set sayle, and anon went to dinner, my Lord and we very merry; and after dinner I went down below and there sang, and took leave of W. Howe, Captain Rolt, and the rest of my friends, then went up and took leave of my Lord, who give me his hand and parted with great respect. So went and Captain Ferrers with me into our wherry, and my Lord did give five guns, all they had charged, which was the greatest respect my Lord could do me, and of which I was not a little proud. So with a sad and merry heart I left them sailing pleasantly from Erith, hoping to be in the Downs to-morrow early.

18th. In the afternoon my wife and I by water to Captain Lambert's where we took great pleasure in their turret-garden, and seeing the fine needleworks of his wife, the best I ever saw in my life, and afterwards had a very handsome treat and good musique that she made upon the harpsicon. So home, where I met Jack Cole, who staid with me a good while, and is still of the old good humour that we were of at school together, and I am very glad to see him. He gone, I went to bed.

22nd. Abroad all the morning about several businesses. At noon went and dined with my Lord Crew, where very much made of by him and his lady. Then to the Theatre, "The Alchymist,"[1] which is a most incomparable play.

23rd. (Lord's Day.) In the morning to church, and my wife not being well, I went with Sir W. Batten home to dinner, my Lady being out of town, where there was Sir W. Pen, Captain Allen and his daughter Rebecca, and Mr. Hempson and his wife. After dinner to church, all of us, and had a very good sermon of a stranger, and so I and the young company to walk first to Graye's Inn Walks, where great store of gallants, but above all the ladies that I there saw, or ever did see, Mrs. Frances Butler (Monsieur L'Impertinent's sister) is the greatest beauty.

24th. (Midsummer-day.) We kept this a holiday, and so went not to the office at all. All the morning at home. At noon my father came to see my house now it is done, which is now very neat. He and I and Dr. Williams (who is come to see my wife, whose soare belly is now grown dangerous as she thinks) to the ordinary over against the Exchange, where we dined.

27th. I took my leave of my father, who is going this morning to my uncle upon my aunt's letter this week that he is not well and so needs my father's help. This day Mr. Holden[2] sent me a bever, which cost me £4 5s.

28th. At home all the morning practising to sing, which is now my great trade, and at noon to my Lady and dined with her. So back and to the office, and there sat till 7 at night, and then Sir W. Pen, and I in his coach went to Moorefields, and there walked, and stood and saw the wrestling, which I never saw so much of before, between the north and west countrymen.

29th. I walked to the Bell at the Maypole[3] in the Strand, and thither came to me by appointment Mr. Chetwind, Gregory, and

[1] By Ben Jonson.
[2] Mr. Holden was Pepys' hatter. It is a sign of Pepys' growing social consequence that he should be able to allow himself a hat of this price—the modern equivalent of £20.
[3] The Maypole was fixed on the present site of St. Mary-le-Strand.

Hartlibb,[1] so many of our old club, and Mr. Kipps, where we staid and drank and talked with much pleasure till it was late, and so I walked home and to bed. Mr. Chetwind by chewing of tobacco is become very fat and sallow, whereas he was consumptive; and in our discourse he fell commending of "Hooker's Ecclesiastical Polity," as the best book, and the only one that made him a Christian, which puts me upon the buying of it, which I will do shortly.

30th. (Lord's Day.) To church. After dinner to Graye's Inn Walk, all alone, and with great pleasure seeing the fine ladies walk there. Myself humming to myself (which now-a-days is my constant practice since I begun to learn to sing) the trillo, and found by use that it do come upon me. This day the Portuguese Embassador came to White Hall to take leave of the King, he being now going to end all with the Queen, and to send her over. The weather now very fair and pleasant, but very hot. My father gone to Brampton to see my uncle Robert, not knowing whether to find him dead or alive. Myself lately under a great expense of money upon myself in clothes and other things, but I hope to make it up this summer by my having to do in getting things ready to send with the next fleet to the Queen. Myself in good health.

July 1st. This morning I went up and down into the city to buy several things, as I have lately done, for my house. Among other things a fair chest of drawers for my own chamber, and an Indian gown for myself. The first cost me 33*s.*, the other 34*s.* Home and dined there, and Theodore Goodgroome,[2] my singing master, with me, and then to our singing. After that to the office, and then home.

3rd. To the office, and that being done to Sir W. Batten's with the Comptroller, where we sat late talking and disputing with Mr. Mills the parson of our parish. This day my Lady Batten and my wife were at the burial of a daughter of Sir John Lawson's, and had rings for themselves and their husbands. Home and to bed.

6th. Waked this morning with news, brought me by a messenger on purpose, that my uncle Robert is dead, and died yesterday; so I rose sorry in some respect, glad in my expectations in another respect. So I made myself ready, went and told my uncle Wight,

[1] Mr. Chetwind, "my old and most ingenious acquaintance." Thomas Gregory was at one time Clerk of the Cheque at Chatham. Samuel Hartlib, the younger (a son of Milton's friend) had been a neighbour of Pepys in Axe Yard.
[2] Pepys had engaged Theodore Goodgroome on June 25 at twenty shillings a month. His first song was "La cruda la bella."

"SO MANY OF OUR OLD CLUB"

my Lady, and some others thereof, and bought me a pair of boots in St. Martin's, and got myself ready; and then to the Post House and set out about eleven and twelve o'clock, taking the messenger with me that came to me. And so we rode and got well by nine o'clock to Brampton, where I found my father well. My uncle's corps in a coffin standing upon joint-stools in the chimney in the hall; but it begun to smell, and so I caused it to be set forth in the yard all night, and watched by two men. My aunt I found in bed in a most nasty ugly pickle, made me sick to see it. My father and I lay together to-night, I greedy to see the will, but did not ask to see it till to-morrow.

7th. (Lord's Day.) In the morning my father and I walked in the garden and read the will; where, though he gives me nothing at present till my father's death, or at least very little, yet I am glad to see that he hath done so well for us all, and well to the rest of his kindred. After that done, we went about getting things, as ribbands and gloves, ready for the burial. Which in the afternoon was done; where, it being Sunday, all people far and near come in; and in the greatest disorder that ever I saw, we made shift to serve them what we had of wine and other things; and then to carry him to the church, where Mr. Taylor buried him.

8th, 9th, 10th, 11th, 12th, 13th. I fell to work, and my father to look over my uncle's papers and clothes, and continued all this week upon that business, much troubled with my aunt's base, ugly humours. We had news of Tom Trice's [1] putting in a caveat against us, in behalf of his mother, to whom my uncle hath not given anything, and for good reason therein expressed, which troubled us also. But above all, our trouble is to find that his estate appears nothing as we expected, and all the world believes; nor his papers so well sorted as I would have had them, but all in confusion, that break my brains to understand them. We missed also the surrenders of his copyhold land, without which the land would not come to us, but to the heir at law; so that what with this, and the badness of the drink, and the ill opinion I have of the meat, and the biting of the gnats by night, and my disappointment in getting home this week, and the trouble of sorting all the papers, I am almost out of my wits with trouble; only I appear the more contented, because I would not have my father troubled.

[1] The quarrel with Tom Trice which arose out of Robert Pepys' will lasted for a long time and caused Pepys a great deal of trouble. A sister of Robert Pepys had married a man called Trice. Jaspar Trice, mentioned on July 20, was perhaps a brother of Tom Trice.

16th, 17th, 18th, 19th.   These four days we spent in putting things in order, letting of the crop upon the ground, agreeing with Stankes [1] to have a care of our business in our absence, and we think ourselves in nothing happy but in lighting upon him to be our bayly; in riding to Offord and Sturtlow, and up and down all our lands, and in the evening walking, my father and I about the fields talking.

20th.   Up to Huntingdon this morning to Sir Robert Bernard,[2] with whom I met Jasper Trice.   So Sir Robert caused us to sit down together and began discourse very fairly between us; so I drew out the will and show it him, but could come to no issue till Tom Trice comes.   I walked home, and there found Tom Trice come, and he and my father gone to Goody Gorum's, where I found them, and there had some calm discourse, but came to no issue, and so parted.   So home and to bed.

21st.   (Lord's Day.)   At home all the morning, putting my papers in order against my going to-morrow, and doing many things else to that end.   Had a good dinner, and Stankes and his wife with us.   To my business again in the afternoon, and in the evening came the two Trices, Mr. Greene, and Mr. Philips, and so we began to argue.   At last it came to some agreement that for our giving of my aunt £10 she is to quit the house; and for other matters they are to be left to the law, which do please us all; and so we broke up, pretty well satisfyed.

22nd.   Up by three, and going by four on my way to London. To Hatfield before twelve o'clock, where I had a very good dinner. And so to horse again and with much ado got to London.

23rd.   Went to the theatre, and saw "Brenoralt," [3] I never saw before.   It seemed a good play, but ill acted; only I sat before Mrs. Palmer and filled my eyes with her, which much pleased me. Then to my father's, where by my desire I met my uncle Thomas, and discoursed of my uncle's will to him; and so home and to bed. Troubled to hear how proud and idle Pall is grown that I am resolved not to keep her.

24th.   This morning my wife in bed tells me of our being robbed of our silver tankard, which vexed me all day for the negligence of my people to leave the door open.   My wife and I by water to Whitehall, where I left her to her business, and I to my cozen Thomas Pepys, and discoursed with him at large about our busi-

[1] William Stankes, bailiff of Robert Pepys' estates at Brampton.
[2] Sergeant-at-Law, M.P. for Huntingdon.
[3] *Brennoralt, or the Discontented Colonel.* By Sir John Suckling.

ness of my uncle's will. Then to the Wardrobe, but come too late, and so dined with the servants. Then to my Lady, who do shew my wife and me the greatest favour in the world, in which I take great content. Home by water and to the office all the afternoon, which is a great pleasure to me again, to talk with persons of quality and to be in command, and I give it out among them that the estate left me is £200 a year in land, besides moneys, because I would put an esteem upon myself.[1] This afternoon I hear that my man Will hath lost his clock with my tankard, at which I am very glad.

25th. This morning came my box of papers from Brampton of all my uncle's papers, which will now set me at work enough. To my mother's, where I found my wife and my aunt Bell [2] and Mrs. Ramsey, and great store of tattle there was between the old women and my mother, who thinks that there is God knows what fallen to her.

26th. Having the beginning of this week made a vow to myself to drink no wine this week (finding it to unfit me to look after business), and this day breaking of it against my will, I am much troubled for it, but I hope God will forgive me.

27th. To Westminster, where at Mr. Montagu's chamber I heard a Frenchman play, a friend of Monsieur Eschar's, upon the guitar, most extreme well, though at the best methinks it is but a bawble.

August 1st. This morning Sir Williams both, and my wife and I and Mrs. Margarett Pen [3] went by coach to Walthamstow, a-gossiping to Mrs. Browne, where I did give her six silver spoons [4] for her boy.

10th. This morning came the maid that my wife hath lately hired for a chamber maid.[5] She is very ugly, so that I cannot care for her, but otherwise she seems very good. I went to my Lady's and dined with her, and after dinner took the two young gentlemen and the two ladies and carried them and Captain Ferrers to the Theatre, and shewed them "The merry Devill of Edmunton," which is a very merry play, the first time I ever saw it, which pleased me well.

11th. (Lord's Day.) To our own church in the forenoon, and in the afternoon to Clerkenwell Church, only to see the two

---

[1] It proved to be worth about £80 a year.
[2] Mrs. Bell was a sister of Pepys' father and of the deceased uncle.
[3] Only daughter of Sir W. Penn.
[4] But not the porringer of silver. See May 29.　　[5] This maid (Doll) left on November 27.

"TO GRAYE'S INN WALK"

fayre Botelers; [1] and I happened to be placed in the pew where they afterwards came to sit, but the pew by their coming being too full, I went out into the next, and there sat and had my full view of them both, but I am out of conceit now with them, Colonel Dillon being come back from Ireland again, and do still court them, and comes to church with them, which makes me think they are not honest.

24th. At the office all the morning and did business; by and by we are called to Sir W. Batten's to see the strange creature that Captain Holmes hath brought with him from Guiny; it is a great baboon, much like a man in most things. I do believe that it already understands much English, and I am of the mind it might be taught to speak or make signs. Saw "Hamlet, Prince of Denmark," done with scenes very well, but above all, Betterton [2] did the prince's part beyond imagination.

25th. (Lord's Day.) At church in the morning, and dined at home alone with my wife very comfortably, and so again to church with her, and had a very good and pungent sermon of Mr. Mills, discoursing the necessity of restitution. Home, and I found my Lady Batten and her daughter to look something askew upon my wife, because my wife do not buckle to them and is not solicitous for their acquaintance, which I am not troubled at at all. By and by comes in my father (he intends to go into the country to-morrow), and he and I among other discourse at last called Pall up to us, and there in great anger told her before my father that I would keep her no longer, and my father he said he would have nothing to do with her. At last, after we had brought down her high spirit, I got my father to yield that she should go into the country with my mother and him, and stay there awhile to see how she will demean herself.

26th. This morning before I went out I made even with my maid Jane, who has this day been my maid three years, and is this day to go into the country to her mother. The poor girl cried, and I could hardly forbear weeping to think of her going, for though she be grown lazy and spoilt by Pall's coming, yet I shall never have one to please us better in all things, and so harmless, while I live. So I paid her her wages and gave her *2s. 6d.* over, and bade her adieu, with my mind full of trouble at her going.

---

[1] Frances Butler and her sister; sisters of " *Mons. L'Impertinent.*" Colonel Cary Dillon, subsequently fifth Earl of Roscommon, was at this time courting Frances Butler, but the match was broken off.
[2] Thomas Betterton, chief actor in Davenant's company. The character of Hamlet was one of his masterpieces. Sir Wm. Davenant introduced the use of scenery.

30th. At noon my wife and I met at the Wardrobe, and there dined with the children, and after dinner up to my Lady and talked and laughed a good while. Then my wife and I to Drury Lane to the French comedy,[1] which was so ill done, and the scenes and company and everything else so nasty and out of order and poor that I was sick all the while in my mind to be there. Here my wife met with a son of my Lord Somersett, whom she knew in France, a pretty man; I showed him no great countenance, to avoyd further acquaintance.

31st. To Bartholomew fair[2] and there met with my Ladies Jemimah and Paulina,[3] with Mr. Pickering and Madamoiselle, at seeing the monkeys dance, which was much to see, when they could be brought to do so, but it troubled me to sit among such nasty company. After that with them into Christ's Hospitall, and there Mr. Pickering bought them some fairings, and I did give every one of them a bauble, which was the little globes of glass with things hanging in them, which pleased the ladies very well. After that home with them in their coach, and there was called up to my Lady, and she would have me stay to talk with her, which I did I think a full hour.

Thus ends the month. My maid Jane newly gone, and Pall left now to do all the work till another maid comes. Myself and wife in good health. My Lord Sandwich in the Straits and newly recovered of a great sickness at Alicante. My father gone to settle at Brampton, and myself under much business and trouble for to settle things in the estate to our content. But what is worst, I find myself lately too much given to seeing of plays, and expense, and pleasure, which makes me forget my business, which I must labour to amend. No money comes in, so that I have been forced to borrow a great deal for my own expenses, and to furnish my father, to leave things in order. I have some trouble about my brother Tom, who is now left to keep my father's trade, in which I have great fears that he will miscarry for want of brains and care. At Court things are in very ill condition, there being so much emulacion, poverty, and the vices of drinking, swearing, and loose amours, that I know not what will be the end of it, but confusion. And the Clergy so high, that all people that I meet

---

[1] The French comedians acted at the Cockpit.
[2] Held on St. Bartholomew's day in West Smithfield, near to the priory church of St. Bartholomew; it ceased in 1855. In Pepys' time it lasted for a fortnight and was so large as to involve four parishes. During its early history the fair grew to be a vast national market, and the chief cloth sale in the kingdom.
[3] Lady Paulina Montagu, daughter of Lord Sandwich, and Lady Jem's sister.

with do protest against their practice. In short, I see no content or satisfaction any where, in any one sort of people. We are at our Office quiet, only for lack of money all things go to rack. The season very sickly every where of strange and fatal fevers.

September 2nd. My wife has been busy all the day making of pies, and has been abroad and bought things for herself, and tells me that she met at the Change with my young ladies of the Wardrobe, and there helped them to buy things; and also with Mr. Somersett, who did give her a bracelet of rings, which did a little trouble me, though I know there is no hurt yet in it, but only for fear of further acquaintance.

5th. To the Privy Seal this morning about business, in my way taking leave of my mother, who goes to Brampton to-day. But doing my business at the Privy Seal pretty soon, I took boat and went to my uncle Fenner's, and there I found my mother and my wife and Pall (of whom I had this morning at my own house taken leave, and given her 20s. and good counsel how to carry herself to my father and mother), and so I took them, it being late, to Beard's, where they were staid for, and so I put them into the waggon, and saw them going presently, Pall crying exceedingly.

7th. At the office all the morning. I having appointed the young ladies at the Wardrobe to go with them to a play to-day my wife and I took them to the Theatre, where we seated ourselves close by the King, and Duke of York, and Madame Palmer, which was great content; and indeed I can never enough admire her beauty. And here was "Bartholomew Fayre," [1] with the puppet-show, acted to-day, which had not been these forty years (it being so satyricall against Puritanism, they durst not till now, which is strange they should already dare to do it, and the King do countenance it), but I do never a whit like it the better for the puppets, but rather the worse.

11th. Took Mr. Moore home to my house to dinner, where I found my wife's brother, Balty, as fine as hands could make him, and his servant, a Frenchman, to wait on him, and come to have my wife to visit a young lady which he is a servant to, and have hope to trepan [2] and get for his wife. I did give way for my wife to go with him, and so after dinner they went, and Mr. Moore and I out again, he about his business and I to Dr. Williams [3] to talk with him again; and he and I walking through Lincoln's

[1] By Ben Jonson.
[2] To entice.
[3] Dr. John Williams, Pepys' lawyer, who was advising him in his dispute with Tom Trice.

Inn Fields observed at the Opera "Twelfth Night," was acted there, and the King there; so I, against my own mind and resolution, could not forbear to go in, which did make the play seem a burthen to me, and I took no pleasure at all in it; and so after it was done went home with my mind troubled for my going thither, after my swearing to my wife that I would never go to a play without her.

25th. Much against my nature and will, yet such is the power of the Devil over me I could not refuse it, to the Theatre, and saw "The Merry Wives of Windsor," ill done.

29th. (Lord's Day.) To church in the morning, and so to dinner, and Sir W. Pen and daughter, and Mrs. Poole, his kinswoman, Captain Poole's wife, came by appointment to dinner with us, and a good dinner we had for them, and were very merry, and so to church again; and then to Sir W. Pen's and there supped, where his brother, a traveller, and one that speaks Spanish very well, and a merry man, supped with us; and what at dinner and supper I drink I know not how, of my own accord, so much wine that I was even almost foxed, and my head aked all night; so home and to bed without prayers, which I never did yet since I came to the house, of a Sunday night: I being now so out of order that I durst not read prayers for fear of being perceived by my servants in what case I was. So to bed.

30th. This morning up by moon-shine at 5 o'clock, to White Hall, to meet Mr. Moore at the Privy Seal; but he not being come as appointed, I went into King Street to the Red Lyon to drink my morning draft; and there I heard of a fray between the two Embassadors of Spain and France, and that this day, being the day of the entrance of an Embassador from Sweden, they intended to fight for the precedence. Our King, I heard, ordered that no Englishman should meddle in the business, but let them do what they would. And to that end all the soldiers in the town were in arms all the day long, and some of the train-bands in the City; and a great bustle through the City all the day. To the Wardrobe, and dined there, and then abroad, and in Cheapside hear that the Spanish hath got the best of it and killed three of the French coach-horses and several men, and is gone through the City next to our King's coach; at which, it is strange to see how all the City did rejoice. And indeed we do naturally all love the Spanish, and hate the French. At the Mewes I saw the Spanish coach go, with fifty drawn swords at least to guard it, and our soldiers shouting for joy.

October 1st. This morning my wife and I lay long in bed, and among other things fell into talk of musique, and desired that I would let her learn to sing, which I did consider, and promised her she should. So before I rose, word was brought me that my singing master, Mr. Goodgroome, was come to teach me; and so she rose and this morning began to learn also.

7th. About business all day, troubled in my mind till I can hear from Brampton, how things go on at Sturtlow, at the Court, which I was cleared in at night by a letter, which tells me that my cozen Tom was there to be admitted in his father's name as heir-at-law, but that he was opposed, and I was admitted by proxy, which put me out of great trouble of mind.

8th. At the office all the morning. After office done, went and eat some Colchester oysters with Sir W. Batten at his house, and there, with some company, dined and staid there talking all the afternoon; and late after dinner took Mrs. Martha out by coach, and carried her to the Theatre in a frolique, to my great expense, and there shewed her part of the "Beggar's Bush," [1] without much pleasure, but only for a frolique, and so home again.

9th. This morning went out about my affairs, among others to put my Theorbo [2] out to be mended, and then at noon home again, thinking to go with Sir Williams both to dinner by invitation to Sir W. Rider's, but at home I found Mrs. Pierce la belle, and Madam Clifford, with whom I was forced to stay, and made them the most welcome I could; and I was (God knows) very well pleased with their beautiful company, and after dinner took them to the Theatre, and so saw them both at home.

19th. At the office all the morning, and at noon Mr. Coventry, who sat with us all the morning, and Sir G. Carteret, Sir W. Pen, and myself, by coach to Captain Marshe's, at Limehouse, to a house that hath been their ancestors' for this 250 years, close by the lime-house which gives the name to the place. Here they have a design to get the King to hire a dock for the herring busses, [3] which is now the great design on foot, to lie up in. We had a very good and handsome dinner, and excellent wine. I not being neat in clothes, which I find a great fault in me, could not be so merry as otherwise, and at all times I am and can be, when I am in good habitt; which makes me remember my father Osborne's [4] rule

---

[1] By Beaumont and Fletcher.   [2] A bass lute.   [3] A herring-boat of ten or fifteen tons.
[4] Francis Osborn, *Advice to a Son* (Pepys had bought a copy on January 23). Osborn says: Wear your Cloaths neat; exceeding, rather than comming short of others of like fortune; a Charge born out by Acceptance where ever you come; Therefore spare all other ways rather than prove defective in this.

for a gentleman to spare in all things rather than in that. So by coach home, and so to write letters by post, and so to bed.

26th. In the evening news was brought that Sir R. Slingsby, our Comptroller (who hath this day been sick a week), is dead; which put me into so great a trouble of mind, that all the night I could not sleep, he being a man that loved me, and had many qualitys that made me to love him above all the officers and commissioners in the Navy.

27th. (Lord's Day.) At church in the morning; where in the pew both Sir Williams and I had much talk about the death of Sir Robert, which troubles me much; and them in appearance, though I do not believe it, because I know that he was a cheque to their engrossing the whole trade of the Navy-office.

November 2nd. At the office all the morning; where Sir John Minnes, our new Comptroller,[1] was fetched by Sir Wm. Pen and myself from Sir Wm. Batten's, and led to his place in the office. The first time that he had come hither, and he seems a good fair condition man and one that I am glad hath the office.

7th. This morning came one Mr. Hill (sent by Mr. Hunt, the Instrument maker), to teach me to play on the Theorbo, but I do not like his play nor singing, and so I found a way to put him off. So to the office.

9th. At the office all the morning. After dinner I to the Wardrobe, and there staid talking with my Lady all the afternoon till late at night. Among other things my Lady did mightily urge me to lay out money upon my wife, which I perceived was a little more earnest than ordinary, and so I seemed to be pleased with it, and do resolve to bestow a lace upon her.

11th. Captain Ferrers carried me, the first time that ever I saw any gaming house, to one, entering into Lincoln's-Inn-Fields, at the end of Bell Yard; where strange the folly of men to lay and lose so much money, and very glad I was to see the manner of a gamester's life, which I see is very miserable, and poor, and unmanly. And thence he took me to a dancing school in Fleet Street, where we saw a company of pretty girls dance, but I do not in myself like to have young girls exposed to so much vanity. So to the Wardrobe, where I found my Lady had agreed upon a lace for my wife of £6, which I seemed much glad of that it was no more, though in my mind I think it too much, and I pray God keep me

---

[1] Sir John Minnes was at this time sixty-three years of age. He had been a great traveller and a noted seaman.

so to order myself and my wife's expenses that no inconvenience in purse or honour follow this my prodigality. So by coach home.

13th. By appointment, we all went this morning to wait upon the Duke of York, which we did in his chamber, as he was dressing himself in his riding suit to go this day by sea to the Downs. He is in mourning for his wife's grandmother, which is thought a great piece of fondness.[1] After, I to Whitehall and to see la belle Pierce, and so on foot to my Lord Crew's, where I found him come to his new house, which is next to that he lived in last. From thence to the Theatre, and there saw "Father's own Son," and so it raining very hard I went home by coach, with my mind very heavy for this my expensefull life, which will undo me, I fear, after all my hopes, if I do not take up, for now I am coming to lay out a great deal of money in clothes for my wife I must forbear other expenses.

17th. (Lord's Day.) To church and heard a simple fellow upon the praise of Church musique, and exclaiming against men's wearing their hats on in the church, but I slept part of the sermon, till latter prayer and blessing and all was done, without waking, which I never did in my life. So home.

27th. This morning our maid Dorothy and my wife parted, which though she be a wench for her tongue not to be borne with, yet I was loth to part with her, but I took my leave kindly of her and went out to Savill's, the painter, and there sat the first time for my face with him. Thence to dinner with my Lady.

December 1st. (Lord's Day.) There hath lately been great clapping up of some old statesmen, such as Ireton, Moyer,[2] and others, and they say upon a great plot, but I believe no such thing; but it is but justice that they should be served as they served the poor Cavaliers; and I believe it will oftentimes be so as long as I live, whether there be cause or no.

7th. To the Privy Seal, and sealed there the first time this month; and, among other things that passed, there was a patent for Roger Palmer (Madam Palmer's husband) to be Earl of Castlemaine and Baron of Limbricke in Ireland; but the honour is tied up to the males got of the body of this wife, the Lady Barbary: the reason whereof every body knows.

13th. With my wife to the Paynter's, and there she sat the first time to be drawn, while I all the while stood looking on a

---

[1] Fondness, foolishness.
[2] Sir John Ireton, brother of the General, and Samuel Moyer, one of the Council of State.

"AT MY BOOKSELLER'S IN PAUL'S CHURCHYARD I MET WITH MR. CRUMLUM"

pretty lady's picture, whose face did please me extremely. At last, he having done, I found that the dead colour of my wife is good, above what I expected, which pleased me exceedingly. So home and to the office.

14th. All the morning at home lying in bed with my wife till 11 o'clock. Such a habit we have got this winter of lying long abed. Dined at home, and in the afternoon to the office. There sat late, and so home and to bed.

23rd. At my bookseller's[1] in Paul's Churchyard I met with Mr. Crumlum and the second matter of Paul's School, and thence I took them to the Starr, and there we sat and talked, and I had great pleasure in their company, and very glad I was of meeting him so accidentally, I having omitted too long to go to see him. Here in discourse of books I did offer to give the school what books he would choose of £5.

29th. I carried my wife to Westminster, and she went to see Mrs. Hunt, and I to the Abbey, and there meeting with Mr. Hooper, he took me in among the quire, and there I sang with them their service. To the Wardrobe and supped, and staid very long talking with my Lady, who seems to doat every day more and more upon us. So home and to prayers, and to bed.

30th. At the office, and so with my wife and Sir W. Pen to see our pictures, which do not much displease us, and so back again; and I staid at the Mitre, whither I had invited all my old acquaintance of the Exchequer to a good chine of beef, which with three barrels of oysters and three pullets, and plenty of wine and mirth, was our dinner, and there was about twelve of us. I made them a foolish promise to give them one this day twelvemonth, and so forever while I live; but I do not intend it.

31st. My wife and I this morning to the Paynter's, and there she sat the last time. After supper, and my barber had trimmed me, I sat down to end my journell for this year, and my condition at this time, by God's blessing, is thus: my health is very good, and so my wife's in all respects: my servants, W. Hewer, Sarah, Nell,[2] and Wayneman: my house at the Navy Office. I suppose myself to be worth about £500 clear in the world, and my goods of my house my own, and what is coming to me from Brampton when my father dies, which God defer. My chiefest thought is now to get a good wife for Tom, there being one offered by the

---

[1] Joseph Kirton.
[2] Sarah had come on November 28, she stayed a year. She found more favour with **Pepys** than with his wife. Nell had been engaged a month earlier; but she only stayed six months.

Joyces, a cozen of theirs, worth £200 in ready money. But my greatest trouble is that I have for this last half year been a very great spendthrift in all manner of respects, that I am afeard to cast up my accounts, though I hope I am worth what I say above. But I will cast them up very shortly. I have newly taken a solemn oath about abstaining from plays and wine, which I am resolved to keep according to the letter of the oath which I keep by me. The fleet hath been ready to sail for Portugall, but hath lacked wind this fortnight, and by that means my Lord is forced to keep at sea all this winter till he brings home the Queen, which is the expectation of all now, and the greatest matter of publique talk.

THIRD YEAR

1662

January 1st. Waking this morning out of my sleep on a sudden, I did with my elbow hit my wife a great blow over her face and nose, which waked her with pain, at which I was sorry, and to sleep again.

4th. At home most of the morning hanging up pictures, and seeing how my pewter sconces that I have bought will become my stayres and entry, and then with my wife by water to Westminster, whither she to her father's and I to Westminster Hall.

13th. All the morning at home, and Mr. Berkenshaw[1] (whom I have not seen a great while, came to see me), who staid with me a great while talking of musique, and I am resolved to begin to learn of him to compose, and to begin to-morrow, he giving of me so great hopes that I shall soon do it. Before twelve o'clock comes, by appointment, Mr. Peter and the Dean,[2] and Côllonel Honiwood, brothers, to dine with me; and so we dined very merry, at least I seemed so, but the dinner does not please me, and less the Dean and Collonel, whom I found to be pitiful sorry gentlemen, though good-natured. But Mr. Peter after dinner did show us the experiment (which I had heard talk of) of the chymicall glasses, which break all to dust by breaking off a little small end; which is a great mystery to me.[3] They being gone, my aunt Wight and my wife and I to cards, she teaching of us how to play at gleeke,[4] which is a pretty game; but I have not my head so free as to be troubled with it.

16th. Towards Cheapside; and in Paul's Churchyard saw the funeral of my Lord Cornwallis, late Steward of the King's House, a bold profane talking man, go by, and thence I to the Paynter's, and there paid him £6 for the two pictures, and 36s. for the two frames. In the afternoon at the office, and at night to Sir W.

---

[1] John Berkenshaw, an Irish music-teacher, living at Southwark.
[2] Michael Honywood was Dean of Lincoln.
[3] Still called after Prince Rupert, who introduced them from Bohemia. They consist of glass drops with long and slender tails; when these are snapped the whole drop falls into powder.
[4] A card game for three persons.

Batten, and there saw him and Captain Cock and Stokes [1] play at cards, and afterwards supped with them. Stokes told us that notwithstanding the country of Gambo is so unhealthy yet the people of the place live very long, so as the present king there is 150 years old, which they count by rains, because every year it rains continually four months together. He also told us that the kings there have above 100 wives a-piece, and offered him the choice of any of his wives, and so he did Captain Holmes. So home and to bed.

20th. This morning Sir Wm. Batten and Pen and I did begin the examining the Treasurer's [2] accounts, and we were all at it till noon. Then to dinner, he providing a fine dinner for us, there being at table the wine cooper, who this day did divide the two butts, which we did send for, of sherry from Cales.[3] Mine was put into a hogshead, and the vessel filled up with four gallons of malaga wine; but what it will stand us in I know not, but it is the first great quantity of wine that I ever bought.

23rd. By invitacon to my uncle Fenner's, where I found his new wife, a pitiful, old, ugly, ill-bred woman in a hatt, a midwife. Here were many of his, and as many of her relations, sorry, mean people; and after choosing our gloves, we all went over to the Three Crane Tavern, and though the best room in the house, in such a narrow dogg-hole we were crammed, and I believe we were near forty, that it made me loathe my company and victuals; and a sorry poor dinner it was too. After dinner, I took aside the two Joyce's, and took occasion to thank them for their kind thoughts for a wife for Tom: but that considering the possibility there is of my having no child, and what then I shall be able to leave him, I do think he may expect in that respect a wife with more money, and so desired them to think no more of it. This done with my wife by coach to my aunt Wight's, where I left her, and I to the office, and that being done to her again, and sat playing at cards after supper till 12 at night, and so by moonshine home and to bed.

25th. At home and the office all the morning. Walking in the garden to give the gardener directions what to do this year (for I intend to have the garden handsome), Sir W. Pen came to me, and did break a business to me about removing his son from Oxford to Cambridge to some private college. I proposed Magda-

---

[1] Capt. George Cock, a merchant. He became later steward for sick and wounded seamen. John Stokes was Captain of the *Royal James*. Gambo is of course Gambia.
[2] Sir George Carteret.   [3] Cadiz.

lene, but cannot name a tutor at present; but I shall think and write about it.

27th. This morning, going to take water upon Towerhill, we met with three sleddes standing there to carry my Lord Monson and Sir H. Mildmay and another[1] to the gallows and back again, with ropes about their necks; which is to be repeated every year, this being the day of their sentencing the King.

February 2nd. (Lord's Day.) To church in the morning, and then home and dined with my wife, and so both of us to church again, where we had an Oxford man give us a most impertinent sermon upon "Cast your bread upon the waters," &c. So home to read, supper, and to prayers, and then to bed.

3rd. After musique practice I went to the office, and there with the two Sir Williams all the morning about business, and at noon I dined with Sir W. Batten with many friends more, it being his wedding-day; and among other froliques, it being their third year, they had three pyes, whereof the middlemost was made of an ovall form, in an ovall hole within the other two, which made much mirth, and was called the middle piece; and above all the rest, we had great striving to steal a spooneful out of it; and I remember Mrs. Mills, the minister's wife, did steal one for me and did give it me; and to end all, Mrs. Shippman[2] did fill the pye full of white wine, it holding at least a pint and a half, and did drink it off for a health to Sir William and my Lady, it being the greatest draft that ever I did see a woman drink in my life.

4th. At noon to my Lord Crew's, where one Mr. Templer dined; and, discoursing of the nature of serpents, he told us some that in the waste places of Lancashire do grow to a great bigness, and that do feed upon larks, which they take thus:—They observe when the lark is soared to the highest, and do crawl till they come to be just underneath them; and there they place themselves with their mouths uppermost, and there, as is conceived, they do eject poyson up to the bird; for the bird do suddenly come down again in its course of a circle, and falls directly into the mouth of the serpent; which is very strange.

8th. All the morning in the cellar with the colliers, removing the coles out of the old cole hole into the new one, which cost me 8*s.* the doing; but now the cellar is done and made clean it do please me exceedingly, as much as any thing that was ever yet

---

[1] Robert Wallop.

[2] Mrs. Shipman was a friend of the Battens at Walthamstow, where she owned a large dairy. She had stood godmother to Sir W. Batten's niece when Pepys and Sir W. Penn were godfathers.

done to my house. I pray God keep me from setting my mind too much upon it. About 3 o'clock, the colliers having done, I went up to dinner (my wife having often urged me to come, but my mind is so set upon these things that I cannot but be with the workmen to see things done to my mind, which if I am not there is seldom done); and so to the office.

9th. (Lord's Day.) I took physique this day, and was all day in my chamber, talking with my wife about her laying out of £20, which I had long since promised her to lay out in clothes against Easter for herself, and composing some ayres, God forgive me! At night to prayers and to bed.

10th. Musique practice a good while, then to Paul's Church-yard, and there I met with Dr. Fuller's "England's Worthys," the first time that I ever saw it; and so I sat down reading in it, till it was two o'clock before I thought of the time going; and so I rose and went home to dinner, being much troubled that (though he had some discourse with me about my family and arms) he says nothing at all, nor mentions us either in Cambridgeshire or Norfolk. But I believe, in deed, our family were never consider-able. At home all the afternoon, and at night to bed.

15th. With the two Sir Williams to the Trinity-house, and there to dinner, and after dinner I was sworn a Younger Brother,[1] and after I was sworn all the Elder Brothers shake me by the hand: it is their custom, it seems.

23rd. (Lord's Day.) This day by God's mercy I am 29 years of age, and in very good health, and like to live and get an estate; and if I have a heart to be contented, I think I may reckon myself as happy a man as any is in the world, for which God be praised.

24th. Long with Mr. Berkenshaw in the morning at my musique practice, finishing my song of "Gaze not on Swans," in two parts, which pleases me well, and I did give him £5 for this month or five weeks that he hath taught me, which is a great deal of money and troubled me to part with it.

28th. The boy failing to call us up as I commanded, I was angry, and resolved to whip him for that and many other faults, to-day. Early with Sir W. Pen by coach to Whitehall, to the Duke of York's chamber, and staid a great while with the Duke. Home, and to be as good as my word, I bade Will get me a rod, and he and I called the boy up to one of the upper rooms of the Comptroller's

---

[1] Pepys became Master of the Trinity House in 1676.

house towards the garden, and there I reckoned all his faults, and whipped him soundly; but the rods were so small that I fear they did not much hurt to him, but only to my arm, which I am already, within a quarter of an hour, not able to stir almost. After supper to bed.

March 1st. After supper I settled to what I had long intended, to cast up my accounts with myself, and after much pains to do it and great fear, I do find that I am £500 in money beforehand in the world, which I was afraid I was not; but I find that I had spent above £250 this last half year, which troubles me much.

2nd. (Lord's Day.) Talking long in bed with my wife about our frugall life for the time to come, proposing to her what I could and would do if I were worth £2,000, that is, be a knight, and keep my coach, which pleased her; and so I do hope we shall hereafter live to save something, for I am resolved to keep myself by rules from expenses. To church in the morning: none in the pew but myself.

3rd. All the morning at home about business with my brother Tom, and then with Mr. Moore; and then I set to make some strict rules for my future practice in my expenses, which I did bind myself in the presence of God by oath to observe upon penalty therein set down. I am told that this day the Parliament hath voted 2*s.* per annum for every chimney in England, as a constant revenue for ever to the Crown.[1]

5th. To the pewterer's, to buy a poore's-box to put my forfeits in, upon breach of my late vows.

13th. All day, either at the office or at home, busy about business till late at night, I having lately followed my business much, find great pleasure in it, and a growing content.

16th. (Lord's Day.) This morning, till churches were done, I spent going from one church to another and hearing a bit here and a bit there. So to the Wardrobe to dinner with the young Ladies, and then into my Lady's chamber and talked with her a good while; and so walked to White Hall, an hour or two in the Park, which is now very pleasant. Here the King and Duke came to see their fowl play.[2] The Duke took very civil notice of me. So walked home, calling at Tom's, giving him my resolution about my boy's livery.

[1] This Act was repealed in William and Mary's reign.
[2] Water-fowl appear to have been kept in St. James's Park since the reign of Queen Elizabeth.

19th. This noon came a letter from T. Pepys,[1] the turner, in answer to one of mine the other day to him, wherein I did cheque him for not coming to me, as he had promised, with his and his father's resolucion about the difference between us. But he writes to me in the very same slighting terms that I did to him, without the least respect at all, but word for word as I did him, which argues a high and noble spirit in him. Though it troubles me a little that he should make no more of my anger, yet I cannot blame him for doing so, he being the elder brother's son, and not depending upon me at all.

22nd. At the office all the morning. At noon Sir Williams both and I by water down to the "Lewes," Captain Dekins, his ship, a merchantman, where we met the owners and several other great merchants; among others one Jefferys, a merry man that is a fumbler,[2] and he and I called brothers, and he made all the mirth in the company. We had a very fine dinner, and all our wives' healths, with seven or nine guns apiece; and exceeding merry we were, and so home by barge again, and I vexed to find Griffin leave the office door open, and had a design to have carried away the screw or the carpet in revenge to him, but at last I would not, but sent for him and chid him, and so to supper and to bed, having drank a great deal of wine.

23rd. (Lord's Day.) This morning was brought me my boy's fine livery, which is very handsome, and I do think to keep to black and gold lace upon gray, being the colour of my arms, for ever. To church in the morning, and so home with Sir W. Batten, and there eat some boiled great oysters, and so home; and while I was at dinner with my wife I was sick.

24th. Comes La Belle Pierce to see my wife, and to bring her a pair of peruques of hair, as the fashion now is for ladies to wear; which are pretty, and are of my wife's own hair, or else I should not endure them. After a good whiles stay I went to see if any play was acted, and I found none upon the post, it being Passion Week. So home again, and took water with them towards Westminster.

26th. To the office and Sir G. Carteret's all the morning about business. At noon come my good guests, Madame Turner, The., and Cozen Norton,[3] and a gentleman, one Mr. Lewin of the King's Life Guard. I had a pretty dinner for them, viz., a brace of stewed carps, six roasted chickens, and a jowl of salmon, hot,

[1] Son of Pepys' uncle Thomas. He and his father had been disputing Pepys' right to the Brampton estates ever since the death of "Uncle Robert."
[2] Possibly a stammerer. [3] Joyce Norton, a cousin both of Pepys and of the Turners.

for the first course; a tanzy and two neats' tongues, and cheese the second; and were very merry all the afternoon, talking and singing and piping upon the flageolette. In the evening they went with great pleasure away, and I with great content and my wife walked half an hour in the garden, and so home to supper and to bed.

27th. Early Sir G. Carteret, both Sir Williams and I by coach to Deptford, it being very windy and rainy weather, taking a codd and some prawnes in Fish Street with us. We settled to pay the Guernsey a small ship, but come to a great deal of money, it having been unpaid ever since before the King came in; by which means not only the King pays wages while the ship has lain still, but the poor men have most of them been forced to borrow all the money due for their wages before they receive it (and that at a dear rate, God knows) so that many of them had very little to receive at the table, which grieved me to see it. To dinner, very merry.

30th. (Easter Day.) Having my old black suit new furbished, I was pretty neat in clothes to-day, and my boy, his old suit new trimmed, very handsome. To church in the morning, and so home, leaving the two Sir Williams to take the Sacrament, which I blame myself that I have hitherto neglected all my life, but once or twice at Cambridge.[1] My wife and I to church in the afternoon and seated ourselves, she below me; and by that means the precedence of the pew which my Lady Batten and her daughter takes is confounded; and after sermon she and I did stay behind them in the pew, and went out by ourselves a good while after them, which we judge a very fine project hereafter to avoyd contention. So my wife and I to walk an hour or two on the leads, which begins to be very pleasant, the garden being in good condition.

April 2nd. Mr. Moore came to me, and he and I walked to the Spittle an hour or two before my Lord Mayor and the blew-coat boys come, which at last they did, and a fine sight of charity it is indeed. We got places and staid to hear a sermon; but, it being a Presbyterian one, it was so long that after above an hour of it we went away, and I home and dined; and then my wife and I by water to the Opera, and there saw "The Bondman"[2] most excellently acted; and though we had seen it so often, yet I never liked it better than to-day. We are resolved to see no more plays till Whitsuntide.

---

[1] This conflicts with a certificate given in 1681 by Dr. Mills, which says that Pepys was a regular communicant at St. Olave's from 1660 onwards.   [2] By Massinger.

5th. At the office till almost noon, and then broke up. Then came Sir G. Carteret, and he and I walked together alone in the garden taking notice of some faults in the office, particularly of Sir W. Batten's, and he seemed to be much pleased with me.

11th. Up early to my lute and a song, then about six o'clock with Sir W. Pen by water to Deptford. So to Greenwich; and had a fine pleasant walk to Woolwich, having in our company Captn. Minnes. Among other things he tells me that negroes drowned look white and lose their blackness, which I never heard before.

14th. Being weary last night I lay very long in bed to-day, talking with my wife, and persuaded her to go to Brampton, and take Sarah with her, next week, to cure her ague by change of ayre, and we agreed all things therein. We rose, and at noon dined. Then to Paternoster Row to buy things for my wife against her going. So home and walked upon the leads with my wife; and whether she suspected anything or no I know not, but she is quite off of her going to Brampton, which something troubles me; and yet all my design was that I might the freer go to Portsmouth when the rest go to pay off the yards there, which will be very shortly. But I will get off if I can. So to supper and to bed.

19th. This morning before we sat I went to Aldgate; and at the corner shop, a draper's, I stood, and did see Barkestead, Okey, and Corbet drawn towards the gallows at Tiburne; and there they were hanged and quartered.[1] They all looked very cheerful; but I hear they all die defending what they did to the King to be just; which is very strange.

21st. This morning I attempted to persuade my wife in bed to go to Brampton this week, but she would not, which troubles me; and seeing that I could keep it no longer from her I told her that I was resolved to go to Portsmouth to-morrow.

22nd. After taking leave of my wife, which we could hardly do kindly because of her mind to go along with me, Sir W. Pen and I took coach and so over the bridge to Lambeth. Here we got a dish of buttered eggs, and there staid till Sir G. Carteret came to us from White Hall, who brought Dr. Clerke with him, at which I was very glad; and so we set out, and I was very much pleased with his company, and were very merry all the way. We came to Gilford and there passed our time in the garden, cutting of sparagus for supper, the best that ever I eat in my life but in the house last year.

---

[1] Three regicides, captured at Delfe, in Holland, by Sir G. Downing.

23rd. Up early and to Petersfield; [and thence to Portsmouth].

24th. To the Pay all the afternoon.

26th. Rode to Southampton, where we went to the Mayor's and there dined, and had sturgeon of their own catching the last week, which do not happen in twenty years, and it was well ordered. They brought us also some caveare, which I attempted to order, but all to no purpose, for they had neither given it salt enough, nor are the seedes of the roe broke, but are all in berryes.

27th. (Sunday.) After dinner by coach to the Yard, and there on board the Swallow in the dock hear our navy chaplain preach a sad sermon, full of nonsense and false Latin; but prayed for the Right Honourable the principall officers. After sermon took him to Mr. Tippets's to drink a glass of wine, and so at 4 back again by coach to Portsmouth.

30th. This afternoon after dinner comes Mr. Stephenson, one of the burgesses of the town, to tell me that the Mayor and burgesses did desire my acceptance of a burgess-ship, and were ready at the Mayor's to make me one. So I went, and there they were all ready, and did with much civility give me my oath, and after the oath, did by custom shake me all by the hand. So I took them to a tavern and made them drink, and paying the reckoning, went away.

May 1st. Set out this morning from Portsmouth very early and got by noon to Petersfield, several officers of the Yard accompanying us so far. Here we dined and were merry. To horse again after dinner, and got to Gilford, where after supper I to bed, having this day been offended by Sir W. Pen's foolish talk, and I offending him with my answers. Among others he in discourse complaining of want of confidence, did ask me to lend him a grain or two, which I told him I thought he was better stored with than myself. So that I see I must keep a greater distance than I have done. The Duchess of York is brought to bed of a girl,[1] at which I find nobody pleased.

2nd. Early to coach again and to Kingston, where we baited a little, and presently to coach again and got early to London, and I found all well at home. After I had washed myself, it having been the hottest day that has been this year, by coach to Dr. Clerke's lady. She is a very fine woman, and what with her person and the number of fine ladies that were with her, I was much out of countenance, and could hardly carry myself like a man

---

[1] Mary, afterwards Queen of England.

among them; but however, I staid till my courage was up again, and talked to them, and viewed her house, which is most pleasant; and so drank and good-night.

3rd. To dinner to my Lady Sandwich, and Sir Thomas Crew's children coming thither, I took them and all my Ladys to the Tower and showed them the lions and all that was to be shown; and so took them to my house, and there made much of them, and so saw them back to my Lady's. Sir Thomas Crew's children being as pretty and the best behaved that ever I saw of their age.[1]

4th. (Lord's Day.) Lay long talking with my wife. Then Mr. Holliard came to me and let me blood, about sixteen ounces, I being exceedingly full of blood and very good. I begun to be sick; but lying upon my back I was presently well again, and did give him 5s. for his pains; and so we parted, and I to my chamber to write down my journall from the beginning of my late journey to this house. Dined well, and after dinner, my arm tied up with a black ribbon, I walked with my wife to my brother Tom's; our boy waiting on us with his sword, which this day he begins to wear, to outdo Sir W. Pen's boy, who this day, and Sir W. Batten's too, begin to wear new livery; but I do take mine to be the neatest of them all. My wife and I walked to Grays Inn, to observe fashions of the ladies, because of my wife's making some clothes.

10th. By myself at the office all the morning drawing up instructions for Portsmouth yard in those things wherein we at our late being there did think fit to reform, and got them signed this morning to send away to-night, the Duke being now there.

15th. To Westminster; and at the Privy Seal I saw Mr. Coventry's seal for his being Commissioner with us, at which I know not yet whether to be glad or otherwise. At night, all the bells of the town rung, and bonfires made for the joy of the Queen's arrival, who landed at Portsmouth last night. But I do not see much thorough joy but only an indifferent one in the hearts of people, who are much discontented at the pride and luxury of the Court, and running in debt.

20th. My wife and I by coach to the Opera, and there saw the 2nd part of "The Siege of Rhodes." [2] Thence to Tower-wharf, and there took boat, and we all walked to Halfeway House, and there eat and drank, and were pleasant, and so finally home again in the evening, and so good night, this being a very pleasant life that

[1] They were first cousins to the Sandwich children, Sir Thomas Crew being a brother of Lady Sandwich.   [2] By Sir William Davenant.

we now lead, and have long done; the Lord be blessed, and make us thankful. But, though I am much against too much spending, yet I do think it best to enjoy some degree of pleasure now that we have health, money, and opportunity, rather than to leave pleasures to old age or poverty, when we cannot have them so properly.

23rd. At the office good part of the morning, and then about noon with my wife on foot to the Wardrobe. In the parler, while I was reading, news was brought me that my Lord Sandwich is come and gone up to my Lady, which put me into great suspense of joy; so I went up waiting my Lord's coming out of my Lady's chamber, which by and by he did, and looks very well, and my soul is glad to see him. He very merry, and hath left the King and Queen at Portsmouth, and is come up to stay here till next Wednesday, and then to meet the King and Queen at Hampton Court. So to dinner, and my Lord mighty merry; among other things, saying that the Queen is a very agreeable lady, and paints still. There coming much company after dinner to my Lord, my wife and I slunk away to the Opera, where we saw "Witt in a Constable," [1] the first time that it is acted; but so silly a play I never saw I think in my life. After it was done, my wife and I to the puppet play in Covent Garden, and indeed it is very pleasant. Here among the fidlers I first saw a dulcimere played on with sticks knocking of the strings, and is very pretty. So by water home, and supped with Sir William Pen very merry, and so to bed.

25th. (Lord's Day.) To trimming myself, which I have this week done every morning, with a pumice stone, which I learnt when I was last at Portsmouth; and I find it very easy, speedy, and cleanly, and shall continue the practice of it. To church, and heard a good sermon of Mr. Woodcocke's at our church; only in his latter prayer for a woman in childbed, he prayed that God would deliver her from the hereditary curse of child-bearing, which seemed a pretty strange expression. With Captn. Ferrers in Mr. George Montagu's coach to Charing Cross; and there at the Triumph tavern he showed me some Portugall ladys, which are come to town before the Queen. They are not handsome, and their farthingales [2] a strange dress. Many ladies and persons of quality come to see them. I find nothing in them that is pleasing; and I see they have learnt to kiss and look freely up and down already, and I do believe will soon forget the recluse practice of

[1] By Henry Glapthorne.
[2] A kind of crinoline, introduced by Queen Elizabeth, and by this time out of fashion in England.

"TO THE TOWER AND SHOWED THEM THE LIONS"

their own country. They complain much for lack of good water to drink.

26th. Up by four o'clock in the morning and fell to the preparing of some accounts for my Lord of Sandwich. By and by by appointment comes Mr. Moore, and we found that my Lord is above £7,000 in debt, and that he hath money coming into him that will clear all, and so we think him clear, but very little money in his purse. So to my Lord's, and after he was ready we spent an hour with him, giving him an account thereof; and he having some £6,000 in his hands, remaining of the King's, he is resolved to make use of that.

28th. My father by appointment to dine with me, which we did very merrily, I desiring to make him as merry as I can while the poor man is in town.

29th. With my wife and the two maids and the boy took boat and to Foxhall,[1] where I had not been a great while. To the Old Spring Garden, and there walked long, and the wenches gathered pinks. Here we staid, and seeing that we could not have anything to eat, but very dear, and with long stay, we went forth again without any notice taken of us, and so we might have done if we had had anything. Thence to the New one, where I never was before, which much exceeds the other; and here we also walked, and the boy crept through the hedge and gathered abundance of roses; and, after a long walk, passed out of doors as we did in the other place, and here we had cakes and powdered beef and ale; and so home again by water with much pleasure. This day, being the King's birth-day, was very solemnly observed, and the more, for that the Queen this day comes to Hampton Court. In the evening bonfires were made, but nothing to the great number that was heretofore at the burning of the Rump. So to bed.

30th. This morning I made up my accounts, and find myself *de claro* worth about £530, and no more, so little have I increased it since my last reckoning; but I confess I have laid out much money in clothes.

31st. Had Sarah to comb my head clean, which I found so foul with powdering and other troubles, that I am resolved to try how I can keep my head dry without powder; and I did also in a suddaine fit cut off all my beard,[2] which I had been a great while bringing up, only that I may with my pumice-stone do my whole

---

[1] Vauxhall Gardens.
[2] Used in the old sense of hair growing on the face. Pepys wore a moustache only.

face, as I now do my chin, and to save time, which I find a very easy way and gentile. So she also washed my feet in a bath of herbs, and so to bed.

June 2nd. My wife and I to Mrs. Clarke's at Westminster, the first visit that ever we both made her yet. We found her in a dishabillée, intending to go to Hampton Court to-morrow. We had much pretty discourse, and a very fine lady she is. This day my wife put on her slasht wastecoate, which is very pretty.

3rd. At the office all the morning, and Mr. Coventry brought his patent and took his place with us this morning. Upon our making a contract, I went, as I use to do, to draw the heads thereof; but Sir W. Pen most basely told me that the Comptroller is to do it, and so begun to employ Mr. Turner about it, at which I was much vexed, and begun to dispute; and it was ruled for me. What Sir J. Minnes will do when he comes I know not, but Sir W. Pen did it like a base raskall, and so I shall remember him while I live.

7th. To the office, where all the morning, and I find Mr. Coventry is resolved to do much good, and to enquire into all the miscarriages of the office. At noon with him and Sir W. Batten to dinner at Trinity House. My mind in great trouble whether I should go as I intended to Hampton Court to-morrow or no. At last resolved the contrary, because of the charge thereof, and I am afraid now to bring in any accounts for journeys, and so will others I suppose be, because of Mr. Coventry's prying into them. Thence sent for to Sir G. Carteret's, and there talked with him a good while. I perceive, as he told me, were it not that Mr. Coventry had already feathered his nest in selling of places, he do like him very well, and hopes great good from him.

8th. (Lord's Day.) To my Lady's, and there supped with her; and merry, among other things, with the parrott which my Lord hath brought from the sea, which speaks very well, and cries Pall so pleasantly that made my Lord give it my Lady Paulina; but my Lady her mother do not like it. Home, and observe my man Will to walk with his cloak flung over his shoulder like a Ruffian, which, whether it was that he might not be seen to walk along with the footboy I know not, but I was vexed at it; and coming home, and after prayers, I did ask him where he learned that immodest garb, and he answered me that it was not immodest, or some such slight answer, at which I did give him two boxes on the ears, which I never did before, and so was after a little troubled at it.

12th. This morning I tried on my riding cloth suit with close knees, the first that I ever had; and I think they will be very convenient, if not too hot to wear any other open knees after them. At the office all the morning, where we had a full Board, viz., Sir G. Carteret, Sir John Mennes, Sir W. Batten, Mr. Coventry, Sir W. Pen, Mr. Pett, and myself. Among many other businesses, I did get a vote signed by all, concerning my issuing of warrants, which they did not smell the use I intend to make of it; but it is to plead for my clerks to have their right of giving out all warrants, at which I am not a little pleased. But a great difference happened between Sir G. Carteret and Mr. Coventry, about passing the Victualler's account; it ended in anger, and I believe will come to be a question before the King and Council. I did what I could to keep myself unconcerned in it, having some things of my own to do before I would appear high in anything.[1]

13th. Up 4 o'clock in the morning, and read Cicero's Second Oration against Catiline, which pleased me exceedingly; and more I discern therein than ever I thought was to be found in him; but I perceive it was my ignorance, and that he is as good a writer as ever I read in my life. By and by to Sir G. Carteret's, to talk with him about yesterday's difference at the office, and offered my service to look into any old books or papers that I have that may make for him. He was well pleased therewith, and did much inveigh against Mr. Coventry. Upon the whole I do find that he do much esteem of me and is my friend, and I may make good use of him.

14th. Up by four o'clock in the morning and upon business at my office. Then we sat down to business, and about 11 o'clock, having a room got ready for us, we all went out to the Tower-hill; and there, over against the scaffold, made on purpose this day, saw Sir Henry Vane[2] brought. A very great press of people. He made a long speech, many times interrupted by the Sheriff and others there; and they would have taken his paper out of his hand, but he would not let it go. But they caused all the books of those that writ after him to be given the Sheriff; and the trumpets were brought

---

[1] A sidelight upon the manner in which Pepys' official salary was augmented is afforded by the minutes of a Privy Council meeting on May 19, 1677. It appears that about 1000 ships per annum were issued with Passes by the Secretary of the Admiralty, who was entitled to a fee of 25*s.* upon each Pass. "[Mr. Pepys] humbly submitted himself to His Majesty as to the Continuance of his said Fee, or allowing him Compensation for it in case he thinks it for His Service to have it taken away. Upon which His Majesty was pleased to say, that he saw no reason for the having it taken away." One recalls Lord Sandwich's aphorism (Aug. 16, 1660) "that it was not the salary of any place that did make a man rich, but the opportunity of getting money while he is in the place."
[2] Sir Harry Vane, the younger, an inflexible Republican. He was charged with complicity in the death of King Charles I.

under the scaffold that he might not be heard. Then he prayed, and so fitted himself, and received the blow; but the scaffold was so crowded that we could not see it done.   He had a blister, or issue, upon his neck, which he desired them not hurt: he changed not his colour or speech to the last, but died justifying himself and the cause he had stood for; and spoke very confidently of his being presently at the right hand of Christ; and in all things appeared the most resolved man that ever died in that manner, and showed more of heat than cowardize, but yet with all humility and gravity.

15th. (Lord's Day.) To church but my wife not being dressed as I would have her, I was angry, and she, when she was out of doors in her way to church, returned home again vexed. But I to church; Mr. Mills, an ordinary sermon. So home, and found my wife and Sarah gone to a neighbour church, at which I was not much displeased.

18th. To Lilly's, the painter's, where we saw among other rare things, the Duchess of York,[1] her whole body, sitting in state in a chair, in white sattin, and another of the King, that is not finished; most rare things. I did give the fellow something that showed them us, and promised to come some other time, and he would show me Lady Castlemaine's, which I could not then see, it being locked up! Home, and after some merry discourse in the kitchen with my wife and maids as I now-a-days often do, I being well pleased with both my maids, to bed.

23rd. Up early this morning, and my people are taking down the hangings and things in my house because of the great dust that is already made by the pulling down of Sir W. Batten's house, and will be by my own when I come to it. To my office, and there hard at work all the morning. Home, and after a little dinner to my office again, and in the evening Sir W. Warren came to me about business, and that being done, discoursing of deals, I did offer to go along with him among his deal ships, which we did to half a score; where he showed me the difference between Dram, Swinsound, Christiania, and others, and told me many pleasant notions concerning their manner of cutting and sawing them by watermills, and the reason how deals become dearer and cheaper; among others, when the snow is not so great as to fill up the vallies that they may pass from hill to hill over the snow, then it is dear carriage. From on board he took me to his yard, where vast and

---

[1] This portrait, by Sir Peter Lely, is now at Hampton Court.

many places of deals, sparrs, and bulks, &c., the difference between which I never knew before, and indeed am very proud of this evening's work. He had me into his house, which is most pretty and neat and well furnished. After a glass, not of wine, for I would not be tempted to drink any, but a glass of mum, I well home by water.

28th. This day a genteel woman came to me, claiming kindred of me, as she had once done before, and borrowed 10*s.* of me, promising to repay it at night, but I hear nothing of her. I shall trust her no more.

30th. Up betimes, and to my office, where I fell upon boring holes for me to see from my closet into the great office, without going forth, wherein I please myself much. So settled to business, and at noon with my wife to the Wardrobe, and there dined and staid talking all the afternoon with my Lord, and about four o'clock took coach with my wife and Lady, and went to my house, where I took great pride to lead her through the Court by the hand, she being very fine, and her page carrying up her train. She staid a little at my house, and then walked through the garden, and took water, and went first on board the King's pleasure boat, which pleased her much. Then to Greenwich Park; and up to the top of the hill, and so down again, and took boat, and so through bridge to Blackfryers, and home, she being much pleased with the ramble in every particular of it. So we supped with her, and then walked home, and to bed.

OBSERVATIONS.

This I take to be as bad a juncture as ever I observed. The King and his new Queen minding their pleasures at Hampton Court. All people discontented; some that the King do not gratify them enough; and the others, Fanatiques of all sorts, that the King do take away their liberty of conscience; and the height of the Bishops, who I fear will ruin all again. They do much cry up the manner of Sir H. Vane's death, and he deserves it. They clamour against the chimney-money, and say they will not pay it without force. And in the mean time, like to have war abroad; and Portugall to assist, when we have not money to pay for any ordinary layings-out at home. Myself all in dirt about building of my house and Sir W. Batten's a story higher. Into a good way, fallen on minding my business and saving money, which God encrease; and I do take great delight in it, and see the benefit of it.

July 4th. Up by five o'clock, and after my journall put in order, to my office about my business, which I am resolved to follow, for every day I see what ground I get by it. By and by comes Mr. Cooper, mate of the Royall Charles, of whom I intend to learn mathematiques, and do begin with him to-day, he being a very able man, and no great matter, I suppose, will content him. After an hour's being with him at arithmetique (my first attempt being to learn the multiplication-table); then we parted till to-morrow. And so to my business at my office again till 4 in the afternoon, without eating or drinking all day, and then parted, and I home to eat a bit, and so back again to my office.

5th. To my office all the morning, to get things ready against our sitting, and by and by we sat and did business all the morning, and at noon had Sir W. Pen (who I hate with all my heart for his base treacherous tricks, but yet I think it not policy to declare it yet), and his son William, to my house to dinner.

6th. (Lord's Day.) Lay long in bed to-day with my wife merry and pleasant, and then rose and settled my accounts with my wife for housekeeping, and do see that my kitchen, besides wine, fire, candle, sope, and many other things, comes to about 30*s*. a week, or a little over.

9th. Up by four o'clock, and at my multiplicacion-table hard, which is all the trouble I meet withal in my arithmetique. So made me ready and to the office, where busy till night. Then came Mr. Mills, the minister, to see me, which he hath but rarely done to me, though every day almost to others of us; but he is a cunning fellow, and knows where the good victuals is, and the good drink, at Sir W. Batten's. However, I used him civilly, though I love him as I do the rest of his coat.

12th. Up by five o'clock, and put things in my house in order to be laid up, against my workmen come on Monday to take down the top of my house, which trouble I must go through now, but it troubles me much to think of it. So to my office, where till noon we sat, and then I to dinner and to the office all the afternoon with much business. At night with Cooper at arithmetique, and then came Mr. Creed about my Lord's accounts to even them, and he gone I to supper and to bed.

14th. Up by 4 o'clock and to my arithmetique, and so to my office till 8; then to Thames Street along with old Mr. Green, among the tarr-men, and did instruct myself in the nature and prices of tarr.

20th. (Lord's Day.) My wife and I lay talking long in bed, and at last she is come to be willing to stay two months in the country. It has rained all this morning so furiously that there is not one dry-footing above nor below in my house. So I fitted myself for dirt, and removed all my books to the office, and all day putting up and restoring things, it raining all day long as hard within doors as without. At night read my oaths, as I am obliged every Lord's day.

21st. To Woolwich, to the Rope-Yard. Thence to the dock, where we walked in Mr. Shelden's[1] garden, drinking and eating figs, which were very good, and talking while the Royal James was bringing towards the dock; and then we went out and saw the manner and trouble of docking such a ship, which yet they could not do, but only brought her head into the Dock, and so shored her up till next tide. But, good God! what a deal of company was there from both yards to help to do it, when half the company would have done it as well. But I see it is impossible for the King to have things done as cheap as other men.

28th. Up early, and by six o'clock, after my wife was ready, I walked with her to the George, at Holborn Conduit, where the coach stood ready to carry her and her maid to Bugden, [2] and so I took a troubled though willing good-bye, because of the bad condition of my house to have a family in it.

31st. Up early and among my workmen, I ordering my rooms above, which will please me very well. So to my office, and there we sat all the morning, where I begin more and more to grow considerable there. At noon Mr. Coventry and I by his coach to the Exchange together; and so took boat to Billingsgate, and went down on board the Rosebush at Woolwich, and found all things out of order; but after frightening the officers there we left them, and so on shore to the yard, and did the same to the officers of the yard. Here we found Sir W. Batten going about his survey, but so poorly and unlike a survey of the Navy, that I am ashamed of it, and so is Mr. Coventry. We found fault with many things; and so by water home again, all the way talking of the office business and other very pleasant discourse, and much proud I am of getting thus far into his books, which I think I am very much in. So home late; and it being the last day of the month, I did make up my accounts before I went to bed, and found myself worth about £650, for which

---

[1] William Shelden, Clerk of the Cheque at Woolwich.
[2] Buckden, a village in Huntingdonshire, close to Brampton.

"WHAT A DEAL OF COMPANY WAS THERE"

the Lord God be praised, and so to bed. I drank but two glasses of wine this day, and yet it makes my head ake all night, and indisposed me all the next day, of which I am glad.

August 8th. Up by four o'clock in the morning, and at five by water to Woolwich, there to see the manner of tarring, and all the morning looking to see the several proceedings in making of cordage, and other things relating to that sort of works, much to my satisfaction. At noon came Mr. Coventry on purpose from Hampton Court to see the same, and dined with Mr. Falconer, and after dinner to several experiments of Hemp, and particularly some Milan hemp that is brought over ready dressed. Thence we walked talking, very good discourse all the way to Greenwich, and I do find most excellent discourse from him. Among other things, his rule of suspecting every man that proposes any thing to him to be a knave; or, at least, to have some ends of his own in it. Another rule is a proverb that he hath been taught, which is that a man that cannot sit still in his chamber (the reason of which I did not understand him), and he that cannot say no (that is, that is of so good a nature that he cannot deny any thing, or cross another in doing any thing), is not fit for business. The last of which is a very great fault of mine, which I must amend in. Thence by boat to Deptford, and there surprised the Yard, and called them to a muster, and discovered many abuses, which we shall be able to understand hereafter and amend. Thence walked to Redriffe, and so to London Bridge, where I parted with him, and walked home and did a little business, and to supper and to bed.

17th. (Lord's Day.) Up very early, this being the last Sunday that the Presbyterians are to preach, unless they read the new Common Prayer, and renounce the Covenant,[1] and so I had a mind to hear Dr. Bates's farewell sermon, and walked to St. Dunstan's, where, it not being seven o'clock yet, the doors were not open; and so I went and walked an hour in the Temple-garden, reading my vows, which it is a great content to me to see how I am a changed man in all respects for the better since I took them, which the God of Heaven continue to me, and make me thankful for. At eight o'clock I went, and crowded in at a back door among others, the church being half-full almost before any doors were open publicly; which is the first time that I have done so these many years since I used to go with my father and mother; and so

[1] On St. Bartholomew's Day. August 24, 1662, the Act of Uniformity took effect, and about 200 Presbyterian and Independent ministers lost their preferments. The Book of Common Prayer referred to is that of 1662, now in use.

got into the gallery, beside the pulpit, and heard very well. His text was, "Now the God of Peace ——;" the last Hebrews, and the 20th verse: he making a very good sermon, and very little reflections in it to anything of the times. Besides the sermon, I was very well pleased with the sight of a fine lady that I have often seen walk in Graye's Inn Walks, and it was my chance to meet her again at the door going out, and very pretty and sprightly she is, and I believe the same that my wife and I some years since did meet at Temple Bar gate and have sometimes spoke of. So to Madam Turner's, and dined with her.

20th. Up early, and to my office, and thence to my Lord Sandwich, whom I found in bed, and he sent for me in. Among other talk, he do tell me that he hath put me into commission with a great many great persons in the business of Tangier,[1] which is a very great honour to me, and may be of good concernment to me. By and by comes in Mr. Coventry to us, whom my Lord tells that he is also put into the commission, and that I am there, of which he said he was glad; and did tell my Lord that I was indeed the life of this office, and much more to my commendation beyond measure. And that, whereas before he did bear me respect for his sake, he do do it now much more for my own; which is a great blessing to me. Sir G. Carteret having told me what he did yesterday concerning his speaking to my Lord Chancellor about me. So that on all hands, by God's blessing, I find myself a very rising man.

I went to Westminster Hall and there meeting Mr. Townsend, he would needs take me to Fleet Street, to one Mr. Barwell, squire sadler to the King, and there we and several other Wardrobemen dined. We had a venison pasty, and other good plain and handsome dishes; the mistress of the house a pretty, well-carriaged woman, and a fine hand she hath; and her maid a pretty brown lass. But I do find my nature ready to run back to my old course of drinking wine and staying from my business, and yet, thank God, I was not fully contented with it, but did stay at little ease, and after dinner hastened home by water, and so to my office till late at night.

22nd. About three o'clock this morning I waked with the noise of the rayne, having never in my life heard a more violent shower; and then the catt was lockt in the chamber, and kept a

---

[1] The Portuguese had recovered Tangiers from the Spaniards in 1656, and now passed it to the English as part of Queen Catherine's dowry. The English defended it against the Moors in 1680; but in 1684 it was decided on grounds of expense to abandon it.

great mewing, and leapt upon the bed, which made me I could not sleep a great while. Then to sleep, and about five o'clock rose, and up to my office, and about 8 o'clock went down to Deptford.

23rd. Up early and to my office till noon. After sitting, Mr. Creed by appointment being come, he and I went out together. It being the day of the Queen's coming to town from Hampton Court, we walked to White Hall, and through my Lord's lodgings we got into White Hall garden, and so to the Bowling-green, and up to the top of the new Banqueting House there, over the Thames, which was a most pleasant place as any I could have got; and all the show consisted chiefly in the number of boats and barges; and two pageants, one of a King, and another of a Queen, with her Maydes of Honour sitting at her feet very prettily; and they tell me the Queen is Sir Richard Ford's daughter. Anon come the King and Queen in a barge under a canopy with 10,000 barges and boats, I think, for we could see no water for them, nor discern the King nor Queen. And so they landed at White Hall Bridge,[1] and the great guns on the other side went off. But that which pleased me best was that my Lady Castlemaine stood over against us upon a piece of White Hall, where I glutted myself with looking on her. There happened a scaffold below to fall, and we feared some hurt, but there was none, but she of all the great ladies only run down among the common rabble to see what hurt was done, and did take care of a child that received some little hurt, which methought was so noble.

The show being over, I went away, not weary with looking on her, and to my Lord's lodgings, where my brother Tom and Dr. Thomas Pepys were to speak with me. So I walked with them in the garden, and they told me the business, which was to see a gentlewoman for a wife for Tom, of Mr. Cooke's providing, worth £500, of good education, her name Hobell, and lives near Banbury, demands £40 per annum joynter. Tom likes her, and, they say, had a very good reception.

September 3rd. After dinner by water to the office, and there we met and sold the Weymouth, Successe, and Fellowship hulkes, where pleasant to see how backward men are at first to bid; and yet when the candle is going out, how they bawl and dispute afterwards who bid the most first. And here I observed one man cunninger than the rest that was sure to bid the last man, and to carry

---

[1] The landing stairs at Whitehall. Pepys was watching from what is now the United Services Museum, in Whitehall.

it; and inquiring the reason, he told me that just as the flame goes out the smoke descends, which is a thing I never observed before, and by that he do know the instant when to bid last, which is very pretty.[1]

7th. (Lord's Day.) Meeting Mr. Pierce, the chyrurgeon, he took me into Somersett House; and there carried me into the Queen-Mother's presence-chamber, where she was with our own Queen sitting on her left hand (whom I did never see before); and though she be not very charming, yet she hath a good, modest, and innocent look, which is pleasing. Here I also saw Madam Castlemaine, and, which pleased me most, Mr. Crofts,[2] the King's bastard, a most pretty spark of about 15 years old, who I perceive do hang much upon my Lady Castlemaine, and is always with her; and I hear the Queens, both of them, are mighty kind to him. By and by in comes the King, and anon the Duke and his Duchess; so that, they being all together, was such a sight as I never could almost have happened to see with so much ease and leisure. They staid till it was dark, and then went away; the King and his Queen, and my Lady Castlemaine and young Crofts, in one coach and the rest in other coaches. Here were great store of great ladies, but very few handsome. The King and Queen were very merry; and he would have made the Queen-Mother believe that his Queen was with child, and said that she said so. And the young Queen answered, "You lye;" which was the first English word that I ever heard her say: which made the King good sport; and he would have taught her to say in English, "Confess and be hanged."

9th. This afternoon Sir John Minnes, Mr. Coventry, and I went into Sir John's lodgings, where he showed us how I have blinded all his lights, and stopped up his garden door, and other things he takes notice of that he resolves to abridge me of; which do vex me so much that for all this evening and all night in my bed, so great a fool I am, and little master of my passion, that I could not sleep for the thoughts of my losing things which in themselves are small and not worth half the trouble. The more fool am I, and must labour against it for shame, especially I that used to preach up Epictetus's rule of τὰ ἐφ' ἡμῖν καὶ τὰ οὐκ ἐφ' ἡμῖν.[3] Late at my office, troubled in mind, and then to bed, but could hardly sleep.

[1] The old way of conducting an auction, by inch of candle.
[2] James, the son of Charles II. by Lucy Walter, daughter of William Walter, of Rock Castle, Pembrokeshire. He was created Duke of Monmouth in 1663, married the only child of the second Earl of Buccleuch, and was made Duke of Buccleuch in 1673, taking the name of Scott. Actually, he was at this time only 13½ years old.
[3] Epictetus, *Encheiridion*, i. 1. "Some things are for us, others not." A quotation which Pepys frequently uses when he finds himself fretting at matters beyond his control.

27th. In the afternoon got my wife's chamber put into readiness against her coming, which she did at night. I found her and her maid and dogg very well, and herself grown a little fatter than she was. I was very well pleased to see her and had her company with great content and much mutual love, only I do perceive that there has been falling out between my mother and she, and a little between my father and she; but I hope all is well again; and I perceive she likes Brampton House and seat better than ever I did myself, and tells me how my Lord hath drawn a plot of some alteracions to be made there, and hath brought it up, which I saw and like well. I perceive my Lord and Lady have been very kind to her, and Captn. Ferrers so kind that I perceive I have some jealousy of him, but I know what is the Captain's manner of carriage, and therefore it is nothing to me.

29th. (Michaelmas Day.) This day my oaths for drinking of wine and going to plays are out, and so I do resolve to take a liberty to-day, and then to fall to them again. To the King's Theatre, where we saw "Midsummer's Night's Dream," which I had never seen before, nor shall ever again, for it is the most insipid ridiculous play that ever I saw in my life. I saw, I confess, some good dancing and some handsome women, and which was all my pleasure.

30th. To my office where we sat till noon, and then I to dinner with Sir W. Pen; and while we were at it coming my wife to the office, and so I sent for her up, and after dinner we took coach and to the Duke's playhouse, where we saw "The Duchess of Malfy"[1] well performed, but Betterton and Ianthe to admiration. I have made up this evening my monthly ballance, and find that, notwithstanding the loss of £30 to be paid to the loyall and necessitous cavaliers by act of Parliament,[2] yet I am worth about £680, for which the Lord God be praised. My condition at present is this:—I have long been building, and my house to my great content is now almost done. My mind is somewhat troubled about my best chamber, which I question whether I shall be able to keep or no. I am also troubled for the journey which I must needs take suddenly to the Court at Brampton; but most of all for that I am not provided to understand my business, having not minded it a great while, and at the best shall be able but to make a bad matter of it; but God, I hope, will guide all to the best, and I am resolved

---

[1] By Webster. Ianthe (Mary Saunderson) married Betterton shortly afterwards.
[2] Two Acts for the relief of necessitous royalist soldiers were passed in 1662.

to-morrow to fall hard to it. I pray God help me therein, for my father and mother and all our well-doings do depend upon my care therein. My brother Tom is gone out of town this day, to make a second journey to his mistress at Banbury, of which I have good expectacions, and pray God to bless him therein.

October 5th. (Lord's Day.) Lay long in bed talking with my wife, and among other things fell out about my maid Sarah, whom my wife would fain put away, when I think her as good a servant as ever came into a house, but it seems my wife would have one that would dress a head well; but we were friends at last. I to church. Dined with my wife, and then to talk again above, chiefly about her learning to dance against her going next year into the country, which I am willing she shall do.

8th. Up and by water to my Lord Sandwich's, and was with him a good while in his chamber, and among other things to my extraordinary joy, he did tell me how much I was beholding to the Duke of York, who did yesterday of his own accord tell him that he did thank him for one person brought into the Navy, naming myself, and much more to my commendation; which is the greatest comfort and encouragement that ever I had in my life, and do owe it all to Mr. Coventry's goodness and ingenuity. Hither this might my scallop,[1] bought and got made by Captain Ferrers' lady, is sent, and I brought it home, a very neat one. It .cost me about £3, and £3 more I have given him to buy me another. I do find myself much bound to go handsome, which I shall do in linen, and so the other things may be all the plainer.

9th. Up early about my business to get me ready for my journey. But first to the office; where we sat all the morning till noon, and then broke up; and I bid them adieu for a week, having the Duke's leave got me by Mr. Coventry. And so between one and two o'clock got on horseback at our back gate, with my man Will with me, both well-mounted on two grey horses. We rode and got to Ware before night; and so resolved to ride on to Puckeridge.

10th. Up, and between eight and nine mounted again; and so rid to Cambridge. Dr. Fairbrother telling me that this day there is a Congregation for the choice of some officers in the University, he after dinner gets me a gown, cap, and hood, and carries me to the Schooles, where Mr. Pepper, my brother's tutor, and this day chosen Proctor, did appoint a M.A. to lead me into the Regent

---

[1] A lace neck-band, the edges of which were scalloped.

House, where I sat with them, and did [vote] by subscribing papers thus: "Ego Samuel Pepys eligo Magistrum Bernardum Skelton (and which was more strange, my old schoolfellow and acquaintance, and who afterwards did take notice of me, and we spoke together), alterum è taxatoribus hujus Academiæ in annum sequentem." The like I did for one Biggs, for the other Taxor, and for other officers, as the Vice-Proctor (Mr. Covell), for Mr. Pepper, and which was the gentleman that did carry me into the Regent House. This being done, and the Congregation dissolved by the Vice-Chancellor, I to Trinity Hall, and there stayed a good while with Dr. John Pepys,[1] and so to Impington, to take such advice as my old uncle and his son Claxton could give me.

11th. Up betimes, and after a little breakfast, and a very poor one, like our supper, and such as I cannot feed on, because of my she-cozen Claxton's gouty hands, I mounted and rode to Huntingdon, and so to Brampton; where I found my father and two brothers, and Mr. Cooke, my mother and sister. So we are now all together, God knows when we shall be so again. I walked up and down the house and garden, and find my father's alteracions very handsome.

13th. With my father took a melancholy walk to Portholme, seeing the country-maids milking their cows there, they being there now at grass, and to see with what mirth they come all home together in pomp with their milk, and sometimes they have musique gc before them. So back home again, and to supper. And so waiting with much impatience and doubt the issue of to-morrow's Court, I to bed, but hardly slept half an hour the whole night, my mind did so run with fears of to-morrow.

14th. Up, and did digest into a method all I could say in our defence, in case there should be occasion, and so about nine o'clock to the court at the Lordshipp where the jury was called; they being sworn and the charge given them, they fell tò our business, finding the heir-at-law to be my uncle Thomas. But the steward, as he promised me, did find pretensions very kindly and readily to put off their admittance, and my father and I [were] admitted to all the lands; he for life, and I for myself and my heirs in reversion. That being done and taken leave of the steward, I did with most compleat joy of mind go from the Court with my father home, and in a quarter of an hour did get on horseback,

---

[1] Brother of Roger. Their father was Talbot Pepys of Impington. Claxton had married their sister.

"WITH WHAT MIRTH THEY COME ALL HOME TOGETHER IN POMP WITH THEIR MILK"

with my brother Tom, Cooke, and Will, all mounted, and without eating or drinking, take leave of father, mother, Pall, to whom I did give 10*s*., but have shown no kindness since I come, for I find her so very ill-natured that I cannot love her, and she so cruel a hypocrite that she can cry when she pleases, and John and I away, calling in at Hinchingbroke, and taking leave in three words of my Lady, and the young ladies; and so by moonlight most bravely all the way to Cambridge, with great pleasure, whither we come at about nine o'clock, and took up at the Bear.

15th. Waked very early; and, when it was time, did call up Will, and we rose, and musique (with a bandore [1] for the base) did give me a levett; [2] and so we got ready; and while breakfast was providing, I went forth and showed Mr. Cooke King's College Chapel, Trinity College, and St. John's College Library; and that being done, to our inn again: where I met Dr. Fairbrother brought thither by my brother Tom, and he did breakfast with us. A very good-natured man he is, and told us how the room we were in was the room where Cromwell and his associated officers did begin to plot and act their mischiefs in these counties. Having eat well, only our oysters proving bad, we mounted about nine o'clock. We came to Ware about three o'clock, and the night being pretty light, made shift to reach London. So to bed being very hot and feverish by being weary.

16th. I rose in good temper, finding a good chimney-piece made in my upper dining-room chamber, and the dining-room wainscot in a good forwardness, at which I am glad, and then to the office.

21st. To Mr. Smith, the scrivener, upon Ludgate Hill, to whom Mrs. Butler do committ her business concerning her daughter and my brother.

22nd. I to Mr. Smith's, where I was last night, and there by appointment met Mrs. Butler, with whom I plainly discoursed and she with me. I find she will give but £400, and no more, and is not willing to do that without a joynture, which she expects and I will not grant for that portion. I perceive she had much greater expectations of Tom's house and being than she finds. But however we did break off the business wholly, but with great love and kindness between her and me, and would have been glad we had known one another's minds sooner. After taking a kind farewell, I to Tom's, and there did give him a full account of this sad news. Hence, it raining hard, by coach home, being first

---

[1] An old form of banjo.   [2] A reveille.

trimmed here by Benier, who being acquainted with all the players, do tell me that Betterton is a very sober, serious man, and studious and humble, following of his studies, and is rich already with what he gets and saves.

26th. (Lord's Day.) Up and put on my new Scallop, and is very fine. To church, and there saw the first time Mr. Mills in a surplice; but it seemed absurd for him to pull it over his ears in the reading-pew, after he had done, before all the church, to go up to the pulpitt, to preach without it.

November 3rd. Up and with Sir J. Minnes in his coach to White Hall, to the Duke's; but found him gone out a-hunting. Thence to my Lord Sandwich, who tells me how the Duke of York is smitten in love with my Lady Chesterfield (a virtuous lady, daughter to my Lord of Ormond); and so much, that the duchess of York hath complained to the King and her father about it, and my Lady Chesterfield is gone into the country for it. At all which I am sorry; but it is the effect of idleness, and having nothing else to employ their great spirits upon.

22nd. This morning, from some difference between my wife and Sarah, her maid, my wife and I fell out cruelly, to my great discontent. But I do see her set so against the wench, whom I take to be a most extraordinary good servant, that I was forced for the wench's sake to bid her get her another place, which shall cost some trouble to my wife, however, before I suffer to be.

25th. Great talk among people how some of the Fanatiques do say that the end of the world is at hand, and that next Tuesday is to be the day.

27th. At my waking I found the tops of the houses covered with snow, which is a rare sight that I have not seen these three years. Up, and put my people to perfect the cleaning of my house, and so to the office, where we sat till noon; and then we all went to the next house upon Tower Hill, to see the coming by of the Russia Embassador; for whose reception all the City trained-bands do attend in the streets, and the King's life-guards, and most of the wealthy citizens in their black velvet coats, and gold chains (which remain of their gallantry at the King's coming in), but they staid so long that we went down again home to dinner. And after I had dined, I heard they were coming, and so I walked to the Conduit in the Quarrefowr,[1] at the end of Gracious-street and

[1] French *carrefour*, four cross-roads, called *temp.* Edward III. Carfukes: cf. "Carfax" at Oxford. Gracious Street is Gracechurch Street.

Cornhill; and there (the spouts thereof running very near me upon all the people that were under it) I saw them pretty well go by. I could not see the Embassador in his coach; but his attendants in their habits and fur caps very handsome, comely men, and most of them with hawkes upon their fists to present to the King. But Lord! to see the absurd nature of Englishmen, that cannot forbear laughing and jeering at every thing that looks strange.

30th. (Lord's Day.) This day I first did wear a muffe, being my wife's last year's muffe, and now have bought her a new one; this serves me very well.

December 1st. I to my Lord Sandwich's, to Mr. Moore, to talk a little about business; and then over the Parke (where I first in my life, it being a great frost, did see people sliding with their skeates, which is a very pretty art), to Mr. Coventry's chamber to St. James's, where we all met to a venison pasty and were very merry. Here we staid till three or four o'clock; and so to the Council Chamber, where there met the Duke of York, Prince Rupert, Duke of Albemarle, my Lord Sandwich, Sir Wm. Compton, Mr. Coventry, Sir J. Minnes, Sir R. Ford, Sir W. Rider, myself, and Captain Cuttance, as Commissioners for Tangier. And after our Commission was read by Mr. Creed, who I perceive is to be our Secretary, we did fall to discourse of matters. This done we broke up, and I to the Cockpitt, with much crowding and waiting, where I saw "The Valiant Cidd" [1] acted, a play I have read with great delight; but is a most dull thing acted, which I never understood before, there being no pleasure in it, though done by Betterton and by Ianthe, and another fine wench that is come; nor did the King or Queen once smile all the whole play, nor any of the company seem to take any pleasure but what was in the greatness and gallantry of the company.

5th. Up, it being a snow and hard frost, and being up I did call up Sarah, who do go away to-day or to-morrow. I paid her her wages, and gave her 10*s.* myself, and my wife 5*s.* to give her. For my part I think never servant and mistress parted upon such foolish terms in the world as they do, only for an opinion in my wife that she is ill-natured, in all other things being a good servant. The wench cried, and I was ready to cry too, but to keep peace I am content she should go.

---

[1] Translated from Corneille.

7th. (Lord's Day.) A great snow, and so to church this morning with my wife, which is the first time she hath been at church since her going to Brampton. So home, and we dined above in our dining room, the first time since it was new done. In the afternoon to my aunt Wight's, where great store of her usuall company, and here we staid a pretty while talking, I differing from my aunt, as I commonly do, in our opinion of the handsomeness of the Queen, which I oppose mightily, saying that if my nose be handsome, then is her's, and such like.

18th. Up and to the office; Mr. Coventry and I alone sat till two o'clock, and then he inviting himself to my house to dinner, of which I was proud; but my dinner being a legg of mutton and two capons, they were not done enough, which did vex me, but we made shift to please him, I think. But I was, when he was gone, very angry with my wife and people.

23rd. Slept hard till 8 o'clock this morning, and so up and to the office. Sat all the morning, and at noon home to dinner with my wife alone, and after dinner sat by the fire; and then up to make up my accounts with her, and find that my ordinary housekeeping comes to £7 a month, which is a great deal.

25th. (Christmas Day.) Up pretty early, leaving my wife not well in bed, and with my boy walked, it being a most brave cold and dry frosty morning, and had a pleasant walk to White Hall, where I intended to have received the Communion with the family, but I came a little too late. So I walked up into the house and spent my time looking over pictures, particularly the ships in King Henry the VIIIth's Voyage to Bullen; [1] marking the great difference between their build then and now. By and by down to the chappell again where Bishopp Morley preached upon the song of the Angels, "Glory to God on high, on earth peace, and good will towards men." The sermon done, a good anthem followed, with vialls, and then the King came down to receive the Sacrament. But I staid not. Dined by my wife's bed-side with great content, having a mess of brave plum-porridge and a roasted pullet for dinner, and I sent for a mince-pie abroad, my wife not being well to make any herself yet.

26th. Up, my wife to the making of Christmas pies all day, being now pretty well again, and I abroad to the Wardrobe. Hither come Mr. Battersby; and we falling into a discourse of a new book

---

[1] Boulogne. These pictures are now at Hampton Court.

of drollery in verse called Hudebras,[1] I would needs go find it out, and met with it at the Temple: cost me 2s. 6d. But when I came to read it, it is so silly an abuse of the Presbyter Knight going to the warrs, that I am ashamed of it; and by and by meeting at Mr. Townsend's at dinner, I sold it to him for 18d.

31st. At noon took my wife to Mrs. Pierce's by invitacion to dinner, where there came Dr. Clerke and his wife and sister and Mr. Knight, chief chyrurgeon to the King and his wife. We were pretty merry, the two men being excellent company, but I confess I am wedded from the opinion either of Mrs. Pierce's beauty upon discovery of her naked neck to-day, being undrest when we came in, or of Mrs. Clerke's genius, which I so much admired, I finding her to be so conceited and fantastique in her dress this day and carriage, though the truth is, witty enough. After dinner with much ado the doctor and I got away to follow our business for a while, he to his patients and I to the Tangier Committee, where the Duke of York was. Thence Mr. Povy, [2] in his coach, carried Mr. Gauden and I into London to Mr. Bland's, the merchant, where we staid discoursing. Then to eat a dish of anchovies and drink wine and syder, and very merry, but above all things pleased to hear Mrs. Bland talk like a merchant in her husband's business very well, and it seems she do understand it and perform a great deal. Thence merry back, Mr. Povy and I, to White Hall; he carrying me thither on purpose to carry me into the ball this night before the King. All the way he talking very ingeniously, and I find him a fine gentleman, and one that loves to live nobly and neatly, as I perceive by his discourse of his house, pictures, and horses. He brought me first to the Duke's chamber, where I saw him and the Duchess at supper; and thence into the room where the ball was to be, crammed with fine ladies, the greatest of the Court. By and by comes the King and Queen, the Duke and Duchess, and all the great ones: and after seating themselves, the King takes out the Duchess of York; and the Duke, the Duchess of Buckingham; the Duke of Monmouth, my Lady Castlemaine; and so other lords other ladies: and they danced the Bransle.[3] After that, the King led a lady a single Coranto; and then the rest of the lords, one after another, other ladies: very noble it was, and great pleasure to see. Then to country dances; the King leading the first, which he called for; which was, says he, "Cuckolds all

---

[1] Butler's *Hudibras.* He bought another copy later on.
[2] Treasurer of the Duke of York.   [3] A country dance.

THE DUKE OF MONMOUTH AND MY LADY CASTLEMAINE

awry," [1] the old dance of England. The manner was, when the King dances, all the ladies in the room, and the Queen herself, stand up: and indeed he dances rarely, and much better than the Duke of York. Having staid here as long as I thought fit, to my infinite content, it being the greatest pleasure I could wish now to see at Court, I went out, leaving them dancing.

Thus ends this year with great mirth to me and my wife. Our condition being thus:—we are at present spending a night or two at my Lord's lodgings at White Hall. Our home at the Navy-office, which is and hath a pretty while been in good condition, finished and made very convenient. My purse is worth about £650, besides my goods of all sorts, which yet might have been more but for my late layings out upon my house and public as-sessment, and yet would not have been so much if I had not lived a very orderly life all this year by virtue of the oaths that God put into my heart to take against wine, plays, and other expenses, and to observe for these last twelve months, and which I am now going to renew, I under God owing my present content thereunto. My family is myself and wife, William, my clerk; Jane, my wife's upper mayde, but, I think growing proud and negligent upon it: we must part, which troubles me; Susan, our cook-mayde, a pretty willing wench, but no good cook; and Wayneman, my boy, who I am now turning away for his naughty tricks. We have had from the beginning our healths to this day, very well, blessed be God! Our late mayde Sarah going from us (though put away by us) to live with Sir W. Pen do trouble me, though I love the wench, so that we do make ourselves a little strange to him and his family for it, and resolve to do so. The same we are for other reasons to my Lady Batten and hers. We have lately had it in our thoughts to find out a woman to my wife that can sing or dance, and yet finding it hard to save anything at the year's end as I now live, I think I shall not be such a fool till I am more warm in my purse, besides my oath of entering into no such expenses till I am worth £1000. By my last year's diligence in my office, blessed be God! I am come to a good degree of knowledge therein; and am acknowl-edged so by all the world, even the Duke himself, to whom I have good access: and by that, and my being Commissioner with him for Tangier, he takes much notice of me; and I doubt not but, by the continuance of the same endeavours, I shall in a little time come to be a man much taken notice of in the world, especially

---

[1] Awry, i.e. a row.

being come to so great an esteem with Mr. Coventry. The only weight that lies heavy upon my mind is the ending the business about my dead uncle's estate, which is very ill on our side, and I fear when all is done I must be forced to maintain my father myself, or spare a good deal towards it out of my own purse, which will be a very great pull back to me in my fortune. But I must be contented and bring it to an issue one way or other.

Publique matters stand thus: The King is bringing, as is said, his family, and Navy, and all other his charges, to a less expence. In the mean time, himself following his pleasures more than with good advice he would do; at least, to be seen to all the world to do so. His dalliance with my Lady Castlemaine being publique, every day, to his great reproach; and his favouring of none at Court so much as those that are the confidants of his pleasure; which, good God! put it into his heart to mend, before he makes himself too much contemned by his people for it! The Duke of Monmouth is in so great splendour at Court, and so dandled by the King that some doubt, if the King should have no child by the Queen (which there is yet no appearance of), whether he would not be acknowledged for a lawful son, and that there will be a difference follow upon it between the Duke of York and him; which God prevent! My Lord Chancellor is threatened by people to be questioned, the next sitting of the Parliament by some spirits that do not love to see him so great: but certainly he is a good servant to the King. The Queen-Mother is said to keep too great a Court now; and her being married to my Lord St. Alban's is commonly talked of; and that they had a daughter between them in France, how true, God knows. The Bishopps are high, and go on without any diffidence in pressing uniformity; and the Presbyters seem silent in it, and either conform or lay down, though without doubt they expect a turn, and would be glad these endeavours of the other Fanatiques would take effect; there having been a plot lately found, for which four have been publickly tried at the Old Bayley and hanged. My Lord Sandwich is still in good esteem, and now keeping his Christmas in the country; and I in good esteem, I think, as any man can be, with him. In fine, for the good condition of myself, wife, family, and estate, in the great degree that it is, and for the public state of the nation, so quiett as it is, the Lord God be praised!

FOURTH YEAR

1663

January 1st. Rose and to White Hall, where I spent a little time walking among the courtiers, which I perceive I shall be able to do with great confidence, being now beginning to be pretty well known among them. Then to my wife again, and found Mrs. Sarah with us in the chamber we lay in. Among other discourse Mrs. Sarah tells us how the King sups at least four or [five] times every week with my Lady Castlemaine; and most often stays till the morning with her, and goes home through the garden all alone privately, and that so as the very centrys take notice of it and speak of it.

4th. (Lord's Day.) Up and to church, where a lazy sermon, and so home to dinner to a good piece of powdered beef, but a little too salt. At dinner my wife did propound my having of my sister Pall at my house again to be her woman, since one we must have, hoping that in that quality possibly she may prove better than she did before; which I take very well of her, and will consider of it, it being a very great trouble to me that I should have a sister of so ill a nature that I must be forced to spend money upon a stranger when it might better be upon her, if she were good for anything.

5th. To the King's chamber, whither by and by the Russia Embassadors come; who, it seems, have a custom that they will not come to have any treaty with our or any King's Commissioners, but they will themselves see at the time the face of the King himself, be it forty days one after another; and so they did to-day only go in and see the King. To the Cockpitt, where we saw "Claracilla,"[1] a poor play, done by the King's house (but neither the King nor Queen were there, but only the Duke and Duchess, who did show some impertinent and, methought, unnaturall dalliances there, before the whole world, such as kissing, and leaning upon one another); but to my very little content, they not acting in any degree like the Duke's people.

6th. (Twelfth Day.) Up and Mr. Creed brought a pot of chocolate ready made for our morning draft, and then he and I

[1] By Killigrew.

140

to the Duke's, but I was not very willing to be seen at this end of the town, and so returned to our lodgings. Thence into Wood Street, and there bought a fine table for my dining-room, cost me 50s.; and while we were buying it there was a scare-fire in an ally over against us, but they quenched it. So to my brother's, where Creed and I and my wife dined with Tom; and after dinner to the Duke's house,[1] and there saw "Twelfth Night" acted well, though it be but a silly play, and not related at all to the name or day. Thence my wife and I home, and found all well, only myself somewhat vexed at my wife's neglect in leaving of her scarf, waistcoat, and night-dressings in the coach to-day that brought us from Westminster; though, I confess, she did give them to me to look after, yet it was her fault not to see that I did take them out of the coach. I believe it might be as good as 25s. loss or thereabouts.

This night making an end wholly of Christmas, with a mind fully satisfied with the great pleasures we have had by being abroad from home; and I do find my mind so apt to run to its old want of pleasures, that it is high time to betake myself to my late vows, which I will to-morrow, God willing, perfect and bind myself to; that so I may for a great while, do my duty, as I have well begun, and increase my good name and esteem in the world, and get money, which sweetens all things, and whereof I have much need. So home to supper and to bed, blessing God for his mercy to bring me home, after much pleasure, to my house and business with health and resolution to fall hard to work again.

7th. Up pretty early, that is by seven o'clock, it being not yet light before or then. So to my office all the morning, signing the Treasurer's ledger, part of it where I have not put my hand, and then eat a mouthful of pye at home to stay my stomach; and so by water to Deptford.

8th. Up pretty early, and sent my boy to the carrier's with some wine for my father, for to make his feast among his Brampton friends this Christmas, and my muff to my mother, sent as from my wife. But before I sent my boy out with them I beat him for a lie he told me; at which his sister, with whom we have of late been highly displeased and warned her to be gone, was angry; which vexed me to see the girl I loved so well, and my wife, should at last turn so much a fool and unthankful to us.

Dined at home; and there being the famous new play acted the

[1] During the Commonwealth all theatres had been suppressed. After the Restoration two distinct companies were established by royal authority: one called the King's Company, under Thomas Killigrew; the other called the Duke's Company, under Sir William Davenant, who engaged Betterton.

first time to-day, which is called "The Adventures of Five Hours,"
at the Duke's house, being, they say, made or translated by Colonel
Tuke,[1] I did long to see it; and so made my wife to get her ready,
though we were forced to send for a smith to break open her
trunk, her mayde Jane being gone forth with the keys, and so we
went; and though early, were forced to sit almost out of sight, at
the end of one of the lower forms, so full was the house. And the
play, in one word, is the best, for the variety and the most excellent continuance of the plot to the very end, that ever I saw or
think ever shall, and all possible, not only to be done in the time,
but in most other respects very admittable, and without one word
of ribaldry; and the house, by its frequent plaudits, did show their
sufficient approbation. So home; with much ado in an hour getting a coach home; and after writing letters at my office I went home
to supper and to bed, now resolving to set up my rest as to plays
till Easter, if not Whitsuntide next, excepting plays at Court.

   9th. Waking in the morning, my wife I found also awake,
and begun to speak to me with great trouble and tears of the necessity of her keeping somebody to bear her company; for her familiar-
ity with her other servants is it that spoils them all, and other
company she hath none, which is too true; and called for Jane to
reach her out of her trunk, giving her the keys to that purpose, a
bundle of papers: and pulls out a paper, a copy of what, a pretty
while since, she had wrote in a discontent to me, which I would
not read, but burnt. She now read it, and it was so piquant, and
wrote in English, and most of it true, of the retiredness of her life
and how unpleasant it was; that being wrote in English, and so
in danger of being met with and read by others, I was vexed at
it, and desired her and then commanded her to tear it. When she
desired to be excused it I forced it from her and tore it, and withal
took her other bundle of papers from her, and leapt out of the bed,
and in my shirt clapped them into the pocket of my breeches
that she might not get them from me; and having got on my stockings and breeches and gown I pulled them out one by one and tore
them all before her face, though it went against my heart to do it,
she crying and desiring me not to do it; but such was my passion
and trouble to see the letters of my love to her, and my will wherein
I had given her all I have in the world when I went to sea with my
Lord Sandwich, to be joyned with a paper of so much disgrace to
me and dishonour if it should have been found by any body.

---

[1] Adapted by Sir Samuel Tuke from a Spanish play by Calderon.

Having torn them all, saving a bond of my uncle Robert's which she hath long had in her hands, and our marriage license, and the first letter that ever I sent her when I was her servant, I took up the pieces and carried them into my chamber; and there, after many disputes with myself whether I should burn them or no, and having picked up the pieces of the paper she read to-day, and of my will which I tore, I burnt all the rest, and so went out of my office troubled in mind.

There coming a letter to me from Mr. Pierce, the surgeon, by my desire appointing his and Dr. Clerke's coming to dine with me next Monday, I went to my wife and agreed upon matters; and at last for my honour am forced to make her presently a new Moyre[1] gown to be seen by Mrs. Clerke, which troubles me to part with so much money; but however it sets my wife and I to friends again, though I and she never were so heartily angry in our lives as to-day almost, and I doubt the heart-burning will not [be] soon over; and the truth is I am sorry for the tearing of so many poor loving letters of mine from sea and elsewhere to her. So to my office again. So home, and mighty friends with my wife again, and so to bed.

13th. My poor wife rose by five o'clock in the morning, before day, and went to market and bought fowls and many other things for dinner, with which I was highly pleased; and the chine of beef was down also before six o'clock, and my own jack, of which I was doubtfull, do carry it very well. Things being put in order, and the cook come, I went to the office, where we sat till noon and then broke up, and I home; whither by and by comes Dr. Clerke and his lady, his sister and a she-cozen, and Mr. Pierce and his wife; which was all my guests. I had for them, after oysters, at first course a hash of rabbits, a lamb, and a rare chine of beef. Next a great dish of roasted fowl, cost me about 30*s.*, and a tart; and then fruit and cheese. My dinner was noble and enough. I had my house mighty clean and neat; my room below with a good fire in it; my dining-room above, and my chamber being made a withdrawing-chamber; and my wife's a good fire also. I find my new table very proper, and will hold nine or ten people well, but eight with great room. After dinner the women to cards in my wife's chamber, and the Dr. and Mr. Pierce in mine, because the dining-room smokes unless I keep a good charcoal fire, which

---

[1] Moyre is mohair. When they had first proposed inviting these guests, Pepys had been ashamed that his wife should only have a taffeta gown, when all the world was wearing winter gowns of Moyre.

I was not then provided with. At night to supper, had a good sack posset and cold meat, and sent my guests away about ten o'clock at night, both them and myself highly pleased with our management of this day; and indeed their company was very fine, and Mrs. Clerke a very witty, fine lady, though a little conceited and proud. So weary, so to bed. I believe this day's feast will cost me near £5.

19th. This noon I did find out Mr. Dixon at Whitehall, and discoursed with him about Mrs. Wheatly's daughter for a wife for my brother Tom,[1] and have committed it to him to enquire the pleasure of her father and mother concerning it. I demanded £300.

22nd. Mr. Dixon by agreement came to dine, to give me an account of his success with Mr. Wheatly for his daughter for my brother; and in short it is that his daughter cannot fancy my brother because of his imperfection in his speech, which I am sorry for; but there the business must die, and we must look out for another.

27th. I have news this day from Cambridge that my brother hath had his bachelor's cap put on; but that which troubles me is that he hath the pain of the stone, it beginning just as mine did. I pray God help him.

28th. To my Lord Sandwich's, whom I find playing at dice; and by this I see how time and example may alter a man, he being now acquainted with all sorts of pleasures and vanities which heretofore he never thought of nor loved, nor it may be hath allowed. So home, and there found my wife seeming to cry; for bringing home in a coach her new ferrandin[2] waistecoate, in Cheapside a man asked her whether that was the way to the Tower; and while she was answering him, another on the other side snatched away her bundle out of her lap and could not be recovered, but ran away with it; which vexes me cruelly, but it cannot be helped. So to my office, and there till almost 12 at night with Mr. Lewes,[3] learning to understand the manner of a purser's account, which is very hard and little understood by my fellow officers, and yet mighty necessary. So at last with great content broke up and home to supper and bed.

February 1st. (Lord's Day.) Up and to church, where Mr. Mills, a good sermon; and so home and had a good dinner with

---

[1] The preliminary reconnaissances for this match had taken place in the previous August—at the instance of the Wheatlys, who were at that time offering " £200 down with her."
[2] A stuff made of silk mixed with some other material.   [3] A clerk in the Victualling Office.

"MY POOR WIFE . . . WENT TO MARKET"

my wife, with which I was pleased to see it neatly done; and this troubled me to think of parting with Jane, that is come to be a very good cook. After dinner walked to my Lord Sandwich, and staid with him talking almost all the afternoon. It being a fine frost, my boy lighting me I walked home, and after supper up to prayers; and then alone with my wife and Jane did fall to tell her what I did expect would become of her since, after so long being my servant, she had carried herself so as to make us be willing to put her away; and desired God to bless [her], but bid her never to let me hear what became of her, for that I could never pardon ingratitude.

2nd. Up, and after paying Jane her wages I went away, because I could hardly forbear weeping, and she cried, saying it was not her fault that she went away, and indeed it is hard to say what it is, but only her not desiring to stay that she do now go. This day at my Lord's I sent for Mr. Ashwell,[1] and his wife came to me, and by discourse I perceive their daughter is very fit for my turn if my family may be as much for hers; but I doubt it will be to her loss to come to me for so small wages, but that will be considered of.

4th. To Paul's School, it being Apposition-day there. I heard some of their speeches, and they were just as schoolboys' used to be, of the seven liberal sciences; but I think not so good as ours were in our time. Went up to see the head forms posed in Latin, Greek, and Hebrew, but I think they did not answer in any so well as we did; only in geography they did pretty well. So down to the school, where Dr. Crumlum did me much honour by telling many what a present I had made to the school, shewing my Stephanus, in four volumes, cost me £4 10*s.*[2] He also shewed us, upon my desire, an old edition of the grammar of Colett's, where his epistle to the children is very pretty; and in rehearsing the creed it is said "borne of the cleane Virgin Mary." Thence with Mr. Elborough [3] (he being all of my old acquaintance that I could meet with here) to a cook's shop to dinner, but I found him a fool, as he ever was, or worse. So to the office, where after doing some business I went home, where I found our new mayde Mary, that is come in Jane's place.

5th. Up and to the office, where we sat all the morning, and then home to dinner, and found it so well done, above what I did

---

[1] A clerk in the Exchequer, and old friend of Pepys'.
[2] Stephens' *Thesaurus Linguae Latine.* Dean Colet was the founder of St. Paul's School.
[3] Thomas Elborough, curate of St. Laurence, Poultney; a school-fellow of Pepys'.

"CREED AND I AND CAPTN. FERRERS TO THE PARK"

expect from my mayde Susan, now Jane is gone, that I did call her in and give her sixpence.

6th. To a Bookseller's in the Strand, and there bought Hudibras again, it being certainly some ill humour to be so against that which all the world cries up to be the example of wit; for which I am resolved once again to read him, and see whether I can find it or no.

8th. (Lord's Day.) Up, and it being a very great frost, I walked to White Hall, and to my Lord Sandwich's by the fireside till chapel time; and so to chappell, where there preached little Dr. Duport,[1] of Cambridge. But though a great scholler he made the most flat dead sermon, both for matter and manner of delivery, that ever I heard, and very long beyond his hour, which made it worse. Creed and I and Captn. Ferrers to the Park, and there walked finely, seeing people slide. The little Duke of Monmouth, it seems, is ordered to take place of all Dukes, and so to follow Prince Rupert now, before the Duke of Buckingham or any else. Whether the wind and the cold did cause it or no I know not, but having been this day or two mightily troubled with an itching all over my body which I took to be a louse or two that might bite me, I found this afternoon that all my body is inflamed, and my face in a sad redness and swelling and pimpled, so that I was before we had done walking not only sick but ashamed of myself to see myself so changed in my countenance, so that after we had thus talked we parted; and I walked home with much ado, the ways being so full of ice and water by peoples' trampling. At last got home and to bed presently, and had a very bad night of it, in great pain in my stomach, and in great fever.

9th. Could not rise and go to the Duke as I should have done, but keep my bed and by the Apothecary's advice I am to sweat soundly, it being some disorder given the blood, but by what I know not, unless it be by my late quantitys of Dantzic-girkins that I have eaten. Sir J. Minnes advises me to the same thing but would not have me take anything from the apothecary, but from him, his Venice treacle being better, which I did consent to and fell into a great sweat; and about 10 or 11 o'clock came out of it, and slept pretty well.

12th. My wife's brother brought Mary Ashwell, whom we find a very likely person to please us, both for person, discourse, and other qualitys. She dined with us, and after dinner went

---

[1] Dr. James Duport, Professor of Greek and Vice-Master of Trinity College. He became Master of Magdalene in 1668.

away again, being agreed to come to us about three weeks or a
month hence. My wife and I well pleased with our choice, only
I pray God I may be able to maintain it.

23rd. Resolved to take my wife to a play at Court to-night,
and the rather because it is my birthday, being this day thirty
years old, for which let me praise God. While my wife dressed
herself, Creed and I walked out to see what play was acted to-day,
and we find it "The Slighted Mayde." [1] We saw it well acted,
though the play hath little good in it, being most pleased to see
the little girl dance in boy's apparel, she having very fine legs;
only bends in the hams, as I perceive all women do. The play
being done, we took coach and to Court, and there got good
places and saw "The Wilde Gallant," [2] performed by the King's
house, but it was ill acted, and the play so poor a thing as I never
saw in my life almost; and so little answering the name that
from beginning to end I could not, nor can at this time, tell certainly which was the Wild Gallant. The King did not seem
pleased at all, all the whole play, nor any body else, though Mr.
Clerke whom we met here did commend it to us. My Lady Castlemaine was all worth seeing to-night, and little Steward. [3]

It being done, we got a coach and got well home about 12 at
night. Now as my mind was but very ill satisfied with these two
plays themselves, so was I in the midst of them sad to think of the
spending so much money and venturing upon the breach of my
vow, which I found myself sorry for, I bless God, though my
nature would well be contented to follow the pleasure still. But
I did make payment of my forfeiture presently, though I hope to
save it back again by forbearing two plays at Court for this one
at the Theatre, or else to forbear that to the Theatre which I am
to have at Easter. But it being my birthday and the last play
that is likely to be acted at Court before Easter, because of the
Lent coming in, I was the easier content to fling away so much
money. So to bed. This day I was told that my Lady Castlemaine hath all the King's Christmas presents, made him by the
peers, given to her, which is a most abominable thing; and that at
the great ball she was much richer in jewells than the Queen and
Duchess put both together.

27th. Up and to my office, whither several persons came to
me about office business. About 11 o'clock, Commissioner Pett

[1] By Sir Robert Stapylton.   [2] Dryden's first play.
[3] "La belle Stuart"; she married Charles Stuart, 6th Duke of Lennox and 3rd Duke of Richmond.

and I walked to Chyrurgeon's Hall (we being all invited thither, and promised to dine there), where we were led into the Theatre; and by and by comes the reader, with the Master and Company, in a very handsome manner, and all being settled, he begun his lecture, this being the second upon the kidneys, ureters, &c., which was very fine; and his discourse being ended we walked into the Hall, and there being great store of company we had a fine dinner and good learned company, many Doctors of Physique, and we used with extraordinary great respect. Among other observables we drank the King's health out of a gilt cup given by King Henry VIII. to this Company, with bells hanging at it, which every man is to ring by shaking after he hath drunk up the whole cup. There is also a very excellent piece of the King, done by Holbein, stands up in the Hall, with the officers of the Company kneeling to him to receive their Charter. Thence we went into a private room, and there were the kidneys, ureters [&c.] upon which he read to-day; and Dr. Scarborough upon my desire and the company's did show very clearly the manner of the disease of the stone and the cutting, and all other questions that I could think of. Thence with great satisfaction to me, back to the company, where I heard good discourse, and so to the afternoon Lecture upon the heart and lungs, &c.; and that being done we broke up, took leave, and back to the office. Here late, and to Sir W. Batten's to speak upon some business, where I found Sir J. Minnes pretty well fuddled I thought: he took me aside to tell me how being at my Lord Chancellor's to-day, my Lord told him that there was a Great Seal passing for Sir W. Pen, through the impossibility of the Comptroller's duty to be performed by one man, to be as it were joynt-comptroller with him; at which he is stark mad, and swears he will give up his place, and do rail at Sir W. Pen the cruellest. But to see how the old man do strut, and swear that he understands all his duty as easily as crack a nut (and easier, he told my Lord Chancellor, for his teeth are gone); and that he understands it as well as any man in England, and that he will never leave to record that he should be said to be unable to do his duty alone; though, God knows, he cannot do it more than a child. All this I am glad to see fall out between them, and myself safe; and yet I hope the King's service well done for all this, for I would not that should be hindered by any of our private differences. So to my office, and then home to supper and to bed.

March 2nd. Up early and by water with Commissioner Pett to Deptford, and there took the Jemmy yacht (that the King and the Lords virtuosos[1] built the other day) down to Woolwich, where we discoursed of several matters both there and at the Rope-yard; and so to the yacht again, and went down four or five miles with extraordinary pleasure, it being a fine day and a brave gale of wind, and had some oysters brought us aboard newly taken, which were excellent, and ate with great pleasure. There also coming into the river two Dutchmen, we sent a couple of men on board and bought three Hollands cheeses, cost 4*d.* a piece, excellent cheeses. So back again to Woolwich. We dined at the White Hart with several officers with us, and after dinner went and saw the Royal James brought down to the stern of the Docke (the main business we came for), and then to the Ropeyard, and saw a trial between Riga hemp and a sort of Indian grass, which is pretty strong, but no comparison between it and the other for strength, and it is doubtful whether it will take tarre or no. So to the yacht again, and so home where I found my poor wife all alone at work, and the house foul, it being washing day.

3rd. (Shrove Tuesday.) At noon, by promise, Mrs. Turner and her daughter came along with Roger Pepys to dinner. We were as merry as I could be, having but a bad dinner for them; but so much the better, because of the dinner which I must have at the end of this month. And here Mrs. The. shewed me my name upon her breast as her Valentine, which will cost me 20*s.* After dinner I took them down into the wine-cellar, and broached my tierce of claret for them.

10th. Dined upon a poor Lenten dinner at home, my wife being vexed at a fray this morning with my Lady Batten about my boy's going thither to turn the watercock with their maydes' leave, but my Lady was mighty high upon it and she would teach his mistress better manners, which my wife answered aloud that she might hear, that she could learn little manners of her.

12th. Sat late, and having done I went home, where I found Mary Ashwell come to live with us, of whom I hope well, and pray God she may please us; which, though it cost me something, yet will give me much content.

15th. (Lord's Day.) Up and with my wife and her woman Ashwell the first time to church, where our pew was so full with Sir J. Minnes's sister and her daughter that I perceive when we

---

[1] The Royal Society.

come all together some of us must be shut out; but I suppose we shall come to some order what to do therein. Dined at home, and to church again in the afternoon, and so home, and I to my office till the evening. So home to supper and talk; and Ashwell is such good company that I think we shall be very lucky in her. So to prayers and to bed.

17th. Sir W. Batten and I to my Lord Mayor's;[1] and by and by comes in Sir Richard Ford. In our drinking, which was always going, we had many discourses, but from all of them I do find Sir R. Ford a very able man of his brains and tongue, and a scholler. But my Lord Mayor I find to be a talking, bragging Bufflehead, a fellow that would be thought to have led all the City in the great business of bringing in the King, and that nobody understood his plots, and the dark lanthorn he walked by; but led them and plowed with them as oxen and asses (his own words) to do what he had a mind: when in every discourse I observe him to be as very a coxcomb as I could have thought had been in the City. Here we staid talking till eleven at night, Sir R. Ford breaking to my Lord our business of our patent to be Justices of the Peace in the City, which he stuck at mightily; but however, Sir R. Ford knows him to be a fool, and so in his discourse he made him appear, and cajoled him into a consent to it: but so as I believe when he comes to his right mind to-morrow he will be of another opinion; and though Sir R. Ford moved it very weightily and neatly, yet I had rather it had been spared now. But to see how he do rant, and pretend to sway all the City in the Court of Aldermen, and says plainly that they cannot do, nor will he suffer them to do, any thing but what he pleases nor is there any officer of the City but of his putting in nor any man that could have kept the City for the King thus well and long but him. And if the country can be preserved, he will undertake that the City shall not dare to stir again. When I am confident there is no man almost in the City cares for him, nor hath he brains to outwit any ordinary tradesman.

18th. Wake betimes and talk a while with my wife about a wench that she has hired yesterday, which I would have enquired of before she comes, she having lived in great families, and so up and to my office, where all the morning, and at noon home to dinner. After dinner by water to Redriffe, my wife and Ashwell with me, and so walked, and left them at Halfway house; I to Deptford, where up and down the store-houses, and on board two or three

[1] Sir John Robinson, a clothworker.

ships now getting ready to go to sea, and so back, and find my wife
walking in the way.   So home again, merry with our Ashwell,
who is a merry jade; and so awhile to my office, and then home to
supper and to bed.   This day my tryangle, which was put in tune
yesterday, did please me very well, Ashwell playing upon it pretty
well.[1]

19th.   Up betimes and to Woolwich all alone by water, where
took the officers most abed.   I walked and enquired how all matters and businesses go, and by and by to the Clerk of the Cheque's
house, and there eat some of his good Jamaica brawne, and so
walked to Greenwich.   So to Deptford, where I did the same to
great content, and see the people begin to value me as they do
the rest.

23rd.   This day Greatorex brought me a very pretty weather-
glass for heat and cold.

April 1st.   Up betimes and abroad to my brother's, but they
tell me that my brother is abroad, and that my father is not yet
up.   At which I wondered, not thinking that he was come, though
I expected him, because I looked for him at my house.   So I up
to his bedside and staid an hour or two talking with him.   Among
other things he tells me how unquiett my mother is grown, that
he is not able to live almost with her, if it were not for Pall.   I
left him in bed, being very weary, to come to my house to-night
or to-morrow, when he pleases; and so I home to dinner.   My
wife being lazily in bed all this morning, Ashwell and I dined
below together; and a pretty girl she is, and I hope will give my
wife and myself good content, being very humble and active.

2nd.   Up by very betimes and to my office, where all the morning till towards noon, and then by coach to Westminster Hall
with Sir W. Pen.   I took occasion to speak about my wife's strange-
ness to him and his daughter, and that believing at last that it
was from his taking of Sarah to be his maid, he hath now put her
away, at which I am glad.

3rd.   Going out of White Hall I met Captain Grove, who did
give me a letter directed to myself from himself.   I discerned money
to be in it, and took it, knowing, as I found it to be, the proceed
of the place I have got him to be, the taking up of vessels for
Tangier.   But I did not open it till I came home to my office;
and there I broke it open, not looking into it till all the money was
out, that I might say I saw no money in the paper if ever I should

[1] Probably a triangular spinet.

be questioned about it. There was a piece in gold and £4 in silver. So home to dinner with my father and wife; and after dinner up to my tryangle, where I found that above my expectation Ashwell has very good principles of musique and can take out a lesson herself with very little pains, at which I am very glad.

4th. Up betimes and to my office. Home, whither comes Roger Pepys, Mrs. Turner her daughter, Joyce Norton, and a young lady, a daughter of Coll. Cockes, my uncle Wight, his wife and Mrs. Anne Wight: this being my feast in lieu of what I should have had a few days ago for my cutting of the stone, for which the Lord make me truly thankful. Very merry at, before, and after dinner, and the more for that my dinner was great, and most neatly dressed by our own only maid. We had a fricasee of rabbits and chickens, a leg of mutton boiled, three carps in a dish, a great dish of a side of lamb, a dish of roasted pigeons, a dish of four lobsters, three tarts, a lamprey pie (a most rare pie), a dish of anchovies, good wine of several sorts, and all things mighty noble and to my great content. After dinner to Hide Park, my aunt, Mrs. Wight and I in one coach, and all the rest of the women in Mrs. Turner's.

At the Park was the King, and in another coach my Lady Castlemaine, they greeting one another at every tour.[1] Here about an hour, and so leaving all by the way we home and found the house as clean as if nothing had been done there to-day from top to bottom, which made us give the cook 12*d.* a piece, each of us. So to my office about writing letters by the post, one to my brother John at Brampton telling him (hoping to work a good effect by it upon my mother) how melancholy my father is, and bidding him use all means to get my mother to live peaceably and quietly, which I am sure she neither do nor I fear can ever do; but frightening her with his coming down no more, and the danger of her condition if he should die, I trust may do good. So home and to bed.

5th. (Lord's Day.) To church, where a simple bawling young Scot preached.

6th. Took my wife by coach and left her at Madam Clerk's, to make a visit there, and I to the Committee of Tangier, where I found to my great joy my Lord Sandwich, the first time I have seen him abroad these some months; and by and by he rose and took leave, being, it seems, this night to go to Kensington or

----

[1] The company drove round and round the Ring in Hyde Park.

"MY WIFE COULD NOT GET HER TO BE CONTENTED TO HAVE IT DRAWN AFTER THE
FIRST TWITCH"

Chelsey, where he hath taken a lodging for a while to take the ayre.

7th. Up very betimes, and angry with Will that he made no more haste to rise after I called him. So to my office, and all the morning there. At noon to the Exchange, and so home to dinner, where I found my wife had been with Ashwell to La Roche's to have her tooth drawn, which it seems aches much; but my wife could not get her to be contented to have it drawn after the first twitch, but would let it alone, and so they came home with it undone, which made my wife and me good sport.

8th. Up betimes and to my office, and by and by, about 8 o'clock, to the Temple. Thence by water to White Hall to chappell. After sermon I went up and saw the ceremony of the Bishop of Peterborough's paying homage upon the knee to the King, while Sir H. Bennet,[1] Secretary, read the King's grant of the Bishopric of Lincoln, to which he is translated. His name is Dr. Lany. Here I also saw the Duke of Monmouth, with his Order of the Garter. I am told that the University of Cambridge did treat him a little while since with all the honour possible, with a comedy at Trinity College, and banquet, and made him Master of Arts there. All which, they say, the King took very well. Dr. Raynbow, Master of Magdalen, being now Vice-Chancellor. Home by water to dinner, and with my father, wife and Ashwell after dinner by water towards Woolwich.

12th. (Lord's Day.) To Gray's Inn walks, where some handsome faces. Coming home, a drunken boy was carrying by our constable to our new pair of stocks to handsel them, being a new pair and very handsome.

17th. Up by five o'clock as I have long done, and to my office all the morning. At noon home to dinner with my father with us. Our dinner, it being Good Friday, was only sugar-sopps and fish; the only time that we have had a Lenten dinner all this Lent. This morning Mr. Hunt, the instrument maker, brought me home a Basse Viall to see whether I like it, which I do not very well; besides I am under a doubt whether I had best buy one yet or no, because of spoiling my present mind and love to business.

19th. (Easter Day.) Up and this day put on my close-kneed coloured suit which, with new stockings of the colour, with belt and new gilt-handled sword, is very handsome. After supper fell in discourse of dancing, and I find that Ashwell hath a very fine

---

[1] Sir Henry Bennet, Secretary of State. Later Earl of Arlington.

carriage, which makes my wife almost ashamed of herself to see
herself so outdone; but to-morrow she begins to learn to dance for
a month or two. So to prayers and to bed.

20th. This day the little Duke of Monmouth was married at
White Hall, in the King's chamber; and to-night is a great supper
and dancing at his lodgings near Charing-Cross. I observed his
coat at the tail of his coach: he gives the arms of England, Scotland, and France, quartered upon some other fields, but what
it is that speaks his being a bastard I know not.

23rd. St. George's day and Coronacion, the King and Court
being at Windsor, at the installing of the King of Denmark by
proxy, and the Duke of Monmouth. I up betimes, and with my
father, having a fire made in my wife's new closet above, it being
a wet and cold day, we sat there all the morning looking over his
country accounts ever since his going into the country. I find his
spending hitherto has been (without extraordinary charges) at
full £100 per annum, which troubles me, and I did let him apprehend it, so as that the poor man wept, though he did make it well
appear to me that he could not have saved a farthing of it. I
did tell him how things stand with us and did shew my distrust of
Pall, both for her good nature and house wifery, which he was
sorry for, telling me that indeed she carries herself very well and
carefully; which I am glad to hear, though I doubt it was but his
doting and not being able to find her miscarriages so well nowa-
days as he could heretofore have done. We resolve upon sending
for Will Stankes up to town to give us a right understanding in
all that we have in Brampton. To my office and put a few things
in order, and so home to spend the evening with my father. At
cards till late; and being at supper, my boy being sent for some
mustard to a neat's tongue, the rogue staid half an hour in the
streets, it seems at a bonfire; at which I was very angry, and resolve
to beat him to-morrow.

24th. Up betimes, and with my salt eel[1] went down in the
parler and there got my boy and did beat him till I was fain to
take breath two or three times. Yet for all I am afeard it will
make the boy never the better, he is grown so hardened in his
tricks; which I am sorry for, he being capable of making a brave
man, and is a boy that I and my wife love very well. So made me
ready, and to my office, where all the morning, and at noon home,
sending my boy to enquire after two dancing masters at our end

---

[1] Rope's end.

of the town for my wife to learn, of whose names the boy brought word. After dinner all the afternoon fiddling upon my viallin (which I have not done many a day) while Ashwell danced, above in my upper best chamber, which is a rare room for musique.

25th. My wife hath begun to learn this day of Mr. Pembleton, but I fear will hardly do any great good at it, because she is conceited that she do well already, though I think no such thing. So to bed.

26th. (Lord's Day.) Lay pretty long in bed talking with my wife, and then up and set to the making up of my monthly accounts. But Tom coming, with whom I was angry for botching my camlott coat, to tell me that my father and he would dine with me, and that my father was at our church, I got me ready and had a very good sermon of a country minister upon "How blessed a thing it is for brethren to live together in unity!" So home and all to dinner. In the evening my wife, Ashwell, and the boy and I and the dogg over the water, and walked to Half-way house and beyond into the fields, gathering of cowslipps; and so to Half-way house with some cold lamb we carried with us, and there supped; and had a most pleasant walk back again, Ashwell all along telling us some parts of their mask at Chelsey School, which was very pretty; and I find she hath a most prodigious memory, remembering so much of things acted six or seven years ago. So home, and after reading my vows, being sleepy, without prayers to bed, for which God forgive me!

29th. Up betimes, and after having at my office settled some accounts for my Lord Sandwich, I went forth, and taking up my father at my brother's, took coach and towards Chelsey, 'lighting at an alehouse near the Gatehouse at Westminster to drink our morning draught; and so up again and to Chelsey, where we found my Lord all alone at a little table with one joynt of meat at dinner. We sat down and very merry talking, and mightily extolling the manner of his retirement and the goodness of his diet, which indeed is so finely dressed: the mistress of the house, Mrs. Beeke, having been a woman of good condition heretofore, a merchant's wife, and hath all things most excellently dressed; among others her cakes admirable, and so good that my Lord's words were, they were fit to present to my Lady Castlemaine. From ordinary discourse my Lord fell to talk of other matters to me. My father staid a good while at the window and then sat down by himself while my Lord and I were thus an hour togther or two after dinner discoursing; and by and by he took his leave, and told me he would stay below for me. Anon I took leave, and coming down found my father unexpectedly in great pain and desiring for God's sake to get him a bed to lie upon, which I did; and W. Howe and I staid by him, in so great pain as I never saw, poor wretch, and with that patience, crying only: "Terrible, terrible pain, God help me, God help me," with the mournful voice that made my heart ake. He desired to rest a little alone to see whether it would abate, and W. Howe and I went down and walked in the gardens, which are very fine, and a pretty fountayne with which I was finely wetted; and up to a banquetting house, with a very fine prospect. And so back to my father, who I found in such pain that I could not bear the sight of it without weeping, never thinking that I should be able to get him from thence; but at last, finding it like to continue, I got him to go to the coach, with great pain; and driving hard, he all the while in a most unsufferable torment, not staying the coach to speak with anybody, at last we got home; and all helping him we got him to bed presently, and after half an hour's lying in his naked bed (it being a rupture with which he is troubled, and has been this 20 years), he was at good ease, and so continued, and so fell to sleep; and we went down, whither W. Stankes was come with his horses. But it is very pleasant to hear how he rails at the rumbling and ado that is in London over it is in the country, that he cannot endure it. He supped with us, and very merry; and then he to his lodgings at the Inne with the horses, and so we to bed, I to my father who is very well again, and both slept very well.

30th. Up, and after drinking my morning draft with my father and W. Stankes, to my office, where till towards noon; and then to the Exchange, and back home to dinner, where Mrs. Hunt, my father, and W. Stankes. But, Lord! what a stir Stankes makes with his being crowded in the streets and wearied in walking in London, and would not be wooed by my wife and Ashwell to go to a play, nor to White Hall, or to see the lyons, though he was carried in a coach. I never could have thought there had been upon earth a man so little curious in the world as he is. At the office all the afternoon till 9 at night; so home to cards with my father, wife, and Ashwell, and so to bed.

May 1st. Up betimes and my father with me, and he and I all the morning and Will Stankes private in my wife's closet above, settling our matters concerning our Brampton estate, &c.; and

I find that there will be £50 per annum clear coming towards my father's maintenance. I advised my father to good husbandry and to living within the compass of £50 a year, and all in such kind words as not only made them but myself to weep, and I hope it will have a good effect. That being done and all things agreed on, we went down, and after a glass of wine we all took horse; and I, upon a horse hired of Mr. Game, saw him out of London at the end of Bishopsgate Street; and so I turned and rode with some trouble through the fields, and then Holborn, &c., towards Hide Park, whither all the world, I think, are going. At the Chequer at Charing Cross I put up my own dull jade, and saddled a delicate stone-horse, and with that rid in state to the Park, where none better mounted than I almost; but being in a throng of horses, seeing the King's riders showing tricks with their managed horses,[1] which were very strange, my stone-horse was very troublesome, and begun to fight with other horses, to the dangering him and myself; and with much ado I got out, and kept myself out of harm's way. And so home to see Sir J. Minnes, and after staying talking with him awhile I took leave and went to hear Mrs. Turner's daughter play on the harpsicon. But, Lord! it was enough to make any man sick to hear her; yet I was forced to commend her highly. So home to supper and to bed, Ashwell playing upon the tryangle very well before I went to bed.

2nd. Being weary last night I slept till almost seven o'clock, a thing I have not done many a day. So up and to my office (being come to some angry words with my wife about neglecting the keeping of the house clean, I calling her beggar, and she me pricklouse,[2] which vexed me), and there all the morning. So to the Exchange and then home to dinner, and very merry and well pleased with my wife, and so to the office again.

3rd. My wife not being very well did not dress herself but staid at home all day; and so I to church in the afternoon and so home again, and up to teach Ashwell the grounds of time and other things on the tryangle, and made her take out a Psalm very well, she having a good ear and hand. And so a while to my office, and then home to supper and prayers, to bed, my wife and I having a little falling out because I would not leave my discourse below with her and Ashwell to go up and talk with her alone upon something she has to say. She reproached me but I had rather

---

[1] *i.e.* horses trained to the *manège* or riding-school.
[2] Pricklouse, *i.e.* a tailor: an acid reference to Pepys' extraction.

talk with any body than her, by which I find I think she is jealous of my freedom with Ashwell, which I must avoid giving occasion of.

4th. The dancing-master came, whom standing by, seeing him instructing my wife, when he had done with her he would needs have me try the steps of a coranto; and what with his desire and my wife's importunity I did begin, and then was obliged to give him entry-money 10*s.*, and am become his scholler. The truth is I think it a thing very useful for a gentleman, and sometimes I may have occasion of using it; and though it cost me what I am heartily sorry it should, besides that I must by my oath give half as much more to the poor, yet I am resolved to get it up some other way; and then it will not be above a month or two in a year. So though it be against my stomach yet I will try it a little while; if I see it comes to any great inconvenience or charge I will fling it off.

8th. Took my wife and Ashwell to the Theatre Royall,[1] being the second day of its being opened. The play was "The Humerous Lieutenant," a play that hath little good in it, nor much in the very part which, by the King's command, Lacy now acts instead of Clun. In the dance the tall devil's actions was very pretty. The play being done, we home by water, having been a little shamed that my wife and woman were in such a pickle, all the ladies being finer and better dressed in the pitt than they used, I think, to be. To my office to set down this day's passage; and though my oath against going to plays do not oblige me against this house, because it was not then in being, yet believing that at the time my meaning was against all publique houses, I am resolved to deny myself the liberty of two plays at Court which are in arreare to me for the months of March and April, which will more than countervail this excess; so that this month of May is the first that I must claim a liberty of going to a Court play according to my oath.

9th. To Westminster, where at Mr. Jervas's, my old barber, I did try two or three borders and perriwiggs, meaning to wear one; and yet I have no stomach for it, but that the pains of keeping my hair clean is so great. He trimmed me, and at last I parted, but my mind was almost altered from my first purpose from the trouble that I foresee will be in wearing them also. Thence by water home and to the office, where busy late; and so home to supper and bed.

[1] This was the first Drury Lane Theatre. The play was by Beaumont and Fletcher.

10th. (Lord's Day.) Up betimes and put on a black cloth suit with white lynings under all, as the fashion is to wear, to appear under the breeches. So being ready walked to St. James's and was there at mass, and was forced in the crowd to kneel down. And mass being done, to the King's Head ordinary, whither I sent for Mr. Creed and there we dined, where many Parliament-men. Among other things, talking of the way of ordinaries, that it is very convenient because a man knows what he hath to pay, one did wish that, among many bad, we could learn two good things of France; which were that we would not think it below the gentleman or person of honour at a tavern to bargain for his meat before he eats it; and next to take no servant without certificate from some friend or gentleman of his good behaviour and abilities.

11th. Up betimes and by water to Woolwich, and thence on foot to Greenwich, where going I was set upon by a great dogg, who got hold of my garters and might have done me hurt; but, Lord, to see in what a maze I was, that having a sword about me I never thought of it or had the heart to make use of it, but might for want of that courage have been worried.

12th. A little angry with my wife for minding nothing now but the dancing-master, having him come twice a day, which is a folly. To my office till late.

13th. After dinner Pembleton[1] came, and I practised. But, Lord! to see how my wife will not be thought to need telling by me or Ashwell, and yet will plead that she has learnt but a month, which causes many short fallings out between us. So to my office, whither one-eyed Cooper came to see me, and I made him to show me the use of platts,[2] and to understand the lines, and how to find how lands bear, &c., to my great content.

15th. Up betimes and walked to St. James's, where Mr. Coventry being in bed I walked in the Park, discoursing with the keeper of Pell Mell, who was sweeping of it; who told me of what the earth is mixed that do floor the Mall, and that over all there is cockle-shells powdered and spread to keep it fast; which however in dry weather turns to dust and deads the ball.[3]   Home, where I found my wife and the dancing-master alone above, not dancing but talking.   Now so deadly full of jealousy I am that my heart and head did so cast about and fret that I could not do any busi-

---

[1] The dancing master.   [2] Sea-charts.
[3] Pall Mall was so called from the game which was played along it.   In this a boxwood ball was driven through an iron ring suspended at some height above the ground in a long alley; the player who, starting from one end, could drive the ball through the ring with the fewest strokes won the game.

ness possibly, but went out to my office; and anon late home again and ready to chide at every thing, and then suddenly to bed and could hardly sleep yet durst not say any thing, but was forced to say that I had bad news from the Duke as an excuse to my wife, who by my folly has too much opportunity given her with the man, who is a pretty neat black man, but married.

16th. Up with my mind disturbed and with my last night's doubts upon me, for which I deserve to be beaten if not really served as I am fearful of being; especially since God knows that I do not find honesty enough in my own mind but that upon a small temptation I could be false to her, and therefore ought not to expect more justice from her; but God pardon both my sin and my folly herein. To my office and there sitting all the morning, and at noon dined at home. After dinner comes Pembleton, and I being out of humour would not see him, pretending business. But, Lord! with what jealousy did I walk up and down my chamber listening to hear whether they danced or no, which they did, notwithstanding I afterwards knew and did then believe that Ashwell was with them. So to my office awhile; and my jealousy still reigning I went in and, not out of any pleasure but from that only reason, did go up to them to practise, and did make an end of "La Duchesse," which I think I should, with a little pains, do very well. So broke up and saw him gone.

21st. At dinner, my wife and I had high words about her dancing, to that degree that I did enter and make a vow to myself not to oppose her or say anything to dispraise or correct her therein as long as her month lasts, in pain of 2s. 6d. for every time; which, if God pleases, I will observe, for this roguish business has brought us more disquiett than anything that has happened a great while. After dinner to my office, where late, and then home; and Pembleton being there again we fell to dance a country dance or two, and so to supper and bed. But being at supper my wife did say something that caused me to oppose her in; she used the word devil, which vexed me, and among other things I said I would not have her to use that word; upon which she took me up most scornfully, which, before Ashwell and the rest of the world, I know not now-a-days how to check as I would heretofore, for less than that would have made me strike her. So that I fear without great discretion I shall go near to lose too my command over her, and nothing do it more than giving her this occasion of dancing and other pleasures, whereby her mind is taken up from her business and finds other sweets besides pleasing of me, and so makes her that she begins not at all to take pleasure in me or study to please me as heretofore. But if this month of her dancing were but out (as my first was this night, and I paid off Pembleton for myself) I shall hope with a little pains to bring her to her old wont.

24th. (Lord's Day.) My wife telling me that there was a pretty lady come to church with Peg Pen to-day, I against my intention had a mind to go to church to see her, and did so; and she is pretty handsome. But over against our gallery I espied Pembleton, and saw him leer upon my wife all the sermon, I taking no notice of him, and my wife upon him; and I observed she made a curtsey to him at coming out without taking notice to me at all of it, which with the consideration of her being desirous these two last Lord's days to go to church both forenoon and afternoon do really make me suspect something more than ordinary, though I am loth to think the worst; but yet it put and do still keep me at a great loss in my mind, and makes me curse the time that I consented to her dancing, and more my continuing it a second month, which was more than she desired, even after I had seen too much of her carriage with him. But I must have patience and get her into the country, or at least to make an end of her learning to dance as soon as I can. So home, and read to my wife a fable or two in Ogleby's Æsop, and so to supper, and then to prayers and to bed. My wife this evening discoursing of making clothes for the country, which I seem against, pleading lack of money; but I am glad of it in some respects because of getting her out of the way from this fellow, and my own liberty to look after my business more than of late I have done. So to prayers and to bed.

25th. Sarah Kite my cozen, poor woman, came to see me and borrow 40*s.* of me, telling me she will pay it at Michaelmas again to me. I was glad it was no more, being indifferent whether she pays it me or no; but it will be a good excuse to lend her nor give her any more. So I did freely at first word do it, and give her a crown more freely to buy her child something, she being a good-natured and painful wretch, and one that I would do good for as far as I can that I might not be burdened. My wife was not ready, and she coming early did not see her, and I was glad of it.

26th. Lay long in bed talking with my wife. So up and to my office a while and then home, where I found Pembleton; and by many circumstances I am led to conclude that there is something more than ordinary between my wife and him, which do so trouble

"SHE MADE A CURTSEY TO HIM AT COMING OUT WITHOUT TAKING NOTICE TO ME AT ALL OF IT"

me that I know not at this very minute that I now write this almost what either I write or am doing, nor how to carry myself to my wife in it, being unwilling to speak of it to her for making of any breach and other inconveniences, nor let it pass for fear of her continuing to offend me and the matter grow worse thereby. So that I am grieved at the very heart; but I am very unwise in being so. There dined with me Mr. Creed and Captain Grove, and before dinner I had much discourse, in my chamber with Mr. Deane,[1] the builder of Woolwich, about building of ships. But nothing could get the business out of my head, I fearing that this afternoon, by my wife's sending every one abroad and knowing that I must be at the office, she has appointed him to come. This is my devilish jealousy, which I pray God may be false; but it makes a very hell in my mind, which the God of heaven remove or I shall be very unhappy. So to the office, where we sat awhile. By and by my mind being in great trouble I went home to see how things were, and there I found as I doubted Mr. Pembleton with my wife, and nobody else in the house, which made me almost mad; and, going up to my chamber, after a turn or two I went out again and called somebody on pretence of business and left him in my little room at the door, telling him I would come again to him to speak with him about his business. So in great trouble and doubt to the office, and made a quick end of our business and desired leave to be gone, pretending to go to the Temple; but it was home, and so up to my chamber, and continued in my chamber vexed and angry till he went away, pretending aloud, that I might hear, that he could not stay, and Mrs. Ashwell not being within they could not dance. But I staid all the evening walking, and though anon my wife came up to me and would have spoke of business to me, yet I construed it to be but impudence, and though my heart full yet I did say nothing, being in a great doubt what to do. So at night suffered them to go all to bed, and late put myself to bed in great discontent, and so to sleep.

27th. So I waked by 3 o'clock, my mind being troubled, and so took occasion to wake my wife, and after having lain till past 4 o'clock seemed going to rise, though I did it only to see what she would do, and so going out of the bed she took hold of me and would know what ailed me, and after many kind and some cross words I began to tax her discretion in yesterday's business; but she quickly

---

[1] Afterwards Sir Anthony Deane, F.R.S., a celebrated shipbuilder, Member of Parliament for Harwich and for Shoreham in later years.

told me my own, knowing well enough that it was my old disease of jealousy, which I denied, but to no purpose. After an hour's discourse, sometimes high and sometimes kind, I found very good reason to think that her freedom with him is very great and more than was convenient, but with no evil intent; and so after awhile I caressed her and parted seeming friends, but she crying in a great discontent. So I up and by water to the Temple. Thence to Westminster Hall, where I met with my cozen Roger Pepys, and walked a good while with him; and among other discourse as a secret he hath committed to nobody but myself, he tells me that he thinks it fit to marry again, and would have me, by the help of my uncle Wight or others, to look him out a widow between thirty and forty years old, without children and with a fortune, which he will answer in any degree with a joynture fit for her fortune. A woman sober, and no highflyer, as he calls it.

This day there was great thronging to Banstead Downs, upon a great horse-race and foot-race. I am sorry I could not go thither. So home back as I came, to London Bridge, and so home, where I find my wife in a musty humour, and tells me before Ashwell that Pembleton had been there, and she would not have him come in unless I was there, which I was ashamed of; but however, I had rather it should be so than the other way. So to my office to put things in order there, and by and by comes Pembleton, and word is brought me from my wife thereof, that I might come home. So I sent word that I would have her go dance, and I would come presently. So being at a great loss whether I should appear to Pembleton or no, and what would most proclaim my jealousy to him, I at last resolved to go home, and there we danced country dances and single, my wife and I; and my wife paid him off for this month also, and so he is cleared. After dancing we took him down to supper and were very merry, and I made myself so, and kind to him as much as I could, to prevent his discourse, though I perceive to my trouble that he knows all, and may do me the disgrace to publish it as much as he can. Which I take very ill, and if too much provoked shall witness it to her. After supper and he gone we to bed.

28th. To the Duke's House, and there saw "Hamlett" done, giving us fresh reason never to think enough of Betterton. Who should we see come upon the stage but Gosnell,[1] my wife's maid?

---

[1] Mrs. Gosnell had entered Mrs. Pepys' service in the previous December, but had only stayed a few days.

but neither spoke, danced, nor sung, which I was sorry for. But she becomes the stage very well. Thence by water home.

30th. To my brother's, and there I found my aunt James, a poor, religious, well-meaning, good soul, talking of nothing but God Almighty, and that with so much innocence that mightily pleased me. Here was a fellow that said grace so long like a prayer; I believe the fellow is a cunning fellow, and yet I by my brother's desire did give him a crown, he being in great want, and, it seems, a parson among the fanatiques, and a cozen of my poor aunt's, whose prayers she told me did do me good among the many good souls that did by my father's desires pray for me when I was cut of the stone, and which God did hear; which I also in complaisance did own, but, God forgive me, my mind was otherwise.

June 2nd. To-night I took occasion with the vintner's man, who came by my direction to taste again my tierce of claret, to go down to the cellar with him to consult about the drawing of it; and there to my great vexation I find that the cellar door hath long been kept unlocked, and above half the wine drunk. I was deadly mad at it, and examined my people round, but nobody would confess it: but I did examine the boy, and afterwards Will, and told him of his sitting up after we were in bed with the maids; but as to that business he denies it, which I can not remedy, but I shall endeavour to know how it went. My wife did also this evening tell me a story of Ashwell stealing some new ribbon from her, a yard or two, which I am sorry to hear, and I fear my wife do take a displeasure against her, that they will hardly stay together, which I should be sorry for because I know not where to pick such another out anywhere.

3rd. In the evening to the office and did some business, then home, and, God forgive me, did from my wife's unwillingness to tell me whither she had sent the boy, presently suspect that he was gone to Pembleton's, and from that occasion grew so discontented that I could hardly speak or sleep all night.

4th. I did by a wile get out of my boy that he did not yesterday go to Pembleton's or thereabouts, but only was sent all that time for some starch, and I did see him bringing home some; and yet all this cannot make my mind quiet.

5th. Up and to read a little, and by and by the carver coming, I directed him how to make me a neat head for my viall that is making. About 10 o'clock my wife and I, not without some discontent, abroad by coach, and I set her at her father's; but their condition is such that she will not let me see where they live, but goes by herself when I am out of sight.

6th. Walked, drinking my morning draft of whay by the way, to York House, where the Russia Embassador do lie; and there I saw his people go up and down louseing themselves. They are all in a great hurry, being to be gone the beginning of next week.

9th. Up and after ordering some things towards my wife's going into the country, to the office, where I spent the morning upon my measuring rules very pleasantly till noon, and then comes Creed and he and I talked about mathematiques, and he tells me of a way found out by Mr. Jonas Moore which he calls duodecimal arithmetique, which is properly applied to measuring, where all is ordered by inches, which are 12 in a foot, which I have a mind to learn.

11th. Spent the evening with my wife, and she and I did jangle mightily about her cushions that she wrought with worsteds the last year, which are too little for any use; but were good friends by and by again. But one thing I must confess I do observe which I did not before, which is that I cannot blame my wife to be now in a worse humour than she used to be, for I am [so] taken up in my talk with Ashwell, who is a very witty girl, that I am not so fond of her as I used and ought to be; which now I do perceive I will remedy, but I would to the Lord I had never taken any, though I cannot have a better than her. To supper and to bed. The consideration that this is the longest day in the year [1] is very unpleasant to me.

12th. Up and my office, there conning my measuring Ruler, which I shall grow a master of in a very little time. At noon to the Exchange and so home to dinner, and abroad with my wife by water to the Royall Theatre; and there saw "The Committee,"[2] a merry but indifferent play, only Lacey's part, an Irish footman, is beyond imagination. Here I saw my Lord Falconbridge, and his Lady, my Lady Mary Cromwell, who looks as well as I have known her, and well clad; but when the House began to fill she put on her vizard, and so kept it on all the play; which of late is become a great fashion among the ladies, which hides their whole face. So to the Exchange to buy things with my wife, among others a vizard for herself.

13th. After dinner by water to the Royall Theatre, where I resolve to bid farewell, as shall appear by my oaths to-morrow

---

[1] According to the old style.　　　　[2] By Sir Robert Howard.

against all plays either at publique houses or Court till Christmas be over. Here we saw "The Faithfull Sheepheardesse," [1] a most simple thing, and yet much thronged after and often shown, but it is only for the scenes' sake, which is very fine indeed and worth seeing. Saw my Lady Castlemaine, who I fear is not so handsome as I have taken her for, and now she begins to decay something. This is my wife's opinion also, for which I am sorry. Thence by coach, with a mad coachman that drove like mad, and down bye-ways through Bucklersbury home, everybody through the street cursing him, being ready to run over them.

15th. Up betimes, and anon my wife rose and did give me her keys, and put other things in order and herself against going this morning into the country. I am troubled to see her forced to sit in the back of the coach, though pleased to see her company none but women and one parson; she I find is troubled at all, and I seemed to make a promise to get a horse and ride after them; and so, kissing her often, and Ashwell once, I bid them adieu. That done, to the Trinity House where among others I found my Lords Sandwich and Craven, and my cousin Roger Pepys, and Sir Wm. Wheeler.[2]   Anon we sat down to dinner, which was very great, as they always have. Great variety of talk. Sometimes they talked of handsome women, and Sir J. Minnes saying that there was no beauty like what he sees in the country-markets (and specially at Bury, in which I will agree with him that there is a prettiest women I ever saw), my Lord replied thus: "Sir John, what do you think of your neighbour's wife?" looking upon me. "Do you not think that he hath a great beauty to his wife? Upon my word he hath." Which I was not a little proud of. Thence by barge with my Lord to Blackfriars, where we landed and I thence walked home. My head akeing with the healths I was forced to drink to-day I sent for the barber, and he having done, I up to my wife's closett and there played on my viallin a good while, and without supper anon to bed, sad for want of my wife, whom I love with all my heart, though of late she has given me some troubled thoughts.

21st. (Lord's Day.) Up betimes, and fell to reading my Latin grammar, which I perceive I have great need of, having lately found it by my calling Will to the reading of a chapter in Latin, and I am resolved to go through it. To church and slept all the sermon, the Scott, to whose voice I am not to be reconciled, preaching.

[1] By John Fletcher.   [2] M.P. for Queenborough.

22nd. Up betimes and to my office, reading over all our letters of the office that we have wrote since I came into the Navy, whereby to bring the whole series of matters into my memory, and to enter in my manuscript some of them that are needful and of great influence. Thence to the Park, and there walked up and down with Creed, talking, who is so knowing, and a man of that reason, that I cannot but love his company, though I do not love the man, because he is too wise to be made a friend of, and acts all by interest and policy, but is a man fit to learn of.

23rd. Up by four o'clock, and so to my office; but before I went out, calling as I have of late done for my boy's copy-book, I found that he had not done his task; so I beat him, and then went up to fetch my rope's end, but before I got down the boy was gone. I searched the cellar with a candle, and from top to bottom could not find him high nor low. So to the office. Home to dinner alone, and there I found that my boy had got out of doors, and came in for his hat and band, and so is gone away to his brother; but I do resolve even to let him go away for good and all.

25th. This noon I received a letter from the country from my wife, wherein she seems much pleased with the country; God continue that she may have pleasure while she is there. She, by my Lady's advice, desires a new petticoat of the new silk striped stuff, very pretty. So I went to Paternoster Row presently and bought her one, with Mr. Creed's help, a very fine rich one, the best I did see there, and much better than she desires or expects.

26th. Sir W. Batten, Sir J. Minnes, my Lady Batten and I by coach to Bednall Green to Sir W. Rider's[1] to dinner, where a fine place, good lady mother, and their daughter, Mrs. Middleton, a fine woman. A noble dinner, and a fine merry walk with the ladies alone after dinner in the garden, which is very pleasant; the greatest quantity of strawberrys I ever saw, and good, and a collation of great mirth, Sir J. Minnes reading a book of scolding very prettily. This very house was built by the Blind Beggar of Bednall Green, so much talked of and sang in ballads; but they say it was only some of the outhouses of it. We drank great store of wine, and a beer glass at last which made me almost sick.

30th. Thus, by God's blessing, ends this book of two years; I being in all points in good health and a good way to thrive and do well. Some money I do and can lay up, but not much, being worth now above £700 besides goods of all sorts. My wife in

[1] Master of the Trinity House.

the country with Ashwell, her woman, with my father; myself at home with W. Hewer and my cooke-maid Hannah, my boy Wayneman being lately run away from me. In my office my repute and understanding good, especially with the Duke and Mr. Coventry; only the rest of the officers do rather envy than love me, I standing in most of their lights, specially Sir W. Batten, whose cheats I do daily oppose to his great trouble, though he appears mighty kind and willing to keep friendship with me, while Sir J. Minnes, like a dotard, is led by the nose by him.

July 4th. This day in the Duke's chamber, there being a Roman story in the hangings, and upon the standards written these four letters S. P. Q. R., Sir G. Carteret came to me to know what the meaning of those four letters were; which ignorance is not to be borne in a Privy Counsellor, methinks, that a schoolboy should be whipt for not knowing.

5th. (Lord's Day.) Lady Batten had sent twice to invite me to go with them to Walthamstow to-day, Mrs. Martha being married already this morning to Mr. Castle, at this parish church. I got a horse and rode thither very pleasantly, and had two pair of gloves as the rest, and walked up and down with my Lady in the garden, she mighty kind to me; and I have the way to please her. A good dinner and merry, but methinks none of the kindness nor bridall respect between the bridegroom and bride that was between my wife and I, but as persons that marry purely for convenience. After dinner to church by coach. An old doting parson preached. So home again, Sir J. Minnes and I in his coach together, talking all the way of chymistry, wherein he do know something, at least seems so to me that cannot correct him.

9th. Abroad, it raining, to Blackfriars, and there went into a little alehouse, and here I kissed three or four times the maid of the house, who is a pretty girl but very modest. By water to Deptford, and there mustered the Yard, purposely, God forgive me, to find out Bagwell, a carpenter, whose wife is a pretty woman, that I might have some occasion of knowing him, which I did so luckily that going thence he and his wife did of themselves meet me in the way. But I spoke little to her, but shall give occasion for her coming to me.

13th. Walked to St. James's, and finding many coaches at the Gate, I found upon enquiry that the Duchess is brought to bed of a boy;[1] and hearing that the King and Queen are rode abroad

---

[1] James Stuart, Duke of Cambridge, second son of the Duke of York. He only lived four years.

with the Ladies of Honour to the Park, and seeing a great crowd of gallants staying here to see their return, I also staid walking up and down. By and by the King and Queen, who looked in this dress (a white laced waistcoat and a crimson short pettycoat, and her hair dressed *à la négligence*) mighty pretty; and the King rode hand in hand with her. Here was also my Lady Castlemaine rode among the rest of the ladies, but the King took, methought, no notice of her; nor when they 'light did any body press (as she seemed to expect, and staid for it) to take her down, but was taken down by her own gentleman. She looked mighty out of humour and had a yellow plume in her hat (which all took notice of), and yet is very handsome, but very melancholy: nor did any body speak to her, or she so much as smile or speak to any body. I followed them up into White Hall and into the Queen's presence, where all the ladies walked, talking and fiddling with their hats and feathers, and changing and trying one another's by one another's heads, and laughing. But it was the finest sight to me, considering their great beautys and dress, that ever I did see in all my life. But above all, Mrs. Stewart in this dress, with her hat cocked and a red plume, with her sweet eye, little Roman nose, and excellent taille, is now the greatest beauty I ever saw, I think, in my life; and, if ever woman can, do exceed my Lady Castlemaine, at least in this dress: nor do I wonder if the King changes, which I verily believe is the reason of his coldness to my Lady Castlemaine.

19th. (Lord's Day.) Read over my vows and increased them by a vow against all strong drink till November next of any sort or quantity, by which I shall try how I can forbear it. God send it may not prejudice my health, and then I care not.

22nd. To my brother Tom's barber and had my hair cut, while his boy played on the viallin, a plain boy, but has a very good genius. Thence to my Lord Crew's. My Lord not being come home, I met and staid below with Captain Ferrers who was come to wait upon my Lady Jemimah to St. James's, she being one of the four ladies that hold up the mantle at the christening this afternoon of the Duke's child. In discourse, Captain Ferrers tells me that my Lord Sandwich finds some pleasure in the country where he now is, whether he means one of the daughters of the house or no I know not, but hope the contrary; that he thinks he is very well pleased with staying there, but yet upon breaking up of the Parliament, which the King by a message to-day says shall be on Monday next, he resolves to go.

24th. To Mr. Bland's,[1] where Mr. Povy and Gauden and I
were invited to dinner, which we had very finely and great plenty,
but for drink, though many and good, I drank nothing but small
beer and water, which I drank so much that I wish it may not do
me hurt. They had a kinswoman they call daughter in the house,
a short, ugly, red-haired slut, that plays upon the virginalls and
sings, but after such a country manner I was weary of it, but
yet could not but commend it. So by and by after dinner comes
Monsr. Gotier, who is beginning to teach her, but, Lord! what a
droll fellow it is to make her hold open her mouth, and telling this
and that so drolly would make a man burst; but himself I perceive
sings very well. Anon we sat down again to a collacõn of cheese
cakes, tarts, custards, and such like, very handsome, and so up
and away home.

27th. By water to Westminster, and there came most luckily
to the Lords' House as the House of Commons were going into the
Lords' House, and there I crowded in along with the Speaker,[2]
and got to stand close behind him, where he made his speech to
the King (who sat with his crown on and robes, and so all the Lords
in their robes, a fine sight); wherein he told his Majesty what they
have done this Parliament and now offered for his royall consent.
The Clerk of the House reads the title of the bill, and then looks
at the end and there finds (writ by the King I suppose) "Le Roy
le veult," and that he reads. And to others he reads, "Soit fait
comme vous désirez." And to the Subsidys, as well that for the
Commons, I mean the layety, as for the Clergy, the King writes,
"Le Roy remerciant les Seigneurs, &c., Prélates, &c., accepte
leur bénévolences." The Speaker's speech was far from any oratory, but was as plain (though good matter) as any thing could be,
and void of elocution. After the bills passed, the King, sitting on
his throne, with his speech writ in a paper which he held in his lap,
and scarce looked off of it, I thought, all the time he made his
speech to them, giving them thanks for their subsidys, of which,
had he not need, he would not have asked or received them; and
that need, not from any extravagancys of his, he was sure, in any
thing, but the disorders of the times compelling him to be at greater
charge than he hoped for the future, by their care in their country,
he should be; and that for his family expenses and others, he would
labour however to retrench in many things convenient, and would

1 A merchant concerned in business with Tangiers.
2 Sir Edward Turner, M.P. for Hertford.

"HAD MY HAIR CUT, WHILE HIS BOY PLAYED ON THE VIALLIN"

have all others to do so too. He desired that nothing of old faults should be remembered, or severity for the same used to any in the country, it being his desire to have all forgot as well as forgiven. But, however, to use all care in suppressing any tumults, &c. So he concluded that for the better proceeding of justice he did think fit to make this a Session, and to prorogue them to the 16th of March next: His speech was very plain, nothing at all of spirit in it, nor spoke with any; but rather on the contrary imperfectly, repeating many times his words though he read all; which I was sorry to see, it having not been hard for him to have got all the speech without book. So they all went away, the King out of the House at the upper end, he being by and by to go to Tunbridge to the Queen.

31st. Up early to my accounts this month, and I find myself worth clear £730, the most I ever had yet, which contents me though I encrease but very little.   Thence to my office doing business, and at noon to the Exchange, where I met Dr. Pierce, who tells me as a friend the great injury that he thinks I do myself by being so severe in the Yards, and contracting the ill-will of the whole Navy for those offices singly upon myself.   Now I discharge a good conscience therein, and I tell him that no man can (nor do he say any say it) charge me with doing wrong; but rather do as many good offices as any man.   They think, he says, that I have a mind to get a good name with the King and Duke, who he tells me do not consider any such thing; but I shall have as good thanks to let all alone, and do as the rest.   But I believe the contrary; and yet I told him I never go to the Duke alone, as others do, to talk of my own services.   However, I will make use of his council and take some course to prevent having the single ill-will of the office.

August 1st. Mr. Coventry and I by water to Gravesend, and there eat a bit and so mounted, I upon one of his horses which met him there, a brave proud horse, all the way talking of businesses of the office and other matters to good purpose. Being come to Chatham, we put on our boots and so walked to the yard, where we met Commissioner Pett, and there walked up and down looking and inquiring into many businesses.

2nd. (Lord's Day.) Up and after the barber had done we walked to the Docke, and so on board the Mathias, where Commissioner Pett and he and I and a good many of the officers and others of the yard did hear an excellent sermon of Mr. Hudson's.

We took him with us to the Hill-house, and there we dined, and an officer or two with us. Then to the parish church, and there heard a poor sermon with a great deal of false Greek in it. Thence to the Docke and by water to view St. Mary Creeke, but do not find it so proper for a wet docks as we would have it, it being uneven ground and hard in the bottom and no great depth of water in many places. Returned and walked from the Docke home, Mr. Coventry and I very much troubled to see how backward Commissioner Pett is to tell any of the faults of the officers, and to see nothing in better condition here for his being here than they are in other yards where there is none. After some discourse to bed. But I sat up an hour after Mr. Coventry was gone to read my vows, it raining a wonderful hard showre about 11 at night for an hour together. So to bed.

3rd. Up both of us very betimes and to the Yard, and see the men called over and choose some to be discharged. Then to the Ropehouses and viewed them all, and made an experiment which was the stronger, English or Riga hemp; the latter proved the stronger, but the other is very good, and much better we believe than any but Riga. We did many other things, and I caused the Timber measurer to measure some timber, where I found much fault and with reason, which we took public notice of, and did give them admonition for the time to come. At noon Mr. Pett did give us a very great dinner, too big in all conscience, so that most of it was left untouched. After dinner Commissioner Pett, Mr. Coventry and I sat close to our business all the noon in his parler. And then in the evening walked in the garden, where we conjured him to look after the yard, and for the time to come that he would take the whole faults and ill management of the yard upon himself, he having full power and our concurrence to suspend or do anything else that he thinks fit to keep people and officers to their duty. He having made good promises, though I fear his performance, we parted (though I spoke so freely that he could have been angry) good friends, and in some hopes that matters will be better for the time to come. So walked to the Hill-house and there made ourselves ready and mounted and rode to Gravesend.

4th. We were called up about four a-clock, and took boat, and to London by nine a-clock. So to the office, where we sat all the morning. My brother John I find come to town to my house, as I sent for him, on Saturday last. This day I received a letter from my wife which troubles me mightily, wherein she tells me how Ashwell did give her the lie to her teeth, and that thereupon my wife giving her a box on the eare, the other struck her again, and a deal of stir which troubles me; and that my Lady has been told by my father or mother something of my wife's carriage, which altogether vexes me, and I fear I shall find a trouble of my wife when she comes home to get down her head again. But if Ashwell goes I am resolved to have no more, but to live poorly and low again for a good while, and save money and keep my wife within bounds if I can, or else I shall bid Adieu to all content in the world.

5th. All the morning at the office. In the afternoon to Westminster hall, and there found Mrs. Lane,[1] and by and by by agreement we met at the Parliament stairs (in my way down to the boat who should meet us but my lady Jemimah, who saw me lead her but said nothing to me of her, though I ought to speak to her to see whether she would take notice of it or no) and off to Stangate and so to the King's Head at Lambeth march, and had variety of meats and drinks. Staid pretty late, and so over with her by water, and took coach; and at home my brother and I fell upon Des Cartes, and I perceive he has studied him well, and I cannot find but he has minded his book, and do love it. This evening came a letter about business from Mr. Coventry, and with it a silver pen he promised me to carry inke in, which is very necessary. So to prayers and to bed.

7th. Up and to my office a little, and then to Brown's for my measuring rule, which is made, and is certainly the best and the most commodious for carrying in one's pocket, and most useful that ever was made, and myself have the honour of being as it were the inventor of this form of it. After dinner, I walked to Deptford and there found Sir W. Pen, and I fell to measuring of some planks that was serving into the yard, which the people took notice of, and the measurer himself was amused at, for I did it much more ready than he, and I believe Sir W. Pen would be glad I could have done less or he more. By and by walked back again, and on my way young Bagwell and his wife waylayd me to desire my favour about getting him a better ship, which I shall pretend to be willing to do for them, but my mind is to know his wife a little better. So home, and my brother John and I up and I to my musique, and then to discourse with him, and I find him not so thorough a philosopher, at least in Aristotle, as I took him for,

[1] Mrs. Betty Lane: a seamstress who had a stall in Westminster Hall.

he not being able to tell me the definition of final nor which of the
4 Qualitys belonged to each of the 4 Elements.

8th. In the afternoon took my brother John and Will down to
Woolwich by water, and after being there a good while, and eating
of fruit in Sheldon's garden, we began our walk back again, I asking
many things in physiques of my brother John, to which he gives
me so bad or no answer at all; as in the regions of the ayre he told
me that he knew of no such thing, for he never read Aristotle's
philosophy and Des Cartes ownes no such thing, which vexed me
to hear him say. But I shall call him to task, and see what it
is that he has studied since his going to the University.

10th. After dinner I went to Greatorex's, whom I found in
his garden, and set him to work upon my ruler, to engrave an
almanac and other things upon the brasses of it, which a little before night he did; but the latter part he slubbered over, that I
must get him to do it over better, or else I shall not fancy my rule.
Which is such a folly that I am come to now, that whereas before
my delight was in multitude of books and spending money in
that and buying alway of other things, now that I am become a
better husband[1] and have left off buying, now my delight is in the
neatness of everything, and so cannot be pleased with anything
unless it be very neat, which is a strange folly. Hither came W.
Howe about business, and he and I had a great deal of discourse
about my Lord Sandwich, and I find by him that my Lord do dote
upon one of the daughters of Mrs. Becke where he lies, so that he
spends his time and money upon her. He tells me she is a woman
of a very bad fame and very imprudent, and has told my Lord
so; yet for all that my Lord do spend all his evenings with her,
though he be at court in the day time, and that the world do take
notice of it.

11th. Dr. Pierce tells me that the King comes to towne this
day from Tunbridge, to stay a day or two, and then fetch the Queen
from thence, who he says is grown a very debonnaire lady, and
now hugs him, and meets him galloping upon the road, and all the
actions of a fond and pleasant lady that can be.

12th. A little to my office, to put down my yesterday's journall,
and so abroad to buy a bedstead and do other things. So home
again, and having put up the bedstead and done other things in
order to my wife's coming, I went out to several places and to
Mrs. Turner's, she inviting me last night, and there dined. By

[1] *i.e.* saver.

water to my brother's, and there I hear my wife is come, and gone home, and my father is come to town also.

16th. (Lord's Day.) After dinner to church, and there, looking up and down, I found Pembleton to stand in the isle against us, he coming too late to get a pew. Which, Lord! into what a sweat did it put me!

17th. Fell into discourse, my wife and I, to Ashwell, and much against my will I am fain to express a willingness to Ashwell that she should go from us, and yet in my mind I am glad of it, to ease me of the charge. So she is to go to her father this day.

20th. This evening the girle that was brought to me to-day for so good a one, being cleansed of lice this day by my wife and good new clothes put on her back, she run away from Goody Taylour that was shewing her the way to the bakehouse, and we heard no more of her.

22nd. Mr. Castle and I to Greenwich, and in our way met some gypsys, who would needs tell me my fortune, and I suffered one of them, who told me many things common as others do, but bade me beware of a John and a Thomas, for they did seek to do me hurt, and that somebody should be with me this day se'nnight to borrow money of me, but I should lend him none. She got ninepence of me. And so I left them and to Greenwich and so to Deptford, and thence home by water. This day Sir W. Batten tells me that Mr. Newburne is dead of eating cowcumbers, of which the other day I heard another, I think.

September 3rd. To Sir W. Batten, who is going this day for pleasure down to the Downes. I eat a breakfast with them, and at my Lady's desire with them by coach to Greenwich, where I went aboard with them on the Charlotte yacht. The wind very fresh, and I believe they will all be sicke enough, besides that she is mighty troublesome on the water. I left them under sayle, and I to Deptford, and, after a word or two with Sir J. Minnes, walked to Redriffe and so home. In my way it coming into my head, overtaking of a beggar or two on the way that looked like Gypsys, what the Gypsys 8 or 9 days ago had foretold, and looking when I came to my office upon my journall, that my brother John had brought a letter that day from my brother Tom to borrow £20 more of me, it pleased me mightily to see how, contrary to my expectations, having so lately lent him £20, and belief that he had money by him to spare, and that after some days not thinking

"IT WAS THE CONSTABLE AND HIS WATCH"

of it, I should look back and find what the Gypsy had told me to be so true. After dinner at home to my office and there till late doing business.

4th. [St. Bartholomew's Day.] Mrs. Harper sent for a maid for me to come to live with my wife. I like the maid's looks well enough, and I believe may do well, she looking very modestly and speaking so too. I directed her to speak with my wife. After dinner done, by coach with my wife to Bartholemew Fayre and showed her the monkeys dancing on the ropes, which was strange. There was also a horse with hoofs like rams hornes, a goose with four feet, and a cock with three. Thence to another place, and saw some German Clocke works, the Salutation of the Virgin Mary, and several Scriptural stories; but above all there was at last represented, the sea, with Neptune, Venus, mermaids, and Ayrid[1] on a dolphin, the sea rocking, so well done that had it been in a gaudy manner and place, and at a little distance, it had been admirable.

8th. Dined at home with my wife. It being washing day we had a good pie baked of a leg of mutton; and then to my office, and then abroad, and among other places to Moxon's and there bought a payre of globes cost me £3 10*s.*, with which I am well pleased, I buying them principally for my wife who has a mind to understand them, and I shall take pleasure to teach her.

10th. Up betimes and to my office, and there sat all the morning making a great contract with Sir W. Warren for £3,000 worth of masts; but, good God! to see what a man might do were I a knave, the whole business from beginning to end being done by me out of the office, and signed to by them upon the once reading of it. But I hope my pains was such as the King has the best bargain of masts has been bought these 27 years in this office. This day our cook maid (we have no luck in maids now-a-days), which was likely to prove a good servant, though none of the best cooks, fell sick and is gone to her friends, having been with us but 4 days.

11th. This morning about two or three o'clock, knocked up in our back yard, and rising to the window, being moonshine, I found it was the constable and his watch, who had found our back yard door open and so came in to see what the matter was. So I desired them to shut the door and bid them good night, and so to bed again.

[1] Ayrid, *i.e.* Arion.

12th. To my office, where all the morning; and so to the 'Change at noon, and there by appointment met and bring home my uncle Thomas, who resolves to go with me to Brampton on Monday next. I wish he may hold his mind; the truth is I do find him a much more cunning fellow than I ever took him for, nay in his very drink he has his wits about him.

14th. Up betimes, and my wife, and by coach to Bishop's Gate, it being a very promising fair day. There at the Dolphin we met my uncle Thomas and his son-in-law and Mr. Moore. Set out and after a little bayte (I paying all the reckonings the whole journey) at Ware, to Buntingford, where my wife, by drinking some cold beer, being hot herself, presently after 'lighting begins to be sick, and became so pale, and I alone with her in a great chamber there, that I thought she would have died; and so in great horror, and having a great tryall of my true love and passion for her, called the mayds and mistresse of the house, and so with some strong water, and after a little vomit, she came to be pretty well again; and so to bed.

15th. Up pretty betimes and rode as far as Godmanchester, Mr. Moore having two falls, once in water and another in dirt, and there 'light and eat and drunk, being all of us very weary, but especially my uncle and wife. Thence to Brampton to my father's, and there found all well. So my father, cozen Thomas and I up to Hinchingbroke, where I find my Lady and the young ladies; and there I alone with my Lady two hours, she carrying me through every part of the house and gardens, which are and will be mighty noble indeed.

17th. Up, and my father being gone to bed ill last night and continuing so this morning, I was forced to come to a consideration whether it was fit for to let my uncle and his son go to Wisbeach about my uncle Day's estate alone or no, and concluded it unfit; and so resolved to go with them myself. Leaving my wife there I begun a journey with them, and with much ado through the fens, along dikes where sometimes we were ready to have our horses sink to the belly, we got by night with great deal of stir and hard riding to Parson's Drove,[1] a heathen place, where I found my uncle and aunt Perkins and their daughters, poor wretches! in a sad poor thatched cottage like a poor barn or stable, peeling of hemp, in which I did give myself good content to see their manner of preparing of hemp; and in a poor condition of habitt took them

[1] A village about five miles from Wisbeach.

to our miserable inn, and there after long stay and hearing of Frank their son, the miller, play upon his treble, as he calls it, with which he earns part of his living, and singing of a country song, we sat down to supper; the whole crew, and Frank's wife and child, a sad company of which I was ashamed, supped with us. And so about twelve at night, or more, to bed in a sad, cold, nasty chamber; only the mayde was indifferent handsome, and so I had a kiss or two of her, and I to bed, and so to sleep till the morning, but was bit cruelly, and nobody else of our company, which I wonder at, by the gnatts.

18th. Up, and got our people together as soon as we could; and after eating a dish of cold cream, which was my supper last night too, we took leave of our beggarly company, though they seem good people, too; and over most sad Fenns, all the way observing the sad life which the people of the place (which if they be born there, they do call the Breedlings of the place) do live, sometimes rowing from one spot to another, and then wadeing, to Wisbeach, a pretty town, and a fine church and library, where sundry very old abbey manuscripts; and a fine house, built on the church ground by Secretary Thurlow, and a fine gallery built for him in the church, but now all in the Bishop of Ely's hands. After visiting the church, &c., we went out of the towne, by the help of a stranger, to find out one Blinkhorne, a miller, of whom we might inquire something of old Day's disposal of his estate, and in whose hands it now is; and by great chance we met him and brought him to our inn to dinner; and instead of being informed in his estate by this fellow we find that he is the next heir to the estate, which was matter of great sport to my cozen Thomas and me, to see such a fellow prevent us in our hopes, he being Day's brother's daughter's son, whereas we are but his sister's sons and grandsons[1]; so that after all we were fain to propose our matter to him, and to get him to give us leave to look after the business, and so he to have one-third part and we two to have the other two-third parts of what should be recovered of the estate, which he consented to; and after some discourse and paying the reckoning, we mounted again and rode, being very merry at our defeat, to Chatteris.

19th. Up pretty betimes, and after eating something, we set out, they going straight to London and I to Brampton, where I

[1] From this it appears that Pepys' paternal grandfather had married a Miss Day. The miller Blinkhorne would therefore be second cousin both to Pepys and his cousin Thomas.

find my father ill in bed still, and Madam Norbery[1] (whom and her fair daughter and sister I was ashamed to kiss, but did, my lip being sore with riding in the wind and bit with the gnatts), lately come to town, come to see my father and mother, and they after a little stay being gone, I told my father my success. And after dinner my wife and I took horse, and rode with marvellous and the first and only hour of pleasure that ever I had in this estate since I had to do with it, to Brampton woods; and through the wood rode, and gathered nuts in my way, and then at Graffam to an old woman's house to drink, where my wife used to go; and being in all circumstances highly pleased, and in my wife's riding and good company at this time, I rode and she showed me the river behind my father's house, which is very pleasant, and so saw her home, and I straight to Huntingdon. Thence walked to Hinching-broke, where my Lord and ladies all. And so I in among them, and my Lord glad to see me, and the whole company. Here I staid and supped with them, but yet observing my Lord not to be so mightily ingulphed in his pleasure in the country as I expected and hoped.

20th. (Lord's Day.) My wife and I mounted, and with my father's boy we rode to Bigglesworth[2] by the help of a couple of countrymen that led us through the very long and dangerous waters because of the ditches on each side, though it begun to be very dark; and there we had a good breast of mutton roasted for us, and supped, and to bed.

21st. Up very betimes by break of day, and got my wife up, whom the thought of this day's journey do discourage; and after eating something, and changing of a piece of gold to pay the reckoning, we mounted, and through Baldwicke,[3] where a fayre is kept to-day, and a great one for cheese and other such commodities, and so to Hatfield, it being most curious weather from the time we set out to our getting home, and here we dined; and my wife being very weary I took the opportunity of an empty coach that was to go to London, and left her to come in it for half-a-crown, and so I and the boy home as fast as we could drive, and it was even night before we got home. By and by comes my wife by coach well home, and having got a good fowl ready for supper against her coming we eat heartily, and so with great content and ease to our own bed, there nothing appearing so to our content as to be at our own home after being abroad awhile.

---

[1] Mrs. Norbury appears to have been a sister of Pepys' Aunt Wight.   She owned some property in Brampton.   [2] Biggleswade.   [3] Baldock.

22nd. This day my wife showed me bills printed, wherein her father has got a patent for curing of smoky chimneys, but I fear it will prove but a poor project.

30th. I sat late making up my month's accounts, and blessed be God do find myself £760 creditor, notwithstanding that for clothes for myself and wife and layings out on her closett I have spent this month £47.

October 14th. After dinner my wife and I to the Jewish Synagogue, where the men and boys in their vayles, and the women behind a lattice out of sight; and some things stand up, which I believe is their Law, in a press to which all coming in do bow; and at the putting on their vayles do say something, to which others that hear him do cry Amen, and the party do kiss his vayle. Their service all in a singing way, and in Hebrew. And anon their Laws that they take out of the press are carried by several men, four or five several burthens in all, and they do relieve one another; and (whether it is that every one desires to have the carrying of it I cannot tell), thus they carried it round about the room while such a service is singing. And in the end they had a prayer for the King, which they pronounced his name in Portugall; but the prayer, like the rest, in Hebrew. But, Lord! to see the disorder, laughing, sporting, and no attention, but confusion in all their service, more like brutes than people knowing the true God, would make a man forswear ever seeing them more. Away thence with my mind strongly disturbed with them.

17th. Had some discourse of the Queen's being very sick, if not dead, the Duke and Duchess of York being sent for betimes this morning to come to White Hall to her.

19th. Waked with a very high wind, and said to my wife, "I pray God I hear not of the death of any great person, this wind is so high!" fearing that the Queen might be dead. So up, and going by coach with Sir W. Batten and Sir J. Minnes to St. James's, they tell me that Sir W. Compton[1] died yesterday: at which I was most exceedingly surprised, he being, and so all the world saying that he was, one of the worthyest men and best officers of State now in England. Coming to St. James's I hear that the Queen did sleep five hours pretty well to-night, and that she waked and gargled her mouth, and to sleep again. It seems she was so ill as to be shaved and pidgeons put to her feet, and to have the extreme unction given her by the priests, who

[1] M.P. for Cambridge, and a member of the Tangier Commission.

were so long about it that the doctors were angry. The King, they all say, is most fondly disconsolate for her and weeps by her, which makes her weep; which one this day told me he reckons a good sign, for that it carries away some rheume from the head.

20th. Up and to the office, where we sat; and at noon Sir G. Carteret, Sir J. Minnes, and I to dinner to my Lord Mayor's, being invited, where was the Farmers of the Customes, my Lord Chancellor's three sons, and other great and much company, and a very great noble dinner, as this Mayor is good for nothing else. No extraordinary discourse of anything, every man being intent upon his dinner, and myself willing to have drunk some wine to have warmed my belly, but I did for my oath's sake willingly refrain it, but am so well pleased and satisfied afterwards thereby, for it do keep me always in so good a frame of mind that I hope I shall not ever leave this practice. Thence home by coach, calling at several places by the way. Among others at Paul's Churchyard, and while I was in Kirton's shop a fellow came to offer kindness or force to my wife in the coach, but she refusing he went away, after the coachman had struck him and he the coachman. So I being called went thither, and the fellow coming out again of a shop I did give him a good cuff or two on the chops, and seeing him not oppose me I did give him another; at last found him drunk, of which I was glad, and so left him, and home, and so to my office awhile, and so home to supper and to bed. This evening at my Lord's lodgings Mrs. Sarah tells us that the Queen's sickness is the spotted fever; that she was as full of the spots as à leopard: which is very strange that it should be no more known; but perhaps it is not so. And that the King do seem to take it much to heart, for that he hath wept before her; but for all that that he hath not missed one night since she was sick, of supping with my Lady Castlemaine; which I believe is true, for she [Sarah] says that her husband hath dressed the suppers every night.

21st. This evening after I came home I begun to enter my wife in arithmetique in order to her studying of the globes, and she takes it very well and I hope, with great pleasure, I shall bring her to understand many fine things.

23rd. To Mr. Rawlinson's [1] and saw some of my new bottles made with my crest upon them, filled with wine, about five or six dozen.

[1] Daniel Rawlinson kept the "Mitre" in Fenchurch Street.

29th. Up, it being my Lord Mayor's day, Sir Anthony Bateman. This morning was brought home my new velvet cloake, that is, lined with velvet, a good cloth the outside, the first that ever I had in my life, and I pray God it may not be too soon now that I begin to wear it. I had it this day brought thinking to have worn it to dinner, but I thought it would be better to go without it because of the crowde, and so I did not wear it; and wanting a band, I found all my bands that were newly made clean so ill smoothed that I crumpled them and flung them all on the ground and was angry with Jane, which made the poor girle mighty sad, so that I were troubled for it afterwards. At noon I went forth, and by coach to Guild Hall. Went up and down to see the tables, where under every salt there was a bill of fare, and at the end of the table the persons proper for the table. Many were the tables, but none in the Hall but the Mayor's and the Lords of the Privy Council that had napkins or knives, which was very strange. Wine was offered, I only drinking some hypocras,[1] which do not break my vowe, it being to the best of my present judgment only a mixed compound drink, and not any wine. If I am mistaken, God forgive me! but I hope and do think I am not. By and by come into the Hall the Lord Chancellor (Archbishopp before him), with the Lords of the Council and other Bishopps, and they to dinner. Anon comes the Lord Mayor, who went up to the lords and then to the other tables to bid wellcome; and so all to dinner. I sat at the Merchant Strangers' table, where ten good dishes to a messe, with plenty of wine of all sorts, of which I drunk none; but it was very unpleasing that we had no napkins nor change of trenchers, and drunk out of earthen pitchers and wooden dishes. It happened that after the lords had half dined came the French Embassador, up to the lords' table, where he was to have sat; but finding the table set he would not sit down nor dine with the Lord Mayor, who was not yet come, nor have a table to himself, which was offered, but in a discontent went away again. After I had dined, I and Creed rose and went up and down the house, and up to the lady's room, and there stayed gazing upon them. But though there were many and fine, both young and old, yet I could not discern one handsome face there. I expected musique, but there was none but only trumpets and drums, which displeased me. The dinner, it seems, is made by the Mayor and two Sheriffs for the time being, the Lord Mayor paying one half and they the other.

---

[1] Spiced and sweetened wine.

And the whole is reckoned to come to about 7 or £800 at most. Being wearied with looking upon a company of ugly women, Creed and I went away, and took coach and through Cheapside, and there saw the pageants, which were very silly, and thence I by coach home. By and by came my brother Tom, with whom I was very angry for not sending me a bill with my things, so as that I think never to have more work done by him if ever he serves me so again, and so I told him.

31st. Up and to the office, where we sat all the morning, and at noon home to dinner, where Creed came and dined with me, and after dinner he and I upstairs, and I showed him my velvet cloake and other things of clothes that I have lately bought, which he likes very well, and I took his opinion as to some things of clothes. Thence to the office, where busy till night, and then to prepare my monthly account, about which I staid till 10 or 11 o'clock at night, and to my great sorrow find myself £43 worse than I was the last month. But it hath chiefly arisen from my layings-out in clothes for myself and wife; viz., for her about £12, and for myself £55 or thereabouts; having made myself a velvet cloake, two new cloth suits, black, plain both, a new shagg[1] gowne, trimmed with gold buttons and twist, with a new hat, and silk tops for my legs, and many other things. I hope I shall not need now to lay out more money a great while; but I hope I shall with more comfort labour to get more, and with better successe than when for want of clothes I was forced to sneake like a beggar. My greatest trouble and my wife's is our family, mighty out of order by this fellow Will's corrupting the mayds by his idle talke and carriage, which we are going to remove by hastening him out of the house, which his uncle Blackburne is upon doing, and I am to give him £20 per annum toward his maintenance.

November 2nd. Up, and by coach to White Hall, and there in the long Matted Gallery I find Sir G. Carteret, Sir J. Minnes, and Sir W. Batten; and by and by comes the King to walk there with three or four with him; and soon as he saw us, says he, "Here is the Navy Office," and there walked twenty turns the length of the gallery, talking methought but ordinary talke. I heard the Duke say that he was going to wear a perriwigg; and they say the King also will. I never till this day observed that the King is mighty gray.

[1] A stuff resembling plush.

3rd. Comes Chapman, the periwigg-maker, and upon my liking it, without more ado I went up, and there he cut off my haire, which went a little to my heart at present to part with it; but it being over and my periwigg on, I paid him £3 for it, and away went he with my owne haire to make up another of, and I by and by, after I had caused all my mayds to look upon it; and they conclude it do become me, though Jane was mightily troubled for my parting of my own haire, and so was Besse. I went abroad to the coffee house, and coming back went to Sir W. Pen and there sat with him till late at night. Sir W. Pen observed mightily and discoursed much upon my cutting off my haire, as he do of every thing that concerns me, but it is over, and so I perceive after a day or two it will be no great matter.

7th. To Westminster Hall, where, seeing Howlett's daughter going out of the other end of the Hall, I followed her [as] if I would to have offered talk to her and dallied with her a little, but I could not overtake her. Then calling at Unthank's for something of my wife's not done, a pretty little gentlewoman, a lodger there, came out to tell me that it was not yet done, which though it vexed me yet I took opportunity of taking her by the hand with the boot, and so found matter to talk a little the longer to her, but I was ready to laugh at myself to see how my anger would not operate, my disappointment coming to me by such a messenger.

8th. (Lord's Day.) Up, and it being late, to church without my wife, and there I found that my coming in a perriwigg did not prove so strange to the world as I was afeard it would, for I thought that all the church would presently have cast their eyes all upon me, but I found no such thing.

12th. After dinner Mr. Moore and I discoursing of my Lord's negligence in attendance at Court, and the discourse the world makes of it with the too great reason that I believe there is for it, I resolved and took coach to his lodgings, thinking to speak with my Lord about it without more ado. Here I met Mr. Howe, and he and I [spoke] largely about it, and he very soberly acquainted me how things are with my Lord, that my Lord do not do anything like himself, but follows his folly, and spends his time either at cards at Court with the ladies, when he is there at all, or else at Chelsy with the slut to his great disgrace, and indeed I do see and believe that my Lord do apprehend that he do grow less too at Court. Anon my Lord do come in, and I begun to fall in discourse with him, but my heart did misgive me

"HEARING OF THE MAYDS READ IN THE BIBLE"

that my Lord would not take it well, and then found him not in a humour to talk; and so after a few ordinary words, my Lord not talking in the manner as he uses to do, I took leave, and spent some time with W. Howe again, and told him how I could not do what I had so great a mind and resolution to do, but that I thought it would be as well to do it in writing, which he approves of; and so I took leave of him, and by coach home, my mind being full of it, and in pain concerning it. So to my office busy very late, the nights running on faster than one thinks, and so to supper and to bed.

14th. After dinner Will told me if I pleased he was ready to remove his things, and so before my wife I did give him good counsel, and that his going should not abate my kindnesse for him if he carried himself well, and so bid "God bless him," and left him to remove his things, the poor lad weeping; but I am apt to think matters will be the better both for him and us. This night, I think, is the first that I have lain without ever a man in my house besides myself since I came to keep any. By the way I hear to-day that my boy Waynman has been put into a Barbadoes ship to be sent away; and though he sends to me to get a release for him I will not, out of love to the boy, for I doubt to keep him here were to bring him to the gallows.

15th. (Lord's Day.) In the afternoon to my office and there drew up a letter to my Lord, stating to him what the world talks concerning him. So home to supper. After a good supper with my wife, and hearing of the mayds read in the Bible, we to prayers, and to bed.

17th. With Mr. Moore to my office, and there I read to him the letter I have wrote to send to my Lord. Which Mr. Moore do conclude so well drawn that he would not have me by any means to neglect sending it, and did offer to take the same words and send them as from him with his hand to him, which I am not unwilling should come (if they are at all fit to go) from any body but myself; and so, he being gone, I did take a copy of it to keep by me in shorthand and sealed them up to send to-morrow by my Will.

18th. This morning I sent Will with my great letter of reproof to my Lord Sandwich, who did it give into his owne hand. I pray God give a blessing to it, but confess I am afeard what the consequence may be to me of good or bad, which is according to the ingenuity that he do receive it with. However, I am satisfied that it will do him good, and that he needs it.

MY LORD,

I do verily hope that neither the manner nor matter of this advice will be condemned by your Lordship, when for my defence in the first I shall alledge my double attempt, since your return from Hinchinbroke, of doing it personally, in both of which your Lordship's occasions, no doubtfulnesse of mine, prevented me, and that being now fearful of a sudden summons to Portsmouth, for the discharge of some ships there, I judge it very unbecoming the duty which every bit of bread I eat tells me I owe to your Lordship to expose the safety of your honour to the uncertainty of my return. For the matter, my Lord, it is such as could I in any measure think safe to conceal from, or likely to be discovered to you by any other hand, I should not have dared so far to owne what from my heart I believe is false, as to make myself but the relater of other's discourse; but, sir, your Lordship's honour being such as I ought to value it to be, and finding both in city and court that discourses pass to your prejudice, too generally for mine or any man's controllings but your Lordship's, I shall, my Lord, without the least greatening or lessening the matter, do my duty in laying it shortly before you.

People of all conditions, my Lord, raise matter of wonder from your Lordship's so little appearance at Court: some concluding thence their disfavour thereby, to which purpose I have had questions asked me, and endeavouring to put off such insinuations by asserting the contrary, they have replied, that your Lordship's living so beneath your quality, out of the way, and declining of Court attendance, hath been more than once discoursed about the King. Others, my Lord, when the chief ministers of State, and those most active of the Council have been reckoned up, wherein your Lordship never used to want an eminent place, have said, touching your Lordship, that now your turn was served, and the King had given you a good estate, you left him to stand or fall as he would, and, particularly in that of the Navy, have enlarged upon your letting fall all service there.

Another sort, and those the most, insist upon the bad report of the house wherein your Lordship, now observed in perfect health again, continues to sojourne, and by name have charged one of the daughters for a common courtizan, alledging both places and persons where and with whom she hath been too well known, and how much her wantonnesse occasions, though unjustly, scandal to your Lordship, and that as well to gratifying of some enemies as to the wounding of more friends I am not able to tell.

Lastly, my Lord, I find a general coldness in all persons towards your Lordship, such as, from my first dependence on you, I never yet knew, wherein I shall not offer to interpose any thoughts or advice of mine, well knowing your Lordship needs not any. But with a most faithful assurance that no person nor papers under Heaven is privy to what I here write, besides myself and this, which I shall be careful to have put into your owne hands, I rest confident of your Lordship's just construction of my dutifull intents herein, and in all humility take leave, may it please your Lordship,

Your Lordship's most obedient Servant,

S. P.

22nd (Lord's Day.) Up pretty early to my Lord's lodgings, whom I found ready to go to chappell; but I coming, he begun with a very serious countenance to tell me that he had received my late letter, wherein first he took notice of my care of him and his honour, and did give me thanks for that part of it where I say that from my heart I believe the contrary of what I do there relate to be the discourse of others; but since I intended it not a reproach, but matter of information, and for him to make a judgment of it for his practice, it was necessary for me to tell him the persons of whom I have gathered the several particulars which I there insist on. I would have made excuses in it, but seeing him so earnest in it I found myself forced to it. When I spoke of the tenderness that I have used in declaring this to him, there being nobody privy to it, he told me that I must give him leave to except one. I told him that possibly somebody might know of some thoughts of mine, I having borrowed some intelligence in this matter from them, but nobody could say they knew of the thing itself what I writ.[1] This, I confess, however, do trouble me, for that he seemed to speak it as a quick retort, and it must sure be Will. Howe, who did not see anything of what I writ, though I told him indeed that I would write; but in this, I think, there is no great hurt. I find him, though he cannot but owne his opinion of my good intentions, and so he did again and again profess it, that he is troubled in his mind at it; and I confess, I think I may have done myself an injury for his good,

[1] See 17th, *ante.*

which, were it to do again, and that I believed he would take it no better, I think I should sit quietly without taking any notice of it, for I doubt there is no medium between his taking it very well or very ill. I could not forbear weeping before him at the latter end, which since I am ashamed of, though I cannot see what he can take it to proceed from but my tenderness and good will to him.

December 10th. To St. Paul's Church Yard, to my bookseller's, and having gained this day in the office by my stationer's bill to the King about 40s. or £3, I did here sit two or three hours calling for twenty books to lay this money out upon, and found myself at a great losse where to choose, and do see how my nature would gladly return to laying out money in this trade. I could not tell whether to lay out my money for books of pleasure, as plays, which my nature was most earnest in; but at last, after seeing Chaucer, Dugdale's History of Paul's, Stow's London, Gesner, History of Trent, besides Shakespeare, Jonson, and Beaumont's plays, I at last chose Dr. Fuller's Worthys, the Cabbala or Collections of Letters of State, and a little book, Délices de Hollande, with another little book or two, all of a good use or serious pleasure: and Hudibras, both parts, the book now in greatest fashion for drollery, though I cannot I confess see enough where the wit lies.

15th. Before I was up, my brother's man came to tell me that my cozen Edward Pepys[1] was dead, died at Mrs. Turner's, for which my wife and I are very sorry, and the more for that his wife was the only handsome woman of our name.

21st. I did go to Shoe Lane to see a cocke-fighting at a new pit there, a sport I was never at in my life; but, Lord! to see the strange variety of people, from Parliament-man to the poorest 'prentices, bakers, brewers, butchers, draymen, and what not: and all these fellows one with another in swearing, cursing and betting. I soon had enough of it, and yet I would not but have seen it once, it being strange to observe the nature of these poor creatures, how they will fight till they drop down dead upon the table, and strike after they are ready to give up the ghost, not offering to run away when they are weary or wounded past doing further; whereas where a dunghill brood comes he will, after a sharp stroke that pricks him, run off the stage, and then they wring off his neck without more ado, whereas the other they pre-

---

[1] Of Broomsthorpe, Norfolk, and of the Middle Temple. He was brother to Mrs. Turner.

serve, though their eyes be both out, for breed only of a true cock of the game. The rule is if any man will bet £10 to a crowne, and nobody take the bet, the game is given over, and not sooner. One thing more it is strange to see how people of this poor rank, that look as if they had not bread to put in their mouths, shall bet three or four pounds at one bet and lose it, and yet bet as much the next battle (so they call every match of two cocks); so that one of them will lose £10 or £20 at a meeting. Thence, having enough of it, by coach to my Lord Sandwich's, where I find him within with Captain Cooke and his boys, playing and singing over my Lord's anthem which he hath made to sing in the King's Chappell. My Lord saluted me kindly and took me into the withdrawing-room to hear it at a distance; and indeed it sounds very finely, and is a good thing I believe to be made by him, and they all commend it.

27th. Up and to church alone, and so home to dinner with my wife, very pleasant and pleased with one another's company, and in our general enjoyment one of another better we think than most other couples do. So after dinner to the French church, but came too late, and so back to our owne church, where I slept all the sermon, the Scott preaching, and so home.

31st. Sat till 4 o'clock in the morning making up my accounts and writing this last Journall of the year. And first I bless God I do find that I am worth in money above £800, whereof in my Lord Sandwich's hand £700, and the rest in my hand. For which the good God be pleased to give me a thankful heart and a mind careful to preserve this and increase it. I do live at my lodgings in the Navy Office, my family being, besides my wife and I, Jane Gentleman, Besse, our excellent, good-natured cook-mayde, and Susan, a little girle; having neither man nor boy, nor like to have again a good while, living now in most perfect content and quiett, and very frugally also. My wife's brother come to great unhappiness by the ill-disposition, my wife says, of his wife, and her poverty, which she now professes after all her husband's pretence of a great fortune; but I see none of them, at least they come not to trouble me. At present I am concerned for my cozen Angier, of Cambridge, lately broke in his trade, and this day am sending his son John, a very rogue, to sea. Pall with my father, and God knows what she do there, or what will become of her, for I have not anything yet to spare her, and she grows now old, and must be disposed of one way or other. The Duchesse of York at this time sicke of the meazles, but is growing well again. Myself, blessed be God! in a good way and design and resolution of sticking to my business to get a little money with doing the best service I can to the King also; which God continue! So ends the old year.

FIFTH YEAR

1664

January 1st. My wife and I went to the Duke's house, the first play I have been at these six months, according to my last vowe, and here saw the so much cried-up play of "Henry the Eighth"; which, though I went with resolution to like it, is so simple a thing made up of a great many patches, that besides the shows and processions in it there is nothing in the world good or well done.

2nd. I come to a new vowe, that I will not see above one play in a month at any of the publique theatres till the sum of 50s. be spent, and then none before New Year's Day next, unless that I do become worth £1,000 sooner than then. So to the King's house, and saw "The Usurper,"[1] which is no good play, though better than what I saw yesterday. However we rose unsatisfied, and took coach and home.

4th. To the Tennis Court and there saw the King play at Tennis, and others: but to see how the King's play was extolled without any cause at all was a loathsome sight, though sometimes indeed he did play very well and deserved to be commended; but such open flattery is beastly. Afterwards to St. James's Parke and there spent an hour or two, it being a pleasant day, seeing people play at Pell Mell; where it pleased me mightily to hear a gallant, lately come from France, swear at one of his companions for suffering his man (a spruce blade) to be so saucy as to strike a ball while his master was playing on the Mall. Thence took coach at White Hall and took up my wife, who is mighty sad to think of her father, who is going into Germany against the Turkes: but what will become of her brother I know not; he is so idle, and out of all capacity I think to earn his bread. Home and at my office till 12 at night making my solemn vowes for the next year, which I trust in the Lord I shall keep; but I fear I have a little too severely bound myself in some things, and in too many, for I fear I may forget some. But however I know the worst, and shall

[1] By Edward Howard.

198

by the blessing of God observe to perform, or pay my forfeits punctually.

6th. (Twelfth Day.) This morning I began a practice which I find by the ease I do it with that I shall continue, it saving me money and time; that is, to trimme myself with a razer, which pleases me mightily.

8th. Upon the 'Change a great talke there was of one Mr. Tryan, an old man, a merchant in Lyme-Streete, gagged and robbed of £1,050 in money and about £4,000 in jewells.

10th. (Lord's Day.) All our discourse to-night was Mr. Tryan's late being robbed; and that Collonell Turner (a mad, swearing, confident fellow, well known by all, and by me), was the man that either did or plotted it; and he and his wife now in Newgate for it, of which we are all glad, so very a known rogue he was.

11th. At home I found the house full of the washing and my wife mighty angry about Will's being here to-day talking with her mayds. At which I was angry, and after directing her to beat at least the little girl, I went to the office and there reproved Will, who told me that he went thither by my wife's order, she having commanded him to come thither on Monday morning. Now God forgive me! how apt I am to be jealous of her as to this fellow, and that she must needs take this time, when she knows I must be gone out to the Duke. But this cursed humour I cannot cool in myself by all the reason I have, which God forgive me for, and convince me of the folly of it, and the disquiet it brings me.

19th. Up, without any kindness to my wife, and so to the office, where we sat all the morning. After dinner to my office again till very late, and my eyes began to fail me and be in pain, which I never felt to now-a-days; which I impute to sitting up late writing and reading by candlelight. So home to supper and to bed.

20th. To White Hall, and meeting Mr. Pierce walked with him an hour in the Matted Gallery. Among other things he tells me that the Duke of Monmouth the King do still doat on beyond measure, insomuch that the King only, the Duke of York, and Prince Rupert, and the Duke of Monmouth, do now wear deep mourning, that is, long cloaks, for the Duchesse of Savoy; so that he mourns as a Prince of the Blood, while the Duke of York do no more, which gives great offence. But that the Duke of York do give himself up to business, and is like to prove a noble Prince; and so indeed I do from my heart think he will. Then my Lord

Sandwich came upon me, to speak with whom my business of coming again to-night to this ende of the town chiefly was, in order to the seeing in what manner he received me. He treated me, though with respect, yet as a stranger, without any of the intimacy or friendship which he used to do.

21st. Up, and after sending my wife to my aunt Wight's to get a place to see Turner hanged, I to the office, where we sat all the morning. And at noon going to the 'Change, and seeing people flock in the city, I enquired and found that Turner was not yet hanged. And so I went among them to Leadenhall Street, and to St. Mary Axe, where he lived, and there I got for a shilling to stand upon the wheel of a cart, in great pain, above an houre before the execution was done, he delaying the time by long discourses and prayers one after another, in hopes of a reprieve; but none came, and at last was flung off the ladder in his cloake. A comely-looked man he was, and kept his countenance to the end: I was sorry to see him. It was believed there were at least 12 or 14,000 people in the street. So I home all in a sweat, and dined by myself.

30th. Up, and a sorry sermon of a young fellow I knew at Cambridge; but the day kept solemnly for the King's murder, and all day within doors making up my Brampton papers; and in the evening Mr. Commander came and we made perfect and signed and sealed my last will and testament, which is so to my mind, and I hope to the liking of God Almighty, that I take great joy in myself that it is done, and by that means my mind in a good condition of quiett. This evening, being in a humour of making all things even and clear in the world, I tore some old papers; among others, a romance which (under the title of "Love a Cheate") I begun ten years ago at Cambridge; and at this time reading it over to-night I like it very well, and wondered a little at myself at my vein at that time when I wrote it, doubting that I cannot do so well now if I would try.

February 1st. To the Duke's chamber, where the King came and stayed an hour or two laughing at Sir W. Petty, who was there about his boat,[1] and at Gresham College in general; at which poor Petty was, I perceive, at some loss; but did argue discreetly, and bear the unreasonable follies of the King's objections and other bystanders with great discretion, and offered to take oddes against

---

[1] Sir William Petty had designed a double-keeled ship, and the Royal Society were interesting themselves in his invention, of which great things were expected.

the King's best boates; but the King would not lay, but cried him down with words only. Gresham College he mightily laughed at for spending time only in weighing of ayre, and doing nothing else since they sat. To the Coffee-house, where I heard Lt.-Coll. Baron tell very good stories of his travels over the high hills in Asia above the clouds; how clear the heaven is above them, how thicke like a mist the way is through the cloud that wets like a sponge one's clothes, the ground above the clouds all dry and parched; nothing in the world growing, it being only a dry earth, yet not so hot above as below the clouds. The stars at night most delicate bright and a fine clear blue sky, but cannot see the earth at any time through the clouds, but the clouds look like a world below you.

2nd. To the Sun Taverne with Sir W. Warren, and he did give me a payre of gloves for my wife wrapt up in paper, which I would not open, feeling it hard, but did tell him that my wife should thank him, and so went on in discourse. When I came home, Lord! in what pain I was to get my wife out of the room without bidding her go, that I might see what these gloves were; and by and by, she being gone, it proves a payre of white gloves for her and forty pieces in good gold, which did so cheer my heart that I could eat no victuals almost for dinner for joy to think how God do bless us every day more and more; and more yet I hope he will upon the increase of my duty and endeavours. I was at great losse what to do, whether tell my wife of it or no, which I could hardly forbear, but yet I did and will think of it first before I do, for fear of making her think me to be in a better condition or in a better way of getting money than yet I am.

3rd. In Covent Garden to-night I stopped at the great Coffee-house,[1] where I never was before; where Dryden the poet (I knew at Cambridge), and all the wits of the town, and Harris the player, and Mr. Hoole of our College. And had I had time then, or could at other times, it will be good coming thither; for there I perceive is very witty and pleasant discourse. But I could not tarry, and as it was late they were all ready to go away.

9th. Up and to the office, where sat all the morning. Thence home, and there found Captain Grove in mourning for his wife, and he dined with me. He being gone, my wife and I did walk an houre or two above in our chamber, seriously talking of businesses.

---

[1] At this coffee-house, later known as Will's, Dryden had a chair reserved for him near the fireplace in winter and in the balcony in summer.

She and I did cast about how to get Captain Grove for my sister, in which we are mighty earnest at present, and I think it would be a good match, and will indeavour it. So to my office a while, then home to supper and to bed.

10th. Up, and by coach to my Lord Sandwich, to his new house, a fine house, but deadly dear, in Lincoln's Inne Fields, where I found and spoke a little to him. He is high and strange still, but did ask me how my wife did, and at parting remembered him to his cozen, which I thought was pretty well, being willing to flatter myself that in time he will be well again.

15th. This afternoon Sir Thomas Chamberlin came to the office to me, and showed me several letters from the East Indys, showing the height that the Dutch are come to there, showing scorn to all the English, even in our only Factory there of Surat, beating several men, and hanging the English Standard St. George under the Dutch flagg in scorn; saying that whatever their masters do or say at home they will do what they list, and will be masters of all the world there; and have so proclaimed themselves Soveraigne of all the South Seas, which certainly our King cannot endure, if the Parliament will give him money. But I doubt and yet do hope they will not yet, till we are more ready for it.

17th. At my office till 3 o'clock in the morning, having resolved to sit up, and did till now it is ready to strike 4 o'clock, all alone, cold, and my candle not enough left to light me to my owne house; and so, with my business however brought to some good understanding, and set it down pretty clear, I went home to bed with my mind at good quiet, and the girl sitting up for me (the rest all a-bed). I eat and drank a little, and to bed, weary, sleepy, cold, and my head akeing.

March 4th. Up and by coach to my Lord Sandwich, with whom I spoke, walking a good while with him in his garden. We did talk long and freely that I hope the worst is past and all will be well. There were several people by, trying a new-fashion gun brought my Lord this morning to shoot off often, one after another, without trouble or danger, very pretty. Home to dinner, and I to White Hall, and there being met by the Duke of Yorke, he called me to him and discoursed a pretty while with me about the new ship's dispatch building at Woolwich, and talking of the charge did say that he finds always the best the most cheape. I never had so much discourse with the Duke before, and till now did ever fear to meet him. Thence to my Lord's, and took up my wife, whom my Lady hath received with her old good nature and kindnesse, and so homewards.

8th. Up with some little discontent with my wife upon her saying that she had got and used some puppy-dog water, being put upon it by a desire of my aunt Wight to get some for her, who hath a mind, unknown to her husband, to get some for her ugly face. "Heraclius"[1] being acted, which my wife and I have a mighty mind to see, we do resolve, though not exactly agreeing with the letter of my vowe, yet altogether with the sense, to see another this month, by going hither instead of that at Court. The play hath one very good passage well managed in it, about two persons pretending, and yet denying themselves, to be son to the tyrant Phocas, and yet heire of Mauricius to the crowne. The garments like Romans very well. The little girle is come to act very prettily, and spoke the epilogue most admirably. But at the beginning, at the drawing up of the curtaine, there was the finest scene of the Emperor and his people about him, standing in their fixed and different postures in their Roman habitts, above all that ever I yet saw at any of the theatres. Walked home, calling to see my brother Tom, who is in bed, and I doubt very ill of a consumption. To the office a while, and so home to supper and to bed.

10th. Home to dinner with my wife, to a good hog's harslet,[2] a piece of meat I love, but have not eat of I think these seven years; and after dinner abroad by coach to White Hall, and at the Privy Seale I enquired and found the Bill come for the Corporation of the Royall Fishery; whereof the Duke of Yorke is made present Governor, and several other very great persons, to the number of thirty-two, made his assistants for their lives: whereof by my Lord Sandwich's favour I am one, and take it not only as a matter of honour, but that that may come to be of profit to me.

13th. (Lord's Day.) Comes Mrs. Turner's boy with a note to me to tell me that my brother Tom was so ill as they feared he would not long live, and that it would be fit I should come and see him so I walked along with them.

15th. Up and to the office, where we sat all the morning. After dinner took coach and to my brother's, where contrary to my expectation he continues as bad or worse, talking idle, and now not at all knowing any of us as before. Here staid a great while,

---

[1] Translated from Corneille.   [2] The heart, liver, and other edible offal, especially of the hog.

I going up and down the house looking after things. In the evening Dr. Wiverley came again. About 8 o'clock having no mind to see him die, as we thought he presently would, I withdrew and led Mrs. Turner home; but before I came back, which was in half a quarter of an hour, my brother was dead, which put me into a present very great transport of grief and cries; and indeed it was a most sad sight.

18th. Up betimes, and walked to my brother's, where a great while putting things in order against anon; then to Madam Turner's and eat a breakfast there, and so to Wotton, my shoemaker, and there got a pair of shoes blacked on the soles against anon for me. So to church, and with the grave-maker chose a place for my brother to lie in, just under my mother's pew. But to see how a man's tombes are at the mercy of such a fellow, that for sixpence he would, (as his owne words were), "I will justle them together but I will make room for him;" speaking of the fulness of the middle isle, where he was to lie; and that he would, for my father's sake, do my brother that is dead all the civility he can. At noon home, where I dressed myself, and so did Besse; and so to my brother's again, whither, though invited, as the custom is, at one or two o'clock, they came not till four or five. But at last one after another they come, many more than I bid, and my reckoning that I bid was one hundred and twenty; but I believe there was nearer one hundred and fifty. Their service was six biscuits a-piece, and what they pleased of burnt claret. My cosen Joyce Norton kept the wine and cakes above, and did give out to them that served, who had white gloves given them. The men sat by themselves in some rooms, and women by themselves in others, very close, but yet room enough. Anon to church, walking out into the streete to the Conduit and so across the streete, and had a very good company along with the corps. And being come to the grave as above, Dr. Pierson, the minister of the parish, did read the service for buriall, and so I saw my poor brother laid into the grave; and so all broke up, and I and my wife and Madam Turner and her family to my brother's, and by and by fell to a barrell of oysters, cake, and cheese, being too merry for so late a sad work. But, Lord! to see how the world makes nothing of the memory of a man an houre after he is dead! And, indeed, I must blame myself; for though at the sight of him dead and dying, I had real grief for a while, while he was in my sight, yet presently after, and ever since, I have had very little grief indeed for him. By and by I took my wife and Besse (who hath done me very good service in cleaning and getting ready every thing and serving the wine and things to-day, and is indeed a most excellent good-natured and faithful wench, and I love her mightily), by coach home, and so after being at the office to set down the day's work home to supper and to bed.

19th. My father and my brother John came to towne by coach. I sat till night with him, giving him an account of things. He, poor man, very sad and sickly.

25th. After dinner to the office; thence with my wife to see my father and discourse how he finds Tom's matters, which he do very ill, and that he finds him to have been so negligent that he used to trust his servants with cutting out of clothes, never hardly cutting out any thing himself; and by the abstract of his accounts we find him to owe above £290, and to be coming to him under £200. Thence home with my wife, it being very dirty on foot, and bought some fowl in Gracious Street and some oysters against our feast to-morrow.

26th. My solemn feast for my cutting of the stone, it being now, blessed be God! this day six years since the time; and I bless God I do in all respects find myself free from that disease or any signs of it. It hath pleased the Lord in six years time to raise me from a condition of constant and dangerous and most painfull sicknesse and low condition and poverty to a state of constant health almost, great honour and plenty, for which the Lord God of heaven make me truly thankfull. My wife found her gowne come home laced, which is indeed very handsome, but will cost me a great deal of money, more than ever I intended, but it is but for once.

April 3rd. (Lord's Day.) Being weary last night lay long, and called up by W. Joyce. So I rose, and his business was to ask advice of me, he being summonsed to the House of Lords to-morrow for endeavouring to arrest my Lady Peters for a debt. I did give him advice, and will assist him.

4th. To Westminster, to the Painted Chamber, and there met the two Joyces. Will in a very melancholy taking. After a little discourse I to the Lords' House before they sat, and stood within it a good while, while the Duke of York came to me and spoke to me a good while about the new ship at Woolwich. And so staid without a good while, and saw my Lady Peters, an impudent jade, soliciting all the Lords on her behalf.

5th. Coming home I find my wife dressed as if she had been abroad, but I think she was not; but she answering me some way that I did not like I pulled her by the nose, indeed to offend her; though afterwards to appease her I denied it, but only it was done in haste. The poor wretch took it mighty ill, and I believe besides wringing her nose she did feel pain, and so cried a great while; but by and by I made her friends, and so after supper to my office a while, and then home to bed.

12th. My father come to lie at our house, poor man, my heart never being fuller of love to him, nor admiration of his prudence and pains heretofore in the world than now, to see how Tom hath carried himself in his trade; and how the poor man hath his thoughts going to provide for his younger children and my mother. But I hope they shall never want.

14th. Up betimes, and after my father's eating something I walked out with him as far as Milk Streete, he turning down to Cripplegate to take coach; and at the end of the streete I took leave, being much afeard I shall not see him here any more, he do decay so much every day.

17th. (Lord's Day.) Up, and I put on my best cloth black suit and my velvet cloake, and with my wife in her best laced suit to church, where we have not been these nine or ten weeks. The truth is, my jealousy hath hindered it, for fear she should see Pembleton. He was here to-day, but I think sat so as he could not see her, which did please me, God help me! mightily, though I know well enough that in reason this is nothing but my ridiculous folly.

18th. Up and by coach to Westminster, and there solicited W. Joyce's business again and did speake to the Duke of Yorke about it, who did understand it very well. I afterwards did without the House fall in company with my Lady Peters and endeavoured to mollify her; but she told me she would not, to redeem her from hell, do any thing to release him, but would be revenged while she lived, if she lived the age of Methusalem. At last it was ordered by the Lords that it should be referred to the Committee of Privileges to consider. So I, after discoursing with the Joyces, away by coach to the 'Change; and there, among other things, do hear that a Jew hath put in a policy of four per cent. to any man, to insure him against a Dutch warr for four months; I could find in my heart to take him at this offer, but however will advise first. To Hide Parke, where I have not been since last year; where I saw the King with his periwigg, but not altered at all; and my Lady Castlemayne in a coach by herself, in yellow satin and a pinner [1] on; and many brave persons. And myself being in a hackney and full of people was ashamed to be seen by the world, many of them knowing me.

21st. To Westminster Hall, and there at the Lords' House heard that it is ordered that, upon submission upon the knee both to the House and my Lady Peters, W. Joyce shall be released. I forthwith made him submit, and aske pardon upon his knees, which he did before several Lords. But my Lady would not hear it, but swore she would post the Lords, that the world might know what pitifull Lords the King hath; and that revenge was sweeter to her than milk; and that she would never be satisfied unless he stood in a pillory and demand pardon there. But I perceive the Lords are ashamed of her.

The House this day have voted that the King be desired to demand right for the wrong done us by the Dutch, and that they will stand by him with their lives and fortunes, which is a very high vote, and more than I expected. What the issue will be, God knows!

23rd. (Coronation Day.) To the 'Change, where I met with Mr. Coventry, who himself is now full of talke of a Dutch warr, for it seems the Lords have concurred in the Commons' vote about it; and so the next week it will be presented to the King, insomuch that he do desire we would look about to see what stores we lack, and buy what we can. Home to dinner, where I and my wife much troubled about my money that is in my Lord Sandwich's hand, for fear of his going to sea and be killed; but I will get what of it out I can.

25th. Up, and with Sir W. Pen by coach to St. James's and there up to the Duke, where most of our talke about a Dutch warr, and discoursing of things indeed now for it. In the Duke's chamber there is a bird, given him by Mr. Pierce, the surgeon, comes from the East Indys, black the greatest part, with the finest collar of white about the neck; but talks many things and neyes like the horse, and other things, the best almost that ever I heard bird in my life. I walked to my Lord Sandwich's, where by agreement I met my wife, and there dined with the young ladies; my Lady, being not well, kept her chamber. Much simple discourse at table among the young ladies. After dinner I took my wife by coach out through the city, discoursing how to spend the after-

[1] A headdress of nightcap form, with a long flap pinned to either side and depending over the breast.

noon; and conquered, with much ado, a desire of going to a play; but took her out at White Chapel, and to Bednal Green; so to Hackney, where I have not been many a year, since a little child I boarded there. Thence to Kingsland, by my nurse's house, Goody Lawrence, where my brother Tom and I was kept when young. Then to Newington Green, and saw the outside of Mrs. Herbert's house, where she lived, and my Aunt Ellen with her; but, Lord! how in every point I find myself to over-value things when a child.

26th. My wife gone this afternoon to the burial of my she-cozen Scott,[1] a good woman; and it is a sad consideration how the Pepys's decay, and nobody almost that I know in a present way of encreasing them. At night late at my office, and so home to my wife to supper and to bed.

29th. After dinner my wife and I by coach to see my Lady Sandwich, where we find all the children and my Lord removed, and the house so melancholy that I thought my Lady had been dead, knowing that she was not well; but it seems she hath the meazles, and I fear the small pox, poor lady. It grieves me mightily, for it will be a sad houre to the family should she miscarry. Thence straight home and to the office; and in the evening comes Mr. Hill the merchant and another with him that sings well, and we sung some things, and good musique it seemed to me, only my mind too full of business to have much pleasure in it. But I will have more of it.

May 2nd. My wife and I to see "The Labyrinth,"[2] the poorest play, methinks, that ever I saw, there being nothing in it but the odd accidents that fell out, by a lady's being bred up in man's apparel, and a man in a woman's. Home and to my office, whither comes Mr. Bland and pays me the debt he acknowledged he owed me for my service in his business of the Tangier Merchant,[3] twenty pieces of new gold, a pleasant sight. It cheered my heart, and he being gone, I home to supper, and shewed them my wife; and she, poor wretch, would fain have kept them to look on, without any other design but a simple love to them, but I thought it not convenient, and so took them into my own hand. So after supper to bed.

3rd. Up, and being ready went by agreement to Mr. Bland's and there drank my morning draft in good chocollatte, and slabbering my band sent home for another; and so by water to White

---

[1] Judith Scott, daughter of Richard Pepys, Lord Chief-Justice of Ireland.
[2] Translated from Corneille.   [3] A ship freighted by the Navy Office.

Hall, and walked to St. James's and so to Mr. Coventry's chamber, and there upon my Lord Peterborough's [1] accounts, where I endeavoured to shew the folly and punish it as much as I could of Mr. Povy; for of all the men in the world I never knew any man of his degree so great a coxcomb in such imployments. I see I have lost him for ever, but I value it not; for he is a coxcomb, and I doubt not over honest, by some things which I see; and yet for all his folly he hath the good lucke, now and then, to speak his follies in as good words and with as good a show as if it were reason and to the purpose, which is really one of the wonders of my life.

9th. To my Lady Sandwich's, who, good lady, is now, thanks be to God! so well as to sit up, and sent to us, if we were not afeard, to come up to her. So we did; but she was mightily against my wife's coming so near her, though, poor wretch! she is as well as ever she was as to the meazles, and nothing can I see upon her face. There we sat talking with her above three hours, till six o'clock, of several things with great pleasure and so away, and home by coach.

16th. After supper my wife and I talked and concluded upon sending my father an offer of having Pall come to us to be with us for her preferment, if by any means I can get her a husband here, which, though it be some trouble to us, yet it will be better than to have her stay there till nobody will have her, and then be flung upon my hands.

29th. (Whitsunday. King's Birth and Restauration Day.) Up, and walked to St. James's, and there Mr. Coventry and I did long discourse together of the business of the office and the warr with the Dutch. He desired to know whether I do understand my Lord Sandwich's intentions as to going to sea with this fleete, saying that the Duke, if he desires it, is most willing to it; but, thinking that twelve ships is not a fleete fit for my Lord to be troubled to go out with, he is not willing to offer it to him till he hath some intimations of his mind to go or not. He spoke this with very great respect as to my Lord, though methinks it is strange they should not understand one another better at this time than to need another's mediation. Thence walked over the Parke to White Hall, Mr. Povy with me, to the King's closett. By and by my Lord Sandwich came forth and called me to him: and we fell into discourse a great while about his business, wherein

[1] Lord Peterborough had been Governor of Tangier.

he seems to be very open with me and to receive my opinion as he used to do; and I hope I shall become necessary to him again. He desired me to think of the fitness or not for him to offer himself to go to sea, and to give him my thoughts in a day or two. With Mr. Povy home to dinner, where extraordinary cheer. And after dinner up and down to see his house. And in a word, methinks, for his perspective upon his wall in his garden, and the springs rising up with the perspective in the little closett; his room floored above with woods of several colours, like but above the best cabinet-work I ever saw; his grotto and vault, with his bottles of wine, and a well therein to keep them cool; his furniture of all sorts; his bath at the top of his house, good pictures, and his manner of eating and drinking; do surpass all that ever I did see of one man in all my life.

31st. To my Lord Sandwich's to discourse about his going to sea. We concluded it wholly inconsistent with his honour not to go with this fleete, nor with the reputation which the world hath of his interest at Court; and so he did give me commission to tell Mr. Coventry that he is most willing to receive any commands from the Duke in this fleete, were it less than it is, and that particularly in this service. With this message I parted, and by coach to the office, where I found Mr. Coventry and told him this. Methinks, I confess, he did not seem so pleased with it as I expected, or at least could have wished, and asked me whether I had told my Lord that the Duke do not expect his going, which I told him I had. But now whether he means really that the Duke, as he told me the other day, do think the fleete too small for him to take, or that he would not have him go, I swear I cannot tell. I was told to-day that upon Sunday night last, being the King's birth-day, the King was at my Lady Castlemayne's lodgings dancing with fiddlers all night almost, and all the world coming by taking notice of it, which I am sorry to hear.

June 1st. Mr. Holliard came to me, and to my great sorrow, after his great assuring me that I could not possibly have the stone again, he tells me that he do verily fear that I have it again, and has brought me something to dissolve it, which do make me very much troubled and pray to God to ease me.

3rd. At the Committee for Tangier all the afternoon, where a sad consideration to see things of so great weight managed in so confused a manner, the Duke of York and Mr. Coventry, for aught I see, being the only two that do anything like men; Prince Rupert do nothing but swear and laugh a little, with an oathe or two, and that's all he do.

4th. To the Duke, and was with him giving him an account how matters go, and of the necessity there is of a power to presse seamen, without which we cannot really raise men; besides that it will assert the King's power of pressing, which at present is somewhat doubted, and will make the Dutch believe that we are in earnest.

Mr. Coventry discoursing this noon about Sir W. Batten (what a sad fellow he is!) told me how the King told him the other day how Sir W. Batten, being in the ship with him and Prince Rupert when they expected to fight, did walk up and down sweating with a napkin under his throat to dry up his sweat; and that Prince Rupert being a most jealous man, and particularly of Batten, do walk up and down swearing bloodily to the King that Batten had a mind to betray them to-day, and that the napkin was a signal; "but, by God," says he, "if things go ill, the first thing I will do is to shoot him." He discoursed largely and bravely to me concerning the different sort of valours, the active and passive valour. For the latter he brought as an instance General Blake, who, in the defending of Taunton and Lime for the Parliament, did through his stubborn sort of valour defend it the most *opiniastrément* that ever any man did any thing; and yet never was the man that ever made any attaque by land or sea, but rather avoyded it on all, even fair, occasions. On the other side, Prince Rupert, the boldest attaquer in the world for personal courage; and yet in the defending of Bristol no man ever did anything worse, he wanting the patience and seasoned head to consult and advise for defence, and to bear with the evils of a siege.

He tells me above all of the Duke of Yorke, that he is more himself and more of judgment is at hand in him in the middle of a desperate service than at other times, as appeared in the business of Dunkirke, wherein no man ever did braver things, or was in hotter service in the close of that day, being surrounded with enemies; and then, contrary to the advice of all about him, his counsel carried himself and the rest through them safe, by advising that he might make his passage with but a dozen with him; "For," says he, "the enemy cannot move after me so fast with a great body, and with a small one we shall be enough to deal with them;" and though he is a man naturally martiall to the highest degree, yet a man that never in his life talks one word of himself or service of his owne, but only that he saw such or such a thing, and lays it down for maxime that a Hector can have no courage.

14th. After dinner by coach to Kensington to my Lady Sandwich, who hath lain this fortnight here. Much company came hither to-day, above all Mr. Becke of Chelsy, and wife and daughter, my Lord's mistress, and one that hath not one good feature in her face, and yet is a fine lady, of a fine *taille* and very well carriaged, and mighty discreet. I took all the occasion I could to discourse with the young ladies in her company to give occasion to her to talk, which now and then she did, and that mighty finely; and is, I perceive, a woman of such an ayre as I wonder the less at my Lord's favour to her, and I dare warrant him she hath brains enough to entangle him. Giving them occasion to invite themselves to-morrow to me to dinner to my venison pasty, I got their mother's leave, and so good night, very well pleased with my day's work, and above all that I have seen my Lord's mistresse. So home to supper, and a little at my office, and to bed.

15th. At noon comes Mr. Creed by chance, and by and by the three young ladies: and very merry we were with our pasty, very well baked, and a good dish of roasted chickens, pease, lobsters, strawberries. And after dinner to cards; and about five o'clock by water down to Greenwich, and up to the top of the hill, and there played upon the ground at cards. And so to the Cherry Garden, and then by water singing finely to the Bridge,[1] and there landed; and so took boat again and to Somersett House. And by this time, the tide being against us, it was past ten of the clock; and such a troublesome passage in regard of my Lady Paulina's fearfullness that in all my life I never did see any poor wretch in that condition. I sent my wife home by coach with Mr. Creed's boy; and myself and Creed in the coach home with them. But, Lord! the fear that my Lady Paulina was in every step of the way; and indeed at this time of the night it was no safe thing to go that road; so that I was even afeard myself, though I appeared otherwise. We came safe, however, to their house, where all were abed; we knocked them up, my Lady and all the family being in bed. Creed and I, it being about twelve o'clock and past, to several houses, inns, but could get no lodging, all being in bed. At last we found some people drinking and roaring, and there got in, and after drinking got an ill bed, where

---

[1] Old London Bridge. They had to get out owing to the swirl of water between the piers.

16th. I lay in my drawers and stockings and wastecoate till five of the clock, and so up; and being well pleased with our frolique walked to Knightsbridge, and there eat a messe of creame, and so to St. James's, and there walked a little, and so I to White Hall and took coach, and found my wife well got home last night, and now in bed.

24th. After dinner to White Hall; and there met with Mr. Pierce, and he showed me the Queene's bed-chamber and her closett, where she had nothing but some pretty pious pictures and books of devotion; and her holy water at her head as she sleeps, with her clock by her bed-side, wherein a lamp burns that tells her the time of the night at any time. Thence with him to the Parke, and there met the Queene coming from Chappell with her Mayds of Honour all in silver-lace gowns again, which is new to me, and that which I did not think would have been brought up again. Thence he carried me to the King's closett, where such variety of pictures and other things of value and rarity that I was properly confounded, and enjoyed no pleasure in the sight of them; which is the only time in my life that ever I was so at a loss for pleasure, in the greatest plenty of objects to give it me. Thence doing abundance of errands to my great content, at night weary home, where Mr. Creed waited for me; and he told me he is now in a hurry fitting himself for sea, and that it remains that he deals as an ingenuous man with me in the business I wot of, which he will do before he goes. But I perceive he will have me do many good turns for him first, which I promise, and as he acquits himself to me I will willingly do.

27th. Our new mayd Jane come, a cook-mayd.

28th. Up, and this day put on a half shirt first this summer, it being very hot; and yet so ill-tempered I am grown that I am afeard I shall catch cold, while all the world is ready to melt away.

July 1st. Busy till the evening, and then by agreement came Mr. Hill and Andrews and one Cheswicke, a maister who plays very well upon the Spinette, and we sat singing Psalms till 9 at night, and so broke up with great pleasure; and very good company it is, and I hope I shall now and then have their company. They being gone, I to my office till towards twelve o'clock, and then home and to bed.

4th. Find my wife this day of her own accord to have lain out 25*s.* upon a pair of pendantes for her eares, which did vex me and brought both me and her to very high and very foule words from her to me, such as trouble me to think she should have in her mouth; and reflecting upon our old differences, which I hate to have remembered. I vowed to breake them, or that she should go and get what she could for them again. I went with that resolution out of doors; the poor wretch afterwards in a little while did send out to change them for her money again. I followed Besse her messenger at the 'Change, and there did consult and sent her back; I would not have them changed, being satisfied that she yielded.

7th. To White Hall, and there found the Duke and twenty more reading their commission (of which I am, and was also sent to, to come) for the Royall Fishery, which is very large, and a very serious charter it is; but the company generally so ill fitted for so serious a worke that I do much fear it will come to little. So home, calling by the way for my new bookes, viz., Sir H. Spillman's "Whole Glossary," "Scapula's Lexicon," and Shakespeare's plays, which I have got money out of my stationer's bills to pay for.

8th. To Paul's Churchyarde about my books, and to the binder's and directed the doing of my Chaucer, though they were not full neate enough for me, but pretty well it is; and thence to the clasp-maker's to have it clasped and bossed.

10th. (Lord's Day.) To my Lord Sandwich's and there dined with my Lady and the children. After dinner took our leaves and my wife her's in order to her going into the country to-morrow. To Kate Joyce's christening where much company; good service of sweetmeates.

11th. Betimes up this morning, and by coach to Holborne, where, at nine o'clock, they set out, and I and my man Will on horseback, by my wife, to Barnett; a very pleasant day; and there dined with her company, which was very good; a pretty gentlewoman with her, that goes but to Huntington, and a neighbour to us in towne. Here we staid two hours and then parted for all together, and my poor wife I shall soon want I am sure. Thence I and Will to see the Wells,[1] half a mile off, and there I drank three glasses, and went and walked and came back and drunk two more; the woman would have had me drink three more, but I could not, my belly being full. And so we rode round by Kingsland, Hackney, and Mile End, and so home weary. And not being very well, I betimes to bed, and there fell into a most mighty sweat

[1] Mineral wells on Barnet Common.

in the night, about eleven o'clock; and there, knowing what money I have in the house and hearing a noyse, I begun to sweat worse and worse, till I melted almost to water.   I rung, and could not in half an houre make either of the wenches hear me, and this made me fear the more, lest they might be gag'd; and then I begun to think that there was some design in a stone being flung at the window over our stayres this evening, by which the thiefes meant to try what looking there would be after them, and know our company.   These thoughts and fears I had, and do hence apprehend the fears of all rich men that are covetous and have much money by them.   At last Jane rose, and then I understand it was only the dogg wants a lodging and so made a noyse.   So to bed, but hardly slept; at last did, and so till morning.

13th.   Mr. Moore was with me late to desire me to come to my Lord Sandwich to-morrow morning, which I shall, but I wonder what my business is.

14th.   Walked to my Lord's.   He did begin with a most solemn profession of the same confidence in and love for me that he ever had, and then told me what a misfortune was fallen upon me and him: in me, by a displeasure which my Lord Chancellor did show to him last night against me, in the highest and most passionate manner that ever any man did speak.   And what should the business be, but that I should be forward to have the trees in Clarendon Park marked and cut down which he, it seems, hath bought of my Lord Albemarle; when, God knows! I am the most innocent man in the world in it, and did nothing of myself, nor knew of his concernment therein, but barely obeyed my Lord Treasurer's warrant for the doing thereof.   My Lord do seem most nearly affected; he is partly, I believe, for me, and partly for himself. So he advised me to wait presently upon my Lord and clear myself in the most perfect manner I could, with all submission and assurance that I am his creature both in this and all other things; and that I do owne that all I have is derived through my Lord Sandwich from his Lordship.

So, full of horror, I went to my Lord Chancellor's; and there coming out after dinner I accosted him, telling him that I was the unhappy Pepys that had fallen into his high displeasure, and come to desire him to give me leave to make myself better understood to his Lordship, assuring him of my duty and service.   He answered me very pleasingly and desired me to call upon him some evening: I named to-night and he accepted of it.   So with my heart light I to White Hall. Thence to the Half Moone and thence to my Lord Chancellor's and there heard several tryals, wherein I perceive my Lord is a most able and ready man. After all done, he called, "Come, Mr. Pepys, you and I will take a turn in the garden." So he was led down stairs, having the goute, and there walked with me, I think, above an houre, talking most friendly, yet cunningly. I told him clearly how things were; how ignorant I was of his Lordship's concernment in it; how I did not do nor say one word singly, but what was done was the act of the whole Board. He told me by name that he was more angry with Sir G. Carteret than with me, and also with the whole body of the Board. I think I did thoroughly appease him, till he thanked me for my desire and pains to satisfy him. Lord! to see how we poor wretches dare not do the King good service for fear of the greatness of these men. I parted with great assurance how I acknowledged all I had to come from his Lordship; which he did not seem to refuse, but with great kindness and respect parted. So I by coach home. At my office late, and so home to eat something, being almost starved for want of eating my dinner to-day; and so to bed, my head being full of great and many businesses of import to me.

15th. With Creed to White Hall, where, staying for him in one of the galleries, there comes out of the chayre-room Mrs. Stewart, in a most lovely form, with her hair all about her eares, having her picture taken there. There was the King and twenty more, I think, standing by all the while, and a lovely creature she in this dress [1] seemed to be. Thence to the 'Change by coach, and so home to dinner and then to my office.

20th. Dined with a good pig, and then out by coach to White Hall, it being a great day to-day there upon drawing at the Lottery of Sir Arthur Slingsby. I got in and stood by the two Queenes and the Duchesse of Yorke, and just behind my Lady Castlemayne, whom I do heartily adore; and good sport it was to see how most that did give their ten pounds did go away with a pair of globes only for their lot, and one gentlewoman, one Mrs. Fish, with the only blanke. And one I staid to see drew a suit of hangings valued at £430, and they say are well worth the money, or near it. One other suit there is better than that; but very many lots of three and fourscore pounds. I observed the King and Queenes did get but as poor lots as any else. But the wisest man I met with was Mr.

---

[1] The dress of a cavalier.

"MRS. STEWART IN A MOST LOVELY FORM"

Cholmley,[1] who insured as many as would from drawing of the one blank for 12*d*.; in which case there was the whole number of persons to one, which I think was three or four hundred. And so he insured about 200 for 200 shillings, so that he could not have lost if one of them had drawn it, for there was enough to pay the £10; but it happened another drew it, and so he got all the money he took.

21st. This morning to the office comes Nicholas Osborne, Mr. Gauden's clerke, to desire of me what piece of plate I would choose to have a £100 or thereabouts bestowed upon me in, he having order to lay out so much. I a great while urged my unwillingnesse to take any, not knowing how I could serve Mr. Gauden, but left it wholly to himself; so at noon I find brought home in fine leather cases a pair of the noblest flaggons that ever I saw all the days of my life; whether I shall keepe them or no I cannot tell, for it is to oblige me to him in the business of the Tangier victualling, wherein I doubt I shall not; but glad I am to see that I shall be sure to get something on one side or other, have it which will: so, with a merry heart, I looked upon them, and locked them up. To Westminster and to Mrs. Lane's lodgings, and by and by her husband comes, a sorry, simple fellow, and his letter to her which she proudly showed me a simple, nonsensical thing. A man of no discourse, and I fear married her to make a prize of, which he is mistaken in, and a sad wife I believe she will prove to him.

25th. Mr. Cole (my old Jack Cole) comes to see me; so I made him stay with me till 11 at night, talking of old school stories, and very pleasing ones; and truly I find that we did spend our time and thoughts then otherwise than I think boys do now, and I think as well as methinks that the best are now. And strange to see how we are all divided that were bred so long at school together, and what various fortunes we have run, some good, some bad.

26th. Great discourse of the fray yesterday in Moorefields, how the butchers at first did beat the weavers (between whom there hath been ever an old competition for mastery), but at last the weavers rallied and beat them. At first the butchers knocked down all for weavers that had green or blue aprons, till they were fain to pull them off and put them in their breeches. At last the butchers were fain to pull off their sleeves, that they might not be known, and were soundly beaten out of the field, and some deeply

---

[1] Hugh Cholmeley, afterwards the third baronet, a member of the Tangier Commission.

wounded and bruised; till at last the weavers went out tryumphing, calling £100 for a butcher. I to Mr. Reeves to see a microscope, he having been with me to-day morning, and three chose one which I will have. Thence back and took up young Mrs. Harman, a pretty bred and pretty humoured woman whom I could love well, though not handsome, yet for her person and carriage, and black.

28th. To Westminster, to my barbers; and strange to think how when I find that Jervas himself did intend to bring home my periwigg and not Jane, his maid, I did desire not to have it at all. All our discourse is of a Dutch warr, and I find it is likely to come to it, for they are very high and desire not to compliment us at all, as far as I hear, but to send a good fleet to Guinny to oppose us there. My Lord Sandwich newly gone to sea, and I, I think, fallen into his very good opinion again.

31st. (Lord's Day.) Up, and to church, where I have not been these many weeks. So home, and thither, inviting him yesterday, comes Mr. Hill, and to musique all the afternoon. He being gone, in the evening I to my accounts; and to my great joy and with great thanks to Almighty God I do find myself most clearly worth £1,014, the first time that ever I was worth £1,000 before, which is the height of all that ever I have for a long time pretended to. So with praise to God for this state of fortune that I am brought to as to wealth, I home to supper and to bed, desiring God to give me the grace to make good use of what I have, and continue my care and diligence to gain more.

August 3rd. Up betimes and set some joyners on work to new lay my floor in our wardrobe, which I intend to make a room for musique.

4th. At noon dined with Sir W. Pen, a piece of beef only, and I counterfeited a friendship and mirth which I cannot have with him; yet out with him by his coach, and he did carry me to a play and pay for me at the King's house, which is "The Rivall Ladys,"[1] a very innocent and most pretty witty play. I was much pleased with it and, it being given me, I look upon it as no breach to my oathe. Here we hear that Clun, one of their best actors, was the last night set upon and murdered; one of the rogues taken, an Irish fellow. It seems most cruelly butchered and bound. The house will have a great miss of him.

5th. Up very betimes and set my plaisterer to work about whiting and colouring my musique roome, which having with great

[1] By Dryden.

pleasure seen done, about ten o'clock I dressed myself, and so mounted upon a very pretty mare sent me by Sir W. Warren, and so through the City, not a little proud, God knows, to be seen upon so pretty a beast, and to my cozen W. Joyce's, and he and I out of towne toward Highgate. Thence forward to Barnett, and there drank, and so by night to Stevenage, it raining a little, but not much, and there to my great trouble find that my wife was not come. So vexed and weary, I after supper to bed.

6th. At eight o'clock comes my wife in the coach, and a coach full of women, only one man riding by, gone down last night to meet a sister of his coming to town. So very joyful drank there, not 'lighting, and we mounted and away with them to Welling,[1] and there 'light, and dined very well, and merry and glad to see my poor wife. Here very merry as being weary I could be, and after dinner out again, and to London. In our way all the way the mightiest merry at a couple of young gentlemen, come down to meet the same gentlewoman, that ever I was in my life, and so W. Joyce too, to see how one of them was horsed upon a hard-trotting sorrell horse, and both of them soundly weary and galled. But it is not to be set down how merry we were all the way. We 'light in Holborne, and by another coach my wife and mayde home, and I by horseback, and found all things well and most mighty neate and clean.

7th. (Lord's Day.) Lay long caressing my wife and talking, she telling me sad stories of the ill, improvident, disquiett and sluttish manner that my father and mother and Pall live in the country, which troubles me mightily and I must seek to remedy it. So up and ready, and my wife also, and then down, and I showed my wife to her great admiration and joy Mr. Gauden's present of plate, the two flaggons, which indeed are so noble that I hardly can think that they are yet mine. So blessing God for it, we down to dinner mighty pleasant, and so up after dinner for a while, and I then to White Hall. Walked homeward and met with Mr. Spong, and he with me as far as the Old Exchange talking of many ingenuous things, musique, and at last of glasses, and I find him still the same ingenuous man that ever he was, and do among other fine things tell me that by his microscope of his owne making he do discover that the wings of a moth is made just as the feathers of the wing of a bird, and that most plainly and certainly.

[1] Welwyn.

13th. Up, and before I went to the office comes my taylor with a coate I have made to wear within doors, purposely to come no lower than my knees, for by my wearing a gowne within doors comes all my tenderness about my legs. There comes also Mr. Reeve, with a microscope and scotoscope. For the first I did give him £5 10*s*., a great price, but a most curious bauble it is, and he says as good nay, the best he knows in England; and he makes the best in the world. The other he gives me, and is of value; and a curious curiosity it is to look objects in a darke room with. Mr. Creed dining with me I got him to give my wife and me a play this afternoon, lending him money to do it, which is a fallacy that I have found now once, to avoyde my vowe with, but never to be more practised I swear; and to the new play at the Duke's house of "Henry the Fifth;" a most noble play, writ by my Lord Orrery; wherein Betterton, Harris, and Ianthe's parts are most incomparably wrote and done, and the whole play the most full of height and raptures of wit and sense, that ever I heard; having but one incongruity, or what did not please me in it, that is, that King Harry promises to plead for Tudor to their Mistresse, Princesse Katherine of France, more than when it comes to it he seems to do; and Tudor refused by her with some kind of indignity, not with a difficulty and honour that it ought to have been done in to him.

15th. Up, and with Sir J. Minnes by coach to St. James's, and there did our business with the Duke, who tells us more and more signs of a Dutch warr, and how we must presently set out a fleete for Guinny, for the Dutch are doing so, and there I believe the warr will begin. At Charing Crosse I saw the great Dutchman that is come over, under whose arm I went with my hat on, and could not reach higher than his eyebrows with the tip of my fingers, reaching as high as I could. He is a comely and well-made man, and his wife a very little but pretty comely Dutch woman.

20th. I forth to bespeak a case to be made to keep my stone which I was cut in, which will cost me 25*s*.

26th. This day my wife tells me Mr. Pen,[1] Sir William's son, is come back from France, and come to visit her. A most modish person, grown, she says, a fine gentleman.

27th. Home, and there find my boy Tom Edwards come, sent me by Captain Cooke, having been bred in the King's Chappell these four years. I propose to make a clerke of him, and if he deserves well to do well by him. I find him a very schoole boy, that

---

1 Afterwards the famous Quaker.

talks innocently, and impertinently, but at present it is a sport to us, and in a little time he will leave it. All the newes this day is that the Dutch are, with twenty-two sayle of ships of warr, crewsing up and down about Ostend, at which we are alarmed. My Lord Sandwich is come back into the Downes with only eight sayle, which is or may be a prey to the Dutch, if they knew our weakness and inability to set out any more speedily.

28th. (Lord's Day.) Up, and with my boy alone to church, the first time I have had anybody to attend me to church a great while. Home to dinner, and there met Creed, who dined; and we merry together, as his learning is such, and judgment, that I cannot but be pleased with it.

30th. After dinner comes Mr. Pen to visit me, and staid an houre talking with me. I perceive something of learning he hath got, but a great deale, if not too much, of the vanity of the French garbe and affected manner of speech and gait. I fear all real profit he hath made of his travel will signify little.

September 4th. (Lord's Day.) All the morning looking over my old wardrobe and laying by things for my brother John and my father, by which I shall leave myself very bare in clothes, but yet as much as I need, and the rest would but spoile in the keeping.

5th. Up and to St. James's, and there did our business with the Duke, where all our discourse of warr in the highest measure. Prince Rupert was with us, who is fitting himself to go to sea in the Heneretta.[1] And afterwards in White Hall I met him and he spoke to me, and in other discourse, says he, "God damn me, I can answer but for one ship, and in that I will do my part; for it is not in that as in an army, where a man can command every thing." And so home, and thither came W. Bowyer and dined with us; but strange to see how he could not endure onyons in sauce to lamb, but was overcome with the sight of it, and so was forced to make his dinner of an egg or two. My aunt James here to-day with Kate Joyce twice to see us. The second time my wife was at home, and they it seems are going down to Brampton, which I am sorry for, for the charge that my father will be put to; but it must be borne with, and my mother has a mind to see them. But I do condemn myself mightily for my pride and contempt of my aunt and kindred that are not so high as myself, that I have not seen, nor invited her all this while.

[1] *Henrietta.*

"MR. PEN . . . A MOST MODISH PERSON"

6th. Called upon Doll, our pretty 'Change woman, for a pair of gloves trimmed with yellow ribbon to match the petticoate my wife bought yesterday, which cost me 20s.; but she is so pretty that, God forgive me! I could not think it too much: which is a strange slavery that I stand in to beauty, that I value nothing near it. This day Mr. Coventry did tell us how the Duke did receive the Dutch Embassador the other day; by telling him that, whereas they think us in jest, he believes that the Prince (Rupert) which goes in this fleete to Guinny will soon tell them that we are in earnest.

8th. My [wife] this afternoon being very well dressed by her new woman, Mary Mercer, a decayed merchant's daughter that our Will helps us to, did go to the christening of Mrs. Mills the parson's wife's child, where she never was before.

9th. Up, and to put things in order against dinner. I out and bought several things, among others a dozen of silver salts. Home and to the office, where some of us met a little, and then home. And at noon comes my company, namely Anthony and Will Joyce and their wives, my aunt James newly come out of Wales, and my cosen Sarah Gyles. Her husband did not come, and by her I did understand afterwards that it was because he was not yet able to pay me the 40s. she had borrowed a year ago of me. I was as merry as I could, giving them a good dinner. I forgot there was Mr. Harman and his wife, my aunt, a very good harmlesse woman. They eyed mightily my great cupboard of plate, I this day putting my two flaggons upon my table; and indeed it is a fine sight, and better than ever I did hope to see of my owne. Mercer dined with us at table, this being her first dinner in my house. After dinner left them and to White Hall, where a small Tangier Committee, and so back again home, and there my wife and Mercer and Tom and I sat till eleven at night singing and fiddling; and a great joy it is to see me master of so much pleasure in my house that it is and will be still, I hope, a constant pleasure to me to be at home. The girle plays pretty well upon the harpsicon, but only ordinary tunes, but hath a good hand; sings a little, but hath a good voyce and eare. My boy, a brave boy, sings finely, and is the most pleasant boy at present, while his ignorant boy's tricks last, that ever I saw. So to supper, and with great pleasure to bed.

10th. Up and to the office, where we sate all the morning, and I much troubled to think what the end of our great sluggishness will be, for we do nothing in this office like people able to carry on a warr. We must be put out, or other people put in.

12th. To St. James's, and there did our business as usual with the Duke; and saw him with great pleasure play with his little girle,[1] like an ordinary private father of a child.

16th. After dinner I forth with my boy to buy severall things, stools and andirons and candlesticks, &c., household stuff, and walked to the mathematical instrument maker in Moorefields and bought a large pair of compasses, and there met Mr. Pargiter; and he would needs have me drink a cup of horse-radish ale, which he and a friend of his troubled with the stone have been drinking of, which we did; and then walked into the fields, all the way talking of Russia, which he says is a sad place, and though Moscow is a very great city, yet it is from the distance between house and house; and few people compared with this, and poor, sorry houses, the Emperor himself living in a wooden house, his exercise only flying a hawk at pigeons and carrying pigeons ten or twelve miles off and then laying wagers which pigeon shall come soonest home to her house. All the winter within doors, some few playing at cheese, but most drinking their time away. Women live very slavishly there, and it seems in the Emperor's court no room hath above two or three windows, and those the greatest not a yard wide or high, for warmth in winter time; and that the general cure for all diseases there is their sweating houses, or people that are poor they get into their ovens, being heated, and there lie. Little learning among things of any sort. Not a man that speaks Latin, unless the Secretary of State by chance.

This day old Hardwicke came and redeemed a watch he had left with me in pawne for 40*s*. seven years ago, and I let him have it.

19th. Up, my wife and I having a little anger about her woman already, she thinking that I take too much care of her at table to mind her (my wife) of cutting for her; but it soon over, and so up and with Sir W. Batten and Sir W. Pen to St. James's, and there did our business with the Duke.

21st. To Povy's to dinner, where great and good company; among others Sir John Skeffington whom I knew at Magdalen College, a fellow-commoner, my fellow-pupil, but one with whom I had no great acquaintance, he being then, God knows, much above me.

---

[1] Afterwards Queen Mary II., then aged two years and four months.

23rd. In the morning comes Mr. Fuller, that was the wit of Cambridge in my time, and staid all the morning with me discoursing, and his business to get a man discharged, which I did do for him. Dined with little heart at noon. In the afternoon against my will to the office, where Sir G. Carteret and we met about an order of the Council for the hiring him a house, giving him £1,000 fine, and £70 per annum for it. Here Sir J. Minnes took occasion in the most childish and most unbeseeming manner to reproach us all, but most himself, that he was not valued as Comptroller among us, nor did anything but only set his hand to paper, which is but too true; and every body had a palace, and he no house to lie in, and wished he had but as much to build him a house with as we have laid out in carved worke. It was to no end to oppose, but all bore it, and after laughed at him for it.

29th. Newes come of our beating the Dutch at Guinny quite out of all their castles almost, which will make them quite mad here at home, sure. Nay they say that we have beat them out of the New Netherlands[1] too; so that we have been doing them mischief for a great while in several parts of the world, without publique knowledge or reason. Coming home to-night I did go to examine my wife's house accounts, and finding things that seemed somewhat doubtful I was angry, though she did make it pretty plain; but confessed that when she do misse a sum she do add something to other things to make it, and upon my being very angry she do protest she will here lay up something for herself to buy her a necklace with, which madded me and do still trouble me, for I fear she will forget by degrees the way of living cheap and under sense of want.

30th. Up, and all day both morning and afternoon at my accounts, it being a great month both for profit and layings out, the last being £89 for kitchen and clothes for myself and wife, and a few extraordinaries for the house; and my profits, besides salary, £239; so that this weeke my balance come to £1,203, for which the Lord's name be praised!

October 2nd. (Lord's Day.) I walked through the City, putting in at several churches. And so over Moorefields, and thence to Clerkenwell church; and there, as I wished, sat next pew to the fair Butler, who indeed is a most perfect beauty still, and one I do very much admire myself for my choice of her for a beauty, she having the best lower part of her face that ever I saw all days

[1] Afterwards renamed New York.

of my life. After church I walked to my Lady Sandwich's, and
dined with her. So away back to Clerkenwell Church, thinking
to have got sight of la belle Boteler again, but failed, and so after
church walked all over the fields home, and there my wife was
angry with me for not coming home, and for gadding abroad to
look after beauties, she told me plainly; so I made all peace, and to
supper. This evening came Mrs. Lane (now Martin) with her
husband to desire my helpe about a place for him.

3rd. Up with Sir J. Minnes by coach to St. James's, and there
all the newes now of very hot preparations for the Dutch: and
being with the Duke, he told us he was resolved to make a tripp
himself, and that Sir W. Pen should go in the same ship with him.
Which honour, God forgive me! I could grudge him, for his
knavery and dissimulation, though I do not envy much the having
the same place myself. Talke also of great haste in the getting out
another fleete, and building some ships; and now it is likely we
have put one another by each other's dalliance past a retreate.
Thence with our heads full of business we broke up, and I to my
barber's, and there only saw Jane and stroked her under the chin,
and away to the Exchange, and thence home to dinner. But
meeting Bagwell's wife at the office before I went home I took her
into the office and there kissed her. She rebuked me for doing it,
saying that did I do so much to many bodies else it would be a
stain to me. But I do not see but she takes it well enough.

5th. Comes Mr. Cocker[1] to see me, and I discoursed with him
about his writing and ability of sight, and how I shall do to get
some glasse or other to helpe my eyes by candlelight; and he tells
me he will bring me the helps he hath within a day or two, and shew
me what he do. Thence to the Musique-meeting at the Post-
office, where I was once before. And thither anon come all the
Gresham College, and a great deal of noble company: and the new
instrument was brought called the Arched Viall. But after three
hours' stay it could not be fixed in tune; and so they were fain
to go to some other musique of instruments, which I am grown
quite out of love with, and so I home.

10th. Sir W. Batten do raile against Mr. Turner and his
wife, telling me he is a false fellow, and his wife a false woman,
and has rotten teeth and false, set in with wire; and as I know they
are so, so I am glad he finds it so. This day, by the blessing of
God, my wife and I have been married nine years: but my head

---

[1] Edward Cocker, the great writing-master.

being full of business, I did not think of it to keep it in any extraordinary manner. But bless God for our long lives and loves and health together, which the same God long continue, I wish from my very heart!

13th. I met with Mr. White,[1] Cromwell's chaplin that was, and had a great deale of discourse with him. Among others he tells me that Richard is, and hath long been, in France, and is now going into Italy. He hath been in some straits at the beginning, but relieved by his friends. That he goes by another name, but do not disguise himself, nor deny himself to any man that challenges him. He tells me for certain that offers had been made to the old man of marriage between the King and his daughter, to have obliged him, but he would not. He thinks (with me) that it never was in his power to bring in the King with the consent of any of his officers about him; and that he scorned to bring him in as Monk did, to secure himself and deliver every body else.

24th. To a Committee at White Hall of Tangier, where I had the good lucke to speak something to very good purpose about the Mole at Tangier, which was well received even by Sir J. Lawson and Mr. Cholmely, the undertakers, against whose interest I spoke; that I believe I shall be valued for it. Thence into the galleries to talk with my Lord Sandwich; among other things about the Prince's [2] writing up to tell us of the danger he and his fleete lie in at Portsmouth of receiving affronts from the Dutch; which my Lord said he would never have done, had he lain there with one ship alone: nor is there any great reason for it, because of the sands. However the fleete will be ordered to go and lay themselves up at the Cowes. Much beneath the prowesse of the Prince, I think, and the honour of the nation, at the first to be found to secure themselves.

25th. To the Committee of the Fishery, and there did make my report of the late public collections for the Fishery, much to the satisfaction of the Committee, and I think much to my reputation, for good notice was taken of it and much it was commended. So home, in my way taking care of a piece of plate for Mr. Christopher Pett, against the launching of his new great ship to-morrow at Woolwich, which I singly did move to his Royall Highness, and did obtain it for him, to the value of twenty pieces.

[1] It is of Jeremiah White that the story is told of his so far presuming upon his popularity in Cromwell's household as to aspire to the hand of one of Cromwell's daughters. Being caught on his knees before her, he had the wit to say that he was seeking her help in his suit to one of her servants: whereupon Cromwell, equally resourceful, sent for the servant and another chaplain, and married them on the spot.   [2] Prince Rupert.

And he, under his hand, do acknowledge to me that he did never receive so great a kindness from any man in the world as from me herein.

30th. (Lord's Day.) Up, and this morning put on my new, fine, coloured cloth suit, with my cloake lined with plush, which is a dear noble suit, costing me about £17. To church, and then home to dinner, and after dinner to a little musique with my boy; and so to church with my wife, and so home and with her all the evening reading, and at musique with my boy with great pleasure. And so to supper, prayers, and to bed.

November 3rd. Sir W. Pen came to take his leave of me, being to-morrow, which is very sudden to us, to go on board, to lie on board, but I think will come ashore again before the ship, the Charles, can go away. So home to supper and to bed. This night Sir W. Batten did among other things tell me strange newes, which troubles me, that my Lord Sandwich will be sent Governor to Tangier; which in some respects, indeed, I should be glad of, for the good of the place and the safety of his person, but I think his honour will suffer, and it may be his interest fail by his distance.

4th. Up and to St. James's, where I find Mr. Coventry full of business packing up for his going to sea with the Duke. Walked with him, talking about the management of our office. He tells me the weight of dispatch will lie chiefly on me, and told me freely his mind touching Sir W. Batten and Sir J. Minnes, the latter of whom, he most aptly said, was like a lapwing; that all he did was to keepe a flutter, to keepe others from the nest that they would find.

5th. Up and to the office, where all the morning. At noon to the 'Change, and thence home to dinner; and so with my wife to the Duke's house to a play, "Macbeth," a pretty good play, but admirably acted. Thence home, the coach being forced to go round by London Wall home because of the bonefires, the day being mightily observed in the City. To my office late at business, and then home to supper and to bed.

7th. Up and with Sir W. Batten to White Hall, where mighty thrusting about the Duke now upon his going. We were with him long. He advised us to follow our business close, and to be directed in his absence by the Committee of the Council for the Navy. To my barber's, but Jane not being in the way I to my Lady Sandwich's, and there met my wife and dined. But I find that I dine as well myself, that is as neatly, and my meat as good and well-dressed, as my good Lady do in the absence of my Lord.

9th. To White Hall, and there the King being in his Cabinet Council I was called in, and demanded by the King himself many questions, to which I did give him full answers. There were at this Council my Lord Chancellor, Archbishop of Canterbury, Lord Treasurer, the two Secretarys, and Sir G. Carteret. Not a little contented at this chance of being made known to these persons, and called often by my name by the King. The Duke of York is this day gone away to Portsmouth.

13th. (Lord's Day.) This morning to church, where mighty sport to hear our clerke sing out of tune, though his master sits by him that begins and keeps the tune aloud for the parish. Dined at home very well, and spent all the afternoon with my wife within doors and getting a speech out of Hamlett, "To bee or not to bee," without book. In the evening to sing psalms, and in come Mr. Hill to see me; and then he and I and the boy finely to sing, and so anon broke up after much pleasure. He gone I to supper, and so prayers and to bed.

18th. This day I had a letter from Mr. Coventry that tells me that my Lord Brunkard[1] is to be one of our Commissioners, of which I am very glad, if any more must be.

21st. To the Lords at White Hall, where they do single me out to speak to and to hear, much to my content, and received their commands. This day for certain newes is come that Teddiman[2] hath brought in eighteen or twenty Dutchmen, merchants, their Bourdeaux fleete, and two men of warr to Portsmouth. And I had letters this afternoon that three are brought into the Downes and Dover, so that the warr is begun: God give a good end to it!

25th. Up and at my office all the morning to prepare an account of the charge we have been put to extraordinary by the Dutch already, and I have brought it to appear £852,700; but God knows this is only a scare to the Parliament, to make them give the more money. In the evening took my wife out by coach, leaving her at Unthanke's while I to Westminster Hall, where I hear that Mrs. Lane and her husband live a sad life together, and he is gone to be a paymaster to a company to Portsmouth to serve at sea. Thence I home, calling my wife, and at Sir W. Batten's hear that the House have given the King £2,500,000 to be paid for this warr, only for

---

[1] William, 2nd Viscount Brouncker, first President of the Royal Society.
[2] Captain Sir Thomas Teddiman had been appointed Rear-Admiral of Lord Sandwich's squadron.

the Navy, in three years' time; which is a joyfull thing to all the King's party I see, but was much opposed that it should be so much.

28th. To Westminster, and there to Jervas's and was a little while with Jane, and so to London by coach and to the Coffeehouse. Home to dinner, then come Dr. Clerke to speak with me about sick and wounded men, wherein he is like to be concerned.

30th. Up, and with Sir W. Batten and Sir J. Minnes to the Committee of the Lords, and there did our business; but, Lord! what a sorry dispatch these great persons give to business.

December 2nd. After dinner with my wife and Mercer to the Duke's House, and there saw "The Rivalls,"[1] which I had seen before; but the play not good, nor anything but the good actings of Betterton and his wife and Harris.

3rd. The Duke of Yorke expected to-night with great joy from Portsmouth, after his having been abroad at sea three or four days with the fleete; and the Dutch are all drawn into their harbours. But it seems like a victory: and a matter of some reputation to us it is, and blemish to them, but in no degree like what it is esteemed at, the weather requiring them to do so.

10th. At the office all the morning, where comes my Lord Brunkard with his patent in his hand; a modest civil person he seems to be, but wholly ignorant in the business of the Navy as possible; but I hope to make a friend of him, being a worthy man.

11th. (Lord's Day.) I to the French church, where much pleased with the three sisters of the parson, very handsome, especially in their noses, and sing prettily. I heard a good sermon of the old man touching duty to parents. Here was Sir Samuel Morland[2] and his lady very fine, with two footmen in new liverys (the church taking much notice of them), and going into their coach after sermon with great gazeing.

14th. Up, and after a while at the office, I abroad in several places, among others to my bookseller's, and there spoke for several books against New Year's Day, I resolving to lay out about £7 or £8, God having given me some profit (extraordinary of late; and bespoke also some plate, spoons, and forks. I pray God keep me from too great expenses. To-night spoke for some fruit for the

---

[1] By Sir William Davenant.
[2] Samuel Morland had been Pepys' tutor at Magdalene College. He was sent by Cromwell to protest to the Duke of Savoy against the massacre of the Protestants in Piedmont. He played a double game, however, and his services towards the King in exile brought him a baronetcy at the Restoration. He was a mathematician and a distinguished inventor, being perhaps the first to propose the use of steam as a prime mover in engines and vessels.

country for my father against Christmas, and where should I do it but at the pretty woman's that used to stand at the doore in Fanchurch Streete, I having a mind to know her.

15th. This night I begun to burn wax candles in my closett at the office, to try the charge, and to see whether the smoke offends like that of tallow candles.

17th. Up and to the office, where we sat all the morning. At noon I to the 'Change, and there, among others, had my first meeting with Mr. L'Estrange,[1] who hath endeavoured several times to speak with me. It is to get now and then some newes of me, which I shall, as I see cause, give him. He is a man of fine conversation, I think, but I am sure most courtly and full of compliments. Thence home to dinner, and then come the looking-glass man to set up the looking-glass I bought yesterday in my dining-room, and very handsome it is. Mighty talke there is of this Comet that is seen a'nights: and the King and Queene did sit up last night to see it, and did, it seems. And to-night I thought to have done so too, but it is cloudy, and so no stars appear. But I will endeavour it.

19th. Going to bed betimes last night we waked betimes, and from our people's being forced to take the key to go out to light a candle, I was very angry and begun to find fault with my wife for not commanding her servants as she ought. Thereupon she giving me some cross answer I did strike her over her left eye such a blow as the poor wretch did cry out and was in great pain, but yet her spirit was such as to endeavour to bite and scratch me. But I coying with her made her leave crying, and sent for butter and parsley, and friends presently one with another, and I up, vexed at my heart to think what I had done, for she was forced to lay a poultice or something to her eye all day, and is black, and the people of the house observed it. But I was forced to rise, and up and with Sir J. Minnes to White Hall, and there we waited on the Duke. Thence to the 'Change and there walked up and down, and then home. After going up to my wife (whose eye is very bad, but she is in very good temper to me), and after dinner, I to the 'Change, and there found Bagwell's wife waiting for me and took her away, and to an alehouse, and there made I much of her. Then away and I to the office. Thence to supper with my wife, very pleasant, and then a little to my office and to bed.

---

[1] Sir Roger L'Estrange, at this time proprietor of the *Public Intelligencer*, published twice a week. This paper was superseded a month later by the *London Gazette*.

20th.   Up and walked to Deptford, where after doing something at the yard I walked, without being observed, with Bagwell home to his house, and there was very kindly used, and the poor people did get a dinner for me in their fashion, of which I also eat very well.   After dinner I found occasion of sending him abroad, and then alone *avec elle.*   By and by he coming back again I took leave and walked home.

22nd.   To the 'Change; and there, among the merchants, I hear fully the news of our being beaten to dirt at Guinny by De Ruyter with his fleete; it being most wholly to the utter ruine of our Royall Company, and reproach and shame to the whole nation.   After dinner tooke boat down to Redriffe; and just in time within two minutes, and saw the new vessel of Sir William Petty's launched, the King and Duke being there.   It swims and looks finely, and I believe will do well.

24th.   This evening I being informed did look and saw the Comet which is now, whether worn away or no I know not, but appears not with a tail, but only is larger and duller than any other star, and is come to rise betimes and to make a great arch.

26th.   To Sir W. Batten's, where Mr. Coventry and all our families here, women and all, and Sir R. Ford and his, and a great feast and good discourse and merry.   There all the afternoon and evening till late; so home to bed, where my people and wife innocently at cards very merry, and I to bed, leaving them to their sport and blindman's buff.[1]

28th.   Abroad with Sir W. Batten to the Council Chamber, where it was strange methought to hear so poor discourses among the Lords themselves, and most of all to see how a little empty matter delivered gravely by Sir W. Pen was taken mighty well, though nothing in the earth to the purpose.   But clothes, I perceive more and more every day, is a great matter.   Thence home to dinner.   After dinner abroad, and among other things visited my Lady Sandwich, and was there with her and the young ladies playing at cards till night.   Then home and to my office late, then home to bed, leaving my wife and people up to more sports, but without any great satisfaction to myself therein.

31st.   After dinner to my accounts of the whole yeare, and was at it till past twelve at night, it being bitter cold.   But yet I was well satisfied with my worke, and above all to find myself, by the great blessing of God, worth £1,349, for which the Lord make

---

[1] Pepys had been ashamed to take his wife to the party owing to her black eye.

me for ever thankful to his holy name for it! Thence home to eat a little, and so to bed. Soon as ever the clock struck one I kissed my wife in the kitchen by the fireside, wishing her a merry new yeare, observing that I believe I was the first proper wisher of it this year, for I did it as soon as ever the clock struck one.

So ends the old yeare, I bless God, with great joy to me. I bless God I never have been in so good plight as to my health in so very cold weather as this is, nor indeed in any hot weather, these ten years as I am at this day and have been these four or five months. But I am at a great losse to know whether it be my hare's foote,[1] or taking every morning of a pill of turpentine, or my having left off the wearing of a gowne. My family is: my wife, in good health, and happy with her; her woman Mercer, a pretty, modest, quiett mayde; her chamber-mayde Besse, her cook mayde Jane, the little girl Susan, and my boy Tom Edwards, and a pretty and loving quiett family I have as any man in England. My credit in the world and my office grows daily, and I am in good esteeme with everybody, I think.

[1] A charm against the colic. See *post*, January 20.

"I KISSED MY WIFE IN THE KITCHEN"

SIXTH YEAR

1665

January 2nd. Being forced to pay a great deale of money away
in boxes (that is, basins at White Hall), I to my barber's, Gervas,
and there had a little opportunity of speaking with my Jane alone.
Thence to the Swan, and there did sport a good while with Herbert's young kinswoman. Then to the Hall, and there with Mrs.
Martin, and to her lodgings which she has now taken to lie in, in
Bow Streete, pitiful poor things, yet she thinks them pretty,
and so they are for her condition I believe good enough. Having
spent 2*s.* in wine and cake upon her, I away sick of her impudence,
and by coach to my Lord Brunker's, by appointment, in the Piazza
in Covent-Guarding; where I occasioned much mirth with a ballet
I brought with me, made from the seamen at sea to their ladies in
town.[1] Here a most noble French dinner and banquet, the best I
have seen this many a day, and good discourse. Thence to the
office, and then very late home; where thinking to be merry was
vexed with my wife's having looked out a letter in Sir Philip Sidney about jealousy for me to read, which she industriously and
maliciously caused me to do; and the truth is my conscience told
me it was most proper for me, and therefore was touched at it,
but tooke no notice of it, but read it out most frankly. But it
stucke in my stomach. However, to cards with my wife a good
while, and then to bed.

9th. Up and walked to White Hall, it being a brave frost, and I
in perfect good health, blessed be God! In my way saw a woman
that broke her thigh, in her heels slipping up upon the frosty
streete. To the Duke, and there did our usual worke. Here I
saw the Royal Society bring their new book, wherein is nobly
writ their charter and laws, and comes to be signed by the Duke
as a Fellow; and all the Fellows' hands are to be entered there,
and lie as a monument; and the King hath put his with the word
Founder. Thence I to Westminster, to my barber's, and found

---

[1] Prior to the publication of this passage it had been held that Lord Dorset's famous ballad "To
all you ladies now at land" was written on the eve of the great victory of June 3 of this year.

236

occasion to see Jane, and then to the Swan to Herbert's girl, and lost time a little with her; and so took coach to my Lord Crew's and dined with him, who receives me with the greatest respect that could be; telling me that he do much doubt of the successe of this warr with Holland, we going about it, he doubts, by the instigation of persons that do not enough apprehend the consequences of the danger of it, and therein I do think with him.

11th. This night when I come home I was much troubled to hear my poor canary bird, that I have kept these three or four years, is dead.

13th. Up betimes and walked to my Lord Bellasses's [1] lodgings in Lincolne's Inne Fieldes, and there he received and discoursed with me in the most respectful manner that could be, telling me what a character of my judgment and care and love to Tangier he had received of me, that he desired my advice and my constant correspondence, which he much values; and in my courtship, in which, though I understand his designe very well, and that it is only a piece of courtship, yet it is a comfort to me that I am become so considerable as to have him need to say that to me, which, if I did not do something in the world, would never have been.

14th. With my wife to the King's house, there to see "Vulpone," [2] a most excellent play, the best I think I ever saw, and well acted. So with Sir W. Pen home in his coach, and then to the office. So home to supper and bed, resolving by the grace of God from this day to fall hard to my business again, after some weeke or fortnight's neglect.

15th. (Lord's Day.) Up, and after a little at my office to prepare a fresh draught of my vows for the next yeare, I to church, where a most insipid young coxcomb preached. Then home to dinner. At four o'clock with Sir W. Pen in his coach to my Lord Chancellor's, where by and by Mr. Coventry, Sir W. Pen, Sir J. Lawson, Sir G. Ascue,[3] and myself were called in to the King, there being several of the Privy Council, and my Lord Chancellor lying at length upon a couch (of the goute I suppose).

19th. This day was buried (but I could not be there) my cozen Percivall Angier; and yesterday I received the newes that Dr. Tom Pepys is dead, at Impington, for which I am but little

---

[1] John, Lord Belasyse, Governor of Tangier.   [2] Ben Jonson's *Volpone.*
[3] Admiral Sir George Ayscue. He was knighted by King Charles I., but continued to serve in the Commonwealth and the Restoration periods.

sorry, not only because he would have been troublesome to us, but a shame to his family and profession; he was such a coxcomb.

20th. With my wife to the New Exchange. So homeward in my way buying a hare and taking it home; which arose upon my discourse to-day with Mr. Batten in Westminster Hall, who showed me my mistake that my hare's foote hath not the joynt to it; and assures me he never had his cholique since he carried it about him: and it is a strange thing how fancy works, for I no sooner almost handled his foote but whereas I was in some pain yesterday and tother day and in fear of more to-day, I became very well, and so continue. At home to my office a while, and so to supper, read, and to cards, and to bed.

23rd. Up, and with Sir W. Batten and Sir W. Pen to the Duke and there did our usual business. And here I met the great newes confirmed by the Duke's own relation, by a letter from Captain Allen. First, of our own loss of two ships, the Phœnix and Nonesuch, in the Bay of Gibraltar: then of Captain Allen and his seven ships with him, in the Bay of Cales, or thereabouts, fighting with the 34 Dutch Smyrna fleete, sinking the King Salamon, a ship worth a £150,000 or more, and another, and taking of three merchant-ships. Two of our ships were disabled by the Dutch unfortunately falling against their will against them. The Dutch men-of-war did little service. The Spaniards on shore at Cales did stand laughing at the Dutch to see them run away and flee to the shore, 34 or thereabouts, against eight Englishmen at most. I do purpose to get the whole relation, if I live, of Captain Allen himself. Thence to Jervas's, my mind, God forgive me, running too much after some folly, but *elle* not being within I away by coach to the 'Change, and thence home to dinner. And finding Mrs. Bagwell waiting at the office after dinner, away she and I to a cabaret where she and I have eat before. So to my office a little and to Jervas's again, thinking *avoir rencontrais* Jane, *mais elle n'etait pas dedans.* So I back again and to my office, where I did with great content *ferais* a vow to mind my business, and *laisser aller les femmes* for a month, and am with all my heart glad to find myself able to come to so good a resolution, that thereby I may follow my business which, and my honour, thereby lies a bleeding. So home to supper and to bed.

24th. To the office, where all the afternoon and at night till very late, and then home to supper and bed, having a great cold, got on Sunday last by sitting too long with my head bare for Mercer to comb my hair and wash my eares.

30th. At night at my office, being late at it, comes Mercer to me, to tell me that my wife was in bed and desired me to come home; for they hear, and have night after night lately heard, noises over their head upon the leads. Now it is strange to think how, knowing that I have a great sum of money in my house, this puts me into a most mighty affright, that for more than two hours I could not almost tell what to do or say, but feared this and that, and remembered that this evening I saw a woman and two men stand suspiciously in the entry in the darke. I calling to them, they made me only this answer: the woman said that the men came to see her. But who she was I could not tell. The truth is my house is mighty dangerous, having so many ways to be come to; and at my windows over the stairs to see who goes up and down; but if I escape to-night I will remedy it. God preserve us this night safe! So at almost two o'clock I home to my house and in great fear to bed, thinking every running of a mouse really a thiefe; and so to sleep very brokenly all night long, and found all safe in the morning.

February 3rd. Up and walked with my boy (whom, because of my wife's making him idle, I dare not leave at home). Walked first to Salsbury court, to Mrs. Turner; she was dressing herself by the fire in her chamber, and there took occasion to show me her leg, which indeed is the finest I ever saw, and she not a little proud of it. Thence to my bookseller's. My bill for the rebinding of some old books to make them suit with my study cost me, besides other new books in the same bill, £3; but it will be very handsome. At the 'Change did several businesses. Thence, being invited, to my uncle Wight's, where the Wights all dined; and, among the others, pretty Mrs. Margaret, who indeed is a very pretty lady; and though by my vowe it costs me 12*d.* a kiss after the first, yet I did adventure upon a couple. So home, and then took coach and to visit my Lady Sandwich, where she discoursed largely to me her opinion of a match, if it could be thought fit by my Lord, for my Lady Jemimah with Sir G. Carteret's eldest son; but I doubt he hath yet no settled estate in land. But I will inform myself, and give her my opinion.

4th. To my office, and there all the morning. At noon to dinner to my Lord Belasses, where he told us a very handsome passage of the King's sending him his message about holding out the town of Newarke, of which he was then governor for the King. This message he sent in a slugg-bullet, being writ in cypher, and wrapped up in lead and swallowed. So the messenger come to my Lord and told him he had a message from the King but it was yet in his belly; so they did give him some physique, and out it come. This was a month before the King's flying to the Scotts; and therein he told him that at such a day, being the 3d or 6th of May, he should hear of his being come to the Scotts; and at the just day he did come to the Scotts. He told us another odd passage: how the King having newly put out Prince Rupert of his generallshipp, upon some miscarriage at Bristoll, the great officers of the King's army mutinyed, and come in that manner with swords drawn into the market-place of the towne where the King was; which the King hearing, says, "I must to horse." And there himself personally, when every body expected they should have been opposed, the King come, and cried to the head of the mutineers, which was Prince Rupert, "Nephew, I command you to be gone." So the Prince, in all his fury and discontent, withdrew, and his company scattered; which they say was the greatest piece of mutiny in the world.

9th. Sir William Petty tells me that Mr. Barlow[1] is dead; for which, God knows my heart, I could be as sorry as is possible for one to be for a stranger, by whose death he gets £100 per annum, he being a worthy, honest man; but after having considered that when I come to consider the providence of God by this means unexpectedly to give me £100 a year more in my estate, I have cause to bless God, and do it from the bottom of my heart.

14th. (St. Valentine.) This morning comes betimes Dicke Pen,[2] to be my wife's Valentine, and come to our bedside. By the same token I had him brought to my side, thinking to have made him kiss me; but he perceived me and would not, so went to his Valentine: a notable, stout, witty boy. I up about business, and opening the door, there was Bagwell's wife, with whom I talked afterwards, and she had the confidence to say she came with a hope to be time enough to be my Valentine; and so indeed she did, but my oath preserved me from loosing any time with her. And so I and my boy abroad by coach to Westminster, where did two or three businesses, and then home to the 'Change and did much business there.

---

[1] Pepys' predecessor as Clerk of the Acts, to whom he paid part of the salary.
[2] Second son of Sir William. He died young.

15th. With Creed to Gresham College, where I had been by Mr. Povy the last week proposed to be admitted a member; and was this day admitted by signing a book and being taken by the hand by the President, my Lord Brunkard, and some words of admittance said to me. But it is a most acceptable thing to hear their discourse, and see their experiments; which were this day upon the nature of fire. After this being done, they to the Crowne Taverne behind the 'Change, and there my Lord and most of the company to a club supper. Here excellent discourse till ten at night, and then home.

19th. At supper, hearing by accident of my mayds letting in a rogueing Scotch woman to helpe them to washe and scoure in our house, I fell mightily out, and made my wife, to the disturbance of the house and neighbours, to beat our little girle, and then we shut her down into the cellar, and there she lay all night.

20th. At the office I found Bagwell's wife, whom I directed to go home, and I would do her business, which was to write a letter to my Lord Sandwich for her husband's advance into a better ship as there should be occasion; which I did. My wife tells me that she hath hired a chamber mayde, one of the prettiest maydes that ever she saw in her life, and that she is really jealous of me for her, but hath ventured to hire her from month to month; but I think she means merrily.

21st. My wife busy in going with her woman to a hot-house to bathe herself, after her long being within doors in the dirt, so that she now pretends to a resolution of being hereafter very clean. How long it will hold I can guess. I dined with Sir W. Batten and my Lady, they being now a'days very fond of me. After office to Lincolne's Inne Fields, and there I with my Lady Sandwich (good lady) talking of innocent discourse of good house-wifery and husbands for her daughters, and the luxury and loose-ness of the times: what mad freaks the Mayds of Honour at Court have; that one or the Duchesse's mayds the other day dressed herself like an orange wench, and went up and down and cried oranges, till falling down, or by such accident, though in the even-ing, her fine shoes were discerned, and she put to a great deale of shame; that such as these tricks being ordinary, and worse among them, thereby few will venture upon them for wives. This day my Lord Sandwich writ me word from the Downes that he is like to be in towne this week.

22nd. Lay last night alone, my wife after her bathinge lying alone in another bed. So cold all night. Up and to the office, where busy all the morning.

23rd. This day, by the blessing of Almighty God, I have lived thirty-two years in the world, and am in the best degree of health at this minute that I have been almost in my life time, and at this time in the best condition of estate that ever I was in, the Lord make me thankfull. At noon to the 'Change, where I hear the most horrid and astonishing newes that ever was yet told in my memory, that De Ruyter with his fleete in Guinny hath proceeded to the taking of whatever we have, forts, goods, ships, and men, and tied our men back to back and thrown them all into the sea, even women and children also. This a Swede or Hamburgher is come into the River and tells that he saw the thing done.

25th. At noon to the 'Change; where just before I come the Swede that had told the King and the Duke so boldly this great lie was whipt round the 'Change: he confessing it a lie, and that he did it in hopes to get something. It is said the Judges, upon demand, did give it their opinion that the law would judge him to be whipt, to lose his eares, or to have his nose slit: but I do not hear that anything more is to be done to him. They say he is delivered over to the Dutch Embassador to do what he pleased with him. At night late home, and to clean myself with warm water, (my wife will have me, because she do herself), and so to bed.

27th. To a Committee of the Council to discourse concerning pressing of men[1] : but, Lord! how they meet; never sit down: one comes, now another goes, then comes another; one complaining that nothing is done, another swearing that he hath been there these two hours and nobody come. At last it come to this, my Lord Annesly, says he, "I think we must be forced to get the King to come to every committee; for I do not see that we do any thing at any time but when he is here." And I believe he said the truth: and very constant he is at the council table on council-days, which his predecessors it seems very rarely did; but thus I perceive the greatest affair in the world at this day is likely to be managed by us.

By coach to Sir Philip Warwicke's;[2] and there he did contract with me a kind of friendship and freedom of communication,

---

[1] Conditions of service in the Navy were in all respects so poor that recruits had to be forcibly collected by the methods of the press-gang. See June 4, *ante.*
[2] Secretary to the Treasurer, formerly secretary to King Charles I.

wherein he assures me to make me understand the whole business of the Treasurer's business of the Navy, that I shall know as well as Sir G. Carteret what money he hath; and will needs have me come to him sometimes, or he meet me, to discourse of things tending to the serving the King: and I am mighty proud and happy in becoming so known to such a man, and I hope shall pursue it. Thence back home to the office a little tired and out of order, and then to supper and to bed.

March 2nd. Begun this day to rise betimes before six o'clock, and going down to call my people, found Besse and the girle with their clothes on, lying within their bedding upon the ground close by the fireside, and a candle burning all night, pretending they would rise to scoure. This vexed me, but Besse is going and so she will not trouble me long.

5th. (Lord's Day.) To my Lord Sandwich's and dined with my Lord, it being the first time he hath dined at home since his coming from sea: and a pretty odd demand it was of my Lord to my Lady before me: "How do you, sweetheart? How have you done all this week?" himself taking notice of it to me that he had hardly seen her the week before. At dinner he did use me with the greatest solemnity in the world, in carving for me and nobody else, and calling often to my Lady to cut for me, and all the respect possible.

6th. To St. James's, and there did our business with the Duke. Great preparations for his speedy return to sea. So home, and there find our new chamber-mayde, Mary, come, which instead of handsome, as my wife spoke and still seems to reckon, is a very ordinary wench, I think, and therein was mightily disappointed.

9th. To Paule's Schoole, where I visited Mr. Crumlum at his house; and, Lord! to see how ridiculous a conceited pedagogue he is, though a learned man, he being so dogmaticall in all he do and says. But among other discourse, we fell to the old discourse of Paule's Schoole; and he did, upon my declaring my value of it, give me one of Lilly's grammars of a very old impression, as it was in the Catholique times, which I shall much set by. And so, after some small discourse, away and called upon my wife at a linen draper's shop buying linen, and so home and to my office, where late, and home to supper and to bed. This night my wife had a new suit of flowered ash-coloured silke, very noble.

13th. This day my wife begun to wear light-coloured locks, quite white almost, which, though it makes her look very pretty, yet not being natural vexes me, that I will not have her wear them.

17th. To the Committee of Tangier. A very great Committee, the Lords Albemarle, Sandwich, Barkely, Fitzharding, Peterborough, Ashley, Sir Thos. Ingram, Sir G. Carteret and others. The whole business was the stating of Povy's accounts, of whom to say no more, never could man say worse himself nor have worse said of him than was by the company to his face; I mean, as to his folly, and very reflecting words to his honesty. Broke up with the most open shame to him, and high words to him of disgrace that they would not trust him with any more money till he had given an account of this. Then he took occasion to desire me to step aside, and he and I by water to London together. In the way of his owne accord he proposed to me that he would surrender his place of Treasurer to me to have half the profit. The thing is new to me; but the more I think the more I like it, and do put him upon getting it done by the Duke. Whether it takes or no I care not, but I think at present it may have some convenience in it.

18th. Povy and Creed and I to do some business upon Povy's accounts all the afternoon till late at night, where, God help him! never man was so confounded, and all his people about him, in this world as he and his are. After we had done something to the purpose we broke up, and Povy acquainted me before Creed what he had done in speaking to the Duke and others about his making me Treasurer, and has carried it a great way, so as I think it cannot well be set back.

19th. (Lord's Day.) Mr. Povy sent his coach for me betimes, and I to him. So we went to Creed's new lodging in the Mewes,[1] and there we found Creed with his parrot upon his shoulder, which struck Mr. Povy coming by, just by the eye, very deep, which, had it hit his eye, had put it out. I to Mr. Coventry, and there had his most friendly and ingenuous advice, advising me not to decline the thing, it being that that will bring me to be known to great persons, while now I am buried among three or four of us, says he, in the Navy. To my Lord Sandwich's to dinner, and after dinner to Mr. Povy's, who hath been with the Duke of Yorke, and, by the mediation of Mr. Coventry, the Duke told him that the business shall go on. Being very glad of this news, Mr. Povy and I in his coach to Hyde Parke, being the first day of the tour

[1] On the site of the present National Gallery.

"WITH HIS PARROT . . . WHICH STRUCK MR. POVY COMING BY"

there. Where many brave ladies; among others, Castlemayne lay impudently upon her back in her coach asleep, with her mouth open.

20th. Povy and I to St. James's, where the Duke did direct Secretary Bennet to declare his mind to the Tangier Committee, that he approves of me for Treasurer; and with a character of me to be a man whose industry and discretion he would trust soon as any man's in England. So to White Hall to the Committee of Tangier, where there were present my Lord of Albemarle, my Lord Peterborough, Sandwich, Barkeley, FitzHarding, Secretary Bennet, Sir Thomas Ingram, Sir John Lawson, Povy and I. Where, after other business, Povy did declare his business very handsomely; that he was sorry he had been so unhappy in his accounts as not to give their Lordships the satisfaction he intended, and that he was sure his accounts are right, and continues to submit them to examination, and is ready to lay down in ready money the fault of his account; and that for the future, that the work might be better done and with more quiet to him, he desired, by approbation of the Duke, he might resign his place to Mr. Pepys. Whereupon, Secretary Bennet did deliver the Duke's command, which was received with great content and allowance beyond expectation; the Secretary repeating also the Duke's character of me. And there I received their constitution under all their hands presently; so that I am already confirmed their Treasurer, and put into a condition of striking of tallys;[1] and all without one harsh word or word of dislike, but quite the contrary; which is a good fortune beyond all imagination. Here we rose, and Povy and Creed and I, all full of joy, thence to dinner.

21st. Up, and my taylor coming to me, did consult all my wardrobe how to order my clothes against next summer. To the office, where busy all the morning. Home and there found a couple of state cups, very large, coming, I suppose, each to about £6 a piece, from Burrows the slopseller.

22nd. To Mr. Coventry, whose profession of love and esteem for me to myself was so large and free that I never could expect or wish for more, nor could have it from any man in England, that I should value it more.

23rd. Up and to my Lord Sandwich, who follows the Duke this day by water down to the Hope,[2] where "The Prince" lies.

---

[1] Pieces of wood, notched or scored with the record of any payment made; they were then split in two, and each party to the account kept one half.
[2] A reach of the Thames, near Tilbury.

He received me, busy as he was, with mighty kindness and joy at my promotions, telling me most largely how the Duke hath expressed on all occasions his good opinion of my service and love for me. I paid my thanks and acknowledgement to him, and so back home, where at the office all the morning.

26th. (Lord's Day and Easter Day.) Up (and with my wife, who has not been at church a month or two) to church. At noon home to dinner, my wife and I (Mercer staying to the Sacrament) alone. This is the day seven years which, by the blessing of God, I have survived of my being cut of the stone, and am now in very perfect good health and have long been; and though the last winter hath been as hard a winter as any have been these many years, yet I never was better in my life, nor have not, these ten years, gone colder in the summer than I have done all this winter, wearing only a doublet and a waistcoate cut open on the back; abroad a cloake, and within doors a coate I slipped on. Now I am at a losse to know whether it be my hare's foot which is my preservative, for I never had a fit of the collique since I wore it, or whether it be my taking of a pill of turpentine every morning, or all together; but this I know, with thanks to God Almighty, that I am now as well as ever I can wish or desire to be; only I do find that my backe grows very weak, that I cannot stoop to write or tell money without sitting but I have pain for a good while after it.

27th. To the Duke of Albemarle, the first time that we officers of the Navy have waited upon him since the Duke of Yorke's going, who hath deputed him to be Admirall in his absence. And I find him a quiet heavy man, that will help business when he can and hinder nothing, and am very well pleased with our attendance on him. I did afterwards alone give him thanks for his favour to me about my Tangier business, which he received kindly, and did speak much of his esteem of me. So to my Lord Peterborough's, where mighty merry to see how plainly my Lord and Povy did abuse one another about their accounts, each thinking the other a foole, and I thinking they were not either of them in that point much in the wrong.

April 3rd. With Creed, my wife, and Mercer to a play at the Duke's of my Lord Orrery's, called "Mustapha," which being not good made Betterton's part and Ianthe's but ordinary too, so that we were not contented with it at all. Thence home and to the office a while, and then home to supper and to bed. All the pleasure of the play was, the King and my Lady Castlemayne were there; and pretty witty Nell,[1] at the King's house, sat next us, which pleased me mightily.

4th. All the morning at the office busy. At noon to the 'Change, and then went up to the' Change to buy a pair of cotton stockings, which I did at the husband's shop of the most pretty woman there, who did also invite me to buy some linnen of her; and I was glad of the occasion, and bespoke some bands of her, intending to make her my seamstress, she being one of the prettiest and most modest looked women that ever I did see. Dined at home; and to the office, where very late till I was ready to fall down asleep, and did several times nod in the middle of my letters.

5th. This day was kept publiquely by the King's command as a fast day against the Dutch warr, and I betimes to Woolwich and Deptford, where by business I have been hindered a great while of going. Did a very great deale of business, and then home, and there by promise find Creed, and he and my wife, Mercer and I by coach to take the ayre; and, where we had formerly been, at Hackney, did there eat some pullets we carried with us, and some things of the house; and after a game or two at shuffle-board, home, and Creed lay with me; but, being sleepy, he had no mind to talk about business, which indeed I intended by inviting him to lie with me, but I would not force it on him, and so to bed, he and I, and to sleep, being the first time I have been so much at my ease and taken so much fresh ayre these many weeks or months.

7th. Up betimes to the Duke of Albemarle about money to be got for the Navy, or else we must shut up shop.

12th. Sir G. Carteret, my Lord Brunkard, Sir Thomas Harvy,[2] and myself, down to my Lord Treasurer's chamber to him and the Chancellor, and the Duke of Albemarle; and there I did give them a large account of the charge of the Navy, and want of money. But strange to see how they held up their hands crying, "What shall we do?" Says my Lord Treasurer,[3] "Why, what means all this, Mr. Pepys? This is true, you say; but what would you have me to do? I have given all I can, for my life. Why will not people lend their money? Why will they not trust the King as well as Oliver? Why do our prizes come to nothing, that yielded so

---

[1] Nell Gwynne.
[2] Sir Thomas Harvey had bought his place as an Extra Commissioner for the Navy from his predecessor, Lord Berkeley.   [3] Lord Southampton.

much heretofore?" And this was all we could get, and went away without other answer; which is one of the saddest things that at such a time as this, with the greatest action on foot that ever was in England, nothing should be minded, but let things go on of themselves, do as well as they can. So home vexed, and going to my Lady Batten's, there found a great many women with her in her chamber merry, my Lady Pen and her daughter, among others; where my Lady Pen flung me down upon the bed, and herself and others one after another upon me, and very merry we were.

24th. To my Lady Sandwich's to dinner, where my wife by agreement. After dinner alone, my Lady told me, with the prettiest kind of doubtfullnesse whether it would be fit for her with respect to Creed to do it that is in the world, that Creed had broke his desire to her of being a servant to Mrs. Betty Pickering,[1] and placed it upon encouragement which he had from some discourse of her ladyship, commending of her virtues to him, which, poor lady, she meant most innocently. She did give him a cold answer, but not so severe as it ought to have been; and, it seems, as the lady since to my Lady confesses, he had wrote a letter to her, which she answered slightly, and was resolved to contemn any motion of his therein. My Lady takes the thing very ill, as it is fit she should; but I advise her to stop all future occasions of the world's taking notice of his coming thither so often as of late he hath done. But to think that he should have this devilish presumption to aime at a lady so near to my Lord is strange, both for his modesty and discretion. Thence to the Cockepitt, and there walked an houre with my Lord Duke of Albemarle alone in his garden, where he expressed in great words his opinion of me; that I was the right hand of the Navy here, nobody but I taking any care of any thing therein; so that he should not know what could be done without me. At which I was (from him) not a little proud. With my wife and Mercer to the Parke; but the King being there, and I now-a-days being doubtfull of being seen in any pleasure, did part from the tour, and away out of the Parke to Knightsbridge, and there eat and drank in the coach, and so home; and after a while at my office, home to supper and to bed, having got a great cold I think by my pulling off my periwigg so often.

---

[1] Lord Sandwich's sister had married Sir Gilbert Pickering, and this was a daughter. She did marry Creed, and bore him eleven children.

28th. Down the river to visit the victualling-ships, where I find all out of order. And come home to dinner, and then to write a letter to the Duke of Albemarle about the victualling-ships, and carried it myself to the Council-chamber, where it was read; and when they rose, my Lord Chancellor passing by stroked me on the head, and told me that the Board had read my letter, and taken order for the punishing of the watermen for not appearing on board the ships. And so did the King afterwards, who do now know me so well, that he never sees me but he speaks to me about our Navy business.

30th. (Lord's Day.) I with great joy find myself to have gained this month above £100 clear, and in the whole to be worth above £1,400. Thus I end this month in great content as to my estate and gettings: in much trouble as to the pains I have taken and the rubs I expect yet to meet with about the business of Tangier. The fleete, with about 106 ships, upon the coast of Holland in sight of the Dutch, within the Texel. Great fears of the sickenesse here in the City, it being said that two or three houses are already shut up. God preserve us all!

May 1st. At noon going to the 'Change I met my Lord Brunkard, Sir Robert Murry, Deane Wilkins, and Mr. Hooke, going by coach to Colonell Blunt's to dinner.[1] So they stopped and took me with them. Landed at the Tower-wharf, and thence by water to Greenwich, and there coaches met us; and to his house, a very stately sight for situation and brave plantations; and among others, a vineyard, the first that ever I did see. No extraordinary dinner, nor any other entertainment good; but only after dinner to the tryall of some experiments about making of coaches easy. And several we tried; but one did prove mighty easy (not here for me to describe, but the whole body of the coach lies upon one long spring), and we all, one after another, rid in it; and it is very fine and likely to take. These experiments were the intent of their coming, and pretty they are. Thence back by coach to Greenwich, and in his pleasure boat to Deptford, and there stopped and into Mr. Evelyn's,[2] which is a most beautiful place, but it being dark and late, I staid not, but Deane Wilkins and Mr. Hooke and I walked to Redriffe, and noble discourse all day long did please me; and it being late did take them to my

---

[1] This was a committee of the Royal Society, appointed to investigate Col. Blunt's invention.
[2] This is the first mention in the Diary of John Evelyn, the other seventeenth-century diarist, himself a member of the Royal Society. A warm personal friendship developed in later years between the two men.

"MY LORD CHANCELLOR . . . STROKED ME ON THE HEAD"

house to drink, and did give them some sweetmeats, and thence sent them with a lanthorn home, two worthy persons as are in England, I think, or the world.

3rd. To Gresham College, and saw a cat killed with the Duke of Florence's poyson, and saw it proved that the oyle of tobacco drawn by one of the Society do the same effect, and is judged to be the same thing with the poyson both in colour and smell and effect.

5th. To Woolwich and back to Blackewall, and after dinner to Mr. Evelyn's. He being abroad we walked in his garden, and a lovely noble ground he hath indeed. And among other rarities a hive of bees, so as being hived in glass you may see the bees making their honey and combs mighty pleasantly. This day, after I had suffered my owne hayre to grow long in order to wearing it, I find the convenience of periwiggs is so great that I have cut off all short again, and will keep to periwiggs.

7th. (Lord's Day.) My wife begun to learn to limn; and, by her beginning upon some eyes, I think she will do very fine things, and I shall take great delight in it.

10th. To the Guard in Southwarke, there to get some soldiers, by the Duke's order, to go keep pressmen on board our ships. So to the 'Change and did much business, and them home to dinner; and there find my poor mother come out of the country to-day in good health, and I am glad to see her. But my business, which I am sorry for, keeps me from paying the respect I ought to her at her first coming, she being grown very weak in her judgement, and doating again in her discourse through age and some trouble in her family. I left her and my wife to go abroad to buy something, and then I to my office.

12th. By water to the Exchequer, and there up and down through all the offices to strike my tallys for £17,500; which me-thinks is so great a testimony of the goodness of God to me, that I, from a mean clerke there, should come to strike tallys myself for that sum, and in the authority that I do now, is a very stupendous mercy to me. I shall have them struck to-morrow. But to see how every little fellow looks after his fees, and to get what he can for everything, is a strange consideration; the King's fees that he must pay himself for this £17,500 coming to above £100. Thence called my wife at Unthanke's to the New Exchange and elsewhere to buy a lace band for me, but we did not buy; but I find it so necessary to have some handsome clothes that I cannot but lay out some money thereupon. To the 'Change, and thence to my watchmaker, where he has put it in order, and a good and brave piece it is, and he tells me worth £14, which is a greater present than I valued it.[1]

13th. Lord! to see how much of my old folly and childish-nesse hangs upon me still that I cannot forbear carrying my watch in my hand in the coach all this afternoon, and seeing what o'clock it is one hundred times, and am apt to think with myself, how could I be so long without one; though I remember since, I had one, and found it a trouble, and resolved to carry one no more about me while I lived. Mr. Cholmeley advises me from Tangier how people are at worke to overthrow our Victualling business, by which I shall lose £300 per annum. I am much obliged to him for this secret kindnesse.

14th. (Lord's Day.) Up, and with my wife to church, it being Whitsunday; my wife very fine in a new yellow bird's-eye hood, as the fashion is now. We had a most sorry sermon; so home to dinner, my mother having her new suit brought home, which makes her very fine. After dinner my wife and she and Mercer to Thomas Pepys's wife's christening of his first child, and I took a coach, and to Walthamstow, where (failing at the old place) Sir W. Batten by and by come home, I walking up and down the house and garden with my Lady very pleasantly, then to supper very merry, and then back by coach by dark night. As soon as I come home, upon a letter from the Duke of Albemarle, I took boat at about 12 at night, and down the River in a gally, my boy and I, down to the Hope and so up again, sleeping and waking, with great pleasure, my business to call upon every one of

15th. Our victualling ships to set them agoing, and so home, and after dinner to the King's playhouse, all alone, and saw "Love's Maistresse." [2] Some pretty things and good variety in it, but no or little fancy in it. Thence to the Duke of Albemarle to give him account of my day's works, where he shewed me letters from Sir G. Downing,[3] of four days' date, that the Dutch are come out and joyned, well-manned and resolved to board our best ships, and fight for certain they will. Thence to the Swan at Herbert's, and there the company of Sarah a little while, and so away and called at the Harp and Ball, where the mayde, Mary, is very *formosa*. Thence home, and being sleepy to bed.

---

[1] The watch had been given him a month previously by "one Briggs, a scrivener and sollicitor." [2] By Thomas Heywood.   [3] Then Resident at the Hague.

17th. To Langford's,[1] where I never was since my brother died there. I find my wife and Mercer, having with him agreed upon two rich silk suits for me, which is fit for me to have, but yet the money is too much, I doubt, to lay out altogether; but it is done, and so let it be, it being the expense of the world that I can the best bear with and the worst spare.

28th. (Lord's Day.) To Sir Philip Warwicke's to dinner, where abundance of company come in unexpectedly; and here I saw one pretty piece of household stuff, as the company increaseth, to put a larger leaf upon an ovall table. After dinner much good discourse with Sir Philip, who I find, I think, a most pious, good man, and a professor of a philosophicall manner of life and principles like Epictetus, whom he cites in many things. Thence to my Lady Sandwich's, where to my shame I had not been a great while before. Here, upon my telling her a story of my Lord Rochester's running away on Friday night last with Mrs. Mallett, the great beauty and fortune of the North, who was at Charing Cross seized on by both horse and foot men, and forcibly taken and put into a coach with six horses, and two women provided to receive her, and carried away. Upon immediate pursuit, my Lord of Rochester was taken at Uxbridge; but the lady is not yet heard of, and the Lord sent to the Tower. Hereupon my Lady did confess to me as a great secret her being concerned in this story; for if this match breaks between my Lord Rochester and her, then by the consent of all her friends my Lord Hinchingbroke stands fair, and is invited for her. She is worth, and will be at her mother's death (who keeps but a little from her), £2,500 per annum. Pray God give a good success to it![2] Thence home and to see my Lady Pen, where my wife and I were shown a fine rarity, of fishes kept in a glass of water, that will live so for ever; and finely marked they are, being foreign.

30th. In the evening by coach with my wife and mother Mercer, our usual tour by coach, and eat at the old house at Islington; but, Lord! to see how my mother found herself talk upon every object to think of old stories. Here I met with one that tells me that Jack Cole, my old schoole-fellow, is dead and buried lately of a consumption, who was a great crony of mine.

---

[1] Langford had taken on the Pepys' tailor's shop after Tom Pepys' death.
[2] In August of the following year the proposed match was broken off, Lord Hinchingbroke "not being fully pleased with the vanity and liberty of her carriage," and "she declaring her affections to be settled." Six months later she married Lord Rochester.

June 1st. I put on my new silke camelott sute; the best that ever I wore in my life, the sute costing me above £24. In this I went with Creed to Goldsmiths' Hall, to the burial of Sir Thomas Viner [1]; which Hall and Haberdashers' also, was full of people. We saw all the funeral, which was with the blue-coat boys and old men, all the Aldermen and Lord Mayor, etc., and the number of the company very great. The show being over, I took coach and to Westminster Hall, where I took the fairest flower, and by coach to Tothill Fields for the ayre till it was dark. I 'light, and in with the fairest flower to eat a cake. Away without any notice, and after delivering the rose where it should be, I to the Temple and 'light, and there took another coach, and so home to write letters, but very few, God knows, being by my pleasure made to forget everything that is. The coachman that carried us cannot know me again, nor the people at the house where we were.

3rd. All this day by all people upon the River, and almost every where else hereabouts were heard the guns, our two fleets for certain being engaged, which was confirmed by letters from Harwich, but nothing particular: and all our hearts full of concernment for the Duke, and I particularly for my Lord Sandwich and Mr. Coventry, after his Royal Highnesse.

6th. To my Lady Sandwich's, who, poor lady, expects every hour to hear of my Lord; but in the best temper, neither confident nor troubled with fear, that I ever did see in my life.

7th. This morning my wife and mother rose about two o'clock; and with Mercer, Mary, the boy, and W. Hewer, as they had designed, took boat and down to refresh themselves on the water to Gravesend. To the office, and meeting Creed away with him to my Lord Treasurer's. Thence, it being the hottest day that ever I felt in my life, we to the New Exchange and there drunk whey, with much entreaty getting it for our money, and they would not be entreated to let us have one glasse more. So took water and to Fox-Hall, to the Spring garden, and there walked an houre or two with great pleasure, saving our minds ill at ease concerning the fleete and my Lord Sandwich, that we have no newes of them, and ill reports run up and down of his being killed, but without ground. Here staid pleasantly walking and spending but *6d.* till nine at night, and then by water to White Hall, and there I stopped to hear news of the fleete, but none come, which

[1] Lord Mayor, 1654; a goldsmith.

is strange; and so by water home, where weary with walking and with the mighty heat of the weather, and for my wife's not coming home, I staying walking in the garden till twelve at night, when it begun to lighten exceedingly, through the greatness of the heat. Then despairing of her coming home, I to bed. This day, much against my will, I did in Drury Lane see two or three houses marked with a red cross upon the doors, and "Lord have mercy upon us" writ there; which was a sad sight to me, being the first of the kind that, to my remembrance, I ever saw. It put me into an ill conception of myself and my smell, so that I was forced to buy some roll-tobacco to smell to and chaw, which took away the apprehension.

8th. About five o'clock my wife come home, it having lightened all night hard, and one great shower of rain. She come and lay upon the bed; I up and to the office, where all the morning. Alone at home to dinner, my wife, mother and Mercer dining at W. Joyce's, I giving her a caution to go round by the Half Moone to his house, because of the plague. At the Goldsmiths I met with the great news at last newly come from the Duke of Yorke that we have totally routed the Dutch; that the Duke himself, the Prince, my Lord Sandwich and Mr. Coventry are all well, which did put me into such joy that I forgot almost all other thoughts. Thence with great joy to the Cockepitt, where the Duke of Albemarle, like a man out of himself with content, new-told me all; and by and by comes a letter from Mr. Coventry's own hand to him. A great[er] victory never known in the world. They are all fled, some 43 got into the Texell and others elsewhere, and we in pursuit of the rest. Thence with my heart full of joy, home, and to my office a little; then to my Lady Pen's, where they are all joyed and not a little puffed up at the good successe of their father; and good service indeed is said to have been done by him. Had a great bonefire at the gate; and I with my Lady Pen's people and others to Mrs. Turner's great room, and then down into the streete. I did give the boys 4*s.* among them, and mighty merry. So home to bed, with my heart at great rest and quiett.

9th. Up and to White Hall, and in my way met with Mr. Moore, who tells me that the King did say that my Lord Sandwich had done nobly and worthily. At noon eat a small dinner at home, and so abroad to buy several things, and among others with my taylor to buy a silke suit, which though I had one lately, yet I do, for joy of the good newes we have lately had of our victory over the

Dutch, which makes me willing to spare myself something extraordinary in clothes; and after long resolution of having nothing but black, I did buy a coloured silk ferrandin.

10th. In the evening home; and there to my great trouble hear that the plague is come into the City: but where should it begin but in my good friend and neighbour's, Dr. Burnett, in Fanchurch Street, which in both points troubles me mightily. To the office to finish my letters and then home to bed, being troubled at the sicknesse, and my head filled also with other business enough; and particularly how to put my things and estate in order, in case it should please God to call me away, which God dispose of to his glory!

11th. (Lord's Day.) Up, and expected long a new suit; but, coming not, dressed myself in my late new black silke camelott suit; and, when fully ready, comes my new one of coloured ferrandin, which my wife puts me out of love with, which vexes me, but I think it is only my not being used to wear colours which makes it look a little unusual upon me. At noon by invitation comes my two cozen Joyces and their wives, my aunt James and he-cozen Harman. I had a good dinner for them, and as merry as I could be in such company. They being gone I out of doors a little to shew, forsooth, my new suit, and back again, and in going I saw poor Dr. Burnett's door shut; but he hath, I hear, gained great goodwill among his neighbours, for he discovered it himself first and caused himself to be shut up of his own accord, which was very handsome.

14th. To my Lord Treasurer's, there to speak with him, and waited in the lobby three long hours for to speake with him, to the trial of my utmost patience; but missed him at last, and forced to go home without it, which may teach me how I make others wait. This day met with a letter of Captain Ferrers, wherein he tells my Lord was with his ship in all the heat of the day, and did most worthily.

15th. Up, and put on my new stuff suit with close knees, which becomes me most nobly, as my wife says. At the office all day. At noon put on my first laced band, all lace, and to Kate Joyce's to dinner, where my mother, wife, and abundance of their friends, and good usage. Thence wife and Mercer and I to the Old Exchange, and there bought two lace bands more, one of my semstresse, whom my wife concurs with me to be a pretty woman. So down to Deptford and Woolwich, my boy and I. At Woolwich discoursed with Mr. Sheldon about my bringing my wife down for a month or two to his house, which he approves of, and I think will be very convenient. The towne grows very sickly, and people to be afeard of it, there dying this last week of the plague 112, from 43 the week before.

16th. Up and to the office, where I set hard to business, but was informed that the Duke of Yorke is come, and hath appointed us to attend him this afternoon. So after dinner and doing some business at the office I to White Hall, where the Court is full of the Duke and his courtiers returned from sea. All fat and lusty and ruddy by being in the sun. I kissed his hands, and we waited all the afternoon. By and by saw Mr. Coventry, which rejoiced my very heart. Anon he and I, from all the rest of the company, walked into the Matted Gallery, where after many expressions of love we fell to talk of business. Strange to hear how the Dutch do relate, as the Duke says, that they are the conquerors, and bonefires are made in Dunkirke in their behalf, though a clearer victory can never be expected. Mr. Coventry thinks they cannot have lost less than 6,000 men, and we not dead above 200, and wounded about 400.

17th. At the office find Sir W. Pen come home, who looks very well; and I am gladder to see him than otherwise I should be, because of my hearing so well of him for his serviceablenesse in this late great action. It struck me very deep this afternoon going with a hackney coach from my Lord Treasurer's down Holborne, the coachman I found to drive easily and easily, at last stood still, and come down hardly able to stand, and told me that he was suddenly struck very sicke, and almost blind, he could not see. So I 'light and went into another coach with a sad heart for the poor man and trouble for myself lest he should have been struck with the plague, being at the end of the towne that I took him up; but God have mercy upon us all!

21st. To the Cross Keys at Cripplegate, where I find all the towne almost going out of towne, the coaches and waggons being all full of people going into the country.

22nd. In great pain whether to send my mother into the country to-day or no, I hearing that she, poor wretch, hath a mind to stay a little longer. At last I resolved to put it to her, and she agreed to go, so I would not oppose it, because of the sicknesse in the towne, and my intentions of removing my wife. So I did give her money and took a kind leave of her, and left my wife and people to see her out of town, and I at the office all the morning. At noon my wife tells me that she is with much ado gone, and I pray God bless her, but it seems she was to the last unwilling to go, but would not say so, but put it off till she lost her place in the coach, and was fain to ride in the waggon part. After dinner to the office again till night, very busy, and so home not very late to supper and to bed.

23rd. Up and to White Hall to a Committee for Tangier, where his Royal Highness was. At this Committee, unknown to me, comes my Lord of Sandwich, who, it seems, come to towne last night. After the Committee was up my Lord Sandwich did take me aside and we walked an hour alone together in the robe-chamber, the door shut, telling me how much the Duke and Mr. Coventry did both in the fleete and here make of him, and that in some opposition to the Prince: yet that all the discourse of the towne, and the printed relation, should not give him one word of honour my Lord thinks mighty strange; he assuring me that though by accident the Prince was in the van the beginning of the fight for the first pass, yet all the rest of the day my Lord was in the van, and continued so. That notwithstanding all this noise of the Prince he had hardly a shot in his side nor a man killed, whereas he hath above 30 in her hull, and not one mast whole nor yard, but the most battered ship of the fleet, and lost most men, saving Captain Smith of "The Mary." It therefore troubles my Lord that Mr. Coventry should not mention a word of him in his relation. I did in answer offer that I was sure the relation was not compiled by Mr. Coventry but by L'Estrange, out of several letters, as I could witness; and that Mr. Coventry's letter that he did give the Duke of Albemarle did give him as much right as the Prince, for I myself read it first and then copied it out, which I promised to show my Lord, with which he was somewhat satisfied. From that discourse my Lord did begin to tell me how much he was concerned to dispose of his children, and would have my advice and help; and propounded to match my Lady Jemimah to Sir G. Carteret's eldest son, which I approved of, and did undertake the speaking with him about it as from myself, which my Lord liked. So parted, with my head full of care about this business.

24th. (Midsummer-day.) To Sir G. Carteret at his chamber, and in the best manner I could, and most obligingly, moved the business. He received it with great respect and content and thanks to me, and promised that he would do what he could possibly for his son to render him fit for my Lord's daughter, and shewed great kindness to me and sense of my kindness to him herein.   Sir William Pen told me this day that Mr. Coventry is to be sworn a Privy Counsellor, at which my soul is glad.[1]

25th.   (Lord's Day.)   To White Hall, where, after I had again visited Sir G. Carteret and received his (and now his Lady's) full content in my proposal, I went to my Lord Sandwich; and having told him how Sir G. Carteret received it, he did direct me to return to Sir G. Carteret and give him thanks for his kind reception of this offer, and that he would the next day be willing to enter discourse with him about the business.   Which message I did presently do, and so left the business with great joy to both sides.   So by water home and to supper and bed, being weary with long walking at Court; but had a Psalm or two with my boy and Mercer before bed, which pleased me mightily.

26th.   With Creed to the King's Head and there dined with him at the ordinary, and good sport with one Mr. Nicholls, a prating coxcomb, that would be thought a poet but would not be got to repeat any of his verses.   Thence I home, and there find my wife's brother and his wife, a pretty little modest woman, where they dined with my wife.   He did come to desire my assistance for a living; and upon his good promises of care, and that it should be no burden to me, I did say and promise I would think of finding something for him.   And the rather because his wife seems a pretty discreet young thing and humble, and he above all things desirous to do something to maintain her, telling me sad stories of what she endured with him in Holland; and I hope it will not be burdensome.

28th.   This morning I met with Sir G. Carteret, who tells me how all things proceed between my Lord Sandwich and himself to full content, and both sides depend upon having the match finished presently, and professed great kindnesse to me, and said that now we were something akin.   I am mightily, both with respect to myself and much more of my Lord's family, glad of this alliance.   After dinner to White Hall.   Thence by coach to several places, and so home; and all the evening with Sir J. Minnes and all the women of the house (excepting my Lady Batten) late in the garden chatting.   At 12 o'clock home to supper and to bed.

---

[1] Mr. Coventry was knighted and sworn a Privy Councillor two days later.

"SHE IS WITH MUCH ADO GONE"

My Lord Sandwich is gone towards the sea to-day, it being a sudden resolution, I having taken no leave of him.

29th. Up and by water to White Hall, where the Court full of waggons and people ready to go out of towne. To the Harp and Ball, and there drank and talked with Mary. This end of the towne every day grows very bad of the plague.

30th. In the afternoon I down to Woolwich and after me my wife and Mercer, whom I led to Mr. Sheldon's to see his house, and I find it a very pretty place for them to be at. So I back again, walking both forward and backward, and left my wife to come by water. Thus this book of two years ends. Myself and family in good health, consisting of myself and wife, Mercer, her woman, Mary, Alce and Susan our maids, and Tom my boy. In a sickly time of the plague growing on. Having upon my hands the troublesome care of the Treasury of Tangier, with great sums drawn upon me and nothing to pay them with; also the business of the office great. Consideration of removing my wife to Woolwich; she lately busy in learning to paint, with great pleasure and success.

July 5th. Up and advised about sending of my wife's bedding and things to Woolwich, in order to her removal thither. In the afternoon I abroad to St. James's, and there with Mr. Coventry a good while. From thence walked round to White Hall, the Parke being quite locked up. To Sir G. Carteret, and mighty glad he is to see me, and begun to talk of our great business of the match, how matters are quite concluded with all possible content between my Lord and him and signed and sealed, so that my Lady Sandwich is to come thither to-morrow or next day; and the young lady is sent for, and all likely to be ended between them in a very little while, with mighty joy on both sides, and the King, Duke, Lord Chancellor, and all mightily pleased. By water to Woolwich, where I found my wife come and her two mayds, and very prettily accommodated they will be; and I left them going to supper, grieved in my heart to part with my wife. Late home and to bed, very lonely.

6th. By coach to several places, among others to see my Lord Brunkerd, who is not well, but was at rest when I come. I could not see him, nor had much mind, one of the great houses within two doors of him being shut up: and, Lord! the number of houses visited, which this day I observed through the town quite round in my way by Long Lane and London Wall.

7th. Up, and having set wine coopers at work drawing out a tierce of wine for the sending of some of it to my wife, I abroad, only taking notice to what a condition it hath pleased God to bring me that at this time I have two tierces of Claret, two quarter casks of Canary, and a smaller vessel of Sack; a vessel of Tent, another of Malaga, and another of white wine, all in my wine cellar together; which I believe none of my friends of my name now alive ever had of his owne at one time.[1]

8th. All day very diligent at the office. Ended my letters by 9 at night, and then fitted myself to go down to Woolwich to my wife, which I did.

9th. (Lord's Day.) Very pleasant with her and among my people, while she made her ready; and about 10 o'clock by water to Sir G. Carteret, and there find my Lady in her chamber not very well, but looks the worst almost that ever I did see her in my life. It seems her drinking of the water at Tunbridge did almost kill her before she could with most violent physique get it out of her body again. We are received with most extraordinary kindnesse by my Lady Carteret and her children, and dined most nobly. After dinner I took occasion to have much discourse with Mr. Ph. Carteret,[2] and find him a very modest man; and I think verily of mighty good nature, and pretty understanding. He did give me a good account of the fight with the Dutch. My Lady Sandwich dined in her chamber. About three o'clock I, leaving my wife there, took boat and home.

13th. By water at night late to Sir G. Carteret's, but there being no oars to carry me I was fain to call a skuller that had a gentleman already in it, and he proved a man of love to musique, and he and I sung together the way down with great pleasure, and an incident extraordinary to be met with. Thence after long discourse I and my wife, who by agreement met here, took leave, and I saw my wife a little way down (it troubling me that this absence makes us a little strange instead of more fond), and so parted, and I home to some letters, and then home to bed. Above 700 died of the plague this week.

---

[1] Tent, or *vino tinto*, was a sweet red wine from southern Spain; malaga was a white wine from the port of that name in a neighbouring district. Canary was a light sweet wine, and sack, which came either from Spain or the Canaries, probably corresponded to our sherry. A tierce is one-third of a pipe, say 200 bottles.

[2] This meeting took place at the Treasurer's house at Deptford, Sir George Carteret's official residence. Philip Carteret was at this time twenty-four and she seventeen. He was subsequently knighted, but perished in 1672 with Lord Sandwich, when the latter's flag-ship was blown up at the battle of Solebay.

14th. Up, and all the morning at the Exchequer. Thence to the Old Exchange by water and there bespoke two fine shirts of my pretty seamstress. Upon the 'Change all the news is that guns have been heard and that news is come by a Dane that my Lord was in view of De Ruyter, and that since his parting from my Lord of Sandwich he hath heard guns; but little of it do I think true. In the evening I by water to Sir G. Carteret's, and there find my Lady Sandwich buying things for my Lady Jem.'s wedding; and my Lady Jem. is beyond expectation come to Dagenhams,[1] where Mr. Carteret is to go to visit her to-morrow; and my proposal of waiting on him, he being to go alone to all persons strangers to him, was well accepted, and so I go with him. But, Lord! to see how kind my Lady Carteret is to her! Sends her most rich jewells, and provides bedding and things of all sorts most richly for her, which makes my Lady and me out of our wits almost to see the kindnesse she treats us all with, as if they would buy the young lady. Thence away home, and foreseeing my being abroad two days did sit up late making of letters ready against to-morrow, and other things, and so to bed, to be up betimes by the helpe of a larum watch, which by chance I borrowed of my watchmaker to-day, while my owne is mending.

15th. After dinner at Sir G. Carteret's, Mr. Carteret and I by and by set out, and so toward Dagenhams. But, Lord! what silly discourse we had by the way as to love-matters, he being the most awkerd man I ever met with in my life as to that business. Thither we come (by that time it begun to be dark), and were kindly received by Lady Wright and my Lord Crew. And to discourse they went, my Lord discoursing with him, asking of him questions of travell, which he answered well enough in a few words; but nothing to the lady from him at all. To supper, and after supper to talk again, he yet taking no notice of the lady. My Lord would have had me have consented to leaving the young people together to-night to begin their amours, but I advised against it, lest the lady might be too much surprised. So they led him up to his chamber, where I staid a little to know how he liked the lady, which he told me he did mightily; but, Lord! in the dullest insipid manner that ever lover did. So I bid him good-night.

16th. (Lord's Day.) I up, having lain with Mr. Moore in the chaplin's chamber, and having trimmed myself, down to Mr.

---

[1] Near Romford: the home of Lady Wright, sister to Lady Sandwich. Her brother, Lord Crew, was also there at this time.

"HERE I TAUGHT HIM WHAT TO DO"

Carteret; and he being ready we down and walked in the gallery
an hour or two, it being a most noble and pretty house that ever,
for the bigness, I saw. Here I taught him what to do: to take the
lady always by the hand to lead her, and telling him that I would
find opportunity to leave them two together, he should make these
and these compliments, and also take a time to do the like to Lord
Crew and Lady Wright. After I had instructed him, which he
thanked me for, owning that he needed my teaching him, my
Lord Crew come down and family, the young lady among the
rest; and so by coaches to church four miles off, where a pretty
good sermon, and a declaration of penitence of a man that had
undergone the Churche's censure for his wicked life. Thence
back again by coach, Mr. Carteret having not had the confidence
to take his lady once by the hand, coming or going, which I told
him of when we come home, and he will hereafter do it. So to
dinner. My Lord excellent discourse. Then to walk in the gallery,
and to sit down. By and by my Lady Wright and I go out (and
then my Lord Crew, he not by design), and left the young people
together. And a little pretty daughter of my Lady Wright's
most innocently come out afterward, and shut the door to, as if
she had done it, poor child, by inspiration; which made us without, have good sport to laugh at. They together an hour, and
by and by church-time, whither he led her into the coach and into
the church, and so at church all the afternoon. Several handsome
ladies at church; but it was most extraordinary hot that ever I
knew it. So home again and to walk in the gardens, where we left
the young couple a second time. Anon to supper, and excellent
discourse and dispute between my Lord Crew and the chaplin,
who is a good scholler, but a nonconformist.

   17th. Up all of us, and to billiards; my Lady Wright, Mr.
Carteret, myself, and every body. By and by the young couple
left together. Anon to dinner; and after dinner Mr. Carteret
took my advice about giving to the servants, and I led him to give
£10 among them, which he did, by leaving it to the chief man-
servant, Mr. Medows, to do for him. Before we went I took my
Lady Jem. apart, and would know how she liked this gentleman,
and whether she was under any difficulty concerning him. She
blushed, and hid her face awhile; but at last I forced her to tell me.
She answered that she could readily obey what her father and
mother had done; which was all she could say, or I expect. So
anon I took leave, and for London. But, Lord! to see, among

other things, how all these great people here are afeard of London, being doubtfull of anything that comes from thence or that hath lately been there, that I was forced to say that I lived wholly at Woolwich. In our way Mr. Carteret did give me mighty thanks for my care and pains for him, and is mightily pleased.

To London to my office, and there took letters from the office, where all well, and so to the Bridge, and there he and I took boat and to Deptford, where mighty welcome, and brought the good newes of all being pleased to them. Mighty mirth at my giving them an account of all; but the young man could not be got to say one word before me or my Lady Sandwich of his adventures.

21st. Abroad to several places, among others to Anthony Joyce's, and there broke to him my desire to have Pall married to Harman, whose wife, poor woman, is lately dead, to my trouble, I loving her very much; and he will consider it. So home and late at my chamber setting some papers in order; the plague growing very raging, and my apprehensions of it great. So very late to bed.

26th. To Greenwich to the Park, where I hear the King and Duke are come by water this morn from Hampton Court. They asked me several questions. The King mightily pleased with his new buildings there. I followed them to Castle's ship in building, and there met Sir W. Batten, and thence to Sir G. Carteret's, where all the morning with them. Great variety of talk, and was often led to speak to the King and Duke. By and by they to dinner, and all to dinner and sat down to the King saving myself, which, though I could not in modesty expect, yet, God forgive my pride! I was sorry I was there, that Sir W. Batten should say that he could sit down where I could not, though he had twenty times more reason than I; but this was my pride and folly. The King having dined, he come down, and I went in the barge with him, I sitting at the door. Down to Woolwich (and there I just saw and kissed my wife, and away again to the King) and back again with him in the barge, hearing him and the Duke talk, and seeing and observing their manner of discourse. And God forgive me! though I admire them with all the duty possible, yet the more a man considers and observes them the less he finds of difference between them and other men, though (blessed be God!) they are both princes of great nobleness and spirits. The Duke of Monmouth is the most skittish leaping gallant that ever I saw, always in action, vaulting or leaping or clambering. Thence, mighty full of the honour of this day, I took coach and to Kate Joyce's; but she not within, I back to the Exchange, where I went up and sat talking with my beauty, Mrs. Batelier,[1] a great while, who is indeed one of the finest women I ever saw in my life. The sicknesse is got into our parish this week.

27th. To Hampton Court and dispatched all my business, and so staid and saw the King and Queene set out toward Salisbury,[2] and after them the Duke and Duchesse, whose hands I did kiss. And it was the first time I did ever, or did see any body else, kiss her hand; and it was a most fine white and fat hand. It was pretty to see the young pretty ladies dressed like men, in velvet coats, caps with ribbands, and with laced bands, just like men. Only the Duchesse herself it did not become.

30th. (Lord's Day.) Up, and in my night gowne, cap and neckcloth, undressed all day long, lost not a minute, but in my chamber setting my Tangier accounts to rights. Which I did by night to my very heart's content, not only that it is done, but I find every thing right, and even beyond what, after so long neglecting them, I did hope for. The Lord of Heaven be praised for it! It was a sad noise to hear our bell to toll and ring so often to-day, either for deaths or burials; I think five or six times. At night weary with my day's work, but full of joy at my having done it, I to bed, being to rise betimes to-morrow to go to the wedding at Dagenhams.

31st. Up, and very betimes by six o'clock at Deptford, and there find Sir G. Carteret and my Lady ready to go I being in my new coloured silk suit, and coat trimmed with gold buttons and gold broad lace round my hands, very rich and fine. By water to the Ferry, where, when we come, no coach there and tide of ebb so far spent as the horseboat could not get off on the other side the river to bring away the coach. So we were fain to stay there in the unlucky Isle of Doggs, in a chill place, the morning cool and wind fresh, above two if not three hours to our great discontent. Yet being upon a pleasant errand, and seeing that it could not be helped, we did bear it very patiently. Anon the coach comes. We, fearing the canonicall hour would be past before we got thither, did with a great deal of unwillingness send away the license and wedding ring. So that when we come, though we drove hard with six horses, yet we found them gone from home; and, going

---

[1] She was the lady behind the counter at which Pepys bought his linen.
[2] The Court moved to Salisbury on account of the plague.

towards the church, met them coming from church, which troubled us. But however that trouble was soon over, hearing it was well done. The young lady mighty sad, which troubled me; but yet I think it was only her gravity in a little greater degree than usual. All saluted her, but I did not till my Lady Sandwich did ask me whether I had saluted her or no. So to dinner, and very merry we were, but yet in such a sober way as never almost any wedding was in so great families: but it was much better.

After dinner company divided, some to cards, others to talk. At night to supper, and so to talk; and which, methought, was the most extraordinary thing, all of us to prayers as usual, and the young bride and bridegroom too. And so after prayers soberly to bed; only I got into the bridegroom's chamber while he undressed himself, and there was very merry till he was called to the bride's chamber, and into bed they went. I kissed the bride in bed, and so the curtaines drawne with the greatest gravity that could be, and so good night.

Whereas I feared I must have sat up all night, we did here all get good beds, and I lay in the same I did before with Mr. Brisband, who is a good scholler and sober man. Speaking of enchantments and spells, I telling him some of my charms, he told me this of his owne knowledge, at Bourdeaux in France. The words these:

Voyci un Corps mort,
Royde come un Baston,
Froid comme Marbre,
Leger come un esprit,
Levons te au nom de Jesus Christ.

He saw four little girles, very young ones, all kneeling, each of them upon one knee; and one begun the first line, whispering in the eare of the next, and the second to the third, and the third to the fourth, and she to the first. Then the first begun the second line, and so round quite through, and putting each one finger only to a boy that lay flat upon his back on the ground as if he was dead. At the end of the words they did with their four fingers raise this boy as high as they could reach; and he being there and wondering at it, did, for feare there might be some sleight used in it by the boy, or that the boy might be light, call the cook of the house, a very lusty fellow, and they did raise him in just the same manner. This is one of the strangest things I ever heard, but he tells it me of his owne knowledge, and I do heartily believe it to be true. I enquired of him whether they were Protestant or Catholique girles, and he told me they were Protestant, which made it the more strange to me. Thus we end this month, after the greatest glut of content that ever I had; only under some difficulty because of the plague, which grows mightily upon us, the last week being about 1,700 or 1,800 of the plague.

August 1st. Slept and lay long; then up and my Lord [Crew] and Sir G. Carteret being gone abroad, I first to see the bridegroom and bride, and found them both up and he gone to dress himself. Both red in the face, and well enough pleased this morning with their night's lodging. About five o'clock Sir G. Carteret and his lady and I took coach. Drove hard home, and it was night ere we got to Deptford, where, with much kindnesse from them to me, I left them, and home to the office, where I find all well.

8th. Up and to the office, where all the morning we sat. At noon I home to dinner alone, and after dinner to Sir W. Batten's, and there sat the most of the afternoon talking and drinking too much with my Lord Bruncker and others, very merry. So to my office a little, and then to the Duke of Albemarle's about some business. The streets mighty empty all the way now even in London, which is a sad sight. And to Westminster Hall, where talking, hearing very sad stories. Poor Will, that used to sell us ale at the Hall-door, his wife and three children died, all I think in a day. So home through the City again, wishing I may have taken no ill in going; but I will go I think no more thither. Late at the office.

10th. To the office, in great trouble to see the Bill this week rise so high, to above 4,000 in all, and of them above 3,000 of the plague. After writing letters, home to draw over anew my will, which I had bound myself by oath to dispatch by to-morrow night, the town growing so unhealthy that a man cannot depend upon living two days to an end. So having done something of it, I to bed.

12th. The people die so that now it seems they are fain to carry the dead to be buried by day-light, the nights not sufficing to do it in. And my Lord Mayor commands people to be within at nine at night, all as they say that the sick may have liberty to go abroad for ayre.

14th. By water to Woolwich where supped with my wife and then to bed betimes. I did present her with the dyamond ring awhile since given me by Mr. Dicke Vines's brother for helping him to be a purser, valued at about £10; the first thing of that nature I did ever give her.

15th. Up by 4 o'clock and walked to Greenwich, where called at Captain Cocke's and to his chamber, he being in bed, where something put my last night's dream into my head, which I think is the best that ever was dreamt, which was that I had my Lady Castlemayne in my armes; and then dreamt that this could not be awake, but that it was only a dream: but that since it was a dream, and that I took so much real pleasure in it, what a happy thing it would be if when we are in our graves (as Shakespeere resembles it) we could dream, and dream but such dreams as this, that then we should not need to be so fearful of death as we are this plague time. By water to the Duke of Albemarle, with whom I spoke a great deale in private. It was dark before I could get home, and so land at Churchyard stairs, where to my great trouble I met a dead corps of the plague in the narrow ally just bringing down a little pair of stairs. But I thank God I was not much disturbed at it. However, I shall beware of being late abroad again.

19th. Slept till 8 o'clock, and then up, and met with letters from the King and Lord Arlington, for the removal of our office to Greenwich.

26th. I down by water to Greenwich, where we met the first day, my Lord Bruncker, Sir J. Minnes and I, and I think we shall do well there. Walked toward my Lord Brunker's where I went in, having never been there before, and there he made a noble entertainment for Sir J. Minnes, myself and Captain Cocke, none else saving some painted lady that dined there, I know not who she is. But very merry we were, and after dinner into the garden,

28th. Up, and being ready I out to the goldsmith's, having not for some days been in the streets; but now how few people I see, and those looking like people that had taken leave of the world. In the afternoon I sent down my boy to Woolwich with some things before me, in order to my lying there for good and all.

31st. Up; and, after putting several things in order to my removal, to Woolwich. Thus this month ends with great sadness upon the publick, through the greatness of the plague every where through the kingdom almost. In the City died this week 7,496, and of them 6,102 of the plague. But it is feared that the true number of the dead this week is near 10,000; partly from the poor that cannot be taken notice of through the greatness of the number, and partly from the Quakers and others that will not have

"RECEIVED STARK-NAKED INTO THE ARMS OF A FRIEND"

any bell ring for them. Our fleete gone out to find the Dutch; all our fear is that the Dutch should be got in before them, which would be a very great sorrow to the publick, and to me particularly for my Lord Sandwich's sake. A great deal of money being spent, and the kingdom not in a condition to spare, nor a parliament without much difficulty to meet to give more. As to myself I am very well, only in fear of the plague, and as much of an ague by being forced to go early and late to Woolwich, and my family to lie there continually. My late gettings have been very great to my great content, and am likely to have yet a few more profitable jobbs in a little while; for which Tangier and Sir W. Warren I am wholly obliged to.

September 3rd. (Lord's Day.) Up; and put on my coloured silk suit very fine, and my new periwigg, bought a good while since but durst not wear because the plague was in Westminster when I bought it; and it is a wonder what will be the fashion after the plague is done as to periwiggs, for nobody will dare to buy any haire for fear of the infection, that it had been cut off of the heads of people dead of the plague. To church, where a sorry dull parson. I up to the Vestry at the desire of the Justices of the Peace, in order to the doing something for the keeping of the plague from growing; but Lord! to consider the madness of the people of the town, who will (because they are forbid) come in crowds along with the dead corps to see them buried; but we agreed on some orders for the prevention thereof. Among other stories one was very passionate, methought, of a complaint brought against a man in the towne for taking a child from London from an infected house. Alderman Hooker told us it was the child of a very able citizen in Gracious Street, a saddler, who had buried all the rest of his children of the plague, and himself and wife now being shut up and in despair of escaping, did desire only to save the life of this little child; and so prevailed to have it received stark-naked into the arms of a friend, who brought it (having put it into new fresh clothes) to Greenwich; where upon hearing the story, we did agree it should be permitted to be received and kept in the towne.

4th. After dinner to Greenwich where I found my Lord Bruncker. We to walk in the Park, and there eat some fruit out of the King's garden, and thence walked home, my Lord Bruncker giving me a very neat cane to walk with; but it troubled me to pass by Coome farme where about twenty-one people have died of the plague, and three or four days since I saw a dead corps in a coffin lie in the Close unburied; and a watch is constantly kept there night and day to keep the people in, the plague making us cruel as doggs one to another.

5th. Up, and walked with some Captains and others talking to me to Greenwich. Here we sat very late and for want of money, which lies heavy upon us, did nothing of business almost. Thence home with my Lord Bruncker to dinner. After dinner comes Colonell Blunt in his new chariot made with springs, and he hath rode, he says, now this journey, many miles in it with one horse, and out-drives any coach, and out-goes any horse, and so easy, he says. So for curiosity I went into it to try it, and up the hill to the heath, and over the cart-rutts and found it pretty well, but not so easy as he pretends.

6th. Busy all the morning writing letters to several, so to dinner, to London, to pack up more things thence; and there I looked into the street and saw fires burning in the street, as it is through the whole City, by the Lord Mayor's order. Thence by water to the Duke of Albemarle's: all the way fires on each side of the Thames, and strange to see in broad daylight two or three burials upon the Banke-side, one at the very heels of another: doubtless all of the plague, and yet at least forty or fifty people going along with every one of them.

7th. Up by 5 of the clock, mighty full of fear of an ague, but was obliged to go; and so by water, wrapping myself up warm, to the Tower, and there sent for the Weekely Bill and find 8,252 dead in all, and of them 6,978 of the plague, which is a most dreadfull number. Thence to Brainford, reading "The Villaine,"[1] a pretty good play, all the way. There a coach of Mr. Povy's stood ready for me, and he at his house ready to come in, and so we together merrily to Swakely,[2] Sir R. Viner's. He took us up and down with great respect, and showed us all his house and grounds; and it is a place not very moderne in the garden nor house, but the most uniforme in all that ever I saw; and some things to excess. Pretty to see over the screene of the hall (put up by Sir J. Harrington, a Long Parliament-man) the King's head, and my Lord of Essex on one side, and Fairfax on the other; and upon the other side of the screene the parson of the parish and the lord of the manor and his sisters. The window-cases, door-cases and chimnys of all the house are marble. He showed me a black boy

---

[1] By T. Porter.   [2] At Ickenham, Middlesex.

that he had that died of a consumption, and being dead he caused him to be dried in an oven, and lies there entire in a box. By and by to dinner, where his lady I find yet handsome, but hath been a very handsome woman; now is old. Hath brought him near £100,000 and now he lives, no man in England in greater plenty, and commands both King and Council with his credit he gives them. After dinner Sir Robert led us up to his long gallery, very fine, above stairs, and better, or such, furniture I never did see. After all this, and ending the chief business to my content about getting a promise of some money of him, we took leave, being exceedingly well treated here, and a most pleasant journey we had back.

10th. (Lord's Day.) My wife told me the ill news that she hears that her father is very ill, and then I told her I feared of the plague, for that the house is shut up. There happened newes to come to me by an expresse from Mr. Coventry telling me the most happy news of my Lord Sandwich's meeting with part of the Dutch; his taking two of their East India ships and six or seven others, and very good prizes: and that he is in search of the rest of the fleet, with the loss only of the Hector, poor Captain Cuttle. This news do so overjoy me that I know not what to say enough to express it; but the better to do it I did walk to Greenwich, and there I to Captain Cocke's, where I find my Lord Bruncker and Sir J. Minnes. Where we supped (there was also Mr. Evelyn); but the receipt of this newes did put us all into such an extacy of joy that it inspired into Sir J. Minnes and Mr. Evelyn such a spirit of mirth that in all my life I never met with so merry a two hours as our company this night was. Among other humours, Mr. Evelyn's repeating of some verses made up of nothing but the various acceptations of *may* and *can*, and doing it so aptly upon occasion of something of that nature, and so fast, did make us all die almost with laughing, and did so stop the mouth of Sir J. Minnes in the middle of all his mirth (and in a thing agreeing with his own manner of genius) that I never saw any man so out-done in all my life; and Sir J. Minnes's mirth too to see himself out-done was the crown of all our mirth. In this humour we sat till about ten at night, and so we to bed, it being one of the times of my life wherein I was the fullest of true sense of joy.

15th. Up, it being a cold misling morning, and so by water to the office, where very busy upon several businesses. At noon got the messenger, Marlow, to get me a piece of bread and butter and cheese and a bottle of beer and ale, and so I went not out of the office but dined off that. Then to my business again. Thence with Captain Cocke, and drank a cup of good drink, which I am fain to allow myself during this plague time, by advice of all, and not contrary to my oathe, my physician being dead and chyrurgeon out of the way, whose advice I am obliged to take; and so by water home and eat my supper, and to bed, being in much pain to think what I shall do this winter time, for go every day to Woolwich I cannot without endangering my life; and staying from my wife at Greenwich is not handsome.

20th. Up, and after being trimmed, the first time I have been touched by a barber these twelvemonths, I think, and more, went to Sir J. Minnes's and thence to the Duke of Albemarle. But, Lord! what a sad time it is to see no boats upon the River; and grass grows all up and down White Hall court, and nobody but poor wretches in the streets! And, which is worst of all, the Duke showed us the number of the plague this week, brought in the last night from the Lord Mayor; that it is encreased about 600 more than the last, which is quite contrary to all our hopes and expectations, from the coldness of the late season.

22nd. Up betimes and to the office. Was called away by my Lord Bruncker and Sir J. Minnes, and to Blackwall, there to look after the storehouses, and that being done, we into Johnson's house and were much made of, eating and drinking. But here it is observable what he tells us, that in digging his late Docke, he did 12 foot under ground find perfect trees over-covered with earth. Nut trees, with the branches and the very nuts upon them; some of whose nuts he showed us. Their shells black with age, and their kernell, upon opening, decayed, but their shell perfectly hard as ever. And a yew tree he showed us (upon which, he says, the very ivy was taken up whole about it), which upon cutting with an addes we found to be rather harder than the living tree usually is.

30th. Up and to the office, where busy all the morning. The great burden we have upon us at this time at the office is the providing for prisoners and sicke men that are recovered, they lying before our office doors all night and all day, poor wretches. Having been on shore, the captains won't receive them on board, and other ships we have not to put them on, nor money to pay them off or provide for them. God remove this difficulty! In the evening by agreement took ship in the Bezan and the tide carried us no further than Woolwich, and so I on shore to my wife. She took me downstairs and there alone did tell me her falling out with both her mayds and particularly Mary; and how Mary had to her teeth told her she would tell me of something that should stop her mouth, and words of that sense, which do make me mightily out of temper. So to bed.

October 1st. (Lord's Day.) Called up about 4 of the clock and so dressed myself and so on board the Bezan. Spent most of the morning talking and reading of "The Siege of Rhodes," [1] which is certainly (the more I read it the more I think so) the best poem that ever was wrote. Breakfasted betimes and come to the fleete about two of the clock in the afternoon, having a fine day and a fine winde. My Lord received us mighty kindly, and after discourse with us in general left us to our business, and he to his officers, having called a council of warr. Anon called down to my Lord, and there with him till supper talking. So to supper, and there my Lord the kindest man to me, before all the table talking of me to my advantage, and with tenderness too that it overjoyed me.

2nd. We having sailed all night (and I do wonder how they in the dark could find the way) we got by morning to Gillingham, and thence walked to Chatham; and there with Commissioner Pett viewed the Yard. Thence to Rochester, walked to the Crowne, and while dinner was getting ready, I did there walk to visit the old Castle ruines, which hath been a noble place; and there going up I did upon the stairs overtake three pretty mayds, or women, and took them up with me, and I did *baiser sur mouches, et toucher leurs mains* to my great pleasure. But, Lord! to see what a dreadfull thing it is to look down the precipices, for it did fright me mightily, and hinder me of much pleasure which I would have made to myself in the company of these three, if it had not been for that. The place hath been very noble and great and strong in former ages. So to walk up and down the Cathedral, and thence to the Crowne, whither Mr. Fowler, the Mayor of the towne, was come in his gowne and is a very reverend magistrate. After I had eat a bit I went away, and so took horses and to Gravesend, and there staid not, but got a boat, the sicknesse being very much in the towne still. About 8 o'clock got to Woolwich and there supped and mighty pleasant with my wife, who is, for ought I see, all friends with her mayds; and so in great joy and content to bed.

[1] By Sir William Davenant.

5th. Lay long in bed talking among other things of my sister Pall, and my wife of herself is very willing that I should give her £400 to her portion, and would have her married as soon as we could; but this great sicknesse time do make it unfit to send for her up. I abroad to the office and thence to the Duke of Albemarle, all my way reading a book of Mr. Evelyn's translating and sending me as a present, about directions for gathering a Library, but the book is above my reach. But his epistle to my Lord Chancellor is a very fine piece. So away to Mr. Evelyn's to discourse of our confounded business of prisoners and sick and wounded seamen, wherein he and we are so much put out of order.[1] And here he showed me his gardens, which are for variety of evergreens, and hedge of holly, the finest things I ever saw in my life. Thence in his coach to Greenwich, and there to my office, all the way having a fine discourse of trees and the nature of vegetables. Being come to my lodging [2] I got something to eat, having eat little all the day, and so to bed, having this night renewed my promises of observing my vowes as I used to do; for I find that, since I left them off, my mind is run a' wool-gathering and my business neglected.

7th. Up and to the office. Did business, though not much, because of the horrible crowd and lamentable moan of the poor seamen that lie starving in the streets for lack of money, which do trouble and perplex me to the heart; and more at noon when we were to go through them, for then a whole hundred of them followed us, some cursing, some swearing, and some praying to us. And that that made me more troubled was a letter come this afternoon from the Duke of Albemarle, signifying the Dutch to be in sight with 80 sayle yesterday morning off of Solebay, coming right into the bay. God knows what they will and may do to us, we having no force abroad able to oppose them, but to be sacrificed to them.

11th. Up, and so in my chamber staid all the morning doing something toward my Tangier accounts, for the stating of them, and also comes up my landlady, Mrs. Clerke, to make an agreement for the time to come; and I, for the having room enough, and to keepe out strangers, and to have a place to retreat to for my wife if the sicknesse should come to Woolwich, am contented to pay

---

[1] Evelyn was Commissioner for sick and wounded for Kent and Sussex.
[2] A lodging at Greenwich which Pepys found it convenient to occupy occasionally, and where later (see October 11 and December 31, *post*) he made his temporary home. Mrs. Pepys returned to London (from Woolwich) on December 2nd, but Pepys himself remained at Greenwich until January 7.

dear; so for three rooms and a dining-room, and for linen and bread and beer and butter at nights and mornings, I am to give her £5 10*s*. per month, and I wrote and we signed to an agreement.

To Woolwich, where we had appointed to keepe the night merrily; and so, by Captain Cocke's coach, had brought a very pretty child, a daughter of one Mrs. Tooker's, next door to my lodging, and so she and a daughter and kinsman of Mrs. Pett's made up a fine company at my lodgings at Woolwich, where my wife and Mercer and Mrs. Barbara danced, and mighty merry we were; but especially at Mercer's dancing a jigg, which she does the best I ever did see, having the most natural way of it, and keeps time the most perfectly I ever did see. This night is kept in lieu of yesterday for my wedding day of ten years; for which God be praised! being now in an extreme good condition of health and estate and honour, and a way of getting more money. Though at this houre under some discomposure, rather than damage, about some prize goods that I have bought off the fleete in partnership with Captain Cocke; and for the discourse about the world concerning my Lord Sandwich, that he hath done a thing so bad, besides the precedent for a General to take what prizes he pleases, and the giving a pretence to take away much more than he intended, and all will lie upon him.[1] Having danced with my people as long as I saw fit to sit up, I to bed and left them to do what they would.

16th. Took boat and down to the Tower, where I hear the Duke of Albemarle is. To Lumbarde Street, but can get no money. So upon the Exchange. The newes for certain that the Dutch are come with their fleete before Margett, and some men were endeavouring to come on shore when the post come away, perhaps to steal some sheep. Thence I walked to the Tower. But, Lord! how empty the streets are and melancholy, so many poor sick people in the streets full of sores; and so many sad stories overheard as I walk, every body talking of this dead, and that man sick, and so many in this place, and so many in that. And they tell me that in Westminster there is never a physician and but one apothecary left, all being dead; but that there are great hopes of a great decrease this week: God send it! At the Tower found my Lord Duke

---

[1] On September 3 and 4 Lord Sandwich had captured a number of Dutch ships, including several merchantmen loaded with valuable goods from the East Indies. He had ill-advisedly allowed the hatches to be broken and a valuable distribution of prizes to be made among the captains in his fleet: his own share appears to have been worth £5000. In the storm of protest which ensued (fanned by Albemarle and Coventry) Lord Sandwich was deprived of his command. To screen him, however, from public disgrace he was appointed Ambassador to Spain.

and Duchesse at dinner; so I sat down. And much good cheer, the Lieutenant and his lady and several officers with the Duke. But, Lord! to hear the silly talk that was there, would make one mad, the Duke having none almost but fools about him.

19th. Up, and to my accounts. After dinner I went to the Duke of Albemarle's; and among other things, spoke to him for my wife's brother, Balty, to be of his guard, which he kindly answered that he should. My business of the Victualling goes on as I would have it; and now my head is full how to make some profit of it to myself or people. To that end when I came home I wrote a letter to Mr. Coventry offering myself to be the Surveyor Generall, and am apt to think he will assist me in it, but I do not set my heart much on it, though it would be a good helpe.

26th. Up, and to the office, and thither comes Sir Christopher Mings to see me, and he and I together by water to the Tower; and I find him a very witty well-spoken fellow, and mighty free to tell his parentage, being a shoemaker's son, to whom he is now going.[1] And I to the 'Change, where I hear how the French have taken two and sunk one of our merchantmen in the Streights and carried the ships to Toulon, so that there is no expectation but we must fall out with them. The 'Change pretty full, and the town begins to be lively again, though the streets very empty, and most shops shut. So down to Greenwich and to the office till night, and then they come and tell me my wife is come, so I to her, vexed at her coming. But it was upon innocent business, so I was pleased and made her stay.

27th. By water to the Duke of Albemarle's, and there much company, but I staid and dined, and he makes mighty much of me. Here he proposed to me from Mr. Coventry, as I had desired of Mr. Coventry, that I should be Surveyor-Generall of the Victualling business, which I accepted.

28th. The King and Court, they say, have now finally resolved to spend nothing upon clothes but what is of the growth of England; which, if observed, will be very pleasing to the people, and very good for them.

31st. About nine at night I come home, and there find Mrs. Pierce come and little Fran. Tooker, and Mr. Hill, and other people, a great many dancing, and anon comes Mrs. Coleman with her husband and Laneare.[2] The dancing ended and to sing,

---

[1] Sir Christopher Mings, who rose to the rank of Admiral, was killed in the action against the Dutch in June of the following year.
[2] Edward Coleman and Nicholas Lanier, both musical composers.

which Mrs. Coleman do very finely, though her voice is decayed as to strength but mighty sweet though soft, and a pleasant jolly woman, but in mighty good humour was to-night. At it till past midnight, and then broke up and to bed. Hill and I together.

November 1st. Lay very long in bed discoursing with Mr. Hill of most things of a man's life, and how little merit do prevail in the world, but only favour; and that, for myself, chance without merit brought me in; and that diligence only keeps me so, and will, living as I do among so many lazy people that the diligent man becomes necessary, that they cannot do anything without him.

5th. (Lord's Day.) Made a visit to Mr. Evelyn, who among other things showed me most excellent painting in little, in distemper, Indian incke, water colours, graveing; and above all, the whole secret of mezzo-tinto and the manner of it, which is very pretty, and good things done with it. He read to me very much also of his discourse he hath been many years and now is about, about Guardenage, which will be a most noble and pleasant piece. He read me part of a play or two of his making, very good, but not as he conceits them, I think, to be. He showed me his Hortus Hyemalis; leaves laid up in a book of several plants kept dry, which preserve colour, however, and look very finely, better than any Herball. In fine, a most excellent person he is, and must be allowed a little for a little conceitedness; but he may well be so, being a man so much above others. He read me, though with too much gusto, some little poems of his own, that were not transcendant, yet one or two very pretty epigrams; among others, of a lady looking in at a grate, and being pecked at by an eagle that was there.

6th. Sir G. Carteret and I did talk of my Lord Sandwich's business; what enemies he hath, and how they have endeavoured to bespatter him. He says it was purposed by some hot-heads in the House of Commons, at the same time when they voted a present to the Duke of Yorke, to have voted £10,000 to the Prince and half-a-crowne to my Lord of Sandwich; but nothing come of it.

15th. Up and all the morning at the office busy, and at noon to the King's Head taverne, where all the Trinity House dined to-day to choose a new Master; but, Lord! to see how Sir W. Batten governs all. After dinner who comes in but my Lady Batten, and a troop of a dozen women almost, and expected as I found afterward to be made mighty much of; but nobody minded them. But the best jest was that when they saw themselves not regarded they would go away, and it was horrible foule weather; and my Lady Batten walking through the dirty lane with new spicke and span white shoes, she dropped one of her galoshes in the dirt, where it stuck, and she forced to go home without one, at which she was horribly vexed, and I led her; and after vexing her a little more in mirth I parted, and to Glanville's, where I knew Sir John Robinson, Sir G. Smith and Captain Cocke were gone; and there I made them, against their resolutions, to stay from houre to houre till it was almost midnight, and a furious, darke and rainy, and windy, stormy night; and which was best, I, with drinking small beer, made them all drunk drinking wine, at which Sir John Robinson made great sport. The plague, blessed be God! is decreased.

17th. Down to Quinbrough water, where all the great ships are now come, and there on board my Lord, and was soon received with great content. We fell to publique discourse, wherein was principally this: he cleared it to me beyond all doubt that Coventry is his enemy, and has been long so. I shewed him how advisable it were upon almost any terms for him to get quite off the sea employment. He answers me again that he agrees to it, but thinks the King will not let him go off. As an infinite secret my Lord tells me the factions are high between the King and the Duke, and all the Court are in an uproare with their loose amours; the Duke of Yorke being in love desperately with Mrs. Stewart. Nay, that the Duchesse herself is fallen in love with her new Master of the Horse and another. So that God knows what will be the end of it.

22nd. This day the first of the Oxford Gazettes[1] come out, which is very pretty, full of newes and no folly in it. To my office, and at night home to my lodgings, and took T. Willson and T. Hater with me, and there spent the evening till midnight. Among other things it pleased me to have it demonstrated that a Purser without professed cheating is a professed loser, twice as much as he gets.

24th. Up, and after doing some business at the office, I to London, and there in my way, at my old oyster shop in Gracious

---

[1] So called because the King and Court were at this time at Oxford, having moved there from Salisbury on September 23. No. xxiv. of the *Oxford Gazette* was the first London Gazette.

"MY LADY BATTEN . . . DROPPED ONE OF HER GALOSHES"

Streete, bought two barrels of my fine woman of the shop, who is alive after all the plague, which now is the first observation or inquiry we make at London concerning everybody we knew before it. So to the 'Change, where very busy with several people, and mightily glad to see the 'Change so full. Off the 'Change I went home with Sir G. Smith to dinner, sending for one of my barrels of oysters, which were good, though come from Colchester where the plague hath been so much. Here a very brave dinner, though no invitation; and, Lord! to see how I am treated, that come from so mean a beginning, is matter of wonder to me. But it is God's great mercy to me, and His blessing upon my taking pains and being punctual in my dealings.

30th. Great joy we have this week in the weekly Bill, it being come to 544 in all, and but 333 of the plague; so that we are encouraged to get to London soon as we can.

December 2nd. Up, and discoursing with my wife, who is resolved to go to London for good and all this day, we did agree upon giving Mr. Sheldon £10, and Mrs. Barbary two pieces; and so I left her to go down thither to fetch away the rest of the things and pay him the money, and so I to the office. Dined with my wife at noon and took leave of her, and I to the office busy till past one in the morning.

4th. Several people to me about business. So out and by water to London and home to my house at the office, where my wife had got a dinner for me: and it was a joyfull thing for us to meet here, for which God be praised! Here was her brother come to see her, and speake with me about business. It seems my recommending of him hath not only obtained his presently being admitted into the Duke of Albemarle's guards, and present pay, but also to be put as a right-hand man, and other marks of special respect, at which I am very glad, partly for him, and partly to see that I am reckoned something in my recommendations; but wish he may carry himself that I may receive no disgrace by him. Late by water home, taking a barrel of oysters with me, and at Greenwich went and sat with Madam Penington, and so away to my lodging.

6th. Up betimes, it being fast-day; and by water to the Duke of Albemarle, who come to towne from Oxford last night. He is mighty brisk, and very kind to me, and asks my advice principally in everything. He surprises me with the news that my Lord Sandwich goes Embassador to Spayne speedily; though I know not whence this arises, yet I am heartily glad of it. So home by water again, thinking to have met Mrs. Pierce; but she not there I home and dined, and comes presently by appointment my wife. I spent the afternoon upon a song [1] of Solyman's words to Roxalana that I have set; and so with my wife walked and Mercer to Mrs. Pierce's, where Captain Rolt and Mrs. Knipp,[2] Mr. Coleman and his wife, and Laneare, Mrs. Worshipp and her singing daughter, met; and by and by unexpectedly comes Mr. Pierce from Oxford. Here the best company for musique I ever was in in my life, and wish I could live and die in it, both for musique and the face of Mrs. Pierce, and my wife and Knipp, who is pretty enough, but the most excellent mad-humoured thing, and sings the noblest that ever I heard in my life, and Rolt with her, some things together most excellently. I spent the night in extasy almost; and having invited them to my house a day or two hence we broke up.

8th. By water to London to the Navy office, there to give order to my mayde to buy things to send down to Greenwich for supper to-night; and I also to buy other things, as oysters, and lemons 6*d.* per piece, and oranges 3*d.* So by water to White Hall, where we found Sir G. Carteret with the Duke, and also Sir G. Downing, whom I had not seen in many years before. He greeted me very kindly, and I him. Thence by water down to Greenwich, and there found all my company come; that is, Mrs. Knipp, and an ill, melancholy, jealous-looking fellow, her husband, that spoke not a word to us all the night; Pierce and his wife, and Rolt, Mrs. Worshipp and her daughter, Coleman and his wife, and Laneare; and to make us perfectly happy there comes by chance to towne Mr. Hill to see us. Most excellent musique we had in abundance, and a good supper, dancing, and a pleasant scene of Mrs. Knipp's rising sicke from table, but whispered me it was for some hard word or other her husband gave her just now when she laughed and was more merry than ordinary. But we got her in humour again, and mighty merry; spending the night till two in the morning with most complete content as ever in my life. Then broke up, and we to bed, Mr. Hill and I, whom I love more and more, and he us.

9th. Called up betimes by my Lord Bruncker to go with him to the Duke of Albemarle, which by his coach I did. Our discourse

---

[1] The original music of Pepys' song "Beauty retire" is in the Pepys' Library at Magdalene College. The words are taken from "The Siege of Rhodes," by Sir William Davenant.
[2] An actress at the King's House.

upon the ill posture of the times through lacke of money. At the Duke's did some business, and I believe he was not pleased to see all the Duke's discourse and applications to me and every body else. Here my Lord and I staid and dined. At table the Duchesse, a damned ill-looked woman, complaining of her Lord's going to sea the next year, said these cursed words: "If my Lord had been a coward he had gone to sea no more: it may be then he might have been excused, and made an Embassador" (meaning my Lord Sandwich). This made me mad, and I believed she perceived my countenance change, and blushed herself very much. Thence after dinner to the office, where late writing letters, and then home to Mr. Hill, and sang among other things my song of "Beauty retire," which he likes, only excepts against two notes in the base; but likes the whole very well. So late to bed.

18th. To London and there visited my wife, and was a little displeased to find she is so forward all of a spurt to make much of her brother and sister since my last kindnesse to him in getting him a place; but all ended well presently.

21st. At the office all the morning. At noon all of us dined at Captain Cocke's. Mr. Evelyn there, in very good humour. All the afternoon till night pleasant, and then I took my leave of them and to the office, where I wrote my letters, and away home, my head full of business and some trouble for my letting my accounts go so far that I have made an oathe this night for the drinking no wine, &c., on such penalties till I have passed my accounts and cleared all. Coming home and going to bed, the boy tells me his sister has provided me a supper of little birds killed by her husband, and I made her sup with me; and after supper I had the pleasure of her lips, she being a pretty woman. She gone, I to bed.

22nd. To my Lord Bruncker's, and there spent the evening by my desire in seeing his Lordship open to pieces and make up again his watch, thereby being taught what I never knew before; and it is a thing very well worth my having seen, and am mightily pleased and satisfied with it. So I sat talking with him till late at night, somewhat vexed at a snappish answer Madam Williams[1] did give me to herself, upon my speaking a free word to her in mirthe, calling her a mad jade. She answered, we were not so well acquainted yet.

25th. (Christmas-day.) To church in the morning and there saw a wedding in the church, which I have not seen many a day;

[1] Lord Brouncker's mistress.

and the young people so merry one with another. And strange to see what delight we married people have to see these poor fools decoyed into our condition, every man and woman gazing and smiling at them. Thence to my Lord Bruncker's by invitation and dined there, and so home.

30th. Up and to the office; at noon home to dinner, and all the afternoon to my accounts, and there find myself to my great joy a great deal worth above £4,000, for which the Lord be praised! and is principally occasioned by my getting £500 of Cocke for my profit in his bargains of prize goods, and from Mr. Gawden's making me a present of £500 more when I paid him £8,000 for Tangier. So to my office to write letters, then to my accounts again, and so to bed, being in great ease of mind.

31st. (Lord's Day.) All the morning in my chamber, writing fair the state of my Tangier accounts, and so dined at home. In the afternoon to the Duke of Albemarle and thence back again by water, and so to my chamber to finish the entry of my accounts and to think of the business I am next to do; and upon this late and with my head full of this business to bed. Thus ends this year, to my great joy, in this manner. I have raised my estate from £1,300 in this year to £4,400. I have got myself greater interest, I think, by my diligence, and my employments encreased by that of Treasurer for Tangier and Surveyour of the Victualls. It is true we have gone through great melancholy because of the great plague, and I put to great charges by it by keeping my family long at Woolwich, and myself and another part of my family, my clerks, at my charge at Greenwich, and a mayde at London; but I hope the King will give us some satisfaction for that. But now the plague is abated almost to nothing, and I intending to get to London as fast as I can. My family, that is my wife and maids, having been there these two or three weeks. The Dutch war goes on very ill by reason of lack of money.

I have never lived so merrily (besides that I never got so much) as I have done this plague time, by my Lord Bruncker's and Captain Cocke's good company, and the acquaintance of Mrs. Knipp, Coleman and her husband, and Mr. Laneare, and great store of dancings we have had at my cost (which I was willing to indulge myself and wife) at my lodgings. The great evil of this year, and the only one indeed, is the fall of my Lord of Sandwich.[1] The Duke of Albemarle goes with the Prince to sea this next year, and

[1] See note, p. 311.

my Lord very meanly spoken of; and, indeed, his miscarriage about the prize goods is not to be excused, to suffer a company of rogues to go away with ten times as much as himself, and the blame of all to be deservedly laid upon him.   My whole family hath been well all this while, and all my friends I know of, saving my aunt Bell, who is dead, and some children of my cozen Sarah's, of the plague. But many of such as I know very well, dead; yet to our great joy the town fills apace, and shops begin to be open again.   Pray God continue the plague's decrease! for that keeps the Court away from the place of business, and so all goes to rack as to publick matters, they at this distance not thinking of it.

SEVENTH YEAR

1666

January 2nd. To my Lord Bruncker's, and there find Sir J. Minnes and all his company, and above all my dear Mrs. Knipp, with whom I sang; and in perfect pleasure I was to hear her sing, and especially her little Scotch song of "Barbary Allen"; and to make our mirthe the completer Sir J. Minnes was in the highest pitch of mirthe and his mimicall tricks that ever I saw, and most excellent pleasant company he is.

5th. I with my Lord Bruncker and Mrs. Williams by coach with four horses to London to my Lord's house in Covent-Guarden. But, Lord! what staring to see a nobleman's coach come to town. And porters every where bow to us, and such begging of beggars! And a delightfull thing it is to see the towne full of people again as now it is; and shops begin to open, though in many places seven or eight together and more all shut, but yet the towne is full compared with what it used to be: I mean the City end, for Covent-Guarden and Westminster are yet very empty of people, no Court nor gentry being there. So I to the 'Change and there met Mr. Povy newly come to town, and he and I to Sir George Smith's and there dined nobly. Away to Cornhill to expect my Lord Bruncker's coming back again, and by and by comes my Lord, and did take me up and so to Greenwich; and after sitting with them a while at their house, home, thinking to get Mrs. Knipp, but could not, she being busy with company, but sent me a pleasant letter, writing herself "Barbary Allen."

6th. Up betimes and by water to the Cockepitt. Thence with Lord Bruncker to Greenwich by water to a great dinner and much company, hoping to get Mrs. Knipp to us, having wrote a letter to her in the morning, calling myself "Dapper Dicky," in answer to her's of "Barbary Allen," but could not. After dinner to cards, and then comes notice that my wife is come unexpectedly to me to towne. So I to her. It is only to see what I do, and why I come not home.

7th. (Lord's Day.) Up, and being trimmed I was invited by Captain Cocke, and dined with him. Thence to my lodging, and considering how I am hindered by company there to do any thing among my papers I did resolve to go away to-day rather than stay to no purpose till to-morrow, and so got all my things packed up. So took leave of my landlady and daughters, having paid dear for what time I have spent there, but yet having been quiett; and my health, I am very well contented therewith. So with my wife and Mercer took boat and away home; but in the evening before I went comes Mrs. Knipp, just to speake with me privately to excuse her not coming to me yesterday, complaining how like a devil her husband treats her, but will be with us in towne a weeke hence, and so I kissed her and parted. Being come home, my wife and I to look over our house and consider of laying out a little money to hang our bedchamber better than it is, and so resolved to go and buy something to-morrow; and so after supper, with great joy in my heart for my coming once again hither, to bed.

8th. Up, and my wife and I by coach to Bennett's, in Paternoster Row, few shops there being yet open, and there bought velvett for a coate, and camelott for a cloake for myself; and thence to a place to look over some fine counterfeit damasks to hang my wife's closett, and pitched upon one, and so by coach home again, I calling at the 'Change. And so home to dinner, and all the afternoon look after my papers at home and my office against tomorrow; and so after supper and considering the uselessness of laying out so much money upon my wife's closett, but only the chamber, to bed.

9th. Up, and then to the office, where we met first since the plague, which God preserve us in!

10th. To the office and anon to the Duke of Albemarle by coach. Here, which vexes me, I heard the damned Duchesse say again to twenty gentlemen publiquely in the room that she would have Montagu sent once more to sea before he goes to his Embassy; and wishing her lord had been a coward, for then perhaps he might have been made an Embassador and not been sent now to sea. But one good thing, she said; she cried mightily out against the having of gentlemen Captains with feathers and ribbands, and wished the King would send her husband to sea with the old plain sea Captains that he served with formerly, that would make their ships swim with blood, though they could not make legs[1] as Captains now-a-days can.

---

[1] *i.e.* bow and play the courtier.

12th. By coach to the Duke of Albemarle, where Sir W. Batten and I only met. Thence back by coach and called at Wotton's, my shoemaker, lately come to towne, and bespoke shoes, as also got him to find me a taylor to make me some clothes, my owne being not yet in towne, nor Pym, my Lord Sandwich's taylor. So he helped me to a pretty man, one Mr. Penny, against St. Dunstan's Church.

17th. Busy all the morning settling things against my going out of towne this night. After dinner late took horse and so rode to Dagenhams in the dark. There find the whole family well. It was my Lord Crew's desire that I should come, and chiefly to discourse with me of Lord Sandwich's matters. By and by to supper, my Lady Wright very kind. After supper up to wait on my Lady Crew, who is the same weake silly lady as ever, asking such saintly questions. Down to my Lord again and sat talking all houre or two; and anon to prayers the whole family, and then an to bed, I handsomely used, lying in the chamber Mr. Carteret formerly did, but sat up an houre talking sillily with Mr. Carteret, and so to bed.

18th. Up before day and thence rode to London before office time, where I met a note at the doore to invite me to supper to Mrs. Pierce's because of Mrs. Knipp, who is in towne and at her house. After dinner to the office. Anon comes to me thither my Lord Bruncker, Mrs. Williams, and Knipp. I brought down my wife in her night-gowne, she not being indeed very well, to the office to them and there by and by they parted all, and my wife and I anon and Mercer by coach to Pierce's, where mighty merry, and sing and dance with great pleasure; and I danced, who never did in company in my life.

20th. To the office, where I sent my boy home for some papers; where, he staying longer than I would have him, and being vexed at the business and to be kept from my fellows in the office longer than was fit, I become angry, and boxed my boy when he came, that I do hurt my thumb so much that I was not able to stir all the day after, and in great pain.

22nd. To the Crowne taverne behind the Exchange by appointment, and there met the first meeting of Gresham College since the plague. What among other fine discourse pleased me most was about Respiration: that it is not to this day known, or concluded on among physicians, nor to be done either, how the action is managed by nature, or for what use it is. Here late till poor Dr. Merriot was drunk; and so all home, and I to bed.

23rd. Up and to the office. After dinner to the office again all the afternoon, and much business with me. Good newes beyond all expectation of the decrease of the plague, being now but 79. So home with comfort to bed. A most furious storme all night and morning.

25th. I to the office, where I did much business, and set my people to work against furnishing me to go to Hampton Court, where the King and Duke will be on Sunday next. It is now certain that the King of France hath publickly declared war against us, and God knows how little fit we are for it. At night comes Sir W. Warren, and he and I into the garden, and talked over all our businesses. He gives me good advice not to embarke into trade (as I have had it in my thoughts), so as to be seen to mind it, for it will do me hurte, and draw my mind off from my business and embroile my estate too soon. So to the office business, and I find him as cunning a man in all points as ever I met with in my life, and mighty merry we were in the discourse of our owne trickes.

26th. Up, and pleased mightily with what my poor wife hath been doing these eight or ten days with her owne hands like a drudge, in fitting the new hangings of our bedchamber of blue and putting the old red ones into my dressing-room; and so by coach to White Hall.

28th. Up about six (Lord's Day), and being dressed in my velvett coate and plain cravatte took a hackney coach provided ready for me by eight o'clock, and so to my Lord Bruncker's with all my papers, and there took his coach with four horses and away to Hampton Court, where we find the King, and Duke, and Lords, all in council; so we walked up and down: there being none of the ladies come, and so much the more business I hope will be done. The Council being up, out comes the King, and I kissed his hand, and he grasped me very kindly by the hand. The Duke also, I kissed his, and he mighty kind. I found my Lord Sandwich there, poor man! I see with a very melancholy face. After changing a few words with Sir W. Coventry, who assures me of his respect and love to me, and his concernment for my health in all this sickness, I went down into one of the Courts, and there met the King and Duke; and the Duke called me to him. And the King come to me of himself and told me, "Mr. Pepys," says he, "I do give you thanks for your good service all this year, and I assure you I am very sensible of it." And the Duke of Yorke did tell me with pleasure that he had read over my discourse about pursers and would have it ordered in my way, and so fell from one discourse to another. I walked with them quite out of the Court into the fields.

29th. Up, and to Court by coach, where to Council before the Duke of Yorke, the Duke of Albemarle with us; and after Sir W. Coventry had gone over his notes I went over all mine with good successe. My Lord Sandwich come in in the middle of the business, and, poor man, very melancholy, methought, and said little at all, or to the business, and sat at the lower end, just as he come, no roome being made for him, only I did give him my stoole, and another was reached me. After council done, I walked to and again up and down the house, discoursing with this and that man.

February 2nd. Up betimes, and knowing that my Lord Sandwich is come to towne with the King and Duke, I to wait upon him, which I did, and having received his commands I among other things did look over some pictures at Cade's for my house, and did carry home a silver drudger for my cupboard of plate, and did call for my silver chafing dishes. So home, and with my wife looked over our plate, and picked out £40 worth, I believe, to change for more usefull plate, to our great content, and then we shall have a very handsome cupboard of plate.

4th. Lord's day; and my wife and I the first time together at church since the plague, and now only because of Mr. Mills his coming home to preach his first sermon, expecting a great excuse for his leaving the parish before any body went, and now staying till all are come home; but he made but a very poor and short excuse, and a bad sermon.

5th. My Lord [Bruncker] invited me to dinner to-day to dine with Sir W. Batten and his Lady, who were invited before; but lest he should thinke so little an invitation would serve me my turne I refused and to Westminster about business.

7th. It being fast day I staid at home all day long to set things to rights in my chamber by taking out all my books, and putting my chamber in the same condition it was before the plague. But in the morning doing of it and knocking up a nail I did bruise my left thumb so as broke a great deal of my flesh off, that it hung by a little. It was a sight frighted my wife, but I put some balsam of Mrs. Turner's to it; and though in great pain, yet went on with my business and did it to my full content, setting every thing in order.

10th. Up, and to the office. At noon, full of business, to dinner. This day comes first Sir Thomas Harvy after the plague, having been out of towne all this while. He was coldly received by us, and he went away before we rose also, to make himself appear yet a man less necessary. Home and late at my letters, and so to supper and to bed, being now-a-days for these four or five months mightily troubled with my snoring in my sleep, and know not how to remedy it.

14th. (St. Valentine's day.) I took Mr. Hill to my Lord Chancellor's new house that is building, and went with trouble up to the top of it, and there is there the noblest prospect that ever I saw in my life, Greenwich being nothing to it; and in every thing is a beautiful house, and most strongly built in every respect; and as if, as it hath, it had the Chancellor for its master.[1] Thence with him to his paynter, Mr. Hales, who is drawing his picture, which will be mighty like him, and pleased me so that I am resolved presently to have my wife's and mine done by him, he having a very masterly hand.[2]

18th. (Lord's Day.) Lay long in bed discoursing with pleasure with my wife, among other things about Pall's coming up, for she must be here a little to be fashioned; and my wife hath a mind to go down for her, which I am not much against. And so I rose and to my chamber to settle several things.

21st. Up, and with Sir J. Minnes to White Hall by his coach, by the way talking of my brother John to get a spiritual promotion for him, which I am now to looke after, for as much as he is shortly to be Master in Arts, and writes me this weeke a Latin letter that he is to go into orders this Lent.

23rd. Up betimes, and out of doors by 6 of the clock, and walked (W. Howe with me) to my Lord Sandwich's, who did lie the last night at his house in Lincoln's Inne Fields. The house full of people come to take leave of my Lord, who this day goes out of towne upon his embassy towards Spayne. I promised to wait upon him on Sunday at Cranbourne.[3] At noon dined at home, and to the office again. Anon comes Mrs. Knipp to see my wife, who is gone out; so I fain to entertain her, and took her out by

1 Clarendon House, Piccadilly, stood on the present site of Albemarle Street.
2 Pepys' portrait, by John Hales, now hangs in the National Portrait Gallery.
3 Cranbourne was a Royal Lodge in Windsor Forest; it was the official residence of Sir George Carteret, as Vice-Chamberlain. The Sandwich family were staying there with Lady Jemima, now married to Philip Carteret.

coach to look [for] my wife at Mrs. Pierce's and Unthanke's, but find her not. So back again, and then my wife comes home, having been buying of things, and at home I spent all the night talking with this baggage. So I supped, and was merry at home all the evening, and the rather it being my birthday, 33 years, for which God be praised that I am in so good a condition of healthe and estate, and every thing else as I am, beyond expectation, in all.

25th. (Lord's Day.) My wife up between three and four of the clock in the morning to dress herself, and I about five. Then with our coach of four horses I hire on purpose, to Cranborne. All the company glad to see us, and mighty merry to dinner. After dinner to walke in the Parke, my Lord and I alone, and my Lady Carteret not suffering me to go back again to-night, in a-doors and to talke with all and with my Lady Carteret; and I with the young ladies and gentlemen, who played on the guittar, and mighty merry, and anon to supper. And then my Lord going away to write, the young gentlemen to flinging of cushions, and other mad sports; at this late till towards twelve at night; and then being sleepy, I and my wife in a passage-room to bed, and slept not very well because of noise.

26th. Called up about five in the morning, and my Lord up, and took leave, a little after six, very kindly of me and the whole company. I and my wife staid till 9 o'clock almost, and then took coach to Windsor, t'o the Garter, and thither sent for Dr. Childe, who come to us and carried us to St. George's Chappell, and there placed us among the Knights' stalls (and pretty the observation, that no man, but a woman may sit in a Knight's place, where any brass-plates are set); and hither come cushions to us, and a young singing-boy to bring us a copy of the anthem to be sung. And here, for our sakes, had this anthem and the great service sung extraordinary, only to entertain us. It is a noble place indeed, and a good Quire of voices. Great bowing by all the people, the poor Knights particularly, to the Alter. After prayers, we to see the plate of the chappell and the robes of Knights, and a man to shew us the banners of the several Knights in being, which hang up over the stalls. And so to other discourse very pretty, about the Order. Was shewn where the late [King] is buried, and King Henry the Eighth and my Lady Seymour. This being done, to the King's house, and to observe the neatness and contrivance of the house and gates: it is the most romantique castle that is in the world. But, Lord! the prospect that is in the balcone in the Queene's lodgings, and the terrace and walk, are strange things to consider, being the best in the world, sure. Infinitely satisfied I and my wife with all this, she being in all points mightily pleased too, which added to my pleasure; and so giving a great deal of money to this and that man and woman, we to our taverne, and there dined, the Doctor with us; and so took coach and away to Eton, the Doctor with me.

At Eton I left my wife in the coach, and he and I to the College, and there find all mighty fine. The school good, and the custom pretty of boys cutting their names in the struts of the window when they go to Cambridge, by which many a one hath lived to see himself Provost and Fellow, that had his name in the window standing. To the Hall, and there find the boys' verses, "De Peste"; it being their custom to make verses at Shrove-tide. I read several, and very good ones they were, and better, I think, than ever I made when I was a boy, and in rolls as long and longer than the whole Hall, by much. Thence to the porter's, in the absence of the butler, and did drink of the College beer, which is very good; and went into the back fields to see the scholars play. Thence took leave of the Doctor, and so took coach, and finely, but sleepy, away home, and got thither about eight at night, and after a little at my office, I to bed; and an houre after, was waked with my wife's quarrelling with Mercer, at which I was angry, and my wife and I fell out. But with much ado to sleep again, I beginning to practise more temper, and to give her her way.

March 2nd. Up as I have of late resolved before 7 in the morning, and to the office, where all the morning, among other things setting my wife and Mercer with much pleasure to worke upon the ruling of some paper for the making of books for pursers, which will require a great deale of worke and they will earn a good deale of money by it, the hopes of which makes them worke mighty hard. Mr. Hill come to sup and take his last leave of me. God give him a good voyage and successe in his business. Thus we parted and my wife and I to bed, heavy for the losse of our friend.[1]

8th. Up betimes and to the office, where all the morning sitting, and did discover three or four fresh instances of Sir W. Pen's old cheating dissembling tricks, he being as false a fellow as ever was born. After dinner I took coach and away to Hales's, where my wife is sitting; and, indeed, her face and necke, which are now

---

[1] Mr. Hill was going to Tangier.

finished, do so please me that I am not myself almost, nor was not all the night after in writing of my letters, in consideration of the fine picture that I shall be master of.

9th. To Sir W. Batten's and there Mrs. Knipp coming we did spend the evening together very merry. She and I singing, and, God forgive me! I do still see that my nature is not to be quite conquered, but will esteem pleasure above all things, though yet in the middle of it it has reluctances after my business, which is neglected by my following my pleasure. However, musique and women I cannot but give way to, whatever my business is.

12th. After dinner comes my uncle and aunt Wight; the latter I have not seen since the plague; a silly, froward, ugly woman she is. We made mighty much of them, and she talks mightily of her fear of the sicknesse, and so a deale of tittle tattle; and I left them and to my office where late, and so home to supper and to bed. This day I hear my Uncle Talbot Pepys died the last week, and was buried.

15th. I and my cozen Anthony Joyce to discourse of our proposition of marriage between Pall and Harman, and he and I to Harman's house and took him to a taverne hard by, and I offered £500, and he declares most ingenuously that his trade is not to be trusted on, that he however needs no money, but would have her money bestowed on her, which I like well, he saying that he would adventure 2 or £300 with her. I like him as a most good-natured, and discreet man, and, I believe, very cunning. We come to this conclusion for us to meete one another the next weeke, and then we hope to come to some end, for I did declare myself well satisfied with the match.

17th. At noon home to dinner and presently with my wife out to Hales's, where I am still infinitely pleased with my wife's picture. I paid him £14 for it, and 25s. for the frame, and I think it is not a whit too deare for so good a picture. This day I begun to sit, and he will make me, I think, a very fine picture. He promises its hall be as good as my wife's, and I sit to have it full of shadows, and do almost break my neck looking over my shoulder to make the posture for him to work by.

19th. This day by letter from my father he propounds a match in the country for Pall, which pleased me well, of one that hath seven score and odd pounds land per annum in possession, and expects £1,000 in money by the death of an old aunt. He hath neither father, mother, sister, nor brother, but demands £600

down, and £100 on the birth of first child, which I had some in-
clination to stretch to.   But my wife tells me he is a drunken,
ill-favoured, ill-bred country fellow, which sets me off of it again,
and I will go on with Harman.

23rd.   Up, and going out of my dressing-room when ready to
go down stairs, I spied little Mrs. Tooker, my pretty little girle,
which, it seems, did come yesterday to our house to stay a little
while with us, but I did not know of it till now.   I was glad of her
coming, she being a very pretty child, and now grown almost a
woman.   I out by six o'clock by appointment to Hales's, where
we fell to my picture presently very hard.   By coach to Anthony
Joyce to receive Harman's answer, which did trouble me to receive, for he now demands £800, whereas he never made exception at the portion, but accepted of £500.   This I do not like;
but however I cannot much blame the man if he thinks he can get
more of another than of me.

24th.   Up and to the office, where all the morning.   At noon
home to dinner, where Anthony Joyce, and I did give my final
answer: I would give but £500 with my sister, and did show him
the good offer made us in the country, to which I did now more
and more incline, and intend to pursue that.

29th.   This day poor Jane, my old, little Jane, came to us
again, to my wife's and my great content; and we hope to take
mighty pleasure in her, she having all the marks and qualities of
a good and loving and honest servant; she coming by force away
from the other place, where she hath lived ever since she went
from us, and at our desire, her late mistresse having used all the
stratagems she could to keepe her.

30th.   My wife and I mighty pleased with Jane's coming to us
again.   Up, and away goes Alce, our cooke-mayde, a good servant,
whom we loved and did well by her, and she an excellent servant,
but would not bear being told of any faulte in the fewest and
kindest words, and would go away of her owne accord after having given her mistresse warning fickly for a quarter of a yeare
together.   So we shall take another girle.

31st.   All the morning at the office busy.   At noon to dinner,
and thence to the office and did my business there as soon as I
could, and then home and to my accounts, where very late at them;
but, Lord! what a deale of do I have to understand any part of
them, and in short, do what I could, I could not come to any understanding of them.   But after I had throughly wearied myself

I was forced to go to bed and leave them much against my will, and vowe too; but I hope God will forgive me, for I have sat up these four nights till past twelve at night to master them, but cannot. Thus ends this month, with my head and mind mighty full and disquiett because of my accounts, which I have let go too long, and confounded my publique with my private that I cannot come to any liquidating of them. However, I do see that I must be grown richer than I was by a good deale last month.

April 3rd. After dinner I to my accounts hard all the afternoon till it was quite darke, and I thank God I do come to bring them very fairly to make me worth £5,000 stocke in the world.

5th. To the office, where the falsenesse and impertinencies of Sir W. Pen would make a man mad to think of. After dinner home, where I find my wife hath on a sudden, upon notice of a coach going away to-morrow, taken a resolution of going in it to Brampton, we having lately thought it fit for her to go to satisfy herself and me in the nature of the fellow that is there proposed to my sister. So she to fit herself for her journey and I to the office all the afternoon till late, and so home and late putting notes to "It is decreed, nor shall thy fate, &c.,"[1] and then to bed.

13th. Up, being called up by my wife's brother, for whom I have got a commission from the Duke of Yorke for Muster-Master of one of the divisions, of which I am glad as well as he. Called upon an old woman in Pannier Ally to agree for ruling of some paper for me and she will do it pretty cheap. Here I found her have a very comely black mayde [Nan] to her servant, which I liked very well.

15th. (Easter Day.) Walked into the Park to the Queene's chappell, and there heard a good deal of their mass, and some of their musique, which is not so contemptible, I think, as our people would make it, it pleasing me very well; and, indeed, better than the anthem I heard afterwards at White Hall, at my coming back. I staid till the King went down to receive the Sacrament, and stood in his closett with a great many others, and there saw him receive it, which I did never see the manner of before. But I do see very little difference between the degree of the ceremonies used by our people in the administration thereof and that in the Roman church, saving that methought our Chappell was not so fine, nor the manner of doing it so glorious, as it was in the Queene's

[1] Ben Jonson's lines: "It is decreed—nor shall thy fate, O Rome! Resist my vow, though hills were set on hills." There was always a bombastic quality about Pepys' songs. The third, "Gaze not on swans!" has not been preserved. "It is decreed" is in the Pepys Library.

chappell. Thence walked to Mr. Pierce's, and there dined, I alone with him and her and their children. After a great deale of discourse I walked thence into the Parke with her little boy James with me, who is the wittiest boy and the best company in the world; and so back again through White Hall both coming and going, and people did generally take him to be my boy.

19th. Anon comes home my wife from Brampton, not looked for till Saturday, which will hinder me of a little pleasure, but I am glad of her coming. She tells me Pall's business is like to go on, but I must give, and she consents to it, another £100. She says she doubts my father is in want of money, for rents come in mighty slowly. My mother grows very unpleasant and troublesome and my father mighty infirm, which altogether makes me mighty thoughtfull.

20th. Up, and after an houre or two's talke with my poor wife, who gives me more and more content every day than other, I abroad by coach to Westminster, and there met with Mrs. Martin, and she and I over the water and after a walke in the fields to the King's Head, and there spent an houre or two with her, and eat a tansy and so parted; and I to the New Exchange, there to get a list of all the modern plays which I intend to collect and to have them bound up together.

23rd. The plague, I hear, encreases in the towne much, and exceedingly in the country everywhere. Walked to Westminster Hall, and after a little stay, I took coach and away home, in my way asking in two or three places the worth of pearles, I being now come to the time that I have long ago promised my wife a necklace. There find a girle sent at my desire by Mrs. Michell of Westminster Hall, to be my girle under the cooke-mayde, Susan. But I am a little dissatisfied that the girle, though young, is taller and bigger than Su, and will not, I fear, be under her command, which will trouble me.

24th. Up, and presently am told that the girle that came yesterday hath packed up her things to be gone home again to Enfield, whence she come, which I was glad of, that we might be at first rid of her altogether rather than be liable to her going away hereafter. The reason was that London do not agree with her. So I did give her something, and away she went.

25th. Abroad to my ruler's of my books, having, God forgive me! a mind to see Nan there, which I did; and so back again. And then out again to see Mrs. Bettons, who were looking out of the window as I come through Fenchurch Street: so that indeed I am not, as I ought to be, able to command myself in the pleasures of my eye. So home, and with my wife and Mercer spent our evening upon our new leads by our bedchamber singing, while Mrs. Mary Batelier looked out of the window to us. It is a convenience I would not want for anything in the world, it being methinks better than almost any room in my house.

28th. Very busy all the afternoon till night, among other things, writing a letter to my brother John, the first I have done since my being angry with him,[1] and that so sharpe a one too that I was sorry almost to send it when I had wrote it, but it is preparatory to my being kind to him, and sending for him up hither when he hath passed his degree of Master of Arts.

30th. Dined alone, my wife gone abroad to conclude about her necklace of pearle. My wife comes home by and by, and hath pitched upon a necklace with three rows, which is a very good one, and £80 is the price. In the evening with my wife and Mercer by coach to take the ayre as far as Bow, and eat and drank in the coach by the way and with much pleasure and pleased with my company. So ends this month with great layings-out. Good health and gettings, and advanced well in the whole of my estate, for which God make me thankful!

May 4th. Had a great fray with my wife again about Browne's coming to teach her to paynt, and sitting with me at table, which I will not yield to. I do thoroughly believe she means no hurte in it; but very angry we were, and I resolved all into my having my will done without disputing, be the reason what it will; and so I will have it. This evening, being weary of my late idle courses, and the little good I shall do the King or myself in the office, I bound myself to very strict rules till Whitsunday next.

5th. At the office till 10 at night busy about letters and other necessary matter of the office. About 11 I home, it being a fine moonshine and so my wife and Mercer come into the garden, and, my business being done, we sang till about twelve at night, with mighty pleasure to ourselves and neighbours, by their casements opening, and so home to supper and to bed.

9th. Up by five o'clock, which I have not a long time done, and down the river by water to Deptford. Walked back again reading of my Civill Law Book, and so home and by coach to White

---

[1] John Pepys had written in slighting terms about Samuel to his brother Tom, and Samuel had found the letters among Tom's papers after the death of the latter two years previously. Pepys had taken occasion to reprimand John before his father with great severity.

Hall. Thence by water to Westminster, so away home and to dinner. After dinner away to my Lord Treasurer's, and thence to Pierce's, where I find Knipp, and I took them to Hales's to see our pictures finished. So home, where my wife in mighty pain and mightily vexed at my being abroad with these women; and when they were gone called them I know not what, which vexed me. So I with them to Mrs. Turner's and there sat with them a while. Anon my wife sends for me; I come, and what was it but to scold at me, and she would go abroad to take the ayre presently, that she would. So I left my company and went with her to Bow, but was vexed and spoke not one word to her all the way going nor coming, or being come home, but went up straight to bed. Half an hour after (she in the coach leaning on me as being desirous to be friends) she comes up mighty sicke with a fit of the cholique and in mighty pain and calls for me out of the bed. I rose and held her; she prays me to forgive her, and in mighty pain we put her to bed, where the pain ceased by and by; and so had some asparagus to our bed side for supper and very kindly afterward to sleepe and good friends in the morning.

10th. Busy till past six o'clock, and then abroad with my wife by coach, who is now at great ease. We took with us Mrs. Turner, who was come to visit my wife just as we were going out. A great deale of tittle tattle discourse to little purpose, I finding her, though in other things a very discreete woman, as very a gossip speaking of her neighbours as any body. Going out towards Hackney by coach for the ayre, the silly coachman carries us to Shoreditch, which was so pleasant a piece of simplicity in him and us, that made us mighty merry. So back again late, it being wondrous hot all the day and night and it lightning exceeding all the way we went and came, but without thunder. Coming home we called at a little ale-house, and had an eele pye, of which my wife eat part and brought home the rest. So being come home we to supper and to bed. This day come our new cook maid Mary.

17th. To the office, where all the morning with fresh occasion of vexing at myself for my late neglect of business, by which I cannot appear half so usefull as I used to do. Home at noon to dinner, and then to my office again, where I could not hold my eyes open for an houre, but I drowsed (so little sensible I apprehend my soul is of the necessity of minding business), but I anon wakened and minded my business, and did a great deale with very great pleasure; and so home at night to supper and to bed, mightily pleased with myself for the business that I have done, and convinced that if I would but keepe constantly to do the same I might have leisure enough and yet do all my business; and by the grace of God so I will. So to bed.

21st. Up between 4 and 5 o'clock and to set several papers to rights, and so to the office. At noon dined at home, and after dinner comes in my wife's brother Balty and his wife, he being stepped ashore from the fleete for a day or two. In discourse I am infinitely pleased with his deportment in his business of Muster-Master, and hope mighty well from him, and am glad with all my heart I put him into this business.

29th. (King's birth-day and Restauration day.) Waked with the ringing of the bells all over the towne; so up before five o'clock, and to the office, where we met. At noon I did, upon a small invitation of Sir W. Pen's, go and dine with Sir W. Coventry at his office and did go with them after dinner to the Victualling office; and there, beyond belief, did acquit myself very well to full content. Being broke up there, I home to my office, and thither my wife comes to me, to tell me that if I would see the handsomest woman in England I shall come home presently: and who should it be but the pretty lady of our parish that did heretofore sit on the other side of our church over against our gallery, that is since married: she with Mrs. Anne Jones, one of this parish, that dances finely, and Mrs. —— sister did come to see her this afternoon; and so I home and there find Creed also come to me. So there I spent most of the afternoon with them, and indeed she is a pretty black woman, her name Mrs. Horsely. But, Lord! to see how my nature could not refrain from the temptation but I must invite them to Foxhall, to Spring Gardens, though I had freshly received minutes of a great deale of extraordinary business. However I could not helpe it, but sent them before with Creed, and I did some of my business; and so after them and find them there in an arbour, and had met with Mrs. Pierce and some company with her. So here I spent 20*s.* upon them and were pretty merry. Among other things, had a fellow that imitated all manner of birds and doggs and hogs with his voice, which was mighty pleasant. Staid here till night, and then home.

30th. Toward noon word is brought me that my father and my sister are come. I expected them to-day, but not so soon. I to them, and am heartily glad to see them.

31st. Waked very betimes in the morning by extraordinary thunder and rain, which did keep me sleeping and waking till very late. So up, and so saw all my family up, and my father and sister, who is a pretty good-bodied woman, and not over thicke, as I thought she would have been, but full of freckles, and not handsome in face. And so I out by water among the ships, and to Deptford and Blackewall about business, and so home and to dinner with my father and sister and family, mighty pleasant all of us; and among other things with a sparrow that our Mercer hath brought up now for three weeks, which is so tame that it flies up and down, and upon the table, and eats and pecks, and do everything so pleasantly that we are mightily pleased with it.

June 2nd. Up, and to the office, where certain newes is brought us of a letter come to the King this morning from the Duke of Albemarle,[1] dated yesterday at eleven o'clock, as they were sailing to the Gunfleete, that they were in sight of the Dutch fleete, and were fitting themselves to fight them; so that they are, ere this, certainly engaged; besides, several do averr they heard the guns all yesterday in the afternoon. This put us at the Board into a tosse. Presently come orders for our sending away to the fleete a recruite of 200 soldiers. So I rose from the table, and to the Victualling-office, and thence upon the River among several vessels to consider of the sending them away; and lastly down to Greenwich, and there appointed two yachts to be ready for them, and did order the soldiers to march to Blackewall. Walked to the waterside, and there seeing the King and Duke come down in their barge to Greenwich-house, I to them, and did give them an account of what I was doing. They went up to the Parke to hear the guns of the fleete go off. After dinner, having nothing else to do till flood, I went and saw Mrs. Daniel, to whom I did not tell that the fleets were engaged, because of her husband, who is in the R. Charles. Very pleasant with her half an hour, and so away and down to Blackewall, and there saw the soldiers (who were by this time gotten most of them drunk) shipped off. But, Lord! to see how the poor fellows kissed their wives and sweethearts in that simple manner at their going off, and shouted, and let off their guns, was strange sport.

4th. Up, and with Sir J. Minnes and Sir W. Pen to White Hall in the latter's coach, where, when we come, we find the Duke at St. James's, whither he is lately gone to lodge. So walk-

[1] The Duke and Prince Rupert had gone to sea on April 23.

ing through the Parke we saw hundreds of people listening to hear the guns. After wayting upon the Duke, Sir W. Pen and I home in his new fine coach, where no sooner come, but newes is brought me of a couple of men come to speak with me from the fleete; so I down, and who should it be but Mr. Daniel, all muffled up, and his face as black as the chimney, and covered with dirt, pitch, and tarr, and powder, and muffled with dirty clouts, and his right eye stopped with okum. He is come last night at five o'clock from the fleete, with a comrade of his that hath endangered another eye. I went presently into the coach with them, and carried them to Somerset-House-stairs, and there took water (all the world gazing upon us and concluding it to be newes from the fleete, and every body's face appeared expecting of newes) to the Privy-stairs, and left them at Mr. Coventry's lodging (he, though, not being there); and so I into the Parke to the King, and told him my Lord Generall was well the last night at five o'clock, and the Prince come with his fleete and joyned with his about seven. The King was mightily pleased with this newes, and so took me by the hand and talked a little of it; and then he bid me to fetch the two seamen to him, and there he heard the whole account.

5th. Up, and to the office, where all the morning, expecting every houre more newes of the fleete and the issue of yesterday's fight, but nothing come.

6th. To St. James's. There we all met and did our business as usual with the Duke. Thence after the Duke into the Parke, walking through to White Hall, and there every body listening for guns, but none heard, and every creature is now overjoyed and concludes upon very good grounds that the Dutch are beaten because we have heard no guns nor no newes of our fleete. By and by an expresse to Sir W. Coventry, being the narration of Captain Hayward of The Dunkirke, gives a very serious account; how upon Monday the two fleetes fought all day till seven at night, and then the whole fleete of Dutch did betake themselves to a very plain flight, and never looked back again. That Sir Christopher Mings is wounded in the leg; that the Generall is well. That it is conceived reasonably, that of all the Dutch fleete, which, with what recruits they had, come to one hundred sayle, there is not above fifty got home; and of them, few if any of their flags. We were all so overtaken with this good newes that the Duke ran with it to the King, who was gone to chappell, and there all the Court was in a hubbub, being rejoiced over head and ears in this good newes.

Away go I by coach to the New Exchange, and there did spread this good newes a little, though I find it had broke out before. And so home to our own church, it being the common Fast-day, and it was just before sermon; but, Lord! how all the people in the church stared upon me to see me whisper to Sir John Minnes and my Lady Pen. Here after sermon comes to our office 40 people almost of all sorts and qualities to hear the newes, which I took great delight to tell them. Then home and found my wife at dinner, not knowing of my being at church, and after dinner my father and she out to Hales's, where my father is to begin to sit to-day for his picture, which I have a desire to have. Bonefires were lighted all the towne over. The joy of the city was this night exceeding great.

7th. Up betimes, and to my office about business. My Lord Bruncker and Sir T. H.[1] that come from Court, tell me quite contrary newes which astonishes me, that we are beaten, lost many ships and good commanders; have not taken one ship of the enemy's. The Duke of Albemarle writes that he never fought with worse officers in his life, not above twenty of them behaving themselves like men. It was as great an alteration to find myself required to write a sad letter instead of a triumphant one to my Lady Sandwich this night, as ever on any occasion I had in my life. So late home and to bed.

8th. To the Exchequer about some Tangier businesses, and then home, where to my very great joy I find Balty come home without any hurt, after the utmost imaginable danger he hath gone through in the Henery, being upon the quarter-deck with Harman all the time.

10th. (Lord's Day.) Up very betimes, and down the river to Deptford, and did a good deale of business in sending away and directing several things to the Fleete. That being done, back to London to my office. At noon home to dinner, where my cozen Joyces, both of them, they and their wives and little Will, come by invitation to dinner to me, and I had a good dinner for them; but, Lord! how sicke was I of W. Joyce's company, both the impertinencies of it and his ill manners before me at my table to his wife, which I could hardly forbear taking notice of; but being at my table and for his wife's sake, I did, though I will prevent his giving me the like occasion again at my house I will warrant him. After dinner I took leave and by water to White Hall, and

---

[1] Sir Thomas Harvey.

"AND THERE TOOK WATER"

there spent all the afternoon in the Gallery, till the Council was up, to speake with Sir W. Coventry. Walking here I met with Pierce the surgeon, who is lately come from the fleete, and tells me that all the commanders, officers, and even the common seamen do condemn every part of the late conduct of the Duke of Albemarle: both in his fighting at all, in his manner of fighting, running among them in his retreat, and running the ships on ground; so as nothing can be worse spoken of. This evening we hear that Sir Christopher Mings is dead of his late wounds; and Sir W. Coventry did commend him to me in a most extraordinary manner.

12th. Up, and to the office, where we sat all the morning. At noon to dinner, and then to White Hall. Walking here in the galleries I find the Ladies of Honour dressed in their riding garbs, with coats and doublets with deep skirts, just for all the world like mine, and buttoned their doublets up the breast, with perriwigs and with hats; so that, only for a long petticoat dragging under their men's coats, nobody could take them for women in any point whatever; which was an odde sight, and a sight did not please me.

13th. In my way homeward did buy a couple of lobsters, and so home to dinner, where I find my wife and father had dined and were going out to Hales's to sit there. So Balty and I alone to dinner; and in the middle of my grace, praying for a blessing upon (these his good creatures), my mind fell upon my lobsters: upon which I cried, Odd zooks! and Balty looked upon me like a man at a losse what I meant, thinking at first that I meant only that I had said the grace after meat instead of that before meat. But then I cried, what is become of my lobsters? Whereupon he run out of doors to overtake the coach, but could not, so came back again, and mighty merry at dinner to thinke of my surprize.

Being invited to Sir Christopher Mings's funeral, I into the church and there heard the service, and staid till they buried him, and then out. And there met with Sir W. Coventry (who was there out of great generosity, and no person of quality there but he) and went with him into his coach, and being in it with him there happened this extraordinary case. About a dozen able, lusty, proper men come to the coach-side with tears in their eyes, and one of them that spoke for the rest begun and says to Sir W. Coventry, "We are here a dozen of us that have long known and loved, and served our dead commander Sir Christopher Mings, and have now done the last office of laying him in the ground. We would be glad we had any other to offer after him, and in revenge of him. All we have is our lives; if you will please to get His Royal Highness to give us a fire-ship among us all, here is a dozen of us, out of all which choose you one to be commander, and the rest of us, whoever he is, will serve him, and if possible do that that shall show our memory of our dead commander, and our revenge." Sir W. Coventry was herewith much moved (as well as I, who could hardly abstain from weeping), and took their names, and so parted; telling me that he would move His Royal Highness as in a thing very extraordinary, which was done.

20th. Up, but in some pain of the collique. I have of late taken too much cold by washing my feet and going in a thin silke waistcoate without any other coate over it, and open-breasted, but I hope it will go over. I did this morning (my father being to go away to-morrow) give my father some money to buy him a horse, and for other things. In Cheapside I met Mrs. Williams in a coach, and she called me, so I must needs 'light and go along with her and Knipp as far as Paternoster Row, which I did do and there staid in Bennett's shop with them, and was fearful lest the people of the shop, knowing me, should ask after my father and give Mrs. Williams any knowledge of me to my disgrace.

24th. Sunday. Midsummer day. By water to Deptford, and there did a great deale of business, being in a mighty hurry, Sir W. Coventry writing to me that there was some thoughts that the Dutch fleete were out or coming out. Business being done, I away back home, and after dinner by water to White Hall, and there waited till the councill rose, in the boarded gallery. By and by Sir W. Coventry comes out, and he and I took his coach, and to Hide-Parke. He do, I perceive, forbear saying any thing to the reproach of the Duke of Albemarle; but I do as plainly see that he do not like the Duke of Albemarle's proceedings. He concurs with me, that the next bout will be a fatal one to one side or other, because if we be beaten we shall not be able to set out our fleete again. Back to White Hall, and there I left him, being in a little doubt whether I had behaved myself in my discourse with the policy and circumspection which ought to be used to so great a courtier as he is, and so wise and factious a man.

26th. Up and to my office betimes, and there all the morning, very busy to get out the fleete, the Dutch being now for certain out. At noon to the 'Change about business, and so home to dinner, and after dinner to the setting my Journall to rights. And so to the office again, where all the afternoon full of business, and there till night, that my eyes were sore that I could not write no longer. Then into the garden, then my wife and Mercer and my Lady Pen and her daughter with us, and here we sung in the darke very finely half an houre, and so home to supper and to bed.

29th. To the office, where I met with a letter from Dover, which tells me (and it did come by expresse) that newes is brought over by a gentleman from Callice that the Dutch fleete, 130 sail, are come upon the French coast, and that the country is bringing in picke-axes and shovells and wheel-barrows into Callice; that there are 6,000 men armed with head, back and breast (Frenchmen) ready to go on board the Dutch fleete, and will be followed by 12,000 more; that they pretend they are to come to Dover, and that thereupon the Governor of Dover Castle is getting the victuallers' provision out of the towne into the Castle to secure it. But I do think this is a ridiculous conceit; but a little time will show.

30th. Up and to the office, and mightily troubled all this morning with going to my Lord Mayor (Sir Thomas Bludworth, a silly man, I think), and other places, about getting shipped some men that they have these two last nights pressed in the City out of houses: the persons wholly unfit for sea, and many of them people of very good fashion, which is a shame to think of; and carried to Bridewell they are, yet without being impressed with money legally as they ought to be. But to see how the King's business is done; my Lord Mayor himself did scruple at this time of extremity to do this thing because he had not money to pay the pressed-money to the men; he told me so himself. Nor to take up boats to carry them down through bridge to the ships I had prepared to carry them down in; insomuch that I was forced to promise to be his paymaster, and he did send his City Remembrancer afterwards to the office, and at the table, in the face of the officers, I did there out of my owne purse disburse £15 to pay for their pressing and diet last night and this morning; which is a thing worth record of my Lord Mayor. Busy about this all the morning; at noon dined and then to the office again, and all the afternoon till twelve at night full of this business and others. Home to supper and to bed. But before I was in bed, while I was undressing myself, our new ugly mayde, Luce, had like to have broke her necke in the darke, going down our upper stairs. But, which I was glad of, the poor girle did only bruise her head; but at first did lie on the ground groaning and drawing her breath like one a-dying.

July 1st. (Sunday.) To Deptford to the yard, and so back to the Tower several times about the business of the pressed men, and late at it till twelve at night, shipping of them. But, Lord! how some poor women did cry; and in my life I never did see such natural expression of passion as I did here in some women's be-wailing themselves, and running to every parcel of men that were brought, one after another, to look for their husbands; and wept over every vessel that went off, thinking they might be there, and looking after the ship as far as ever they could by moonlight, that it grieved me to the heart to hear them. Besides, to see poor patient labouring men and housekeepers leaving poor wives and families, taking up on a sudden by strangers, was very hard, and that without press-money, but forced against all law to be gone. It is a great tyranny.

4th. To the office, where busy all day; and in the evening Sir W. Pen come to me, and we walked together and talked of the late fight. He told me that our very commanders, nay, our very flag-officers, do stand in need of exercising among themselves; and discoursing the business of commanding a fleete, he telling me that even one of our flag-men in the fleete did not know which tacke lost the wind or which kept it, in the last engagement. He did talk very rationally to me, insomuch that I took more pleasure this night in hearing him discourse than I ever did in my life in any thing that he said.

6th. Up, and after doing some business at my office, abroad to Lumbard Street about the getting of a good sum of money thence home, in preparation for my having some good sum in my hands for fear of a trouble in the State, that I may not have all I have in the world out of my hands and so be left a beggar. Dined with Sir G. Carteret, and after dinner had much discourse about our publique business; and he plainly answering me to the question, who is it that the weight of the warr depends upon? that it is only Sir W. Coventry. He tells me too the Duke of Albemarle is dissatisfied, and that the Duchesse do curse Coventry as the man that betrayed her husband to the sea; though I believe that it is not so. Thence to Lumbard Streete and received £2,000, and carried it home, whereof £1,000 in gold; the greatest quantity not only that I ever had of gold, but that ever I saw together.

Being at home, I there met with a letter from Bab Allen,[1] to invite me to be godfather to her boy, which I consented to, but know not the time when it is to be.

7th. At the office all the morning; at noon dined at home, and Creed with me. He tells me he finds all things mighty dull at Court, and that they now begin to lie long in bed; it being, as we suppose, not seemly for them to be found playing and gaming as they used to be, nor that their minds are at ease enough to follow those sports; and yet not knowing how to employ themselves (though there be work enough for their thoughts and councils and pains), they keep long in bed.

9th. After dinner to my office, where busy till come to by Lovett and his wife. Home with them, and there find my aunt Wight with my wife; and there was also Mrs. Mary Batelier and her sister, newly come out of France, a black, very black woman, but mighty good-natured people both, as ever I saw. Here I made the black one sing a French song, which she did mighty innocently; and then Mrs. Lovett play on the lute, which she do very well; and then Mercer and I sang; and so with great pleasure I left them, having shewed them my chamber, and £1,000 in gold, which they wondered at, and given them sweetmeats, and shewn my aunt Wight my father's picture, which she admires.

10th. To the office, the yarde being very full of women (I believe above three hundred) coming to get money for their husbands and friends that are prisoners in Holland; and they lay clamouring and swearing and cursing us, that my wife and I were afeard to send a venison-pasty that we have for supper to-night to the cook's to be baked, for fear of their offering violence to it; but it went, and no hurt done. Then I took an opportunity when they were all gone into the fore-yarde and slipt into the office, and there busy all the afternoon. But by and by the women got into the garden and come all to my closett window, and there tormented me; and I confess their cries were so sad for money, and laying down the condition of their families and their husbands, and what they have done and suffered for the King, and how ill they are used by us, and how well the Dutch are used here by the allowance of their masters, and what their husbands are offered to serve the Dutch abroad, that I do most heartily pity them, and was ready to cry to hear them, but cannot helpe them. However when the rest were gone I did call one to me that I heard

[1] Mrs. Knipp; see entry for January 5, *ante.*

complaine only and pity her husband, and did give her some money, and she blessed me and went away. Anon, my business at the office being done, I home and there find my wife and the two Mrs. Bateliers walking in the garden. Had a good supper, and very merry, Mistresses Bateliers being both very good-humoured. We sang and talked, and then led them home, and there they made us drink; and among other things did show us in cages some birds brought from about Bourdeaux that are all fat; and, examining one of them, they are so, almost all fat. Their name is [Ortolans],[1] which are brought over to the King for him to eat, and indeed are excellent things.

11th. Up, and by water to Sir G. Downing's. Away by coach to St. James's. By and by called to wait on the Duke, the King being present. Thence to Westminster Hall and there staid a while, and then to the Swan and kissed Sarah, and so home to dinner, and after dinner out again to Sir Robert Viner. Thence to Westminster, doing several things by the way; so by coach took up my wife at her sister's, and so away to Islington, and home late. But when I come to the office I there met with a command from my Lord Arlington to go down to a galliott at Greenwich, by the King's particular command, that is going to carry the Savoy Envoye over, and we fear there may be many Frenchmen there on board; and so I have a power and command to search for and seize all that have not passes from one of the Secretarys of State. So I to the Tower, and got a couple of musquetiers with me, and Griffen and my boy Tom, and so down; and being come found none on board. I staid not long there, but away, and on shore at Greenwich, the night being late and the tide against us; so, having sent before, to Mrs. Clerke's, and there I had a good bed and well received, the whole people rising to see me; and among the rest young Mrs. Daniel, whom I kissed again and again alone, and so by and by to bed and slept pretty well.

12th. But was up again by five o'clock, and was forced to rise, having much business, and so up and dressed myself. At the office all the morning. At noon home and thought to have slept, my head all day being full of business and yet sleepy and out of order, and so I lay down on my bed in my gowne to sleep, but I could not. Therefore about three o'clock up and to dinner, and thence to the office, where Mrs. Burroughs, my pretty widow, was; and so I sent her away by agreement, and presently I by

[1] There is a blank space here in the MS.

coach after, and took her up in Fenchurch Streete and away through the City, hiding my face as much as I could, but she being mighty pretty and well enough clad I was not afeard, but only lest somebody should see me and think me idle. And so into the fields Uxbridge way, a mile or two beyond Tyburne, and then back to Charing Crosse, and there I set her down. All the way most excellent pretty company. I had her lips as much as I would, and a mighty pretty woman she is and very modest, and yet kinde in all fair ways. All this time I passed with mighty pleasure, it being what I have for a long time wished for, and did pay this day 5s. forfeite for her company. She being gone, I to White Hall and there to Lord Arlington's. So home, where at the office did the most in that wearied and sleepy state I could, and so home to supper. And after supper falling to singing with Mercer did however sit up with her, she pleasing me with her singing of "Helpe, helpe," till past midnight and I not a whit drowsy; and so to bed.

14th. To the office very late, very busy, and did indeed dispatch much business; and so to supper and to bed. After a song in the garden, which, and after dinner, is now the greatest pleasure I take, and indeed do please me mightily, to bed, after washing my legs and feet with warm water in my kitchen. This evening I had Davila[1] brought home to me, and find it a most excellent history as ever I read.

18th. Up in good case, and so by coach to St. James's and there did our business, which is mostly every day to complain of want of money; and that only will undo us in a little time. Thence with Sir W. Pen home, calling at Lilly's to have a time appointed when to be drawn among the other Commanders of Flags the last year's fight.[2] And so full of work Lilly is that he was fain to take his table-book out to see how his time is appointed, and appointed six days hence for him to come between seven and eight in the morning. I to the office, where busy all the afternoon, and in the evening with Sir W. Pen, walking with whom in the garden I am of late mighty great; and it is wisdom to continue myself so, for he is of all the men of the office at present most manifestly usefull and best thought of. He and I supped together upon the seat in the garden, and thence, he gone, my wife and Mercer come and walked and sang late, and then home to bed.

---

[1] *Storia delle guerre civili di Francia,* by Enrico Caterino Davila.
[2] This portrait by Sir Peter Lely is now at Greenwich Hospital.

21st. Up and to the office, where all the morning sitting. At noon walked in the garden with Commissioner Pett (newly come to towne), who tells me how infinite the disorders are among the commanders and all officers of the fleete. No discipline; nothing but swearing and cursing, and every body doing what they please; and the Generalls, understanding no better, suffer it, to the reproaching of this Board, or whoever it will be. Sir W. Pen is gone down to Sheernesse to-day to see things made ready against the fleete shall come in again, which makes Pett mad, and calls him dissembling knave, and that himself takes all the pains and is blamed, while he do nothing but hinder business and takes all the honour of it to himself, and tells me plainly he will fling up his commission rather than bear it.

23rd. Up, and to my chamber doing several things there of moment, and then comes Sympson, the Joyner; and he and I with great pains contriving presses to put my books up in, they now growing numerous, and lying one upon another on my chairs. After dinner to the office and there till five or six o'clock, and then by coach to St. James's, and there with Sir W. Coventry and Sir G. Downing to take the ayre in the Parke.

25th. Up betimes. At White Hall we find the Court gone to Chappell, it being St. James's-day. And by and by, while they are at chappell, and we waiting chappell being done, come people out of the Parke, telling us that the guns are heard plain. And so every body to the Parke; and by and by the chappell done, and the King and Duke into the bowling-green and upon the leads, whither I went, and there the guns were plain to be heard; though it was pretty to hear how confident some would be in the loudnesse of the guns, which it was as much as ever I could do to hear them. By and by the King to dinner, and I waited there his dining; but, Lord! how little I should be pleased, I think, to have so many people crowding about me; and among other things it astonished me to see my Lord Barkeshire[1] waiting at table and serving the King drink, in that dirty pickle as I never saw man in my life. Here I met Mr. Williams, who would have me to dine where he was invited to dine, at the Backe-stayres. So after the King's meat was taken away, we thither; but he could not stay, but left me there among two or three of the King's servants, where we dined with the meat that come from his table; which was most excellent, with most brave drink cooled in ice (which

---

[1] Thomas Howard, 1st Earl of Berkshire, was then aged about eighty-five.

at this hot time was welcome), and I drinking no wine had metheglin [1] for the King's own drinking, which did please me mightily.

28th. With my Lord Bruncker went to my Lord Lauderdale's [2] house to speake with him. We find [him] and his lady and some Scotch people at supper. Pretty odd company. But at supper there played one of their servants upon the viallin some Scotch tunes only; several, and the best of their country, as they seemed to esteem them by their praising and admiring them, but, Lord! the strangest ayre that ever I heard in my life, and all of one cast. But strange to hear my Lord Lauderdale say himself that he had rather hear a cat mew than the best musique in the world, and the better the musique the more sicke it makes him; and that of all instruments he hates the lute most, and next to that the baggpipe.

29th. (Lord's Day.) A letter from Sir W. Coventry tells me that we have the victory, and had taken two of their great ships. Mr. Spong and Reeves dined with me by invitation, and after dinner to our business of my microscope to be shown some of the observables of that; and then down to my office to looke in a darke room with my glasses and tube, and most excellently things appeared indeed beyond imagination.

31st. To a Committee of Tangier, and did come thither time enough to meet Povy and Creed and none else. The Court being empty, the King being gone to Tunbridge and the Duke of York a-hunting. I had some discourse with Povy, who is mightily discontented I find about his disappointments at Court, and says of all places, if there be hell, it is here. No faith, no truth, no love, nor any agreement between man and wife, nor friends. He would have spoke broader but I put it off to another time, and so parted. Then with Creed and read over with him the narrative of the late fight, which he makes a very poor thing of, as it is indeed.

August 1st. Up betimes to the settling of my last month's accounts, and I bless God I find them very clear, and that I am worth £5,700, the most that ever my book did yet make out. So prepared to attend the Duke of Yorke as usual, but Sir W. Pen just as I was going out comes home from Sheernesse, and held me in discourse about publique business, till I come by coach too late to St. James's, and there find that every thing stood still and noth-

---

[1] A liquor made of honey and water, boiled and fermenting.
[2] Secretary of State for Scotland. His house was on Highgate Hill (now included in Waterlow Park).

ing done for want of me. Thence walked over the Parke with Sir W. Coventry, who I clearly see is not thoroughly pleased with the late management of the fight, nor with any thing that the Generalls do. I left him going to Chappell, and after dinner to Mrs. Martin's, and there find Mrs. Burroughs, and by and by comes a pretty widow, one Mrs. Eastwood, and one Mrs. Fenton, a maid; and here merry kissing and all the innocent pleasure in the world. But, Lord! to see the dissembling of this widow, how upon the singing of a certain jigg by Doll, Mrs. Martin's sister, she seemed to be sick and fainted and God knows what, because the jigg which her husband (who died this last sickness) loved.

5th. (Lord's Day.) To the church by Merchant-tailors' Hall, and there I find in the pulpit Elborough, my old schoolfellow and a simple rogue, and yet I find him preaching a very good sermon, and in as right a parson-like manner, and in good manner too, as I have heard any body; and the church very full, which is a surprising consideration. So home and had a good dinner, and after dinner with my wife and Mercer and Jane by water all the afternoon up as high as Morclacke with great pleasure, and a fine day, reading over the second part of the "Siege of Rhodes," with great delight. We landed and walked at Barne-elmes, and then at the Neat Houses I landed and bought a millon; and we did also land and eat and drink at Wandsworth, and so to the Old Swan and thence walked home, it being a mighty fine cool evening. And there being come, my wife and I spent an houre in the garden talking.

6th. After dinner in comes Mrs. Knipp. I very pleasant with her, but perceive my wife hath no great pleasure in her being here, she not being pleased with my kindnesse to her. By and by comes Mr. Pierce and his wife, and here we talked and were pleasant, only my wife in a chagrin humour, she not being pleased with my kindnesse to either of them: and by and by she fell into some silly discourse wherein I checked her, which made her mighty pettish, and discoursed mighty offensively to Mrs. Pierce, which did displease me. But I would make no words, but put the discourse by as much as I could (it being about a report that my wife said was made of herself and meant by Mrs. Pierce, that she was grown a gallant, when she had but so few suits of clothes these two or three years, and a great deale of that silly discourse). But by this means we had little pleasure in their visit; however Knipp and I sang, and then I offered them to carry them home and to take my wife with me, but she would not go. However I would not be removed from my civility to them, but sent for a coach and went with them; and in our way, Knipp saying that she come out of doors without a dinner to us, I took them to Old Fish Streete, to the very house and woman where I kept my wedding dinner, where I never was since, and there I did give them a jole of salmon and what else was to be had. I set them both at home, and so home, and there find my wife mightily out of order, and reproaching of Mrs. Pierce and Knipp as wenches, and I know not what. But I did give her no words to offend her, and quietly let all pass; and so to bed without any good looke or words to or from my wife.

7th. Up, and to the office, where we sat all the morning, and home to dinner, and then to the office again, being pretty good friends with my wife again, no angry words passed. In the evening comes Mr. Reeves with a twelve-foote glasse, so I left the office and home, where I met Mr. Batelier with my wife, in order to our going to-morrow by agreement to Bow to see a dancing meeting. But, Lord! to see how soon I could conceive evil fears and thoughts concerning them; so Reeves and I and they up to the top of the house, and there we endeavoured to see the moon and Saturne and Jupiter; but the heavens proved cloudy, and so we lost our labour, having taken pains to get things together, in order to the managing of our long glasse. So down to supper and then to bed, Reeves lying at my house.

8th. Up, and with Reeves walk as far as the Temple, and there parted, and I took coach, having first discoursed with Mr. Hooke[1] a little, whom we met in the streete, about the nature of sounds, and he did make me understand the nature of musicall sounds made by strings, mighty prettily; and told me that having come to a certain number of vibrations proper to make any tone, he is able to tell how many strokes a fly makes with her wings (those flies that hum in their flying) by the note that it answers to in musique during their flying. That, I suppose, is a little too much refined; but his discourse in general of sound was mighty fine. There I left them, and myself by coach to St. James's, where we attended with the rest of my fellows on the Duke, whom I found with two or three patches upon his nose and about his right eye, which come from his being struck with the bough of a tree the other day in his hunting; and it is a wonder it did not strike out his eye. To my Lady Pooly's where my wife was with Mr. Batelier and his sisters, and there I found

---

[1] Dr. Robert Hooke, a distinguished experimentalist in the early history of the Royal Society.

a noble supper, and every thing exceeding pleasant. About
ten o'clock we rose from table and sang a song, and so home in
two coaches; and being there come, and sent away Mr. Batelier
and his sister, I find Reeves there, it being a mighty fine bright
night; and so upon my leads, though very sleepy, till one in the
morning, looking on the moon and Jupiter with this twelve-foote
glasse and another of six foote that he hath brought with him to-
night, and the sights mighty pleasant, and one of the glasses I
will buy, it being very usefull. So to bed mighty sleepy, Reeves
lying at my house again; and mighty proud I am (and ought to be
thankfull to God Almighty) that I am able to have a spare bed
for my friends.

12th. (Lord's Day.) Up and to my chamber, where busy
all the morning, and my thoughts very much upon the manner of
my removal of my closett things the next weeke into my present
musique room, if I find I can spare or get money to furnish it.
In the evening I and my wife up to her closett to consider how to
order that the next summer, if we live to it; and then down to
my chamber at night to examine her kitchen accounts, and
there I took occasion to fall out with her for her buying a laced
handkercher and pinner without my leave. Though the thing is
not much, yet I would not permit her begin to do so, lest worse
should follow. From this we began both to be angry, and so continued till bed, and did not sleep friends.

13th. Up, without being friends with my wife, nor great
enemies, being both quiet and silent. So out to Paul's Churchyarde, to treat with a bookbinder to come and gild the backs of
all my books, to make them handsome to stand in my new presses
when they come.

14th. (Thanksgiving day.[1]) After dinner with my wife and
Mercer to the Beare-garden,[2] where I have not been, I think, of
many years, and saw some good sport of the bull's tossing of the
dogs, one into the very boxes. But it is a very rude and nasty
pleasure. We had a great many hectors in the same box with us
(and one very fine went into the pit and played his dog for a wager,
which was a strange sport for a gentleman), where they drank
wine, and drank Mercer's health first, which I pledged with my
hat off; and who should be in the house but Mr. Pierce the surgeon,
who saw us and spoke to us. Thence home, well enough satisfied

---

[1] For the late victory at sea over the Dutch.
[2] On the south bank of the river, near the present site of Southwark Bridge.

however with the variety of this afternoon's exercise; and so I to
my chamber, till in the evening our company come to supper. We
had invited to a venison pasty Mr. Batelier and his sister Mary,
Mrs. Mercer, her daughter Anne, Mr. Le Brun and W. Hewer;
and so we supped, and very merry. And then about nine o'clock
to Mrs. Mercer's gate, where the fire and boys expected us, and
her son had provided abundance of serpents and rockets; and there
mighty merry (my Lady Pen and Pegg going thither with us, and
Nan Wright), till about twelve at night, flinging our fireworks,
and burning one another and the people over the way. And at
last our businesses being most spent, we into Mrs. Mercer's, and
there mighty merry, smutting one another with candle grease and
soot, till most of us were like devils. And that being done, then
we broke up, and to my house, and there I made them drink; and
upstairs we went, and then fell into dancing (W. Batelier dancing
well) and dressing, him and I and one Mr. Banister (who with his
wife come over also with us) like women; and Mercer put on a suit
of Tom's, like a boy, and mighty mirth we had, and Mercer danced
a jigg; and Nan Wright and my wife and Pegg Pen put on perriwigs.
Thus we spent till three or four in the morning, mighty merry; and
then parted, and to bed.

15th. Mighty sleepy; slept till past eight of the clock, and was
called up by a letter from Sir W. Coventry, which among other
things tells me how we have burned one hundred and sixty ships
of the enemy. I up, and with all possible haste, and in pain for
fear of coming late, it being our day of attending the Duke of
Yorke, to St. James's, where they are full of the particulars; how
they are generally good merchant ships, some of them laden and
supposed rich ships. We spent five fire-ships upon them. We
landed on the Schelling and burned a town, and so come away.
All this will make the Duke of Albemarle in repute again, I doubt,
though there is nothing of his in this. But, Lord! to see what
successe do, whether with or without reason, and making a man
seem wise notwithstanding never so late demonstration of the
profoundest folly in the world.

16th. To the office, where all the afternoon and very busy and
doing much business; but here I had a most eminent experience
of the evil of being behindhand in business. I was the most backward to begin any thing, and would fain have framed to myself
an occasion of going abroad, and should, I doubt, have done it,
but some business coming in one after another kept me there,

"AND MIGHTY MIRTH WE HAD"

and I fell to the ridding away of a great deale of business; and when my hand was in it was so pleasing a sight to see my papers disposed of and letters answered, which troubled my book and table, that I could have continued there with delight all night long; and did till called away by my Lady Pen and Pegg and my wife to their house to eat with them; and there I went, and exceeding merry. So mighty merry home and to bed.

17th. Up and betimes by water to Woolwich. Back with Captain Erwin, discoursing about the East Indys, where he hath often been. And among other things he tells me how the King of Syam seldom goes out without thirty or forty thousand people with him, and not a word spoke, nor a hum or cough in the whole company to be heard. He tells me the punishment frequently there for malefactors is cutting off the crowne of their head, which they do very dexterously, leaving their brains bare, which kills them presently. He told me what I remember he hath once done heretofore: that every body is to lie flat down at the coming by of the King, and nobody to look upon him upon pain of death. So to my house, and there I find one of my new presses for my books brought home, which pleases me mightily.[1]

20th. All the afternoon till almost midnight upon my Tangier accounts, getting Tom Wilson to help me in writing as I read, and at night W. Hewer, and find myself most happy in the keeping of all my accounts, for that after all the changings and turnings necessary in such an account, I find myself right to a farthing in an account of £127,000.

22nd. To the Exchequer and so home, and there find Mrs. Knipp and my wife going to dinner. She tells me my song of "Beauty Retire" is mightily cried up, which I am not a little proud of; and do think I have done "It is Decreed" better, but I have not finished it. My closett is doing by upholsters, which I am pleased with. After dinner and doing something at the office, I with my wife, Knipp and Mercer by coach to Moorefields, and there saw "Polichinello," which pleases me mightily.[2]

23rd. At the office all the morning, whither Sir W. Coventry sent me word that the Dutch fleete is certainly abroad; and so we are to hasten all we have to send to our fleete with all speed. But, Lord! to see how my Lord Bruncker undertakes the despatch of the fire-ships, when he is no more fit for it than a porter.

---

[1] Twelve of these presses or bookcases are now at Magdalene College. Pepys' books, 3000 in number, stand on the shelves in the order in which he left them.
[2] Polichinello was a puppet-show of Italian origin, the forerunner of Punch and Judy.

PEPYS AT WORK

24th. Up, and dispatched several businesses at home in the morning, and then comes Sympson to set up my other new presses for my books, and so he and I fell in to the furnishing of my new closett, and taking out the things out of my old, and I kept him with me all day, and he dined with me, and so all the afternoon till it was quite darke hanging things, that is my maps and pictures and draughts, and setting up my books, and as much as we could do, to my most extraordinary satisfaction; so that I think it will be as noble a closett as any man hath, and light enough; though indeed it would be better to have had a little more light. He gone, my wife and I to talk, and sup.

28th. To the office, where we sat all the morning. At noon I with my wife and Mercer to Philpott Lane, a great cook's shop, to the wedding of Mr. Longracke, our purveyor, a good, sober, civil man, and hath married a sober, serious mayde. Here I met much ordinary company, I going thither at his great request. A good dinner, and, what was best, good musique. After dinner the young women went to dance; among others Mr. Christopher Pett his daughter, who is a very pretty, modest girle, I am mightily taken with her. And so we broke up mightily civilly, the bride and bridegroom going to Greenwich (they keeping their dinner here only for my sake) to lie, and we home, where I to the office; and anon am on a sudden called to meet Sir W. Pen and Sir W. Coventry at the Victualling Office, which did put me out of order to be so surprised. But I went, and there Sir William Coventry did read me a letter from the Generalls to the King, a most scurvy letter, reflecting most upon Sir W. Coventry, and then upon me for my accounts (not that they are not true, but that we do not consider the expence of the fleete), and then of the whole office, in neglecting them and the King's service, and this in very plain and sharp and menacing terms.

29th. To St. James's, and there Sir W. Coventry took Sir W. Pen and me apart, and read to us his answer to the Generalls' letter to the King that he read last night; wherein he is very plain, and states the matter in full defence of himself and of me with him, which he could not avoid; which is a good comfort to me, that I happen to be involved with him in the same cause. And then, speaking of the supplies which have been made to this fleete more than ever in all kinds to any, even that wherein the Duke of Yorke himself was, "Well," says he, "if this will not do, I will say, as Sir J. Falstaffe did to the Prince, 'Tell your father that

"HE AND I FELL IN TO THE FURNISHING OF MY NEW CLOSETT"

if he do not like this let him kill the next Piercy himself,'[1] " and
so we broke up and to the Duke, and there did our usual business.
No newes where the Dutch are. We think our fleete sayled yesterday, but we have no newes of it.

September 2nd. (Lord's Day.) Some of our mayds sitting up
late last night to get things ready against our feast to-day, Jane
called us up about three in the morning to tell us of a great fire they
saw in the City. So I rose and slipped on my night-gowne and went
to her window, and thought it to be on the back-side of Marke-
lane at the farthest; but, being unused to such fires as followed, I
thought it far enough off; and so went to bed again and to sleep.
About seven rose again to dress myself, and there looked out at
the window and saw the fire not so much as it was, and further off.
So to my closett to set things to rights after yesterday's cleaning.
By and by Jane comes and tells me that she hears that above
300 houses have been burned down to-night by the fire we saw,
and that it is now burning down all Fish-street, by London Bridge.
So I made myself ready presently and walked to the Tower, and
there got up upon one of the high places, Sir J. Robinson's little
son going up with me; and there I did see the houses at that end of
the bridge all on fire, and an infinite great fire on this and the
other side the end of the bridge. So with my heart full of trouble,
I down to the water-side, and there got a boat and through bridge,
and there saw a lamentable fire. Poor Michell's house, as far as
the Old Swan, already burned that way, and the fire running
further. Everybody endeavouring to remove their goods, and
flinging into the river or bringing them into lighters that lay off;
poor people staying in their houses as long as till the very fire
touched them, and then running into boats, or clambering from
one pair of stairs by the water-side to another. And among other
things the poor pigeons, I perceive, were loth to leave their houses,
but hovered about the windows and balconys till they were, some of
them burned, their wings, and fell down. Having staid, and in
an hour's time seen the fire rage every way, and nobody, to my
sight, endeavouring to quench it, but to remove their goods and
leave all to the fire; and having seen it get as far as the Steele-
yard, and the wind mighty high and driving it into the City, and
every thing after so long a drought proving combustible, even the
very stones of churches, I to White Hall and there up to the King's

[1] *King Henry IV.*, part i. v. 4. The letter from Prince Rupert and the Duke of Albemarle is preserved among the State Papers. The Generals observe that Mr. Pepys' accounts and Sir Wm. Coventry's computations are of less interest to the fleet than the actual provisions of which they are short.

closett in the Chappell, where people come about me and I did give them an account dismayed them all, and word was carried in to the King. So I was called for and did tell the King and Duke of Yorke what I saw, and that unless his Majesty did command houses to be pulled down nothing could stop the fire. They seemed much troubled, and the King commanded me to go to my Lord Mayor from him and command him to spare no houses, but to pull down before the fire every way. The Duke of York bid me tell him that if he would have any more soldiers he shall. Here meeting with Captain Cocke, I in his coach which he lent me, and Creed with me to Paul's, and there walked along Watling-street as well as I could, every creature coming away loaden with goods to save, and here and there sicke people carried away in beds. Extraordinary good goods carried in carts and on backs. At last met my Lord Mayor in Canning-street like a man spent, with a handkercher about his neck. To the King's message he cried, like a fainting woman, "Lord! what can I do? I am spent: people will not obey me. I have been pulling down houses, but the fire overtakes us faster than we can do it." That he needed no more soldiers; and that, for himself, he must go and refresh himself, having been up all night. So he left me, and I him, and walked home, seeing people all almost distracted; and no manner of means used to quench the fire. The houses, too, so very thick thereabouts, and full of matter for burning, as pitch and tarr, in Thames-street; and warehouses of oyle, and wines, and brandy and other things. I saw Mr. Isaake Houblon, the handsome man, prettily dressed and dirty, at his door at Dowgate receiving some of his brothers' things, whose houses were on fire; and, as he says have been removed twice already, and he doubts (as it soon proved) that they must be in a little time removed from his house also, which was a sad consideration. And to see the churches all filling with goods by people who themselves should have been quietly there at this time. By this time it was about twelve o'clock; and so home, and soon as dined, away and walked through the City, the streets full of nothing but people and horses and carts loaden with goods. They now removing out of Canning-streete (which received goods in the morning) into Lumbard-streete, and further. Met with the King and Duke of York in their barge, and with them to Queenhithe, and there called Sir Richard Browne to them. Their order was only to pull down houses apace; and so below bridge at the water-side, but little was or could be done, the fire coming upon them so fast. River full of lighters and boats taking in goods, and good goods swimming in the water, and only I observed that hardly one lighter or boat in three that had the goods of a house in, but there was a pair of Virginalls in it.

Having seen as much as I could now, I away to White Hall by appointment, and there walked to St. James's Parke, and there met my wife and Creed, and walked to my boat; and there upon the water again, and to the fire up and down, it still encreasing, and the wind great. So near the fire as we could for smoke; and all over the Thames, with one's face in the wind, you were almost burned with a shower of fire-drops. This is very true; so as houses were burned by these drops and flakes of fire, three or four, nay, five or six houses, one from another. When we could endure no more upon the water, we to a little ale-house on the Bankside, over against the Three Cranes, and there staid till it was dark almost, and saw the fire grow; and, as it grew darker, appeared more and more, and in corners and upon steeples, and between churches and houses as far as we could see up the hill of the City, in a most horrid malicious bloody flame, not like the fine flame of an ordinary fire. We staid till, it being darkish, we saw the fire as only one entire arch of fire from this to the other side the bridge, and in a bow up the hill for an arch of above a mile long: it made me weep to see it. The churches, houses and all on fire and flaming at once; and a horrid noise the flames made, and the cracking of houses at their ruine. So home with a sad heart, and there find poor Tom Hater come with some few of his goods saved out of his house, which is burned. I invited him to lie at my house and did receive his goods, but was deceived in his lying there, the newes coming every moment of the growth of the fire; so as we were forced to begin to pack up our owne goods and prepare for their removal; and did by moonshine (it being brave dry and moonshine and warm weather) carry much of my goods into the garden, and Mr. Hater and I did remove my money and iron chests into my cellar, as thinking that the safest place. And got my bags of gold into my office ready to carry away, and my chief papers of accounts also there, and my tallys into a box by themselves. So great was our fear, as Sir W. Batten hath carts come out of the country to fetch away his goods this night. We did put Mr. Hater, poor man, to bed a little; but he got but very little rest, so much noise being in my house taking down of goods.

3rd. About four o'clock in the morning my Lady Batten sent me a cart to carry away all my money and plate and best things to Sir W. Rider's at Bednall-greene: which I did, riding myself in my night-gowne in the cart, and, Lord! to see how the streets and the high-ways are crowded with people running and riding, and getting of carts at any rate to fetch away things. I find Sir W. Rider tired with being called up all night and receiving things from sev-eral friends. His house full of goods, and much of Sir W. Batten's and Sir W. Pen's. I am eased at my heart to have my treasure so well secured. Then home, with much ado to find a way, nor any sleep all this night to me nor my poor wife, but then, and all this day, she and I and all my people labouring to get away the rest of our things. The Duke of Yorke come this day by the office and spoke to us, and did ride with his guard up and down the City to keep all quiet (he being now Generall, and having the care of all). This day, Mercer being not at home but against her mistress's order gone to her mother's, and my wife going thither to speak with W. Hewer met her there, and was angry; and her mother saying that she was not a 'prentice girl, to ask leave every time she goes abroad, my wife with good reason was angry, and when she came home bid her be gone again. And so she went away, which troubled me; but yet less than it would, because of the condition we are in fear of coming into in a little time of being less able to keepe one in her quality. At night lay down a little upon a quilt of W. Hewer's in the office, all my owne things being packed up or gone; and after me my poor wife did the like, we having fed upon the remains of yesterday's dinner, having no fire nor dishes, nor any opportunity of dressing any thing.

4th. Up by break of day to get away the remainder of my things. Sir W. Batten not knowing how to remove his wine did dig a pit in the garden and laid it in there; and I took the oppor-tunity of laying all the papers of my office that I could not other-wise dispose of. And in the evening Sir W. Pen and I did dig another and put our wine in it, and I my Parmazan cheese as well as my wine and some other things. This afternoon, sitting melan-choly with Sir W. Pen in our garden, and thinking of the certain burning of this office without extraordinary means, I did propose for the sending up of all our workmen from Woolwich and Dept-ford yards (none whereof yet appeared), and to write to Sir W. Coventry to have the Duke of Yorke's permission to pull down houses rather than lose this office, which would much hinder the King's business. So Sir W. Pen he went down this night, in order to the sending them up to-morrow morning; and I wrote to Sir W. Coventry about the business, but received no answer. This night Mrs. Turner (who, poor woman, was removing her goods all this day, good goods into the garden, and knows not how to dispose of them) and her husband supped with my wife and I at night in the office, upon a shoulder of mutton from the cook's, without any napkin or any thing, in a sad manner, but were merry. Only now and then walking into the garden, and saw how horridly the sky looks, all on a fire in the night, was enough to put us out of our wits; and indeed it was extremely dreadful, for it looks just as if it was at us, and the whole heaven on fire. I after supper walked in the darke down to Tower-streete, and there saw it all on fire. Now begins the practice of blowing up of houses in Tower-streete, those next the Tower, which at first did frighten people more than any thing. W. Hewer this day went to see how his mother did, and comes late home, telling us how he hath been forced to remove her to Islington, her house in Pye-corner being burned; so that the fire is got so far that way, and all the Old Bayly, and was running down to Fleete-streete; and Paul's is burned, and all Cheapside. I wrote to my father this night, but the post-house being burned, the letter could not go.

5th. I lay down in the office again upon W. Hewer's quilt, being mighty weary and sore in my feet with going till I was hardly able to stand. About two in the morning my wife calls me up and tells me of new cryes of fire, it being come to Barkeing Church, which is the bottom of our lane.[1] I up, and finding it so resolved presently to take her away, and did, and took my gold, which was about £2,350, W. Hewer and Jane down by Proundy's boat to Woolwich; but, Lord! what a sad sight it was by moone-light to see the whole City almost on fire, that you might see it plain at Woolwich as if you were by it. There when I come I find the gates shut, but no guard kept at all, which troubled me because of discourse now begun that there is plot in it and that the French had done it. I got the gates open, and to Mr. Sheldon's, where I locked up my gold and charged my wife and W. Hewer never to leave the room without one of them in it, night or day. So back again, by the way seeing my goods well in the lighters at Deptford and watched well by people. Home, and whereas I expected to have seen our house on fire, it being now about seven o'clock, it was not. But to the fyre, and there find greater hopes than I expected; for my

[1] Allhallows Barking, in Great Tower Street, nearly opposite the end of Seething Lane.

"HE HATH BEEN FORCED TO REMOVE HER"

confidence of finding our Office on fire was such that I durst not ask any body how it was with us till I come, and saw it not burned. But going to the fire I find, by the blowing up of houses and the great helpe given by the workmen out of the King's yards sent up by Sir W. Pen, there is a good stop given to it, as well as at Marke-lane end as ours; it having only burned the dyall of Barking Church and part of the porch, and was there quenched. I up to the top of Barking steeple and there saw the saddest sight of desolation that I ever saw; every where great fires, oyle-cellars and brimstone and other things burning. I became afeard to stay there long, and therefore down again as fast as I could, the fire being spread as far as I could see it; and to Sir W. Pen's, and there eat a piece of cold meat, having eaten nothing since Sunday, but the remains of Sunday's dinner. And having removed all my things and received good hopes that the fire at our end is stopped, I walked into the town, and find Fanchurch-streete, Gracious-streete, and Lumbard-streete all in dust. The Exchange a sad sight, nothing standing there of all the statues or pillars but Sir Thomas Gresham's picture[1] in the corner. Walked into Moorefields (our feet ready to burn, walking through the towne among the hot coles), and find that full of people, and poor wretches carrying their goods there, and every body keeping his goods together by themselves (and a great blessing it is to them that it is fair weather for them to keep abroad night and day). Drank there, and paid twopence for a plain penny loaf; thence homeward, having passed through Cheapside and Newgate Market, all burned, and seen Anthony Joyce's house in fire. I also did see a poor cat taken out of a hole in the chimney joyning to the wall of the Exchange, with the hair all burned off the body and yet alive. So home at night, and find there good hopes of saving our office, but great endeavours of watching all night, and having men ready; and so we lodged them in the office and had drink and bread and cheese for them. And I lay down and slept a good night about midnight.

   6th. Up about five o'clock, and there met Mr. Gawden at the gate of the office to call our men to Bishop's-gate, where no fire had yet been near, and there is now one broke out. I went with the men, and we did put it out in a little time; so that that was well again. It was pretty to see how hard the women did work in the cannells, sweeping of water; but then they would scold for drink, and be as drunk as devils. I saw good butts of sugar broke

[1] Statue.

open in the street, and people go and take handsfull out and put into beer and drink it. And now all being pretty well I took boat and over to Southwarke, and took boat on the other side the bridge and so to Westminster thinking to shift myself, being all in dirt from top to bottom; but could not there find any place to buy a shirt or pair of gloves, Westminster Hall being full of people's goods, those in Westminster having removed all their goods; but to the Swan, and there was trimmed, and then to White Hall, but saw nobody, and so home. A sad sight to see how the River looks, no houses nor church near it, to the Temple, where it stopped. To Sir R. Ford's and there dined on an earthen platter; a fried breast of mutton; a great many of us, but very merry, and indeed as good a meal, though as ugly a one, as I ever had in my life. Thence down to Deptford, and there with great satisfaction landed all my goods at Sir G. Carteret's safe, and nothing missed I could see, or hurt. This being done to my great content, I home and to Sir W. Batten's, and there supped well and mighty merry, and our fears over. From them to the office, and there slept with the office full of labourers, who talked and slept and walked all night long there. But strange it was to see Cloath-workers' Hall on fire these three days and nights in one body of flame, it being the cellar full of oyle.

7th. Up by five o'clock, and blessed be God! find all well; and by water to Paul's Wharfe. Walked thence and saw all the towne burned, and a miserable sight of Paul's church, with all the roofs fallen, and the body of the quire fallen into St. Fayth's;[1] Paul's school also, Ludgate, and Fleet-street, my father's house and the church and a good part of the Temple the like. So to Creed's lodging near the New Exchange, and there find him laid down upon a bed, the house all unfurnished, there being fears of the fire's coming to them. There borrowed a shirt of him and washed. To Sir W. Coventry at St. James's, who lay without curtains, having removed all his goods, as the King at White Hall and every body had done and was doing. He hopes we shall have no publique distractions upon this fire, which is what every body fears, because of the talke of the French having a hand in it. And it is a proper time for discontents; but all men's minds are full of care to protect themselves and save their goods. The militia is in armes every where. Our fleetes, he tells me, have been in sight one of another, and most unhappily by fowle weather were parted, to our great

---

[1] St. Faith's church was in the crypt under the choir of old St. Paul's.

losse. So home and did give orders for my house to be made clean.

This day our Merchants first met at Gresham College, which, by proclamation, is to be their Exchange. Strange to hear what is bid for houses all up and down here, a friend of Sir W. Rider's having £150 for what he used to let for £40 per annum. Much dispute where the Custome-house shall be; thereby the growth of the City again to be foreseen. I home late to Sir W. Pen's, who did give me a bed, but without curtains or hangings, all being down. So here I went the first timé into a naked bed, only my drawers on, and did sleep pretty well; but still both sleeping and waking had a fear of fire in my heart, that I took little rest. People do all the world over cry out of the simplicity of my Lord Mayor in generall; and more particularly in this business of the fire, laying it all upon him. A proclamation is come out for markets to be kept at Leadenhall and Mile-end-greene and several other places about the towne, and Tower-hill; and all churches to be set open to receive poor people.

8th. To St. James, where we met first at Sir W. Coventry's chamber, and there did what business we can without any books. Our discourse, as every thing else, was confused. Thence with Sir W. Batten to the Cock-pit, whither the Duke of Albemarle is come. It seems the King holds him so necessary at this time that he hath sent for him, and will keep him here. We to him; he is courted in appearance by every body. He very kind to us; I perceive he lays by all business of the fleete at present and minds the City, and is now hastening to Gresham College to discourse with the Aldermen. Sir W. Batten and I home (where met by my brother John, come to town to see how things are with us), and then presently he with me to Gresham College, where infinity of people, partly through novelty to see the new place and partly to find out and hear what is become one man of another. I met with many people undone, and more that have extraordinary great losses. People speaking their thoughts variously about the beginning of the fire and the rebuilding of the City. Then to Sir W. Batten's and took my brother with me, and there dined with a great company of neighbours, and much good discourse; among others of the low spirits of some rich men in the City in sparing any encouragement to the poor people that wrought for the saving their houses. Among others Alderman Starling, a very rich man without children, the fire at next door to him in our lane, after our men had saved his house did give 2s. 6d. among thirty of them, and did quarrel with some that would remove the rubbish out of the way of the fire, saying that they come to steal. Sir W. Coventry told me of another this morning in Holborne, which he shewed the King: that when it was offered to stop the fire near his house for such a reward that came but to 2s. 6d. a man among the neighbours he would give but 18d. Thence to Bednall Green by coach, my brother with me, and saw all well there, and fetched away my journall-book to enter for five days past, and then back to the office.

9th. (Sunday.) Up, and was trimmed, and sent my brother to Woolwich to my wife, to dine with her. I walked to Bednall Green and there dined well, but a bad venison pasty at Sir W. Rider's. Good people they are, and good discourse; and his daughter, Middleton, a fine woman, discreet. Thence home and to church, and there preached Dean Harding, but methinks a bad, poor sermon, though proper for the time; nor eloquent in saying at this time that the City is reduced from a large folio to a decimo-tertio. So to my office, and take leave of my brother whom I sent back this afternoon. I was very kind to him and did give him 40s. for his pocket. Anon to Sir W. Pen's to bed, and made my boy Tom to read me asleep.

10th. All the morning clearing our cellars, and breaking in pieces all my old lumber to make room and to prevent fire. And then to Sir W. Batten's and dined; and there hear that Sir W. Rider says that the towne is full of the report of the wealth that is in his house, and would be glad that his friends would provide for the safety of their goods there. This made me get a cart, and thither, and there brought my money all away. Took a hackney-coach myself (the hackney-coaches now standing at Allgate). Much wealth indeed there is at his house. Blessed be God, I got all mine well thence and lodged it in my office; but vexed to have all the world see it. By and by comes brother Balty from sea, which I was glad of; and so got him and Mr. Tooker and the boy to watch with them all in the office all night, while I upon Jane's coming went down to my wife to Woolwich, and there find my wife out of humour and indifferent, as she uses upon her having much liberty abroad.

13th. Up, and down to Tower Wharfe; and there, with Balty and labourers from Deptford, did get my goods housed well at home. After supper to bed in my house, the first time I have lain there; and lay with my wife in my old closett upon the ground, and Balty and his wife in the best chamber, upon the ground also.

14th. Up, and to work, having carpenters come to helpe in setting up bedsteads and hangings; and at that trade my people and I all the morning till pressed by publique business to leave them against my will in the afternoon: and yet I was troubled in being at home to see all my goods lie up and down the house in a bad condition, and strange workmen going to and fro might take what they would almost. All the afternoon busy; and Sir W. Coventry come to me, and found me as God would have it in my office, and people about me setting my papers to rights; and there discoursed about getting an account ready against the Parliament, and thereby did create me infinite of business, and to be done on a sudden, which troubled me: but however, he being gone, I about it late and to good purpose. And so home, having this day also got my wine out of the ground again and set in my cellar; but with great pain to keep the porters that carried it in from observing the money-chests there. So to bed as last night, only my wife and I upon a bedstead with curtains in that which was Mercer's chamber, and Balty and his wife (who are here and do us good service), where we lay last night. This day poor Tom Pepys, the turner, was with me, and Kate Joyce, to bespeake places; one for himself, the other for her husband. She tells me he hath lost £140 per annum, but have seven houses left.

15th. All the morning at the office. Dined with Sir W. Batten; mighty busy about this account, and while my people were busy, wrote near thirty letters and orders with my owne hand. At it till eleven at night; and it is strange to see how clear my head was, being eased of all the matter of all these letters, whereas one would think that I should have been dazed; I never did observe so much of myself in my life. In the evening there comes to me Captain Cocke, and walked a good while in the garden. He says he hath computed that the rents of houses lost by this fire in the City comes to £600,000 per annum. That certainly never so great a loss as this was borne so well by citizens in the world, he believing that not one merchant upon the 'Change will break upon it: that he do not apprehend there will be any disturbances in State upon it, for that all men are busy in looking after their owne business to save themselves. He gone, I to finish my letters and home to bed, and find to my infinite joy many rooms clean; and myself and wife lie in our own chamber again. But much terrified in the nights now-a-days with dreams of fire and falling down of houses.

16th. (Lord's Day.) Lay with much pleasure in bed talking with my wife. At noon with my wife, against her will, all undressed and dirty, dined at Sir W. Pen's, where was all the company of our families in towne; but, Lord! so sorry a dinner (venison baked in pans) that the dinner I have had for his lady alone hath been worth four of it. Thence after dinner, displeased with our entertainment, to my office again and there till almost midnight and my people with me, and then home, my head mightily akeing about our accounts.

17th. Up betimes and shaved myself after a week's growth; but, Lord! how ugly I was yesterday and how fine to-day! By water, seeing the City all the way, a sad sight indeed, much fire being still in. To Sir W. Coventry, and thence by coach over the ruins down Fleete Streete and Cheapside to Broad Streete, to Sir G. Carteret.

22nd. To my closet, and had it new washed, and now my house is so clean as I never saw it or any other house in my life, and every thing in as good condition as ever before the fire; but with, I believe, about £20 cost one way or other, besides about £20 charge in removing my goods; and do not find that I have lost any thing but two little pictures of ships and sea and a little gold frame for one of my sea-cards. To the office, and there my Lord Bruncker come. He do now give me a watch, a plain one, in the roome of my former watch with many motions which I did give him. If it goes well, I care not for the difference in worth, though I believe there is above £5. Till past midnight at our accounts, and have brought them to a good issue so as to be ready to meet Sir G. Carteret and Sir W. Coventry to-morrow: but must work to-morrow, which Mr. T. Hater had no mind to, it being the Lord's day; but being told the necessity submitted, poor man! This night writ for brother John to come to towne. Among other reasons, my estate lying in money, I am afeard of any sudden miscarriage.

23rd. (Lord's Day.) Up, and after being trimmed, all the morning at the office with my people about me till about one c'clock, and then home, and my people with me, and eat a bit of victuals in my old closet, now my little dining-room, which makes a pretty room; and my house being so clean makes me mightily pleased, but only I do lacke Mercer or somebody in the house to sing with. Soon as eat a bit by water to White Hall, and there at Sir G. Carteret's lodgings Sir W. Coventry met, and we did debate the whole business of our accounts to the Parliament; where it appears to us that the charge of the war from September 1st 1664 to this Michaelmas will have been but £3,200,000, and we have paid in that time somewhat about £2,200,000, so that we owe above £900,000: but our method of accounting, though it cannot I believe be far wide from the mark, yet will not abide a strict examination if the Parliament should be troublesome.

26th. To White Hall. Here, at night, I met with good Mr. Evelyn, who observes that none of the nobility come out of the country at all to help the King or comfort him or prevent commotions at this fire, but do as if the King were nobody; nor ne'er a priest comes to give the King and Court good council or to comfort the poor people that suffer; but all is dead, nothing of good in any of their minds. He bemoans it, and says he fears more ruin hangs over our heads. Thence away by coach, and called away my wife at Unthanke's, where she tells me she hath bought a gowne of 15s. per yard (the same, before her face, my Lady Castlemayne this day bought also), which I seemed vexed for, though I do not grudge it her, but to incline her to have Mercer again, which I believe I shall do; but the girle, I hear, has no mind to come to us again, which vexes me. Being come home, I to Sir W. Batten, and there hear our business was tendered to the House to-day, and a Committee of the whole House chosen to examine our accounts; and a great many Hotspurs enquiring into it and likely to give us much trouble and blame, and perhaps (which I am afeard of) will find faults enow to demand better officers. This I truly fear.

27th. Up, and with my wife by coach as far as the Temple, and there she to the mercer's again and I to look out Penny, my tailor, to speak for a cloak and cassock for my brother, who is coming to town; and I will have him in a canonical dress, that he may be the fitter to go abroad with me.

28th. Lay long in bed, and am come to agreement with my wife to have Mercer again on condition she may learn this winter two months to dance, and she promises me she will endeavour to learn to sing; and all this I am willing enough to. So up, and by and by the glazier comes to finish the windows of my house, which pleases me, and the bookbinder to gild the backs of my books. I got the glass of my book-presses to be done presently, which did mightily content me, and to setting my study in a little better order; and so to my office to my people, busy about our Parliament accounts; and so to dinner, and then at them again close.

October 1st. Up, and all the morning at the office. At noon to Sir W. Coventry's chamber and dined with him. Thence to White Hall, and there did hear Betty Michell was at this end of the towne, and so without breach of vowe did stay to endeavour to meet with her and carry her home; but she did not come, so I lost my whole afternoon. But pretty! how I took another pretty woman for her, taking her a clap on the breech, thinking verily it had been her. My wife do tell me that W. Hewer tells her that Mercer hath no mind to come. So I was angry at it, and resolved with her to have Falconbridge's girle.

2nd. To White Hall to the House, and spoke to Sir W. Coventry, where he told me I must attend the Committee in the afternoon. So away home and eat a short dinner, and then with Sir W. Pen to White Hall. By and by the Committee met, and I walked out; and anon they rose and called me in, and appointed me to attend a Committee of them to-morrow at the office to examine our lists. This put me into a mighty fear and trouble, they doing it in a very ill humour, methought. So I away and called on my Lord Bruncker to desire him to be there to-morrow, and so home, full of trouble in mind to think what I shall be obliged to answer, that am neither fully fit, nor in any measure concerned, to take the shame and trouble of this office upon me, but only from the inability and folly of the Comptroller that occasions it.

3rd. Waked betimes. So up, and with Mr. Hater and W. Hewer and Griffin to consider of our business; and by and by, by eight o'clock, comes Birch, the first, with the lists and books of accounts delivered in. He calls me to work, and there he and I begun, when by and by comes Garraway, the fi, st time I ever saw him, and Sir W. Thompson and Mr. Boscawen.[1] They to it, and I did make shift to answer them better than I expected. Sir W. Batten, Lord Bruncker, W. Pen, come in, but presently went out; and J. Minnes come in and said two or three words from the purpose, but to do hurt; and so away he went also, and left me all the morning with them alone to stand or fall. At noon Sir W. Batten comes to them to invite them (though fast day) to dinner, which they did, and good company they were, but especially Garraway. After dinner to work again, only the Committee

---

[1] Three Parliament-men, William Garway (Chichester), Alderman Sir Wm. Thompson (London), and Edward Boscawen (Truro).

and I, till dark night, and ended with good peace, and much seeming satisfaction; but I find them wise and reserved, and instructed to hit all our blots.

5th. This day, coming home, Mr. Kirton's kinsman, my bookseller, come in my way. He do believe all the great booksellers almost undone: not only these, but their warehouses at their Hall and under Christchurch and elsewhere being all burned. A great want thereof there will be of books, specially Latin books and foreign books.

7th. (Lord's Day.) After dinner I with Sir J. Minnes to White Hall, where met by W. Batten and Lord Bruncker, to attend the King and Duke of York at the Cabinet; but nobody had determined what to speak of, but only in general to ask for money. So I was forced immediately to prepare in my mind a method of discoursing. And anon we were called in to the Green Room, where the King, Duke of York, Prince Rupert, Lord Chancellor, Lord Treasurer, Duke of Albemarle, G. Carteret, W. Coventry, Morrice. Nobody beginning, I did, and made a current and I thought a good speech, laying open the ill state of the Navy by the greatness of the debt, greatness of work to do against next yeare, the time and materials it would take, and our incapacity through a total want of money. I had no sooner done but Prince Rupert rose up and told the King in a heat that, whatever the gentleman had said, he had brought home his fleete in as good a condition as ever any fleete was brought home. I therefore did only answer that I was sorry for his Highness's offence, but that what I said was but the report we received from those entrusted in the fleete to inform us. He muttered and repeated what he had said; and so, after a long silence on all hands, nobody, not so much as the Duke of Albemarle, seconding the Prince, nor taking notice of what he said, we withdrew. I was not a little troubled at this passage, and the more when speaking with Jacke Fenn about it he told me that the Prince will be asking now who this Pepys is, and find him to be a creature of my Lord Sandwich's, and therefore this was done only to disparage him. I made my brother in his cassocke to say grace this day, but I like his voice so ill that I begin to be sorry he hath taken this order upon him.

8th. The King hath yesterday in Council declared his resolution of setting a fashion for clothes, which he will never alter. It will be a vest, I know not well how; but it is to teach the nobility thrift, and will do good.

12th. My wife hath brought her new girle I have helped her to, of Mr. Falconbridge's. She is wretched poor, and but ordinary favoured; and we fain to lay out seven or eight pounds worth of clothes upon her back, which methinks do go against my heart; and I do not think I can ever esteem her as I could have done another that had come fine and handsome; and which is more, her voice, for want of use, is.so furred that it do not at present please me; but her manner of singing is such that I shall, I think, take great pleasure in it. Well, she is come, and I wish us good fortune in her.

13th. To White Hall, and there the Duke of York (who is gone over to all his pleasures again) was just come in from hunting. So I stood and saw him dress himself and try on his vest, which is the King's new fashion, and will be in it for good and all on Monday next, and the whole Court: it is a fashion the King says he will never change. He being ready, he and my Lord Chancellor and Duke of Albemarle and Prince Rupert, Lord Bellasses, Sir H. Cholmly, Povy and myself met at a Committee for Tangier. I am mad in love with my Lord Chancellor, for he do comprehend and speak out well, and with the greatest easinesse and authority that ever I saw man in my life. I did never observe how much easier a man do speak when he knows all the company to be below him, than in him; for though he spoke indeed excellent well, yet his manner and freedom of doing it, as if he played with it and was informing only all the rest of the company, was mighty pretty. At the end Sir W. Coventry come. He says he thinks the House may say no more to us for the present, but that we must mend our manners against the next tryall; and mend them we will.

14th. (Lord's Day.) Lay long in bed, among other things talking of my wife's renewing her acquaintance with Mrs. Pierce, which, by my wife's ill using her when she was here last, hath been interrupted. Herein we were a little angry together, but presently friends again; and so up, and I to church, which was mighty full, and my beauties, Mrs. Lethulier and fair Batelier both there.

15th. This day the King begins to put on his vest, and I did see several persons of the House of Lords and Commons too, great courtiers, who are in it; being a long cassocke close to the body, of black cloth, and pinked with white silke under it, and a coat over it, and the legs ruffled with black riband like a pigeon's leg; and upon the whole I wish the King may keep it, for it is a very fine and handsome garment. I with Sir G. Carteret to his lodgings at White Hall to dinner, where my Lady Carteret is, and mighty kind, both of them, to me. Their son and my Lady Jemimah will be here very speedily. She tells me the ladies are to go into a new fashion shortly, and that is to wear short coats, above their ancles; which she and I do not like, but conclude this long trayne to be mighty graceful. But she cries out of the vices of the Court.

17th. All the morning at the office. At noon home to dinner, alone with my brother, with whom I had now the first private talke I have had, and find he hath preached but twice in his life. I did give him some advice to study pronunciation; but I do fear he will never make a good speaker, nor, I fear, any general good scholar, for I do not see that he minds optickes or mathematiques of any sort, nor anything else that I can find. I know not what he may be at divinity and ordinary school-learning. However he seems sober, and that pleases me.

19th. With Sir G. Carteret, Sir W. Coventry, Lord Bruncker and myself I did lay the state of our condition before the Duke of York, that the fleete could not go out without several things it wanted and we could not have without money. Sir G. Carteret asked me whether £50 or £60 would do us any good, and when I told him the very rum man must have £200 he held up his eyes as if we had asked a million. Sir W. Coventry told the Duke of York plainly he did rather desire to have his commission called in than serve in so ill a place, where he cannot do the King service, and I did concur in saying the same. The Duke of York did confess that he did not see how he could do anything without a present supply of £20,000, and that he would speak to the King next Council day. Sir W. Batten was at the pay to-day and tells me how rude the men were, but did go away quietly being promised pay on Wednesday next. God send us money for it!

20th. Up, and all the morning at the office, where none met but myself. There comes to me Commissioner Middleton. He says that the fleete was in such a condition as to discipline as if the Devil had commanded it; so much wickedness of all sorts. He being gone, comes Sir G. Carteret, and he and I walked together awhile, discoursing upon the sad condition of the times.

25th. After dinner I out with my wife to Mrs. Pierce's. She received us with mighty respect and discretion, and was making herself mighty fine to go to a great ball to-night at Court, being the Queene's birthday. Thence I to my Lord Bruncker's, and with him to Mrs. Williams's, where we met Knipp. I was glad to

MRS. KNIPP

see the jade. Made her sing; and she told us they begin at both houses to act on Monday next. But I fear, after all this sorrow, their gains will be but little.

26th. Up, and all the morning and most of the afternoon within doors, beginning to set my accounts in order from before this fire, I being behindhand with them ever since; and this day I got most of my tradesmen to bring in their bills and paid them.

28th. (Lord's Day.) Up, and to church with my wife, and then home; and there is come little Michell and his wife (I sent for them), and also comes Captain Guy to dine with me, and he and I much talk together. He cries out of the discipline of the fleete, and confesses really that the true English valour we talk of is almost spent and worn out, few of the commanders doing what they should do; and he much fears we shall therefore be beaten the next year. He assures me we were beaten home the last June fight, and that the whole fleete was ashamed to hear of our bonefires.

29th. By coach (having in the Hall bought me a velvet riding cap, cost me 20s.) to my taylor's, and there bespoke a plain vest, and so to my goldsmith to bid him look out for some gold for me; and he tells me that ginnys,[1] which I bought 2,000 of not long ago, and cost me but 18½d. change, will now cost me 22d.; and but very few to be had at any price. However some more I will have, for they are very convenient and of easy disposal. So home to dinner and to discourse with my brother upon his translation of my Lord Bacon's "Faber Fortunæ," which I gave him to do and he has done it, but meanely; I am not pleased with it at all, having done it only literally, but without any life at all. About five o'clock I took my wife (who is mighty fine, and with a new fair pair of locks, which vex me, though like a foole I helped her the other night to buy them) to Mrs. Pierce's, and there staying a little I away before to White Hall and into the new play-house there, the first time I ever was there, and the first play I have seen since before the great plague. By and by Mr. Pierce comes, bringing my wife and his, and Knipp. By and by the King and Queene, Duke and Duchesse, and all the great ladies of the Court; which indeed was a fine sight. But the play being "Love in a Tub,"[2] a silly play, and though done by the Duke's people, yet having neither Betterton nor his wife, and the whole thing done ill, and being ill also, I had no manner of pleasure in the play.

---

[1] Guineas took their name from the gold brought by the African Company from the Gold Coast. When first coined they were worth 20s., but the value rose to 30s. in 1695.
[2] By Sir George Etherege.

The sight of the ladies was exceeding noble, and above all my Lady Castlemayne.

30th. Up, and to the office, where sat all the morning, and at noon home to dinner, and then to the office again, where late very busy and dispatching much business. At night home to supper and singing with my wife, who hath lately begun to learn and I think will come to do something, though her eare is not good.

31st. I bless God I do find that I am worth more than ever I yet was, which is £6,200, for which the Holy Name of God be praised!

November 4th. (Lord's Day.) Comes my taylor's man in the morning and brings my vest home, and coate to wear with it, and belt and silver-hilted sword. So I rose and dressed myself, and I like myself mightily in it, and so do my wife. Then, being dressed, to church; and after church pulled my Lady Pen and Mrs. Markham into my house to dinner, and after dinner to White Hall. Here I waited in the gallery till the Council was up, and among others did speak with Mr. Cooling, my Lord Chamberlain's secretary, who tells me my Lord Generall is become mighty low in all people's opinion, and that he hath received several slurs from the King and Duke of York. The people at Court do see the difference between his and the Prince's management, and my Lord Sandwich's. That he is grown a drunken sot, and drinks with nobody but Troutbecke,[1] whom nobody else will keep company with. Of whom he told me this story: That once the Duke of Albemarle in his drink taking notice of a wonder that Nan Hide should ever come to be Duchesse of York, "Nay," says Troutbecke, "ne'er wonder at that; for if you will give me another bottle of wine I will tell you as great if not greater a miracle." And what was that but that our dirty Besse (meaning his Duchesse) should come to be Duchesse of Albemarle?

5th. (A holyday.) To my Lord Crew's and there dined, and mightily made of, having not, to my shame, been there in 8 months before. The best family in the world for goodness and sobriety. After dinner I and Sir Thomas Crew went aside to discourse of public matters, and do find by him that all the country gentlemen are publickly jealous of the courtiers in the Parliament, and that they do doubt every thing that they propose. He do, from what he hath heard at the Committee for examining the burn-

---

[1] John Troutbeck had been surgeon to the Duke of Albemarle's troop of Life Guards; he was now chief surgeon to the King.

ing of the City, conclude it as a thing certain that it was done by plots; it being proved by many witnesses that endeavours were made in several places to encrease the fire, and that both in City and country it was bragged by several Papists that upon such a day or in such a time we should find the hottest weather that ever was in England, and words of plainer sense.

9th. Upon the 'Change, where I seldom have of late been, I find all people mightily at a losse what to expect, but confusion and fears in every man's head and heart. Whether war or peace all fear the event will be bad. Thence home and with my brother to dinner, my wife being dressing herself against night; after dinner I to my closett all the afternoon till the porter brought my vest back from the taylor's, and then to dress myself very fine about 4 or 5 o'clock; and by that time comes Mr. Batelier and Mercer, and away by coach to Mrs. Pierce's, by appointment, where we find good company. After some trifling discourse, we to dancing, and very good sport, and mightily pleased I was with the company. After our first bout of dancing, Knipp and I to sing, and Mercer and Captain Downing (who loves and understands musique) would by all means have my song of "Beauty, retire", which Knipp had spread abroad, and he extols it above any thing he ever heard, and, without flattery, I know it is good in its kind. This being done and going to dance again, comes news that White Hall was on fire; and presently more particulars, that the Horse-guard was on fire; and so we run up to the garret and find it so, a horrid great fire; and by and by we saw and heard part of it blown up with powder. The ladies begun presently to be afeard; one fell into fits. The whole town in an alarme. Drums beat and trumpets, and the guards every where spread, running up and down in the street. And I begun to have mighty apprehensions how things might be at home, and so was in mighty pain to get home. By and by comes news that the fire has slackened; so then we were a little cheered up again, and to supper, and pretty merry. After supper another dance or two, and then newes that the fire is as great as ever, which put us all to our wit's-end; and I mightily anxious to go home, but the coach being gone, and it being about ten at night and rainy dirty weather, I knew not what to do, but to walk out with Mr. Batelier, myself resolving to go home on foot and leave the women there. And so did; but at the Savoy got a coach, and come back and took up the women; and so, having, by people come from the fire, understood that the fire was overcome and all well, we

merrily parted, and home. Stopped by several guards and con-
stables quite through the town round the wall as we went, all being
in armes. Being come home, we to cards till two in the morning,
and drinking lamb's-wool.[1] So to bed.

10th. Up and to the office, where Sir W. Coventry come to
tell us that the Parliament did fall foul of our accounts again yesterday, and we must arme to have them examined, which I am
sorry for: it will bring great trouble to me, and shame upon the
office. At noon with my Lord Bruncker and Sir Thomas Harvy
to Cocke's house, and there Mrs. Williams and other company,
and an excellent dinner. Mr. Temple's wife,[2] after dinner, fell
to play on the harpsicon till she tired everybody, that I left the
house without taking leave, and no creature left standing by her to
hear her. This is the fatal day that every body hath discoursed
for a long time to be the day that the Papists, or I know not who,
had designed to commit a massacre upon; but however I trust in
God we shall rise to-morrow morning as well as ever.

11th. (Lord's Day.) My wife and brother and I to my uncle
Wight's, where my aunt is grown so ugly and their entertainment
so bad that I am in pain to be there; nor will go thither again a
good while if sent for: for we were sent for to-night; we had not gone
else.

14th. To the Exchange for some things for my wife, and then
to Knipp's, and there staid reading of Waller's verses while she
finished dressing, her husband being by. Her lodging very mean,
and the condition she lives in; yet makes a shew without doors,
God bless us! I carried him along with us into the City and set
him down in Bishopsgate Street, and then home with her. After
dinner I to teach her my new recitative of "It is decreed," of which
she learnt a good part, and I do well like it and believe shall be
well pleased when she hath it all, and that it will be found an agreeable thing.

At the meeting at Gresham College to-night, which it seems they
now have every Wednesday again, there was a pretty experiment
of the blood of one dogg let out, till he died, into the body of another
on one side, while all his own run out on the other side. The first
died upon the place, and the other very well and likely to do well.
This did give occasion to many pretty wishes, as of the blood of
a Quaker to be let into an Archbishop, and such like; but may if it

---

[1] Ale, mixed with sugar, nutmeg, and the pulp of roasted apples.
[2] Wife of Sir Robert Viner's chief clerk.

takes be of mighty use to man's health, for the mending of bad blood by borrowing from a better body.

15th. Took coach to Mrs. Pierce's, where I find her as fine as possible, and himself going to the ball at night at Court. So I carried them in my coach, and having set them into the house, and gotten Mr. Pierce to undertake the carrying in my wife, I to Unthanke's, where she appointed to be, and there told her, and back again about business to White Hall, while Pierce went and fetched her and carried her in. I, after I had met with Sir W. Coventry and given him some account of matters, I also to the ball, and with much ado got up to the loft, where with much trouble I could see very well. Anon the house grew full, and the candles light, and the King and Queen and all the ladies set: and it was indeed a glorious sight to see Mrs. Stewart in black and white lace, and her head and shoulders dressed with dyamonds, and the like a great many great ladies more, only the Queen none; and the King in his rich vest of some rich silke and silver trimming, as the Duke of York and all the dancers were, some of cloth of silver, and others of other sorts, exceeding rich. Mrs. Stewart danced mighty finely, and many French dances, specially one the King called the New Dance, which was very pretty; but upon the whole matter, the business of the dancing of itself was not extraordinary pleasing. But the clothes and sight of the persons was indeed very pleasing, and worth my coming, being never likely to see more gallantry while I live, if I should come twenty times. About twelve at night it broke up.

20th. After dinner by coach to Barkeshire-house, and there did get a very great meeting; the Duke of York being there, and much business done, though not in proportion to the greatness of the business, and my Lord Chancellor sleeping and snoring the greater part of the time.

22nd. To the office, where we sat all the morning. At noon home to dinner, where my wife and I fell out, I being displeased with her cutting away a lace handkercher sewed about her neck down to her breasts almost, out of a belief, but without reason, that it is the fashion. Here we did give one another the lie too much, but were presently friends; and then I to my office, where very late and did much business, and then home, and there find Mr. Batelier, and did sup and play at cards awhile. But he tells me the newes how the King of France hath, in defiance to the King of England, caused all his footmen to be put into vests, and that the noblemen

"SHE TIRED EVERYBODY"

of France will do the like; which, if true, is the greatest indignity ever done by one Prince to another, and would incite a stone to be revenged. This makes me mighty merry, it being an ingenious kind of affront; but yet it makes me angry to see that the King of England is become so little as to have the affront offered him.

28th. At noon comes my Lord Hinchingbroke, Sir Thomas Crew, Mr. John Crew, Mr. Carteret, and Brisband. I had six noble dishes for them, dressed by a man-cook, and commended, as indeed they deserved, for exceeding well done. We eat with great pleasure, and I enjoyed myself in it with reflections upon the pleasures which I at best can expect, yet not to exceed this; eating in silver plates, and all things mighty rich and handsome about me. A great deal of fine discourse, sitting almost till dark at dinner, and then broke up with great pleasure, especially to myself; and they away, only Mr. Carteret and I to Gresham College, and here they had good discourse how this late experiment of the dog, which is in perfect good health, may be improved for good uses to men, and other pretty things, and then broke up. Here was Mr. Henry Howard, that will hereafter be Duke of Norfolke.

29th. Up, and to the office, where busy all the morning. At noon home to dinner, where I find Balty come out to see us, but looks like death, and I do fear he is in a consumption; he has not been abroad many weeks before.

To shew how mad we are at home here, and unfit for any troubles: my Lord St. John did, a day or two since, openly pull a gentleman in Westminster Hall by the nose while the Judges were upon their benches, and the other gentleman did give him a rap over the pate with his cane, of which fray the Judges, they say, will make a great matter.

December 3rd. At noon home, and there find Kate Joyce, who dined with me. Her husband and she are weary of their new life of being an Innkeeper, and will leave it, and would fain get some office; but I know none the foole is fit for, but would be glad to help them if I could, though they have enough to live on, God be thanked!

6th. Harman dined with us, and great sport to hear him tell how Will Joyce grows rich by the custom of the City coming to his end of the towne, and how he rants over his brother and sister for their keeping an Inne, and goes thither and tears like a prince, calling him hosteller and his sister hostess. Then after dinner,

"AND IN A MIGHTY HEAT I WAS"

my wife and brother, in another habit[1] go out to see a play; but I am not to take notice that I know of my brother's going.

7th.   Home to dinner, where finding the cloth laid and much crumpled, but clean, I grew angry and flung the trenchers about the room, and in a mighty heat I was.   So a clean cloth was laid, and my poor wife very patient, and so to dinner, and in comes Mrs. Barbara Sheldon, now Mrs. Wood, and dined with us; she mighty fine and lives, I perceive, mighty happily, which I am glad [of] for her sake, but hate her husband for a block-head in his choice.

8th.   Up, and to the office, where we sat all the morning, and at noon home to dinner, and there find Mr. Pierce and his wife and Betty, a pretty girle; who in discourse at table told me the great Proviso passed the House of Parliament yesterday.   It is a Proviso to the Poll Bill, that there shall be a Committee of nine persons that shall have the inspection upon oath, and power of giving others, of all the accounts of the money given and spent for this warr.   To the King's playhouse (which troubles me since, and hath cost me a forfeit of 10*s*., which I have paid), and there did see a good part of "The English Monsieur,"[2] which is a mighty pretty play, very witty and pleasant.   And the women do very well, but above all little Nelly, that I am mightily pleased with the play; and much with the House, more than ever I expected, the women doing better than ever I expected, and very fine women.   Here I was in pain to be seen, and hid myself; but as God would have it Sir John Chichly come, and sat just by me.

10th.   Up, and at my office all the morning, and several people with me.   Captain Cocke tells me how angry the Court is at the late Proviso brought in by the House.   How still my Lord Chancellor is, not daring to do or say any thing to displease the Parliament; that the Parliament is in a very ill humour, and grows every day more and more so.

12th.   Sir H. Cholmly did with grief tell me how the Parliament hath been told plainly that the King hath been heard to say that he would dissolve them rather than pass this Bill with the Proviso; but tells me that the Proviso is removed, and now carried that it shall be done by a Bill by itself.   He tells me how the King hath lately paid about £30,000 to clear debts of my Lady Castlemayne's.   He says that he hears £400,000 hath gone into the Privy purse

---

[1] *i.e.* not in canonical dress.
[2] By the Hon. James Howard. Nell Gwyn appeared as Lady Wealthy.

since this warr, and that that hath consumed so much of our money, and makes the King and Court so mad to be brought to discover it. Newes this day from Brampton, of Mr. Ensum, my sister's sweetheart, being dead: a clowne.

13th. Up, and to the office, where we sat. At noon to the 'Change and there met Captain Cocke, and had a second time his direction to bespeak £100 of plate, which I did at Sir R. Viner's, being twelve plates more, and something else I have to choose. This afternoon Sir W. Warren and Mr. Moore, one after another, walked with me in the garden, and they both tell me that my Lord Sandwich is called home, and that he do grow more and more in esteem everywhere, and is better spoken of, which I am mighty glad of. For these three or four days I perceive my overworking of my eyes by candlelight do hurt them as it did the last winter; that by day I am well and do get them right, but then after candlelight they begin to be sore and run, so that I intend to get some green spectacles.

14th. To Westminster Hall, and there met my good friend Mr. Evelyn, and walked with him a good while. The house sat till three o'clock, and then up: and I home with Sir Stephen Fox to his house to dinner, and the Cofferer [1] with us. There I find Sir S. Fox's lady, a fine woman, and seven the prettiest children of their's that ever I knew almost. A very genteel dinner, and in great state and fashion, and excellent discourse; and nothing like an old experienced man and a courtier, and such is the Cofferer Ashburnham.

17th. Up, and several people to speak with me, and then comes Mr. Cæsar, [2] and then Goodgroome, and, what with one and the other, nothing but musique with me this morning, to my great content; and the more to see that God Almighty hath put me into condition to bear the charge of all this. So out to the 'Change and did a little business, and then home. To dinner, and then to my chamber to do several things; among other things to write a letter to my Lord Sandwich, it being one of the burdens upon my mind that I have not writ to him since he went into Spain. Spent the evening in fitting my books, to have the number set upon each, in order to my having an alphabet of my whole, which will be of great ease to me.

[1] William Ashburnham, Cofferer to the King's Household.
[2] William Cæsar (*alias* Smegergill) was a composer of songs which appear in several seventeenth-century collections. He is often mentioned in the Diary.

19th. Up to the Lords' House to enquire for Lord Bellasses; and there hear how at a conference this morning between the two Houses about the business of the Canary Company, my Lord Buckingham leaning rudely over my Lord Marquis Dorchester, my Lord Dorchester removed his elbow. Duke of Buckingham asked him whether he was uneasy; Dorchester replied, yes, and that he durst not do this were he any where else: Buckingham replied, yes he would, and that he was a better man than himself; Dorchester answered that he lyed. With this Buckingham struck off his hat, and took him by his periwigg and pulled it aside, and held him. My Lord Chamberlain and others interposed, and upon coming into the House the Lords did order them both to the Tower, whither they are to go this afternoon.

20th. At noon home to dinner, where was Balty come, who is well again, and the most recovered in his countenance that ever I did see.

23rd. (Lord's Day.) Up and alone to church, and meeting Nan Wright at the gate had opportunity to take two or three baisers, and so to church, where a vain fellow with a periwigg preached, Chaplain, as by his prayer appeared, to the Earl of Carlisle. Home, and there dined with us Betty Michell and her husband. After dinner to White Hall by coach, and took them with me. And in the way I would have taken su main as I did the last time, but she did in a manner withhold it.

24th. To dinner, where Mercer with us, and very merry. After dinner she goes and fetches a little son of Mr. Backeworth's, the wittiest child and of the most spirit that ever I saw in my life for discourse of all kind, and so ready and to the purpose, not above four years old. I this evening did buy me a pair of green spectacles, to see whether they will help my eyes or no.

25th. (Christmas Day.) Lay pretty long in bed, and then rose, leaving my wife desirous to sleep, having sat up till four this morning seeing her mayds make mince-pies. I to church, where our parson Mills made a good sermon. Then home, and dined well on some good ribs of beef roasted and mince pies; only my wife, brother, and Barker;[1] and plenty of good wine of my owne, and my heart full of true joy and thanks to God Almighty for the goodness of my condition at this day. After dinner I begun to teach my wife and Barker my song, "It is decreed," which pleases

---

[1] Barker was the maid whom Mrs. Pepys had obtained through Mr. Falconbridge. See October 12th, *ante.*

me mightily. Then out and walked alone on foot to the Temple, it being a fine frost, and so back home. My head a little thought-full how to behave myself in the business of the victualling, which I think will be prudence to offer my service in doing something in passing the pursers' accounts, thereby to serve the King, get honour to myself, and confirm me in my place in the victualling, which at present yields not work enough to deserve my wages.

31st. Rising this day with a full design to mind nothing else but to make up my accounts for the year past, I did take money and walk forth to several places in the towne as far as the New Exchange to pay all my debts, it being still a very great frost and good walking. I staid at the Fleece Tavern in Covent Garden while my boy Tom went to W. Joyce's to pay what I owed for candles there. Thence to the New Exchange to clear my wife's score, and so going back again I met Doll Lane (Mrs. Martin's sister), with another young woman of the Hall, one Scott, and took them to the Half Moon Taverne and there drank some burnt wine with them. And so away home by coach, and there to dinner, and then to my accounts, wherein at last I find them clear and right, but to my great discontent do find that my gettings this year have been £573 less than my last. And then again my spendings this year have exceeded my spendings the last by £644: this year it appears I have spent £1,154, which is a sum not fit to be said that ever I should spend in one year before I am master of a better estate than I am. Yet, blessed be God! and I pray God make me thankful for it, I do find myself worth in money, all good, above £6,200. This, I trust in God, will make me thankfull for what I have, and carefull to make up by care next year what by my neg-ligence and prodigality I have lost and spent this year. The doing of this, and entering of it fair, with the sorting of all my expenses to see how and in what points I have exceeded, did make it late work, till my eyes become very sore and ill; and then did give over, and supper, and to bed. Thus ends this year of publick wonder and mischief to this nation, and therefore generally wished by all people to have an end. Myself and family well, having four mayds and one clerk, Tom, in my house; and my brother now with me to spend time in order to his preferment. Our healths all well, only my eyes with overworking them are sore as candlelight comes to them, and not else. Publick matters in a most sad condition; seamen discouraged for want of pay, and are become not to be governed: nor, as matters are now, can any fleete go out next year.

Our enemies, French and Dutch, great, and grow more by our poverty. The Parliament backward in raising because jealous of the spending of the money; the City less and less likely to be built again, every body settling elsewhere and nobody encouraged to trade. A sad, vicious, negligent Court, and all sober men there fearful of the ruin of the whole kingdom this next year; from which, good God deliver us! One thing I reckon remarkable in my owne condition is that I am come to abound in good plate, so as at all entertainments to be served wholly with silver plates, having two dozen and a half.

EIGHTH YEAR

1667

January 4th. Up, and seeing things put in order for a dinner at my house to-day, I to the office awhile, and about noon home, and there saw all things in good order. Anon comes our company; my Lord Bruncker, Sir W. Pen, his lady and Pegg, and her servant Mr. Lowther,[1] my Lady Batten (Sir W. Batten being forced to dine at Sir R. Ford's, being invited), Mr. Turner and his wife. Here I had good room for ten, and no more would my table have held well had Sir J. Minnes, who was fallen lame, and his sister and niece and Sir W. Batten come, which was a great content to me to be without them. I did make them all gaze to see themselves served so nobly in plate, and a neat dinner, indeed, though but of seven dishes. Mighty merry I was and made them all, and they mightily pleased. My Lord Bruncker went away after dinner to the ticket-office; the rest staid, only my Lady Batten home, her ague-fit coming on her at table. The rest merry, and to cards, and then to sing and talk, and at night to sup, and then to cards; and last of all to have a flaggon of ale and apples, drunk out of a wood cupp as a Christmas draught, made all merry; and they full of admiration at my plate, particularly my flaggons (which indeed are noble). And so late home, all with great mirth and satisfaction to them, as I thought, and to myself to see all I have and do so much outdo for neatness and plenty anything done by any of them. They gone, I to bed much pleased, and do observe Mr. Lowther to be a pretty gentleman, and I think too good for Peg; and by the way Peg Pen seems mightily to be kind to me, and I believe by her father's advice, who is also himself so; but I believe not a little troubled to see my plenty.

8th. At night to Sir W. Batten's. Among other things he tells me that he hears for certain that Sir W. Coventry hath resigned to the King his place of Commissioner of the Navy, the thing he hath often told me that he had a mind to do; but I am surprised

[1] Anthony Lowther, F.R.S., later M.P. for Appleby; he subsequently married Sir W. Penn's daughter Peg.

357

to think that he hath done it, and am full of thoughts all this evening after I heard it what may be the consequences of it to me.

9th. To Arundell House, where first the Royall Society meet
by the favour of Mr. Harry Howard, who was there and has given
us his grandfather's library, a noble gift, and a noble favour and
undertaking it is for him to make his house the seat for this college. Here was an experiment shown about improving the use
of powder for creating of force in winding up of springs, and other
uses of great worth. And here was a great meeting of worthy
noble persons. Thence to the office and then home to supper,
Mercer and her sister there.

11th. Up, being troubled at my being found abed adays by
all sorts of people, I having got a trick of sitting up later than I
need, never supping, or very seldom, before 12 at night. Then to
the office, there busy all the morning; and among other things
comes Sir W. Warren and walked with me awhile, whose discourse
I love, he being a very wise man and full of good counsel, and his
own practices for wisdom much to be observed. And among other
things he tells me how he is fallen in with my Lord Bruncker,
who has promised him most particular inward friendship, and yet
not to appear at the board to do so; and he tells me how my Lord
Bruncker should take notice of the two flaggons he saw at my house
at dinner at my late feast, and merrily, yet I know enviously, said
I could not come honestly by them. This I am glad to hear,
though vexed to see his ignoble soul, but I shall beware of him;
and yet it is fit he should see I am no mean fellow, but can live
in the world and have something.

16th. Prince Rupert, I hear to-day, is very ill. This day before the Duke of York the business of the Muster-Masters was
reported and Balty found the best of the whole number, so as the
Duke enquired who he was and whether he was a stranger by his
two names, both strange; and offered that he and one more who
hath done next best should have not only their owne but part of
the others' salary, but that I having said he was my brother-in-
law he did stop. But they two are ordered their pay which I am
glad of, and some of the rest will lose their pay and others be laid
by the heels. So home to dinner and found Balty; told him the
good news, and then after dinner away. Home to supper with my
wife, and after supper my wife told me how she had moved to W.
Hewer the business of my sister for a wife to him, which he received with mighty acknowledgements, as she says, above any-

thing, but says he hath no intention to alter his condition. So that I am in some measure sorry she ever moved it; but I hope he will think it only come from her. So after supper a little to the office to enter my journall, and then home to bed. Talk there is of a letter to come from Holland desiring a place of treaty; but I do doubt it. This day I observe still in many places the smoking remains of the late fire.

20th. (Lord's Day.) Up betimes and down to the Old Swan; there called on Michell and his wife, which in her night linen appeared as pretty almost as ever to my thinking I saw woman. Here I drank some burnt brandy. I invited them to dine with me, and so away to White Hall to Sir W. Coventry, with whom I have not been alone a good while; and very kind he is, and tells me how the business is now ordered by order of council for my Lord Bruncker to assist Sir J. Minnes in all matters of accounts relating to the Treasurer, and Sir W. Pen in all matters relating to the victuallers' and pursers' accounts, which I am very glad of; and the more for that I think it will not do me any hurt at all. Other discourse, much especially about the heat the House was in yesterday about the ill management of the Navy, which I was sorry to hear; though I think they were well answered, both by Sir G. Carteret and W. Coventry, as he informs me the substance of their speeches. Having done with him, I home mightily satisfied with my being with him; and coming home I to church, and there, beyond expectation, find our seat and all the church crammed by twice as many people as used to be: and to my great joy find Mr. Frampton[1] in the pulpit; so to my great joy I hear him preach, and I think the best sermon for goodness and oratory, without affectation or study, that ever I heard in my life. The truth is he preaches the most like an apostle that ever I heard man; and it was much the best time that ever I spent in my life at church. His text, Ecclesiastes xi., verse 8th—the words, "But if a man live many years, and rejoice in them all; yet let him remember the days of darkness; for they shall be many. All that cometh is vanity."

23rd. Up, and with Sir W. Batten and Sir W. Pen to White Hall, and there to the Duke of York and did our usual business. Having done there, I to St. James's to see the organ Mrs. Turner told me of the other night, of my late Lord Aubigney's; and I took my Lord Bruncker with me, he being acquainted with my present

---

[1] Robert Frampton, later Bishop of Gloucester.

Lord Almoner, Mr. Howard, brother to the Duke of Norfolke; so he and I thither and did see the organ. Here we sat and talked with him a good while, and having done with discourse my Lord Almoner took us quite through the whole house and chapel and the new monastery, showing me most excellent pieces in waxworke: a crucifix given by a Pope to Mary Queen of Scotts, where a piece of the Cross is; and several fine pictures. I saw the dortoire and the cells of the priests, and we went into one, a very pretty little room, very clean, hung with pictures, set with books. The Priest was in his cell, with his hair clothes to his skin, bare-legged, with a sandall only on, and his little bed without sheets; and no feather bed, but yet I thought soft enough. His cord about his middle; but in so good company, living with ease, I though it a very good life. A pretty library they have. And I was in the refectoire, where every man his napkin, knife, cup of earth, and basin of the same; and a place for one to sit and read while the rest are at meals. And into the kitchen I went, where a good neck of mutton at the fire and other victuals boiling: I do not think they fared very hard. Their windows all looking into a fine garden and the Park, and mighty pretty rooms all. I wished myself one of the Capuchins. Having seen what we could here, and all with mighty pleasure, so away with the Almoner in his coach, talking merrily about the difference in our religions, to White Hall, and there we left him. I in my Lord Bruncker's coach, he carried me to the Savoy, and there we parted.

After dinner to the New Exchange, there to take up my wife and Mercer, and thence to the King's house, and there saw "The Humerous Lieutenant" [1]: a silly play, I think. Here in a box above we spied Mrs. Pierce; and going out they called us, and so we staid for them; and Knipp took us all in and brought to us Nelly, a most pretty woman, who acted the great part of Cœlia to-day very fine, and did it pretty well: I kissed her, and so did my wife, and a mighty pretty soul she is. Knipp made us stay in a box and see the dancing preparatory to to-morrow for "The Goblins," a play of Suckling's, not acted these twenty-five years, which was pretty; and so away thence, pleased with this sight also, and especially kissing of Nell. So away with my wife and Mercer home preparing against to-morrow night to have Mrs. Pierce and Knipp and a great deal more company to dance.

24th. Up, and to the office. We sat all the afternoon. Being

---

[1] By Beaumont and Fletcher.

rose, I entering my letters and getting the office swept and a good fire made and abundance of candles lighted, I home, where most of my company come of this end of the town: Mercer and her sister, Mr. Batelier and Pembleton, my Lady Pen and Pegg and Mr. Lowther (but did not stay long, and I believe it was by Sir W. Pen's order, for they had a great mind to have staid), and also Captain Rolt. And anon, at about seven or eight o'clock, comes Mr. Harris, of the Duke's playhouse, and brings Mrs. Pierce with him, and also one dressed like a country-mayde with a straw hat on; which at first I could not tell who it was, though I expected Knipp: but it was she coming off the stage just as she had acted this day in "The Goblins"; a merry jade. Now my house is full, and four fiddlers that play well. Harris I first took to my closet, and I find him a very curious and understanding person in all pictures and other things, and a man of fine conversation, and so is Rolt. So away with all my company down to the office, and there fell to dancing and continued at it an hour or two, there coming Mrs. Anne Jones, a merchant's daughter hard by, who dances well, and all in mighty good humour, and danced with great pleasure; and then sung and then danced, and then sung many things of three voices, both Harris and Rolt singing their parts excellently. Among other things Harris sung his Irish song, the strangest in itself and the prettiest sung by him that ever I heard. Then to supper in the office, a cold, good supper, and wondrous merry. Here was Mrs. Turner also, and Mrs. Markham. After supper to dancing again and singing, and so continued till almost three in the morning, and then, with extraordinary pleasure, broke up. Only towards morning Knipp fell a little ill and so my wife home with her to put her to bed, and we continued dancing and singing; and among other things our Mercer unexpectedly did happen to sing an Italian song I know not, of which they two sung the other two parts to, that did almost ravish me, and made me in love with her more than ever with her singing. As late as it was, yet Rolt and Harris would go home to-night, and walked it, though I had a bed for them. The company being all gone to their homes, I up with Mrs. Pierce to Knipp, who was in bed; and we waked her, and I did sing a song, lying by her on the bed, and then left my wife to see Mrs. Pierce in bed to her in our best chamber, and so to bed myself, my mind mightily satisfied with all this evening's work, and thinking it to be one of the merriest enjoyment I must look for in the world; only the musique did not please me, they not being contented with less than 30*s.*

25th. This afternoon I saw the Poll Bill, now printed; wherein I do fear I shall be very deeply concerned, being to be taxed for all my offices, and then for my money that I have, and my title, as well as my head. It is a very great tax; but yet I do think it is so perplexed it will hardly ever be collected duly. After dinner to the office again, where Lord Bruncker, W. Batten, and W. Pen and I met to talk again about the Controller's office, and there W. Pen would have a piece of the great office cut out to make an office for him, which I opposed to the making him very angry, but I think I shall carry it against him, and then I care not.

30th. Fast-day for the King's death. I all the morning at my chamber making up my month's accounts. In the evening my wife and I and Mercer and Barker to little Michell's, walked, with some neats' tongues and cake and wine, and there sat with the little couple with great pleasure, and talked and eat and drank, and saw their little house, which is very pretty; and I much pleased therewith. And so walked home about eight at night, it being a little moonshine and fair weather, and so into the garden, and, with Mercer, sang till my wife put me in mind of its being a fast day; and so I was sorry for it and stopped, and home to cards awhile, and had opportunity para baiser Mercer several times, and so to bed.

February 2nd. This night comes home my new silver snuffle-dish which I do give myself for my closet, which is all I purpose to bestow in plate of myself or shall need many a day, if I can keep what I have. I am very well pleased this night with reading a poem I brought home with me last night from Westminster Hall, of Dryden's[1] upon the present war; a very good poem.

3rd. (Lord's Day.) Up, and with Sir W. Batten and W. Pen to White Hall, and there to Sir W. Coventry's chamber, and there staid till he was ready, talking, and among other things of the Prince's being trepanned, which was in doing just as we passed through the Stone Gallery, we asking at the door of his lodgings, and were told so. We are all full of wishes for the good success; though I dare say but few do really concern ourselves for him in our hearts. Up to the Duke of York, and with him did our business.

4th. My wife and I to the Duke's playhouse, and there saw "Heraclius,"[2] an excellent play, to my extraordinary content;

---

[1] *Annus mirabilis.*
[2] Translated from Corneille.

and the more from the house being very full, and great company; among others Mrs. Steward, very fine, with her locks done up with puffs, as my wife calls them: and several other great ladies had their hair so, though I do not like it; but my wife do mightily. But it is only because she sees it is the fashion.

7th. To the office, where all the morning, and then home to dinner. And before dinner I went into my green dining room, and there talking with my brother upon matters relating to his journey to Brampton to-morrow and giving him good counsel about spending the time when he shall stay in the country with my father, I looking another way heard him fall down, and turned my head and he was fallen down all along upon the ground dead, which did put me into a great fright; and to see my brotherly love! I did presently lift him up from the ground, he being as pale as death; and being upon his legs he did presently come to himself, and said he had something come into his stomach very hot. I never was so frighted but once, when my wife was ill at Ware upon the road,[1] and I did continue trembling a good while and ready to weepe to see him, he continuing mighty pale all dinner and melancholy, that I was loth to let him take his journey to-morrow, but he began to be pretty well. And after dinner my wife and Barker fell to singing, which pleased me pretty well, my wife taking mighty pains and proud that she shall come to trill; and indeed I think she will. So to the office, and there all the afternoon late doing business, and then home, and find my brother pretty well. So to write a letter to my Lady Sandwich for him to carry, I having not writ to her a great while. Then to supper and so to bed. I did this night give him 20*s.* for books, and as much for his pocket, and 15*s.* to carry him down, and so to bed.

8th. This morning my brother John come up to my bedside and took his leave of us. My wife loves him mightily as one that is pretty harmless, and I do begin to fancy him from yesterday's accident, it troubling me to think I should be left without a brother or sister, which is the first time that ever I had thoughts of that kind in my life.

9th. To the office, where we sat all the morning busy. At noon home to dinner, and then to my office again, where also busy, very busy late, and then went home and read a piece of a play,

---

[1] See *ante,* September 14th, 1663.

"Every Man in his Humour," [1] wherein is the greatest propriety of speech that ever I read in my life: and so to bed.

10th. (Lord's Day.) Up and with my wife to church, where Mr. Mills made an unnecessary sermon upon Original Sin, neither understood by himself nor the people. Home, where Michell and his wife, and also there come Mr. Carter, my old acquaintance of Magdalene College, who hath not been here of many years. After dinner he went away, and awhile after them Michell and his wife, whom I love mightily.

11th. To Westminster Hall and after walking a good while in the Hall, it being Term time, I home by water, calling at Michell's and giving him a fair occasion to send his wife to the New Exchange to meet my wife and me this afternoon. So home to dinner, and after dinner by coach to Lord Bellasses', and with him to Povy's house. Having done what we had to do there, my Lord carried me and set me down at the New Exchange, where I staid at Pottle's shop till Betty Michell come, which she did about five o'clock, and was surprised not to trouver my muger [2] there; but I did make an excuse good enough, and so I took elle down, and over the water to the cabinet-maker's, and there bought a dressing-box for her for 20*s.*, but would require an hour's time to make fit. We staid in the shop and above seeing the workmen work, which was pretty, and some exceeding good work, and very pleasant to see them do it, till it was late quite dark, and the mistresse of the shop took us into the kitchen and there talked and used us very prettily, and took her for my wife, which I owned, and there very merry till my thing done, and then took coach and home. But now comes our trouble, I did begin to fear that su marido might go to my house to enquire pour elle, and there, trouvant my muger at home, would not only think himself, but give my femme occasion to think strange things. This did trouble me mightily, so though elle would not seem to have me trouble myself about it, yet did agree to the stopping the coach at the streete's end, and je allois con elle home, and there presently hear by him that he had newly sent su mayde to my house to see for her mistresse. This do much perplex me, and I did go presently home (Betty whispering me behind the tergo de her mari, that if I would say that we did come home by water, elle could make up la cose well satis), and there in a sweat did walk in the entry ante

[1] By Ben Jonson.
[2] Spanish for wife.

my door, thinking what I should say à my femme; and as God would have it, while I was in this case (the worst in reference à my femme that ever I was in in my life), a little woman comes stumbling to the entry steps in the dark; whom asking who she was, she enquired for my house. So knowing her voice, and telling her su donna is come home she went away. But, Lord! in what a trouble was I when she was gone to recollect whether this was not the second time of her coming, but at last concluding that she had not been here before, I did bless myself in my good fortune in getting home before her, and do verily believe she had loitered some time by the way, which was my great good fortune, and so I in a-doors and there find all well. So my heart full of joy, I to the office awhile and then home, and after supper and doing a little business in my chamber I to bed, after teaching Barker a little of my song.

12th. With Lord Bruncker by coach to his house, there to hear some Italian musique: and here we met Tom Killigrew, Sir Robert Murray, and the Italian Signor Baptista,[1] who hath composed a play in Italian for the Opera, which T. Killigrew do intend to have up; and here he did sing one of the acts. He himself is the poet as well as the musician, which is very much, and did sing the whole from the words without any musique prickt, and played all along upon a harpsicon most admirably, and the composition most excellent. This done, T. Killigrew and I to talk: and he tells me how the audience at his house is not above half so much as it used to be before the late fire. That Knipp is like to make the best actor that ever come upon the stage, she understanding so well that they are going to give her £30 a-year more. That the stage is now by his pains a thousand times better and more glorious than ever heretofore. Now wax-candles, and many of them; then not above 3 lbs. of tallow: now all things civil, no rudeness anywhere; then as in a bear-garden: then two or three fiddlers; now nine or ten of the best: then nothing but rushes upon the ground, and every thing else mean; and now all otherwise: then the Queen seldom and the King never would come; now not the King only for state, but all civil people do think they may come as well as any. He tells me that he hath gone several times, eight or ten times, he tells me, hence to Rome to hear good musique; so much he loves it, though he never did sing or play a note. That he hath ever endeavoured in the late King's time and in this

---

[1] Giovanni Baptista Draghi, an Italian composer in the service of Queen Catherine.

to introduce good musique, but he never could do it, there never having been any musique here better than ballads. Nay, says "Hermitt poore" and "Chevy Chese"[1] was all the musique we had; and yet no ordinary fiddlers get so much money as ours do here, which speaks our rudenesse still. That he hath gathered our Italians from several Courts in Christendome to come to make a concert for the King, which he do give £200 a-year a-piece to: but badly paid, and do come in the room of keeping four ridiculous gundilows,[2] he having got the King to put them away and lay out money this way; and indeed I do commend him for it, for I think it is a very notle undertaking.

14th. After dinner by coach to my Lord Chancellor's, and there a meeting: the Duke of York, Duke of Albemarle, and several other Lords of the Commission of Tangier. And there I did present a state of my accounts, and managed them well; and my Lord Chancellor did say, though he was in other things in an ill humour, that no man in England was of more method, nor made himself better understood than myself. Thence away by coach to Sir H. Cholmly, and he and I to the Temple, and there walked in the dark in the walks talking of newes; and he surprises me with the certain newes that the King did last night in Council declare his being in treaty with the Dutch. This morning come up to my wife's bedside, I being up dressing myself, little Will Mercer to be her Valentine; and brought her name writ upon blue paper in gold letters, done by himself, very pretty; and we were both well pleased with it. But I am also this year my wife's Valentine, and it will cost me £5; but that I must have laid out if we had not been Valentines.

17th. (Lord's Day.) This evening, going to the Queen's side to see the ladies, I did find the Queene, the Duchesse of York and another or two at cards, with the room full of great ladies and men; which I was amazed at to see on a Sunday, having not believed it; but, contrarily, flatly denied the same a little while since to my cozen Roger Pepys.

18th. With my wife by coach to the Duke of York's play-house expecting a new play, and so stayed not no more than other people, but to the King's house, to "The Mayd's Tragedy";[3] but vexed all the while with two talking ladies and Sir Charles Sedley; yet pleased to hear their discourse, he being a stranger. And one

---

[1] "Like hermit poor in pensive place obscure," set by Ferrabosco, was a favourite song of Isaak Walton. "Chevy Chase" is of course a famous ballad.
[2] Gondolas.   [3] By Beaumont and Fletcher.

"LITTLE WILL MERCER TO BE HER VALENTINE"

of the ladies would and did sit with her mask on all the play, and, being exceeding witty as ever I heard woman, did talk most pleasantly with him; but was, I believe, a woman of quality. He would fain know who she was, but she would not tell; yet did give him many pleasant hints of her knowledge of him, by that means setting his brains at work to find out who she was, and did give him leave to use all means to find out who she was but pulling off her mask. He was mighty witty, and she also making sport with him very inoffensively, that a more pleasant rencontre I never heard. But by that means lost the pleasure of the play wholly, to which now and then Sir Charles Sedley's exceptions against both words and pronouncing were very pretty.

21st. Up, and to the Office, where sat all the morning, and there a most furious conflict between Sir W. Pen and I, in few words, and on a sudden occasion, of no great moment, but very bitter, and stared on one another, and so broke off, and to our business, my heart as full of spite as it could hold, for which God forgive me and him!

22nd. At dinner to Sir W. Pen's house, where some other company. It is instead of a wedding dinner for his daughter, whom I saw in palterly clothes, nothing new but a bracelet that her servant had given her, and ugly she is, as heart can wish. A sorry dinner, not anything handsome or clean but some silver plates they borrowed of me. My wife was here too. So a great deal of talk, and I seemingly merry, but took no pleasure at all. We had favours given us all, and we put them in our hats, I against my will, but that my Lord and the rest did.

23rd. This day I am, by the blessing of God, 34 years old, in very good health and mind's content, and in condition of estate much beyond whatever my friends could expect of a child of their's, this day 34 years. The Lord's name be praised! and may I be ever thankful for it.

25th. Lay long in bed, talking with pleasure with my poor wife, how she used to make coal fires, and wash my foul clothes with her own hand for me, poor wretch! in our little room at my Lord Sandwich's; for which I ought for ever to love and admire her, and do; and persuade myself she would do the same thing again if God should reduce us to it. So up and by coach abroad to the Duke of Albemarle's about sending soldiers down to some ships, and so home, calling at a belt-maker's to mend my belt, and so home and to dinner, where pleasant with my wife; and then to the office, where mighty busy all the day, saving going forth to the 'Change to pay for some things. And at my gold-smith's did observe the King's new medall, where, in little, there is Mrs. Steward's face as well done as ever I saw anything in my whole life, I think: and a pretty thing it is, that he should choose her face to represent Britannia by.[1] So at the office late very busy and much business with great joy dispatched, and so home to supper and to bed.

27th. Up by candle-light about six o'clock, it being bitter cold weather, and by water down to Woolwich ropeyard. Home about noon; there find Mr. Hunt newly come out of the country, who tells me the country is much impoverished by the greatness of taxes: the farmers do break every day almost, and £1,000 a-year become not worth £500. He dined with us, and we had good discourse of the general ill state of things; and by the way he told me some ridiculous pieces of thrift of Sir G. Downing's, who is his countryman, in inviting some poor people at Christmas last to charm the country people's mouths; but did give them nothing but beef, porridge, pudding and pork; and nothing said all dinner, but only his mother would say, "It's good broth, son." He would answer, "Yes, it is good broth." Then says his lady, "Confirm all, and say, 'Yes, very good broth.'" By and by she would begin and say, "Good pork:" "Yes," says the mother, "good pork." Then he cries, "Yes, very good pork." And so they said of all things; to which nobody made any answer, they going there not out of love or esteem of them, but to eat his vict-uals, knowing him to be a niggardly fellow; and with this he is jeered now all over the country. Met Mr. Cooling, who tells me of my Lord Duke of Buckingham's being sent for last night by a Serjeant at Armes to the Tower for treasonable practices, and that the King is infinitely angry with him and declared him no longer one of his Council.[2] I know not the reason of it, or occasion.

28th. Up, and there comes to me Drumbleby with a flageolet made to suit with my former, and brings me one Greeting, a master, to teach my wife. I agree by the whole with him to teach her to take out any lesson of herself for £4. She was not ready to begin to-day, but do to-morrow.

---

[1] This was a large silver medal with the King's head on one side and on the other Frances Stuart, afterwards Duchess of Richmond, as Britannia.

[2] Buckingham had lost this round in his continual contest with Clarendon; but he was released on the Lord Chancellor's fall six months later, and became for a while the King's chief adviser.

March 1st. To the office till dinner-time and then home to dinner, and before dinner making my wife to sing. Poor wretch! her ear is so bad that it made me angry, till the poor wretch cried to see me so vexed at her, that I think I shall not discourage her so much again, but will endeavour to make her understand sounds and do her good that way; for she hath a great mind to learn, only to please me; and therefore I am mighty unjust to her in discouraging her so much, but we were good friends, and to dinner; and were it not Friday (on which in Lent there are no plays) I had carried her to a play.

2nd. Up, and to the office, where sitting all the morning; and among other things did agree upon a distribution of £30,000 and odd, which is the only sum we hear of like to come out of all the Poll Bill for the use of this office for buying of goods. I did herein some few courtesies for particular friends I wished well to, and for the King's service also, and was therefore well pleased with what was done. After dinner with my wife to the King's house to see "The Mayden Queene," a new play of Dryden's, mightily commended for the regularity of it, and the strain and wit; and the truth is there is a comical part done by Nell, which is Florimell, that I never can hope ever to see the like done again, by man or woman. The King and Duke of York were at the play. But so great performance of a comical part was never I believe in the world before as Nell do this, both as a mad girle, then most and best of all when she comes in like a young gallant; and hath the motions and carriage of a spark the most that ever I saw any man have. It makes me, I confess, admire her. Thence home and to the office, where busy a while, and then home to read the lives of Henry 5th and 6th, very fine, in Speede,[1] and so to bed.

3rd. (Lord's Day.) To my Lord Chancellor's, and there, meeting Sir H. Cholmly, he tells me that the Duke of Buckingham hath provoked, by his ill-carriage, the Duke of York, my Lord Chancellor, and all the great persons; and therefore most likely will die. He tells me, too, many practices of treachery against this King; as betraying him in Scotland, and giving Oliver an account of the King's private councils, which the King knows very well, and hath yet pardoned him.

5th. To the office, and there all the afternoon late doing much business, and then to see Sir W. Batten. I by discourse do perceive he and his Lady are to their hearts out with my Lord Brunc-

[1] John Speed's Chronicle.

ker and Mrs. Williams. But, Lord! to see to what a poor content any acquaintance among these people, or the people of the world as they now-a-days go is worth; for my part I and my wife will keep to one another and let the world go hang, for there is nothing but falseness in it.

6th. Sir W. Pen told me, going with me this morning to White Hall, that for certain the Duke of Buckingham is brought into the Tower. To Westminster Hall. There bought some newsbooks, and as every where else hear every body complain of the dearness of coals, being at £4 per chaldron; the weather, too, being become most bitter cold, the King saying to-day that it was the coldest day he ever knew in England. Thence by coach to my Lord Crew's, where very welcome. Here I find they are in doubt where the Duke of Buckingham is; which makes me mightily reflect on the uncertainty of all history, when, in a business of this moment, and of this day's growth, we cannot tell the truth.

9th. To Sir W. Batten's, where W. Pen and others, and mighty merry, only I have got a great cold. This did most certainly come by my staying a little too long bare-legged yesterday morning when I rose, while I looked out fresh socks and thread stockings, yesterday's having in the night, lying near the window, been covered with snow within the window, which made me I durst not put them on.

11th. Up, and with my cold still upon me and hoarseness, but I was forced to rise and to the office, where all the morning busy. At noon with Sir W. Pen by coach to the Sun in Leadenhall Streete, where Sir R. Ford, Sir W. Batten and Commissioner Taylor (whose feast it was) were, and we dined and had a very good dinner. Among other discourses Sir R. Ford did tell me that he do verily believe that the city will in few years be built again in all the greatest streets, and answered the objections I did give to it. Here we had the proclamation this day come out against the Duke of Buckingham, commanding him to come in to one of the Secretaries, or to the Lieutenant of the Tower. A silly, vain man to bring himself to this. Then to discourse of the business of the day, that is, to see Commissioner Taylor's accounts for his ship he built, The Loyall London. Thence away to the office, where late busy, and then home to supper, mightily pleased with my wife's trill, and so to bed.

12th. This day a poor seaman, almost starved for want of food, lay in our yard a-dying. I sent him half-a-crown, and we ordered his ticket to be paid.

13th. To Westminster Hall, and there staid and talked, and then to Sir G. Carteret's, where I dined. So home by water, and stepped into Michell's, and there did baiser my Betty. At home find Mr. Holliard, and made him eat a bit of victuals. Mr. Holliard advises me to have my father come up to town, for he doubts else in the country he will never find ease, for, poor man, his grief is now grown so great upon him that he is never at ease, so I will have him up at Easter. By and by by coach, set down Mr. Holliard near his house at Hatton Garden and myself to Lord Treasurer's, and sent my wife to the New Exchange. I staid not here, but to Westminster Hall, and thence to Martin's, where he and she both within; but there being so much company I had no pleasure here, and so away to the Hall again, and there met Doll Lane coming out, and par contrat did hazer bargain para aller to the cabaret de vin, called the Rose, and ibi I staid two hours, sed she did not venir, lequel troubled me, and so away by coach and took up my wife, and away home. Late at my office preparing a speech against to-morrow morning, before the King at my Lord Treasurer's, and the truth is it run in my head all night. So home to supper and to bed. The Duke of Buckingham is concluded gone over sea, and it is thought to France.

14th. Up, and with Sir W. Batten and W. Pen to my Lord Treasurer's, where we met with my Lord Bruncker an hour before the King come, and had time to talk a little of our business. Then come much company, among others Sir H. Cholmly. Here we fell into talk with Sir Stephen Fox, and among other things of the Spanish manner of walking when three together, and shewed me how, which was pretty, to prevent differences. By and by comes the King and Duke of York, and presently the officers of the Ordnance were called; then we, my Lord Bruncker, W. Batten, W. Pen, and myself, where we find only the King and Duke of York, and my Lord Treasurer and Sir G. Carteret; where I only did speak, laying down the state of our wants, which the King and Duke of York seemed very well pleased with, and we did get what we asked. So we gone out, in went others; viz., one after another, Sir Stephen Fox for the army, Captain Cocke for sick and wounded, Mr. Ashburnham for the household. Thence W. Batten, W. Pen and I back again; I mightily pleased with what I had said and done, and the success thereof. But, it being a fine clear day, I did, en gayeté de cœur, propose going to Bow for ayre sake, and dine there, which they embraced, and so W. Batten and I straight to

Bow, to the Queen's Head, and there bespoke our dinner, carrying meat with us from London; and anon comes W. Pen with my wife and Lady Batten, and then Mr. Lowder with his mother and wife. They being come, we to oysters and so to talk. Very pleasant I was all day; and anon to dinner, and I made very good company. Here till the evening, so as it was dark almost before we got home.

15th. I do hear that letters this day come to Court do tell us that we are likely not to agree, the Dutch demanding high terms, and the King of France the like, in a most braving manner. The merchants do give themselves over for lost, no man knowing what to do, whether to sell or buy, not knowing whether peace or war to expect.

17th. (Lord's Day.) Up betime with my wife, and by coach to White Hall, there my wife and I the first time that ever we went to my Lady Jemimah's chamber. I confess I have been much to blame and much ashamed of our not visiting her sooner, but better now than never. Here we took her before she was up, which I was sorry for, so only saw her, and away to chapel, leaving further visit till after sermon. I put my wife into the pew below, but it was pretty to see, myself being but in a plain band and every way else ordinary, how the verger took me for her man, I think, and I was fain to tell him she was a kinswoman of my Lord Sandwich's, he saying that none under knights-baronets' ladies are to go into that pew. So she being there I to the Duke of York's lodging. Then to Queene's Chapel and there heard a fryer preach, with his cord about his middle, in Portuguese, something I could understand, showing that God did respect the meek and humble as well as the high and rich. He was full of action, but very decent and good, I thought, and his manner of delivery very good. Then I went back to White Hall, and there up to the closet and spoke with several people till sermon was ended. After Chapel I down and took out my wife from the pew. To Sir G. Carteret's, where we dined and mightily made of, and most extraordinary people they are to continue friendship with for goodness, virtue, and nobleness and interest.

18th. A little before noon comes my old good friend, Mr. Richard Cumberland[1] to see me, being newly come to town, whom I have not seen almost, if not quite, these seven years. In his plain country-parson's dress. I could not spend much time with

[1] A contemporary of Pepys' at St. Paul's and Magdalene, of which college he became a Fellow. He was at this time rector of Pepys' village of Brampton, and later became Bishop of Peterborough.

him, but prayed him come with his brother, who was with him, to dine with me to-day; which he did do, and I had a great deal of his good company, and a most excellent person he is as any I know, and one that I am sorry should be lost and buried in a little country town, and would be glad to remove him thence; and the truth is, if he would accept of my sister's fortune, I should give £100 more with him than to a man able to settle her four times as much as, I fear, he is able to do; and I will think of it, and a way how to move it, he having in discourse said he was not against marrying, nor yet engaged. I shewed him my closet, and did give him some very good musique, Mr. Cæsar being here upon his lute. They gone I to the office, where all the afternoon very busy, and among other things comes Captain Jenifer to me, a great servant of my Lord Sandwich's, who tells me that he do hear for certain, though I do not yet believe it, that Sir W. Coventry is to be Secretary of State, and my Lord Arlington Lord Treasurer. I only wish that the latter were as fit for the latter office as the former is for the former. Anon Sir W. Pen come and talked with me in the garden, and tells me that for certain the Duke of Richmond is to marry Mrs. Stewart, he having this day brought in an account of his estate and debts to the King on that account. At night home to supper and so to bed. My father's letter this day do tell me of his own continued illness, and that my mother grows so much worse that he fears she cannot long continue, which troubles me very much. This day Mr. Cæsar told me a pretty experiment of his, of angling with a minikin, a gut-string varnished over, which keeps it from swelling, and is beyond any hair for strength and smallness. The secret I like mightily.

19th. Up, and to the office, where we sat all the morning. At noon dined at home very pleasantly with my wife, and after dinner with a great deal of pleasure had her sing, which she begins to do with some pleasure to me, more than I expected. Then to the office again, where all the afternoon close, and at night home to supper and to bed. It comes in my mind this night to remember to my shame how I was pleased yesterday to find the righteous maid of Magister Griffin sweeping of nostra office, elle con the Roman nariz, which I did heretofore like, and do still refresh me to think que elle is come to us, that I may voir her aliquando.[1]

20th. To Sir W. Batten to dinner, and had a good dinner of ling and herring pie, very good meat, best of the kind that ever I

---

[1] Nariz=nose (Sp.). Aliquando=sometimes (Latin),

had. Having dined, I by coach to the Temple, and there did buy a little book or two, and it is strange how "Rycaut's Discourse of Turky," which before the fire I was asked but 8s. for, there being all but twenty-two or thereabouts burned, I did now offer 20s., and he demands 50s., and I think I shall give it him, though it be only as a monument of the fire. To the office a little, where I met with a sad letter from my brother, who tells me my mother is declared by the doctors to be past recovery, and that my father is also very ill every hour: so that I fear we shall see a sudden change there. God fit them and us for it!

22nd. Home to dinner, where my wife having dressed herself in a silly dress of a blue petticoat uppermost, and a white satin waistcoat and white hood, though I think she did it because her gown is gone to the tailor's, did, together with my being hungry, which always makes me peevish, make me angry; but when my belly was full were friends again.

23rd. At the office all the morning. At noon home to dinner, and then to the office all the afternoon again, where Mr. Moore come, who tells me that there is now no doubt made of a peace being agreed on, the King having declared this week in Council that they would treat at Bredagh. He gone I to my office, where busy late, and so to supper and to bed. Vexed with our mayde Luce, our cook-mayde, who is a good drudging servant in everything else, and pleases us, but that she will be drunk and hath been so last night and all this day, that she could not make clean the house.

25th. (Lady day.) W. Pen and I to Mr. Povy's about a little business of W. Pen's, where we went over Mr. Povy's house, which lies in the same good condition as ever, which is most extraordinary fine; and he was now at work with a cabinet-maker, making of a new inlaid table. Having seen his house, we away, having in our way thither called at Mr. Lilly's,[1] who was working; and indeed his pictures are without doubt much beyond Mr. Hales's, I think I may say I am convinced: but a mighty proud man he is, and full of state. So home and to the office, and by and by to dinner, a poor dinner, my wife and I, at Sir W. Pen's, and then he and I before to the King's playhouse; and by and by comes Mr. Lowther and his wife and mine, and into a box, forsooth, neither of them being dressed, which I was almost ashamed of. Sir W. Pen and I in the pit, and here saw "The Mayden Queene"; which indeed

---

[1] Sir Peter Lely lived in Drury Lane.

the more I see the more I like, and is an excellent play, and so done by Nell, her merry part, as cannot be better done in nature, I think. Thence home, and there I find letters from my brother which tell me that yesterday when he wrote my mother did rattle in the throat so as they did expect every moment her death, which though I have a good while expected did much surprise me; yet was obliged to sup at Sir W. Pen's, and my wife, and there counterfeited some little mirth, but my heart was sad; and so home after supper and to bed, and much troubled in my sleep of my being crying by my mother's bedside, laying my head over hers and crying, she almost dead and dying, and so waked. But what is strange, methought she had hair over her face, and not the same kind of face as my mother really hath; but yet did not consider that, but did weep over her as my mother, whose soul God have mercy of.

26th. Up with a sad heart in reference to my mother, of whose death I undoubtedly expect to hear the next post, if not of my father's also, who by his pain as well as his grief for her is very ill; but on my own behalf I have cause to be joyful this day, it being my usual feast day for my being cut of the stone this day nine years, and through God's blessing am at this day and have long been in as good condition of health as ever I was in my life or any man in England is, God make me thankful for it! But the condition I am in in reference to my mother makes it unfit for me to keep my usual feast. Unless it shall please God to send her well (which I despair wholly of), and then I will make amends for it by observing another day in its room. So to the office, and at the office all the morning, where I had an opportunity to speak to Sir John Harman about my desire to have my brother Balty go again with him to sea as he did the last year, which he do seem not only contented but pleased with, which I was glad of.

27th. To the Duke of York's lodgings and did our usual business; Sir W. Pen telling me that he had this morning spoke of Balty to Sir W. Coventry, and that the thing was done. I to Westminster Hall and there met Balty, whom I had sent for, and there did break the business of my getting him the place. He is mighty glad of it, and earnest to fit himself for it. Having put him in a way of preparing himself for the voyage I did go to the Swan, and there sent for Jervas, my old periwig maker, and he did bring me a periwig, but it was full of nits, so as I was troubled to see it (it being his old fault), and did send him to make it clean;

"HE FORCING US TO HEAR HIM"

and in the mean time, having staid for him a good while, did go away by water to the Castle Taverne, and there met Sir W. Batten, W. Pen, and several others. Being desirous to be at home to see the issue of my country letters about my mother, which I expect shall give me tidings of her death, I home and there to the office, where I find no letter from my father or brother; but by and by the boy tells me that his mistress sends me word that she hath opened my letter, and that she is loth to send me any more news. So I home, and there up to my wife in our chamber, and there received from my brother the newes of my mother's dying on Monday, about five or six o'clock in the afternoon,[1] and that the last time she spoke of her children was on Friday last, and her last words were, "God bless my poor Sam!" The reading hereof did set me a-weeping heartily, and so weeping to myself awhile, and my wife also to herself, I then spoke to my wife respecting myself, and indeed, having some thoughts how much better both for her and us it is than it might have been had she outlived my father and me or my happy present condition in the world, she being helpless, I was the sooner at ease in my mind; and then found it necessary to go abroad with my wife to look after the providing mourning to send into the country, some to-morrow and more against Sunday, for my family, being resolved to put myself and wife, and Barker and Jane, W. Hewer and Tom, in mourning, and my two under-mayds, to give them hoods and scarfs and gloves. So to my tailor's and up and down, and then home and to my office a little, and then to supper and to bed, my heart sad and afflicted, though my judgment at ease.

28th. With Sir W. Batten, W. Pen, and R. Ford to Mr. Johnson's, to see how some works upon some of our repaired ships go on, and at his house eat and drank and mighty extraordinary merry (too merry for me whose mother died so lately, but they know it not, so cannot reproach me therein, though I reproach myself), and in going home had many good stories of Sir W. Batten and one of Sir W. Pen, the most tedious and silly and troublesome (he forcing us to hear him) that ever I heard in my life. So to the office awhile, troubled with Sir W. Pen's impertinences, he being half foxed at Johnson's, and so to bed.

April 3rd. This day I saw Prince Rupert abroad in the Vane-room, pretty well as he used to be, and looks as well, only something appears to be under his periwigg on the crown of his head.

[1] It was on Monday night (25th) that Pepys dreamed of her.

4th. To the office till noon, busy, and then meeting Balty at my house I took him with me by water, and to the Duke of Albemarle. I find the Duke of Albemarle at dinner with sorry company, some of his officers of the Army; dirty dishes, and a nasty wife at table, and bad meat, of which I made but an ill dinner. I remember he said, had all his captains fought, he would no more have doubted to have beat the Dutch, with all their number, than to eat the apple that lay on his trencher. Dinner being done, I brought Balty to the Duke to kiss his hand and thank him for his kindness the last year to him, and take leave of him. And then Balty and I to walk in the Park; and out of pity to his father told him what I had in my thoughts to do for him about the money; that is, to make him Deputy Treasurer of the fleete, which I have done by getting Sir G. Carteret's consent, and an order from the Duke of York for £1,500 to be paid to him. He promises the whole profit to be paid to my wife, for to be disposed of as she sees fit for her father and mother's relief.

5th. To Sir W. Batten's, where Mr. Young was talking about the building of the City again; and he told me that those few churches that are to be new built are plainly not chosen with regard to the convenience of the City (they stand a great many in a cluster about Cornhill), but that all of them are either in the gift of the Lord Archbishop, or Bishop of London, or Lord Chancellor, or gift of the City. Thus all things, even to the building of churches, are done in this world! This morning come to me the Collectors for my Poll-money; for which I paid for my title as Esquire and place of Clerk of Acts, and my head and wife's, and servants' and their wages, £40. 17s.; and though this be a great deal, yet it is a shame I should pay no more; that is, that I should not be assessed for my pay, as in the Victualling business and Tangier; and for my money (which of my own accord I had determined to charge myself with £1,000 money, till coming to the Vestry and seeing nobody of our ablest merchants to do it I thought it not decent for me to do it, nor would it be thought wisdom to do it unnecessarily, but vain glory).

6th. Up, and betimes in the morning down to the Tower wharfe, there to attend the shipping of soldiers to go down to man some ships going out, and pretty to see how merrily some, and most, go, and how sad others; the leave they take of their friends, and the terms that some wives, and other wenches, asked to part with them: a pretty mixture.

11th. To White Hall, thinking there to have seen the Duchess of Newcastle's coming this night to Court to make a visit to the Queene, the King having been with her yesterday to make her a visit since her coming to town. The whole story of this lady is a romance, and all she do is romantick. Her footmen in velvet coats and herself in an antique dress, as they say; and was the other day at her own play, "The Humourous Lovers"; the most ridiculous thing that ever was wrote, but yet she and her Lord mightily pleased with it; and she at the end made her respects to the players from her box, and did give them thanks. There is as much expectation of her coming to Court, that so people may come to see her, as if it were the Queen of Sweden[1]; but I lost my labour, for she did not come this night.

12th. Up, and when ready, and to my office, to do a little business, and coming homeward again saw my door and hatch open, left so by Luce our cookmayde, which so vexed me that I did give her a kick in our entry, and offered a blow at her, and was seen doing so by Sir W. Pen's footboy, which did vex me to the heart because I know he wili be telling their family of it; though I did put on presently a very pleasant face to the boy and spoke kindly to him, as one without passion, so as it may be he might not think I was angry; but yet I was troubled at it. So away by water to White Hall, and there did our usual business before the Duke of York; but it fell out that, discoursing of matters of money, it rose to a mighty heat, very high words arising between Sir G. Carteret and W. Coventry, the former in his passion saying that the other should have helped things if they were so bad; and the other answered, so he would, and things should have been better had he been Treasurer of the Navy. I was mightily troubled at this heat, and it will breed ill blood, I fear; but things are in that bad condition that I do daily expect when we shall all fly in one another's faces, when we shall be reduced every one to answer for himself. We broke up; and I soon after to Sir G. Carteret's chamber, where I find the poor man telling his lady privately, and she weeping. I went into them and did seem, as indeed I was, troubled for this, and did give the best advice I could, which I think did please them: and they do apprehend me their friend, as indeed I am, for I do take the Vice-chamberlain for a most honest man. He did assure me that he was not, all expences and things paid,

---

[1] The celebrated ex-Queen Christina, whose extraordinary character and conduct were then attracting the attention of all Europe.

clear in estate £15,000, better than he was when the King come in; and that the King and Lord Chancellor did know that he was worth, with the debt the King owed him, £50,000, I think, he said, when the King come into England. I did pacify all I could, and then away by water home, there to write letters and things for the dispatch of Balty away this day to sea; and after dinner he did go, I having given him much good counsell and I have great hopes that he will make good use of it, and be a good man, for I find him willing to take pains and very sober. He being gone, I close at my office all the afternoon getting off of hand my papers, which by the late holidays and my laziness were grown too many upon my hands, to my great trouble; and therefore at it as late as my eyes would give me leave, and then by water down to Redriffe, meaning to meet my wife, who is gone with Mercer, Barker and the boy (it being most sweet weather) to walk; and I did meet with them and walked back, and then by the time we got home it was dark, and we staid singing in the garden till supper was ready, and there with great pleasure. But I tried my girles Mercer and Barker singly one after another, a single song, "At dead low ebb," etc., and I do clearly find that as to manner of singing the latter do much the better, the other thinking herself (as I do myself) above taking pains for a manner of singing, contenting ourselves with the judgment and goodness of eare. So to supper, and then parted and to bed.

13th. Wrote to my father, who, I am glad to hear, is at some ease again, and I long to have him in town that I may see what can be done for him here; for I would fain do all I can that I may have him live, and take pleasure in my doing well in the world.

15th. To the King's house by chance, where a new play, so full as I never saw it; I forced to stand all the while close to the very door till I took cold, and many people went away for want of room. The King and Queene and Duke of York and Duchesse there, and all the Court, and Sir W. Coventry. The play called "The Change of Crownes"; a play of Ned Howard's, the best that ever I saw at that house, being a great play and serious; only Lacy did act the country-gentleman come up to Court, who do abuse the Court with all the imaginable wit and plainness about selling of places, and doing every thing for money. The play took very much.

16th. Up, and to the office, where sat all the morning. At noon home to dinner, and thence in haste to carry my wife to see the new play I saw yesterday, she not knowing it. But there, contrary to expectation, find "The Silent Woman."[1] However, in; and there Knipp come into the pit. Knipp tells me the King was so angry at the liberty taken by Lacy's part to abuse him to his face that he commanded they should act no more, till Moone went and got leave for them to act again, but not this play. The King mighty angry; and it was bitter indeed, but very true and witty.

20th. At noon dined, and with my wife to the King's house, but there found the bill torn down and no play acted; and so being in the humour to see one, went to the Duke of York's house, and there saw "The Witts"[2] again, which likes me better than it did, having much wit in it. Here were many fine ladies this afternoon at this house as I have at any time seen. And so after the play home and there wrote to my father, and then to walk in the garden with my wife, resolving by the grace of God to see no more plays till Whitsuntide, I having now seen a play every day this week, till I have neglected my business and that I am ashamed of being found so much absent; the Duke of York and Sir W. Coventry having been out of town at Portsmouth did the more embolden me thereto. So home, and having brought home with me from Fenchurch Street a hundred of sparrowgrass, cost 18*d.*, we had them and a little bit of salmon, which my wife had a mind to, cost 3*s.*

21st. (Lord's Day.) With my wife to church, and then to dinner, Mercer with us, with design to go to Hackney to church in the afternoon. So after dinner she and I sung "Suo Moro," which is one of the best pieces of musique to my thinking that ever I did hear in my life; then took coach and to Hackney church, where very full, and found much difficulty to get pews, I offering the sexton money and he could not help me. So my wife and Mercer ventured into a pew, and I into another. A knight and his lady very civil to me when they come, and the like to my wife in hers, being Sir G. Viner,[3] and his lady rich in jewells, but most in beauty, almost the finest woman that ever I saw. That which we went chiefly to see was the young ladies of the schools,[4] whereof there is great store, very pretty; and also the organ, which is handsome, and tunes the psalm and plays with the people; which is mighty pretty, and makes me mighty earnest to have a pair

---

[1] By Ben Jonson.
[3] Son of a late Lord Mayor.
[2] By Sir Wm. Davenant.
[4] Hackney was famous for its boarding schools.

at our church, I having almost a mind to give them a pair, if they would settle a maintenance on them for it. I am mightily taken with them. So, church done, we to coach and away to Kingsland and Islington, and there eat and drank at the Old House; and so back, it raining a little, which is mighty welcome, it having not rained in many weeks, so that they say it makes the fields just now mighty sweet. So with great pleasure home by night. This night I do come to full resolution of diligence for a good while, and I hope God will give me the grace and wisdom to perform it.

22nd. Captain Cocke tells me how the King was vexed the other day for having no paper laid him at the Council-table, as was usual; and Sir Richard Browne did tell his Majesty he would call the person whose work it was to provide it. Who being come, did tell his Majesty that he was but a poor man, and was out £400 or £500 for it, which was as much as he is worth; and that he cannot provide it any longer without money, having not received a penny since the King's coming in. So the King spoke to my Lord Chamberlain. And many such mementos the King do now-a-days meet withall, enough to make an ingenuous man mad.

24th. To Sir John Duncomb's [1] lodging in the Pell Mell, and there awhile sat and discoursed: and I find him that he is a very proper man for business, being very resolute and proud, and industrious. He thinks the want of money hath undone the King, for the Parliament will never give the King more money without calling all people to account, nor, as he believes, will ever make war again but they will manage it themselves. He says that he believes but four men (such as he could name) would do the business of both offices, his and ours, and if ever the war were to be again it should be so, he believes. He told me to my face that I was a very good clerk, and did understand the business and do it very well, and that he would never desire a better. He do believe that the Parliament, if ever they meet, will offer some alterations to the King, and will turn some of us out, and I protest I think he is in the right. He thinks that much of our misfortune hath been for want of an active Lord Treasurer, and that such a man as Sir W. Coventry would do the business thoroughly.

26th. Up, and by coach with Sir W. Batten and W. Pen to White Hall, and there saw the Duke of Albemarle, who is not well

---

[1] M.P. for Bury St. Edmunds. A Commissioner for the office of Master of the Ordnance; later a Commissioner of the Treasury, and in 1672 Chancellor of the Exchequer.

and do grow crazy. Took a turn with Mr. Evelyn, with whom I walked two hours. He tells me several of the menial servants of the Court lacking bread, that have not received a farthing wages since the King's coming in. He told me the whole story of Mrs. Stewart's going away from Court, he knowing her well; and believes her, up to her leaving the Court, to be as virtuous as any woman in the world. He did tell me of the ridiculous humour of our King and Knights of the Garter the other day, who, whereas heretofore their robes were only to be worn during their ceremonies and service, these, as proud of their coats, did wear them all day till night, and then rode into the Parke with them on. Nay, and he tells me he did see my Lord Oxford and the Duke of Monmouth in a hackney-coach with two footmen in the Parke, with their robes on; which is a most scandalous thing.

After dinner with Sir W. Batten to White Hall, there to attend the Duke of York. Certain newes of the Dutch being abroad on our coast with twenty-four great ships. This done Sir W. Batten and I back again to London, and in the way met my Lady Newcastle going with her coaches and footmen all in velvet. All the town-talk is now-a-days of her extravagancies, with her velvet-cap, her hair about her ears; many black patches, because of pimples about her mouth; naked-necked, without any thing about it, and a black just-au-corps.[1] She seemed to me a very comely woman: but I hope to see more of her on May-day. My mind is mightily of late upon a coach.

27th. This afternoon I spent some time walking with Mr. Moore in the garden, among other things discoursing of my Lord Sandwich's family, which he tells me is in a very bad condition for want of money and management. It seems Mr. Shebly doubts his accounts are ill kept and every thing else in the family out of order, which I am grieved to hear of.

29th. I hear that the Duke of Cambridge, the Duke of York's son, is very sick; and my Lord Treasurer very bad of the stone, and hath been so some days. Sir G. Carteret as a great secret tells me that he hath made a match for my Lord Hinchingbroke to a daughter of my Lord Burlington's, where there is a great alliance, £10,000 portion; a civil family, and relation to my Lord Chancellor, whose son hath married one of the daughters; and that my Lord Chancellor do take it with very great kindness, so that

---

[1] A close-fitting jacket.

he do hold himself obliged by it.   My Lord Hinchingbroke and
the lady know nothing yet of it.   It will, I think, be very happy.[1]

30th.   Up, and Mr. Malden come to speak with me.   Then comes
Sir John Winter to discourse with me about the forest of Deane,
and then about my Lord Treasurer, and asking me whether, as
he had heard, I had not been cut for the stone, I took him to my
closet and there shewed it to him, of which he took the dimensions
and had some discourse of it, and I believe will shew my Lord
Treasurer it.   Thence to the office, where we sat all the morning.
Met with Mr. Pierce, and he tells me the Duke of Cambridge
is very ill and full of spots about his body, that Dr. Frazier knows
not what to think of it.

May 1st.   Up, it being a fine day, and after doing a little business in my chamber to Westminster; in the way meeting many
milk-maids with their garlands upon their pails, dancing with a
fiddler before them; and saw pretty Nelly standing at her lodgings' door in Drury-lane in her smock sleeves and bodice, looking
upon one: she seemed a mighty pretty creature.   After dinner
to the King's playhouse, by agreement met Sir W. Pen, and saw
"Love in a Maze:"[2] but a sorry play.   We sat at the upper bench
next the boxes; and I find it do pretty well, and have the advantage of seeing and hearing the great people, which may be pleasant when there is good store.   Now was only Prince Rupert and
my Lord Lauderdale, and my Lord ——, the naming of whom
puts me in mind of my seeing at Sir Robert Viner's two or three
great silver flagons, made with inscriptions as gifts of the King to
such and such persons of quality as did stay in town the late great
plague, for the keeping things in order in the town, which is a handsome thing.   Thence Sir W. Pen and I in his coach, Tiburne way,
into the Park, where a horrid dust and number of coaches, without
pleasure or order.   That which we, and almost all went for, was
to see my Lady Newcastle, which we could not, she being followed
and crowded upon by coaches all the way she went, that nobody
could come near her; only I could see she was in a large black
coach, adorned with silver instead of gold, and so white curtains,
and every thing black and white, and herself in her cap, but other
parts I could not make out.   But that which I did see, and wonder at with reason, was to find Pegg Pen in a new coach, with
only her husband's pretty sister with her, both patched and very

[1] This match was brought to a successful issue in 1668. The lady was Lady Mary Boyle, fourth
daughter of Richard, first Earl of Burlington.
[2] The second title of Shirley's play "The Changes."

fine, and in much the finest coach in the park, and I think that ever I did see one or other, for neatness and richness in gold and everything that is noble. My Lady Castlemayne, the King, my Lord St. Albans, nor Mr. Jermyn, have so neat a coach, that ever I saw. And, Lord! to have them have this, and nothing else that is correspondent, is to me one of the most ridiculous sights that ever I did see, though her present dress was well enough; but to live in the condition they do at home and be abroad in this coach astonishes me. When we had spent half an hour in the Park we went out again, weary of the dust, and despairing of seeing my Lady Newcastle; and so back the same way and to St. James's, and then home; where we find the two young ladies come home, and their patches off. I suppose Sir W. Pen do not allow of them in his sight. So to talk a little at Sir W. Batten's, and then home to supper, where I find Mrs. Hewer and her son, who have been abroad with my wife in the Park; and so after supper to read, and then to bed.

3rd. Up, and with Sir J. Minnes, W. Batten and W. Pen in the last man's coach to St. James's, and thence up to the Duke of York's chamber, and when ready into his closet and did our business; where among other things we had a proposition of Mr. Pierce's for being continued in pay, or something done for him, in reward of his pains as Chyrurgeon-Generall. The Duke of York and the whole company did shew most particular kindness to Mr. Pierce, every body moving for him, and the Duke himself most, that he is likely to be a very great man, I believe. Thence I presently to the Excise Office, and there met the Cofferer and Stephen Fox by agreement, and then we three to my Lord Treasurer, who continues still very ill. I had taken my stone with me on purpose, and Sir Philip Warwicke carried it in to him to see, but was not in a condition to talk with me about it, poor man. So I to Westminster Hall, and there took a turn with my old acquaintance Mr. Pechell, whose red nose, makes me ashamed to be seen with him, though otherwise a good-natured man.[1] This day the newes is come that the fleete of the Dutch, of about 20 ships, which come upon our coast, is gone to the Frith,[2] and there lies, perhaps to trouble the Scotch privateers.

6th. Up and angry with my mayds for letting in watermen, and I know not who, anybody that they are acquainted with,

---

[1] John Peachell was a Fellow, and later Master, of Magdalene. At this time he held two country livings. He is known to have been a man of bibulous habits.   [2] Firth of Forth

"PRETTY NELLY STANDING AT HER LODGINGS' DOOR"

into my kitchen to talk and prate with them, which I will not endure.

11th. After dinner my wife and Creed and I being entered a hackney coach to go to the other end of the town, we espied The. Turner coming in her coach to see us, and so 'light and took her and another young lady home. After a little talk, I over Tower Hill with them to a lady's they go to visit, and so away with my wife, whose being dressed this day in fair hair did make me so mad that I spoke not one word to her in our going, though I was ready to burst with anger. So to White Hall to the Committee of Tangier. After that broke up, Creed and I into the Park and walked, a most pleasant evening, and so took coach and took up my wife, and in my way home discovered my trouble to my wife for her white locks, swearing by God, several times, which I pray God forgive me for, and bending my fist, that I would not endure it. She, poor wretch, was surprized with it, and made me no answer all the way home; but there we parted, and I to the office late, and then home, and without supper to bed, vexed.

12th. (Lord's Day.) Up, and to my chamber, to settle some accounts there, and by and by down comes my wife to me in her night-gown, and we begun calmly, that upon having money to lace her gown for second mourning, she would promise to wear white locks no more in my sight; which I, like a severe fool, thinking not enough, begun to except against and made her fly out to very high terms and cry, and in her heat told me of keeping company with Mrs. Knipp, saying that if I would promise never to see her more, of whom she hath more reason to suspect than I had heretofore of Pembleton, she would never wear white locks more. This vexed me, but I restrained myself from saying anything, but do think never to see this woman (at least, to have her here), more. But by and by I did give her money to buy lace and she promised to wear no more white locks while I lived, and so all very good friends as ever, and I to my business, and she to dress herself. Against noon we had a coach ready for us, and she and I to White Hall, where I went to see whether Sir G. Carteret was at dinner or no, our design being to make a visit there, and I found them set down, which troubled me, for I would not then go up, but back to the coach to my wife, and she and I homeward again. And in our way bethought ourselves of going alone, she and I, to go to a French house to dinner, and so enquired out Monsieur Robins, my perriwigg-maker, who keeps an ordinary;

and in an ugly street in Covent Garden did find him at the door, and so we in; and in a moment almost had the table covered, and clean glasses, and all in the French manner, and a mess of potage first, and then a couple of pigeons à la esterve, and then a piece of bœuf-à-la-mode, all exceeding well seasoned, and to our great liking; at least it would have been anywhere else but in this bad street, and in a perriwigg-maker's house; but to see the pleasant and ready attendance that we had, and all things so desirous to please, and ingenious in the people, did take me mightily. Our dinner cost us 6*s.*, and so my wife and I away to Islington, it being a fine day, and thence walked over the fields to Kingsland and back again, a walk, I think, I have not taken these twenty years; but puts me in mind of my boy's time, when I boarded at Kingsland and used to shoot with my bow and arrows in these fields. A very pretty place it is; and little did any of my friends think I should come to walk in these fields in this condition and state that I am. Then took coach again, and home through Shoreditch; and at home my wife finds Barker to have been abroad, and telling her so many lies about it that she struck her, and the wench said she would not stay with her: so I examined the wench, and found her in so many lies myself that I was glad to be rid of her, and so resolved having her go away to-morrow.

14th. To my Lord Chancellor's, where I met Mr. Povy, expecting the coming of the rest of the Commissioners for Tangier. Here I understand how the two Dukes, both the only sons of the Duke of York, are sick even to danger, and that on Sunday last they were both so ill as that the poor Duchess was in doubt which would die first: the Duke of Cambridge of some general disease; the other little Duke, whose title I know not,[1] of the convulsion fits, of which he had four this morning. Fear that either of them might be dead did make us think that it was the occasion that the Duke of York and others were not come to the meeting of the Commission which was designed, and my Lord Chancellor did expect. And it was pretty to observe how, when my Lord sent down to St. James's to see why the Duke of York come not, and Mr. Povy, who went, returned, my Lord (Chancellor) did ask, not how the Princes or the Dukes do, as other people do, but "How do the children?" which methought was mighty great, and like a great man and grandfather. I find every body mightily

---

[1] Duke of Kendal, aged ten months.

concerned for these children, as a matter wherein the State is much concerned that they should live.

16th. At noon, this being Holy Thursday, that is, Ascension Day, when the boys go on procession round the parish, we were to go to the Three Tuns' Tavern to dine with the rest of the parish; where all the parish almost was, and of our house, J. Minnes, W. Batten, W. Pen and myself; and Mr. Mills did sit uppermost at the table. Thence home and to my office, where busy. Anon at 7 at night and I and my wife and Sir W. Pen in his coach to Unthanke's, my wife's tailor, for her to speak one word, and then we to my Lord Treasurer's,[1] where I find the porter crying, and suspected it was that my Lord is dead; and, poor Lord! we did find that he was dead just now; and the crying of the fellow did so trouble me, that considering I was not likely to trouble him any more, nor have occasion to give any more anything, I did give him 3s.; but it may be, poor man, he hath lost a considerable hope by the death of his Lord, whose house will be no more frequented as before, and perhaps I may never come thither again about any business. There is a good man gone; and I pray God that the Treasury may not be worse managed by the hand or hands it shall now be put into; though for certain the slowness, though he was of great integrity, of this man, and remissness, have gone as far to undo the nation as anything else that hath happened; and yet, if I knew all the difficulties that he hath lain under, and his instrument Sir Philip Warwicke, I might be brought to another mind. Thence we to Islington, to the Old House, and there eat and drank, and then it being late and a pleasant evening, we home, and there to my chamber, and to bed.

This day Mr. Sheply is come to town and to see me, and he tells me my father is very well only for his pain, so that he is not able to stir, but is in great pain. I would to God that he were in town that I might have what help can be got for him, for it troubles me to have him live in that condition of misery if I can help it.

19th. (Lord's Day.) After church to White Hall, and there find Sir G. Carteret just set down to dinner, and I dined with them. He says that the Treasury will be managed for a while by a Commission, whereof he thinks my Lord Chancellor for the honour of it, and my Lord Ashly and the two Secretaries will be, and some others he knows not. By water home, and there to read the life of Mr. Hooker,[2] which pleases me as much as any thing

---

[1] Lord Southampton.   [2] Izaak Walton's *Life of Mr. Richard Hooker.*

I have read a great while; and by and by comes Mr. Howe to see us, and after him a little Mr. Sheply, and so we all to talk, and, Mercer being there, we some of us to sing, and so to supper, a great deal of silly talk. Among other things, W. Howe told us how the Barristers and Students of Gray's Inne rose in rebellion against the Benchers the other day, who outlawed them, and a great deal of do; but now they are at peace again. They being gone, I to my book again, and made an end of Mr. Hooker's Life, and so to bed.

22nd. Up, and by water to White Hall to Sir G. Carteret, who tells me for certain how the Commission for the Treasury is disposed of: viz., to Duke of Albemarle, Lord Ashly, Sir W. Coventry, Sir John Duncomb and Sir Thomas Clifford, at which he says all the whole Court is disturbed: but my heart is very glad of it, for I do expect they will do much good, and that it is the happiest thing that hath appeared to me for the good of the nation since the King come in. Thence to St. James's, and so into the Duke of York's closet; and there among other things Sir W. Coventry did take notice of what he told me the other day about a report of Commissioner Pett's dealing for timber in the Navy and selling it to us in other names; and besides his own proof did produce a paper I had given him this morning about it, which was so handled that the Duke of York grew very angry and commanded us presently to fall into the examination of it, saying that he would not trust a man for his sake that lifts up the whites of his eyes. And it was declared that if he be found to have done so he should be reckoned unfit to serve the Navy; and I do believe he will be turned out. So home, and by and by comes my poor father, much better than I expected, being at ease by fits, and at another time in as much pain.

23rd. Up, and to the office, where we sat all the morning. At noon home, and with my father dined, and, poor man! he hath put off his travelling clothes to-day, and is mighty spruce, and I love to see him cheerful. This day I hear that last night the Duke of Kendall, second son of the Duke of York, did die; and that the other, Duke of Cambridge, continues very ill still.

24th. With Sir W. Pen to Islington to the old house, where his lady and Madam Lowther and her mother-in-law, did meet us, and two of Mr. Lowther's brothers, and here dined upon nothing but pigeon-pyes, which was such a thing for him to invite all the company to that I was ashamed of it. But after dinner was all our sport, when there come in a juggler, who indeed did shew us so good tricks as I have never seen in my life, I think, of legerdemaine, and such as my wife hath since seriously said that she would not believe but that he did them by the help of the devil. I discern good parts in one of the sons who, methought, did take me up very prettily in one or two things that I said, and I was so sensible of it as to be a caution to me hereafter how I do venture to speak more than is necessary in any company; though, as I did now, I do think them incapable to censure me.

26th. (Lord's Day.) Up sooner than usual on Sundays, and to walk, it being exceeding hot all night (so as this night I begun to leave off my waistcoat this year) and this morning, and so to walk in the garden till toward church time, when my wife and I to church. After dinner I by water alone to Westminster, towards the parish church,[1] and met with Mr. Howlett, who, offering me a pew in the gallery, I had no excuse but up with him I must go, and then much against my will staid out the whole church; but I did entertain myself with my perspective glass up and down the church, by which I had the great pleasure of seeing and gazing at a great many very fine women; and what with that and sleeping, I passed away the time till sermon was done, and then to Mrs. Martin and there staid an hour or two; and away to my boat, and up with it as far as Barne Elmes, reading of Mr. Evelyn's late new book against Solitude,[2] in which I do not find much excess of good matter, though it be pretty for a bye discourse. I walked the length of the Elmes, and with great pleasure saw some gallant ladies and people come with their bottles, and basket, and chairs and form, to sup under the trees by the waterside, which was mighty pleasant. I to boat again; and so landed at the Old Swan, and so home, where I find my poor father newly come out of an unexpected fit of his pain, that they feared he would have died. They had sent for me to White Hall and all up and down, and for Mr. Holliard also, who did come; but W. Hewer being here did I think do the business in getting my father's bowel, that was fallen down, into his body again; and that which made me more sensible of it was that he this morning did show me the place where his bowel did use to fall down and swell, which did trouble me to see. But above all things the poor man's patience under it and his good heart and humour as soon as he was out of it did so work upon me that my heart was sad to think upon his

[1] St. Margaret's.   [2] *Public Employment and an Active Life, with its Appanages, preferred to Solitude.*

condition, but do hope that a way will be found by a steel truss to relieve him. By and by to supper, all our discourse about Brampton.

27th. The new Commissioners of the Treasury did meet this morning; I do hear that they have chosen Sir G. Downing for their secretary. And I think in my conscience they have done a great thing in it, for he is a business active man, and values himself upon having of things do well under his hand, so that I am mightily pleased in their choice. Abroad, and stopped at the Bear-garden stairs, there to see a prize fought. But the house so full there was no getting in there, so forced to go through an alehouse into the pit, where the bears are baited; and upon a stool did see them fight, which they did very furiously, a butcher and a waterman. The former had the better all along, till by and by the latter dropped his sword out of his hand, and the butcher, whether not seeing his sword dropped I know not, but did give him a cut over the wrist, so as he was disabled to fight any longer. But, Lord! to see how in a minute the whole stage was full of watermen to revenge the foul play, and the butchers to defend their fellow, though most blamed him; and there they all fell to it to knocking down and cutting many on each side. It was pleasant to see, but that I stood in the pit, and feared that in the tumult I might get some hurt. At last the rabble broke up, and so I away to White Hall.

28th. After dinner my wife away down with Jane and W. Hewer to Woolwich, in order to a little ayre and to lie there to-night, and so to gather May-dew to-morrow morning, which Mrs. Turner hath taught her as the only thing in the world to wash her face with; and I am contented with it. Presently comes Creed, and he and I by water to Fox-hall, and there walked in Spring Garden. A great deal of company, and the weather and garden pleasant: that it is very pleasant and cheap going thither, for a man may go to spend what he will, or nothing, all is one. But to hear the nightingale and other birds, and here fiddles, and there a harp, and here a Jew's trump, and here laughing, and there fine people walking, is mighty divertising. Among others, there were two pretty women alone, that walked a great while, which being discovered by some idle gentlemen, they would needs take them up; but to see the poor ladies how they were put to it to run from them, and they after them, and sometimes the ladies put themselves along with other company, then the other drew back; at last, the last did get off out of the house, and took boat and away.

I was troubled to see them abused so, and could have found in my heart, as little desire of fighting as I have, to have protected the ladies. So by water home.

29th. My wife comes home from Woolwich, but did not dine with me, going to dress herself against night to go to Mrs. Pierce's to be merry, where we are to have Knepp and Harris and other good people. I at my accounts all the afternoon, being a little lost in them as to reckoning interest. Anon comes down my wife, dressed in her second mourning, with her black moyre waistcoat and short petticoat, laced with silver lace so basely that I could not endure to see her, and with laced lining, which is too soon; so that I was horrid angry, and went out of doors to the office and there staid, and would not go to our intended meeting, which vexed me to the blood; and my wife sent twice or thrice to me, to direct her any way to dress her but to put on her cloth gown, which she would not venture, which made me mad: and so in the evening to my chamber, vexed, and to my accounts, which I ended to my great content, and did make amends for the loss of our mirth this night by getting this done, which otherwise I fear I should not have done a good while else. So to bed.

30th. Up, and to the office, where all the morning. At noon dined at home, being without any words friends with my wife, though last night I was very angry, and do think I did give her as much cause to be angry with me. After dinner I walked to Arundell House, the way very nasty, the day of meeting of the Society being changed from Wednesday to Thursday, which I knew not before, because the Wednesday is a Council-day, and several of the Council are of the Society and would come but for their attending the King at Council; where I find much company, indeed very much company, in expectation of the Duchesse of Newcastle, who had desired to be invited to the Society; and was, after much debate *pro* and *con.*, it seems many being against it; and we do believe the town will be full of ballads of it. Anon comes the Duchesse with her women attending her; among others the Ferabosco, of whom so much talk is that her lady would bid her show her face and kill the gallants. She is indeed black and hath good black little eyes, but otherwise but a very ordinary woman I do think, but they say sings well. The Duchesse hath been a good, comely woman; but her dress so antick and her deportment so ordinary that I do not like her at all, nor did I hear her say any thing that was worth hearing, but that she was full of admiration,

"SO TO BED"

all admiration. Several fine experiments were shown her of colours, loadstones, microscopes, and of liquors: among others of one that did, while she was there, turn a piece of roasted mutton into pure blood, which was very rare. After they had shown her many experiments, and she cried still she was full of admiration, she departed, being led out and in by several Lords that were there. She gone, I by coach home, and there busy at my letters till night, and then with my wife in the evening singing with her in the garden with great pleasure, and so home to supper and to bed.

31st. By water to White Hall to the Lords Commissioners of the Treasury, the first time I ever was there and I think the second that they have met at the Treasury chamber there. Here I saw Duncomb look as big, and take as much state on him, as if he had been born a lord. I was in with him about Tangier, and at present received but little answer from them, they being in a cloud of business yet, but I doubt not but all will go well under them. Thence to Sir G. Carteret at his lodgings, who I perceive is mightily displeased with this new Treasury; and he hath reason, for it will eclipse him. He says, and I believe, that a great many persons at Court are angry at the rise of this Duncomb. He was a kind of an atturny: but for all this I believe this man will be a great man, in spite of all. Late to supper, and with great quiet to bed; finding by the balance of my account that I am creditor £6,900, for which the Lord of Heaven be praised!

June 2nd. (Lord's Day.) Up betimes, and down to my chamber without trimming myself or putting on clean linen, thinking only to keep to my chamber and do business to-day; but when I come there I find that without being shaved I am not fully awake nor ready to settle to business, and so was fain to go up again and dress myself, which I did, and so down to my chamber, and fell roundly to business. So to dinner, and then to my business again all the afternoon close. Being weary and almost blind with writing and reading so much to-day, I took boat at the Old Swan, and then up the river all alone as high as Putney almost, and then back again, all the way reading, and finishing Mr. Boyle's book of Colours, which is so chymical that I can understand but little of it, but understand enough to see that he is a most excellent man.

3rd. To Westminster Hall, and there walked a turn or two with Sir William Doyly,[1] who did lay a wager with me the Treas-

---

[1] M.P. for Yarmouth.

urer-ship would be in one hand, notwithstanding this present Commission, before Christmas: on which we did lay a poll of ling, a brace of carps, and a pottle of wine. Thence down by water to Deptford, it being Trinity Monday, when the Master is chosen.[1] We had a good dinner of plain meat, and a good company at our table, among others my good Mr. Evelyn, with whom after dinner I stepped aside and talked upon the present posture of our affairs; which is, that the Dutch are known to be abroad with eighty sail of ships of war and twenty fire-ships, and the French come into the Channell with twenty sail of men-of-war and five fire-ships, while we have not a ship at sea to do them any hurt with, but are calling in all we can, while our Embassadors are treating at Bredah; and the Dutch look upon them as come to beg peace, and use them accordingly. So broke up, and Creed and I got out of the room and away by water to White Hall, and there he and I waited in the Treasury-chamber an hour or two. By and by I, upon desire, was called in and delivered in my report of my Accounts. Present, Lord Ashly, Clifford, and Duncomb, who, being busy, did not read it, but committed it to Sir George Downing, and so I was dismissed; but, Lord! to see how Duncomb do take upon him is an eyesore, though I think he deserves great honour; but only the suddenness of his rise, and his pride. But I do like the way of these lords, that they admit nobody to use many words, nor do they spend many words themselves, but in great state do hear what they see necessary, and say little themselves but bid withdraw.

7th. At noon home to dinner, my father, wife and I, and a good dinner. And then to the office again, where busy all the afternoon; also I have a desire to dispatch all business that hath lain long on my hands, and so to it till the evening, and then home to sing and pipe with my wife; then to supper and to bed, my head full of thoughts how to keep if I can some part of my wages as Surveyor of the Victualling, which I see must now come to be taken away among the other places that have been occasioned by this war.

8th. Up, and to the office, where all the news this morning is that the Dutch are come with a fleete of eighty sail to Harwich, and that guns were heard plain by Sir W. Rider's people at Bednall-greene all yesterday even. The King hath sent down my Lord of Oxford to raise the countries there; and all the Westerne barges are taken up to make a bridge over the River about the Hope, for horse to cross the River if there be occasion.

---

[1] Sir W. Pen was elected.

9th. (Lord's Day.) Up, and by water to White Hall, and so walked to St. James's, where I hear that the Duke of Cambridge, who was given over long since by the Doctors, is now likely to recover; for which God be praised! To Sir W. Coventry, and there talked with him a great while. In comes my Lord Barkeley, who is going down to Harwich to look after the militia there: and there is also the Duke of Monmouth, and with him a great many young Hectors. My Lord Barkeley wanting some maps, and Sir W. Coventry recommending the six maps [1] of England that are bound up for the pocket, I did offer to present my Lord with them, which he accepted: and so I will send them him. Being come home I find an order come for the getting some fire-ships presently to annoy the Dutch, who are in the King's Channel and expected up higher. So W. Batten and W. Pen being come this evening from their country houses to town we did issue orders about it, and then home to supper and to bed.

10th. Up; and news brought us that the Dutch are come up as high as the Nore; and more pressing orders for fire-ships.

11th. Up, and more letters still from Sir W. Coventry about more fire-ships, and so Sir W. Batten and I to the office, where Bruncker come to us, who is just now going to Chatham upon a desire of Commissioner Pett's, who is in a very fearful stink for fear of the Dutch, and desires help for God and the King and kingdom's sake. So Bruncker goes down, and Sir J. Minnes also, from Gravesend. This morning Pett writes us word that Sheernesse is lost last night, after two or three hours' dispute. The enemy hath possessed himself of that place, which is very sad, and puts us into great fears of Chatham. Sir W. Batten and I down by water to Deptford, and there Sir W. Pen and we did consider of several matters relating to the dispatch of the fire-ships, and so W. Batten and I home again. To business hiring some fire-ships, and receiving every hour almost letters from Sir W. Coventry calling for more fire-ships, and an order from Council to enable us to take any man's ships; and Sir W. Coventry in his letter to us says he do not doubt but at this time under an invasion, as he owns it to be, the King may by law take any man's goods. At this business late, and then home, where a great deal of serious talk with my wife about the sad state we are in, and especially from the beating up of drums this night for the trainbands upon pain of death to appear in arms to-morrow morning with bullet

[1] Wenceslaus Hollar's map, published in 1644.

and powder, and money to supply themselves with victuals for a fortnight.

12th. Up very betimes to our business at the office, there hiring of more fire-ships; and at it close all the morning. Ill newes is come to Court of the Dutch breaking the Chaine at Chatham, which struck me to the heart. And to White Hall to hear the truth of it; and there, going up the backstairs, I did hear some lacquies speaking of sad newes come to Court, saying that hardly anybody in the Court but do look as if he cried. So home, where all our hearts do now ake; for the newes is true that the Dutch have broken the chaine and burned our ships, and particularly "The Royal Charles": other particulars I know not, but most sad to be sure. And the truth is I do fear so much that the whole kingdom is undone that I do this night resolve to study with my father and wife what to do with the little that I have in money by me, for I give all the rest that I have in the King's hands for Tangier, for lost. So God help us!

13th. No sooner up but hear the sad newes confirmed of the Royall Charles being taken by them, and now in fitting by them (which Pett should have carried up higher by our several orders, and deserves therefore to be hanged for not doing it), and turning several others; and that another fleete is come up into the Hope. Upon which newes the King and Duke of York have been below[1] since four o'clock in the morning to command the sinking of ships at Barking-Creeke and other places, to stop their coming up higher: which put me into such a fear that I presently resolved of my father's and wife's going into the country; and at two hours' warning they did go by the coach this day, with about £1,300 in gold in their night-bag. Pray God give them good passage, and good care to hide it when they come home! but my heart is full of fear. They gone, I continued in fright and fear what to do with the rest. W. Hewer hath been at the banker's and hath got £500 out of Blackewell's hands of his own money; but they are so called upon that they will be all broke, hundreds coming to them for money: and their answer is, "It is payable at twenty days: when the days are out we will pay you;" and those that are not so they make tell over their money, and make their bags false on purpose to give cause to retell it, and so spend time.

Every minute some one or other calls for this or that order; and so I forced to be at the office most of the day. I did, about

---

[1] *i.e.* below London Bridge.

noon, resolve to send Mr. Gibson away after my wife with another 1000 pieces. The King and Duke of York up and down all the day here and there: some time on Tower Hill, where the City militia was, where the King did make a speech to them that they should venture themselves no further than he would himself. I also sent, my mind being in pain, Saunders after my wife and father, to overtake them at their night's lodgings, to see how matters go with them. In the evening I sent for my cousin Sarah and her husband, who come, and I did deliver them my chest of writings about Brampton, and my brother Tom's papers, and my journalls, which I value much; and did send my two silver flaggons to Kate Joyce's. I have also made a girdle by which with some trouble I do carry about me £300 in gold about my body, that I may not be without something in case I should be surprised: for I think in any nation but our's people that appear (for we are not indeed so) so faulty as we, would have their throats cut. Late at night comes Mr. Hudson the cooper, my neighbour, and tells me that he come from Chatham this evening at five o'clock and saw this afternoon "The Royal James," "Oake," and "London," burnt by the enemy with their fire-ships. I made my will also this day, and did give all I had equally between my father and wife, and left copies of it in each of Mr. Hater and W. Hewer's hands, who both witnessed the will.

14th. Up, and to the office. By and by comes a man of Mr. Gawden's, who comes from Chatham last night and saw the three ships burnt, they lying all dry, and boats going from the men-of-war and fire them. But that that he tells me of worst consequence is that he himself, I think he said, did hear many Englishmen on board the Dutch ships speaking to one another in English; and that they did cry and say, "We did heretofore fight for tickets; now we fight for dollars!"[1] and did ask how such and such a one did, and would commend themselves to them: which is a sad consideration. And several seamen come this morning to me to tell me that if I would get their tickets paid they would go and do all they could against the Dutch, but otherwise they would not venture being killed and lose all they have already fought for: so that I was forced to try what I could do to get them paid. And indeed the hearts as well as affections of the seamen are turned away; and in the open streets in Wapping, and up and down, the

[1] The word dollar is a corruption of thaler, a large silver coin of varying value current in the German states from the sixteenth century. Corresponding coins of northern European countries were also called dollars in England.

wives have cried publickly, "This comes of your not paying our husbands; and now your work is undone, or done by hands that understand it not."

We do not hear that the Dutch are come to Gravesend, which is a wonder. But a wonderful thing it is that to this day we have not one word yet from Bruncker, or Peter Pett, or J. Minnes, of any thing at Chatham. The people that come hither to hear how things go make me ashamed to be found unable to answer them; for I am left alone here at the office: and the truth is I am glad my station is to be here near my own home and out of danger, yet in a place of doing the King good service. The dismay that is upon us all in the business of the kingdom and Navy at this day is not to be expressed otherwise than by the condition the citizens were in when the City was on fire, nobody knowing which way to turn themselves. At night come home Sir W. Batten and W. Pen, who only can tell me that they have placed guns at Woolwich and Deptford, and sunk some ships below Woolwich and Blackewall and are in hopes that they will stop the enemy's coming up. But strange our confusion! that among them that are sunk they have gone and sunk without consideration "The Franakin," one of the King's ships, with stores to a very considerable value that hath been long loaden for supply of the ships; and the new ship at Bristoll, and much wanted there; and nobody will own that they directed it, but do lay it on Sir W. Rider. No news to-day of any motion of the enemy either upwards towards Chatham or this way.

15th. All the morning at the office. No newes more than last night; only Purser Tyler comes and tells me that he being at all the passages in this business at Chatham, he says there have been horrible miscarriages, such as we shall shortly hear of: that the want of boats hath undone us; and it is commonly said, and Sir J. Minnes under his hand tells us, that they were employed by the men of the Yard to carry away their goods; and I hear that Commissioner Pett will be found the first man that began to remove. At night comes, unexpectedly so soon, Mr. Gibson, who left my wife well, and all got down well with them, but not with himself. He had one of his bags broke, through his breeches, and some pieces dropped out, not many, he thinks, but two, for he 'light and took them up, and went back and could find no more. But I am not able to tell how many, which troubles me. This afternoon poor Betty Michell, whom I love, sent to tell my wife her child was dying, which I am troubled for, poor girle!

17th. Up, and to my office, where busy all the morning, particularly setting my people to work in transcribing pieces of letters publique and private, which I do collect against a black day to defend the office with and myself. At night comes Captain Cocke to see me, and he and I an hour in the garden together. He says the King and Court are all troubled, and the gates of the Court were shut up upon the first coming of the Dutch to us, but they do mind the business no more than ever: that the bankers, he fears, are broke as to ready-money, though Viner had £100,000 by him when our trouble begun.

18th. To the office, and by and by word was brought me that Commissioner Pett is brought to the Tower and there laid up close prisoner; which puts me into a fright lest they may do the same with us as they do with him. This puts me upon hastening what I am doing with my people, and collecting out of my papers our defence.

19th. Up, and to the office, where all the morning busy. By and by comes an order commanding me this afternoon to attend the Council-board, with all my books and papers touching the Medway. I was ready to fear some mischief to myself, though it appears most reasonable that it is to inform them about Commissioner Pett. I eat a little bit in haste at Sir W. Batten's without much comfort, being fearful, though I shew it not, and to my office and get up some papers, and found out the most material letters and orders in our books, and so took coach and to the Council-chamber lobby, where I met Mr. Evelyn who do miserably decry our follies that bring all this misery upon us. While we were discoursing over our publique misfortunes I am called in to a large Committee of the Council: present the Duke of Albemarle, Anglesey, Arlington, Ashly, Carteret, Duncomb, Coventry, Ingram, Clifford, Lauderdale, Morrice, Manchester, Craven, Carlisle, Bridgewater. And after Sir W. Coventry's telling them what orders His Royal Highness had made for the safety of the Medway I told them to their full content what we had done, and showed them our letters. Then was Peter Pett called in, with the Lieutenant of the Tower. He is in his old clothes, and looked most sillily. His charge was chiefly the not carrying up of the great ships, and the using of the boats in carrying away his goods; to which he answered very sillily, though his faults to me seem only great omissions. Lord Arlington and Coventry very severe against him, the former saying that if he was not guilty the world would think them all guilty. The latter urged that there must be some faults, and that the Admiral must be found to have done his part. I did say an unhappy word, which I was sorry for, when he complained of want of oares for the boats: and there was it seems enough, and good enough, to carry away all the boats with from the King's occasions. After having heard him for an hour or more, they bid him withdraw. I all this while showing him no respect, but rather against him, for which God forgive me! for I mean no hurt to him, but only find that these Lords are upon their own purgation, and it is necessary I should be so in behalf of the office. He being gone, they caused Sir Richard Browne[1] to read over his minutes; and then my Lord Arlington moved that they might be put into my hands to put into form, I being more acquainted with such business; and they were so. So I away back with my books and papers; and when I got into the Court it was pretty to see how people gazed upon me, that I thought myself obliged to salute people and to smile, lest they should think I was a prisoner too; but afterwards I found that most did take me to be there to bear evidence against P. Pett. But my fear was such, at my going in, of the success of the day, that at my going in I did think fit to give T. Hater, whom I took with me to wait the event, my closet-key and directions where to find £500 and more in silver and gold, and my tallys, to remove, in case of any misfortune to me. Thence to Sir G. Carteret's to take my leave of my Lady Jem, who is going into the country to-morrow; but she being now at prayers with my Lady and family, and hearing here by Yorke, the carrier, that my wife is coming to towne, I did make haste home to see her, that she might not find me abroad, it being the first minute I have been abroad since yesterday was se'ennight. I got home, and after being there a little she come, and two of her fellow-travellers with her, with whom we drunk: a couple of merchant-like men, I think, but have friends in our country. They being gone, I and my wife to talk, who did give me so bad an account of her and my father's method in burying of our gold that made me mad; and she herself is not pleased with it, she believing that my sister knows of it. My father and she did it on Sunday, when they were gone to church, in open daylight, in the midst of the garden, where for aught they knew many eyes might

[1] Clerk to the Council.

see them: which put me into such trouble that I was almost mad about it, and presently cast about how to have it back again to secure it here, the times being a little better now, at least at White Hall they seem as if they were; but one way or other I am resolved to free them from the place if I can get them. Such was my trouble at this that I fell out with my wife; that, though new come to towne, I did not sup with her nor speak to her to-night, but to bed and sleep.

20th. Up, and so to the office, where all the morning busy. At noon home to dinner; and there my wife and I very good friends, the care of my gold being somewhat over, considering it was in their hands that have as much cause to secure it as myself almost, and so if they will be mad, let them. But yet I do intend to send for it away. Here dined Mercer with us, and after dinner she cut my hair; and then I into my closet and there slept a little, as I do now almost every day after dinner.

21st. This day comes news from Harwich that the Dutch fleete are all in sight, near 100 sail great and small, they think, coming towards them; where, they think, they shall be able to oppose them. Sir H. Cholmly come to me this day, and tells me the Court is as mad as ever; and that the night the Dutch burned our ships the King did sup with my Lady Castlemayne at the Duchess of Monmouth's, and they were all mad in hunting a poor moth. All the Court afraid of a Parliament; but he thinks nothing can save us but the King's giving up all to a Parliament.

22nd. I hear the Duke of Cambridge is dead, which is a great loss to the nation, having I think never an heyre male now of the King's or Duke's to succeed to the Crown.

23rd. (Lord's Day.) After dinner I by water to Woolwich to see the batterys newly raised; which, indeed, are good works to command the River below the ships that are sunk, but not above them. It is a sad sight to see so many good ships there sunk in the River, while we would be thought to be masters of the sea. No news at all of late from Bredagh what our Treaters do.

26th. To White Hall by water, and there to the Lords Treasurers' chamber and there wait; and here it is every body's discourse that the Parliament is ordered to meet the 25th of July, being as they say St. James's day; which every creature is glad of. But it is pretty to consider how, walking to the Old Swan from my house, I met Sir Thomas Harvy, whom, asking the newes of the Parliament's meeting, he told me it was true, and they would

certainly make a great rout among us. I answered I did not care
for my part, though I was ruined, so that the Commonwealth
might escape ruin by it. He answered, "that is a good one, in
faith; for you know yourself to be secure, in being necessary to
the office." Mr. Povy tells me as a great secret, which none knows
but himself, that Sir G. Carteret hath parted with his place of
Treasurer of the Navy, by consent, to my Lord Anglesey, and is
to be Treasurer of Ireland in his stead; but upon what terms it
is I know not; but Mr. Povy tells it is so, and that it is in his power
to bring me to as great a friendship and confidence in my Lord
Anglesey as ever I was with W. Coventry, which I am glad of.
And so parted, and I to my tailor's about turning my old silk
suit and cloak into a suit and vest.

27th. Wakened this morning about three o'clock by Mr.
Griffin with a letter from Sir W. Coventry to W. Pen, which W.
Pen sent me to see, that the Dutch are come up to the Nore again,
and he knows not whether further or no, and would have, therefore,
several things done (ships sunk, and I know not what), which Sir
W. Pen hath directed Griffin to carry to the Trinity House. So
he went away with the letter, and I tried and with much ado did
get a little sleep more; and so up about six o'clock, full of thought
what to do with the money I have left and my plate, wishing with
all my heart that that was all secured. So to the office, where
much business all the morning, and the more by my brethren
being all out of the way; Sir W. Pen this night taken so ill cannot
stir; W. Batten ill at Walthamstow; Sir J. Minnes the like at
Chatham, and my Lord Bruncker there also upon business. Horrible trouble with the backwardness of the merchants to let us
have their ships, and seamen's running away, and not to be got
or kept without money. At noon to dinner, having a haunch of
venison boiled; and all my clerks at dinner with me. To the office
again. Mr. Pierce, this afternoon coming to me, tells me that
all the town do cry out of our office for a pack of fools and knaves;
but says that everybody speaks either well, or at least the best, of
me, which is my great comfort, and think I do deserve it, and shall
shew I have; but yet do think, and he also, that the Parliament
will send us all going; and I shall be well contented with it, God
knows! He gone, I to business till the evening, and then by chance
home, and find the fellow that come up with my wife, Coleman,
from Brampton, a silly rogue, but one that would seem a gentleman; but I did not stay with him.

28th. By water to White Hall to dinner to Sir G. Carteret, but he not at home, but I dined with my Lady and good company, and good dinner. By coach home, and there find my wife making of tea; a drink which Mr. Pelling, the Potticary, tells her is good for her cold. I to the office, and then in the evening to Sir W. Batten's to see how he did; and he is better than he was. He told me how Mrs. Lowther had her train held up yesterday by her page, at his house in the country; which is so ridiculous a piece of pride as I am ashamed of. I then to Sir W. Pen, who continues a little ill, or dissembles it, the latter of which I am apt to believe. Here I staid but little, not meaning much kindness in it; and so to the office and dispatched more business; and then home at night, and to supper with my wife. We hear that the Dutch are gone down again; and thanks be to God! the trouble they give us this second time is not very considerable.

29th. Having taken a resolution to take a turn to Chatham to-morrow, indeed to do business of the King's, but also to give myself the satisfaction of seeing the place after the Dutch have been here, I have sent to and got Creed to go with me. After having done my business at the office I home, and there I found Coleman come again to my house, and with my wife in our great chamber, which vexed me. I staid there awhile, and then to my study vexed, showing no civility to the man. But he comes on a compliment to receive my wife's commands into the country, whither he is going, and it being Saturday my wife told me there was no other room for her to bring him in, and so much is truth: but I staid vexed in my closet.

30th. (Lord's Day.) Up about three o'clock, and Creed and I down by boat to Chatham-yard, and to Commissioner Pett's house, and after dinner into the garden to shew Creed, and I must confess it must needs be thought a sorrowful thing for a man that hath taken so much pains to make a place neat to lose it as Commissioner Pett must now this. By barge, it raining hard, down to the chaine. Back again to Rochester and thence to the Castle, and had good satisfaction from him that showed it us touching the history of it. Then into the fields, a fine walk, and into the Cherry garden, where we had them fresh gathered, and here met with a young, plain, silly shopkeeper, and his wife, a pretty young woman. We talked and eat cherries together and then to walk in the fields till it was late, and did kiss her. Then to our inne, where I hear my Lord Bruncker hath sent for me to speak with me before I go: so I took his coach, which stands there with two horses, and to him and to his bedside, where he was in bed, and hath a watchman with a halbert at his door; and to him, and did talk a little. So took leave of him, and with Creed back again, it being now about 10 at night, and to our inne to supper; and then to bed, being both sleepy, but could get no sheets to our bed, only linen to our mouths, and so to sleep.

July 1st. Up betimes, about 4 o'clock, waked by a damned noise between a sow gelder and a cow and a dog, nobody after we were up being able to tell us what it was. After being ready we took coach, and being very sleepy droused most part of the way to Gravesend, and there 'light, and down to the new batterys, which are like to be very fine; and there did hear a plain fellow cry out upon the folly of the King's officers above, to spend so much money in works at Woolwich and Deptford, and sinking of good ships loaden with goods, when, if half the charge had been laid out here, it would have secured all that, and this place too, before now. And I think it is not only true in this, but that the best of the actions of us all are so silly that the meanest people begin to see through them and contemn them. Besides, says he, they spoil the river by it. Then informed ourselves where we might have some creame, and they guided us to one Goody Best's, a little out of the towne towards London road, and thither we went with the coach, and find it a mighty clean, plain house, and had a dish of very good creame to our liking, and so away presently very merry, talking and laughing at the folly of our masters in the management of things at this day. Got home by noon.

4th. Up, and in vain expecting Sir R. Ford's calling on me I took coach and to the Sessions-house, and so got up to the Bench, my Lord Chief-Justice Keeling being Judge. Here I stood bare, not challenging, though I might well enough, to be covered. But here were several fine trials; among others several brought in for making it their trade to set houses on fire merely to get plunder; and all proved by two little boys, who did give so good account of particulars that I never heard children in my life.

6th. Up, and to the office, where some of us sat busy all the morning. At noon home to dinner, whither Creed come to dine with us and brings the first word I hear of the news of a peace. The news was so good and sudden that I went with great joy to W. Batten and then to W. Pen to tell it them, and so home to dinner mighty merry.

8th. My wife and Creed and I to Charing Cross, there to see the great boy and girle that are lately come out of Ireland, the latter eight, the former but four years old, of most prodigious bigness for their age. I tried to weigh them in my arms, and find them twice as heavy as people almost twice their age; and yet I am apt to believe they are very young. Their father a little sorry fellow, and their mother an old Irish woman. They have had four children of this bigness, and four of ordinary growth, whereof two of each are dead. If, as my Lord Ormond certifies, it be true that they are no older it is very monstrous.

9th. This day my Lord Anglesey, our new Treasurer, come the first time to the Board, and there sat with us till noon; and I do perceive he is a very notable man, and understanding. This evening news comes for certain that the Dutch are with their fleete before Dover, and that it is expected they will attempt something there. The business of the peace is quite dashed again.

10th. This day our girle Mary did go away declaring that she must be where she might earn something one day, and spend it and play away the next. But a good civil wench, and one neither wife nor I did ever give angry word to, but she has this silly vanity that she must play.

12th. To my Lord Crew's where Sir Thomas Crew was, to dinner, and very good discourse with my Lord. And after dinner Sir Thomas Crew and I alone, and he tells me how I am mightily in esteem with the Parliament, there being harangues made in the House to the Speaker, of Mr. Pepys's readiness and civility to shew them every thing, which I am at this time very glad of. Thence after dinner to St. James's, but missed Sir W. Coventry, and so home, and there find my wife in a dogged humour for my not dining at home, and I did give her a pull by the nose and some ill words, which she provoked me to by something she spoke, that we fell extraordinarily out, insomuch that I going to the office to avoid further anger, she followed me in a devilish manner thither, and with much ado I got her into the garden out of hearing, to prevent shame, and so home and by degrees I found it necessary to calme her, and did.

14th. (Lord's Day.) Up, and my wife, a little before four, and by and by Mrs. Turner come to us by agreement, and she and I staid talking below while my wife dressed herself, which vexed me that she was so long about it, keeping us till past five o'clock before she was ready. She ready; and taking some bottles of wine and beer and some cold fowle with us into the coach, we took coach and four horses, which I had provided last night, and so away. A very fine day, and so towards Epsum. The country very fine, only the way very dusty. We got to Epsum by eight o'clock, to the well; where much company, and there we 'light, and I drank the water: I did drink four pints. Here I met with divers of our town, among others with several of the tradesmen of our office, but did talk but little with them, it growing hot in the sun, and so we took coach again and to the towne, to the King's Head. Here we called for drink, and bespoke dinner. W. Hewer rode with us, and I left him and the women, and myself walked to church, where few people, contrary to what I expected, and none I knew, but all the Houblons, brothers, and them after sermon I did salute. We parted to meet anon, and I to my women, and there to dinner, a good dinner, and were merry. After dinner we all lay down (the day being wonderful hot) to sleep, and each of us took a good nap, and then rose. We took coach and to take the ayre. W. Hewer's horse broke loose, and we had the sport to see him taken again. Then I carried them to see my cozen Pepys's house, and 'light and walked round about it, and they like it, as indeed it deserves, very well, and is a pretty place; and then I walked them to the wood hard by, and there got them in the thickets till they had lost themselves, and I could not find the way into any of the walks in the wood, which indeed are very pleasant, if I could have found them. At last got out of the wood again; and I, by leaping down the little bank, coming out of the wood, did sprain my right foot, which brought me great present pain; but presently, with walking, it went away for the present. And so the women and W. Hewer and I walked upon the Downes, where a flock of sheep was; and the most pleasant and innocent sight that ever I saw in my life. We find a shepherd and his little boy reading, far from any houses or sight of people, the Bible to him; so I made the boy read to me, which he did, with the forced tone that children do usually read, that was mighty pretty, and then I did give him something, and went to the father and talked with him; and I find he had been a servant in my cozen Pepys's house, and told me what was become of their old servants. He did content himself mightily in my liking his boy's reading, and did bless God for him the most like one of the old patriarchs that ever I saw in my life, and it brought those thoughts of the old age of the world in my mind for two or three days after. We took notice of his woolen knit stockings of two colours mixed, and of his shoes shod with iron shoes, both at the toe and heels, and with great nails in the soles of his feet, which was mighty pretty: and, taking notice of them, "Why," says the poor man, "the downes, you see, are full of stones, and we are faine to shoe ourselves thus; and these," says he, "will make the stones fly till they sing before me." I did give the poor man something, for which he was mighty thankful, and I tried to cast stones with his horne crooke. He values his dog mightily, that would turn a sheep any way which he would have him when he goes to fold them: told me there was about eighteen scoare sheep in his flock, and that he hath four shillings a week the year round for keeping of them. So we posted thence with mighty pleasure in the discourse we had with this poor man; and Mrs. Turner, in the common fields here, did gather one of the prettiest nosegays that ever I saw in my life.

So to our coach and through Mr. Minnes's wood, and looked upon Mr. Evelyn's house; and so over the common, and through Epsum towne to our inne, in the way stopping a poor woman with her milk-pail, and in one of my gilt tumblers did drink our bellyfulls of milk, better than any creame; and so to our inne and there had a dish of creame, but it was sour and so had no pleasure in it; and so paid our reckoning and took coach, it being about seven at night, and passed and saw the people walking with their wives and children to take the ayre; and we set out for home, the sun by and by going down, and we in the cool of the evening all the way with much pleasure home, talking and pleasing ourselves with the pleasure of this day's work, Mrs. Turner mightily pleased with my resolution, which, I tell her, is never to keep a country-house, but to keep a coach, and with my wife on the Saturday to go sometimes for a day to this place, and then quit to another place; and there is more variety and as little charge, and no trouble, as there is in a country-house. Anon it grew dark, and as it grew dark we had the pleasure to see several glow-wormes, which was mighty pretty, but my foot begins more and more to pain me, which Mrs. Turner, by keeping her warm hand upon it, did much ease; but so that when we come home, which was just at eleven at night, I was not able to walk from the lane's end to my house without being helped, which did trouble me, and therefore to bed presently; but, thanks be to God, found that I had not been missed, nor any business happened in

"A SHEPHERD AND HIS LITTLE BOY READING"

my absence. So to bed, and there had a cere-cloth laid to my foot and leg alone, but in great pain all night long.[1]

27th. At the office all the morning, and at noon to Sir G. Carteret in Broad Street, and there he and I together, and he is mightily pleased with my Lady's Jem having a son; and a mighty glad man he is. He tells me as to news that the peace is now confirmed, and all that over. He do say that the Court is in a way to ruin all for their pleasures; and says that he himself hath once taken the liberty to tell the King the necessity of having at least a show of religion in the Government, and sobriety; and that it was that that did set up and keep up Oliver though he was the greatest rogue in the world, and that it is so fixed in the nature of the common Englishman that it will not out of him.

28th. (Lord's Day). Up and to my chamber, where all the morning close, to draw up a letter to Sir W. Coventry upon the tidings of peace, taking occasion, before I am forced to it, to resign up to his Royall Highness my place of the Victualling, and to recommend myself to him by promise of doing my utmost to improve this peace in the best manner we may, to save the kingdom from ruin.

29th. To Westminster Hall, where the Hall full of people to see the issue of the day, the King being come to speak to the House to-day. One thing extraordinary was, this day a man, a Quaker, came almost naked through the Hall, and with a chafing-dish of fire and brimstone burning upon his head, did pass through the Hall, crying, "Repent! repent!" Presently comes down the House of Commons, the King, having made a very short speech to them, not at all giving them thanks for their readiness to come up to town at this busy time; but told them that he did think he should have had occasion for them, but had none, and therefore did dismiss them to look after their own occasions till October 10. Here I saw old good Mr. Vaughan,[2] and several of the great men of the Commons, and some of them old men, that are come 200 miles and more to attend this session of Parliament, and have been at great charge and disappointments in their other private business; and now all to no purpose, neither to serve their country, content themselves, nor receive any thanks from the King. It is verily expected by many of them that the King will continue the prorogation in October, so as if it be possible never to have Parliament more.

---

[1] Cere-cloth is cloth treated with wax or other glutinous matter; here clearly used as a surgical plaster.
[2] John Vaughan, M.P. for Cardiganshire.

After having spent an hour or two in the hall, my cozen Roger and I and Creed to the Old Exchange, and so home, and there cozen Roger and Creed to dinner with me, and very merry. After dinner by coach with cozen Roger (who before his going did acquaint me in private with an offer made of his marrying of Mrs. Elizabeth Wiles, whom I know; a kinswoman of Mr. Honiwood's, an ugly old maid, but a good housewife, and is said to have £2,500 to her portion; but if I can find that she hath but £2,000, which he prays me to examine, he says he will have her, she being one he hath long known intimately, and a good housewife and discreet woman, though I am against it in my heart, she being not handsome at all: and it hath been the very bad fortune of the Pepyses that ever I knew, never to marry an handsome woman, excepting Ned Pepys [1]) and Creed, set the former down at the Temple resolving to go to Cambridge to-morrow, and Creed and I to White Hall.

August 1st. Up, and all the morning at the office. At noon my wife and I dined at Sir W. Pen's, only with Mrs. Turner and her husband, on a damned venison pasty that stunk like a devil. However I did not know it till dinner was done. We had nothing but only this and a leg of mutton and a pullet or two. Mrs. Markham was here. I was very merry, and after dinner, upon a motion of the women, I was got to go to the play with them, and so to the King's house, to see "The Custome of the Country." [2] The house mighty empty, more than I ever saw it, and an ill play. After the play we went into the house and spoke with Knepp, who went abroad with us by coach to the Neat Houses [3] in the way to Chelsy; and there, in a box in a tree, we sat and sang and talked and eat, my wife out of humour, as she always is when this woman is by. So, after it was dark, we home. The gates of the City shut, it being so late; and at Newgate we find them in trouble, some thieves having this night broke open prison. So we through, and home; and our coachman was fain to drive hard from two or three fellows which he said were rogues, that he met at the end of Blow-bladder Street, next Cheapside.

2nd. Up, but before I rose my wife fell into angry discourse of my kindness yesterday to Mrs. Knipp, and leading her, and sitting in the coach hand in hand and my arm about her middle, and in some bad words reproached me with it. I was troubled,

[1] Edward Pepys of Broomsthorpe, who married Elizabeth Walpole.
[2] By Beaumont and Fletcher.
[3] Gardens on the north bank of the Thames, west of where Vauxhall Bridge now stands.

but having much business in my head and desirous of peace rose, and did not provoke her. Away to the Office where all the morning I was; only Mr. Gawden come to me, and he and I home to my chamber, and there reckoned, and there I received my profits for Tangier of him, and £250 on my victualling score. He is a most noble-minded man as ever I met with, and seems to own himself much obliged to me, which I will labour to make him, for he is a good man also: we talked on many good things relating to the King's service, and in fine I had much matter of joy by this morning's work, receiving above £400 of him on one account or other and a promise that, though I lay down my victualling place, yet, as long as he continues victualler, I shall be the better by him.

  17th. My wife and I and Sir W. Pen to the King's playhouse, where the house extraordinary full; and there was the King and Duke of York to see the new play, "Queen Elizabeth's Troubles, and the History of Eighty Eight."[1] I confess I have sucked in so much of the sad story of Queen Elizabeth from my cradle that I was ready to weep for her sometimes; but the play is the most ridiculous that sure ever come upon the stage.

  18th. (Lord's Day.) Up, and being ready, walked up and down to Cree Church,[2] to see it how it is; but I find no alteration there, as they say there was, for my Lord Mayor and Aldermen to come to sermon, as they do every Sunday, as they did formerly to Paul's. Walked back home and to our own church, where a dull sermon and our church empty of the best sort of people, they being at their country houses. And so home, and there dined with me Mr. Turner and his daughter Betty. Betty is grown a fine lady as to carriage and discourse. I and my wife are mightily pleased with her. We had a good haunch of venison, powdered and boiled, and a good dinner and merry. After sitting an hour to talk we broke up, and I walked towards White Hall, but being wearied turned into St. Dunstan's Church, where I heard an able sermon of the minister of the place; and stood by a pretty, modest maid, whom I did labour to take by the hand and the body but she would not, but got further and further from me. And at last I could perceive her to take pins out of her pocket to prick me if I should touch her again; which seeing I did forbear, and was glad I did spy her design. And then I fell to gaze upon another pretty maid in a pew close to me, and she on me; and I did go about to take her by the hand, which she suffered a little and then with-

---

[1] By Thomas Heywood.   [2] St. Catherine Cree, by the Minories.

"SICK OF THE STAGGERS"

drew. So the sermon ended and the church broke up, and my amours ended also, and so took coach and home, and there took up my wife, and to Islington with her, our old road. But before we got to Islington, between that and Kingsland, there happened an odd adventure: one of our coach-horses fell sick of the staggers, so as he was ready to fall down. The coachman was fain to 'light and hold him up, and cut his tongue to make him bleed, and his tail. The horse continued shaking every part of him, as if he had been in an ague, a good while, and his blood settled in his tongue, and the coachman thought and believed he would presently drop down dead; then he blew some tobacco in his nose, upon which the horse sneezed, and by and by grows well, and draws us the rest of our way, as well as ever he did; which was one of the strangest things of a horse I ever observed, but he says it is usual. It is the staggers. Staid and eat and drank at Islington, at the old house; and so home and to my chamber to read, and then to supper and to bed.

22nd. Up, and to the office; whence Lord Bruncker, J. Minnes, W. Pen and I, went to examine some men that are put in there, for rescuing of men that were pressed into the service: and we do plainly see that the desperate condition that we put men into for want of their pay makes them mad, they being as good men as ever were in the world, and would as readily serve the King again were they but paid. Two men leapt overboard, among others, into the Thames out of the vessel into which they were pressed, and were shot by the soldiers placed there to keep them, two days since; so much people do avoid the King's service! Returning to the office, did ask whether we might visit Commissioner Pett, to which, I confess, I have no great mind; and it was answered that he was close prisoner and we could not, but the Lieutenant of the Tower would send for him to his lodgings if we would; so we put it off to another time. Returned to the office where we sat all the morning, and at noon to Captain Cocke's to dinner.

23rd. Abroad to White Hall in a hackney-coach with Sir W. Pen; and in our way, in the narrow street near Paul's, going the back-way by Tower Street, and the coach being forced to put back, he was turning himself into a cellar, which made people cry out to us, and so we were forced to leap out, he out of one, and I out of the other boote;[1] *Query,* whether a glass-coach would have

---

[1] The "boot" was originally a projection upon either side of a coach, where the passengers sat with their backs to the carriage.

permitted us to have made the escape? neither of us getting any hurt; nor could the coach have got much hurt had we been in it; but, however, there was cause enough for us to do what we could to save ourselves.

24th. (St. Bartholomew's day.) This morning was proclaimed the peace between us and the States of the United Provinces,[1] and in the afternoon the Proclamations were printed and come out; and at night the bells rung, but no bonfires that I hear of any where, partly from the dearness of firing, but principally from the little content most people have in the peace. All the morning at the office. At noon dined, and Creed with me, at home. After dinner we to a play, and there saw "The Cardinall"[2] at the King's house, wherewith I am mightily pleased: so homeward, leaving Creed at the Temple. So with my wife to Mile End, and there drank of Bide's ale,[3] and so home. Most of our discourse is about our keeping a coach the next year, which pleases my wife mightily; and if I continue as able as now it will save us money.

25th. (Lord's Day.) Up and to church, and thence home. After dinner away by water to White Hall and to Westminster, and there to the parish church thinking to see Betty Michell, and did stay an hour in the crowd, thinking by the end of a nose that I saw that it had been her; but at last the head turned towards me, and it was her mother, which vexed me. And so I back to my boat and up to Putney, and there stepped into the church to look upon the fine people there, whereof there is great store, and the young ladies. And so walked to Barne-Elmes, reading of Boyle's Hydrostatickes, which are of infinite delight. And then leisurely home, with great pleasure to myself.

26th. To the Office, where we sat upon a particular business all the morning, and my Lord Anglesey, with us, who, and my Lord Bruncker, do bring us news how my Lord Chancellor's seal is to be taken away from him to-day. The thing is so great and sudden to me that it put me into a very great admiration what should be the meaning of it; and they do not own that they know what it should be. But this is certain, that the King did resolve it on Saturday and did yesterday send the Duke of Albemarle, the only man fit for those works, to him for his purse: to which the Chancellor answered that he received it from the King and would deliver it to the King's own hand, and so civilly returned the Duke of

---

[1] The peace had been signed at Breda on July 31.
[2] By James Shirley.   [3] Alderman John Bide, brewer.

Albemarle without it; and this morning my Lord Chancellor is to be with the King, to come to an end in the business.[1]

27th. Up, and am invited betimes to be godfather to-morrow to Captain Poole's child with my Lady Pen and Lady Batten, which I accepted out of complaisance to them. Sir J. Minnes, W. Batten and I to White Hall, and there hear how it is like to go well enough with my Lord Chancellor; that he is like to keep his Seal, desiring that he may stand his trial in Parliament if they will accuse him of any thing. This day Mr. Pierce the surgeon was with me, and tells me how this business of my Lord Chancellor's was certainly designed in my Lady Castlemayne's chamber; and that when [my Lord Chancellor] went from the King on Monday morning she was in bed, though about twelve o'clock, and ran out in her smock into her aviary looking into White Hall garden, and thither her woman brought her her nightgown; and stood joying herself at the old man's going away. And several of the gallants of White Hall did talk to her in her birdcage, telling her she was the bird of paradise.

28th. Up; and staid undressed till my tailor's boy did mend my vest in order to my going to the christening anon. Then out and to White Hall to attend the Council, so home, and there to dinner; and in the afternoon with my Lady Batten, Pen, and her daughter, and my wife, to Mrs. Poole's, where I mighty merry among the women, and christened the child, a girl, Elizabeth; which, though a girl, yet my Lady Batten would have me to give the name. After christening comes Sir W. Batten, W. Pen and Mr. Lowther, and mighty merry there, and I forfeited for not kissing the two godmothers presently after the christening before I kissed the mother, which made good mirth; and so anon away, and my wife and I took coach and went twice round Bartholomew fayre, which I was glad to see again after two years missing it by the plague. And so home and to my chamber a little, and so to supper and to bed.

31st. At the office all the morning; where, by Sir W. Pen, I do hear that the Seal was fetched away to the King yesterday from the Lord Chancellor; which puts me into a great horror, to have

---

[1] During his thirty-six years of intimate association with the throne, as chief adviser to Charles II. and his father, Clarendon had made many enemies. Latterly in particular he had been held responsible for the failure of the Dutch War; and he had incurred the anger of Parliament, who suspected him of advising the King to dispense with their services. Moreover, after surviving for many years the personal enmity of Lady Castlemaine, he was now obstructing Charles II.'s liaison with Mrs. Stewart. His continued presence had thus become irksome to the King, who now threw him over. He averted a public trial by a precipitate flight to France, where he spent the remaining seven years of his life.

it done after so much debate, and confidence that it would not be done, at last. This day being dissatisfied with my wife's learning so few songs of Goodgroome I did come to a new bargain with him to teach her songs at so much, viz., 10s. a song, which he accepts of, and will teach her.

September 1st. (Lord's Day.) To White Hall, where I met with several people and had my fill of talk. So home and by water to dinner, where comes Pelling and young Michell and his wife, whom I have not seen a great while, poor girle, and then comes Mr. Howe, and all dined with me very merry, and spent all the afternoon, Pelling, Howe and I and my boy, singing of Lock's response to the Ten Commandments, which he hath set very finely. They parted, in the evening my wife and I to walk in the garden; and there scolded a little, I being doubtful that she had received a couple of fine pinners (one of point de Gesne),[1] which I feared she hath from some or other of a present; but on the contrary I find she hath bought them for me to pay for them, without my knowledge. This do displease me much; but yet do so much please me better than if she had received them the other way that I was not much angry, but fell to other discourse, and so to my chamber and got her to read to me for saving of my eyes, and then, having got a great cold, I know not how, I to bed and lay ill at ease all the night.

2nd. This day is kept in the City as a publick fast for the fire this day twelve month: but I was not at church, being commanded with the rest to attend the Duke of York. When we had done Sir W. Coventry called me down with him to his chamber and there told me that he is leaving the Duke of York's service, which I was amazed at. "But," says he, "I did desire it a good while since, and the Duke of York did with much entreaty grant it, desiring that I would say nothing of it, that he might have time and liberty to choose his successor without being importuned for others whom he should not like:" and that he hath chosen Mr. Wren, which I am glad of, he being a very ingenious man; and so Sir W. Coventry says of him.[2] He tells me the true reason is that he, being a man not willing to undertake more business than he can go through, and being desirous to have his whole time to spend

---

[1] Genoese point lace.
[2] Matthew Wren (1629–72), cousin to the architect, was secretary to Lord Clarendon (1660–67) and to the Duke of York (1667–72). He was an original member of the Council of the Royal Society.

upon the business of the Treasury and a little for his own ease, he did desire this of the Duke of York.[1]

I dined with Sir G. Carteret, with whom dined Mr. Jack Ashburnham. In discourse at dinner concerning the change of men's humours and fashions touching meats, Mr. Ashburnham told us that he remembers since the only fruit in request, and eaten by the King and Queen at table as the best fruit, was the Katharine payre, though they knew at the time other fruits of France and our own country. After dinner comes in Mr. Townsend, and there I was witness of a horrid rateing, which Mr. Ashburnham, as one of the Grooms of the King's Bedchamber, did give him for want of linen for the King's person; which he swore was not to be endured, and that the King would not endure it, and that the King his father, would have hanged his Wardrobe-man should he have been served so, the King having at this day no handkerchers, and but three bands to his neck, he swore. Mr. Townsend answered want of money, and the owing of the linen-draper £5,000; and that he hath of late got many rich things made, beds and sheets and saddles, and all without money, and he can go no further: but still this old man, indeed like an old loving servant, did cry out for the King's person to be neglected. But when he was gone Townsend told me that it is the grooms taking away the King's linen at the quarter's end as their fees which makes this great want; for whether the King can get it or no they will run away at the quarter's end with what he hath had, let the King get more as he can.

From him I went to see a great match at tennis between Prince Rupert and one Captain Cooke against Bab. May and the elder Chichly,[2] where the King was, and Court; and it seems are the best players at tennis in the nation. But this puts me in mind of what I observed in the morning, that the King, playing at tennis, had a steele-yard carried to him, and I was told it was to weigh him after he had done playing; and at noon Mr. Ashburnham told me that it is only the King's curiosity which he usually hath of weighing himself before and after his play to see how much he loses in weight by playing, and this day he lost 4½ lbs. Thence home, and took my wife out to Mile End Green, and there I drank, and so home, having a very fine evening. Then home, and I to

[1] Sir W. Coventry, as M.P. for Yarmouth, had been bitterly attacking Lord Clarendon's administration, and his speeches had assisted to bring about the Chancellor's fall. His position as secretary to the Duke of York, Clarendon's son-in-law, would naturally have become a difficult one.

[2] Captain Thomas Cooke, Master of the Tennis Court at Whitehall; Baptist May, Keeper of the Privy Purse; Sir Thomas Chicheley, Master of the Ordnance.

Sir W. Batten and W. Pen, and there discoursed of Sir W. Coventry's leaving the Duke of York and Mr. Wren's succeeding him. They told me both seriously that they had long cut me out for Secretary to the Duke of York if ever W. Coventry left him; which, agreeing with what I have heard from other hands heretofore, do make me not only think that something of that kind hath been thought on, but do comfort me to see that the world hath such an esteem of my qualities as to think me fit for any such thing. Though I am glad with all my heart that I am not so, for it would never please me to be forced to the attendance that that would require, and leave my wife and family to themselves as I must do in such a case; thinking myself now in the best place that ever man was in to please his own mind in, and therefore I will take care to preserve it. So to bed, my cold remaining, though not so much, upon me. This day Nell, an old tall maid, come to live with us, a cook maid recommended by Mr. Batelier.

7th. Up, and to the office, where all the morning. At noon home to dinner, where Goodgroome was teaching my wife, and dined with us, and I did tell him of my intention to learn to trill, which he will not promise I shall obtain, but he will do what can be done, and I am resolved to learn. All the afternoon at the office, and towards night out by coach with my wife, she to the 'Change, and I to see the price of a copper cisterne for the table,[1] which is very pretty, and they demand £6 or £7 for one; but I will have one. Then called my wife at the 'Change, and bought a nightgown for my wife, cost but 24*s.*; and so out to Mile End to drink, and so home to the office to end my letters, and so home to supper and to bed.

8th. (Lord's Day.) To the King's Chapel to the closet, and there I hear Cresset sing a tenor part along with the Church musick very handsomely, but so loud that people did laugh at him, as a thing done for ostentation. Meeting Creed, I with him to the Parke, there to walk a little, and to the Queen's Chapel and there hear their musique. So to White Hall and saw the King and Queen at dinner; and observe (which I never did before), the formality, but it is but a formality, of putting a bit of bread wiped upon each dish into the mouth of every man that brings a dish; but it should be in the sauce. Here were some Russes come to see the King at dinner. I to Sir G. Carteret's to dinner, where Mr. Cofferer Ash-

---

[1] To rinse the dishes in.

burnham, who told a good story of a prisoner's being condemned at Salisbury for a small matter. While he was on the bench with his father-in-law, and while they were considering to transport him to save his life, the fellow flung a great stone at the Judge, that missed him, but broke through the wainscoat. Upon this he had his hand cut off, and was hanged presently.

11th. Comes Sir W. Batten and his lady, and Mr. Griffith their ward, and Sir W. Pen and his lady and Mrs. Lowther, who is grown, either through pride or want of manners, a fool, having not a word to say almost all dinner; and as a further mark of a beggarly, proud fool, hath a bracelet of diamonds and rubies about her wrist and a sixpenny necklace about her neck, and not one good rag of clothes upon her back; and Sir John Chichly in their company, and Mrs. Turner. I had an extraordinary good and handsome dinner for them, better than any of them deserve or understand, saving Sir John Chichly and Mrs. Turner; and not much mirth, only what I by discourse made, and that against my genius. After dinner I took occasion to break up the company soon as I could, and all parted.

15th. (Lord's Day.) Up to my chamber, there to set some papers to rights. By and by to church. Mr. Mills preached, and after sermon by invitation he and his wife come to dine with me, which is the first time they have been in my house I think these five years, I thinking it not amiss, because of their acquaintance in our country, to shew them some respect. Mr. Turner and his wife and their son dined with me, and I had a very good dinner for them, and very merry, and after dinner, he was forced to go, though it rained, to Stepney, to preach. We also to church and then home, and there comes Mr. Pelling with two men, by promise, one whereof, being a very little fellow, did sing a most excellent bass, and yet a poor fellow, a working goldsmith, that goes without gloves to his hands. Here we sung several good things; but I am more and more confirmed that singing with many voices is not singing, but a sort of instrumental musique, the sense of the words being lost by not being heard, and especially as they set them with Fuges of words, one after another; whereas singing properly, I think, should be but with one or two voices at most and the counterpoint. They supped with me, and so broke up; and then my wife and I to my chamber, where through the badness of my eyes she was forced to read to me, which she do very well, and was Mr. Boyle's discourse upon the style of the Scripture,[1] which is a very fine piece, and so to bed.

19th. Up, and all the morning at the office. At noon home to dinner, W. Hewer and I and my wife, when comes my cozen Kate Joyce and an aunt of ours, Lettice, formerly Haynes and now Howlett, come to town to see her friends, and also Sarah Kite, with her little boy in her armes, a very pretty little boy. The child I like very well, and could wish it my own. My wife being all unready did not appear. I made as much of them as I could such ordinary company; and yet my heart was glad to see them, though their condition was a little below my present state, to be familiar with. They gone, I to the office, where all the afternoon very busy.

22nd. (Lord's Day.) This night I did even my accounts of the house, which I have to my great shame omitted now above two months or more, and therefore am content to take my wife's and mayd's accounts as they give them, being not able to correct them, which vexes me: but the fault being my own, contrary to my wife's frequent desires, I cannot find fault, but am resolved never to let them come to that pass again. The truth is I have indulged myself more in pleasure for these last two months than ever I did in my life before since I come to be a person concerned in business, and I doubt when I come to make up my accounts I shall find it so by the expence.

23rd. To the Exchange and did a little business, and so home and took up my wife, and so carried her to the other end, where I 'light at my Lord Ashly's,[2] by invitation, to dine there, which I did, and Sir H. Cholmly, Creed, and Yeabsly. Away, and with Sir H. Cholmly to Westminster; who by the way told me how merry the King and Duke of York and Court were the other day, when they were abroad a-hunting. They come to Sir G. Carteret's house at Cranbourne, and there were entertained and all made drunk; and that all being drunk, Armerer[3] did come to the King and swore to him: "By God, Sir," says he, "you are not so kind to the Duke of York of late as you used to be." "Not I?" says the King, "why so?" "Why," says he, "if you are, let us drink his health." "Why, let us," says the King. Then he fell on his knees and drank it; and having done, the King began to drink

---

[1] *Some Considerations touching the Style of the Holy Scriptures*, by the Hon. Robert Boyle.
[2] Lord Ashley, afterwards Earl of Shaftesbury, lived in a house built by Inigo Jones on the east side of Aldersgate Street.
[3] Sir William Armourer, Equerry to the King.

it. "Nay, Sir," says Armerer, "by God you must do it on your knees!" So he did, and then all the company: and having done it all fell a-crying for joy, being all maudlin, and kissing one another, the King the Duke of York, and the Duke of York the King, and in such a maudlin pickle as never people were; and so passed the day. But Sir H. Cholmly tells me that the King hath this good luck, that the next day he hates to have any body mention what he had done the day before, nor will suffer any body to gain upon him that way, which is a good quality. Parted with Sir H. Cholmly at White Hall, and there I took coach and took up my wife at Unthanke's, and so out for ayre, it being a mighty pleasant day, as far as Bow; and so drank by the way, and home.

24th. Up, and to the Office, where all the morning very busy. At noon home, where there dined with me Anthony Joyce and his wife, and Will and his wife, and my aunt Lettice, that was here the other day, and Sarah Kite; and I had a good dinner for them, and were as merry as I could be in that company where W. Joyce is, who is still the same impertinent fellow that ever he was. After dinner I away to St. James's, where we had an audience of the Duke of York of many things of weight, about which we stayed till past candle-light; and so Sir W. Batten and W. Pen and I fain to go all in a hackney-coach round by London Wall for fear of cellars,[1] this being the first time I have been forced to go that way this year, though now I shall begin to use it. We tired one coach upon Holborne-Conduit Hill, and got another, and made it a long journey home. Where to the office and then home, and at my business till twelve at night, writing in short hand the draught of a report to make to the King and Council to-morrow. This I did finish to-night to the spoiling of my eyes, I fear. This done, then to bed. This evening my wife tells me that W. Batelier hath been here to-day and brought with him the pretty girl he speaks of, to come to serve my wife as a woman, out of the school at Bow. My wife says she is extraordinary handsome, and inclines to have her, and I am glad of it, at least that if we must have one she should be handsome. But I shall leave it wholly to my wife to do what she will therein.

25th. Up as soon as I could see and to the office to write over fair with Mr. Hater my last night's work, which I did by nine o'clock, and got it signed, and so to White Hall. Here I saw the Duke of Buckingham sit in Council again, where he was re-

---

[1] The city being still in ruins after the Great Fire.

admitted, it seems, the last Council-day: and it is wonderful to see how the man is come again to his places, all of them, after the reproach and disgrace done him. At noon I took coach, and to Sir G. Carteret's in Lincoln's-Inn-Fields, to the house that is my Lord's, which my Lord lets him have: and this is the first day of dining there. And there dined with him and his lady my Lord Privy-seale,[1] who is indeed a very sober man; who, among other talk, did mightily wonder at the reason of the growth of the credit of banquiers, since it is so ordinary a thing for citizens to break, out of knavery. Upon this we had much discourse; and I observed therein, to the honour of this City, that I have not heard of one citizen of London broke in all this war, this plague, this fire, and this coming up of the enemy among us; which he owned to be very considerable. After dinner I to the King's playhouse, my eyes being so bad since last night's straining of them that I am hardly able to see, besides the pain which I have in them. The play was a new play, and infinitely full: the King and all the Court almost there. It is "The Storme," a play of Fletcher's, which is but so-so, methinks; only there is a most admirable dance at the end, of the ladies, in a military manner, which indeed did please me mightily.

27th. While I was busy at the office, my wife sends for me to come home, and what was it but to see the pretty girl which she is taking to wait upon her: and though she seems not altogether so great a beauty as she had before told me, yet indeed she is mighty pretty; and so pretty that I find I shall be too much pleased with it, and therefore could be contented as to my judgement, though not to my passion, that she might not come, lest I may be found too much minding her, to the discontent of my wife. She is to come next week. She seems by her discourse to be grave beyond her bigness and age, and exceeding well bred as to her deportment. To the office again, my head running on this pretty girl, and there till noon, when Creed and Sheres come and dined with me; and we had a great deal of pretty discourse of the cere-moniousness of the Spaniards, whose ceremonies are so many and so known. He says that it is so far from dishonour to a man to give private revenge for an affront that the contrary is a disgrace; they holding that he that receives an affront is not fit to appear in the sight of the world till he hath revenged himself: and therefore that a gentleman there that receives an affront oftentimes never

---

[1] John, second Lord Robartes, later Earl of Radnor.

appears again in the world till he hath by some private way or other revenged himself; and that on this account several have followed their enemies privately to the Indys, thence to Italy, thence to France and back again, watching for an opportunity to be revenged. He says that many ladies in Spain, after they are found to be with child, do never stir out of their beds or chambers till they are brought to bed; so ceremonious they are in that point also. He tells me of their wooing by serenades at the window, and that their friends do always make the match; but yet that they have opportunities to meet at masse at church, and there they make love: that the Court there hath no dancing, nor visits at night to see the King or Queen, but is always just like a cloyster, nobody stirring in it: that my Lord Sandwich wears a beard now, turned up in the Spanish manner. But that which pleases me most indeed is that the peace which he hath made with Spain is now printed here, and is acknowledged by all the merchants to be the best peace that ever England had with them. This I am mighty glad of, and it is the first and only piece of good news or thing fit to be owned that this nation hath done several years.

28th. At noon dined at home and Mr. Hater with me, and Mr. Pierce the surgeon dropped in, who I feared did come to bespeak me to be godfather to his son, which I am unwilling now to be, having ended my liking to his wife since I find she paints.

30th. To Westminster, where to the Swan and drank, and away to the Hall, and thence to Mrs. Martin's to bespeak some linen. So by coach home, and there found our pretty girl Willet come, brought by Mr. Batelier, and she is very pretty, and so grave as I never saw a little thing in my life. Indeed I think her a little too good for my family, and so well carriaged as I hardly ever saw. I wish my wife may use her well. Now I begin to be full of thought for my journey the next week, if I can get leave, to Brampton.

October 4th. To my Lord Crew's, and there did stay with him an hour till almost night, discoursing about the ill state of my Lord Sandwich, that he can neither be got to be called home, nor money got to maintain him there; which will ruin his family. And the truth is he do almost deserve it, for by all relation he hath in a little more than a year and a half spent £20,000 of the King's money and the best part of £10,000 of his own; which is a most prodigious expence, more than ever Embassador spent there, and more than these Commissioners of the Treasury will or do allow.

And they demand an account before they will give him any more money, which puts all his friends to a loss what to answer. But more money we must get him, or to be called home.

5th. Up, and to the Office; and there all the morning, none but my Lord Anglesey and myself; but much surprized with the news of the death of Sir W. Batten, who died this morning, having been but two days sick. Sir W. Pen and I did dispatch a letter this morning to Sir W. Coventry to recommend Colonel Middleton, who we think a most honest and understanding man, and fit for that place. At noon home, and by coach to Temple Bar to a India shop, and there bought a gown and sash, which cost me 26*s.*; and so to my Lord Crew and there dined, and after dinner I to my tailor's, and there took up my wife and Willet, and so to the King's house: and there going in met with Knepp, and she took us up into the tireing-rooms, and to the women's shift, where Nell was dressing herself and was all unready, and is very pretty, prettier than I thought. And so walked all up and down the house above, and then below into the scene-room and there sat down, and she gave us fruit: and here I read the questions to Knepp, while she answered me, through all her part of "Flora's Figary's" [1] which was acted to-day. But, Lord! to see how they were both painted would make a man mad, and did make me loath them; and what base company of men comes among them, and how lewdly they talk! and how poor the men are in clothes, and yet what a shew they make on the stage by candle-light, is very observable.

6th. (Lord's Day.) To White Hall, and there met Sir W. Coventry and discoursed with him, and then with my Lord Bruncker and many others to end my matters in order to my going into the country to-morrow for five or six days, which I have not done for above three years.

7th. Up betimes and did do several things towards the settling all matters both of house and office in order for my journey this day, and did leave my chief care and the key of my closet with Mr. Hater, with directions what papers to secure in case of fire or other accident; and so about nine o'clock I and my wife and Willet set out in a coach I have hired, with four horses; and W. Hewer rode by us on horseback; and so my wife and she in their morning gowns, very handsome and pretty, and to my great liking. We set out, and so out at Allgate, and so to the Green Man, and so on

[1] By Richard Rhodes.

to Enfield. And before night come to Bishop Stafford, to the Raynedeere, and here we stayed and supped and lodged.

8th. Up, and broke our fast, and then took coach and away to Cambridge, it being foul rainy weather, and there did take up at the Rose for the sake of Mrs. Dorothy Drawwater, the vintner's daughter, which is mentioned in the play of Sir Martin Marrall. Here we had a good chamber and bespoke a good supper; and then I took my wife and W. Hewer and Willet, it holding up a little, and shewed them Trinity College and St. John's Library, and went to King's College Chapel to see the outside of it only, and so to our inne; and with much pleasure did this, they walking in their pretty morning gowns, very handsome, and I proud to find myself in condition to do this; and so home to our lodging, and there by and by to supper, with much good sport, talking with the Drawers concerning matters of the town and persons whom I remember; and so after supper to cards, and then to bed.

9th. Up and got ready, and eat our breakfast, and then took coach; and the poor, as they did yesterday, did stand at the coach to have something given them, as they do to all great persons, and I did give them something; and the town musique did also come and play, but, Lord! what sad music they made! However I was pleased with them, being all of us in very good humour, and so through the town, and observed at our College of Magdalene the posts new painted, and understand that the Vice-Chancellor [1] is there this year. And so away for Huntingdon, mightily pleased all along the road to remember old stories; and come to Brampton at about noon, and there find my father and sister and brother all well. And here laid up our things, and up and down to see the garden with my father, and the house, and do altogether find it very pretty, especially the little parlour and the summer-houses in the garden; only the wall do want greens upon it, and the house is too low-roofed; but that is only because of my coming from a house with higher ceilings. But altogether is very pretty, and I bless God that I am like to have such a pretty place to retire to: and I did walk with my father without doors, and do find a very convenient way of laying out money there in building, which will make a very good seat, and the place deserves it, I think, very well. By and by to dinner, and after dinner I walked up to Hinchingbroke where my Lady expected me, and there spent all the afternoon with her: the same most excellent, good, discreet lady that

---

[1] Dr. John Howarth, Master of Magdalene.

"THE TOWN MUSIQUE"

ever she was; and among other things is mightily pleased with the lady that is like to be her son Hinchingbroke's wife, which I am mightily glad of. By and by my wife comes with Willet, my wife in her velvett vest, which is mighty fine and becomes her exceedingly. I am pleased with my Lady Paulina and Anne, who both are grown very proper ladies, and handsome enough. But a thousand questions my Lady asked me, till she could think of no more almost, but walked up and down the house with me. But I do find by her that they are reduced to great straits for money, having been forced to sell her plate, 8 or £900 worth; and she is now going to sell a suit of her best hangings, of which I could almost wish to buy a piece or two if the pieces will be broke. But the house is most excellently furnished, and brave rooms and good pictures. Here we staid till night, walking and talking and drinking, and with mighty satisfaction, my Lady with me alone most of the day talking of my Lord's bad condition to be kept in Spayne without money and at a great expense, which (as we will save the family) we must labour to remove. Night being come, we took leave with all possible kindness, and so home; and there Mr. Shepley staid with us and supped, and full of good country discourse, and when supper done took his leave, and we all to bed; only I a little troubled that my father tells me that he is troubled that my wife shows my sister no countenance, and him but very little, but is as a stranger in the house; and I do observe she do carry herself very high: but I perceive there was some great falling out when she was here last, but the reason I have no mind to enquire after, for vexing myself, being desirous to pass my time with as much mirth as I can while I am abroad. So all to bed. My wife and I in the high bed in our chamber, and Willet in the trundle bed,[1] which she desired to lie in, by us.

10th. Waked in the morning with great pain of the collique, by cold taken yesterday, I believe, with going up and down in my shirt; but with rubbing my belly, keeping of it warm, I did at last come to some ease, and rose, and up to walk up and down the garden with my father to talk of all our concernments: about a husband for my sister, whereof there is at present no appearance, but we must endeavour to find her one now, for she grows old [2] and ugly: then for my brother, and resolve he shall stay here this winter and then I will either send him to Cambridge for a year

---

[1] A low bedstead on castors, which ran in under the principal bed.
[2] She was in fact just upon twenty-seven.

till I get him some church promotion, or send him to sea as a chaplain, where he may study and earn his living. Then walked round about our Greene, to see whether, in case I cannot buy out my uncle Thomas and his son's right in this house, that I can buy another place as good thereabouts to build on; and I do not see that I can. But this, with new building, may be made an excellent pretty thing, and I resolve to look after it as soon as I can and Goody Gorum dies. By this time it was almost noon, and then my father and I and wife and Willet abroad by coach round the towne of Brampton to observe any other place as good as ours, and find none, and so back with great pleasure; and thence went all of us, my sister and brother and W. Hewer, to dinner to Hinchingbroke, where we had a good plain country dinner, but most kindly used; and here dined the Minister of Brampton and his wife, who is reported a very good but poor man. Here I spent alone with my Lady after dinner the most of the afternoon, and anon the two twins[1] were sent for from schoole, at Mr. Taylor's, to come to see me, and I took them into the garden, and there in one of the summer-houses did examine them, and do find them so well advanced in their learning that I was amazed at it: they repeating a whole ode without book out of Horace, and did give me a very good account of any thing almost, and did make me very readily very good Latin, and did give me a good account of their Greek grammar, beyond all possible expectation; and so grave and manly as I never saw, I confess, nor could have believed; so that they will be fit to go to Cambridge in two years at most. They are both little, but very like one another, and well-looked children. Then in to my Lady again, and staid till it was almost night again, and then took leave for a great while again, but with extraordinary kindness from my Lady, who looks upon me like one of her own family and interest.

So thence, my wife and people by the highway, and I walked over the park with Mr. Shepley, and through the grove, which is mighty pretty as is imaginable, and so over their drawbridge to Nun's Bridge, and so to my father's, and there sat and drank and talked a little, and then parted. And he being gone, and what company there was, my father and I, with a dark lantern, it being now night, into the garden with my wife, and there went about our great work to dig up my gold. But, Lord! what a tosse I was for

[1] The third and fourth sons, aged at this time about twelve. Oliver Montagu became Solicitor-General, and John became Master of Trinity and Dean of Durham. Neither married.

some time in, that they could not justly tell where it was; that I begun heartily to sweat and be angry that they should not agree better upon the place, and at last to fear that it was gone: but by and by poking with a spit we found it, and then begun with a spudd to lift up the ground. But, good God! to see how sillily they did it, not half a foot under ground, and in the sight of the world from a hundred places if any body by accident were near hand, and within sight of a neighbour's window and their hearing also, being close by: only my father says that he saw them all gone to church before he begun the work, when he laid the money, but that do not excuse it to me. But I was out of my wits almost, and the more from that upon my lifting up the earth with the spudd I did discern that I had scattered the pieces of gold round about the ground among the grass and loose earth; and taking up the iron head-pieces wherein they were put, I perceive the earth was got among the gold, and wet, so that the bags were all rotten, and all the notes, that I could not tell what in the world to say to it, not knowing how to judge what was wanting, or what had been lost by Gibson in his coming down: which all put together did make me mad; and at last was forced to take up the head-pieces, dirt and all, and as many of the scattered pieces as I could with the dirt discern by the candle-light, and carry them up into my brother's chamber, and there locke them up till I had eat a little supper: and then, all people going to bed, W. Hewer and I did all alone, with several pails of water and basins, at last wash the dirt off of the pieces, and parted the pieces and the dirt, and then begun to tell; and by a note which I had of the value of the whole in my pocket, do find that there was short above a hundred pieces, which did make me mad; and considering that the neighbour's house was so near that we could not suppose we could speak one to another in the garden at the place where the gold lay, especially my father being deaf, but they must know what we had being doing on, I feared that they might in the night come and gather some pieces and prevent us the next morning; so W. Hewer and I out again about midnight, for it was now grown so late, and there by candle-light did make shift to gather forty-five pieces more. And so in, and to cleanse them: and by this time it was past two in the morning; and so to bed, with my mind pretty quiet to think that I have recovered so many. And then to bed, and I lay in the trundle-bed, the girl being gone to bed to my wife, and there lay in some disquiet all night, telling of the clock till it was daylight.

11th. And then rose and called W. Hewer, and he and I, with
pails and a sieve, did lock ourselves into the garden, and there
gather all the earth about the place into pails, and then sift those
pails in one of the summer-houses, just as they do for dyamonds
in other parts of the world; and there, to our great content, did
with much trouble by nine o'clock (and by the time we emptied
several pails and could not find one), we did make the last night's
forty-five up seventy-nine: so that we are come to about twenty
or thirty of what I think the true number should be; and perhaps
within less; and of them I may reasonably think that Mr. Gibson
might lose some: so that I am pretty well satisfied that my loss
is not great, and do bless God that it is so well, and do leave
my father to make a second examination of the dirt, which he
promises he will do, and, poor man, is mightily troubled for this
accident; but I declared myself very well satisfied, and so indeed
I am, and my mind at rest in it, being but an accident, which is
unusual; and so gives me some kind of content to remember how
painful it is sometimes to keep money, as well as to get it, and
how doubtful I was how to keep it all night, and how to secure it
to London: and so got all my gold put up in bags. And so having
the last night wrote to my Lady Sandwich to lend me John Bowles
to go along with me my journey, not telling her the reason that
it was only to secure my gold, we to breakfast, and then about ten
o'clock took coach, and my brother John on horseback. But before we went out the Huntingdon musick come to me and played,
and it was better than that of Cambridge. Here I took leave of
my father, and did give my sister 20*s.* She cried at my going; but
whether it was at her unwillingness for my going, or any unkindness of my wife's or no, I know not; but, God forgive me! I take
her to be so cunning and ill-natured that I have no great love for
her; but only is my sister and must be provided for. My gold
I put into a basket and set under one of the seats; and so my work
every quarter of an hour was to look to see whether all was well,
and I did ride in great fear all the day; but it was a pleasant day
and good company, and I mightily contented. Mr. Shepley saw
me beyond St. Neots, and there parted, and we straight to Stevenage, through Bald Lanes, which are already very bad; and at
Stevenage we come well before night, and all sat; and there with
great care I got the gold up to the chamber, my wife carrying one
bag and the girl another, and W. Hewer the rest in the basket,
and set it all under a bed in our chamber; and then sat down to

talk, and were very pleasant, satisfying myself among other things from John Bowles in some terms of hunting, and about deere, bucks and does. And so anon to supper, and very merry we were, and a good supper, and after supper to bed.

12th. Up and eat our breakfast, and set out about nine o'clock, and so to Barnett, where we staid and baited, the weather very good all day and yesterday; and by five o'clock got home, where I find all well, and did bring my gold, to my heart's content, very safe home, having not this day carried it in a basket, but in our hands: the girl took care of one, and my wife another bag, and I the rest, I being afraid of the bottom of the coach lest it should break; and therefore was at more ease in my mind than I was yesterday. At home we find that Sir W. Batten's burial was to-day carried from hence, with a hundred or two of coaches, to Walthamstow, and there buried. I hear that the Parliament hath met on Thursday last, and adjourned to Monday next. The King did make them a very kind speech, promising them to leave all to them to do, and call to account what and whom they pleased. The Parliament is mightily pleased with the King's speech, and voted giving him thanks for what he said and hath done.

Anon comes home Sir W. Pen from the burial, and he and I to walk in the garden, where he did confirm the most of this news, and so to talk of our particular concernments; and among the rest he says that Lady Batten and her children-in-law are all broke in pieces, and that there is but £800 found in the world, of money.

13th. (Lord's Day.) Evened with W. Hewer for my expenses upon the road this last journey, and do think that the whole journey will cost me little less than £18 or £20, one way or other; but I am well pleased with it, and so after supper to bed.

14th. To Mrs. Martin's, where by appointment comes to me Mrs. Howlett,[1] which I was afraid was to have told me something of my freedom with her daughter; but it was not so, but only to complain to me of her son-in-law, how he abuses and makes a slave of her, and his mother is one that encourages him in it, so that they are at this time upon very bad terms one with another, and desires that I would take a time to advise him and tell him what it becomes him to do, which office I am very glad of, for some ends of my own also con sa fille.

17th. Up, and being sent for by my Lady Batten, I to her, and there she found fault with my not seeing her since her being

[1] Betty Michell's mother.

a widow, which I excused as well as I could, though it is a fault; but it is my nature not to be forward in visits. But here she told me her condition, which is good enough, being sole executrix, to the disappointment of all her husband's children. And here do see what creatures widows are in weeping for their husbands, and then presently leaving off; but I cannot wonder at it, the cares of the world taking place of all other passions. Thence to the office, where all the morning busy, and at noon home to dinner, where Mr. John Andrews and his wife come and dined with me. It was an odd, strange thing to observe of Mr. Andrews what a fancy he hath to raw meat, that he eats it with no pleasure unless the blood run about his chops, which it did now by a leg of mutton that was not above half boiled; but it seems at home all his meat is dressed so, and beef and all, and eats it so at nights also.

After dinner I to the office, where my Lord Anglesey tells us that the House of Commons have this morning run into the inquiry in many things; as, the sale of Dunkirke, the dividing of the fleete the last year, the business of the prizes with my Lord Sandwich, and many other things; so that now they begin to fall close upon it, and God knows what will be the end of it; but a Committee they have chosen to inquire into the miscarriages of the war.

19th. At the office all the morning, where very busy, and at noon home to a short dinner, being full of my desire of seeing my Lord Orrery's new play this afternoon at the King's house, "The Black Prince," the first time it is acted; where, though we come by two o'clock, yet there was no room in the pit, but we were forced to go into one of the upper boxes, at 4*s.* a piece, which is the first time I ever sat in a box in my life. And in the same box come, by and by, behind me, my Lord Barkeley and his lady; but I did not turn my face to them to be known, so that I was excused from giving them my seat; and this pleasure I had, that from this place the scenes do appear very fine indeed, and much better than in the pit. The house infinite full, and the King and Duke of York was there.

20th. (Lord's Day.) Pelling the apothecary supped with me (my wife being gone to bed sick of the cholique). Pelling tells me that my Lady Duchesse Albemarle was at Mrs. Turner's this afternoon, she being ill, and did there publickly talk of business and of our Office, and that she believed that I was safe, and had done well; and so, I thank God! I hear every body speaks of me; and indeed I think without vanity I may expect to be profited rather than injured by this inquiry which the Parliament makes into business.

22nd. Slept but ill all the last part of the night, for fear of this day's success in Parliament: therefore up, and all of us all the morning close till almost two o'clock, collecting all we had to say and had done from the beginning touching the safety of the River Medway and Chatham. And having done this and put it into order we away, I not having time to eat my dinner; and so all in my Lord Bruncker's coach, that is to say, Bruncker, W. Pen, T. Harvy and myself, talking of the other great matter with which they charge us, that is of discharging men by ticket,[1] in order to our defence in case that should be asked. We come to the Parliament-door, and there, after a little waiting till the Committee was sat, we were, the House being very full, called in. Sir W. Pen went in and sat as a Member; and my Lord Bruncker would not at first go in, expecting to have a chair set for him, and his brother had bid him not go in till he was called for; but after a few words I had occasion to mention him, and so he was called in, but without any more chair or respect paid him than myself, and so Bruncker and T. Harvy and I were there to answer: and I had a chair brought me to lean my books upon, and so did give them such an account, in a series of the whole business that had passed the Office touching the matter, and so answered all questions given me about it, that I did not perceive but they were fully satisfied with me and the business as to our Office. My discourse held till within an hour after candle-light, for I had candles brought in to read my papers by. None of my brethren said anything but me there, but only two or three silly words my Lord Bruncker gave, in answer to one question. At last the House dismissed us, and my cozen Pepys did come out and joy me in my acquitting myself so well, and so did several others; and my fellow-officers all very brisk to see themselves so well acquitted, which makes me a little proud. So, with our hearts very light, Sir W. Pen and I in his coach home, it being now near eight o'clock, and so to the office, and did a little business by the post, and so home, hungry, and eat a good supper; and so, with my mind well at ease, to bed.

23rd. Sir W. Pen and I into London; and there saw the King, with his kettle-drums and trumpets, going to the Exchange to lay the first stone of the first pillar of the new building of the Ex-

---

[1] *i.e.* giving men a ticket or voucher for the amount of pay due to them.

change,[1] which, the gates being shut, I could not get in to see: but with Sir W. Pen to Captain Cocke's to drink a dram of brandy, and so he to the Treasury office about Sir G. Carteret's accounts, and I took coach and back again toward Westminster; but in my way stopped at the Exchange, and got in, the King being newly gone, and there find the bottom of the first pillar laid. And here was a shed set up, and hung with tapestry, and a canopy of state, and some good victuals and wine for the King, who, it seems, did it; and so a great many people, as Tom Killigrew and others of the Court, there; and there I did eat a mouthful and drink a little, and do find Mr. Gawden in his gowne as Sheriffe, and understand that the King hath this morning knighted him upon the place, which I am mightily pleased with; and I think the other Sheriffe, who is Davis, the little fellow, my schoolfellow, the bookseller, which is a strange turn methinks. Here mighty merry (there being a good deal of good company) for a quarter of an hour, and so I away and to Westminster Hall, where I come just as the House rose; and there in the Hall met with Sir W. Coventry. He says the House was well satisfied with my Report yesterday. So to the King's playhouse, and here to my great satisfaction I did see my Lord Hinchingbroke and his mistress, with her father and mother; and I am mightily pleased with the young lady, being handsome enough, and indeed to my great liking, as I would have her. I could not but look upon them all the play, being exceeding pleased with my good hap to see them, God bring them together! And they are now already mighty kind to one another, and he is as it were one of their family.

The House did also vote this day thanks to be given to the Prince and Duke of Albemarle for their care and conduct in the last year's war, which is a strange act; but, I know not how, the blockhead Albemarle hath strange luck to be loved, though he be, and every man must know it, the heaviest man in the world, but stout and honest to his country.

November 2nd. Up, and to the office, where busy all the morning; at noon home, and after dinner my wife and Willett and I to the King's playhouse, and there saw "Henry the Fourth:" and contrary to expectation, was pleased in nothing more than Cartwright's speaking of Falstaffe's speech about "What is Honour?" The house full of Parliament-men, it being holyday with them: and it was observable how a gentleman of good habit,

---

[1] This (second) building for the Royal Exchange was burnt down in 1838.

sitting just before us, eating of some fruit in the midst of the play, did drop down as dead, being choked; but with much ado Orange Moll [1] did thrust her finger down his throat and brought him to life again. After the play we home, and I busy at the office late, and then home to supper and to bed.

4th. To Turlington, the great spectacle-maker, for advice, who dissuades me from using old spectacles, but rather young ones, and do tell me that nothing can wrong my eyes more than for me to use reading-glasses which do magnify much.

7th. Up, and at the office hard all the morning, and at noon resolved with Sir W. Pen to go see "The Tempest," an old play of Shakespeare's, acted, I hear, the first day; and so my wife and girl and W. Hewer by themselves, and Sir W. Pen and I afterwards by ourselves; and forced to sit in the side balcone over against the musique-room at the Duke's house. The house mighty full; the King and Court there, and the most innocent play that ever I saw, and a curious piece of musique in an echo of half sentences, the echo repeating the former half, while the man goes on to the latter, which is mighty pretty. The play no great wit, but yet good, above ordinary plays.

10th. (Lord's Day.) Mighty cold, and with my wife to church, where a lazy sermon. Here was my Lady Batten in her mourning at church, but I took no notice of her. At noon comes Michell and his wife to dine with us, and pretty merry. I glad to see her still. After dinner Sir W. Pen and I to White Hall, to speak with Sir W. Coventry, and there do hear that the Duke of York hath got, and is full of, the small-pox; and so we to his lodgings, and there find most of the family going to St. James's, and the gallery doors locked up that nobody might pass to nor fro: and a sad house, I am sure. I am sad to consider the effects of his death if he should miscarry, but Dr. Frazier tells me that he is in as good condition as a man can be in his case. The eruption appeared last night; it seems he was let blood on Friday.

11th. After dinner my wife and I and Willett to the King's play-house, and there saw "The Indian Emperour," [2] a good play, but not so good as people cry it up, I think, though above all things Nell's ill speaking of a great part made me mad. Thence with great trouble and charge getting a coach (it being now and having been all this day a most cold and foggy, dark, thick day), we home; and there I to my office, and saw it made clean from top

---

[1] Moll, the orange-seller at the King's playhouse, was a well-known character.   [2] By Dryden.

to bottom, till I feared I took cold in walking in a damp room while it is in washing, and so home to supper and to bed. This day I had a whole doe sent me, which is a fine present, and I had the umbles of it for dinner. This day I hear Kirton, my bookseller, poor man, is dead, I believe of grief for his losses by the fire.

19th. This night I wrote to my father, in answer to a new match which is proposed (the executor of Ensum, my sister's former servant) for my sister, that I will continue my mind of giving her £500 if he likes of the match. My father did also this week, by Shepley, return me up a guinny, which, it seems, upon searching the ground, they have found since I was there. I was told this day that Lory Hide,[1] second son of my Lord Chancellor, did some time since in the House say that if he thought his father was guilty but of one of the things then said against him, he would be the first that should call for judgement against him: which Mr. Waller, the poet, did say was spoke like the old Roman, like Brutus, for its greatness and worthiness.

20th. Up, and all the morning at my office shut up with Mr. Gibson, I walking and he reading to me the order books of the office from the beginning of the war, for preventing the Parliament's having them in their hands before I have looked them over and seen the utmost that can be said against us from any of our orders, and to my great content all the morning I find none. So at noon home to dinner with my clerks, who have of late dined frequently with me, and I do purpose to have them so still, by that means I having opportunity to talk with them about business, and I love their company very well. This afternoon Mr. Mills come and visited me, and stayed a little with me: and among other talk he told me how fully satisfactory my first Report was to the House in the business of Chatham, which I am glad to hear.

21st. To Arundell House, where the meeting of Gresham College was broke up; but there meeting Creed, I with him to the taverne in St. Clement's Churchyard, where was Deane Wilkins, Dr. Whistler, Dr. Floyd, a divine admitted I perceive this day, and other brave men; and there we fell to discourse, and very good. Among the rest they discourse of a man that is a little frantic, that hath been a kind of minister, that is poor and a debauched man, that the College have hired for 20*s.* to have some of the blood of a sheep let into his body; and it is to be done on Saturday next. They purpose to let in about twelve ounces, which they compute

---

[1] Laurence Hyde, later created Earl of Rochester.

is what will be let in in a minute's time by a watch. They differ
in the opinion they have of the effects of it: some think it may have
a good effect upon him as a frantic man by cooling his blood,
others that it will not have any effect at all. But the man is a
healthy man, and by this means will be able to give an account
what alteration if any he do find in himself, and so may be usefull.
On this occasion Dr. Whistler told a pretty story related by Muf-
fet,[1] a good author, of Dr. Caius, that built Keys College; that,
being very old, and living only at that time upon woman's milk,
he, while he fed upon the milk of an angry, fretful woman, was so
himself; and then, being advised to take it of a good-natured,
patient woman, he did become so, beyond the common temper of
his age. Thus much nutriment, they observed, might do. Their
discourse was very fine; and if I should be put out of my office I
do take great content in the liberty I shall be at of frequenting
these gentlemen's company.

    25th. This morning Sir W. Pen tells me that the House was very
hot on Saturday last upon the business of liberty of speech in
the House, and damned the vote in the beginning of the Long
Parliament against it; so that he fears that there may be some bad
thing which they have a mind to broach, which they dare not do
without more security than they now have. God keep us, for
things look mighty ill!

    29th. Waked about seven o'clock this morning with a noise
I supposed I heard near our chamber, of knocking, which by and
by increased; and I, more awake, could distinguish it better. I
then waked my wife, and both of us wondered at it, and lay so
a great while, while that increased, and at last heard it plainer,
knocking as if it were breaking down a window for people to get
out; and then removing of stools and chairs; and plainly, by and
by, going up and down our stairs. We lay, both of us, afeared;
yet I would have rose, but my wife would not let me. Besides,
I could not do it without making noise; and we did both conclude
that thieves were in the house, but wondered what our people
did, whom we thought either killed or afeared, as we were. Thus
we lay till the clock struck eight, and high day. At last I removed
my gown and slippers safely to the other side of the bed over my
wife: and there safely rose, and put on my gown and breeches,
and then, with a firebrand in my hand, safely opened the door,
and saw nor heard any thing. Then (with fear, I confess), went

---

[1] *Health's Improvement* . . ., by Thomas Muffett, 1655, p. 123.

"OPENED MY CHAMBER DOOR"

to the maid's chamber-car-door, and all quiet and safe. Called Jane up, and went down safely, and opened my chamber door, where all well. Then more freely about, and to the kitchen, where the cook-maid up, and all safe. So up again, and when Jane come, and we demanded whether she heard no noise, she said, "yes, and was afeard," but rose with the other maid, and found nothing; but heard a noise in the great stack of chimnies that goes from Sir J. Minnes through our house; and so we sent, and their chimnies have been swept this morning, and the noise was that, and nothing else. It is one of the most extraordinary accidents in my life, and gives ground to think of Don Quixote's adventures how people may be surprised, and the more from an accident last night, that our young gibb-cat[1] did leap down our stairs from top to bottom at two leaps, and frighted us that we could not tell well whether it was the cat or a spirit, and do sometimes think this morning that the house might be haunted. Glad to have this so well over, and indeed really glad in my mind, for I was much afeard, I dressed myself; and to the office both forenoon and afternoon, mighty hard putting papers and things in order to my extraordinary satisfaction, and consulting my clerks in many things, who are infinite helps to my memory and reasons of things; and so being weary, and my eyes akeing, having overwrought them to-day reading so much shorthand, I home and there to supper, it being late, and to bed.

30th. Up, and to the office, where all the morning, and then by coach to Arundel House, to the election of Officers [2] for the next year; where I was near being chosen of the Council, but am glad I was not, for I could not have attended; though above all things I could wish it, and do take it as a mighty respect to have been named there. The company great and the elections long, and then to Cary House,[3] a house now of entertainment, next my Lord Ashly's; and there we, after two hours' stay sitting at the table with our napkins open, had our dinners brought, but badly done. But here was good company. I choosing to sit next Dr. Wilkins, Sir George Ent, and others whom I value there, talked of several things. Much good discourse we had. But here above all I was pleased to see the person who had his blood taken out. He speaks well, and did this day give the Society a relation thereof in Latin, saying that he finds himself much better since, and as a

[1] A tom-cat. Gibb is contracted from Gilbert.
[2] Of the Royal Society.
[3] Probably Canary House, a much-frequented coffee-house.

new man, but he is cracked a little in his head, though he speaks very reasonably, and very well. He is to have the same again tried upon him: the first sound man that ever had it tried on him in England, and but one that we hear of in France, which was a porter hired by the virtuosos. Here all the afternoon till within night, and saw a pretty deception of the sight by a glass with water poured into it, with a stick standing up with three balls of wax upon it, one distant from the other. How these balls did seem double, and disappear one after another, mighty pretty. Thence, paying our shot, 6s. apiece, I home, and there to the office and wrote my letters, and then home, my eyes very sore with yesterday's work; and so home and tried to make a piece by my eare and viall to "I wonder what the grave," &c., and so to supper and to bed, where frighted a good while and my wife again with noises, and my wife did rise twice; but I think it was Sir John Minnes's people again late cleaning their house, for it was past 1 o'clock in the morning before we could fall to sleep, and so slept. But I perceive well what the care of money and treasure in a man's house is to a man that fears to lose it.

December 3rd. Up by candlelight, the only time I think I have done so this winter, and a coach being got over night, I to Sir W. Coventry's, the first time I have seen him at his new house since he came to lodge there. At noon home to dinner, and busy all the afternoon, and at night home, and there met W. Batelier, who tells me the first great news that my Lord Chancellor is fled this day. By and by to Sir W. Pen's. But here I hear the whole; that my Lord Chancellor is gone, and left a paper behind him for the House of Lords, telling them the reason of him retiring, complaining of a design for his ruin. But the paper I must get: only the thing at present is great, and will put the King and Commons to some new counsels certainly. So home to supper and to bed. Sir W. Pen I find in much trouble this evening, having been called to the Committee this afternoon about the business of prizes. Sir Richard Ford told us this evening an odd story of the basenesse of the late Lord Mayor, Sir W. Bolton, in cheating the poor of the City out of the collections made for the people that were burned, of £1,800; of which he can give no account, and in which he hath forsworn himself plainly, so as the Court of Aldermen have sequestered him from their Court till he do bring in an account; which is the greatest piece of roguery that they say was ever found in a Lord Mayor. He says also that this day hath been made appear to them that the Keeper of Newgate, at this day, hath made his house the only nursery of rogues and pickpockets and thieves in the world, where they were bred and entertained, and the whole society met: and that for the sake of the Sheriffes they durst not this day committ him for fear of making him let out the prisoners, but are fain to go by artifice to deal with him. He tells me also speaking of the new street [1] that is to be made from Guild Hall down to Cheapside, that the ground is already most of it bought. And tells me of one particular, of a man that hath a piece of ground lieing in the very middle of the street that must be; which, when the street is cut out of it, there will remain ground enough, of each side, to build a house to front the street. He demanded £700 for the ground, and to be excused paying any thing for the melioration of the rest of his ground that he was to keep. The Court consented to give him £700, only not to abate him the consideration: which the man denied; but told them, and so they agreed, that he would excuse the City the £700 that he might have the benefit of the melioration without paying any thing for it. So much some will get by having the City burned! But he told me that in other cases ground by this means that was not 4d. a-foot before will now, when houses are built, be worth 15s. a-foot. But he tells me that the common standard now reckoned on between man and man, in places where there is no alteration of circumstances but only the houses burnt, there the ground which, with a house on it, did yield £100 a-year, is now reputed worth £33 6s. 8d.

4th. At the office all the morning. At noon to dinner, and presently with my wife abroad, whom and her girle I leave at Unthanke's, and so to White Hall in expectation of waiting on the Duke of York to-day, but was prevented therein; only at Mr. Wren's chamber there I hear that the House of Lords did send down the paper which my Lord Chancellor left behind him, directed to the Lords, to be seditious and scandalous; and the Commons have voted that it be burned by the hands of the hangman, and that the King be desired to agree to it. I do hear also that they have desired the King to use means to stop his escape out of the nation. Thence into the House, and there spied a pretty woman with spots on her face, well clad, who was enquiring for the guard chamber; I followed her, and there she went up, and turned into the turning towards the chapel, and I after her, and

[1] King Street.

upon the stairs there met her coming up again, and there kissed her twice; and her business was to enquire for Sir Edward Bishop, one of the serjeants at armes.

5th. This day, not for want, but for good husbandry, I sent my father by his desire six pair of my old shoes, which fit him and are good; yet methought it was a thing against my mind to have him wear my old things.

6th. Up, and with Sir J. Minnes to the Duke of York, the first time that I have seen him or we waited on him, since his sickness; and, blessed be God! he is not at all the worse for the smallpox, but is only a little weak yet. We did much business with him, and so parted. By and by home with Sir J. Minnes, who tells me that my Lord Clarendon did go away in a Custom-house boat, and is now at Callis: and I confess nothing seems to hang more heavy than his leaving of this unfortunate paper behind him, that hath angered both Houses, and hath I think reconciled them in that which otherwise would have broke them in pieces; so that I do hence, and from Sir W. Coventry's example and doctrine to me, learn that on these sorts of occasions there is nothing like silence; it being seldom any wrong to a man to say nothing, but, for the most part, it is to say anything.

8th. (Lord's Day.) Captain Cocke tells me, to my great satisfaction, that Sir Robert Brookes [1] did dine with him to-day; and that he told him, speaking of me, that he would make me the darling of the House of Commons, so much he is satisfied concerning me. And this Cocke did tell me that I might give him thanks for it; and I do think it may do me good, for he do happen to be held a considerable person of a young man, both for sobriety and ability.

9th. This morning I was troubled with my Lord Hinchingbroke's sending to borrow £200 of me; but I did answer that I had none, nor could borrow any; for I am resolved I will not be undone for any body, though I would do much for my Lord Sandwich, for it is to answer a bill of exchange of his; and I perceive he hath made use of all other means in the world to do it, but I am resolved to serve him, but not ruin myself, as it may be to part with so much of the little I have by me to keep if I should by any turn of times lose the rest.

[1] M.P. for Aldborough. He had been chairman of the Committee of the House before which Pepys had recently appeared.

13th. After dinner comes Mr. Moore, and he and I alone a while, he telling me my Lord Sandwich's credit is like to be undone if the bill of £200 my Lord Hinchingbroke wrote to me about be not paid to-morrow, and that if I do not help him about it they have no way but to let it be protested. So, finding that Creed hath supplied them with £150 in their straits, and that this is no bigger sum, I am very willing to serve my Lord, though not in this kind; but yet I will endeavour to get this done for them, and the rather because of some plate that was lodged the other day with me by my Lady's order, which may be in part of security for my money, as I may order it; for, for ought I see, there is no other to be hoped for. This do trouble me; but yet it is good luck that the sum is no bigger.

15th. (Lord's Day.) Busy at my chamber all the afternoon, and looking over my plate, which indeed is a very fine quantity, God knows, more than ever I expected to see of my own, and more than is fit for a man of no better quality than I am. In the evening comes Mrs. Turner to visit us, who hath been long sick, and she sat and supped with us; and after supper, her son Francke being there, now upon the point of his going to the East Indys, I did give him "Lex Mercatoria,"[1] and my wife my old pair of tweezers, which are pretty, and my book an excellent one for him. Most of our talk was of the great discourse the world hath against my Lady Batten for getting her husband to give her all and disinherit his eldest son; though the truth is, the son, as they say, did play the knave with his father when time was, and the father no great matter better with him, nor with other people also. So she gone, we to bed.

18th. Up, and to my goldsmith's in the morning, to look after the providing of £60 for Mr. Moore towards the answering of my Lord Sandwich's bill of exchange, he being come to be contented with my lending him £60 in part of it, which pleases me, I expecting to have been forced to answer the whole bill; and this which I do do I hope to secure out of the plate which was delivered into my custody of my Lord's the other day, and which I did get Mr. Stokes, the goldsmith, last night to weigh at my house, and there is enough to secure £100.

19th. Up, and to the Office, where Commissioner Middleton first took place at the Board as Surveyor of the Navy, and indeed I think will be an excellent officer; I am sure much beyond what

---

[1] *Consuetudo vel Lex Mercatoria: or the Ancient Law-Merchant,* by Gerard de Malynes.

his predecessor was. At noon, to avoid being forced to invite him to dinner, it being his first day and nobody inviting him, I did go to the 'Change with Sir W. Pen in his coach, who first went to Guildhall, whither I went with him, he to speak with Sheriff Gawden (I only for company); and did here look up and down this place, where I have not been before since the fire; and I see that the city are got a pace on in the rebuilding of Guildhall.[1] Thence to the 'Change, where I stayed very little, and so home to dinner, and there find my wife mightily out of order with her teeth.

20th. Up, and all the morning at the office. At noon home to dinner, where my poor wife in bed in mighty pain, her left cheek so swelled as that we feared it would break, and so were fain to send for Mr. Hollier, who come, and seems doubtful of the defluxions of humours that may spoil her face, if not timely cured. He laid a poultice to it and other directions, and so away, and I to the office, where very late.

21st. At the office all the morning, and at noon home to dinner with my Clerks and Creed, who among other things all alone after dinner, talking of the times, he tells me that the Nonconformists are mighty high, and their meetings frequented and connived at; and they do expect to have their day now soon, for my Lord of Buckingham is a declared friend to them, and even to the Quakers, who had very good words the other day from the King himself: and what is more, the Archbishop of Canterbury is called no more to the Cabal,[2] nor, by the way, Sir W. Coventry, which I am sorry for; the Cabal at present being, as he says, the King and Duke of Buckingham and Lord Keeper, the Duke of Albemarle and Privy Seale. He gone, I to the office, where busy till late at night, and then home to sit with my wife, who is a little better, and her cheek asswaged. I read to her out of "The History of Algiers," which is mighty pretty reading, and did discourse alone about my sister Pall's match, which is now on foot with one Jackson, another nephew of Mr. Phillips's,[3] to whom he hath left his estate.

22nd. (Lord's Day.) Up, and my wife, poor wretch, still in pain, and then to dress myself and down to my chamber to settle some papers; and thither come to me Willet with an errand from her mistress, and this time I first did give her a little kiss, she

---

[1] The Guildhall, though considerably damaged, was not destroyed by the Fire.
[2] Not the famous Cabal; the word as used here merely means the inner circle of Government officials.
[3] Mr. Ensum, Pall's earlier suitor (see Mar. 19, 1666), was related to Mr. Phillips.

being a very pretty humoured girle, and so one that I do love mightily. Thence to my office and there did a little business, and so to church, where a dull sermon, and then home, and Cozen Kate Joyce come and dined with me and Mr. Holliard; but by chance I offering occasion to him to discourse of the Church of Rome, Lord! how he run on to discourse with the greatest vehemence and importunity in the world, as the only thing in the world that he is full of, and it was good sport to me to see him so earnest on so little occasion. She come to see us and to tell me that her husband is going to build his house again and would borrow of me £300, which I shall upon good security be willing to do, and so told her, being willing to have some money out of my hands upon good security.

28th. Up, and to the office, where busy all the morning. At noon home, and there to dinner with my clerks and Mr. Pelling, and had a very good dinner, among others a haunch of venison boiled, and merry we were; and I rose soon from dinner, and with my wife and girle to the King's house, and there saw "The Mad Couple,"[1] which is but an ordinary play; but only Nell's and Hart's mad parts are most excellently done, but especially her's: which makes it a miracle to me to think how ill she do any serious part, as the other day, just like a fool or changeling, and in a mad part do beyond all imitation almost. It pleased us mightily to see the natural affection of a poor woman, the mother of one of the children brought on the stage: the child crying, she by force got upon the stage and took up her child and carried it away off of the stage from Hart. Many fine faces here to-day. Thence home, and there to the office late, and then home to supper and to bed.

29th. At night comes Mrs. Turner to see us; and there among other talk she tells me that Mr. William Pen, who is lately come over from Ireland, is a Quaker again, or some very melancholy thing; that he cares for no company, nor comes into any: which is a pleasant thing, after his being abroad so long, and his father such a hypocritical rogue, and at this time an Atheist. She gone, I to my very great content do find my accounts to come very even and naturally, and so to supper and to bed.

30th. To White Hall, and there to visit Sir G. Carteret, and there was with him a great while, and my Lady and they seem in very good humour; but by and by Sir G. Carteret and I alone, and there we did talk of the ruinous condition we are in. He tells

---

[1] By the Hon. James Howard.

me that the Duke of Buckingham do rule all now, and the Duke of York comes indeed to the Caball, but signifies little there. That this new faction do not endure, nor the King, Sir W. Coventry; but yet that he is so usefull that they cannot be without him. So after some other little discourse I away to both my booksellers, and there laid out several pounds in books now against the new year. After dinner with Sir Philip Carteret to the King's playhouse, there to see "Love's Cruelty," [1] an old play, but which I have not seen before; and in the first act Orange Moll come to me with one of my porters by my house to tell me that Mrs. Pierce and Knepp did dine at my house to-day, and that I was desired to come home. So I went out presently and by coach home, and they were just gone away: so after a very little stay with my wife I took coach again and to the King's playhouse again, and come in the fourth act. Here telling Moll how I had lost my journey, she told me that Mrs. Knepp was in the house, and so shew me to her, and I went to her and sat out the play. Thence, after sitting and talking a pretty while, I took leave and so to my bookseller's and paid for the books I had bought, and away home, where I told my wife where I had been. But she was as mad as a devil, and nothing but ill words between us all the evening while we sat at cards.

[1] By James Shirley.

NINTH YEAR

1668

January 1st. Up, and all the morning in my chamber making up some accounts against this beginning of the new year, and so about noon abroad with my wife, who was to dine with W. Hewer and Willet at Mrs. Pierce's; but I had no mind to be with them, for I do clearly find that my wife is troubled at my friendship with her and Knepp, and so dined with my Lord Crew. Here they did talk much of the present cheapness of corne, even to a miracle; so as their farmers can pay no rent, but do fling up their lands; and would pay in corne, but, which I did observe to my Lord, and he liked well of it, our gentry are grown so ignorant in every thing of good husbandry that they know not how to bestow this corne: which, did they understand but a little trade, they would be able to joyne together and know what markets there are abroad and send it thither, and thereby ease their tenants and be able to pay themselves. Thence I after dinner to the Duke of York's playhouse, and there saw "Sir Martin Marall;"[1] which I have seen so often. Thence I to White Hall, and there walked up and down the house a while. By and by I met with Mr. Brisband, and having it in my mind this Christmas to go to see the manner of the gaming at the Groome-Porter's,[2] I did tell Brisband of it, and he did lead me thither: where, after staying an hour, they begun to play at about eight at night, where to see how differently one man took his losing from another, one cursing and swearing, and another only muttering and grumbling to himself, a third without any apparent discontent at all; to see how the dice will run good luck in one hand for half an hour together, and another have no good luck at all; to see how easily here, where they play nothing but guinnys, a £100 is won or lost; to see two or three gentlemen come in there drunk, and putting their stock of gold together, one 22 pieces, the second 4, and the third 5 pieces, and these to play one with another, and forget how much each of them brought, but he that brought the 22 thinks

[1] By the Duke of Newcastle, probably adapted by Dryden. Pepys had seen it on August 16 last, and recorded that his head ached all the evening and night with laughing.
[2] The Groom Porter was the Court official in charge of the gaming tables.

"THE GAMESTERS"

that he brought no more than the rest; to see the different humours of gamesters to change their luck when it is bad, how ceremonious they are as to call for new dice, to shift their places, to alter their manner of throwing, and that with great industry, as if there was anything in it; to see how some old gamesters that have no money now to spend as formerly do come and sit and look on as among others, Sir Lewis Dives, who was here, and hath been a great gamester in his time; to hear their cursing and damning to no purpose, as one man being to throw a seven if he could, and failing to do it after a great many throws cried he would be damned if ever he flung seven more while he lived, his despair of throwing it being so great, while others did it as their luck served almost every throw; to see how persons of the best quality do here sit down and play with people of any, though meaner; and to see how people in ordinary clothes shall come hither and play away 100, or 2 or 300 guinnys, without any kind of difficulty; and lastly, to see the formality of the groome-porter, who is their judge of all disputes in play and all quarrels that may arise therein, and how his under-officers are there to observe true play at each table, and to give new dice, is a consideration I never could have thought had been in the world, had I not now seen it.   And mighty glad I am that I did see it, and it may be will find another evening before Christmas be over to see it again, when I may stay later, for their heat of play begins not till about eleven or twelve o'clock; which did give me another pretty observation of a man, that did win mighty fast when I was there.   I think he won £100 at single pieces in a little time.   While all the rest envied him his good fortune he cursed it, saying, "A pox on it, that it should come so early upon me, for this fortune two hours hence would be worth something to me, but then, God damn me, I shall have no such luck."   This kind of prophane, mad entertainment they give themselves.   And so I, having enough for once, refusing to venture, though Brisband pressed me hard, and tempted me with saying that no man was ever known to lose the first time, the devil being too cunning to discourage a gamester; and he offered me also to lend me ten pieces to venture, but I did refuse, and so went away, and took coach and home about 9 or 10 at night.

2nd.   This day my wife shows me a locket of dyamonds worth about £40, which W. Hewer do press her to accept, and hath done for a good while, out of his gratitude for my kindness and her's to him.   But I do not like that she should receive it, it not being honourable for me to do it; and so do desire her to force him to take it back again, he leaving it against her will yesterday with her. And she did this evening force him to take it back, at which she says he is troubled; but however it becomes me more to refuse it than to let her accept of it, and so I am well pleased with her returning it him.

10th. This day I received a letter from my father, and another from my cozen Roger Pepys, who have had a view of Jackson's evidences of his estate, and do mightily like of the man and his condition and estate, and do advise me to accept of the match for my sister and to finish it as soon as I can; and he do it so as, I confess, I am contented to have it done, and so give her her portion.[1]

17th. My Lord Hinchingbroke hath been married this week to my Lord Burlington's daughter, and I mighty glad of it, though I am not satisfied that I have not a Favour sent me. But I am mighty glad that the thing is done.

21st. Up, and while at the office comes news from Kate Joyce that if I would see her husband alive, I must come presently. So after the office was up I to him and W. Hewer with me, and find him in his sick bed (I never was at their house, this Inne, before) very sensible in discourse and thankful for my kindness to him, and his breath rattled in his throate, and they did lay pigeons to his feet while I was in the house, and all despair of him, and with good reason. But the story is that it seems on Thursday last he went sober and quiet out of doors in the morning to Islington, and behind one of the inns, the White Lion, did fling himself into a pond, was spied by a poor woman and got out by some people binding up hay in a barn there, and set on his head and got to life, and known by a woman coming that way; and so his wife and friends sent for. He confessed his doing the thing, being led by the Devil, and do declare his reason to be his trouble that he found in having forgot to serve God as he ought, since he come to this new employment:[2] and I believe that, and the sense of his great loss by the fire, did bring him to it, and so everybody concludes. He stayed there all that night and come home by coach next morning, and there grew sick, and worse and worse to this day. I stayed awhile among the friends that were there, and they being now in fear that the goods and estate would be seized on, though

[1] This time the match succeeded, and the second son of the marriage, John Jackson, became Pepys' heir. The unhappy Pall was the only one of Pepys' family to produce any children.
[2] He kept the Three Stags tavern at Holborn Conduit.

he lived all this while, because of his endeavouring to drown himself, my cozen did endeavour to remove what she could of plate out of the house, and desired me to take my flagons; which I was glad of, and did take them away with me in great fear all the way of being seized; though there was no reason for it, he not being dead, but yet so fearful I was. So home, and there eat my dinner, and busy all the afternoon, and troubled at this business. In the evening with Sir D. Gawden, to Guild Hall, to advise with the Towne-Clerke about the practice of the City and nation in this case: and he thinks that it cannot be found selfe-murder; but if it be, it will fall, all the estate, to the King. So we parted, and I to my cozen's again; where I no sooner come but news was brought down from his chamber that he was departed. So, at their entreaty, I presently took coach to White Hall, and there find Sir W. Coventry; and he carried me to the King, the Duke of York being with him, and there told my story which I had told him: and the King, without more ado granted that, if it was found, the estate should be to the widow and children. So away back again to my cozen's, and when I come thither I find her all in sorrow; but she and the rest mightily pleased with my doing this for them.

22nd. Up, mightily busy all the morning at the office. At noon with Lord Brouncker to Sir D. Gawden's, at the Victualling Office, to dinner, where I have not dined since he was Sheriff. He expected us, and a good dinner, and much good company; and a fine house, and especially two rooms, very fine, he hath built there. His lady a good lady; but my Lord led himself and me to a great absurdity in kissing all the ladies but the finest of all the company, leaving her out, I know not how; and I was loath to do it, since he omitted it. This day come the first demand from the Commissioners of Accounts to us, and it contains more than we shall ever be able to answer while we live, and I do foresee we shall be put to much trouble and some shame, at least some of us. Thence stole away after dinner to my cozen Kate's, and there find the Crowner's jury sitting, but they could not end it, but put off the business. Thence, after sitting with her and company a while, comforting her: though I can find she can, as all other women, cry, and yet talk of other things all in a breath. So home, and there to cards with my wife, Deb.,[1] and Betty Turner and Batelier, and after supper late to sing. But, Lord! how did I please myself to make Betty Turner sing, to see what a beast she is as

[1] Deb. (Deborah) was the Christian name of Mrs. Pepys' maid Willett.

to singing, not knowing how to sing one note in tune; but, only for the experiment, I would not for 40s. hear her sing a tune: worse than my wife a thousand times, so that it do a little reconcile me to her. So late to bed.

27th. Mr. Povy tells me the Duchesse is a devil against him, and do now come like Queen Elizabeth and sits with the Duke of York's Council and sees what they do. And she crosses out this man's wages and prices, as she sees fit, for saving money; but yet he tells me she reserves £5,000 a-year for her own spending. And my Lady Peterborough tells me that the Duchesse do lay up, mightily, jewells.

31st. Up, and by coach, with W. Griffin with me, and our Contract-books, to the Commissioners for Accounts, the first time I ever was there, and staid awhile before I was admitted to them. Presently I was called in, where I found the whole number of Commissioners, and was there received with great respect and kindness, and did give them great satisfaction. They did ask many questions, and demanded other books of me, which I did give them very ready and acceptable answers to; and upon the whole I observe they do go about their business like men resolved to go through with it, and in a very good method, like men of understanding. This day Griffin did in discourse tell me that it is observed, and is true, in the late fire of London, that the fire burned just as many Parish-Churches as there were hours from the beginning to the end of the fire; and next, that there were just as many Churches left standing as there were taverns left standing in the rest of the City that was not burned, being I think he told me, thirteen in all of each: which is pretty to observe.

February 6th. To the Duke of York's playhouse; where a new play of Etherige's,[1] called "She Would if she Could"; and though I was there by two o'clock, there was 1000 people put back that could not have room in the pit: and I at last, because my wife was there, made shift to get into the 18d. box, and there saw; but, Lord! how full was the house, and how silly the play, there being nothing in the world good in it, and few people pleased in it.

7th. To Westminster Hall, and there met my cozen, Roger Pepys, and he tells me that Mr. Jackson, my sister's servant, is come to town. The young man is gone out of the Hall, so I could not now see him. Thence to the Commissioners of Accounts and there presented my books, and was made to sit down and used

---

[1] Sir George Etherege, the celebrated wit and man of fashion.

with much respect. I find these gentlemen to sit all day and only eat a bit of bread at noon, and a glass of wine; and are resolved to go through their business with great severity and method. Thence I about two o'clock to Westminster Hall by appointment, and there met my cozen Roger again, and Mr. Jackson, who is a plain young man, handsome enough for Pall, one of no education nor discourse, but of few words, and one altogether that I think will please me well enough. My cozen had got me to give the odd sixth £100 presently, which I intended to keep to the birth of the first child. And let it go. I shall be eased of the care. And so after little talk we parted, resolving to dine together at my house to-morrow. So there parted, my mind pretty well satisfied with this plain fellow for my sister, though I shall, I see, have no pleasure nor content in him, as if he had been a man of reading and parts, like Cumberland; and to the Swan, and there sent for a bit of meat and eat and drank, and so to White Hall to the Duke of York's chamber, where I find him and my fellows at their usual meeting, discoursing about securing the Medway this year, which is to shut the door after the horse is stole. However, it is good.

10th. With Creed home to my house to dinner, where I met with Mr. Jackson, and find my wife angry with Deb., which vexes me. After dinner by coach away to Westminster, taking up a friend of Mr. Jackson's, a young lawyer, and parting with Creed at White Hall. They and I to Westminster Hall, and there met Roger Pepys, and with him to his chamber, and there read over and agreed upon the Deed of Settlement to our minds. Thence I to the Temple to Charles Porter's lodgings, where Captain Cocke met me, and after long waiting on Pemberton, an able lawyer, about the business of our prizes, left the matter with him to think of against to-morrow.

11th. At the office all the morning, where comes a damned summons to attend the Committee of Miscarriages to-day, which makes me mad that I should by my place become the hackney of this Office, in perpetual trouble and vexation, that need it least. At noon home to dinner, where little pleasure, my head being split almost with the variety of troubles upon me at this time, and cares; and after dinner by coach to Westminster Hall, and sent my wife and Deb. to see "Mustapha" [1] acted. Here I brought a book to the Committee, and do find them mighty hot

[1] By Lord Orrery.

in the business of tickets, which makes me mad to see them bite at the stone, and not at the hand that flings it. To the Temple, to Porter's chamber where Cocke met me, and after a stay there some time, they two and I to Pemberton's chamber and there did read over the Act calling people to account, and did discourse all our business of the prizes. He do make it plainly appear, that there is no avoiding to give these Commissioners satisfaction in everything they will ask; and that there is fear lest they may find reason to make us refund for all the extraordinary profit made by those bargains. It was pretty here to see the heaps of money upon this lawyer's table; and more to see how he had not since last night spent any time upon our business, but begun with telling us that we were not at all concerned in that Act; which was a total mistake, by his not having read over the Act at all.

This morning my wife in bed told me the story of our Tom and Jane: how the rogue did first demand her consent to love and marry him, and then, with pretence of displeasing me, did slight her; but both he and she have confessed the matter to her, and she hath charged him to go on with his love to her and be true to her; and so I think the business will go on, which, for my love to her, because she is in love with him, I am pleased with.

14th. (Valentine's day.) Up, being called up by Mercer, who come to be my Valentine, and so I rose and my wife, and were merry a little, I staying to talk, and did give her a guinny in gold for her Valentine's gift. I to my Office to perfect my Narrative about prize-goods, and did carry it to the Commissioners of Accounts, who did receive it with great kindness, and express great value of, and respect to me: and my heart is at rest that it is lodged there in so full truth and plainness, though it may hereafter prove some loss to me. I was told to-night that my Lady Castlemayne is so great a gamester as to have won £15,000 in one night and lost £25,000 in another night at play, and hath played £1,000 and £1,500 at a cast.

18th. To see Kate Joyce, where I find her in great ease of mind, the Jury having this day given in their verdict that her husband died of a feaver. So all trouble is now over, and she safe in her estate.

23rd. (Lord's Day.) This evening my wife did with great pleasure shew me her stock of jewells, encreased by the ring she hath made lately as my Valentine's gift this year, a Turky stone [1]

---

[1] Turquoise.

set with diamonds: and, with this and what she had, she reckons that she hath above £150 worth of jewells of one kind or other; and I am glad of it, for it is fit the wretch should have something to content herself with.

24th.   Up, and to my office, where most of the morning.   Thence about noon with my wife to the New Exchange, by the way stopping at my bookseller's, and there leaving my Kircher's Musurgia to be bound, and did buy "L'illustre Bassa," [1] in four volumes, for my wife.   Thence to the Exchange and left her, while meeting Dr. Gibbons [2] there; he and I to see an organ at the Dean of Westminster's lodgings at the Abby, the Bishop of Rochester's, where he lives like a great prelate, his lodgings being very good, though at present under great disgrace at Court, being put by his Clerk of the Closet's place.   I saw his lady, of whom the *Terræ Filius* of Oxford was once so merry; [3] and two children, whereof one a very pretty little boy, like him, so fat and black.   Here I saw the organ; but it is too big for my house, and the fashion do not please me enough, and therefore will not have it.   Thence to the 'Change back again, leaving him, and took my wife and Deb. home, and there to dinner alone; and after dinner I took them to the Nursery, [4] where none of us ever were before where the house is better and the musique better than we looked for, and the acting not much worse, because I expected as bad as could be: and I was not much mistaken, for it was so.   Their play was a bad one, called "Jeronimo is Mad Again," a tragedy.   I was prettily served this day at the playhouse-door, where, giving six shillings into the fellow's hand for us three, the fellow by legerdemain did convey one away, and with so much grace faced me down that I did give him but five, that though I knew the contrary yet I was overpowered by his so grave and serious demanding the other shilling, that I could not deny him, but was forced by myself to give it him.

27th.   All the morning at the office, and at noon home to dinner, and thence with my wife and Deb. to the King's House to see "The Virgin Martyr," [5] the first time it hath been acted a great while, and it is mighty pleasant; not that the play is worth much, but it is finely acted by Becke Marshal.   But that which did

[1] By Magdaleine de Scudéri.
[2] Christopher Gibbons, organist of Westminster Abbey.
[3] The *terrae filius* was a scholar appointed to make a satirical and jesting speech at an Act in the University of Oxford.
[4] Killigrew had established a training school for the King's Players at the Barbican; and Davenant had one in Hatton Garden for the Duke's Players.   This play was by James Shirley.
[5] By Massinger and Dekker.

please me beyond any thing in the whole world was the wind-musique when the angel comes down, which is so sweet that it ravished me, and indeed, in a word, did wrap up my soul so that it made me really sick, just as I have formerly been when in love with my wife; that neither then, nor all the evening going home, and at home, I was able to think of any thing, but remained all night transported, so as I could not believe that ever any musick hath that real command over the soul of a man as this did upon me: and makes me resolve to practice wind-musique, and to make my wife do the like.

28th. Up, and to the office, where all the morning doing business, and after dinner with Sir W. Pen to White Hall, where we and the rest of us presented a great letter of the state of our want of money to his Royal Highness. While we were thus together with the Duke of York, comes in Mr. Wren from the House, where, he tells us, another storm hath been all this day almost against the Officers of the Navy upon this complaint; that though they have made good rules for payment of tickets, yet that they have not observed them themselves; which was driven so high as to have it urged that we should presently be put out of our places, and so they have at last ordered that we shall be heard at the bar of the House upon this business on Thursday next. This did mightily trouble me and us all; but me particularly, who am least able to bear these troubles, though I have the least cause to be concerned in it.

March 1st. (Lord's Day.) Up very betimes, and by coach to Sir W. Coventry's; and there, largely carrying with me all my notes and papers, did run over our whole defence in the business of tickets, in order to the answering the House on Thursday next; and I do think, unless they be set without reason to ruin us, we shall make a good defence. Thence home, and there my mind being a little lightened by my morning's work I to talk with my wife; and in lieu of a coach this year I have got my wife to be contented with her closet being made up this summer, and going into the country this summer for a month or two to my father's, and there Mercer and Deb. and Jane shall go with her, which I the rather do for the entertaining my wife and preventing of fallings out between her and my father or Deb., which uses to be the fate of her going into the country.

2nd. This day I have the news that my sister was married on Thursday last to Mr. Jackson; so that work is, I hope, well over.

4th. Fell to my work at the office, shutting the doors, that we, I and my clerks, might not be interrupted; and so, only with room for a little dinner, we very busy all the day till night that the officers met for me to give them the heads of what I intended to say, which I did, with great discontent to see them all rely on me that have no reason at all to trouble myself about it, nor have any thanks from them for my labour; but contrarily Brouncker looked mighty dogged, as thinking that I did not intend to do it so as to save him. This troubled me so much as, together with the shortness of the time and muchness of the business, did let me be at it till but about ten at night, and then quite weary and dull and vexed I could go no further, but resolved to leave the rest to to-morrow morning; and so in full discontent and weariness did give over and went home, without supper vexed and sickish to bed, and there slept about three hours; but then waked, and never in so much trouble in all my life of mind, thinking of the task I have upon me, and upon what dissatisfactory grounds, and what the issue of it may be to me.

5th. With these thoughts I lay troubling myself till six o'clock, restless, and at last getting my wife to talk to me to comfort me, which she at last did, and made me resolve to quit my hands of this Office, and endure the trouble of it no longer than till I can clear myself of it. So with great trouble, but yet with some ease from this discourse with my wife, I up and to my Office, whither come my clerks; and so I did huddle, the best I could, some more notes for my discourse to-day, and by nine o'clock was ready, and did go down to the Old Swan, and there by boat, with T. Hater and W. Hewer with me, to Westminster, where I found myself come time enough, and my brethren all ready. But I full of thoughts and trouble touching the issue of this day; and, to comfort myself did go to the Dog and drink half-a-pint of mulled sack, and in the Hall did drink a dram of brandy at Mrs. Hewlett's; and with the warmth of this did find myself in better order as to courage, truly. So we all up to the lobby; and between eleven and twelve o'clock were called in, with the mace before us, into the House, where a mighty full House; and we stood at the bar, namely, Brouncker, Sir J. Minnes, Sir T. Harvey and myself, W. Pen being in the House, as a Member. I perceive the whole House was full, and full of expectation of our defence what it would be, and with great prejudice. After the Speaker had told us the dissatisfaction of the House and read the Report of the Committee, I began our defence most accept-

PEPYS BEFORE PARLIAMENT

ably and smoothly, and continued at it without any hesitation or losse, but with full scope, and all my reason free about me as if it had been at my own table, from that time till past three in the afternoon, and so ended, without any interruption from the Speaker; but we withdrew. And there all my Fellow-Officers, and all the world that was within hearing did congratulate me, and cry up my speech as the best thing they ever heard; and my Fellow-Officers overjoyed in it. We were called in again by and by to answer only one question, touching our paying tickets to ticket-mongers, and so out; and we were in hopes to have had a vote this day in our favour, and so the generality of the House was; but my speech being so long, many had gone out to dinner and come in again half drunk; and then there are two or three that are professed enemies to us and every body else: these did rise up and speak against the coming to a vote now. So that they put it off to to-morrow come se'nnight. However it is plain we have got great ground, and everybody says I have got the most honour that any could have had opportunity of getting; and so with our hearts mightily overjoyed at this success, we all to dinner to Lord Brouncker's, that is to say myself, T. Harvey and W. Pen, and there dined.

6th. Up betimes, and with Sir D. Gawden to Sir W. Coventry's chamber, where the first word he said to me was, "Good-morrow, Mr. Pepys, that must be Speaker of the Parliament-house:" and did protest I had got honour for ever in Parliament. He said that his brother that sat by him admires me; and another gentleman said that I could not get less than £1,000 a-year if I would put on a gown and plead at the Chancery-bar; but, what pleases me most, he tells me that the Sollicitor-Generall [1] did protest that he thought I spoke the best of any man in England. After several talks with him alone touching his own businesses, he carried me to White Hall and there parted; and I to the Duke of York's lodgings, and find him going to the Park, it being a very fine morning, and I after him; and as soon as he saw me he told me with great satisfaction that I had converted a great many yesterday, and did with great praise of me go on with the discourse with me. And by and by overtaking the King, the King and Duke of York come to me both; and he said, "Mr. Pepys, I am very glad of your success yesterday;" and fell to talk of my well speaking, and many of the Lords there. My Lord Barkeley did cry me up for what they had heard of it; and others, Parliament-men there

---

[1] Sir Heneage Finch.

about the King, did say that they never heard such a speech in their lives delivered in that manner. Progers of the Bedchamber swore to me afterwards before Brouncker in the afternoon that he did tell the King that he thought I might teach the Sollicitor-Generall. Every body that saw me almost come to me, with such eulogys as cannot be expressed. From thence I went to Westminster Hall, where I met Mr. G. Montagu, who come to me and kissed me, and told me that he had often heretofore kissed my hands, but now he would kiss my lips: protesting that I was another Cicero, and said all the world said the same of me. Mr. Ashburnham, and every creature I met there of the Parliament, or that knew anything of the Parliament's actings, did salute me with this honour: Mr. Godolphin; Mr. Sands, who swore he would go twenty mile at any time to hear the like again, and that he never saw so many sit four hours together to hear any man in his life as there did to hear me; Mr. Chichly; Sir John Duncomb; and everybody do say that the kingdom will ring of my abilities and that I have done myself right for my whole life; and so Captain Cocke and others of my friends say that no man had ever such an opportunity of making his abilities known; and, that I may cite all at once, Mr. Lieutenant of the Tower did tell me that Mr. Vaughan did protest to him, and that, in his hearing it, said so to the Duke of Albemarle, and afterwards to W. Coventry, that he had sat twenty-six years in Parliament and never heard such a speech there before: for which the Lord God make me thankful! and that I may make use of it not to pride and vain-glory, but that now I have this esteem I may do nothing that may lessen it.

11th. To my Lady Jem. in Lincoln's Inn Fields to get her to appoint the day certain when she will come and dine with me, and she hath appointed Saturday next.

13th. Up betimes to my office, where to fit myself for attending the Parliament again, not to make any more speech (which while my fame is good I will avoid, for fear of losing it) but only to answer to what objections will be made against us. Thence walked to the Old Swan and drank at Michell's, whose house is going up apace. Here I saw Betty, but could not baiser la, and so to Westminster, there to the Hall, where my Lord Brouncker and the rest waiting till noon and not called for by the House; and at noon all of us to Chatelin's, the French house in Covent Garden, to dinner, Brouncker, J. Minnes, W. Pen, T. Harvey and myself: and there had a dinner cost us 8s. 6d. a-piece, a damned base dinner which did not please us at all, so that I am not fond of this house at all, but do rather choose the Beare. After dinner to White Hall to the Duke of York, and there did our usual business. And I, my head being full of to-morrow's dinner, to my Lord Crew's, there to invite Sir Thomas Crew; and there met with my Lord Hinching-broke and his lady, the first time I spoke to her. I saluted her, and she mighty civil: and, with my Lady Jemimah, do all resolve to be very merry to-morrow at my house. My Lady Hinchingbroke I cannot say is a beauty, nor ugly, but is altogether a comely lady enough and seems very good-humoured, and I mighty glad of the occasion of seeing her before to-morrow. Thence home, and there find one laying of my napkins against to-morrow in figures of all sorts, which is might pretty; and it seems it is his trade and he gets much money by it, and do now and then furnish tables with plate and linen for a feast at so much, which is mighty pretty, and a trade I could not have thought of. Thence I to Mrs. Turner and did get her to go along with me to the French pewterer's, and there did buy some new pewter against to-morrow; and thence to White Hall to have got a cook of her acquaintance, the best in England, as she says. But after we had with much ado found him he could not come, nor was Mr. Gentleman in town, whom next I would have had, nor would Mrs. Stone let her man Lewis come, so that I was at a mighty loss what in the world to do for a cooke, Philips being out of town. At last Levett as a great kindness did resolve he would leave his business and come himself, which set me in great ease in my mind, and so home.

14th. Up very betimes, and with Jane to Levett's, there to conclude upon our dinner, and thence to the pewterer's to buy a pewter sesterne, which I have ever hitherto been without, and so up and down upon several occasions to set matters in order. Anon comes my company, viz., my Lord Hinchingbroke and his lady, Sir Philip Carteret and his lady, Godolphin and my cozen Roger, and Creed: and mighty merry; and by and by to dinner, which was very good and plentifull: (I should have said, and Mr. George Montagu, who come at a very little warning, which was exceeding kind of him). And there among other things my Lord had Sir Samuel Morland's late invention for casting up of sums of £. *s. d.*, which is very pretty, but not very useful. Most of our discourse was of my Lord Sandwich and his family, as being all of us of the family; and with extraordinary pleasure all the afternoon, thus together eating and looking over my closet: and my Lady Hinchingbroke I find a very sweet-natured and well-disposed lady, a lover of books and pictures, and of good understanding.

18th. By coach to my bookseller's and to several places to pay my debts, and to Ducke Lane and there bought Montaigne's Essays in English, and so away home to dinner. And after dinner with W. Pen to White Hall, where we and my Lord Brouncker attended the Council to discourse about the fitness of entering of men presently for the manning of the fleete, before one ship is in condition to receive them; the King crying very sillily, "If ever you intend to man the fleete without being cheated by the captains and pursers you may go to bed and resolve never to have it manned." Before I began to say anything in this matter the King and the Duke of York, talking at the Council-table before all the Lords, of the Committee of Miscarriages, how this entering of men before the ships could be ready would be reckoned a miscarriage, "Why," says the King, "it is then but Mr. Pepys making of another speech to them;" which made all the Lords (and there were by also the Atturny and Sollicitor-General), look upon me. Thence Sir W. Coventry, W. Pen and I by hackney-coach to take a little ayre in Hyde Parke, the first time I have been there this year; and we did meet many coaches going and coming, it being mighty pleasant weather. Thence home, and there, in favour to my eyes, stayed at home, reading the ridiculous History of my Lord Newcastle wrote by his wife, which shews her to be a mad, conceited, ridiculous woman, and he an asse to suffer her to write what she writes to him and of him.[1] Betty Turner sent my wife the book to read, and it being a fair print, to ease my eyes, which would be reading, I read that. Anon comes Mrs. Turner and sat and talked with us. So to bed, my eyes being very bad; and I know not how in the world to abstain from reading.

19th. This afternoon I was surprized with a letter without a name to it, very well writ, in a good stile, giving me notice of my cozen Kate Joyce's being likely to ruin herself by marriage, and by ill reports already abroad of her; and I do fear that this keeping of an inne may spoil her, being a young and pretty comely woman, and thought to be left well. I did answer the letter with thanks and good liking, and am resolved to take the advice he gives me,

---

[1] Mrs. Evelyn, in a letter to Dr. Bohun, writes of her: "Her mien surpasses the imagination of poets . . . ; her gracious bows, seasonable nods, courteous stretching out of her hands, twinkling of her eyes, and various gestures of approbation, show what may be expected from her discourse, which is airy, empty, whimsical, and rambling as her books, aiming at science difficulties, high notions, terminating commonly in nonsense, oaths and obscenity."

and go see her and find out what I can: but if she will ruin herself I cannot help it, though I should be troubled for it.

20th. Saving my eyes at my chamber all the evening pricking down some things, and trying some conclusions upon my viall in order to the inventing a better theory of musique than hath yet been abroad; and I think verily I shall do it.

22nd. (Easter day.) I up, and walked to the Temple, and there got a coach and to White Hall. After hearing the service at the King's chapel, by coach home to dinner, where Kate Joyce was, as I invited her, and had a good dinner, only she and us; and after dinner she and I alone to talk about her business, as I designed; and I find her very discreet, and she assures me she neither do nor will incline to the doing anything towards marriage, without my advice, and did tell me that she had many offers, and that Harman and his friends would fain have her; but he is poor and hath poor friends, and so it will not be advisable: but that there is another, a tobacconist, one Holinshed, whom she speaks well of, to be a plain sober man and in good condition, that offers her very well, and submits to me my examining and inquiring after it if I see good; which I do like of it, for it will be best for her to marry, I think, as soon as she can, at least to be rid of this house, for the trade will not agree with a young widow that is a little handsome: at least ordinary people think her so.

26th. Up betimes to the office, where by and by my Lord Brouncker and I met and made an end of our business. So I away with him to Mrs. Williams's, and there dined, and thence I alone to the Duke of York's house, to see the new play, called "The Man is the Master,"[1] where the house was, it being not above one o'clock, very full. But my wife and Deb. being there before, with Mrs. Pierce and Betty Turner, whom my wife carried with her, they made me room; and there I sat, it costing me 8*s.* upon them in oranges, at 6*d.* a-piece. By and by the King come, and we sat just under him, so that I durst not turn my back all the play. Thence by agreement we all of us to the Blue Balls, hard by, whither Mr. Pierce also goes with us, who met us at the play; and anon comes Manuel and his wife, and Knepp and Harris, who brings with him Mr. Banister, the great master of musique; and after much difficulty in getting of musique, we to dancing, and then to a supper of some French dishes, which yet did not please me, and then to dance and sing; and mighty merry we were till about

[1] By Sir Wm. Davenant.

eleven or twelve at night, with mighty great content in all my company; and I did, as I love to do, enjoy myself in my pleasure as being the height of what we take pains for and can hope for in this world, and therefore to be enjoyed while we are young and capable of these joys. My wife extraordinary fine to-day in her flower tabby suit, bought a year and more ago, before my mother's death put her into mourning, and so not worn till this day, and everybody in love with it; and indeed she is very fine and handsome in it. I having paid the reckoning, which come to almost £4, we parted: my company and William Batelier, who was also with us, home in a coach round by the Wall, where we met so many stops by the Watches that it cost us much time and some trouble, and more money to every Watch to them to drink.

This noon my Lord Brouncker sent to Somersett House to hear how the Duchess of Richmond do, and word was brought him that she is pretty well, but mighty full of the smallpox.

27th. My wife and I had a small squabble, but I first this day tried the effect of my silence and not provoking her when she is in an ill humour, and do find it very good, for it prevents its coming to that height on both sides which used to exceed what was fit between us.

30th. Up betimes, and so to the office, there to do business till about ten o'clock; and then out with my wife and Deb. and W. Hewer by coach to Common-garden Coffee-house, where by appointment I was to meet Harris; which I did, and also Mr. Cooper, the great painter, and Mr. Hales: and thence presently to Mr. Cooper's house,[1] to see some of his work, which is all in little, but so excellent as, though I must confess I do think the colouring of the flesh to be a little forced, yet the painting is so extraordinary as I do never expect to see the like again. Here I did see Mrs. Stewart's [2] picture as when a young maid, and now just done before her having the smallpox: and it would make a man weep to see what she was then and what she is like to be, by people's discourse, now. Here I saw my Lord Generall's picture, and my Lord Arlington and Ashly's, and several others. At noon by appointment to Cursitor's Alley, in Chancery Lane, to meet Captain Cocke and some other creditors of the Navy, and there dined; all concluded that the bane of the Parliament hath been the leaving off the old custom of the places allowing wages to those that served

---

1 Samuel Cooper lived in Henrietta Street, Covent Garden.
2 Duchess of Richmond.

them in Parliament, by which they chose men that understood their business and would attend it, and they could expect an account from, which now they cannot.

31st. Up pretty betimes and to the office, where we sat all the morning, and at noon I home to dinner, where uncle Thomas dined with me, as he do every quarter, and I paid him his pension; and also comes Mr. Hollier a little fuddled, and so did talk nothing but Latin, and laugh, that it was very good sport to see a sober man in such a humour, though he was not drunk to scandal. At dinner comes a summons for this office and the Victualler to attend a Committee of Parliament this afternoon, with Sir D. Gawden, which I accordingly did. Having given them good satisfaction I away thence, up and down, wanting a little to see whether I could get Mrs. Burroughes out, but elle being in the shop ego did speak con her much, she could not then go far and so I took coach and away to Unthanke's, and there took up my wife and Deb., and to the Park, where, being in a hackney, and they undressed, was ashamed to go into the tour, but went round the park; and so with pleasure home, where Mr. Pelling come and sat and talked late with us, and he being gone, I called Deb. to take pen, ink, and paper and write down what things come into my head for my wife to do in order to her going into the country; and the girl, writing not so well as she would do, cried, and her mistress construed it to be sullenness, and so away angry with her too; but going to bed she undressed me, and there I did give her good advice and baiser la, elle weeping still.

April 2nd. Up, after much pleasant talk with my wife, and upon some alterations I will make in my house in her absence, and I do intend to lay out some money thereon. So she and I up, and she got her ready to be gone; and by and by comes Betty Turner and her mother and W. Batelier, and they and Deb., to whom I did give 10s. this morning, to oblige her to please her mistress (and ego did baiser her mouche), and also Jane, and so in two coaches set out about eight o'clock towards the carrier, there for to take coach for my father's. With Lord Brouncker to the Royall Society, where they were just done; but there I was forced to subscribe to the building of a College, and did give £40; and several others did subscribe, some greater and some less sums, but several I saw hang off: and I doubt it will spoil the Society, for it breeds faction and ill-will, and becomes burdensome to some that cannot or would not do it. Here to my great content I did try the use of the Otacousticon,[1] which was only a great glass bottle broke at the bottom, putting the neck to my eare, and there I did plainly hear the dashing of the oares of the boats in the Thames to Arundell gallery window, which without it I could not in the least do, and may, I believe, be improved to a great height, which I am mighty glad of.

4th. Up betimes, and by coach towards White Hall, and took Aldgate Street in my way, and there called upon one Hayward that makes virginalls, and did there like of a little espinette and will have him finish it for me: for I had a mind to a small harpsichon, but this takes up less room, and will do my business as to finding out of chords, and I am very well pleased that I have found it. After dinner Sir W. Pen and I away by water to White Hall, and there did attend the Duke of York, and he did carry us to the King's lodgings: but he was asleep in his closet; so we stayed in the Green-Roome, where the Duke of York did tell us what rules he had of knowing the weather and did now tell us we should have rain before to-morrow, it having been a dry season for some time, and so it did rain all night almost; and pretty rules he hath, and told Brouncker and me some of them, which were such as no reason seems ready to be given.

6th. At noon to Mr. George Montagu's to dinner, being invited by him in the hall, and there mightily made of, even to great trouble to me to be so commended before my face, with that flattery and importunity that I was quite troubled with it. Yet he is a fine gentleman, truly, and his lady a fine woman; and, among many sons that I saw there, there was a little daughter that is mighty pretty, of which he is infinite fond: and after dinner did make her play on the gittar and sing, which she did mighty prettily, and seems to have a mighty musical soul, keeping time with most excellent spirit. Here I met with Mr. Brownlow, my old school-fellow, who come thither I suppose as a suitor to one of the young ladies that were there, and a sober man he seems to be. Here I do hear as a great secret that the King, and Duke of York and Duchesse, and my Lady Castlemayne, are now all agreed in a strict league, and all things like to go very current, and that it is not impossible to have my Lord Clarendon in time here again.

May 6th. Up, and to the office, and thence to White Hall, but come too late to see the Duke of York with whom my business was, and so to Westminster Hall, where met with several

[1] Ear-trumpet.

people and talked with them. Here met with Mrs. Washington, my old acquaintance of the Hall, whose husband has a place in the Excise at Windsor and it seems lives well. I have not seen her these 8 or 9 years, and she begins to grow old, I perceive, visibly. So time do alter, and do doubtless the like in myself. This morning the House is upon the City Bill, and they say hath passed it, though I am sorry that I did not think to put somebody in mind of moving for the churches to be allotted according to the convenience of the people, and not to gratify this Bishop, or that College.

7th. Up, and to the office, where all the morning. At noon home to dinner, and thither I sent for Mercer to dine with me; and after dinner she and I called Mrs. Turner, and I carried them to the Duke of York's house, and there saw "The Man's the Master," which proves a very good play. Thence called Knepp from the King's house, where going in for her, the play being done, I did see Beck Marshall come dressed off of the stage, and looks mighty fine and pretty and noble: and also Nell in her boy's clothes, mighty pretty. But, Lord! their confidence! and how many men do hover about them as soon as they come off the stage, and how confident they are in their talk! Here I did kiss the pretty woman newly come, called Pegg, a mighty pretty woman. Here took up Knepp into our coach, and all of us with her to her lodgings, and thither comes Bannister with a song of her's. Here was also Haynes, the incomparable dancer of the King's house, and a seeming civil man, and sings pretty well, and they gone, we abroad to Marrowbone, and there walked in the garden,[1] the first time I ever was there; and a pretty place it is, and here we eat and drank and stayed till 9 at night, and so home by moonshine. And so set Mrs. Knepp at her lodgings, and so the rest, and I home talking with a great deal of pleasure, and so home to bed.

10th. (Lord's Day.) Up, and to the office, there to do business till church time, when Mr. Shepley, newly come to town, come to see me, and we had some discourse of all matters, and particularly of my Lord Sandwich's concernments. He being gone, I to church, and so home, and there comes W. Hewer and Balty; and by and by I sent for Mercer to come and dine with me, and pretty merry, and after dinner I fell to teach her "Canite Jehovæ," which she did a great part presently, and so she away

---

[1] Marylebone Gardens were situated where Beaumont Street and Devonshire Street now stand.

and I to church, and from church home with my Lady Pen; and after being there an hour or so talking I took her and Mrs. Lowther and old Mrs. Whistler, her mother-in-law, by water with great pleasure as far as Chelsy, and so back to Spring Garden at Fox-hall, and there walked and eat and drank. And so to water again and set down the old woman at home at Durham Yard;[1] and it raining all the way, it troubled us, but however my cloak kept us all dry: and so home, and at the Tower wharf there we did send for a pair of old shoes for Mrs. Lowther, and there I did pull the others off and put them on, elle being peu shy, but do speak con mighty kindness to me that she would desire me pour su mari if it were to be done. Here staid a little at Sir W. Pen's who was gone to bed, it being about eleven at night, and so I home to bed.

11th. Up, and to my office, where alone all the morning. About noon comes to me my cousin Sarah and my aunt Livett, newly come out of Gloucestershire, good woman, and come to see me; I took them home and made them drink, but they would not stay dinner, I being alone. But here they tell me that they hear that this day Kate Joyce was to be married to a man called Hollingshed, whom she indeed did once tell me of and desired me to enquire after him. But, whatever she said of his being rich, I do fear by her doing this without my advice it is not as it ought to be; but as she brews let her bake. They being gone, I to dinner with Balty and his wife, and after dinner I out and took a coach and called Mercer, and she and I to the Duke of York's playhouse, and there saw "The Tempest." There happened one thing which vexed me, which is that the orange-woman did come in the pit and challenge me for twelve oranges which she delivered by my order at a late play, at night, to give to some ladies in a box, which was wholly untrue; but yet she swore it to be true. But however I did deny it and did not pay her; but for quiet did buy 4s. worth of oranges of her at 6d. a-piece.

13th. This morning I hear that last night Sir Thomas Teddiman, poor man! did die by a thrush in his mouth: a good man and stout and able, and much lamented.

15th. To Mrs. Williams's and there dined, and she did shew me her closet, which I was sorry to see for fear of her expecting something from me; and here she took notice of my wife's not once coming to see her, which I am glad of, for she shall not; a prating, vain, idle woman. Thence with Lord Brouncker to Lor-

---

1 By the Adelphi; the Bishops of Durham originally had a palace there.

iners'-hall,[1] by Mooregate, a hall I never heard of before, to Sir Thomas Teddiman's burial, where most people belonging to the sea were. And here we had rings: and here I do hear that some of the last words that he said were that he had a very good King, God bless him! but that the Parliament had very ill rewarded him for all the service he had endeavoured to do them and his country. But, Lord! to see among the young commanders, and Thomas Killigrew and others that come, how unlike a burial this was, O'Brian taking out some ballads out of his pocket, which I read, and the rest come about me to hear! and there very merry we were all, they being new ballets. By and by the corpse went; and I, with my Lord Brouncker and Dr. Clerke and Mr. Pierce, as far as the foot of London-bridge, and there we struck off into Thames Street, the rest going to Redriffe where he is to be buried. And we 'light at the Temple and there parted; and I to the King's house and there saw the last act of "The Committee." [2]

19th. Up, and called on Mr. Pierce. He tells me that since my Lord Ormond's coming over, the King begins to be mightily re-claimed, and sups every night with great pleasure with the Queene. And yet it seems that upon Sunday was se'nnight, at night, he did take a pair of oars or sculler, and all alone (or but one with him), go to Somersett House, and there, the garden-door not being open, himself clamber over the walls to make a visit to [the Duchess of Richmond], which is a horrid shame.

22nd. Up, and all the morning at the office busy. At noon home with my people to dinner, where good discourse and merry. After dinner comes Mr. Martin, the purser, and brings me his wife's starling, which was formerly the King's bird, that do speak and whistle finely, which I am mighty proud of and shall take pleasure in it. Thence to the Duke of York's house to a play, and saw "Sir Martin Marr-all," where the house is full; and though I have seen it I think ten times, yet the pleasure I have is yet as great as ever, and is undoubtedly the best comedy ever was wrote. Thence to my tailor's, and a mercer's for patterns to carry my wife of cloth and silk for a bed, which I think will please her and me, and so home and fitted myself for my journey to-morrow, which I fear will not be pleasant because of the wet weather, it raining very hard all this day; but the less it troubles me because the King and Duke of York and Court are at this day at New-

---

[1] The hall of the Loriners or bit-makers, stood at the junction of Basinghall Street and London Wall.   [2] By Sir Robert Howard.

market, at a great horse-race, and proposed great pleasure for two or three days, but are in the same wet. So from the office home to supper, and betimes to bed.

23rd. Up by four o'clock; and, getting my things ready and recommending the care of my house to W. Hewer, I with my boy Tom whom I take with me, about six took coach, and come to Cambridge, after much bad way, about nine at night; and there at the Rose I met my father's horses, with a man, staying for me. But it is so late and the waters so deep that I durst not go to-night; but after supper to bed, and there lay very ill by reason of some drunken scholars making a noise all night, and vexed for fear that the horses should not be taken up from grass, time enough for the morning.

24th. (Lord's Day.) I up at between two and three in the morning, and calling up my boy and father's boy we set out by three o'clock, it being high day; and so through the waters with very good success, though very deep almost all the way, and got to Brampton, where most of them in bed, and so I weary up to my wife's chamber, whom I find in bed, and fell to talk; and mightily pleased, both of us, and up got the rest, Betty Turner and Willet and Jane, all whom I was glad to see, and very merry. Here I saw my brothers and sister Jackson, she growing fat, and since being married I think looks comelier than before: but a mighty pert woman she is, and I think proud, he keeping her mighty handsome, and they say mighty fond, and are going shortly to live at Ellington of themselves, and will keep malting, and grazing of cattle. At noon comes Mr. Phillips and dines with us, and a pretty odd-humoured man he seems to be; but good withal, but of mighty great methods in his eating and drinking, and will not kiss a woman since his wife's death. After dinner, my Lady Sandwich sending to see whether I was come, I presently took horse, and find her and her family at chapel; and thither I went in to them and sat out the sermon, where I heard their chaplain preach a very good and seraphic kind of sermon, too good for an ordinary congregation. After sermon I with my Lady and my Lady Hinchingbroke and Paulina and Lord Hinchingbroke to the dining-room, saluting none of them, and there sat and talked an hour or two with great pleasure and satisfaction to my Lady about my Lord's matters; but I think not with that satisfaction to her or me that otherwise would, she knowing that she did design to-morrow, and I remaining all the while in fear of being asked to lend her some money; as I was, afterward when I had taken leave of her, by Mr. Shepley, £100, which I will not deny my Lady, and am willing to be found when my Lord comes home to have done something of that kind for them.

25th. Rose, it being the first fair day, and yet not quite fair, that we have had some time, and so up, and to walk with my father again in the garden, consulting what to do with him and this house when Pall and her husband go away; and I think it will be to let it, and he go live with her, though I am against letting the house for any long time, because of having it to retire to ourselves. So I do intend to think more of it before I resolve. At noon to dinner, where Mr. Shepley come and we merry, all being in good humour between my wife and her people about her; and after dinner took horse, I promising to fetch her away about fourteen days hence. And so we away and got well to Cambridge. And here 'lighting, I walked to Magdalene College, and there into the butterys, as a stranger, and there drank my bellyfull of their beer, which pleased me as the best I ever drank; and hear by the butler's man, who was son to Goody Mulliner over against the College that we used to buy stewed prunes of, concerning the College and persons in it, and find very few that were of my time. But I was mightily pleased to come in this condition to see and ask. Thence to our quarters and to bed.

26th. Home, where we find all well, and brother Balty and his wife looking to the house, she mighty fine, in a new gold-laced *just à cour.*[1]

27th. Busy till two o'clock, and then with Sir D. Gawden to his house, with my Lord Brouncker and Sir J. Minnes, to dinner, where we dined very well, and much good company. Thence after dinner to the office and there did a little business, and so to see Sir W. Pen, who I find very ill of the goute, sitting in his great chair made on purpose for persons sick of that disease, for their ease. Home, and made the boy to read to me out of Dr. Wilkins his "Real Character," and particularly about Noah's arke, where he do give a very good account thereof, shewing how few the number of the several species of beasts and fowls were that were to be in the arke, and that there was room enough for them and their food and dung, which do please me mightily and is much beyond what ever I heard of the subject, and so to bed.

---

[1] *Juste-au-corps;* a tight-fitting jacket.

"VERY ILL OF THE GOUTE"

30th. Up, and put on a new summer black bombazin suit,[1] and so to the office; and being come now to an agreement with my barber to keep my perriwig in good order at 20s. a-year, I am like to go very spruce, more than I used to do. All the morning at the office and at noon home to dinner, and so to the King's playhouse, and there saw "Philaster"; [2] where it is pretty to see how I could remember almost all along, ever since I was a boy, Arethusa, the part which I was to have acted at Sir Robert Cooke's, and it was very pleasant to me; but more to think what a ridiculous thing it would have been for me to have acted a beautiful woman. Thence to Mr. Pierce's, and there saw Knepp also, and were merry; and here saw my little Lady Katherine Montagu [3] come to town about her eyes, which are sore, and they think the King's evil, poor pretty lady.

June 3rd. Up, and to the office, where busy till 9 o'clock and then to White Hall to the Council-chamber, where I did present the Duke of York with an account of the charge of the present fleete to his satisfaction; and this being done did ask his leave for my going out of town five or six days, which he did give me, saying that my diligence in the King's business was such that I ought not to be denied when my own business called me any whither. Thence with Sir D. Gawden to Westminster, where I did take a turn or two and met Roger Pepys, who is mighty earnest for me to stay from going into the country till he goes, and to bring my people thither for some time: but I cannot, but will find another time this summer for it.

4th. All the evening to set matters in order against my going to Brampton to-morrow, being resolved upon my journey and having the Duke of York's leave, though I do plainly see that I can very ill be spared now, there being much business.

5th.[4] (Friday.) At Barnet, for milk, 6d. On the highway, to menders of the highway, 6d. Dinner at Stevenage, 5s. 6d.

6th. (Saturday.) Spent at Huntingdon with Bowles and Appleyard and Shepley, 2s.

8th. (Monday.) Father's servants (father having in the garden told me bad stories of my wife's ill words), 14s. Pleasant country to Bedford, where, while they stay, I rode through the town; and a good country-town; and there, drinking, 1s. We on to Newport,

---

[1] Bombazin is a twilled or corded dress material, of worsted, sometimes mixed with silk or cotton.
[2] By Beaumont and Fletcher.
[3] Lord Sandwich's youngest child, then aged seven. She lived to be ninety-six.
[4] The rough notes for the next week are written on loose leaves bound into the book. Then follow blank pages left for the fair copy, which was never made.

and there 'light, and I and W. Hewer to the Church, and there give the boy 1s. So to Buckingham, a good old town. Here I to see the Church, which very good, and the leads, and a school in it: did give the sexton's boy 1s. A fair bridge here, with many arches: vexed at my people's making me lose so much time; reckoning, 13s. 4d. Mighty pleased with the pleasure of the ground all the day. At night to Newport Pagnell, and there a good pleasant country-town, but few people in it. The town, and so most of this country, well watered.

9th. (Tuesday.) To Oxford, a very sweet place. To dinner; and then out with my wife and people and landlord: and to him that showed us the schools and library, 10s.; to him that showed us All Souls' College, and Chichly's picture, 5s. So to see Christ Church with my wife, I seeing several others very fine alone with W. Hewer before dinner, and did give the boy that went with me 1s. Strawberries, 1s. 2d. Dinner and servants, £1 0s. 6d. After come home from the schools, I out with the landlord to Brazen-nose College; to the butteries, and in the cellar find the hand of the Child of Hales,[6] . . . long. Butler, 2s. Thence with coach and people to Physic-garden, 1s. So to Friar Bacon's study: I up and saw it, and give the man 1s. Bottle of sack for landlord, 2s. Oxford mighty fine place, and well seated, and cheap entertainment. At night come to Abingdon.

10th. (Wednesday.) Up, and walked to the Hospitall: very large and fine; and pictures of founders, and the History of the Hospitall; and is said to be worth £700 per annum. So did give the poor, which they would not take but in their box, 2s. 6d. So forth towards Hungerford, led this good way by our landlord, one Heart, an old but very civil and well-spoken man, more than I ever heard, of his quality. He gone, we forward; and I vexed at my people's not minding the way. So come to Hungerford, where very good trouts, eels, and crayfish. Dinner: a mean town. Thence set out with a guide. So all over the Plain by the sight of the steeple, the Plain high and low, to Salisbury, by night; but before I come to the town I saw a great fortification, and there 'light, and to it and in it; and find it prodigious, so as to frighten me to be in it all alone at that time of night, it being dark. I understand, since, it to be that that is called Old Sarum. Come to the

---

[1] John Middleton of Hale, a well-known giant. He was nine feet three inches tall, and his hand measured seventeen by eight and a half inches (width of palm only). Pepys left a blank in his diary meaning to fill in the dimensions.

George Inne, where lay in a silk bed; and very good diet. To supper; then to bed.

11th. (Thursday.) Up, and W. Hewer and I up and down the town and find it a very brave place. The river goes through every street; and a most capacious market-place, the Minster most admirable; as big, I think, and handsomer than Westminster: and a most large Close about it, and houses for the Officers thereof, and a fine palace for the Bishop. I looked in and saw the Bishop, my friend Dr. Ward. Thence to the inne; and there not being able to hire coach-horses, and not willing to use our own, we got saddle-horses, very dear. Boy that went to look for them, 6*d*. So the three women behind W. Hewer, Murford, and our guide, and I single to Stonage, over the Plain and some great hills, even to fright us. Come thither, and find them as prodigious as any tales I ever heard of them, and worth going this journey to see. God knows what their use was! they are hard to tell, but yet may be told. Give the shepherd-woman, for leading our horses, 4*d*. So back by Wilton, my Lord Pembroke's house, which we could not see, he being just coming to town; but the situation I do not like, nor the house promise much, it being in a low but rich valley. So back home. So to dinner; and that being done paid the reckoning, which was so exorbitant, and particular in rate of my horses, and 7*s*. 6*d*. for bread and beer, that I was mad, and resolve to trouble the master about it, and get something for the poor; and come away in that humour: £2 5*s*. 6*d*. Servants, 1*s*. 6*d*.; poor, 1*s*.; guide to the Stones, 2*s*.; poor woman in the street, 1*s*.; ribbands, 9*d*.; washwoman, 1*s*.; sempstress for W. Hewer, 3*s*.; lent W. Hewer, 2*s*. Thence about six o'clock, and with a guide went over the smooth Plain indeed till night; and then by a happy mistake, and that looked like an adventure, we were carried out of our way to a town where we would lye, since we could not go so far as we would. And there with great difficulty come about ten at night to a little inn, where we were fain to go into a room where a pedlar was in bed, and made him rise; and there wife and I lay, and in a truckle-bed Betty Turner and Willett. But good beds, and the master of the house a sober, understanding man, and I had good discourse with him about this country's matters, as wool and corne, and other things. And he also merry, and made us mighty merry at supper about manning the new ship at Bristol with none but men whose wives do master them; and it seems it is become in reproach to some men of estate that are such hereabouts, that this is become

common talk. By and by to bed, glad of this mistake, because, it
seems, had we gone on as we intended we could not have passed
with our coach, and must have lain on the Plain all night. This
day from Salisbury I wrote by the post my excuse for not coming
home, which I hope will do, for I am resolved to see the Bath, and
it may be Bristol.

12th. (Friday.) Up, finding our beds good but lousy, which
made us merry. Rode a very good way, led to my great content
by our landlord to Philips-Norton, with great pleasure, being now
come into Somersetshire; where my wife and Deb. mightily joyed
thereat,[1] I commending the country, as indeed it deserves. And
the first town we came to was Brekington, where, we stopping for
something for the horses, we called two or three little boys to us,
and pleased ourselves with their manner of speech, and did make
one of them kiss Deb., and another say the Lord's Prayer (hallowed
be thy kingdom come). At Philips-Norton I walked to the Church
and there saw a very ancient tomb of some Knight Templar, I
think; and here saw the tombstone whereon there were only two
heads cut, which, the story goes, and credibly, were two sisters,
called the Fair Maids of Foscott, that had two bodies upward and
one belly, and there lie buried. Here is also a very fine ring of
six bells, and they mighty tuneable. Having dined very well,
10*s.*, we come before night to the Bath; where I presently stepped
out with my landlord and saw the baths, with people in them.
They are not so large as I expected, but yet pleasant; and the town
most of stone, and clean, though the streets generally narrow. I
home, and being weary, went to bed without supper; the rest
supping.

13th. (Saturday.) Up at four o'clock, being by appointment
called up to the Cross Bath,[2] where we were carried one after one
another, myself and wife and Betty Turner, Willet, and W. Hewer.
And by and by, though we designed to have done before company
come, much company come, very fine ladies; and the manner
pretty enough, only methinks it cannot be clean to go so many
bodies together in the same water. Good conversation among
them that are acquainted here and stay together. Strange to see
how hot the water is; and in some places, though this is the most
temperate bath, the springs so hot as the feet not able to endure.
But strange to see, when women and men herein, that live all the

---

[1] They were both natives of Somerset.
[2] So called from an old cross which stood in the centre of the bath.

season in these waters, that cannot but be parboiled, and look like the creatures of the bath! Carried away wrapped in a sheet, and in a chair home; and there one after another thus carried, I staying above two hours in the water, home to bed, sweating for an hour; and by and by comes musick to play to me, extraordinary good as ever I heard at London almost, or anywhere: 5s.

Up, to go to Bristol, about eleven o'clock, and come thither, the way bad but country good, about two o'clock, where set down at the Horseshoe; and there, being trimmed by a very handsome fellow, 2s., walked with my wife and people through the city, which is in every respect another London, that one can hardly know it to stand in the country, no more than that. No carts, it standing generally on vaults, only dogcarts. So to the Three Crowns Tavern I was directed; but when I come in the master told me that he had newly given over the selling of wine, it seems grown rich; and so went to the Sun, and there Deb. going with W. Hewer and Betty Turner to see her uncle, and leaving my wife with the mistress of the house, I to see the quay, which is a most large and noble place. Walked back to the Sun, where I find Deb. come back, and with her her uncle, a sober merchant, very good company; and so like one of our sober, wealthy London merchants as pleased me mightily. Here we dined, and much good talk with him, 7s. 6d. Then walked with him and my wife and company round the quay, and he shewed me the Custom-house and made me understand many things of the place, and led us through Marsh Street, where our girl was born. But, Lord! the joy that was among the old poor people of the place, to see Mrs. Willet's daughter, it seems her mother being a brave woman and mightily beloved! And so brought us a back way by surprize to his house, where a substantial good house and well furnished; and did give us good entertainment of strawberries, a whole vension-pasty cold, and plenty of brave wine, and above all Bristoll milk: where comes in another poor woman, who, hearing that Deb. was here, did come running hither, and with her eyes so full of tears, and heart so full of joy that she could not speak when she come in, that it made me weep too: I protest that I was not able to speak to her, which I would have done, to have diverted her tears. His wife a good woman, and so sober and substantiall as I was never more pleased anywhere. Servant-maid, 2s. So thence took leave, and he with us through the city, where in walking I find the city pay him great respect, and he the like to the meanest, which

"CREATURES OF THE BATH"

pleased me mightily. He shewed us the place where the merchants meet here, and a fine Cross yet standing, like Cheapside. We back, and by moonshine to the Bath again, about ten o'clock: bad way; and giving the coachman 1*s.*, went all of us to bed.

14th. (Sunday.) Up, and walked up and down the town, and saw a pretty good market-place, and many good streets and very fair stone-houses. And so to the great Church, and there saw Bishop Montagu's [1] tomb; and when placed did there see many brave people come, and among others two men brought in in litters and set down in the chancel to hear; but I did not know one face. Here a good organ; but a vain pragmatical fellow preached a ridiculous, affected sermon that made me angry, and some gentlemen that sat next me and sang well. So home, walking round the walls of the City, which are good, and the battlements all whole.

15th. (Monday.) Up, and to look into the baths, and find the King and Queen's full of a mixed sort, of good and bad, and the Cross only almost for the gentry. So to our inne, and there eat and paid reckoning. Before I took coach I went to make a boy dive in the King's bath, 1*s.* Took coach and away, without any of the company of the other stage-coaches that go out of this town to-day; and rode all day with some trouble for fear of being out of our way over the Downes, where the life of the shepherds is, in fair weather only, pretty. In the afternoon come to Abebury, where, seeing great stones like those of Stonage standing up, I stopped and took a countryman of that town, and he carried me and shewed me a place trenched in, like Old Sarum almost, with great stones pitched in it, some bigger than those at Stonage in figure, to my great admiration: and he told me that most people of learning coming by do come and view them, and that the King did so: and that the Mount cast hard by is called Selbury, from one King Seall buried there, as tradition says. I did give this man 1*s.* So took coach again; but about a mile off it was prodigious to see how full the Downes are of great stones. Before night come to Marlborough, and lay at the Hart, a good house, and a pretty fair town for a street or two; and what is most singular is their houses on one side having their pent-houses supported with pillars, which makes it a good walk. My wife pleased with all.

16th. (Tuesday.) So paying the reckoning, 14*s.* 4*d.*, and servants, 2*s.*, poor 1*s.*, set out. So on, and passing through a good

---

[1] Lord Sandwich's uncle, James Montagu, Bishop of Bath and Wells, and later of Winchester. Died 1618. His brother (the father of Lord Sandwich) had married Pepys' great-aunt, Paulina Pepys.

part of this county of Wiltshire, saw a good house of Alexander Popham's,[1] and another of my Lord Craven's, I think in Barkeshire. Come to Newbery and there dined, which cost me (and musick, which, a song of the old courtier of Queen Elizabeth's and how he was changed upon the coming in of the King, did please me mightily,[2] and I did cause W. Hewer to write it out), 3s. 6d. So out, and lost our way, which made me vexed, but come into it again; and in the evening betimes come to Reading, and then to supper, and then I to walk about the town, which is a very great one, I think bigger than Salsbury: a river runs through it in seven branches, and unite in one in one part of the town, and runs into the Thames half-a-mile off: one odd sign of the Broad Face. W. Hewer troubled with the headake; we had none of his company last night, nor all this day nor night to talk.

17th. (Wednesday.) Rose, and paying the reckoning, 12s. 6d.; servants and poor, 2s. 6d.; musick, the worst we have had, coming to our chamber-door, but calling us by wrong names, we lay; so set out with one coach in company, and through Maydenhead, which I never saw before, to Colebrooke by noon, the way mighty good; and there dined, and fitted ourselves a little to go through London, and on. Somewhat out of humour all day, reflecting on my wife's neglect of things and impertinent humour got by this liberty of being from me, which she is never to be trusted with, for she is a fool. Thence pleasant way to London before night and find all very well, to great content; and there to talk with my wife, and saw Sir W. Pen who is well again. By and by home, and there with my people to supper, all in pretty good humour, though I find my wife hath something in her gizzard that only waits an opportunity of being provoked to bring up; but I will not for my content-sake give it. So I to bed, glad to find all so well here, and slept well.

18th. Up betimes and to the office, there to set my papers in order, and books, my office having been new whited and windows made clean; and so to sit, where all the morning, and did receive a hint or two from my Lord Anglesey, as if he thought much of my taking the ayre as I have done, but I care not; but whatever the matter is, I think he hath some ill-will to me, or at least an opinion that I am more the servant of the Board than I am. At noon home to dinner, where my wife still in a melancholy, fusty

[1] Littlecote House, Ramsbury. Lord Craven's house was Hampstead Marshall: actually in Hampshire.
[2] This ballad, first printed in the reign of James I., was the forerunner of "The Fine Old English Gentleman."

humour, and crying, and do not tell me plainly what it is; but I by little words find that she hath heard of my going to plays and carrying people abroad every day in her absence.

22nd. To my Lord Brouncker's, where a Council of the Royall Society; and there heard Mr. Harry Howard's noble offers about ground for our College, and his intentions of building his own house there most nobly. My business was to meet Mr. Boyle, which I did, and discoursed about my eyes; and he did give me the best advice he could, but refers me to one Turberville,[1] of Salsbury, lately come to town, which I will go to.

23rd. Up, and all the morning at the office. At noon home to dinner, and so to the office again all the afternoon, and then to Westminster to Dr. Turberville about my eyes, whom I met with: and he did discourse, I thought, learnedly about them; and takes time before he did prescribe me any thing, to think of it.

29th. Called up by my Lady Peterborough's servant about some business of hers, and so to the office. Thence by and by with Sir J. Minnes toward St. James's, and I stop at Dr. Turberville's, and there did receive a direction for some physic, and also a glass of something to drop into my eyes: who gives me hopes that I may do well. Thence to St. James's, and thence to White Hall. Thence to the Chapel, it being St. Peter's day, and did hear an anthem of Silas Taylor's making; a dull, old-fashioned thing of six and seven parts that nobody could understand: and the Duke of York when he come out told me that he was a better storekeeper than anthem-maker, and that was bad enough, too.

30th. Up, and at the Office all the morning: then home to dinner, where a stinking leg of mutton, the weather being very wet and hot to keep meat in. Then to the Office again all the afternoon. And so up, and to walk all the evening with my wife and Mrs. Turner in the garden till supper, about eleven at night; and so after supper parted and to bed, my eyes bad, but not worse, only weary with working. But however I very melancholy under the fear of my eyes being spoiled and not to be recovered, for I am come that I am not able to read out a small letter; and yet my sight good for the little while I can read as ever they were, I think.

July 6th. To Mr. Cooper's, and there my wife first sat for her picture; but he is a most admirable workman, and good company.

---

[1] Daubigny Turberville, M.D. (Oxon), was an oculist of considerable repute. Pepys had been advised to consult him by the scientist Robert Boyle.

10th. Up, and to attend the Council. So home to dinner, and thence to Haward's to look upon an Espinette, and I did come near the buying one, but broke off. I have a mind to have one. So to Cooper's, and there find my wife and W. Hewer and Deb. sitting and painting; and here he do work finely, though I fear it will not be so like as I expected: but now I understand his great skill in musick, his playing and setting to the French lute most excellently, and speaks French, and indeed is an excellent man. Thence in the evening with my people in a glass hackney-coach to the park, but was ashamed to be seen. So to the lodge and drank milk, and so home to supper and to bed.

14th. This afternoon my Lady Pickering come to see us: I busy, saw her not. But how natural it is for us to slight people out of power, and for people out of power to stoop to see those that while in power they contemned!

19th. (Lord's Day.) Up, and to my chamber, and there I up and down in the house spent the morning getting things ready against noon, when come Mr. Cooper, Hales, Harris, Mr. Butler that wrote Hudibras, and Mr. Cooper's cozen Jacke; and by and by comes Mr. Reeves and his wife whom I never saw before. And there we dined; a good dinner, and company that pleased me mightily, being all eminent men in their way. Spent all the afternoon in talk and mirth, and in the evening parted; and then my wife and I to walk in the garden, and so home to supper, Mrs. Turner and husband and daughter with us, and then to bed.

20th. Up, and to the office, where Mrs. Daniel comes. All the morning at the office. Dined at home. So to visit my Lord Crew, who is very sick, to great danger, by an irisipulus; the first day I heard of it. And so home, and took occasion to buy a rest for my espinette at the ironmonger's by Holborn Conduit, where the fair pretty woman is that I have lately observed there, and she is pretty, and je credo vain enough.

24th. Up, and by water to St. James's, having by the way shewn Symson Sir W. Coventry's chimney-pieces, in order to the making me one; and there after the Duke of York was ready he called me to his closet, and there I did long and largely show him the weakness of our Office, and did give him advice to call us to account for our duties, which he did take mighty well, and desired me to draw up what I would have him write to the Office. I did lay open the whole failings of the Office, and how it was his duty to find them and to find fault with them as Admiral, especially at this time, which he agreed to, and seemed much to rely on what I said.

29th. Busy all the morning at the office. So home to dinner, where Mercer; and there comes Mr. Swan, my old acquaintance, and dines with me, and tells me for a certainty that Creed is to marry Betty Pickering[1] and that the thing is concluded, which I wonder at and am vexed for.

31st. Up, and at my office all the morning. About noon with Mr. Ashburnham to the new Excise Office, and there discoursed about our business, and I made him admire my drawing a thing presently in shorthand: but, God knows! I have paid dear for it, in my eyes.

August 10th. To Cooper's, where I spent all the afternoon with my wife and girl, seeing him make an end of her picture, which he did to my great content, though not so great as I confess I expected, being not satisfied in the greatness of the resemblance, nor in the blue garment: but it is most certainly a most rare piece of work as to the painting. He hath £30 for his work, and the chrystal and case and gold case comes to £8 3s. 4d.; and which I sent him this night, that I might be out of debt. Thence my people home and I to Westminster Hall about a little business, and so by water home to supper, and my wife to read a ridiculous book I bought to-day of the History of the Taylors' Company; and all the while Deb. did comb my head. And so to bed.

14th. To the Duke of York, who enquired for what I had promised him about my observations of the miscarriages of our Office; and I told him he should have it next week, being glad he called for it; for I find he is concerned to do something, and to secure himself thereby, I believe, for the world is labouring to eclipse him, I doubt; I mean, the factious part of the Parliament. The Office met this afternoon as usual, and waited on him; where among other things he talked a great while of his intentions of going to Dover soon, to be sworn as Lord Warden, which is a matter of great ceremony and state.

19th. Up betimes, and all day and afternoon without going out busy upon my great letter to the Duke of York, which goes on to my content. W. Hewer and Gibson I employ with me in it. This week my people wash, over the water, and so I little company at home. In the evening, being busy above, a great cry I hear, and go down; and what should it be but Jane, in a fit of direct raving,

[1] See April 24, 1665, *ante.*

which lasted half-an-hour. Beyond four or five of our strength to keep her down; and, when all come to all, a fit of jealousy about Tom with whom she is in love.

21st. After dinner I by coach to my bookseller's in Duck Lane, and there did spend a little time and regarder su moher,[1] and so to St. James's, where did a little ordinary business; and by and by comes Monsieur Colbert, the French Embassador, to make his first visit to the Duke of York, and then to the Duchess: and I saw it, a silly piece of ceremony, he saying only a few formal words. A comely man, and in a black suit and cloak of silk, which is a strange fashion now it hath been so long left off.

22nd. This afternoon, after I was weary in my business of the office, I went forth to the 'Change, thinking to have spoke with Captain Cocke, but he was not within. So I home and took London-bridge in my way, walking down Fish Street and Gracious Street to see how very fine a descent they have now made down the hill, that it is become very easy and pleasant. And going through Leaden-Hall, it being market-day, I did see a woman catched that had stolen a shoulder of mutton off of a butcher's stall, and carrying it wrapt up in a cloth in a basket. The jade was surprised and did not deny it, and the woman so silly as to let her go that took it, only taking the meat.

23rd. (Lord's Day.) After dinner to the Office, Mr. Gibson and I, to examine my letter to the Duke of York. And I do mightily like what I have therein done; and did make haste to St. James's, and about four o'clock got thither, and there the Duke of York was ready, to expect me, and did hear it all over with extraordinary content; and did give me many and hearty thanks, and in words the most expressive tell me his sense of my good endeavours, and that he would have a care of me on all occasions; and did with much inwardness tell me what was doing, of designs to make alterations in the Navy; and is most open to me in them, and with utmost confidence desires my further advice on all occasions: and he resolves to have my letter transcribed and sent forthwith to the Office.

25th. Up, and by water to St. James's, and there with Mr. Wren did discourse about my great letter, which the Duke of York hath given him, and is much pleased with it, and earnest to have it be; and he and I are like to be much together in the considering how to reform the Office. It is pretty how Lord Brouncker this

[1] Wife.

day did tell me how he hears that a design is on foot to remove us out of the Office: and proposes that we two do agree to draw up a form of a new constitution of the Office, which I agreed to, saying nothing of my design; and the truth is he is the best man of them all, and I would be glad, next myself, to save him.

26th. Met at the Treasury chamber, and there before the Lords did debate our draft of the victualling contract. There till after candle-lighting, and so home by coach with Sir D. Gawden, who by the way tells me how the City do go on in several things towards the building of the public places, which I am glad to hear, and gives hope that in a few years it will be a glorious place; but we met with several stops and new troubles in the way in the streets, so as makes it bad to travel in the dark now through the City. So I to Mr. Batelier's by appointment, where I find my wife and Deb. and Mercer, Mrs. Pierce and her husband, son and daughter, and Knepp and Harris, and W. Batelier, and his sister Mary, and cozen Gumbleton, a good-humoured, fat young gentleman, son to the Jeweller, that dances well; and here danced all night long, with a noble supper; and about two in the morning the table spread again for a noble breakfast beyond all moderation, that put me out of countenance, so much and so good. Mrs. Pierce and her people went home betimes, but Knepp and the rest staid till almost three in the morning, and then broke up.

27th. Knepp home with us, and I to bed, and rose about six, mightily pleased with last night's mirth, and away by water to St. James's, and there with Mr. Wren did correct his copy of my letter, which the Duke of York hath signed in my very words, without alteration of a syllable. And so I by water to the Office, where we sat all the morning; and just as the Board rises comes the Duke of York's letter, which I knowing, and the Board not being full, and desiring rather to have the Duke of York deliver it himself to us, I suppressed it for this day, my heart beginning to falsify in this business, as being doubtful of the trouble it may give me by provoking them. But however I am resolved to go through it: and it is too late to help it now.

28th. To White Hall where the Duke of York fell to work with us in the Council-chamber; and there with his own hand did give us his long letter, telling us that he had received several from us, and now did give us one from him, taking notice of our several duties and failures, and desired answer to it, as he therein desired. This pleased me well; and so fell to other business, and then parted.

29th.   Up, and all the morning at the Office, where the Duke of York's long letter was read, to their great trouble, and their suspecting me to have been the writer of it.   And at noon comes by appointment Harris to dine with me, and after dinner he and I to Chyrurgeon's-hall, where they are building it new, very fine; and there to see their theatre, which stood all the fire, and, which was our business, their great picture of Holben's,[1] thinking to have bought it, by the help of Mr. Pierce, for a little money: I did think to give £200 for it, it being said to be worth £1,000; but it is so spoiled that I have no mind to it, and is not a pleasant, though a good picture.

September 1st.   Up, and all the morning at the office busy, and after dinner to the office again busy till about four, and then I abroad to see Betty Michell.   So to [Bartholomew] Fair, and there saw several sights; among others the mare that tells money, and many things to admiration; and among others come to me, when she was bid to go to him of the company that most loved a pretty wench in a corner.   And this did cost me 12*d.* to the horse, which I had flung him before, and did give me occasion to baiser a mighty belle fille that was in the house that was exceeding plain, but fort belle.

3rd.   To the Exchequer and several places, calling on several businesses, and particularly my bookseller's, among others for "Hobbs's Leviathan," which is now mightily called for; and what was heretofore sold for 8*s.* I now give 24*s.* for at the second hand, and is sold for 30*s.*, it being a book the Bishops will not let be printed again.

8th.   This day I received so earnest an invitation from Roger Pepys to come to Sturbridge-Fair [at Cambridge] that I resolve to let my wife go, which she shall do the next week.

9th.   Up, and to the office, and thence to the Duke of Richmond's lodgings by his desire by letter yesterday.   I find him at his lodgings in the little building in the bowling-green at White Hall.   They are fine rooms.   I did hope to see his lady, the beautiful Mrs. Stuart, but she I hear is in the country.   His business was about his yacht, and he seems a mighty good-natured man, and did presently write me a warrant for a doe from Cobham when the season comes, buck season being past.   I shall make much of this acquaintance that I may live to see his lady near.   Thence to Westminster, and going met Mr. George Montagu, who talked

[1] Of King Henry VIII. It is still there.

and complimented me mightily; and long discourse I had with him, who for news tells me that now Buckingham does rule all; and the other day, in the King's journey he is now on, at Bagshot and that way, he caused Prince Rupert's horses to be turned out of an inne and caused his own to be kept there, which the Prince complained of to the King, and the Duke of York seconded the complaint; but the King did over-rule it for Buckingham, by which there are high displeasures among them.

12th. To the Office, where till noon, and I do see great whispering among my brethren about their replies to the Duke of York, which vexed me; though I know no reason for it, for I have no manner of ground to fear them.

13th. (Lord's Day.) About four o'clock walked to the Temple, and there by coach to St. James's, and met, to my wish, the Duke of York and Mr. Wren; and understand the Duke of York hath received answers from Brouncker, W. Pen and J. Minnes; and as soon as he saw me he bid Mr. Wren read them over with me. So having no opportunity of talk with the Duke of York, and Mr. Wren some business to do, he put them into my hands like an idle companion, to take home with me before himself had read them, which do give me great opportunity of altering my answer, if there was cause. So took a hackney and home, and after supper made my wife to read them all over, wherein she is mighty useful to me; and I find them all evasions, and in many things false, and in few to the full purpose. Little said reflective on me, though W. Pen and J. Minnes do mean me in one or two places, and J. Minnes a little more plainly would lead the Duke of York to question the exactness of my keeping my records; but all to no purpose. My mind is mightily pleased by this, if I can but get time to have a copy taken of them for my future use; but I must return them to-morrow. So to bed.

14th. By coach to St. James's, where I find Sir W. Pen and Lord Anglesey, who delivered this morning his answer to the Duke of York, but I could not see it. But after being above with the Duke of York, but said nothing, I down with Mr. Wren; and he and I read all over that I had, and I expounded them to him, and did so order it that I had them home with me, so that I shall, to my heart's wish, be able to take a copy of them.

16th. To the office, and thence to St. James's to the Duke of York, walking it to the Temple, and in my way observe that the

Stockes [1] are now pulled quite down; and it will make the coming into Cornhill and Lumber Street mighty noble. I stopped too at Paul's, and there did go into St. Fayth's Church, and also in the body of the west part of the Church, and do see a hideous sight of the walls of the Church ready to fall, that I was in fear as long as I was in it; and here I saw the great vaults underneath the body of the Church. No hurt, I hear, is done yet, since their going to pull down the Church and steeple; but one man, on Monday this week, fell from the top to a piece of the roof of the east end, that stands next the steeple, and there broke himself all to pieces. It is pretty here to see how the late Church was but a case wrought over the old Church; for you may see the very old pillars standing whole within the wall of this. When I come to St. James's I find the Duke of York gone with the King to see the muster of the Guards in Hyde Park; and their Colonel, the Duke of Monmouth, to take his command this day of the King's Life-Guard, by surrender of my Lord Gerard. So I took a hackney-coach and saw it all: and indeed it was mighty noble, and their firing mighty fine, and the Duke of Monmouth in mighty rich clothes; but the well-ordering of the men I understand not. Here, among a thousand coaches that were there, I saw and spoke to Mrs. Pierce: and by and by Mr. Wren hunts me out and gives me my Lord Anglesey's answer to the Duke of York's letter, where I perceive he do do what he can to hurt me by bidding the Duke of York call for my books: but this will do me all the right in the world, and yet I am troubled at it. So away out of the Park and home, and there Mr. Gibson and I to dinner; and all the afternoon with him writing over anew, and a little altering, my answer to the Duke of York. This day my father's letters tell me of the death of poor Fancy, in the country, big with puppies, which troubles me, as being one of my oldest acquaintances and servants. Also good Stankes is dead.

19th. Up, and to the office, where all the morning busy, and so dined with my people at home, and then to the King's playhouse and there saw "The Silent Woman"; the best comedy, I think, that ever was wrote; and sitting by Shadwell the poet, he was big with admiration of it. Here was my Lord Brouncker and W. Pen and their ladies in the box, being grown mighty kind

---

[1] The Stocks Market, so called from a pair of stocks placed near by, occupied the space now filled by the Mansion House.

of a sudden; but God knows it will last but a little while, I dare swear. Knepp did her part mighty well.

21st. To St. James's, and there the Duke of York did of his own accord come to me and tell me that he had read, and do like of, my answers. By water home to dinner, and so out again and by water to Somerset House; but when come thither I turned back and to Southwarke-Fair, very dirty, and there saw the puppet-show of Whittington, which was pretty to see; and how that idle thing do work upon people that see it, and even myself too! And thence to Jacob Hall's dancing on the ropes, where I saw such action as I never saw before, and mightily worth seeing; and here took acquaintance with a fellow that carried me to a tavern, whither come the musick of this booth, and by and by Jacob Hall himself, with whom I had a mind to speak, to hear whether he had ever any mischief by falls in his time. He told me, "Yes, many; but never to the breaking of a limb." He seems a mighty strong man. So giving them a bottle or two of wine, I away with Payne, the waterman. He, seeing me at the play, did get a link to light me, and so light me to the Beare, where Bland, my water-man, waited for me with gold and other things he kept for me, to the value of £40 and more, which I had about me, for fear of my pockets being cut. So by link-light through the bridge, it being mighty dark, but still weather, and so home.

28th. By water to St. James's. Thence to my Lord Burling-ton's house,[1] the first time I ever was there, it being the house built by Sir John Denham, next to Clarendon House, and here I visited my Lord Hinchingbroke and his lady; Mr. Sidney Mon-tagu[2] being come last night to town unexpectedly from Mount's Bay, where he left my Lord well, eight days since, so as we may now hourly expect to hear of his arrival at Portsmouth. Sidney is mighty grown, and I am glad I am here to see him at his first coming; though it cost me dear, for here I come to be necessitated to supply them with £500 for my Lord. He sent him up with a declaration to his friends of the necessity of his being presently supplied with £2,000; but I do not think he will get one. How-ever I think it becomes my duty to my Lord to do something ex-traordinary in this, and the rather because I have been remiss in writing to him during this voyage, more than ever I did in my life, and more indeed than was fit for me. Here I first saw and

---

[1] In Piccadilly: the home of Lady Hinchingbroke's parents.
[2] Sidney Montagu, the second son of Lord Sandwich, married the heiress Anne Wortley, whose name he assumed. He died in 1727. His son married the celebrated Lady Mary Wortley-Montagu.

saluted my Lady Burlington, a very fine-speaking lady, and a good woman, but old and not handsome; but a brave woman in her parts.   Here my Lady Hinchingbroke tells me that she hath bought most of the wedding-clothes for Mrs. Pickering, so that the thing is gone through and will soon be ended; which I wonder at, but let them do as they will.   Here I also, standing by a candle that was brought for sealing of a letter, do set my periwigg a-fire, which made such an odd noise, nobody could tell what it was till they saw the flame, my back being to the candle.   Thence to Westminster Hall and there walked a little, and to the Exchequer, and so home by water; and after eating a bit I to my vintner's, and there did only look upon su wife, which is mighty handsome; and so to my glove and ribbon shop in Fenchurch Street, and did the like there.   And so by coach towards the King's playhouse, and meeting W. Howe took him with me, and there saw "The City Match;"[1] not acted these thirty years, and but a silly play.   So I to White Hall, and there all the evening on the Queen's side; and it being a most summer-like day and a fine warm evening, the Italians come in a barge under the leads before the Queen's drawing-room, and so the Queen and ladies went out and heard them for almost an hour; and it was indeed very good together, but yet there was but one voice that alone did appear considerable, and that was Seignor Joanni.[2]   This done, by and by they went in.   So home to read and sup, and to bed.

October 12th.   This night my bookseller Shrewsbury comes and brings my books of Martyrs,[3] and I did pay him for them, and did this night make the young women before supper to open all the volumes for me.   So to supper, and after supper to read a ridiculous nonsensical book set out by Will. Pen, for the Quakers; but so full of nothing but nonsense that I was ashamed to read in it.[4]

16th.   Up, and busy all the morning at the office, and before noon I took my wife by coach, and Deb., and shewed her Mr. Wren's hangings and bed at St. James's, and Sir W. Coventry's in the Pell-Mell, for our satisfaction in what we are going to buy; and so by Mr. Crow's, home, about his hangings, and do pitch upon buying his second suit of Apostles, the whole suit, which

---

[1] By Jasper Maine, D.D.   [2] See note, February 12, 1667.   [3] Foxe's *Book of Martyrs.*
[4] This was the first work of Sir W. Penn's son, the well-known Quaker. The title runs: "Truth exalted, in a short but sure testimony against all those religions, faiths and worships that have been formed and followed in the darkness of apostacy; and for that glorious light which is now risen and shines forth in the life and doctrine of the despised Quakers . . . by W. Penn, whom divine love constrains, in holy contempt, to trample on Egypt's glory, not fearing the King's wrath, having beheld the Majesty of Him who is invisible." London, 1668.

come to £83; and this we think the best for us, having now the whole suit to answer any other rooms or service. So home to dinner, and with Mr. Hater by water to St. James's: there Mr. Hater to give Mr. Wren thanks for his kindness about his place that he hath lately granted him, of Petty Purveyor of petty emptions, upon the removal of Mr. Turner to be Storekeeper at Deptford.

17th. Mr. Moore with me this afternoon, who tells me that my Lord Sandwich was received mighty kindly by the King and is in exceeding great esteem with him and the rest about him; but I doubt it will be hard for him to please both the King and the Duke of York, which I shall be sorry for. Mr. Moore tells me the sad condition my Lord is in in his estate and debts; and the way he now lives in, so high and so many vain servants about him that he must be ruined if he do not take up, which by the grace of God I will put him upon, when I come to see him.

20th. Up, and to the office all the morning, and then home to dinner, having this day a new girl come to us in the room of Nell, who is lately, about four days since, gone away, being grown lazy and proud. This girl to stay only till we have a boy, which I intend to keep when I have a coach, which I am now about. At this time my wife and I mighty busy laying out money in dressing up our best chamber, and thinking of a coach and coachman and horses, &c.; and the more because of Creed's being now married to Mrs. Pickering, a thing I could never have expected. At noon home to dinner, and my wife and Harman and girl abroad to buy things, and I walked out to several places to pay debts, and among other things to look out for a coach, and saw many; and did light on one for which I bid £50, which do please me mightily, and I believe I shall have it.

21st. At noon to dinner to Mr. Batelier's, his mother coming this day a-house-warming to him, and several friends of his, to which he invited us. Here mighty merry, and his mother the same; I heretofore took her for a gentlewoman, and understanding. I rose from table before the rest, because under an obligation to go to my Lord Brouncker's, where to meet several gentlemen of the Royal Society to go and make a visit to the French Embassador Colbert, at Leicester House, but I come too late, they being gone before; but I followed to Leicester House,[1] but they are gone in and up before me; and so I away to the New Exchange and there

---

[1] Leicester House occupied the north side of the present Leicester Square.

staid for my wife, and she come, we to Cow Lane, and there I
shewed her the coach which I pitch on, and she is out of herself
for joy almost. But the man not within, so did nothing more
towards an agreement, but to Mr. Crow's about a bed, to have
his advice. From Crow's we went back to Charing Cross, and
there left my people at their tailor's, while I to my Lord Sandwich's
lodgings, who come to town the last night and is come thither
to lye, and met with him within; and among others my new cozen
Creed, who looks mighty soberly; and he and I saluted one another with mighty gravity, till we come to a little more freedom
of talk about it.

24th. This morning comes to me the coachmaker, and agreed
with me for £53, and stand to the courtesy of what more I should
give him upon the finishing of the coach: he is likely also to fit me
with a coachman.

25th. (Lord's Day.) Up, and discoursing with my wife about
our house and many new things we are doing of, and so to church I,
and there find Jack Fenn come, and his wife, a pretty black woman:
I never saw her before, nor took notice of her now. So home and
to dinner, and after dinner all the afternoon got my wife and boy
to read to me, and at night W. Batelier comes and sups with us;
and, after supper, to have my head combed by Deb., which occasioned the greatest sorrow to me that ever I knew in this world,
for my wife, coming up suddenly, did find me embracing the girl.
I was at a wonderful loss upon it, and the girle also, and I endeavoured to put it off, but my wife was struck mute and grew
angry; and so, her voice come to her, grew quite out of order, and
I to say little, but to bed, and my wife said little also, but could
not sleep all night; but about two in the morning waked me and
cried, and fell to tell me as a great secret that she was a Roman
Catholique and had received the Holy Sacrament, which troubled
me, but I took no notice of it, but she went on from one thing to
another till at last it appeared plainly her trouble was at what she
saw; but yet I did not know how much she saw, and therefore said
nothing to her. But after her much crying and reproaching me
with inconstancy and preferring a sorry girl before her, I did give
her no provocation, but did promise all fair usage to her and love,
and foreswore any hurt that I did with her, till at last she seemed
to be at ease again, and so toward morning a little sleep, and so
I with some little repose and rest.

26th. Rose, and up and by water to White Hall, but with my mind mightily troubled for the poor girle, whom I fear I have undone by this, my wife telling me that she would turn her out of doors. However I was obliged to attend the Duke of York. He did press me to prepare what I had to say upon the answers of my fellow-officers to his great letter, which I promised to do against his coming to town again the next week. And so thence to my Lord Sandwich's, where, after long stay, he being in talk with others privately, I to him; and there, he taking physic and keeping his chamber, I had an hour's talk with him. Thence by coach home and to dinner, finding my wife mightily discontented, and the girle sad, and no words from my wife to her. So after dinner they out with me about two or three things, and so home again, I all the evening busy, and my wife full of trouble in her looks, and anon to bed, where about midnight she wakes me, and there falls foul of me again, affirming that she saw me hug and kiss the girle; the latter I denied, and truly, the other I confessed and no more, and upon her pressing me did offer to give her under my hand that I would never see Mrs. Pierce more, nor Knepp, but did promise my true love to her, owning some indiscretions in what I did, but that there was no harm in it. She at last upon these promises was quiet, and very kind we were, and so to sleep, and

27th. In the morning up, but my mind troubled for the poor girle, with whom I could not get opportunity to speak, but to the office, my mind mighty full of sorrow for her, where all the morning, and to dinner with my people, and to the office all the afternoon, and so at night home, and there busy to get some things ready against to-morrow's meeting of Tangier, and that being done, and my clerks gone, my wife did towards bedtime begin to be in a mighty rage from some new matter that she had got in her head, and did most part of the night in bed rant at me in most high terms of threats of publishing my shame, and when I offered to rise would have rose too, and caused a candle to be light to burn by her all night in the chimney while she ranted, while the knowing myself to have given some grounds for it, did make it my business to appease her all I could possibly, and by good words and fair promises did make her very quiet, and so rested all night, and rose with perfect good peace, being heartily afflicted for this folly of mine that did occasion it, but was forced to be silent about the girle, which I have no mind to part with, but much less that the poor girle should be undone by my folly. So up with mighty kindness from my wife and a thorough peace, and being up did by a note advise the girle what I had done and owned, which note I was in pain for till she told me she had burned it. This evening Mr. Spong come, and sat late with me, and first told me of the instrument called parallelogram,[1] which I must have one of, shewing me his practice thereon, by a map of England.

30th. Up betimes; and Mr. Povy comes to even accounts with me, which we did, and then fell to other talk. He tells how the Duke of York is led by the nose by his wife. That W. Coventry is now, by the Duke of York, made friends with the Duchess; and that he is often there, and waits on her. That he do believe that the present great men will break in time, and that W. Coventry will be a great man again; for he do labour to have nothing to do in matters of the State, and is so usefull to the side that he is on that he will stand, though at present he is quite out of play. That my Lady Castlemayne hates the Duke of Buckingham. That the Duke of York hath expressed himself very kind to my Lord Sandwich, which I am mighty glad of. This done, he and I to talk of my coach, and I got him to go see it, where he finds most infinite fault with it, both as to being out of fashion and heavy, with so good reason that I am mightily glad of his having corrected me in it; and so I do resolve to have one of his build, and with his advice, both in coach and horses, he being the fittest man in the world for it, and so he carried me home, and said the same to my wife.

November 3rd. Up, and all the morning at the Office. At noon to dinner, and then to the Office, and there busy till 12 at night without much pain to my eyes, but I did not use them to read or write and so did hold out very well. So home and there to supper, and I observed my wife to eye my eyes whether I did ever look upon Deb., which I could not but do now and then (and to my grief did see the poor wretch look on me and see me look on her, and then let drop a tear or two, which do make my heart relent at this minute that I am writing this with great trouble of mind, for she is indeed my sacrifice, poor girle); and my wife did tell me in bed by the by of my looking on other people, and that the only way is to put things out of sight, and this I know she means by Deb.

4th. Up, and by coach to White Hall; and there I find the King and Duke of York come the last night, and every body's mouth full of my Lord Anglesey's suspension being sealed, which it was,

[1] Now called a pantograph.

it seems, yesterday; and it seems the two new Treasurers did kiss the King's hand this morning, brought in by my Lord Arlington.[1] They walked up and down together the Court this day, and several people joyed them; but I avoided it, that I might not be seen to look either way. Several do tell me that Pen is to be removed, and others that he hath resigned his place; and particularly Spragg tells me for certain that he hath resigned it and is become a partner with Gawden in the Victualling, in which I think he hath done a very cunning thing; but I am sure I am glad of it, and it will be well for the King to have him out of this Office. Thence by coach, doing several errands, home and there to dinner, and then to the Office, where all the afternoon till late at night, and so home. Deb. hath been abroad to-day with her friends, poor girle, I believe toward the getting of a place. This day a boy is sent me out of the country from Impington by my cozen Roger Pepys' getting.

5th. With Mr. Povy spent all the afternoon going up and down among the coachmakers in Cow Lane, and did see several, and at last did pitch upon a little chariott, whose body was framed, but not covered, at the widow's that made Mr. Lowther's fine coach; and we are mightily pleased with it, it being light, and will be very genteel and sober: to be covered with leather, and yet will hold four.

9th. Up, and I did by a little note which I flung to Deb. advise her that I did continue to deny that ever I kissed her, and so she might govern herself. The truth is that I did adventure upon God's pardoning me this lie, knowing how heavy a thing it would be for me to the ruin of the poor girle, and next knowing that if my wife should know all it were impossible ever for her to be at peace with me again, and so our whole lives would be uncomfortable. The girl read, and as I bid her returned me the note, flinging it to me in passing by. And so I abroad by coach to White Hall, and there to the Duke of York to wait on him. Thence to Lord Sandwich's, and there to see him; but was made to stay so long, as his best friends are, and when I come to him so little pleasure, his head being full of his own business, I think, that I have no pleasure to go to him.

10th. Up, and my wife still every day as ill as she is all night, will rise to see me out doors, telling me plainly that she dares not let me see the girle; and so I out to the office, where all the

---

[1] This was a personal action of King Charles II. He had turned out Lord Anglesey and put in Sir Thomas Osborne and Sir Thomas Lyttleton as joint Treasurers.

"RETURNED ME THE NOTE"

morning, and so home to dinner, where I found my wife mightily
troubled again, more than ever, and she tells me that it is from
her examining the girle and getting a confession now from her of
all, which do mightily trouble me. So my wife would not go down
to dinner, but I would dine in her chamber with her, and there
after mollifying her as much as I could we were pretty quiet and
eat. After we had dined, we to talk again and she to be troubled,
reproaching me with my unkindness, as also with all her old kind-
nesses to me, and the many temptations she hath refused out of
faithfulness to me, especially from my Lord Sandwich, and then
afterwards the courtship of my Lord Hinchingbrooke, even to the
trouble of his lady, all of which I did acknowledge and was troubled for, and wept. And at last pretty good friends again; and so I
to my office, and there late, and so home to supper with her; and
so to bed, where after half-an-hour's slumber she wakes me and
cries out that she should never sleep more, and so kept raving
till past midnight, that made me cry and weep heartily all the while
for her, and at last with new vows, and particularly that I would
myself bid the girle be gone, and shew my dislike to her, which
I will endeavour to perform, but with much trouble, and so this
appeasing her, we to sleep as well as we could till morning.

  11th. Having done {at the office] I home to supper and to bed,
where, after lying a little while, my wife starts up, and with expressions of affright and madness, as one frantick, would rise, and I
would not let her, but burst out in tears myself, and so continued
almost half the night, the moon shining so that it was light, and
after much sorrow and reproaches and little ravings (though I
am apt to think they were counterfeit from her), and my promise
again to discharge the girle myself, all was quiet again, and so to
sleep.

  12th. To the Office, where all the morning, and at noon to
dinner, and Mr. Wayth, who, being at my office about business,
I took him with me. So having dined we parted, and I to my wife
and to sit with her a little, and then called her and Willet to my
chamber, and there did, with tears in my eyes, which I could not
help, discharge her and advise her to be gone as soon as she could,
and never to see me, or let me see her more while she was in the
house, which she took with tears too, but I believe understands
me to be her friend, and I am apt to believe by what my wife
hath of late told me is a cunning girle, if not a slut. With Mr.
Gibson late at my chamber making an end of my draught of

a letter for the Duke of York in answer to the answers of this
Office, which I have now done to my mind, so as, if the Duke
likes it, will I think put an end to a great deal of the faults of this
Office, as well as my trouble for them.

13th. Before we went to bed my wife told me she would not
have me to see [Willet] or give her her wages, and so I did give my
wife £10 for her year and half a quarter's wages, which she went
into her chamber and paid her, and so to bed, and there, blessed
be God! we did sleep well and with peace, which I had not done
in now almost twenty nights together.

14th. Up, and my wife would not let me be out of her sight,
and went down before me into the kitchen, and come up and told
me that [Willet] was in the kitchen, and therefore would have me
go round the other way; which she repeating and I vexed at it,
answered her a little angrily, upon which she instantly flew out
into a rage, calling me dog and rogue, and that I had a rotten
heart. All which, knowing that I deserved it, I bore with, and
word being brought presently up that she was gone away by coach
with her things, my wife was friends, and so all quiet. At the
Office all the morning, and merry at noon, at dinner; and after
dinner to the Office, where all the afternoon, doing much business,
late. My mind being free of all troubles, I thank God, but only
for my thoughts of this girl, which hang after her.

16th. To Holborne, about Whetstone's Park, where I never
was in my life before, where I understand by my wife's discourse
that Deb. is gone, which do trouble me mightily that the poor
girle should be in a desperate condition forced to go thereabouts,
and there not hearing of any such man as Allbon, with whom my
wife said she now was, I to the Strand.

17th. At my office all the afternoon and at night busy, and
so home to my wife, and pretty pleasant, and at mighty ease in
my mind, being in hopes to find Deb., and without trouble or
the knowledge of my wife. So to supper at night and to bed.

18th. Lay long in bed talking with my wife, she being unwilling to have me go abroad, saying and declaring herself jealous
of my going out for fear of my going to Deb., which I do deny;
for which God forgive me, for I was no sooner out about noon but
I did go by coach directly to Somerset House, and there enquired
among the porters there for Dr. Allbun; and the first I spoke with
told me he knew him, and that he was newly gone into Lincoln's
Inn Fields, but whither he could not tell me, but that one of his

fellows not then in the way did carry a chest of drawers thither with him, and that when he comes he would ask him. Towards night did meet with the porter that carried the chest of drawers with this Doctor, but he would not tell me where he lived, being his good master, he told me, but if I would have a message to him he would deliver it. At last I told him my business was not with him, but a little gentlewoman, one Mrs. Willet, that is with him, and sent him to see how she did from her friend in London, and no other token. He goes while I walk in Somerset House, in the Court; at last he comes back and tells me she is well, and that I may see her if I will, but no more. So I could not be commanded by my reason, but I must go this very night, and so by coach, it being now dark, I to her, close by my tailor's, and she come into the coach to me, and je did baiser her. I did give her the best council I could, to have a care of her honour, and to fear God. Je did give her 20s. and directions para[1] laisser sealed in paper at any time the name of the place of her being at Herringman's, my bookseller in the 'Change, by which I might go para her, and so bid her good night with much content to my mind, and resolution to look after her no more till I heard from her. And so home, and there told my wife a fair tale, God knows, how I spent the whole day, with which the poor wretch was satisfied, or at least seemed so, and so to supper and to bed, she having been mighty busy all day in getting of her house in order against to-morrow to hang up our new hangings and furnishing our best chamber.

   19th. Up, and at the Office all the morning, with my heart full of joy to think in what a safe condition all my matters now stand between my wife and Deb. and me, and at noon, running up stairs to see the upholsters who are at work upon hanging my best room and setting up my new bed, I find my wife sitting sad in the dining room; which enquiring into the reason of, she began to call me all the false, rotten-hearted rogues in the world, letting me understand that I was with Deb. yesterday, which, thinking it impossible for her ever to understand, I did a while deny, but at last did, for the ease of my mind and hers, and for ever to discharge my heart of this wicked business, I did confess all: and above stairs in our bed chamber there I did endure the sorrow of her threats and vows and curses all the afternoon, and, what was worse, she swore by all that was good that she would slit the nose of this girle, and be gone herself this very night from me, and did there demand 3 or

---

[1] To or for; cf. French *pour.*

£400 of me to buy my peace, that she might be gone without making any noise, or else protested that she would make all the world know of it. So with most perfect confusion of face and heart, and sorrow and shame, in the greatest agony in the world I did pass this afternoon, fearing that it will never have an end; but at last I did call for W. Hewer, who I was forced to make privy now to all, and the poor fellow did cry like a child, and obtained what I could not, that she would be pacified upon condition that I would give it under my hand never to see or speak with Deb. while I live, as I did before with Pierce and Knepp, and which I did also, God knows, promise for Deb. too, but I have the confidence to deny it to the perjury of myself. So before it was late there was, beyond my hopes as well as desert, a durable peace; and so to supper, and pretty kind words, and to bed.

20th. This morning up, with mighty kind words between my poor wife and I; and so to White Hall by water, W. Hewer with me, who is to go with me every where until my wife be in condition to go out along with me herself; for she do plainly declare that she dares not trust me out alone, and therefore made it a piece of our league that I should always take somebody with me, or her herself, which I am mighty willing to, being, by the grace of God, resolved never to do her wrong more. We landed at the Temple, and there I bid him call at my cozen Roger Pepys's lodgings, and I staid in the street for him, and so took water again at the Strand stairs; and so to White Hall, in my way I telling him plainly and truly my resolutions, if I can get over this evil, never to give new occasion for it. He is, I think, so honest and true a servant to us both, and one that loves us, that I was not much troubled at his being privy to all this, but rejoiced in my heart that I had him to assist in the making us friends, which he did truly and heartily; and with good success, for I did get him to go to Deb. to tell her that I had told my wife all of my being with her the other night, that so if my wife should send she might not make the business worse by denying it. While I was at White Hall with the Duke of York, doing our ordinary business with him, here being also the first time the new Treasurers, W. Hewer did go to her and come back again, and so I took him into St. James's Park, and there he did tell me he had been with her, and found what I said about my manner of being with her true, and had given her advice as I desired. I did there enter into more talk about my wife and myself, and he did give me great assurance of several particular cases to which my wife had from time to time made him privy of her loyalty and truth to me after many and great temptations, and I believe them truly. I did this night promise to my wife never to go to bed without calling upon God upon my knees by prayer, and I begun this night, and hope I shall never forget to do the like all my life.

23rd. To visit Lord Sandwich, who is now so reserved, or moped rather, I think, with his own business, that he bids welcome to no man, I think, to his satisfaction. However I bear with it, being willing to give him as little trouble as I can, and to receive as little from him, wishing only that I had my money in my purse that I have lent him; but however I shew no discontent at all. So to White Hall, where a Committee of Tangier expected, but none met. I met with Mr. Povy, who I discoursed with about publick business. Thence with W. Hewer, who goes up and down with me like a jaylour, but yet with great love. I took up my wife and boy to Unthank's, and from there to Hercules Pillars and there dined, and thence to our upholster's about some things more to buy, and so to see our coach, and so to the looking-glass man's by the New Exchange, and so to buy a picture for our blue chamber chimney, and so home; and there I made my boy to read to me most of the night, to get through the Life of Archbishop of Canterbury.[1] At supper comes Mary Batelier, and with us all the evening prettily talking, and very innocent company she is.

27th. Mr. Povy to dine with me; where a pretty good dinner, but for want of thought in my wife it was but slovenly dressed up; however much pleasant discourse with him, and some serious; and he tells me that he would by all means have me get to be a Parliament-man the next Parliament, which he believes there will be one, which I do resolve of.

28th. Up, and all the morning at the Office, where while I was sitting one comes and tells me that my coach is come. So I was forced to go out and to Sir Richard Ford's, where I spoke to him, and he is very willing to have it brought in and stand there; and so I ordered it to my great content, it being mighty pretty, only the horses do not please me, and therefore resolve to have better.

29th. (Lord's Day.) Lay long in bed and my mind is mightily more at ease, and I do mind my business better than ever and am more at peace, and trust in God I shall ever be so, though

[1] Peter Heylin's Life of Archbishop Laud.

I cannot yet get my mind off from thinking now and then of Deb.; but I do ever since my promise a while since to my wife pray to God by myself in my chamber every night, and will endeavour to get my wife to do the like with me ere long, but am in much fear of what she lately frighted me with about her being a Catholique, and I dare not therefore move her to go to church for fear she should deny me; but this morning of her own accord she spoke cf going to church the next Sunday, which pleases me mightily. This morning my coachman's clothes come home, and I like the livery mightily.

December 3rd. To the Office, where we sat all the morning; and at noon home to dinner, and then abroad again with my wife to the Duke of York's playhouse, and saw "The Unfortunate Lovers"; [1] a mean play, I think, but some parts very good, and excellently acted. We sat under the boxes, and saw the fine ladies, among others, my Lady Kerneguy, who is most devilishly painted. And so home, it being mighty pleasure to go alone with my poor wife in a coach of our own to a play, and makes us appear mighty great, I think, in the world; at least, greater than ever I could, or my friends for me, have once expected; or, I think, than ever any of my family ever yet lived in my memory but my cozen Pepys in Salisbury Court.

4th. Up, and with W. Hewer by water to White Hall, and there did wait as usual upon the Duke of York. Thence away, my coach meeting me there and carrying me to several places to do little jobs, which is a mighty convenience; and so home, where by invitation I find my aunt Wight, who looked over all our house and is mighty pleased with it, and indeed it is now mighty handsome and rich in furniture. By and by comes my uncle, and then to dinner, where a vension pasty and very merry; and after dinner I carried my wife and her to Smithfield, where they sit in the coach, while Mr. Pickering, who meets me there, and I and W. Hewer and a friend of his, a jockey, did go about to see several pairs of horses for my coach; but it was late, and we agreed on none, but left it to another time: but here I do see instances of a piece of craft and cunning that I never dreamed of, concerning the buying and choosing of horses. My aunt supped with us, and my uncle also: and a good-humoured woman she is, so that I think we shall keep her acquaintance; but mighty proud she is of her wedding-ring, being lately set with diamonds (cost her about

---

[1] By Sir W. Davenant.

£12), and I did commend it mightily to her, but do not think it very suitable for one of our quality.

6th. (Lord's Day.) Up, and with my wife to church; which pleases me mightily. Here Mills made a lazy sermon upon Moses's meeknesse; and so home, and my wife and I alone to dinner, and then she to read a little book concerning speech in general, a translation late out of French, a most excellent piece as ever I read, proving a soul in man, and all the ways and secrets by which nature teaches speech in man, which do please me most infinitely to read.

11th. To Smithfield, but met not Mr. Pickering, he being not come, and so [Will] and I to a cook's shop in Aldersgate Street and dined well for 19½*d.* upon roast beef; and so having dined, we back to Smithfield and there met Pickering, and up and down all the afternoon about horses, and did see the knaveries and tricks of jockeys. Here I met W. Joyce, who troubled me with his impertinencies a great while, and the like Mr. Knepp, who it seems is a kind of a jockey, and would fain have been doing something for me, but I avoided him, and the more for fear of being troubled thereby with his wife, whom I desire but dare not see, for my vow to my wife. At last went away and did nothing, only concluded upon giving £50 for a fine pair of black horses we saw this day se'nnight, and so set Mr. Pickering down near his house, whom I am much beholden to for his care herein, and he hath admirable skill, I perceive, in this business; and so home, and spent the evening talking and merry.

21st. My wife and W. Hewer and I by appointment out with our coach, but the old horses, not daring yet to use the others too much, but only to enter them; and to the Temple, there to call Talbot Pepys, and took him up, and first went into Holborne and there saw the woman that is to be seen with a beard. She is a little plain woman, a Dane, her name Ursula Dyan, about forty years old; her voice like a little girl's, with a beard as muc'ᵇ as any man I ever saw, black almost, and grizly. It begun to grow at about seven years old and was shaved not above seven months ago, and is now so big as any man's almost that ever I saw; I say, bushy and thick. It was a strange sight to me I confess, and what pleased me mightily. Thence to the Duke's playhouse and saw "Macbeth." The King and Court there; and we sat just under them and my Lady Castlemayne, and close to the woman that comes into the pit, a kind of a loose gossip, that pretends to be like her,

"UP AND DOWN . . . ABOUT HORSES"

and is so, something. And my wife, by my troth, appeared I think as pretty as any of them; I never thought so much before; and so did Talbot and W. Hewer, as they said, I heard, to one another. The King and Duke of York minded me, and smiled upon me, at the handsome woman near me.

25th. (Christmas-day.) Up, and I to church, where Alderman Backewell coming in late, I beckoned to his lady to come up to us, who did, with another lady; and after sermon I led her down through the church to her husband and coach, a noble, fine woman and a good one, and one my wife shall be acquainted with. So home and to dinner alone with my wife, who, poor wretch! sat undressed all day till ten at night, altering and lacing of a noble petticoat: while I by her, making the boy read to me the Life of Julius Cæsar, and Des Cartes' book of Musick, the latter of which I understand not, nor think he did well that writ it, though a most learned man. Then after supper I made the boy play upon his lute, which I have not done twice before since he come to me; and so, my mind in mighty content, we to bed.

28th. Up, called up by drums and trumpets; these things and boxes having cost me much money this Christmas already, and will do more. My wife down by water to see her mother, and I with W. Hewer all day together in my closet, making some advance in the settling of my accounts, which have been so long unevened that it troubles me how to set them right, having not the use of my eyes to help me. My wife at night home and tells me how much her mother prays for me and is troubled for my eyes; and I am glad to have friendship with them and believe they are truly glad to see their daughter come to live so well as she do. So spent the night in talking, and so to supper and to bed.

TENTH YEAR

1669

January 1st. Up, and presented from Captain Beckford [1] with a noble silver warming-pan, which I am doubtful whether to take or no. Up, and with W. Hewer to the New Exchange, and then he and I to the cabinet-shops to look out, and did agree, for a cabinet to give my wife for a New-year's gift; and I did buy one cost me £11, which is very pretty, of walnutt-tree, and will come home to-morrow. So back to the old Exchange, and there met my uncle Wight; and there walked, and met with the Houblons and talked with them, gentlemen whom I honour mightily: and so to my uncle's and met my wife; and there, with W. Hewer, we dined with our family.

4th. Lay long talking with my wife, and did of my own accord come to an allowance of her of £30 a-year for all expences, clothes and everything, which she was mightily pleased with, it being more than ever she asked or expected.

7th. Up, and to the office, where busy all the morning, and then at noon home to dinner, and thence my wife and I to the King's playhouse, and there saw "The Island Princesse," [2] the first time I ever saw it; and it is a pretty good play, many good things being in it, and a good scene of a town on fire. We sat in an upper box, and the jade Nell come and sat in the next box; a bold merry slut, who lay laughing there upon people; and with a comrade of hers of the Duke's house, that come in to see the play. Thence home and to the office to do some business, and so home to supper and to bed.

12th. This evening I observed my wife mighty dull, and I myself was not mighty fond, because of some hard words she did give me at noon, out of a jealousy at my being abroad this morning, which, God knows, it was upon the business of the Office unexpectedly: but I to bed, not thinking but she would come after me. But waking by and by out of a slumber, which I usually fall into presently after my coming into the bed, I found she did not prepare to come

[1] He was the slopseller, and no doubt contracted for clothing the Navy.
[2] By Beaumont and Fletcher.

to bed, but got fresh candles, and more wood for her fire, it being mighty cold, too. At this being troubled, I after a while prayed her to come to bed, all my people being gone to bed; so, after an hour or two, she silent, and I now and then praying her to come to bed, she fell out into a fury, that I was a rogue and false to her. But yet I did perceive that she was to seek what to say, only she invented, I believe, a business that I was seen in a hackney coach with the glasses up with Deb., but could not tell the time, nor was sure I was he. I did, as I might truly, deny it,[1] and was mightily troubled, but all would not serve. At last about one o'clock she come to my side of the bed and drew my curtaine open, and with the tongs red hot at the ends, made as if she did design to pinch me with them, at which in dismay I rose up, and with a few words she laid them down; and did by little and little, very sillily, let all the discourse fall; and about two, but with much seeming difficulty, come to bed, and there lay well all night, and long in bed talking together with much pleasure, it being, I know, nothing but her doubt of my going out yesterday without telling her of my going which did vex her, poor wretch! and I cannot blame her jealousy, though it do vex me to the heart.

15th. To White Hall through the Park, where I met the King and the Duke of York, and so walked with them, and so to White Hall, where the Duke of York met the office and did a little business. Then down with Lord Brouncker into the King's little elaboratory, under his closet, a pretty place; and there saw a great many chymical glasses and things, but understood none of them.

18th. To my Lord Sandwich's, and there walk with him through the garden to White Hall, and I took this occasion to invite him to dinner one day to my house, and he readily appointed Friday next, which I shall be glad to have over to his content, he having never yet eat a bit of my bread.

23rd. Up, and to look after the setting things right against dinner, which I did to very good content. So to the office, where all the morning till noon, when word brought me to the Board that my Lord Sandwich was come; so I presently rose, leaving the Board ready to rise, and there I found my Lord Sandwich, Peterborough, and Sir Charles Harbord;[2] and presently after them comes my

---

[1] The Diary confirms this: Pepys had not seen Deb. for a long time.
[2] Sir Charles Harbord, at this time only twenty-five, was a highly distinguished naval commander under Lord Sandwich (with whom he perished four years after this dinner took place). Mr. Sidney was of course Lord Sandwich's son. Sir William Godolphin was M.P. for Camelford, a great Court favourite; just after this occasion he was sent as Envoy Extraordinary to Spain, whence Lord Sandwich was recently returned.

Lord Hinchingbroke, Mr. Sidney, and Sir William Godolphin. And after greeting them, and some time spent in talk, dinner was brought up, one dish after another, but a dish at a time, but all so good; but above all things the variety of wines, and excellent of their kind I had for them; and all in so good order that they were mightily pleased, and myself full of content at it: and indeed it was, of a dinner of about six or eight dishes, as noble as any man need to have, I think; at least all was done in the noblest manner that ever I had any, and I have rarely seen in my life better anywhere else, even at the Court. After dinner my Lords to cards, and the rest of us sitting about them and talking, and looking on my books and pictures, and my wife's drawings which they commend mightily; and mighty merry all day long with exceeding great content, and so till seven at night; and so took their leaves, it being dark and foul weather. Thus was this entertainment over, the best of its kind, and the fullest of honour and content to me that ever I had in my life, and shall not easily have so good again.

26th. To White Hall, leaving my wife at Unthanke's; and I to the Secretary's chamber, where I was by particular order this day summoned to attend, as I find Sir D. Gawden also was. And here was the King and the Cabinet met; and, being called in, among the rest I find my Lord Privy Seale, whom I never before knew to be in so much play as to be of the Cabinet. The business is that the Algerines have broke the peace with us by taking some Spaniards and goods out of an English ship which had the Duke of York's pass, of which advice come this day; and the King is resolved to stop Sir Thomas Allen's fleete from coming home till he hath amends made him for this affront, and therefore sent for us to advise about victuals to be sent to that fleete, and some more ships; wherein I answered them to what they demanded of me, which was but some few mean things; but I see that on all these occasions they seem to rely most upon me.

February 1st. Meeting Mr. Povy, he carried me to Mr. Streeter's,[1] the famous history-painter over the way, whom I have often heard of, but did never see him before; and there I found him and Dr. Wren and several Virtuosos looking upon the paintings which he is making for the new Theatre at Oxford: and indeed they look as if they would be very fine, and the rest think better than those of Rubens in the Banqueting-house at White Hall,

---

[1] Robert Streater, Serjeant-Painter to King Charles II. Dr. Wren was afterwards famous as Sir Christopher.

but I do not so fully think so. But they will certainly be very noble, and I am mightily pleased to have the fortune to see this man and his work, which is very famous; and he a very civil little man, and lame, but lives very handsomely. So thence to my Lord Bellassis, and met him within: my business only to see a chimney-piece in distemper, with egg to keep off the glaring of the light, which I must have done for my room: and indeed it is pretty, but I must confess I do think it is not altogether so beautiful as the oyle picture; but I will have some of one and some of another.

8th. I to visit my Lord Sandwich; and there, while my Lord was dressing himself, did see a young Spaniard that he hath brought over with him dance, which he is admired for as the best dancer in Spain, and indeed he do with mighty mastery; but I do not like his dancing as the English, though my Lord commends it mightily: but I will have him to my house and show it my wife. So to my wife, took her up at Unthank's, and in our way home did shew her the tall woman in Holborne, which I have seen before; and I measured her, and she is without shoes just six feet five inches high, and they say not above twenty-one years old. This morning also, going to visit Roger Pepys at the potticary's in King's Street, he tells me that Roger is gone to his wife's. So that they have been married, as he tells me, ever since the middle of last week: it was his design upon good reasons to make no noise of it; but I am well enough contented that it is over.[1]

10th. Up, and with my wife and W. Hewer, she set us down at White Hall, where the Duke of York was gone a-hunting: and so, after I had done a little business there, I to my wife, and with her to the plaisterer's at Charing Cross that casts heads and bodies in plaister, and there I had my whole face done; but I was vexed first to be forced to daub all my face over with pomatum: but it was pretty to feel how soft and easily it is done on the face, and by and by, by degrees, how hard it becomes, that you cannot break it, and sits so close that you cannot pull it off, and yet so easy that it is as soft as a pillow, so safe is everything where many parts of the body do bear alike. Thus was the mould made; but when it came off there was little pleasure in it as it looks in the mould nor any resemblance, whatever there will be in the figure when I come to see it cast off, which I am to call for a day or two hence, which I shall long to see. Thence to Hercules Pillars, and there my

[1] Roger Pepys had married the widow Dickinson, of Covent Garden, on February 2. "A wonder-full merry, good-humoured, fat but plain woman," Pepys had thought her. She was not the lady mentioned on July 29, 1667.

"DINNER WAS BROUGHT UP"

wife and W. Hewer and I dined, and back to White Hall, where I staid till the Duke of York come from hunting, which he did by and by, and when dressed did come out to dinner, and there I waited: and he did mightily magnify his sauce which he did then eat with every thing, and said it was the best universal sauce in the world, it being taught him by the Spanish Embassador; made of some parsley and a dry toast, beat in a mortar, together with vinegar, salt, and a little pepper: he eats it with flesh or fowl or fish: and then he did now mightily commend some new sort of wine lately found out, called Navarre wine, which I tasted, and is I think good wine: but I did like better the notion of the sauce, and by and by did taste it, and liked it mightily.

12th. After dinner we away and to Dancre's, and there saw our picture of Greenwich in doing,[1] which is mighty pretty, and so to White Hall, my wife to Unthank's, and I attended with Lord Brouncker the King and Council. Thence I homeward, and calling my wife called at my cozen Turner's, and there met our new cozen Pepys (Mrs. Dickenson), and Bab. and Betty[2] come yesterday to town, poor girls, whom we have reason to love, and mighty glad we are to see them; and there staid and talked a little, being also mightily pleased to see Betty Turner, who is now in town, and her brothers Charles and Will, being come from school to see their father, and there talked a while; and so home, and there Pelling hath got me W. Pen's book against the Trinity.[3] I got my wife to read it to me; and I find it so well writ as, I think, it is too good for him ever to have writ it; and it is a serious sort of book, and not fit for every body to read. So to supper and to bed.

15th. To the plaisterer's, and there saw the figure of my face taken from the mould: and it is most admirably like, and I will have another made before I take it away. After dinner my wife and I to my cozen Roger's lodgings, and there find him pretty well again, and his wife mighty kind and merry, and did make mighty much of us, and I believe he is married to a very good woman. Here was also Bab. and Betty, who have not their clothes yet and therefore cannot go out, otherwise I would have had them abroad to-morrow; but the poor girls mighty kind to us, and we must shew them kindness also.

---

[1] Henry Dankers was a Dutch landscape painter employed by King Charles II. to paint views of his seaports and palaces. Pepys had commissioned him to paint a picture of Greenwich for one of the panels of his dining-room.

[2] Roger Pepys' children by a previous wife; they were aged twenty and eighteen.

[3] "The Sandy Foundation Shaken . . ." Its publication without licence was visited with his committal to the Tower.

"GOOD COMELY GIRLS THEY ARE"

18th. Up, and to the Office, and at noon home, expecting to have this day seen Bab. and Betty Pepys here, but they come not; and so after dinner my wife and I to the Duke of York's house to a play, and there saw "The Mad Lover,"[1] which do not please me so well as it used to do, only Betterton's part still pleases me. But here who should we have come to us but Bab. and Betty and Talbot, the first play they were yet at; and going to see us, and hearing by my boy whom I sent to them that we were here, they come to us hither, and happened all of us to sit by my cozen Turner and The., and we carried them home first, and then took Bab. and Betty to our house, where they lay and supped, and pretty merry, and very fine with their new clothes, and good comely girls they are enough, and very glad I am of their being with us, though I would very well have been contented to have been without the charge. So they to bed and we to bed.

19th. Up, and after seeing the girls, who lodged in our bed, with their maid Martha, who hath been their father's maid these twenty years and more, I with Lord Brouncker to White Hall, where all of us waited on the Duke of York; and after our usual business done, W. Hewer and I to look my wife at the Black Lion, Mercer's, but she is gone home; and so I home and there dined, and W. Batelier and W. Hewer with us. All the afternoon I at the Office, while the young people went to see Bedlam,[2] and at night home to them and to supper, and pretty merry, only troubled with a great cold at this time, and my eyes very bad ever since Monday. So to bed. This morning, among other things, talking with Sir W. Coventry, I did propose to him my putting in to serve in Parliament, if there should, as the world begins to expect, be a new one chose: he likes it mightily, both for the King's and Service's sake and the Duke of York's, and will propound it to the Duke of York: and I confess, if there be one, I would be glad to be in.

21st. (Lord's Day.) Up, and with my wife and two girls to church, they very fine; and so home, where comes my cozen Roger and his wife, I having sent for them, to dine with us; and there comes in by chance also Mr. Shepley. Here we dined with W. Batelier, and W. Hewer with us, these two girls making it necessary that they be always with us, for I am not company light enough to be always merry with them: and so sat talking all the

---

[1] By Beaumont and Fletcher.
[2] Then in Bishopsgate.

afternoon, and then Shepley went away first, and then my cozen Roger and his wife. And so I to my Office, and so home to my chamber and to do a little business there, my papers being in mighty disorder, and likely so to continue while these girls are with us.

23rd. Up, and to the Office, where all the morning, and then home, and put a mouthfull of victuals in my mouth, and by a hackney-coach followed my wife and the girls, who are gone by eleven o'clock, thinking to have seen a new play at the Duke of York's house. But I do find them staying at my tailor's, the play not being to-day, and therefore I now took them to Westminster Abbey and there did show them all the tombs very finely, having one with us alone, there being other company this day to see the tombs, it being Shrove Tuesday; and here we did see, by particular favour, the body of Queen Katherine of Valois;[1] and I had the upper part of her body in my hands, and I did kiss her mouth, reflecting upon it that I did kiss a Queen, and that this was my birth-day, thirty-six years old, that I did first kiss a Queen. But here this man, who seems to understand well, tells me that the saying is not true that says she was never buried, for she was buried, only when Henry the Seventh built his chapel it was taken up and laid in this wooden coffin; but I did there see that, in it, the body was buried in a leaden one, which remains under the body to this day. Thence we homeward to the Glass-House, and there shewed my cozens the making of glass, and had several things made with great content; and among others I had one or two singing-glasses made, which make an echo to the voice, the first that ever I saw; but so thin that the very breath broke one or two of them. So home, and thence to Mr. Batelier's, where we supped, and had a good supper, and here was Mr. Gumbleton; and after supper some fiddles, and so to dance; but my eyes were so out of order that I had little pleasure this night at all, though I was glad to see the rest merry, and so about midnight home and to bed.

24th. To the office, doing of much business, and at night my wife sends for me to W. Hewer's lodging, where I find two best chambers of his so finely furnished and all so rich and neat that I was mightily pleased with him and them: and here only my wife and I and the two girls, and had a mighty neat dish of custards and tarts, and good drink and talk. And so away home to bed,

---

1 Wife of King Henry V.; she was buried in 1457.

with infinite content at this his treat, for it was mighty pretty, and everything mighty rich.

28th. (Lord's Day.) By coach with my cozens to their father's, agreeing to be all merry at my house on Tuesday next.

March 1st. Most surprised this morning by my Lord Bellassis, who by appointment met me at Auditor Woods, at the Temple, and tells me of a duell designed between the Duke of Buckingham and my Lord Halifax or Sir W. Coventry, the challenge being prevented by my Lord Arlington, and the King told of it; and this was all the discourse at Court this day. But I, meeting Sir W. Coventry in the Duke of York's chamber, he would not own it to me, but told me that he was a man of too much peace to meddle with fighting, and so it rested: but the talk is full in the town of the business.[1]

2nd. Up, and at the office till noon, when home, and there I find my company come, namely, Madam Turner, Dyke,[2] The. and Betty Turner, and Mr. Bellwood, formerly their father's clerk but now set up for himself, a conceited, silly fellow, but one they make mightily of, my cozen Roger Pepys and his wife and two daughters. I had a noble dinner for them, as I almost ever had, and mighty merry, and particularly myself pleased with looking on Betty Turner, who is mighty pretty. After dinner we fell one to one talk and another to another, and looking over my house and closet and things; and The. Turner to write a letter to a lady in the country, in which I did now and then put in half a dozen words, and sometimes five or six lines, and then she as much, and made up a long and good letter, she being mighty witty really, though troublesome-humoured with it. And thus till night, that our musick come, and the Office ready and candles, and also W. Batelier and his sister Susan come, and also Will. Howe and two gentlemen more, strangers, which at my request yesterday he did bring to dance, called Mr. Ireton and Mr. Starkey. We fell to dancing and continued, only with intermission for a good supper, till two in the morning, the musick being Greeting and another most excellent violin, and theorbo, the best in town. And so with mighty mirth, and pleased with their dancing of jigs afterwards several of them, and among others Betty Turner who did it mighty prettily; and lastly W. Batelier's "Blackmore

---

[1] The Duke of Buckingham and Sir Robert Howard were contemplating producing a caricature of Coventry on the stage. Coventry thereupon challenged Buckingham, and was accordingly imprisoned in the Tower. He was released on March 20. After this he retired to the country for the rest of his life.

[2] Mrs. Turner was a Pepys; and her sister married a Thomas Dyke.

and Blackmore Mad"; and then to a country-dance again, and so broke up with extraordinary pleasure, as being one of the days and nights of my life spent with the greatest content; and that which I can but hope to repeat again a few times in my whole life. This done, we parted, the strangers home, and I did lodge my cozen Pepys and his wife in our blue chamber. My cozen Turner, her sister and The. in our best chamber; Bab., Betty, and Betty Turner in our own chamber; and myself and my wife in the maid's bed, which is very good. Our maids in the coachman's bed; the coachman with the boy in his settle-bed, and Tom where he uses to lie. And so I did to my great content, lodge at once in my house, with the greatest ease, fifteen; and eight of them strangers of quality. My wife this day put on first her French gown, called a Sac, which becomes her very well, brought her over by W. Batelier.

3rd. Called at my cozen Turner's; and there, meeting Mr. Bellwood, did hear how my Lord Mayor, being invited this day to dinner at the Reader's at the Temple, and endeavouring to carry his sword up, the students did pull it down, and forced him to go and stay all the day in a private Councillor's chamber until the Reader himself could get the young gentlemen to dinner; and then my Lord Mayor did retreat out of the Temple by stealth, with his sword up.[1] This do make great heat among the students; and my Lord Mayor did send to the King, and also I hear that Sir Richard Browne did cause the drums to beat for the Train-bands; but all is over, only I hear that the students do resolve to try the Charter of the City.

4th. To White Hall, where in the first court I did meet Sir Jeremy Smith, who did tell me that Sir W. Coventry was just now sent to the Tower about the business of his challenging the Duke of Buckingham. This news did strike me to the heart, and with reason, for by this I do doubt that the Duke of Buckingham will be so flushed that he will not stop at any thing, but be forced to do any thing now, as thinking it not safe to end here; and, Sir W. Coventry being gone, the King will have never a good counsellor, nor the Duke of York any sure friend to stick to him; nor any good man will be left to advise what is good. To the Treasurer's house, where the Duke of York is, and his Duchess; and there we find them at dinner in the great room, unhung;

---

[1] The question of the authority of the Lord Mayor upon entering the Temple appears to be unsettled to this day.

and there was with them my Lady Duchess of Monmouth, the Countess of Falmouth, Castlemayne, Henrietta Hide (my Lady Hinchingbroke's sister), and my Lady Peterborough. And after dinner Sir Jer. Smith and I were invited down to dinner with some of the Maids of Honour, which did me good to have the honour to dine with and look on; and the Mother of the Maids, and the Duke's housekeeper here. And here drank most excellent and great variety and plenty of wines, more than I have drank at once these seven years, but yet did me no great hurt. Having dined and very merry, we up; and there I did find the Duke of York and Duchess, with all the great ladies, sitting upon a carpet on the ground, there being no chairs, playing at "I love my love with an A, because he is so and so: and I hate him with an A, because of this and that": and some of them, but particularly the Duchess herself and my Lady Castlemayne, were very witty. This done they took barge, and I with Sir J. Smith to Captain Cox's, and there to talk; and left them and other company to drink, while I slunk out to Bagwell's and there saw her and her mother and our late maid Nell, who cried for joy to see me, but I had no time for pleasure then nor could stay. Home, and there my wife mighty angry for my absence, and fell mightily out, but not being certain of any thing, but thinks only that Pierce or Knepp was there, and did ask me (and I perceive, the boy), many questions.

6th. Up, and to the office, where all the morning, only before the Office I stepped to Sir W. Coventry at the Tower and there had a great deal of discourse with him; among others, of the King's putting him out of the Council yesterday, with which he is well contented, as with what else they can strip him of, he telling me, and so hath long done, that he is weary and surfeited of business. He told me the matter of the play that was intended for his abuse, wherein they foolishly and sillily bring in two tables like that which he hath made, with a round hole in the middle, in his closet, to turn himself in; [1] and he is to be in one of them as master, and Sir J. Duncomb in the other as his man, or imitator; and their discourse in those tables about the disposing of their books and papers, very foolish. But that that he is offended with is his being made so contemptible as that any should dare to make a gentleman a subject for the mirth of the world: and that therefore he had told Tom Killigrew that he should tell his actors, whoever they

[1] He had a circular table, at the centre of which he sat.

" I LOVE MY LOVE WITH AN A "

were that did offer at any thing like representing him, that he
would not complain to my Lord Chamberlain, which was too weak,
nor get him beaten, as Sir Charles Sidly is said to do, but that he
would cause his nose to be cut.

7th. (Lord's Day.) To the Tower, to see Sir W. Coventry,
who had H. Jermin and a great many more with him, and more
while I was there come in; so that I do hear that there was not
less than sixty coaches there yesterday and the other day; which
I hear also that there is a great exception taken at, by the King
and the Duke of Buckingham.

9th. Up, and to the Tower; and there find Sir W. Coventry
alone, writing down his Journal, which he tells me he now keeps
of the material things; upon which I told him, and he is the only
man I ever told it to, I think, that I kept it most strictly these
eight or ten years; and I am sorry almost that I told it him, it
not being necessary, nor may be convenient, to have it known.
Here he showed me the petition he had sent to the King by my
Lord Keeper, which was not to desire any admittance to employment, but submitting himself therein humbly to his Majesty;
but prayed the removal of his displeasure, and that he might
be set free. From this to other discourse, and so to the Office,
where we sat all the morning. After dinner with my wife and Bab.
and Betty Pepys and W. Hewer, whom I carried all this day with
me, to my cozen Stradwick's, [1] where I have not been ever since
my brother Tom died, there being some difference between my
father and them upon the account of my cozen Scott; and I was
glad of this opportunity of seeing them, they being good and substantial people, and kind, and here met my cozen Roger and his
wife and my cozen Turner; and here, which I never did before,
I drank a glass, of a pint I believe, at one draught, of the juice of
oranges, of whose peel they make comfits; and here they drink
the juice as wine, with sugar, and it is very fine drink; but it being
new I was doubtful whether it might not do me hurt. Having
staid a while, my wife and I back with my cozen Turner, etc.,
to her house, and there we took our leaves of my cozen Pepys,
who goes with his wife and two daughters for Impington to-morrow. They are very good people, and people I love and am obliged
to, and shall have great pleasure in their friendship; and particu-

[1] The Diarist's father had a first cousin, Richard Pepys (d. 1658), who was Lord Chief Justice of
Ireland. Of his children two had married Scotts and one married a Stradwick; and they were thus
second cousins of Samuel Pepys. Thomas Stradwick appears to have had a substantial business in
London as provision dealer or grocer.

larly in hers, she being an understanding and good woman. So away home, and there after signing my letters, my eyes being bad, to supper and to bed.

13th. Up, and to the Tower to see Sir W. Coventry. So away to the Office, where all the morning, and then home to dinner with my people, and so to the Office again, and there all the afternoon till night, when comes by mistake my cozen Turner and her two daughters, which love such freaks, to eat some anchovies and ham of bacon with me, instead of noon, at dinner, when I expected them. But however I had done my business before they come, and so was in good humour enough to be with them. But that which put me in good humour, both at noon and night, is the fancy that I am this day made a Captain of one of the King's ships, in order to my being of a Court-martiall for examining the loss of "The Defyance" and other things, which do give me occasion of much mirth and may be of some use to me; at least I shall get a little money by it for the time I have it, it being designed that I must really be a Captain to be able to sit in this Court. They staid till about eight at night, and then away, and my wife to read to me; and then to bed in mighty good humour, but for my eyes.

16th. Up, and to the office, after having visited Sir W. Coventry at the Tower. At noon home, where my wife and Jane gone abroad, and Tom, in order to their buying of things for their wedding, which is now resolved to be done upon the 26th of this month, the day of my solemnity for my cutting of the stone. My wife therefore not at dinner; and comes to me Mr. Evelyn, and dined with me, but a bad dinner; who is grieved for, and speaks openly to me his thoughts of, the times, and our ruin approaching; and all by the folly of the King. After dinner we parted, and I away down by water with W. Hewer to Woolwich, where I have not been I think more than a year or two. Thence, after seeing Mr. Sheldon, I to Greenwich by water, and there landed at the King's house,[1] which goes on slow, but is very pretty. I to the Park, there to see the prospect of the hill, to judge of Dancre's picture which he hath made thereof for me: and I do like it very well, and it is a very pretty place.

18th. Up, and to see Sir W. Coventry, and walked with him a good while in the Stone Walk; and thence to the office, where we sat all the morning, and so home to dinner, where my wife mighty

---

[1] Now Greenwich Hospital; it formed one wing of a projected palace for King Charles II.

finely dressed by a maid that she hath taken. After dinner my wife and I going by coach, she went with us to Holborne, where we set her down. She is a mighty proper maid and pretty comely, but so so; but hath a most pleasing tone of voice and speaks handsomely, but hath most great hands, and I believe ugly; but very well dressed, and good clothes, and the maid I believe will please me well enough. Thence to Hyde Park, the first time we were there this year, or ever in our own coach, where with mighty pride rode up and down, and many coaches there; and I thought our horses and coach as pretty as any there, and observed so to be by others. Here staid till night, and so home and to the office, where busy late, and so home to supper and to bed with great content.

20th. Mightily pleased with the news brought me to-night that this afternoon a warrant was sent to the Tower for the releasing Sir W. Coventry, which do put me in some hopes that there may be some accommodation made between the Duke of York and the Duke of Buckingham and Arlington.

22nd. To Mr. Wren's, and then up to the Duke of York, and there with Mr. Wren did propound to him my going to Chatham to-morrow with Commissioner Middleton, and so this week to make pay there and examine the business of "The Defyance," and other businesses. The Duke of York mightily satisfied with it.

23rd. Up, and to my office to do a little business there, and so, my things being all ready, I took coach with Commissioner Middleton, Captain Tinker,[1] and Mr. Huchinson, a hackney coach, and over the bridge, and so out towards Chatham and dined at Dartford, where we staid an hour or two, it being a cold day; and so on, and got to Chatham just at night, with very good discourse by the way, but mostly of matters of religion, wherein Huchinson his vein lies. After supper we fell to talk of spirits and apparitions, whereupon many pretty, particular stories were told, so as to make me almost afeard to lie alone, but for shame I could not help it; and so to bed, and being sleepy fell soon to rest, and so rested well.

24th. To the Hill-House, and there did give order for the coach to be made ready; and got Mr. Gibson, whom I carried with me to go with me, and Mr. Coney the surgeon, towards

---

[1] Captain John Tinker was Master-Attendant at Portsmouth. Hutchinson had just been made paymaster.

Maydstone, which I had a mighty mind to see, and took occasion in my way at St. Margett's, to pretend to call to see Captain Allen, to see whether Mrs. Jowles, his daughter, was there; and there his wife come to the door, he being at London, and through a window I spied Jowles, but took no notice of her, but made excuse till night, and then promised to come and see Mrs. Allen again, and so away, it being a mighty cold and windy but clear day; and had the pleasure of seeing the Medway running, winding up and down mightily, and a very fine country. Thence to Maydstone, which I had a mighty mind to see, having never been there; and walked all up and down the town, and up to the top of the steeple and had a noble view, and then down again: and in the town did see an old man beating of flax, and did step into the barn and give him money, and saw that piece of husbandry which I never saw, and it is very pretty: in the street also I did buy and send to our inne, the Bell, a dish of fresh fish. And so, having walked all round the town and found it very pretty, as most towns I ever saw, though not very big, and people of good fashion in it, we to our inne to dinner and had a good dinner; and after dinner a barber come to me and there trimmed me that I might be clean against night, to go to Mrs. Allen. And so, staying till about four o'clock, we set out, homeward, and stopped again at Captain Allen's, and there 'light, and sent the coach and Gibson home, and I and Coney staid; and there comes to us Mrs. Jowles,[1] who is a very fine, proper lady, as most I know, and well dressed. Here was also a gentleman, one Major Manly and his wife, neighbours; and here we staid and drank and talked, and set Coney and him to play while Mrs. Jowles and I to talk; and there had all our old stories up, and there I had the liberty to salute her often, and pull off her glove, where her hand mighty moist, and she mighty free in kindness to me. Here mightily pleased with Mrs. Jowles, and did get her to the street door and there baiser her. Here staid till almost twelve at night, and then with a lanthorn from thence walked over the fields, as dark as pitch, and mighty cold, and snow, to Chatham.

25th. Up, and by and by, about eight o'clock, come Rear-Admiral Kempthorne and seven Captains more, by the Duke of York's order, as we expected, to hold the Court-martiall about the loss of "The Defyance"; and so presently we by boat to "The Charles," which lies over against Upnor Castle, and there we

[1] This was Rebecca Allen, who had married a Lieut. Jowles. Major Manley was M.P. for Bridport.

fell to the business; and there I did manage the business, the Duke
of York having by special order directed them to take the assistance of Commissioner Middleton and me, forasmuch as there
might be need of advice in what relates to the government of
the ships in harbour. And so I did lay the law open to them, and
rattle the Master-Attendants out of their wits almost; and made
the trial last till seven at night, not eating a bit all the day; only
when we had done examination, and I given my thoughts that
the neglect of the Gunner of the ship was as great as I thought
any neglect could be, which might by the law deserve death, but
Commissioner Middleton did declare that he was against giving
the sentence of death, we withdrew, as not being of the Court,
and so left them to do what they pleased; and while they were
debating it the Boatswain of the ship did bring us out of the kettle
a piece of hot salt beef and some brown bread and brandy; and there
we did make a little meal, but so good as I never would desire to
eat better meat while I live, only I would have cleaner dishes.
By and by they had done, and called us down from the quarter-
deck; and there we find they do sentence that the Gunner of "The
Defyance" should stand upon "The Charles" three hours with
his fault writ upon his breast, and with a halter about his neck,
and so be made incapable of any office.

27th. Up, and did a little business, Middleton and I, then after
drinking a little buttered ale he and Huchinson and I took coach,
and exceeding merry in talk to Dartford: Middleton finding stories
of his own life at Barbadoes, and up and down at Venice and elsewhere, that are mighty pretty and worth hearing; and he is a
strange good companion and droll upon the road, more than ever
I could have thought to have been in him. Got home about
six at night. I find all well, but my wife abroad with Jane, who
was married yesterday, and I to the office busy, till by and by my
wife comes home; and so home, and there hear how merry they
were yesterday, and I glad at it, they being married it seems very
handsomely at Islington; and dined at the old house, and lay in
our blue chamber, with much company, and wonderful merry.
The. Turner and Mary Batelier bridesmaids, and Talbot Pepys
and W. Hewer bridesmen.

28th. (Lord's Day.) Lay long talking with pleasure with my
wife, and so up and to the Office with Tom, who looks mighty
smug upon his marriage, as Jane also do, both of whom I did
give joy.

29th. Up, and by water to White Hall; and there to the Duke of York, to shew myself after my journey to Chatham, but did no business to-day with him only after gone from him, I to Sir T. Clifford's; and there, after an hour's waiting, he being alone in his closet, I did speak with him, and give him the account he gave me to draw up, and he did like it very well: and then fell to talk of the business of the Navy: and giving me good words, did fall foul of the constitution [of the Board], and did then discover his thoughts, that Sir J. Minnes was too old, and so was Colonel Middleton, and that my Lord Brouncker did mind his mathematics too much. I did not give much encouragement to that of finding fault with my fellow-officers; but did stand up for the constitution, and did say that what faults there were in our Office would be found not to arise from the constitution, but from the failures of the officers in whose hands it was. This he did seem to give good ear to; but did give me of myself very good words, which pleased me well, though I shall not build upon them any thing. Thence home; and after dinner by water with Tom down to Greenwich, he reading to me all the way, coming and going, my collections out of the Duke of York's old manuscript of the Navy, which I have bound up, and do please me mightily.

30th. Up, and to Sir W. Coventry to see and discourse with him; and he tells me that he hath lately been with my Lord Keeper and had much discourse about the Navy; and particularly he tells me that he finds they are divided touching me and my Lord Brouncker; some are for removing and some for keeping us. He told my Lord Keeper that it would cost the King £10,000 before he hath made another as fit to serve him in the Navy as I am; which, though I believe it is true, yet I am much pleased to have that character given me by W. Coventry, whatever be the success of it. But I perceive they do think that I know too much and shall impose upon whomever shall come next, and therefore must be removed. After some talk of the business of the navy more with him, I away and to the Office, where all the morning; and Sir W. Pen, the first time that he hath been here since his being last sick, which I think is two or three months; and I think will be the last that he will be here as one of the Board, he now inviting us all to dine with him, as a parting dinner, on Thursday next, which I am glad of, I am sure; for he is a very villain.

April 11th. (Lord's Day. Easter Day.) After dinner my wife and I out by coach, and Balty with us, to a painter, a Dutchman

newly come over, one Evarelst,[1] who took us to his lodging close
by and did shew us a little flower-pot of his doing, the finest thing
that ever I think I saw in my life; the drops of dew hanging on the
leaves so as I was forced again and again to put my finger to it,
to feel whether my eyes were deceived or no. He do ask £70 for
it: I had the vanity to bid him £20; but a better picture I never
saw in my whole life, and it is worth going twenty miles to see it.
Thence, leaving Balty there, I took my wife to St. James's, and
there carried her to the Queen's Chapel. Thence to the Park,
and here Sir W. Coventry did first see me and my wife in a coach
of our own; and so did also this night the Duke of York, who did
eye my wife mightily. But I begin to doubt that my being so
much seen in my own coach at this time may be observed to my
prejudice; but I must venture it now.

   12th. Walked to White Hall, and by and by to my wife at
Unthanke's, and with her was Jane, and so to the Cocke, where
they and I and Tom dined, my wife having a great desire to eat
of their soup made of pease, and dined very well; and thence by
water to the Bear-Garden. Here we saw a prize fought between
a soldier and a country fellow, one Warrell, who promised the
least in his looks, and performed the most of valour in his boldness
and evenness of mind and smiles in all he did that ever I saw; and
we were all both deceived and infinitely taken with him. He did
soundly beat the soldier, and cut him over the head. By our own
coach home, and after sitting an hour thrumming upon my viall
and singing, I to bed and left my wife to do something to a waistcoat and petticoat she is to wear to-morrow. This evening coming
home we overtook Alderman Backewell's coach and his lady
and followed them to their house, and there made them the first
visit, where they received us with extraordinary civility, and owning the obligation. But I do, contrary to my expectation, find
her something a proud and vain-glorious woman, in telling the
number of her servants and family and expences: he is also so,
but he was ever of that strain. But here he showed me the model
of his houses that he is going to build in Cornhill and Lumbard
Street; but he hath purchased so much there that it looks like a
little town, and must have cost him a great deal of money.

   13th. Up, and at the Office a good while; and then, my wife
going down the River to spend the day with her mother at Deptford, I abroad, and first to the milliner's in Fenchurch Street,

   [1] Simon Verelst.

over against Rawlinson's, and there, meeting both him and her
in the shop, I bought a pair of gloves, and fell to talk, and found
so much freedom that I stayed there the best part of the morning
till towards noon, with great pleasure, it being a holiday; and then
against my will away and to the 'Change, where I left W. Hewer,
and I by hackney-coach to the Spittle and heard a piece of a
dull sermon to my Lord Mayor and Aldermen, and thence saw them
all take horse and ride away, which I have not seen together many
a-day; their wives also went in their coaches, and indeed the sight
was mighty pleasing.   Thence took occasion to go back to this
milliner's, whose name I now understand to be Clerke; and there,
her husband inviting me up to the balcony to see the sight go
by to dine at Clothworker's-Hall, I did go up and there saw it
go by: and then, there being a good piece of cold roast beef upon
the table, I staid and eat, and had much good conversation.   After
spending most of the afternoon I away home, and there sent for
W. Hewer, and he and I by water to White Hall to look, among
other things, for Mr. May, to unbespeak his dining with me to-
morrow.   But here being in the court-yard, as God would have it,
I spied Deb., which made my heart and head to work, and I presently could not refrain, but sent W. Hewer away to look for Mr.
Wren (W. Hewer, I perceive, did see her, but whether he did see
me see her I know not, or suspect my sending him away I know not,
but my heart could not hinder me), and I run after her and two
women and a man, more ordinary people, and she in her old clothes;
and after hunting a little, find them in the lobby of the chapel
below stairs, and there I observed she endeavoured to avoid me,
but I did speak to her and she to me, and did get her pour dire
me ou she demeurs now, and did charge her para say nothing of me
that I had vu elle, which she did promise; and so with my heart
full of surprize and disorder I away, and meeting with Sir H.
Cholmley walked into the Park with him and back again, looking
to see if I could spy her again in the Park, but I could not.   And
so back to White Hall, and then back to the Park; and so home to
my wife, who is come home from Deptford.   But, God forgive
me, I hardly know how to put on confidence enough to speak as
innocent, having had this passage to-day with Deb., though only,
God knows, by accident.   But my great pain is lest God Almighty
shall suffer me to find out this girl, whom indeed I love; but I will
pray to God to give me grace to forbear it.   So to supper, where
very sparing in my discourse, not giving occasion of any enquiry

where I have been to-day, or what I have done, and so without any trouble to-night more than my fear, we to bed.

14th. My wife and I to Creed's, and there find him and her together alone in their new house, where I never was before, they lodging before at the next door, and a pretty house it is; but I do not see that they intend to keep any coach. Here they treat us like strangers, quite according to the fashion, nothing to drink or eat, which is a thing that will spoil our ever having any acquaintance with them; for we do continue the old freedom and kindness of England to all our friends.

19th. Up, and with Tom by coach to White Hall, and there having set him work in the Robe Chamber to write something for me, I to Westminster Hall and there walked from 10 o'clock to past 12, expecting to have met Deb.; but she not then appearing, I being tired with walking went home, and my wife being all day at Jane's, helping her, as she said, to cut out linen and other things belonging to her new condition, I after dinner out again, and calling for my coach, which was at the coachmaker's, to be new painted and the window-frames gilt against May-day, went on with my hackney to White Hall, and thence by water to Westminster Hall, and there did beckon to Doll Lane, and went to her sister Martin's lodgings, the first time I have been there these eight or ten months, I think, and her sister being gone to Portsmouth to her husband, I did stay and talk and drink with Doll. So away and to White Hall, and there took my own coach, which was now come, and so away home.

20th. In the afternoon walked to the Old Artillery-Ground [1] near the Spitalfields, where I never was before, but now, by Captain Deane's invitation, did go to see his new gun tryed, this being the place where the Officers of the Ordnance do try all their great guns; and when we come, did find that the trial had been made, and they going away with extraordinary report of the proof of his gun, which, from the shortness and bigness, they do call Punchinello. But I desired Colonel Legg to stay and give us a sight of her performance, which he did, and there, in short, against a gun more than as long and as heavy again, and charged with as much powder again, she carried the same bullet as strong to the mark, and nearer and above the mark at a point blank than their's, and is more easily managed, and recoyles no more than that;

[1] Given by King Henry VIII. to the Fraternity of Artillery: it was where Artillery Lane and Artillery Street now stand, in Bishopsgate Street Without.

which is a thing so extraordinary as to be admired for the happiness of his invention, and to the great regret of the old Gunners and Officers of the Ordnance that were there. And so, having seen this great and first experiment, we parted.

May 1st. Up betimes. Called up by my tailor, and there first put on a summer suit this year; but it was not my fine one of flowered tabby vest and coloured camelott tunique, because it was too fine with the gold lace at the hands, that I was afeard to be seen in it; but put on the stuff suit I made the last year, which is now repaired; and so did go to the Office in it, and sat all the morning, the day looking as if it would be fowle. At noon home to dinner, and there find my wife extraordinary fine, with her flowered tabby gown that she made two years ago, now laced exceeding pretty; and indeed was fine all over, and mighty earnest to go, though the day was very lowering; and she would have me put on my fine suit, which I did. And so anon we went alone through the town with our new liveries of serge, and the horses' manes and tails tied with red ribbons, and the standards there gilt with varnish, and all clean, and green reines, that people did mightily look upon us; and the truth is I did not see any coach more pretty, though more gay, than ours all the day. But we set out, out of humour, I because Betty, whom I expected, was not come to go with us; and my wife that I would sit on the same seat with her, which she likes not, being so fine: the day also being unpleasing, though the Park full of coaches, but dusty and windy and cold, and now and then a little dribbling rain; and, what made it worst, there were so many hackney-coaches as spoiled the sight of the gentlemen's, and so we had little pleasure. But here was W. Batelier and his sister in a borrowed coach by themselves, and I took them and we to the lodge, and at the door did give them a syllabub, and other things, cost me 12s., and pretty merry. And so back to the coaches, and there till the evening, and then home, and after a little supper, to bed.

2nd. (Lord's Day.) Up, and by water to White Hall, and there visit my Lord Sandwich, who, after about two months' absence at Hinchingbroke, come to town last night. I saw him, and very kind; and I am glad he is so, I having not wrote to him all the time, my eyes indeed not letting me.

3rd. To St. James's, where the Duke of York was playing in the Pell Mell; and so he called me to him most part of the time that he played, which was an hour, and talked alone to me; and among other things tells me how the King will not yet be got to name anybody in the room of Pen, but puts it off for three or four days; from whence he do collect that they are brewing something for the Navy, but what he knows not.

5th. To St. James's, and thence with the Duke of York to White Hall, where the Board waited on him all the morning: and so at noon to the Spanish Embassador's, where I dined the first time. There was at the table himself and a Spanish Countess, a good, comely, and witty lady, three Fathers and us. Discourse good and pleasant. And here was an Oxford scholar in a Doctor of Law's gowne, sent from the College where the Embassador lay when the Court was there, to salute him before his return to Spain. This man, though a gentle sort of scholar, yet sat like a fool for want of French or Spanish, but only Latin, which he spoke like an Englishman to one of the Fathers. And by and by he and I to talk, and the company very merry at my defending Cambridge against Oxford: and I made much use of my French and Spanish here, to my great content. But the dinner not extraordinary at all, either for quantity or quality.

8th. At the Office all the morning, and this day, the first time, did alter my side of the table, after above eight years sitting on that next the fire. But now I am not able to bear the light of the windows in my eyes I do begin there, and I did sit with much more content than I had done on the other side for a great while, and in winter the fire will not trouble my back. At noon home to dinner, and after dinner all the afternoon within, with Mr. Hater, Gibson and W. Hewer, reading over and drawing up new things in the Instructions of Commanders. By and by comes Browne, the mathematical instrument maker, and brings me home my instrument for perspective, made according to the description of Dr. Wren's, in the late Transactions; and he hath made it, I think, very well, and that that I believe will do the thing, and therein gives me great content; but I fear all the content that must be received by my eyes is almost lost. So to the office, and there late at business, and then home to supper and to bed.

10th. To my Lord Crew, whom I have not seen since he was sick, which is eight months ago, I think, and there dined with him: he is mightily broke. A stranger, a country gentleman, was with him: and he pleased with my discourse accidentally about the decay of gentlemen's families in the country, telling us that the old rule was that a family might remain fifty miles from London one hundred years, one hundred miles from London two hundred years, and so farther or nearer London more or less years.   He also told us that he hath heard his father say that in his time it was so rare for a country gentleman to come to London that when he did come he used to make his will before he set out.   Thence to St. James's and there met the Duke of York, who told me with great content that he did now think he should master our adversaries, for that the King did tell him that he was satisfied in the constitution of the Navy; but that it was well to give these people leave to object against it, which they having not done, he did give order to give warrant to the Duke of York to direct Sir Jeremy Smith to be a Commissioner of the Navy in the room of Pen; which, though he be an impertinent fellow, yet I am glad of it, it showing that the other side is not so strong as it was.

12th.   After dinner my wife and I to the Duke of York's playhouse, and there in the side balcony over against the musick did hear, but not see, a new play, the first day acted, "The Roman Virgin," [1] an old play, and but ordinary, I thought; but the trouble of my eyes with the light of the candles did almost kill me. Thence to my Lord Sandwich's, and there had a promise from Sidney to come and dine with me to-morrow; and so my wife and I home in our coach, and there find my brother John, as I looked for, come to town from Ellington, where among other things he tells me the first news that my sister Jackson is with child, and far gone, which I know not whether it did more trouble or please me, having no great care for my friends to have children, though I love other people's.   So, glad to see him, we to supper, and so to bed.

14th.   Up, and to St. James's to the Duke of York, and thence to White Hall, where we met about office business, and then at noon with Mr. Wren to Lambeth, to dinner with the Archbishop of Canterbury; the first time I was ever there, and I have long longed for it; where a noble house, and well furnished with good pictures and furniture, and noble attendance in good order, and great deal of company, though an ordinary day; and exceeding great cheer, no where better, or so much, that ever I think I saw for an ordinary table: and the Bishop mighty kind to me, particularly desiring my company another time, when less company there.   So over to White Hall, to a little Committee of Tangier; and thence walking in the Gallery I met Sir Thomas Osborne, who to my great con-

[1] Adapted by Betterton from Webster's *Appius and Virginia*.

tent did of his own accord fall into discourse with me, with so much professions of value and respect, placing the whole virtue of the Office of the Navy upon me, and that for the Comptroller's place no man in England was fit for it but me, when Sir J. Minnes, as he says it is necessary, is removed: but then he knows not what to do for a man in my place; and in discourse, though I have no mind to the other, I did bring in Tom Hater to be the fittest man in the world for it, which he took good notice of. But in the whole I was mightily pleased, reckoning myself now fifty per cent. securer in my place than I did before think myself to be.

15th. Up, and at the Office all the morning. Dined at home, and Creed with me home, and I did discourse about evening some reckonings with him in the afternoon; but I could not, for my eyes, do it, which troubled me, and vexed him that I would not; but yet we were friends, I advancing him money without it, and so to walk all the afternoon together in the garden.

16th. (Lord's Day.) All the afternoon drawing up a foul draught of my petition to the Duke of York about my eyes, for leave to spend three or four months out of the Office drawing it so as to give occasion to a voyage abroad, which I did, to my pretty good liking.

18th. Up, and to St. James's and other places, and then to the office, where all the morning. At noon home and dined in my wife's chamber, she being much troubled with the tooth-ake, and I staid till a surgeon of hers come, one Leeson, who hath formerly drawn her mouth, and he advised her to draw it: so I to the Office, and by and by word is come that she hath drawn it, which pleased me, it being well done. So I home to comfort her, and so back to the office till night, busy, and so home to supper and to bed.

19th. To White Hall, and there I waited upon the King and Queen all dinner-time, in the Queen's lodgings, she being in her white pinner and apron; and she seemed handsomer plain so, than dressed. And by and by, dinner done, I out and to walk in the Gallery, for the Duke of York's coming out; and there, meeting Mr. May, he took me down about four o'clock and all alone did get me a dish of cold chickens, and good wine; and I dined like a prince, being before very hungry and empty. By and by the Duke of York comes, and readily took me to his closet and received my petition, and discoursed about my eyes, and pitied me, and with much kindness did give me his consent to be absent, and approved of my proposition to go into Holland to observe things there of the Navy; but would first ask the King's leave, which he anon did, and did tell me that the King would be a good master to me, these were his words, about my eyes, and do like of my going into Holland; but do advise that nobody should know of my going thither, but pretend that I did go into the country somewhere, which I liked well.

20th. Up and to the Office, where all the morning. At noon, the whole Office (Brouncker, J. Minnes, T. Middleton, Samuel Pepys, and Captain Cox), to dine with the Parish at the Three Tuns, this day being Ascension-day, where exceeding good discourse among the merchants, and thence back home, and after a little talk with my wife, to my office and did a great deal of business; and so with my eyes mighty weary, and my head full of care how to get my accounts and business settled against my journey, home to supper, and to bed.

24th. To White Hall, and there all the morning, and thence home, and giving order for some business and setting my brother to making a catalogue of my books, I back again to W. Hewer to White Hall, where I attended the Duke of York, and was by him led to the King, who expressed great sense of my misfortune in my eyes, and concernment for their recovery.

31st. Up very betimes, and so continued all the morning with W. Hewer upon examining and stating my accounts, in order to the fitting myself to go abroad beyond sea, which the ill condition of my eyes, and my neglect for a year or two, hath kept me behind-hand in, and so as to render it very difficult now, and troublesome to my mind to do it; but I this day made a satisfactory entrance therein. Dined at home, and in the afternoon by water to White Hall, calling by the way at Michell's, where I have not been many a day till just the other day, and now I met her mother there and knew her husband to be out of town. Je did baiser elle, and thence had another meeting with the Duke of York at White Hall, on yesterday's work, and made a good advance: and so, being called by my wife, we to the Park, Mary Batelier, and a Dutch gentleman, a friend of hers, being with us. Thence to "The World's End," a drinking-house by the Park; and there merry, and so home late.

And thus ends all that I doubt I shall ever be able to do with my own eyes in the keeping of my Journal, I being not able to do it any longer, having done now so long as to undo my eyes almost every time that I take a pen in my hand; and therefore whatever comes of it I must forbear: and therefore resolve from this time forward to have it kept by my people in long-hand, and must therefore be contented to set down no more than is fit for them and all the world to know; or if there be any thing (which cannot be much, now my amours to Deb. are past, and my eyes hindering me in almost all other pleasures), I must endeavour to keep a margin in my book open, to add here and there a note in short-hand with my own hand.

And so I betake myself to that course, which is almost as much as to see myself go into my grave: for which, and all the discomforts that will accompany my being blind, the good God prepare me!

S. P.

May 31, 1669.

"AND THUS ENDS ALL"

INDEX

Actors, *Betterton* (Thomas), 94, *n.*, 128 133, 134, 167, 221, 231, 516; *Burt* (Nicholas), 53; *Cartwright* (William), 437; *Clun*, 161, 219; *Harris* (Henry), 201, 221, 231, 360, 361, 394, 467, 485, 488, 489; *Hart* (Charles), 448; *Ianthe* (Mrs. Betterton), 128, 134, 221, 231, 247; *Kynaston* (Edward), 48, 64; *Lacy* (John), 161, 169, 382; *Mohun* (Michael), 58, *n.*, 382; *also* 64, 72, 427, 458, *n.; see Gwynn, Killigrew, Knipp.*

Albemarle (Anne, Duchess of), a damned ill-looked woman, 286; the damned duchess again, 290; speaks well of Pepys, 435; *also* 311, 345, 379.

Albemarle (General George Monk, later Duke of), made General of all the Forces, 8; a dull, heavy man, 16, 247; made Commissioner for the Treasury, 38; considers Pepys the right hand of the Navy, 249; asks Pepys' advice, 284; his conduct condemned, 306; will probably gain in repute, 320; is courted by everybody, 334; mighty low in people's opinion, 345; his dirty dishes, nasty wife and bad meat, 379; is not well and do grow crazy, 383; hath strange luck to be loved, 437; *also* 1, 2, 6, 7, 11, 13, 20, 25, 34, 35, 52, *n.*, 79-81, 82, 215, 245, 246, 248, 253, 256, 259, 270, 271, 274-278, 280, 285, 287, 290, 293, 304, 305, 309, 311, 340, 341, 366, 368, 391, 402, 417, 447, 463, 467.

Allen (Rebecca, later Mrs. Jowles), Pepys intent upon her, 75, 76; mighty free in kindness, 525.

Ambassadors, the Portuguese, 88; fray between Spanish and French, 96; coming of the Russian, 133, 140; the French, and the Lord Mayor's Banquet, 188; the Dutch, 224, 242; the French, 487, 494; the Spanish, his universal sauce, 514; Pepys dines with the Spanish, 532.

Andrews (John), Pepys borrows of him, 1, 9; hath a fancy to raw meat, 435; *also* 213.

Angier (Percival), of Cambridge, Pepys' cousin, lately broke, 196; his burial, 237; *also* 10.

Animals, Pepys disturbed at night by a dog, 2; the King's dog, 34; the Pepys's fall out about a dog, 56; frogs that fall from the sky, 84; dancing monkeys, 94, 182; lions at the Tower, 113; a catt or Pepys' bed, 125; a great dogg sets on Pepys, 162; a brave, proud horse, 176; Pepys' pretty mare, 219; a poor cat saved in the Fire, 332; a damned noise between a sow, a cow and a dog, 407; the shepherd's dog, 410; a coach-horse sick of the staggers, 416; Pepys' gibb-cat frights him, 442; in Noah's arke, 474; a mare that tells money, 489; death of poor Fancy, 491.

Ann (Mrs.), Lady Jem's maid, Pepys makes up her bills, 5; very high with Pepys about a flock bed, 7.

Ashwell (Mary), Mrs. Pepys' woman 146; plays on the tryangle, 153, 160; dances to Pepys' fiddling, 158; Mrs. Pepys jealous of, 160, 161; *also* 148, 151 152, 154, 168, 177, 178, 180.

Bagwell (Mrs.), a carpenter's pretty wife, 172; seeks Pepys' favour, 178; Pepys kisses her, 227; Pepys visits her at Deptford, 233; *also* 238, 240, 241, 520.

Balty, see *St. Michael* (Balthazar).

Barker (Mrs.), Mrs. Pepys' woman, 341; sings better than Mercer, 381; *also* 389.

Barlow (Thomas), Pepys' predecessor as Clerk of the Acts, 41; threatens Pepys, 45; is dead, 240.

Bartholomew Fair, 94, *n.*, 182, 418, 489, 526.

Batelier (Mary), one of the finest women, 268; her sister a very black woman, 312; *also* 301, 313, 318, 320, 341, 504, 526, 531, 535.

Batelier (Will), Pepys jealous of, 318; sends maids to the Pepys's, 421, 424; his house-warming, 494; *also* 301, 348, 361, 443, 488, 516, 517, 518, 519, 531, 535.

Batten (Elizabeth, Lady), with Mrs. Pepys to see executions, 68; Pepys kisses her, 75; a fray with Mrs. Pepys, 151; invites Pepys to her daughter's wedding, 172; drops a galosh in the dirt, 282; a widow all broke in pieces, 434; Pepys takes no notice of her, 438; gossip against her, 446; *also* 60, 67, 68, 70, 93, 106, 110, 138, 171, 241, 249, 253, 328, 357, 373, 418, 434.

Batten (Mrs. Martha), Sir William's daughter, is Pepys' valentine, 70, *n.*, 71; marries Mr. Castle; *also* 98.

Batten (Sir William), Surveyor of the Navy, lives like a prince, 55; his black servant, 70, 74; Pepys daily opposes his cheats, 172; his fear of a sea-fight, 211; Pepys jealous of his dining with the King, 267; removes his goods during the Fire, 328; dies, 427; his burial, 434; *also* 46, *n.*, 51, 58, 71, 72-75, 79, 84, 110, 119, 120, 180, 227, 233, 241, 253, 281, 329, 338-340, 357, 370, 372, 378, 398, 401, 405, 424.

Bear-Garden, a rude and nasty pleasure, 319; prize fights there, 393, 528.

Becke (Mrs. Betty), Lord Sandwich's mistress, well carriaged and discreet, 212; *also* 173, 179, 190, 193.

Bellassis (John, Lord), Governor of Tangier, 237; treats Pepys with respect, 237; his stories of Charles I., 239.

Birds, Mrs. Pepys' turtle-doves, 106; larks fed upon by serpents, 106; water-fowl in the Park, 108; the Duke's bird that neyes like a horse, 207; the Emperor of Russia flies a hawk at pigeons, 225; death of Pepys' canary, 237; ortolans, that are almost all fat, 313; pigeons burned in the Fire, 326; Pepys' starling, formerly the King's, 472.

Black Patches, worn at the Hague, 29; Mrs. Pepys has leave to wear, 56; Lady Newcastle's, because of pimples, 384; *also* 54, 59, 386, 444.

Bland (Mr.), merchant, his kinswoman's singing lesson, 174; *also* 136, 208.

Blount (Blunt, Colonel), his coachsprings, 250; not so easy as he pretends, 274.

Bonfires, the city with a glory of, 8; Pepys beats his boy for staying at, 157; *also* 23, 82, 116, 229, 256, 306.

Books, how the King loves the Bible, 34;

537

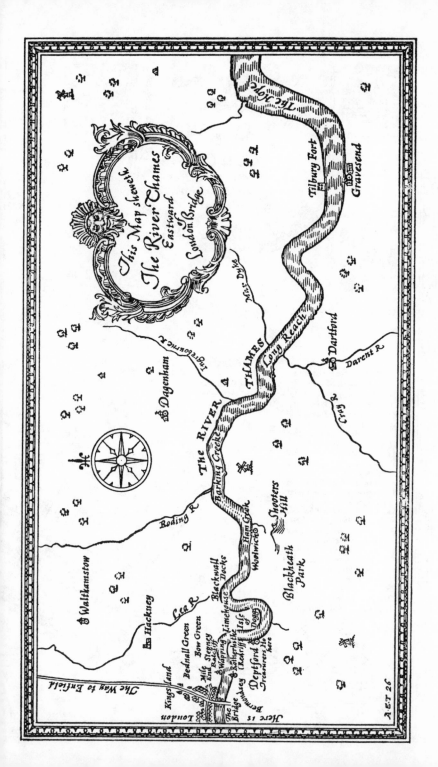

This Map sheweth
The River Thames
Eastward
of
London Bridge

THAMES

The HOPE

Tilbury Fort

Gravesend

Long Reach

Mar. Dyke

Dartford

Darent R.

Ingrebourne R.

Cray R.

Dagenham

THE RIVER

Barking Creek

Shooters Hill

Roding R.

Ham Creek

Woolwich

Blackheath Park

Walthamstow

Hackney

Lea R.

Bednall Green

Bow Green

Mile End
and
Stepney

Blackwall Docks

Limehouse

Wapping

Isle of Dogs

Rotherhithe

Dartford (Redriff)

Kingsland

The Way to Enfield

London

The Bridge

Bermondsey

Here is
Treasure here

A.E.J. 26

Westminster Abbey
& Parliament House

The Piazza in Covent
Garden

A Map
of London in
the Sixteen Sixties
shewing the District West
of Whitefriars

A True Picture of
White Hall

Pasture

The Way to Hampstead

Tyburn
Gibbet

The Way from Paddington

The Area of the Great Fire
is shewn thus §

A Table of References
to this Map

1 Berkeley House, Piccadilly
2 Clarendon House, Piccadilly
3 Burlington House, Piccadilly
4 St Martins in the Fields
5 Wallingford House, Cockspur St.
6 The Cockpit, Whitehall
7 Axe Yard below Tilt Yard, Whall.
8 St Margarets Ch. Westminster
9 The Gate House, Westminster
10 Ashburnham Ho. Westminster
11 Parliament Ho. Westminster
12 St Giles in the Fields
13 Southampton Market W.end of
      Holborn
14 Wills Coffee House, Bow Street
15 Kings Playhouse Drury Lane
16 Maypole in the Strand
17 St Clement Danes Ch. Strand
18 The Dukes House Lincolns Inn
19 Gaming House in Bell Yard
20 Temple Bar
21 St Dunstans in the W. Fleet St.
22 Temple Church
23 St Andrews Ch. Holborn

Pasture & Heath

A Rill

The Way from Knightsbridge

Piccadilly

St James's
Fields

Barkeshire
House

St James
Pallace

Canal
Made by King

Tuttle

Made by

St Peters in Westminster

A Scale of Furlongs
and Yards

Furlongs

Yards   220   440   660

Tootehill Fields

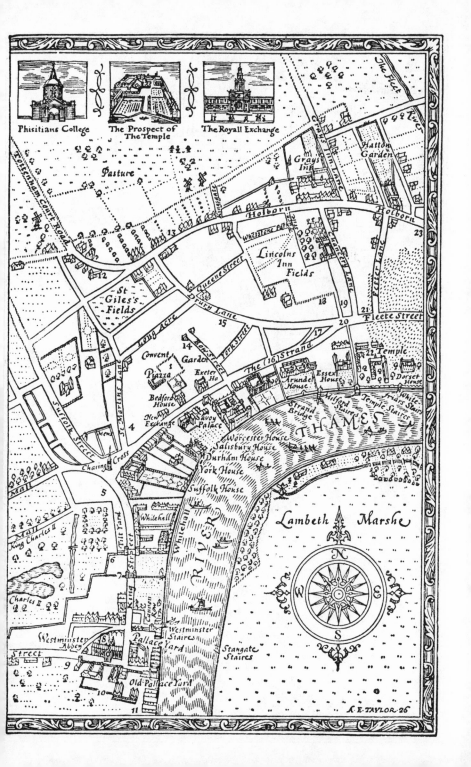

Phisitians College

The Prospect of The Temple

The Royall Exchange

Pasture

Tottenham Court Road

Holborn

Holborn

Grays Inn

Hatton Garden

Whetstone Pk

Grays Inn Lane

Lincolns Inn Fields

Chancery Lane

Fetter Lane

23

St Giles's Fields

Queene Street

Drury Lane

13

12

18

19

21

Fleete Street

Long Acre

15

Bow Street

20

17

Strand

22 Temple

14

Vere Street

The (16) Strand

Convent Garden

Piazza

1

Exeter Ho

Arundel House

Essex House

2 Dorset House

White Friars Stairs

Bedford House

3

St Martins

Menn

4

New Exchange

Savoy Palace

Strand Bridge

Milford Staires

Temple Staires

Suffolk Street

Worcester House

THAMES

Salisbury House

Durham House

York House

Charing Cross

Menn

Suffolk House

Mall

Whitehall

5

Whitehall

RIVER

Lambeth Marshe

King Charles II

Tilt Yard

N

Charles II

6

King Street

7

W   E

Cannon

Westminster Staires

S

Westminster Abbey

8

Pallace Yard

Street

9

Stangate Staires

10

Old Palace Yard

11

A. E. TAYLOR. 26

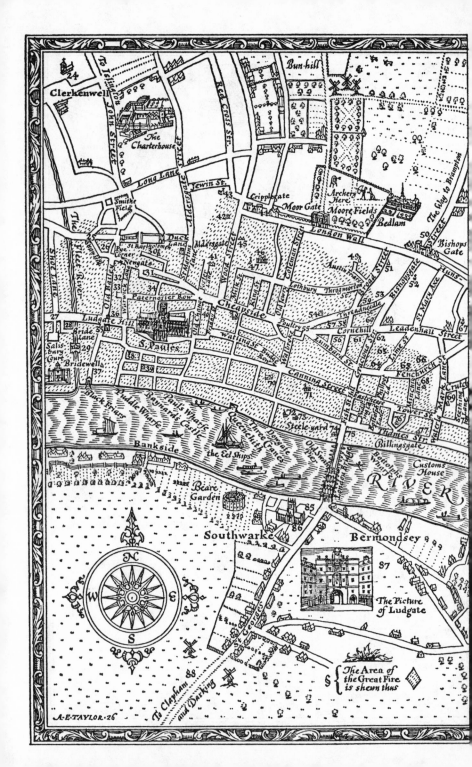

A Map
of London in
the Sixteen Sixties
shewing the District East
of Whitefriars

References continued –

24 St James' Ch. Clerkenwell
25 Holborn Conduit
26 St Sepulchre's Ch. (Newgate)
27 Fleet Conduit
28 St Brides Ch. Fleet Street
29 Bridge in Bridewell
30 Christ Church Newgate
31 Newgate Market
32 Prerogative Office) near
33 Coll. of Physicians } Paternost-
34 Exchequer Office) ter Row
35 Ludgate
36 St Martins Ch. Ludgate
37 Apothecaries Hall also Blackfri- ars Theatre
38 St Andrews in the Wardrobe
39 Doctors Commons
40 St Matthews Ch. Friday St
41 Goldsmiths Hall
42 Barber Chyrurgeons Hall
43 St Giles' Ch Cripplegate
44 Loriners Hall
45 Haberdashers Hall
46 Guildhall
47 St Lawrence Jewry

48 St Mary-le-Bow-Cheapside
49 Dutch Ch. Augustine – Austin- Friars
50 St Botolph's Ch. Bishopsgate
51 Gresham College
52 St Helens Ch. Bishopsgate
53 St Martin Outwich Ch. by Merch- ant Taylors
54 The Posthouse Threadneedle St.
55 Stocks Market, Poultry
56 St Dunstans in the E. Tower St:
57 Royal Exchange
58 Cornehill Conduitt.
59 French Ch. Threadneedle St.
60 Merchant Taylors Hall
61 St Michael's Ch. Cornhill
62 Leadenhall (City Granary &c)
63 Leadenhall Market
64 St Dionis Backchurch by Fencha- rch st.
65 St Gabriels Ch. Fenchurch St.
66 Ironmongers Hall
67 St Katherine Cree
68 Clothworkers Hall Miucing L.
69 St Olave's Ch. Hart St (by Tower)
70 Skinners Hall, Dowgate Hill.
71 St Lawrence Poultney
72 All Hallows the Gt. Thames St.
73 All Hallows the Less, Thames St.
74 Fishmongers Hall. London Edge
75 St Magnus Ch. by London Bdge
76 St Dunstans in the E. Tower St.
77 Trinity Ho. (afterwards at Stepney
78 All Hallows. Barking.
79 Navy Office nr. Tower Hill
80 Site of Scaffold on Tower Hill
81 St Katherines by the Tower
82 St Marys Church Whitechapel
83 Wapping Church
84 Rediff Ch (Rotherhithe)
85 The Bear at the Bridge Foot (A Famous Tavern at the South- wark end of old London Bridge Southwark Fair held hereabouts)
86 St Mary Overies, (now Southwk Cath
87 St Thomass Hospital. Southwark
88 St Margarets Hill Southwark (where The old Admiralty Court was held)

To Shoreditch
Artillery Yard.
To Bowe
Whitechapel
ditch
Aldgate
Here is shewn The Guild-hall
Minories
Red Friars
79
Tower Hill 80
Victualling Office East Smithfield
The Tower
Tower Wharfe
81
Ratcliffe

THAMES
85 Wapping
Redriff 84

The Picture of Greenwich

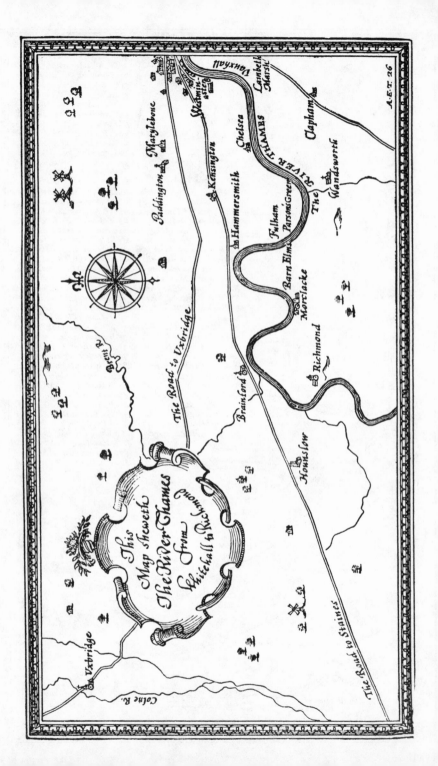

This
Map sheweth
The River Thames
From
Whitehall to Richmond

A.E.T. 26

Colne R.

Uxbridge

The Road to Staines

The Road to Uxbridge

Brent R.

Paddington

Marylebone

Kensington

Hammersmith

Westmin-aster

Vauxhall

Lambeth Marsh

Chelsea

THE RIVER THAMES

Fulham

Barn Elms

Parsons Green

Brainford

Mortlacke

Hounslow

Richmond

The Wandsworth

Clapham

Wapiti